WHEN THE PENTAGON WAS FOR SALE

Inside America's
Biggest Defense Scandal

ANDY PASZTOR

SCRIBNER

NEW YORK   LONDON   TORONTO   SYDNEY
TOKYO   SINGAPORE

SCRIBNER
1230 Avenue of the Americas
New York, NY 10020

Designed by Ellen Sasahara
Manufactured in the United States of America

1 3 5 7 9 10 8 6 4 2

Library of Congress Cataloging-in-Publication Data
Pasztor, Andy.
When the Pentagon was for sale: inside America's biggest defense scan-
dal/Andy Pasztor.
p.   cm.
Includes bibliographical references and index.
1. United States. Defense Dept.—Procurement—Corrupt practices.
2. Defense contracts—United States. 3. United States—Politics and
government—1981–1989. I. Title.
UC263.P37   1995   95-23412
355.6'212'0973—dc20   CIP

ISBN 0-684-19516-X

CONTENTS

CAST OF CHARACTERS

GOVERNMENT OFFICIALS

President Ronald Reagan
President George Bush
Defense Secretary Caspar Weinberger
Defense Secretary Frank Carlucci
Defense Secretary Dick Cheney
Navy Secretary John Lehman, Jr.
Assistant Navy Secretary Melvyn Paisley
William Chappell, chairman of the House defense appropriations
    subcommittee
U.S. Attorney Henry Hudson
Assistant U.S. Attorney Joseph Aronica
Assistant U.S. Attorney Randy Bellows
Senior Federal Bureau of Investigation agent Richard Wade
Senior Defense Criminal Investigative Service agent Michael Costello
Naval Investigative Service agent Steve Fulmer
James Gaines, high-ranking Navy acquisitions official
Victor Cohen, high-ranking Air Force acquisitions official

DEFENSE INDUSTRY PLAYERS

T. A. Wilson, Boeing Company chairman
Benjamin Plymale, senior Boeing Company marketing executive
Thomas Pownall, Martin Marietta Corporation chairman
Malcolm Currie, Hughes Aircraft Company chairman
Robert Daniell, United Technologies Corporation chairman
Eugene Tallia, senior United Technologies Corporation executive
John O'Brien, Grumman Corporation chairman
Bernard Schwartz, Loral Corporation chairman
Michael Blumenthal, Unisys Corporation chairman
Charles Gardner, Unisys Corporation vice-president
Colvin Wellborn, senior Cubic Corporation executive
William Galvin, prominent industry consultant
James Kane, prominent industry consultant
Thomas Muldoon, prominent industry consultant
William Parkin, prominent industry consultant
John Marlowe, federal undercover informant

ACKNOWLEDGMENTS

Writing a book, like almost everything that gives meaning and spice to life, has its highs and lows. To overcome the unavoidable hurdles, every manuscript must have a cadre of champions. Every author, no matter how strongly he or she believes in a topic, needs a group of behind-the-scenes advocates. This project definitely fits that pattern.

Foremost, I wish to acknowledge my beloved father, Erno Pasztor. His indomitable spirit, integrity, wisdom and fervent support are among my greatest treasures. This book is dedicated to him with admiration and utmost respect.

My father-in-law, Jean Mayers, provided the sober analysis, technical expertise and historical perspective that kept me on track. I am indebted to him not only for the days he spent reading drafts, but for his suggestions and exemplary judgment.

In addition, there are many friends and colleagues whose help and kindness I can never repay adequately as they gave generously of their time and advice. Rick Wartzman, with his energy and love of good writing, started me down the road to tell this story. Ed Pound helped me find where the secrets were buried. And Bruce Abell urged me to keep digging. Fred Rose also took time to read parts of the manuscript, as did Susan J. Brite, Christopher Conte, Walter Mossberg, Dick Blome and Wendy Whiting Blome, Bruce Ingersoll, Edwin Rothschild, John Emshwiller, Jeff Cole, Ben Holden, Sarah Lubman and others. Paul Steiger, Steve Sansweet and Albert Hunt of *The Wall Street Journal* gave me the time to pursue leads, for which I am most grateful.

The enthusiasm, loyalty and patience of my editors, Jane Rosenman and Bill Goldstein, and Kris Dahl, my agent, proved absolutely critical. Elizabeth McNamara's legal guidance was superb, and Sean Devlin's care in copyediting was most appreciated. Thanks also are due to Randye Hoder, Susan Smith, Rita Knowlton, Peter Griggs and the excellent manuscript typists at Pro-Typists in Washington, D.C.

Regardless of whether the subjects of this book agree with its conclusions, I express my thanks to them, too, for agreeing to be interviewed. There are too many individuals to list here, but all of them helped lead an outsider through the labyrinthine Pentagon procurement system.

I also thank my aunt, Elizabeth Pasztor, for her encouragement, and my

son, William Robert Pasztor, who helped teach me the value of perseverance and the gift of humor. I hope that those qualities are reflected, at
least in some measure, in the finished product. Finally, above all others,
Eileen Mayers Pasztor, my wife, provided the sustenance that made this
endeavor a reality. Her good sense, marvelous spark and inspiration kept
me from foundering, while her commitment to drawing lessons from the
story helped shape the final narrative.

Whatever missteps I made would have been much greater without the
assistance of all these people. I can only wish that the result justifies their
efforts.

INTRODUCTION

From a distance, it's hard to imagine a more imposing building than the Pentagon. On a bright spring day, its green roof sparkles and its stately limestone walls blend with the cherry blossoms, jogging paths and flower beds hugging the gentle curves of the Potomac River. When the sky is brooding or the setting sun peeks from behind one of its corners, the Pentagon changes character abruptly. It appears larger and more menacing, a dark colossus that dwarfs everything nearby and bristles with the silhouette of communications gear and antennas on almost every side.

The Pentagon has been called everything from "The Puzzle Palace" to a "neoutilitarian rabbit warren," featuring seventeen miles of corridors. For those who have toiled inside, though, there is really only one way to refer to it. They simply call it "The Building." No adjective or other description is necessary. The name, by itself, connotes importance and raw power. Blending patriotism with elements of science fiction, for many people it conjures up scenes of greater mystery and wonder than Washington's other monuments and edifices.

That marvelous image, however, starts to fade the moment you pass through a security check point. A number of corridors are drab or under renovation. Some of the floors are scarred and covered by cracked, discolored tiles. Chipped filing cabinets and faded swivel chairs are piled in hallways, sometimes for months at a time. Except for the spacious, wood-paneled suites reserved for the highest-ranking officers and civilians, offices tend to be cramped and even the signs on many of the doors are worn. There is an aging, surprisingly ragged feel to various corners of the building. Visitors may marvel at the four million square feet of space or the heavily guarded glass doors leading to a supersecret command center in its bowels. But the Pentagon's occupants often end up painting their own cubicles on weekends in order to avoid lengthy delays if the work is done through regular channels. The view from within—frequently through dirty windows or over makeshift partitions—hardly matches the magnificent facade.

The dichotomy also applies to how the armed forces shop for weapons. Like the Pentagon's majestic exterior, its acquisition practices seem unassailable at first glance. The sheer size of the effort is more than impressive: It can be awe-inspiring. During the height of Ronald Reagan's military boom, the Defense Department spent roughly $1 billion a day worldwide. The largest peacetime buildup in history supposedly was too vital not to be carefully managed. In theory, at least, hundreds of thousands of employees had no task other than to keep scrupulously close tabs on contractors. Seventy-nine separate offices issued voluminous acquisition regulations, covering everything from uniforms to submarines. The volume of rules equaled five times the length of Leo Tolstoy's novel *War and Peace*. The Army once promulgated fifteen pages of specifications for sugar cookies alone. And Lockheed, when it submitted a bid to build a new transport plane, delivered a package of papers weighing three tons. Then there were the fifty or so congressional subcommittees that were supposed to be riding herd on the entire procedure. From outside, the organization and its controls seemed beyond reproach.

But upon closer inspection, major shortcomings soon became evident. The same giant companies were caught breaking the law again and again, only to continue receiving new contracts. One midsize electronics contractor was the target of no less than eight separate federal criminal investigations and at least that many civil probes over a five-year period—but the military remained a stalwart customer. The services had nowhere else to turn for the equipment they needed. Executives running defense firms shrugged off the fines and penalties as merely another cost of doing business. Meanwhile, individuals throughout the Pentagon suspected—and some knew all too well—the extent of corruption. Yet they did little, if anything, about it.

The inertia struck me most strongly when I got the chance to work in The Building. I began writing about military acquisition issues for *The Wall Street Journal* in 1985, staying to cover the Defense Department through the collapse of the Soviet Union and the end of President George Bush's administration. Aside from several months in the Middle East reporting on the Persian Gulf conflict, a large portion of my time during those seven years was devoted to tracking criminal investigations and prosecutions of defense suppliers and industry executives. Firms sold substandard parachute cord and improperly tested steel for warships. Even the guidance systems of some *nuclear*-armed missiles were defective. Despite writing hundreds of articles about bribes, overcharges, false bills, phony contracts, fake test results, malfunctioning weapons, suspect parts and other assorted scams to cheat the armed services, I somehow felt that the full story of greed and mismanagement remained untold.

How could such dishonesty exist in a system ostensibly run according to rigid rules and absolute discipline? What combination of personalities and policies allowed petty favors and hefty payoffs to compromise national security? And, most important, what mistakes from those years should we strive to avoid?

In the 1980s, a new breed of high-priced consultants and influence peddlers rose to prominence. Intoxicated with their power and flagrantly breaking laws to snare business for corporate clients, these white-collar hooligans readily found accomplices in The Building and on Capitol Hill.

Reality turned out to be quite different from the high-sounding principles and regulations spelling out how the purchasing machinery was supposed to operate. "There is no conceivable system of procurement we could have concocted," one senator declared, to create an environment "more conducive to temptation and, ultimately, corruption." As an outraged federal judge said when he sentenced one of the notorious middlemen to jail, "I can't believe our government lets a system like this endure."

The phrase stuck in my mind when I set out to identify the most salient lessons from the Reagan era's excesses.

The problem of defense fraud, of course, has grown with the ages. During the Civil War, President Abraham Lincoln groused that his troops found sawdust instead of gunpowder when they pried open ammunition crates at the front. The cavalry discovered it was being charged for the same horses two and three times. One million feet of lumber vanished from the Boston Navy Yard during the corruption-stained administration of Ulysses S. Grant. After World War I, President Warren Harding's administration was sent reeling by the Teapot Dome scandal, which involved payment of bribes for leases of the Navy's oil reserves in the West. Harry Truman, as a senator in 1941, worried that "certain lobbyists were seeking the inside track" on war appropriations, determined to satisfy "only their own selfish interests."

But for all that, the average American held weapons-makers in relatively high regard until the last ten years. Even during Vietnam, critics excoriated contractors for the deadly hardware they built, not for whom they bilked. In the decades following World War II, hardly any major defense contractors were convicted of defrauding the Pentagon.

A few years after President Reagan and his team came to power, fraud and scandal seemed to consume the defense industry almost overnight. Certainly, part of the reason was smarter and more aggressive law enforcement. At the same time, a new generation of congressional watchdogs turned up the heat on suspected companies. Still, the pattern that emerged went beyond isolated examples of avarice, beyond a few "bad apples" shrewd or brazen enough to carry out their illicit schemes. Lawmakers and reformers solemnly promised to "fix" the Defense Department's procurement mess, yet the problems appeared to get worse and the decisions more prone to manipulation. To a large degree, the Pentagon's own rules implicitly encouraged wrongdoing, and its unique culture spawned many of the worst abuses. One veteran Pentagon investigator contends that contractors "in their hearts know that they're taking us to the cleaners. But they say that's not stealing, that's just being smart."

Reagan's arms buildup would have been overtaken anyway by the implosion of the Soviet empire and other world events. But faith in the Pentagon's basic honesty—whether the names at the top belong to Caspar Weinberger and Dick Cheney, or Les Aspin and later William Perry—is a much more important and fragile commodity. Both supporters and critics of Reagan's policies ought to feel betrayed by the crimes that were committed. The revelations undermined trust in the whole defense acquisition process.

Defense Secretary Weinberger's cavalier attitude about the price tag for rearming America was matched by his loose oversight of the procurement bureaucracy. There wasn't time to worry about inefficiencies or possible cost-saving moves, he explains, because "we needed to regain a great deal of military strength very, very quickly." In the end, Weinberger says smugly, "we won the Cold War . . . If we won by too much, if it was overkill, so be it." A Senate wag once quipped that Cap Weinberger was "the first person in history to overdraw a blank check."

The fallout from that spending spree plagues the nation to this day. To begin with, it is making it more difficult for government and industry to adjust to the harsh medicine of leaner defense budgets. Betting that their illegal plots would translate into huge profits, large contractors hustled to set up assembly lines and hired tens of thousands of additional workers. Thousands of smaller subcontractors beefed up their own payrolls and facilities, hoping to ride the coattails of industry giants. The extra capacity wasted hundreds of millions of dollars and saddled companies with a bloated cost structure. The latest estimates indicate that fully one-third of the country's defense industrial base no longer is needed. Now, companies are searching for partners and scrambling to sell assets at fire sale prices. Thanks to the criminal behavior of many, Pentagon suppliers are suffering extra pain and dislocation as the balloon finally deflates.

Sharp cuts in procurement have intensified competition for the Pentagon's leftover business, thereby increasing incentives for thievery and deception. In the mid-1990s, the stakes for each contract and program are higher than ever—often determining which shipyard or aircraft maker will be forced to shut down, or which missile plants will be able to avoid layoffs. Faced with do-or-die struggles in an inexorably shrinking industry, temptations to make payoffs and collect inside bidding information are likely to grow. The same pressures are bound to show up in foreign markets, as U.S. defense firms increasingly look overseas for revenue. "These are Darwinian times in our industry," says the incoming chairman of Lockheed Martin, the country's largest defense firm. After being allowed to overeat during the Reagan years, companies are suddenly being put on a crash diet. Is there any doubt that they will be sorely tempted to cheat and binge?

Shrinking budgets also mean fewer inspectors and auditors to pursue wrongdoers. Already, the pendulum has swung toward much greater reliance on corporate self-disclosure and voluntary ethics compliance efforts. Arms makers are demanding less oversight and more financially rewarding contract terms. Many of the companies leading the charge on these issues—while fighting against tougher criminal sanctions—were among those most heavily investigated during the past decade.

Another lesson of the 1980s revolves around the nomination process.

The White House, the Federal Bureau of Investigation, Congress and senior Pentagon officials all disregarded obvious early warnings about the lifestyle and ethics of Melvyn Paisley, the Navy's corrupt procurement czar from 1981 to 1987. His confirmation hearing was a charade. President Bill Clinton's travails in picking and keeping appointees, both at the Pentagon and in other sensitive slots, illustrate the depth and persistent nature of the personnel problem.

Despite all the rhetoric about vaunted management reforms, the Defense Department doesn't operate all that differently in 1995 than it did a decade ago. The concept of picking contractors based on quality, performance and ethics—rather than simply price—continues to flounder. Ancient interservice rivalries and duplication still warp and bloat military spending plans, providing giant opportunities for chicanery. Legislators generally have stuck with piecemeal and frequently pork-barrel solutions. Six years after the collapse of the Berlin Wall and four years after the disintegration of the Soviet Union, many of the Pentagon's priorities defy logic: The Marines and the Army, for example, still insist on their own tanks, artillery and helicopters. Army radios frequently cannot communicate with those found on ships, while the Marines and the Air Force look askance at refueling each other's choppers in midair. Lacking a unifying vision, each service buys hardware and trains personnel according to its own isolated view of war-fighting.

President Clinton's team is talking about chopping weapons budgets to less than half of what they were in the mid-1980s. But the defense establishment and Republican congressional leaders maintain that such cuts are too radical, too risky in a dangerous and unpredictable world. Nuclear proliferation hazards posed by North Korea, China, Iran, Iraq, Pakistan and various other Third World regimes are used to counter nearly every proposed U.S. defense cutback. Russia's potential to reemerge as a malevolent nuclear power, dominated by a military dictatorship, has become the mainstay of those opposed to unilateral U.S. reductions beyond those already under way. As a hedge against these risks, the Clinton White House has backed away from major reduction and realignment of American nuclear forces. The decision effectively locks in the number of warheads close to current levels and postpones indefinitely further nuclear-arms-reduction talks with Moscow. In short, the unfettered, anything-goes philosophy that produced a Niagara of new money for the armed forces during the 1980s continues in somewhat modified form.

Before the present round of Pentagon trimming concludes, military leaders are preparing for the next buildup. They see it as inevitable. "Reconstitution" of America's defense structure is today's catch-all phrase, referring to speedy expansion of weapons production in the event of a crisis. Republican senators make speeches about plowing an additional ninety billion dollars back into the Pentagon by the end of the decade. Clinton advisers grudgingly agree that billions are required to help improve the readiness of frontline forces. U.S. contractors today account for about 70 percent of the world's arms market, and the Pentagon is thinking about selling top-of-the-line weapons to Argentina, Brazil, Indonesia, and other countries never before offered such deals. Unless we are more vigilant than in the past, the Defense Department may once again be dominated by the go-for-broke views that were at the core of the Reagan spending drive.

At the same time, consultants and contractors working for nondefense departments and agencies have learned a great deal from history. From environmental cleanups to the nation's space program, there is ample evidence that some of the same tricks previously used to defraud the Pentagon are cropping up in civilian arenas. Investigators are discovering inflated overhead accounts, bogus consultant agreements and other familiar criminal activities. As the Clinton domestic agenda takes shape, that trend is bound to accelerate.

Finally, a healthy sense of anger is essential to put the Pentagon scandals that served as a coda to the Cold War into their proper niche. For the most part, the highest-level corporate officers who were implicated escaped unscathed. So did nearly all lawmakers. Justice Department missteps and infighting botched what could have been the most successful probe of congressional corruption since Abscam, the infamous 1980 undercover sting that nabbed seven congressmen and a senator. As one aficionado of scandals puts it: "We've simply lost our will to keep on administering Draconian punishments. It used to be that when you were indicted, it was a big deal. Now when you get indicted, it doesn't even get you uninvited to Washington dinner parties."

So what exactly happened to get us to this point? The pieces came together slowly, as I conducted interviews and burrowed through records looking for explanations. Over two and a half years, I interviewed more than 130 people around the country, from prosecutors and defense lawyers to Pentagon appointees and convicted felons. I wanted to see events from the perspectives of the victims and the accused, as well as through the eyes of investigators who unraveled their misdeeds. To tell the broadest story possible, my goal was to understand the motivations and passions of these individuals before they made national headlines, to describe their lives before and after they became part of the largest procurement scandal that ever rocked the Pentagon.

The narrative is based on firsthand sources whenever feasible, supplemented by grand jury transcripts, sworn depositions, appointment calendars, legal memos, other court documents and, in a number of instances, extensive diaries and informal notes prepared by the criminals themselves. The dialogue is reconstructed from court filings and official transcripts, or the words come directly from the recollections of persons who were involved. Descriptions of physical settings are based primarily on the author's visits to the locations. In most cases, details previously published in newspapers, magazines and books are used exclusively if they have been corroborated by the participants.

This is a cautionary tale: a story of deceit, double-dealing and disregard for the law. It shows the lengths to which large, powerful contractors went to illegally snare military business. It also explores how a flawed system not only survived but managed to thrive and hide its secrets for too long.

Above all, this book seeks to expose the criminals who wrapped themselves in the American flag just to line their own pockets. Close examination of past Pentagon and industry corruption will, I hope, protect us from such scoundrels in coming years. Understanding the mistakes may offer the strongest defense against future outrages.

Chapter I

A DISGRACEFUL AFFAIR

John Marlowe's sex drive kicked into high gear the instant he spotted the two little girls. He must have driven past the rundown Northern Virginia apartment complex hundreds of times over the years, rushing to and from appointments at the Pentagon and nearby Navy and Marine Corps offices. The cluster of three-story buildings, with their pitted red brick, peeling paint and crumbling front steps, seldom warranted a second glance. But on this particular day in March 1984, Marlowe noticed a group of children playing in an alley around the back. He decided business could wait.

Living just a few blocks from one of the busiest highway intersections in suburban Arlington—wedged between fast-food places, discount stores and strip shopping centers—residents of the Barcroft Apartments were used to intrusions. South George Mason Drive, the street that sliced through the grubby, working-class neighborhood, was a favorite shortcut for commuters heading home to the affluent subdivisions and tranquil, gently rolling horse country farther south and west of Washington, D.C. Though it was barely 4:00 P.M., already the street was jammed with impatient drivers hoping to beat rush hour traffic before the rain started again.

Recently, there had been a flurry of muggings and petty thefts around the apartments. Some tenants worried about graffiti-filled basements with unlocked doors. Others complained about boiler rooms with debris piled next to them, and deserted, poorly lit storage areas where strangers could hide. But in spite of the general disrepair—or perhaps because of the potential dangers—folks who lived at the Barcroft Apartments tried to watch out for each other. The adults knew most of the kids, if not by name at least enough to recognize faces. And one or two of the neighbors always seemed to keep an eye on the youngsters' noisy activity.

Marlowe found a parking spot near the front walkway. Making his way around the buildings and down the rear alley, he passed a pickup truck propped up on cinder blocks. The kids were romping on swings and teeter-totters despite the late afternoon chill. He chatted with them for more than half an hour. Then the distinguished-looking businessman in the brown, well-tailored suit strode briskly toward a basement laundry room accompanied by the two little girls.[1]

Preparing dinner in her cramped, two-bedroom apartment overlooking the playground, Betty Lynn McCrocklin daydreamed of the presents she expected from her family. Her father, driving from Pennsylvania with long-promised gifts in the trunk, was supposed to arrive within the hour. But as McCrocklin tidied up and eagerly watched the clock, her eyes kept wandering back to the children. Something bothered her, and the nagging feeling wouldn't disappear. The stranger and his newfound friends edged away from the rest of the youngsters. She saw them outlined clearly against the gray sky as they left the playground, walking up a small hill near the opposite end of the U-shaped courtyard. Suddenly, the figures were coming straight toward her, but still she couldn't fathom what the man wanted. She strained to pick up snatches of conversation until the trio, rattling on about playhouses in the basement, stopped right under her open kitchen window.

Marlowe wanted to be certain that the girls hadn't told anybody what happened the last time. "Did your mother ask you who I was," he kept demanding. Finally, she overheard him almost pleading in the corner of a stairwell, "I want to show you. Can I show you here?" In a furtive voice, one of the girls replied that somebody might see them. He made sure the rooms in the basement next door were deserted, and then waved to the girls to follow him down the steps.[2]

The frantic call came into the Arlington County police department before the girls ducked out of sight. Tuesday, March 6, was a miserably damp, foggy day that meant extra work for police forces throughout the Washington area. In outlying suburbs, the drizzle had turned to sleet a few hours earlier and winds gusted to twenty-three miles per hour. With the temperature dropping, roads were bound to show traces of ice by evening—exactly the type of conditions likely to rattle the region's notoriously nervous foul-weather drivers and keep harried police crews filling out accident reports. The moment McCrocklin breathlessly finished telling her story, however, the dispatcher's instructions crackled over the radio in Officer Joseph Pope's squad car. It was 5:13 P.M., and he had orders to check out the complaint immediately.

The basements of the garden apartments contained the long-forgotten junk of current and former occupants, stuff that even burglars wouldn't contemplate stealing: broken television sets, rusted tools, an ancient pair of ice skates, tattered pieces of furniture and rugs, and remnants of various other belongings nobody could recognize any longer. The spot Marlowe chose was used to store derelict washing machines. Inside the room, behind a closed door safely away from prying eyes, he laid his jacket on the lid of the nearest washer. As he dropped his pants and exposed himself, he asked one of the girls to lift up her blouse and touch him. A tenant interrupted them by coming downstairs to check his laundry in an adjoining room. Marlowe froze, signaling the girls not to make a sound as they followed the unsuspecting man's movements through the peephole left by a missing doorknob. Marlowe tugged up his underwear and zipped his pants once the intruder walked off.[3]

Minutes after receiving the call from headquarters, Officer Pope bounded down the dingy, narrow stairway and listened for motion behind the rickety metal door. Crouching next to a pile of rubbish, he raised his nightstick over his head samurai style, ready to pounce. With a loud cry, he pushed the door open. Startled, hurriedly buttoning his jacket as the policeman burst into the room, was John Pierrepont Marlowe—decorated Vietnam veteran, retired Marine Corps major and successful defense industry consultant. A few steps to his right, transfixed by the commotion, stood Kim P., age ten, and Patricia C., nine. "Nothing is going on in here," Marlowe blurted out before he was arrested.

An off-duty policeman, moonlighting as a security guard at the apartments, was so agitated when he responded to the disturbance that he threatened to pummel the suspect. "Come on, tell us what you did. Come on, tell us," the officer repeated in a menacing tone, but Marlowe remained silent. The two girls, for their part, haltingly began answering questions as soon as Marlowe was handcuffed and taken to the police station in a paddy wagon.[4]

At his trial, the girls described how on two occasions, the six-foot, 205-pound ex-Marine had lured them to basement hideaways with promises of a reward and masturbated in front of them. Their riveting testimony—coupled with the discovery of fresh semen stains at the apartments matching Marlowe's blood type—provided very strong evidence.

The case was tailor-made for Henry Hudson, Arlington County's head prosecutor, who was known for pulling out all the stops to punish sex offenders. Though he was only thirty-six, Hudson's thinning sandy brown hair, unblinking stare and measured southern drawl made him seem older—or maybe it was the combative, humorless way he went about his job. Hudson made his mark by unstinting efforts to crack down on prostitutes, pimps and drug pushers, often accompanying police officers to crime scenes and personally prosecuting the most sensational cases in his booming voice. Tenacious and single-minded were the words invariably used to describe the man. Detractors called him prudish and unyielding. "Henry is the toughest, most unrelenting prosecutor I've ever met," his old friend George Varoutsos likes to say. "But he doesn't have much of a sense of humor."[5]

A courtroom bulldog who worked as a sheriff's deputy before attending law school at night, Henry Hudson was destined for stardom in Virginia's straitlaced Republican party. He adopted a general policy of prosecuting everything to the limit, going so far as to threaten store owners with pornography charges for selling merchandise that would hardly rate a nod from police in neighboring jurisdictions. "Being a prosecutor is my whole life," Hudson once confided in a rare moment of introspection. "I offer no apologies whatsoever."

From his early days at Arlington's Wakefield High School, he dreamed of becoming a street cop over the objections of his parents. They urged him to go to medical school and make money, while he fantasized about the life of a policeman or drug agent carrying out daring undercover raids. The compromise was for him to enroll at American University's law school, where Hudson weighed his options, worked hard and discovered his calling: pursuing felons in a courtroom instead of stalking them on street corners. Working as a prosecutor kept him in touch with the precinct-house camaraderie and sense of excitement he craved, but in other ways it was a bigger thrill than actually arresting criminals. "Presenting evidence and putting a case together combined all my interests and desires," Hudson recalls. "I liked the challenge of it."[6]

Starting as an assistant commonwealth attorney, Hudson, with his rigidly conservative philosophy, raised the hackles of critics. After winning the 1979 election for chief prosecutor of the fast-growing county, Hudson stepped up his battle against street crime and prostitution—twin evils that he perceived were sapping the spirit of his beloved Arlington.

He worked hard to cultivate leaders of civic groups, neighborhood associations and similar organizations, assuring them, for instance, that massage parlors would be rooted out wherever they tried to operate. It certainly made for great publicity. But the motives went deeper. Compared with many recently transplanted northerners—people who flocked to Virginia's sprawling suburbs in search of good jobs and then ran for office pledging to reinvigorate local politics—Hudson enjoyed a tremendous advantage: a homebred, intuitive feel for the most heartfelt concerns of his constituents.

When a distraught group of motel owners complained to him over lunch that hookers loitering in their lounges and bars attracted an unsavory crowd, Hudson quickly instructed the vice squad to run the ladies out of the county. Making good on a campaign pledge, he adopted a similar hard line against residential burglars and other small-time hoods. Anyone convicted of breaking into a home in Arlington County, no matter what was taken or whether the culprit had a previous criminal record, would have to serve at least a few months in jail. "I had an obligation, a social contract with the voters, to take some corrective action; to help fashion what type of community we would have," Hudson explains. "Burglars wouldn't come near Arlington County after the message got out," he now brags. "When people tell me that a prosecutor can't make a difference, I say hogwash."[7]

Hudson's zeal riled defense lawyers, who chastised him as heartless and opportunistic. They grumbled that relatively minor offenses were dealt with as though they were heinous crimes, and that his moral crusade was preoccupied with punishment. Hudson's disdain for plea bargains, they asserted, wasted scarce law-enforcement resources. His assistants "thought nothing of threatening someone in their seventies with jail if they didn't testify against their children," according to attorney Marvin Miller, who tangled with the prosecutor in later years. These younger aides tended to share Hudson's "missionary, messianic view that they are going to save the world," Miller told *The Washington Post*.[8]

In the same vein, civil libertarians groused that some of Hudson's methods reflected a self-righteous, almost careless attitude toward the Constitution. Hudson was lampooned mercilessly by cartoonists and editorial writers nationwide for loyally serving as chairman of Attorney General Edwin Meese's ill-fated antipornography commission. Earlier in his tenure, he sparked a furor in the press by secretly tape recording a conversation between a defendant and his court-appointed defense attorney. (According to the prosecutor, the extreme measure was justified because he suspected an unethical attorney was trying to shake down a destitute client for a larger fee.)

The hubbub faded, but other slipups were more difficult to explain away. The same grand jury that accused Marlowe of sexual misconduct also embroiled Hudson in the dreadful case of David Vasquez. A reclusive and semiretarded janitor, Vasquez was charged with raping a thirty-two-year-old female lawyer in her south Arlington home and then using a piece of rope to hang her from a water pipe in the garage. The crime's brutality and senselessness stunned nearby residents. Hudson pushed hard for prosecution, in the face of contradictory evidence. Detectives failed to read Vasquez his rights and subsequently lied to him that his fingerprints were found at the scene. Hudson argued that the confessions prompted by such trickery were perfectly legal, though two separate confessions ultimately were thrown out by the courts.[9] He persuaded Vasquez to plead guilty to a second-degree murder charge. Five years later, investigators turned up new evidence definitely tying another suspect to the murder, and Virginia's governor pardoned Vasquez.

Still, Hudson kept marching on. The prosecutor's job provided great visibility and solid ties to the county's power brokers. The previous commonwealth attorney, who happened to be one of Hudson's closest friends, was preparing to don the black robes of a federal judge. But disguised by his wooden public speaking style, Hudson nurtured far more sweeping ambitions. He toyed with the idea of running for Congress or state attorney general; eventually, he mused, maybe even getting to the U.S. Senate. For someone bent on climbing so high, a reputation as a ferocious, no-holds-barred prosecutor was essential. Polishing that image was an all-consuming task.

In return, the county's voters cheered his exploits and applauded his aggressive, hands-on approach. They elected him to two consecutive terms. And Hudson reveled in the chummy, small-town atmosphere of the courthouse. He didn't have any children yet, and his grueling work schedule typically brought him to the office on weekends. The people and the constant activity inside the courthouse, to some extent, emerged as a substitute family. Serving as county prosecutor "was the most exciting job I ever had," Hudson says. "I had a very close rapport with the judges.

I knew nearly every police officer by their first name. It was an opportunity to have a really major impact on the community where I was born and raised."[10]

The fact that Marlowe, a defense industry consultant and a retired officer, was arrested down the road from Arlington Cemetery, the Iwo Jima Memorial and other shrines to past warriors also made a difference. On Hudson's turf, the military had the largest payroll and held the greatest allure for young and old alike. Most of his neighbors worked either for the Pentagon or for the multitude of large and small firms that depended on defense contracts. Hudson's wife, for instance, worked as a manpower analyst at Marine Corps headquarters. Both his mother and his father had worked for the Navy as civilians. His father-in-law spent thirty-seven years in the Army, rising to sergeant major. Understandably, Hudson detested corruption of the military's proud tradition. He became incensed with anyone or anything that bred shame or disrespect for people in uniform.

So Marlowe's indictment wasn't likely to get lost among run-of-the-mill cases. Hudson and his staff were primed to pursue such a man with special fervor. The guardian of Arlington County's rectitude couldn't afford to let this one slip away.

Barbara Walker, the Hudson assistant who handled the prosecution, repeatedly reminded the jurors how brazen Marlowe had been in approaching his victims. "Yes, he had a lot to lose," she said during the trial, but "I don't think he thought about all those people" who could identify him. There were potential witnesses in every apartment, easily able to observe him from any of the seventy-one windows that overlooked the courtyard. Common sense presumably would rule out trying to molest kids under such circumstances. But in concluding her case, Walker told the jury that "logical people don't expose themselves and entice children" for illicit basement encounters. "Something compels them to do it . . . and that's what happened here."[11]

Nevertheless, the defense put up a stiff fight. They played up Marlowe's Meritorious Service Medal from two tours in Vietnam and his twenty years of impeccable service in uniform. They emphasized their client's devotion to the community and to his four children, ranging in age from sixteen to twenty-one. There were pointed references to the top-secret Pentagon security clearance Marlowe retained, and ample discussion of the thriving defense consulting firm he ran.

Once he took the stand, with his second wife, Glenna, sitting in the courtroom, Marlowe maintained it was all a case of mistaken identity. He insisted that somebody else, possibly an older man who resembled him, appeared at the playground and later was seen hurrying out of the basement. The girls, he argued, were too frightened or confused to admit it. According to this version of events, he stopped that afternoon only because he happened to be looking for an apartment for his ex-wife. Marlowe went on to explain that the girls actually sought him out, asking help to chase away unidentified prowlers doing unmentionable "bad things" in the basement. After checking out the laundry room and finding nothing untoward, he told the jury, "I didn't particularly want to be involved," and decided to walk out at the precise moment the officer appeared. In any case, Marlowe claimed he wasn't with the girls long enough to have molested them.

Friends and business acquaintances eagerly came forward to vouch for his character. Gerald Mathison, another Pentagon consultant, told the court that the John Marlowe he knew was widely respected as "one of the most intelligent and hard-working and honest men in our business." Part of Marlowe's alibi was provided by Jack Sherman, a longtime friend and veteran Marine Corps procurement official. Sherman testified that during most of the afternoon in question, the two of them had been drinking and swapping stories at the Pawn Shop, a favorite watering hole for civil servants who worked at the Pentagon and their defense industry buddies. Upon learning of the arrest, Sherman explained in rather grandiose terms, he was overcome by "total disbelief and shock," likening the trauma to "the day that John F. Kennedy was assassinated."[12]

Defense lawyer David Sher appealed to the jury's sense of fairness and logic. Would it make sense for a man with no prior criminal record, he wondered, a highly trained, forty-one-year-old former military officer "who thinks in terms of strategy and tactics," to carry out such a crime "in front of the whole world?" In an emotional summation, the lawyer implored the jurors not to demolish everything "this honorable man" had struggled to achieve. "I can assure you," Sher concluded, that a jail sentence would be like sending him "to the gates of hell . . . There is nothing in his past to indicate such bizarre, perverted behavior. He deserves the benefit of the doubt."[13]

But the histrionics fell on deaf ears. Notwithstanding Marlowe's vehement denials and the glowing testimony of friends and associates, jurors found the evidence against him overwhelming. After less than six hours of deliberation, they convicted him on both counts of aggravated sexual battery and related charges of taking indecent liberties with minors. On March 5, 1985, almost twelve months to the day after he was dragged out of the basement at the Barcroft Apartments in disgrace, Marlowe was sentenced to six years confinement in the state correctional center at Craigsville, Virginia.

☆

Scarcely anybody paid attention to Marlowe's plight. Except for those personally involved in the court proceeding, and maybe a small circle of their friends and relatives, the sentence created barely a ripple. In Arlington County, after all, some seven hundred felonies were prosecuted each year.

And at least thirty of them involved rape or sexual attacks just as awful as Marlowe's crimes. Hudson and his prosecutors didn't attach any broader significance to his conviction, nor did the average citizen. Although a couple of brief, perfunctory newspaper stories mentioned the case involving the girls and pointed out Marlowe's military connections, public attention that spring was focused squarely across the Potomac River.

A partisan blood feud was brewing on Capitol Hill, one that dominated the headlines and threatened to spill into every congressional district across the country. President Reagan and his senior Pentagon appointees were locked in a bitter—and increasingly personal—struggle with lawmakers over continuing an unprecedented peacetime defense buildup.

The Reagan administration had pumped a total of well over $1 trillion into Pentagon accounts since taking over the White House, and proudly it projected spending at least another $1.7 trillion through the end of the 1980s. To ensure that America's military strength would be "second to none," the president and Defense Secretary Caspar Weinberger were determined to earmark fully one-third of federal outlays to the Pentagon.[14] Reagan's devotion to such steep increases was visceral—and unshakable. Whenever the president's handlers wanted a friendly crowd for a speech or simply wanted to perk up their boss, they planned a quick trip to a military base or a city dominated by large numbers of military families.[15] Reagan, who so obviously relished the salutes, parades and ceremonies during his visits with the troops, would say, with a quiver in his voice, that serving as commander in chief was "the most sacred, most important task of the presidency." And he translated those sympathies into hard-edged policy.

From the start, Reagan vowed that the Soviet Union's steadily growing military budget would be matched by American resolve and hard cash. In the long run, he could envision arms-control agreements with the Russians. But to safely reach that goal, he argued, immense U.S. defense increases were necessary in the short term. "If you were going to approach the Russians with a dove of peace in one hand," Reagan expounded on his reasoning years later, "you had to have a sword in the other."[16] Accordingly, the president bluntly told his cabinet that U.S. defense spending would be immune from mundane budget concerns. "Nothing can take precedence over rebuilding our defenses. If we have to put up with a deficit to protect our national security, that's what we're going to do."[17]

That unequivocal message soon filtered down to all of the sumptuous, high-ceilinged office suites and stuffy cubbyholes in the Pentagon. At Weinberger's level, it prompted huge increases for virtually all of the expensive weapons in production or on the drawing boards. From nuclear-tipped MX missiles and radar-evading B-2 Stealth bombers to tanks, trucks and everyday military hardware, the secretary swore to Congress that each program was critically important. Not one could be slowed down without gravely endangering national security. As an initial step to reshaping Jimmy Carter's lame-duck budget, Weinberger's staff penciled in higher numbers for nearly every category. They did it partly by rote and partly by intuition, without elaborate analysis.

At his first news conference, the defense chief spoke favorably of deploying neutron bombs able to kill people with high doses of radiation while sparing buildings and vehicles. Soon thereafter, Weinberger emphasized the need for the United States to be prepared to fight at least two major wars simultaneously—rather than the "one-and-a-half-war" doctrine that had served as the bedrock of military planning for decades. (Previous administrations had felt sanguine about coping with a major conflict in Europe as well as a "minor" war, most likely in Asia or the Caribbean.) Weinberger's goal was to double defense spending in five years, particularly, he said, to achieve "a lot bigger, stronger Navy than we had" since the Nixon era.[18] When a new generation of weapons went into production, Weinberger wouldn't tolerate discussion of eliminating purchases of equipment with older designs. He pushed for increases in some areas that even the Joint Chiefs of Staff were willing to forgo. Lawmakers, at the beginning, approved everything he desired.

The first Pentagon budget prepared entirely by Weinberger exceeded the total profits, after taxes, recorded by U.S. corporations for *any* year in history. It set defense spending approximately 50 percent higher than the *combined* federal outlays requested for health, education, job training, agriculture, energy, environmental protection, transportation, natural resources and law enforcement in the same budget.[19]

An intensely loyal man, Weinberger loved wearing presidential cuff links and a tie clip with the president's signature. Twenty-five years after he first met Reagan, then an underdog candidate for governor of California, Weinberger still gushed about the "electrifying nature" of the man's smile, and how it could literally light up an entire room.[20] In his memoirs, Weinberger dwelled on what he called Reagan's "magic"—the president's "extraordinary well honed skills" to put friends and foes at ease with delightful jokes by making them "feel as comfortable and happy as he does."[21]

Weinberger knew little about military issues when he arrived in Washington, but he had a long history of serving as an advocate for Ronald Reagan. He felt his priorities were crystal clear: carry out the Reagan defense mandate at any cost. A prominent presidential biographer has described Weinberger as "a shrewd, articulate and extremely stubborn lawyer" committed to championing whatever cause his boss favored at the moment.[22] From the beginning of his stint at the Pentagon, Weinberger lived up to that reputation. But he preferred to view his role largely in symbolic and public relations terms, leaving technical issues and thorny management problems to be handled by others.

To emphasize the rebirth of pride in the military, for example, the secretary personally ordered officers working at the Pentagon to stop wearing civilian clothes and switch back to full uniform. By contrast, when a spate of news stories blasted substandard tank engines, or reporters wrote about embarrassing glitches with the Navy's newest guided-missile cruiser, he characteristically left it to subordinates to look into the matter. Instead of pressing for specifics or demanding hard-nosed solutions, Weinberger invariably was more concerned with the public's perception of problems than with the causes of the problems themselves.[23] He mostly left it to subordinates to interact with contractors. Regardless of all the high-tech, multibillion-dollar equipment the services succeeded in acquiring under his stewardship, Weinberger remained more comfortable as the fervent salesman of the idea behind the defense buildup than as the architect responsible for drawing up the plans or checking the details.

Like the highly ritualized Japanese Kabuki dance to which he privately compared his budget battles, Weinberger stoically followed the identical moves each year: The strategy was to squeeze as much money as possible out of the House and Senate, without ever forcing senior admirals and generals to set priorities for their wish lists. He refused to budge from that prearranged script. If legislators challenged his judgment, the defense chief snapped that their primary motive was "to launch an attack on me in time for the afternoon and evening editions."[24] If accounting gimmicks fell short and critics insisted that modest cuts were unavoidable, his aides weren't permitted to come forward with a single suggestion of where to trim.

Such intransigence was quite easy to understand, the secretary explained shortly before the end of Reagan's first term: "I did not come back" to Washington "to fight the President" or urge him to temper his basic views on military growth, he said. "I have no reason whatever to believe that any of the things I've done thus far have been things that the President didn't want done."[25]

By 1985, which marked the high point of the Reagan military boom, overall defense budgets had doubled in four years. Defense production was growing three times faster than U.S. industry as a whole. And the Pentagon's "black" budget—consisting of the most highly classified programs with the least congressional oversight—reaped the greatest benefits: The most reliable estimates indicated a nearly 400 percent jump in black programs. The highest-priority research and development projects hidden in those secret accounts grew at an even faster clip.[26]

Neither the White House nor its champions on Capitol Hill described the flush days in such stark terms, but, in fact, the U.S. military was spending some $30 million every hour, twenty-four hours a day, seven days a week.[27] Pentagon expenditures equaled nearly three times the revenues of General Motors. More important, based on the painstakingly prepared graphs Weinberger relied on during his lengthy sessions before Congress, the numbers were headed for astronomical heights. In another few years, the entire bill was supposed to reach nearly $50 million per hour—or roughly $1.1 billion each day, including Sundays and holidays.

"Cappy" Weinberger, as a few close friends affectionately called him, clearly had accomplished the job. His long-term mission, though, entailed more than the impressive "top line" budget numbers he snared year after year through sheer perseverance. He also succeeded in attracting a coterie of true believers to fill other high-ranking Pentagon jobs. They included former Senate aide Richard Perle, whose hard-line Soviet views came to shape U. S. arms control strategy, and former Nixon White House aide Fred Ikle, whose deep-seated distrust of the Soviet Union was embedded in the core of the Pentagon with his confirmation as undersecretary for policy.

These were impassioned Cold War warriors. Their opinions were honed by long years of exile from power, and their convictions were hardened by the ridicule of mainstream foreign policy gurus. Now, the outsiders were sitting at the controls, and their fondest wishes were coming true. Itching to demonstrate America's military resurgence after what they considered a decade of neglect bordering on lunacy, such advisers hardly could be counted on to moderate Weinberger's stubborn streak.

Perhaps the truest believer among his trusted lieutenants—and undoubtedly the youngest and cockiest of them all—was Navy Secretary John F. Lehman, Jr. A protégé of Henry Kissinger, he had a patrician air and the formidable academic credentials to back it up. But along with an honors degree in law from Cambridge University and a Ph.D. in international affairs from the University of Pennsylvania, he possessed the drive and the street savvy of an experienced Washington turf warrior. John Lehman had toiled as head of congressional relations for the National Security Council under President Nixon, and had preached the gospel of maritime superiority ever since. Not yet thirty-nine when he joined the Reagan administration—Lehman always boasted that he landed the "best job in the world"—the dogmatic head of the Navy was the darling of conservative hawks who had President Reagan's ear.

As formal and reserved as Weinberger often was, Lehman tended to be precisely the opposite. With his slim, boyish good looks, penetrating eyes and the dapper, double-breasted blazers he favored, the former Cambridge rowing team captain embodied the assurance and high spirits he wanted to inculcate in the fleet. The jaunty Lehman also thrived on controversy, and his zest for infighting was matched by the size of his ego. The walls of his public relations officer's room were filled with framed pictures of the Navy secretary cut out from magazines and newspapers. Showing the room to visitors, another aide quipped: "This is the secretary's I-love-me room. Every once in a while he comes in here. It's an ego trip for him."[28]

Lehman plotted for over a year to fire Admiral Hyman Rickover, the legendary grandfather of the nuclear Navy, in the process outmaneuvering the service's uniformed leadership and the admiral's wide-ranging network of supporters in Congress. He also openly threatened other admirals, demoting or pushing aside those who wouldn't carry out his wishes. At other times, he was the charming, jovial team player, delighting lawmakers and Pentagon brass with his jokes. Lehman liked to engage in mild horse-play at staff meetings, amusing participants at one of Weinberger's daily morning briefings by tossing around a buoy used to detect submarines.[29]

If Weinberger was the Pentagon's quiet, steadfast chairman of the board, then Lehman was its brash, in-your-face media star. As a lieutenant commander in the Naval Reserves, he loved having his picture taken blasting off carrier decks in the cockpit of an A-6 bomber, or bantering with crew members after flying hours, still dressed in a flight suit and with his close-cropped black hair ruffled by the wind. Frequently, Lehman drove his bodyguards to distraction by ordering limousine drivers to reach breakneck speeds as they whisked him from airports to speeches during out-of-town trips. Stories of his irreverence, propensity for self-promotion and outright arrogance multiplied. The flood of publicity only added to the Navy secretary's thirst for attention. And the heads of the other services found it harder and harder to compete against him, either for public recognition or for procurement dollars.

When it came to attacking the service's Byzantine, tradition-encrusted bureaucracy, Lehman had no peer. Dismissing the acquisition structure he inherited as a "socialist culture," Secretary Lehman ordered wholesale changes designed to enhance competition and centralize control directly under his hand-picked assistants. The results were dramatic. "Lehman's combination of brilliance, brazenness, and guile," according to one veteran journalist tuned in to the Washington power game, "won him more of what he was after than any other major figure in the Pentagon, including Weinberger."[30]

Indeed, the Navy's budget goals under Lehman were strikingly ambitious. For starters, World War II–era battleships were hauled out of moth-balls at great expense. The White House and lawmakers also were persuaded to fund three additional nuclear-powered aircraft carriers—a nearly $40-billion investment considering the cost of building and manning the dozens of smaller ships required to supply and defend these behemoths. No matter where he spoke, the kinetic Navy secretary's message was the same: the glorious promise of the six-hundred-ship fleet he was building.

But lots of money was earmarked for less glamorous purposes as well. According to Lehman, he was profoundly shocked by the magnitude of the service's pent-up needs. "I was aghast to find" during the first weeks in office that "we had less than a week's supply of most major defensive missiles and torpedoes," he wrote years later. "In ships and aircraft spare parts, we had a third of the minimum requirement."[31] Personnel problems were no less daunting in his mind. Recruitment and retention of sailors was so poor, Lehman fumed, that the Navy accepted volunteers "who were illiterate, convicted felons, drug users, and worse."[32] Some ships still didn't have enough crew to leave the dock.

If anyone demanded a justification for the massive buildup, he reeled off the statistics with a vengeance. There was a messianic tinge to his arguments. "Like Paul on the road to Damascus," Lehman explained, he realized his calling was boosting the budget and the self-confidence of the Navy's officer corps. "This outfit is really in trouble," he concluded. "I want to do something about it."[33]

To get his way, Lehman perfected a knack for showmanship. In the middle of high-level Defense Department conclaves, he would pull out a dog-eared copy of the 1980 Republican party platform, which strongly endorsed a six-hundred-ship Navy. While critics attacked one of his pet projects, Lehman carefully laid the document he helped write on the conference table. Flashing a Cheshire grin, Lehman later recounted, he assured the chuckling attendees of the president's "fervent commitment to those simple and beautiful words in the platform."[34]

Much of the Navy chief's time was spent either sweet talking lawmakers in his private dining room or huddling with journalists amid the gleaming antique cabinets and polished brass that filled his office. Lehman's intensity and imperious attitude antagonized the Navy's starchy admirals—the hidebound "blue-suiters," as he disparagingly referred to them—but the approach unquestionably produced results. The Navy's prestige and clout had never been greater. Many pundits in Washington were busy handicapping Lehman's prospects to be secretary of defense in the next Republican administration. *The New York Times* glowingly described "Dr. Lehman" as a "torpedo in Washington budget wars" and "one of the most successful salesmen of the Reagan worldview."[35]

For the Reaganites running the Navy, the debate wasn't merely over dollars. In one fell swoop, Lehman and his cohorts rewrote the service's basic war-fighting doctrine. For the first time, they wanted to rely on aircraft carriers to "take the fight" closer to the Soviet shoreline. Long after departing the Pentagon, Lehman wisecracked that Weinberger graciously encouraged his subordinates to take credit for the defense transformation, even those "like me who were shrinking violets." Everyone "forgets that I really asked for 1,200 ships," Lehman said with a broad grin.[36]

With Weinberger and Lehman taking the lead, "Rearming America" became the overriding message of the early Reagan years. The slogan was embraced by politicians prospecting for votes in every region; it helped Republicans regain control of the Senate after nearly three decades. As James Wade, Jr., the Pentagon's second-ranking research official, sternly lectured lawmakers before they opened the spigot: "There can be no price tag on national survival."[37]

But by the summer of 1985, as John Marlowe appealed his sexual-battery conviction, Weinberger and Lehman were running into serious flak. Many people feared the spectacular cost of the defense expansion. The Pentagon acknowledged that the projected price tag for its eighty-four largest weapons projects rose by $25 *billion* over a three-month period. The Congressional Budget Office reported that while the Pentagon's total aircraft budget had increased by 75 percent since the beginning of the buildup, the number of planes purchased had gone up by less than 10 percent. Roughly the same proportion held true for missiles.[38] Tough questions were raised about the seemingly insatiable appetite of contractors and the lackadaisical controls adopted by their military customers. Legislative hearing rooms reverberated with shouts and accusations of corporate excess. A string of abuses enraged not only critics but also some of the Pentagon's staunchest allies in Congress. After years of docile approval of defense increases, lawmakers from both parties clamored to put a lid on military spending.

Taking advantage of mushy Pentagon rules, contractors had billed the government for babysitters for executives' children, donations to an art gallery and, in one egregious case, kennel fees for an executive's dog. Nothing was off limits for the industry's creative accountants. Boeing sought reimbursement for political contributions, promotional models, decorative key chains for elected officials and sponsoring a paper airplane contest. Firms routinely asked taxpayers to pay country-club fees and lavish entertainment expenses—sometimes to cover food and lodging given to government officials in direct violation of federal laws and rules.

General Dynamics, then the nation's number-one arms supplier, falsified vouchers to purchase gifts for a high-ranking military official. During one nasty six-hour hearing before a House subcommittee, company officials were accused of destroying internal documents to try to throw federal auditors off the trail. In hindsight, company chairman David Lewis said, "there have been some mistakes made" and certain bills "look very wrong to us." One member of the panel lambasted the firm for participating in a "textbook case of fleecing the U.S. taxpayer."[39]

Then came the horror stories of overcharges on spare parts. The $400 hammers, $600 toilet seats, $9,000 wrenches and 500 percent markups on aircraft-engine parts made lawmakers and taxpayer groups apoplectic. So did the idea of the Pentagon paying nearly $18 for a 67-cent bolt. The case of the $2,000 pliers was no less outlandish. An ashtray for a Navy Hawkeye radar plane cost $600, prompting Lehman to take disciplinary action against two officers. A coffee-brewer on the C-5A transport cost $7,400, because Air Force specifications required it to be sturdy enough to survive a crash; the commercial version cost $283 apiece. As if all that weren't enough, billions of dollars worth of spare parts in the Pentagon's inventory were discovered to be outmoded or unnecessary. Suddenly, flogging the Pentagon was the surest way for lawmakers to get press attention and prove their mettle to voters. "It was an eight-year gravy train ride," according to Democratic senator David Pryor of Arkansas. "It was the industry's finest hour in terms of balance sheets."[40]

Coming on top of the spare-parts mess, investigators launched the first wave of felony prosecutions of major defense firms. By the spring of 1985, fully half of the Defense Department's top one hundred suppliers

were under some sort of criminal investigation. The number of new defense fraud cases opened that year was four or five times higher than in
previous years. In March, General Electric was indicted and then pleaded
guilty to charges of defrauding the government by falsifying time cards
for employees working on the Minuteman missile. The legal assault forced
Pentagon damage-control crews to scramble into action. GE and several
other large contractors temporarily were suspended from receiving new
business, while others were barred for a short time from collecting overhead payments.

Senator Barry Goldwater, the feisty chairman of the Armed Services
Committee, usually could be counted on to defend the services and their
favorite suppliers. This time, however, the Arizona Republican was furious
over a $4-billion kitty of unspent funds the Pentagon miraculously found
and then, almost as an afterthought, belatedly disclosed to legislators. This
sleight-of-hand accounting made Goldwater livid. He was quoted describing Secretary Weinberger as a "goddamned fool" for failing to keep
closer track of expenditures. "When you go home, and your wife says
'What about this $600 toilet seat?' and you can't explain it, you're in bad
shape," Goldwater fumed on the Senate floor.[41]

An angry Weinberger struck back. "I was obsessed with the idea that
we might not have much time" to counter the Soviet threat, "not nearly
as much time as we had in World War II," he recalls.[42] Lawmakers had to
be made to understand that the United States was in "an absolutely vital
catch-up situation."[43] No smart-ass critics were going to block him from
carrying out the president's historic, God-given mandate. His credibility
on the line, the secretary promised to do more to eliminate overcharges
and require more thorough audits. But in the same breath, he flatly
warned congressional foes that the defense budget had to keep growing as
quickly as he wanted. Rejecting any portion of the Pentagon's spending
blueprint, Weinberger told lawmakers, would be folly and "the most dangerous thing you could do."[44]

☆

Against this backdrop of political trench warfare, the lurid behavior of
a solitary industry consultant easily could be overlooked. Marlowe wasn't
important enough for his transgressions to raise eyebrows at the Pentagon. Weinberger never heard of him or his case. Lehman had no inkling
of what had happened to the unfortunate girls in the foul basement. Similarly, no warning flags were raised inside the gleaming, modern office
towers along the Potomac—barely a few miles downstream from the
weed-covered playground of the Barcroft Apartments—where some of
the largest military contractors had their Washington headquarters. Marlowe was free on fifty thousand dollars bond and working again while his
appeal was pending. His one-man consulting outfit continued to attract

blue-chip companies such as Boeing, Lockheed, Litton, Sperry and West-inghouse as clients. The entire sordid episode seemed closed. Or so every-body thought.

By early 1986, Hudson had parlayed his law-and-order philosophy and sterling Republican credentials into one of the choicest federal prosecutor jobs in the country: As the U.S. attorney for the Eastern District of Vir-ginia, his jurisdiction extended from the Pentagon to the bustling ship-yards, thriving defense plants and major military bases scattered around Virginia's Tidewater region, more than two hundred miles away. Hudson understood the chance he took by accepting the job. Since he was now the chief federal law-enforcement official in the White House's own backyard, the attorney general and other senior Reagan administration officials would keep an unusually close watch on the cases handled by his district. On the other hand, Hudson reassured himself, lawmakers and most of his bosses in the Justice Department were itching for more Penta-gon fraud prosecutions. There surely wasn't a better place to find and pur-sue such cases—or to further dreams of higher political office—than the Eastern District of Virginia.

Hudson was still feeling his way in the new job when supervisors from the Federal Bureau of Investigation and the Naval Investigative Service showed up at his door to pass on a hot tip from a defense company exec-utive. The whistleblower complained that a small-time industry consul-tant had solicited him for a bribe, promising to deliver a Marine Corps communications contract worth several million dollars. The company of-ficial got angry enough to file a report with the bureau, and then he agreed to secretly tape a few conversations with the person who ap-proached him.

The corrupt consultant's name, incredibly enough, was John P. Mar-lowe.

At first, Hudson didn't recognize the link to his past. But after listening to excited prosecutors describe the situation more thoroughly, he realized the amazing opportunity that had fallen into his lap. Indignant over wrongdoing inside his cherished military, Hudson was determined to play out this string as far as it would go.

Two somber investigators working for Hudson barged into Marlowe's office on September 24, 1986, telling the shocked consultant they knew the details of his payoff scheme. Half an hour later, Marlowe confronted a stunning choice: He could save himself by cooperating and becoming an undercover informant for the government, or the U.S. attorney would move to revoke his bond in the child-molestation case and hit him with a barrage of new fraud charges. Frantic to stay out of jail and too shaken to call an attorney, Marlowe caved in. He secretly taped hundreds of hours of conversations with weapons buyers and fellow consultants over the next nine months. "When you have been accused of something, you do what you have to do," he explained.[45]

Without the sex conviction as leverage, investigators said later, they never would have convinced Marlowe to cooperate with the government. In the end, Marlowe's efforts to pry open the secrets of the defense fraternity were more important than headline-grabbing hearings or congressional chest thumping. Marlowe, the convicted pedophile, became the key that unlocked the cozy ties between the Pentagon, its leading suppliers and a host of elusive middlemen that fed off both.

The investigation Hudson launched with his help—dubbed "Operation Illwind"—had a more profound impact on the Defense Department's relationship with its legion of contractors than anything before or since. Voters could see the pattern of lying, cheating and other gross misdeeds that greased some of the military's buying decisions. The two scared little girls, the frightfully troubled man who accosted them and the tiny puddle of semen on the grimy basement floor turned out to be the catalyst that sparked the biggest Pentagon corruption scandal in history.

Once uncovered, the web of bribery and influence peddling stretched into the Pentagon's inner sanctum and the boardrooms of some of America's largest, most respected corporations. The tremors went all the way to the Oval Office, forcing President Reagan and later President George Bush to acknowledge that dishonesty and greed had tainted what was intended to be their greatest legacy. Ultimately, of course, the revelations devastated public confidence not only in the way the Pentagon acquires its weapons, but also in the quintessential bond of trust that must exist between citizens and the military in a democracy.

The early phases of the probe resembled "a submariner listening to the sounds of the sea" before deciding where to strike, according to Hudson. It took years to score the biggest kills and expose criminality at the highest rungs of the defense establishment. But from the start, Illwind began to lay bare the rot that existed below the glorious veneer of the $3-trillion Reagan arms-buying binge.

To be sure, suspicions of payoffs and crooked contracts had cropped up years before, especially involving the Navy. The upshot was a few low-level criminal investigations and a trickle of minor convictions. Prosecutors had been nibbling at the edges of the problem. Marlowe, at last, provided a chance to pursue major-league targets. Here was an opening to the murky world that Hudson and his investigators had yearned to penetrate for so long.

Steve Fulmer, the Navy criminal investigator who first appreciated Marlowe's potential, remembers the years of frustration trying to decipher the secret code: "Everybody suspected criminal activity was going on, but we could never find a way to break it open. You've got to have one person able to show you where the crack is, so you can start chiseling away. Until you get that, you've got nothing."[46]

The first person Marlowe fingered was none other than Jack Sherman, his favorite drinking partner from the Marine Corps. Sherman admitted collecting over $100,000 in bribes and was responsible for Marlowe's questionable alibi during the child-molestation trial. One of the next culprits caught by Hudson was Thomas Muldoon, a cunning, backslapping industry consultant who had loaned Marlowe fifteen thousand dollars to cover legal fees in that earlier case. But Sherman and Muldoon were merely supporting players in the historic drama, and the bribes that flowed through their fingers were a pittance compared with the ill-gotten fortunes pocketed by others. The names that surfaced in the wiretaps and surveillance films soon read like a *Who's Who* of America's defense community. Besides well-heeled consultants, there were veteran lawmakers, high-flying company executives and the powerful Pentagon acquisition officials with whom they partied. In addition, Hudson's net caught two of Israel's most prominent former military officials.

More than 190 individuals were under full-scale investigation at one point, including a batch of corporate chairmen, presidents and other senior officers of giant defense firms. Sixteen of the Pentagon's top twenty contractors were part of the probe. At the Navy, six of its top ten suppliers came under intense scrutiny. All told, Hudson's team issued more than eight hundred subpoenas and scoured roughly eighty contracts worth tens of billions of dollars for improprieties. Conversations were overheard in the privacy of Pentagon offices. Meanwhile, the capital buzzed with speculation of one hundred or more indictments.

The extent of the government's commitment also set Illwind apart from earlier inquiries: Well over two million documents were collected by the Justice Department; seventy-six thousand phone calls were intercepted on more than three dozen court-approved wiretaps from California to New York; and at the peak of the effort, Hudson controlled an army of nearly one thousand investigators and prosecutors. Leased warehouses were jammed with truckloads of seized evidence, and the FBI developed a sophisticated computer network to keep track of it all. Iowa's Senator Charles Grassley expressed the dismay of many when the investigation blew into the open: "The corruption that will be exposed," he predicted, "will be beyond anyone's wildest imagination."

The schemers were every bit as bold—and in certain respects, just as repulsive—as Marlowe in his attack on the innocent little girls. Like Marlowe, the conspirators thought they could act with impunity; and like him, their drive for self-gratification was so overpowering that they never contemplated the full effect of their actions on others.

Illwind hit the Navy hardest as it blew like a typhoon through the Pentagon. Lehman's confidant and top aide, Assistant Secretary Melvyn Paisley, head of all Navy research and procurement, eventually pleaded guilty to bribery and a bevy of additional felony charges. Under the guise of fostering competition, Paisley and his associates set out to enrich themselves and steer business to their buddies in industry. Not since the infamous Teapot Dome scandal of the 1920s, which cast a pall over President

Warren Harding's final days in office, had such a senior Navy official sold his office for a fee.

A tempestuous, curly-haired ex-fighter pilot, Paisley had a passion for five-star restaurants, younger women and lording it over career officers or civil servants who dared to stand in his way. His impulsive, hard-charging manner and expensive lifestyle created many enemies and fueled gossip in the Pentagon, prompting wails of protest from Navy brass. But inside the industry, intimates liked Mel Paisley for precisely the same reasons. Renowned for his lively stories and off-color gags, Paisley was admired for his panache and sharp business mind. Model airplanes filled the shelves of his office and a worn leather flight jacket hung behind his desk. Friends shrugged off his faults, kidding him for being a World War II ace who never grew up.

Lehman, too, was an ardent fan, skiing, fishing and socializing with him before and after Paisley became an assistant secretary. With his patron's un- wavering support, Paisley ran the Navy's day-to-day acquisition system al- most as a personal fiefdom. He was obdurate and gruff, demanding that contracts be rewritten or firing longtime suppliers seemingly at whim. "I won't change my mind unless John Lehman tells me to," he would bellow in his gravelly voice, jumping up and waving his arms "like a Roman em- peror," recalls one retired Air Force general.

Paisley shamelessly solicited fat consulting contracts and cushy jobs for his friends in industry, giving preferential treatment to contractors that complied. Some firms resisted and cursed him behind his back, but they had nowhere to appeal. With few exceptions, industry leaders adjusted to Paisley's way of doing business because they feared his vengeance. Those who weren't in his good graces worried about ending up on an unofficial blacklist for future Navy work. Paisley's comrade and partner in crime, consultant William Galvin, succinctly told prosecutors why companies were intimidated: "When you're in control you can do anything you want, absolutely anything you want. In some cases, we did."[47]

Before the full extent of Paisley's misdeeds was evident, Lehman called him the Navy's best assistant secretary ever. Paisley was "one of the most effective troubleshooters I have ever worked with" and a man who "spoke with an authority rare among Pentagon civilians," Lehman said.[48] Even now, after everything that has transpired, Lehman is loath to attack his onetime friend. The former Navy secretary's reputation has been stained forever by the scandal. His golden boy image has been equally tarnished, and his political aspirations may never recover. For years after the scandal broke, his mentor George Bush wanted nothing to do with him. Dreams of serving in the cabinet of some future Republican president have all but evaporated. Yet Lehman still talks about originally being attracted to Pais- ley's assertive, can-do personality: "Mel wasn't afraid to break some china to get things done."[49]

The deeper investigators dug into Paisley's conduct, the more they tried to build a case against the boss himself. Though Lehman was never officially designated a target of Illwind, agents questioned his integrity and acumen. They inspected every nuance of his personal and professional life, from fancy dinners and trips with industry executives to the accuracy of the pilot's log he kept to verify reserve training flights. Prosecutors hoped that Paisley's conviction would open up promising new avenues of investigation.

The outrages of Illwind took place, in part, because Secretary Lehman failed to keep closer track of the service's cumbersome procurement machinery. He apparently was too enamored of Paisley's show of loyalty—or perhaps his vision was clouded by the thrill of booming budgets—to pay attention to signs that the Navy was sailing toward treacherous shoals.

In retrospect, Lehman acknowledges that he received ample warnings. Bill Galvin and Mel Paisley's uncommonly close ties, for instance, prompted a rash of whispers along the Pentagon's exclusive "E Ring." Those early, confidential comments later swelled to a buzz among a wider circle of corporate and Navy decision-makers. All over town, tongues were wagging about the unbelievable team of Mel and Bill. Lehman concedes that he should have been more attuned to the potential for fraud once he heard the talk. Even Paisley's admirers, he recalls, warned, "You've got to keep an eye on him, you have to rein him in," because Mel often "erred on the side of too much activism."[50]

When the gossip became too much to ignore, Lehman told his deputy to cut off all dealings with Galvin. "It's time to get separated from that guy," the secretary said.[51] He told Paisley the same thing a number of times over the years. But the orders were halfhearted, and none of them had any effect. The response was pure Paisley: I decide who my friends are, he vowed to himself. Since Lehman also socialized extensively with somebody who worked as a consultant for major defense contractors, "Why is he telling me not to run around with Galvin?" an irate Paisley complained to family and friends.[52] Bill Galvin's instantaneous access to the Navy's hottest secrets remained unchallenged.

While at the helm, Paisley, Galvin and their cronies certainly knew what they wanted: They seemed to have abandoned all distinctions between private gain and public trust. Cocksure that nobody would unravel their plots, they divvied up lucrative Navy contracts over kitchen tables, in elegant hotel suites, amid the posh cabins of the *Queen Elizabeth II* ocean liner and frequently in the offices of industry consultants. Once, Paisley hand-picked the contractor and manager for a supersecret, $1-billion-plus radar project, and then tried to skim off millions of dollars for himself by doling out work to a subcontractor he and Galvin secretly controlled.[53] His audacity knew no bounds. Paisley hoped to snare an honorary degree for himself from Marquette University by having one of the school's administrators appointed to a prestigious Navy advisory board.

The rewards of government service were obvious to those running the scams. When Paisley left the Navy to set up his own consulting firm, he charged some clients as much as $250,000 per year. Nonetheless, one of his acquaintances considered him foolish for returning to the private sector. By surreptitiously helping the same companies from his position as assistant secretary, this admirer reasoned, Paisley "could make more money on the inside than on the outside."[54] To keep him happy, company executives purchased his condominium at an inflated price. In addition, they offered Paisley everything from free home repairs to a free pair of engines for a private plane. "We used him well and paid him," Galvin gloated from his office in Washington's famed Watergate complex, as he chatted about Paisley's complicity with another consultant.[55] It was a remarkably candid comment captured on tape by federal agents—a simple, declarative sentence that, in many ways, summed up an entire era of unchecked greed.

No one will ever know how much the phony contracts and sweetheart deals really cost taxpayers. "Bribery and information-trading were so rife that it was almost like a Third World country," notes one Pentagon veteran.[56] As a consolation, however, the government has extracted substantially more than one quarter of a billion dollars in fines and penalties from the industry, including the largest criminal settlement ever paid by a defense contractor.

In the wake of Paisley's downfall, Hudson's investigators dug up additional damaging information. High-level Air Force procurement officials were implicated in bid rigging and bribery. Prosecutors pursued lawmakers, including the powerful head of one House appropriations subcommittee, who allegedly participated in similar skulduggery. And a related probe uncovered a flourishing, nationwide black market in classified documents spirited out of the Pentagon.

Federal investigators found that a marketing wizard from Boeing, Paisley's former employer, served as the kingpin of an illegal document-swapping gang whose members traded Pentagon secrets as matter-of-factly as schoolboys exchanging baseball cards. This was no casual arrangement to quaff a couple of beers, recount old battlefield exploits and pass along the latest gossip about policy and budget deliberations inside "The Building." From the East Coast to the Pacific shore, defense industry executives secretly but methodically swapped classified documents they weren't entitled to have. Boeing snatched one memo on missile defenses intended only for the chairman of the Joint Chiefs of Staff and two cabinet members. "There were many good old boy networks, not just one," explained Richard Fowler, the Boeing executive who was applauded by superiors for corralling the document. Other contractors illegally secured highly sensitive material as well, frequently getting bootlegged copies before the originals reached their official destinations in the Pentagon. With management's support, firms used phony logs or stashed illicit documents in out-of-the-way places to fool federal inspectors.

Overall, more than ninety companies and individuals were convicted of felonies stemming from the two probes Hudson directed, including eight of the military's fifteen largest suppliers. Some were household names. Boeing, General Electric and United Technologies pleaded guilty. The others that admitted that they violated the law belonged to the cream of the Pentagon's supplier base: Hughes. Unisys. Raytheon. Loral. Litton. Teledyne. Cubic. Hazeltine. Whittaker. LTV. The drumbeat of guilty pleas included some of the nation's proudest and most profitable corporations. Grumman's former chairman and senior executives from several other firms went down the identical path. The Pentagon was forced to tighten its bidding procedures and crack down on the use of consultants. Controls on handling classified materials increased exponentially. Congress rushed to enact new laws to ensure fair competition for contracts. To top it off, the Justice Department quickly began using the same investigative techniques to untangle other areas of government corruption, from medical insurance fraud to municipal payoffs. To combat terrorism, federal prosecutors and the FBI also sought expanded authority to conduct electronic surveillance and use wiretap evidence in court.

For Hudson, however, nothing was as gratifying as nailing Mel Paisley. Three years to the day after Illwind went public, Paisley walked into a packed Alexandria, Virginia, federal courtroom to admit his guilt. Attorney General Richard Thornburgh tried to fit the scandal into a historical context. His press release heaped accolades on the long-running investigation, calling it "the most sweeping and successful operation against white-collar fraud and defense procurement ever carried out by the Justice Department."

Understandably, industry bigwigs bristled at such talk, complaining that the frenzy of news stories was the product of a "lynch mob" mentality. They tried to dismiss Illwind as the fault of a few warped individuals rather than an indictment of the broader procurement system. Corporate chiefs hurriedly organized ethics workshops for employees. They ordered up training programs and hired in-house "ombudsmen" to follow up whistleblower complaints and ferret out wrongdoing. Chastened by the public's anger, defense firms solemnly promised to disclose lawbreaking, promptly and on their own, before government agencies got involved. "I cannot hire auditors and lawyers fast enough," fumed Bernard Schwartz, chairman of Loral, a fast-growing defense electronics powerhouse.

Given the level of government audits, "Our companies are probably the most ethically aware group of any industry," argued Don Fuqua, president of the Aerospace Industries Association. "There has been a total change in the environment . . . we can't even take the folks at the Pentagon out to lunch," he said after Illwind was wrapped up. "During the buildup, government and industry weren't as concerned with some of those things; I guarantee you that they are now."[57]

But the same executives acknowledged that it was impossible to completely root out corruption. How can any large firm, they demanded, possibly be expected to vouch that tens of thousands of workers every day are in full compliance with a staggering number of arcane Pentagon regulations? Lockheed's chairman compared his situation to that of the mayor of a good-sized community. "I don't know of a city with 90,000 people that doesn't have a police force and a jail," he said. "Even in the monasteries, some of the monks are probably misbehaving," snapped William Anders, the chairman of General Dynamics.[58]

In the final analysis, such rationalizations miss the mark. The disgrace of Illwind encompasses much more than the criminals who knowingly violated the law. Military and industry officials at all levels must share the blame. There were some who conveniently looked the other way, and many others who lacked the courage to speak out against the reckless and indecent things they witnessed.

In their unseemly rush to funnel money to the Pentagon, cow the bureaucracy and keep weapons factories humming, Reagan and his acolytes created the perfect breeding ground for the indefensible activities at the heart of this book. The story of Illwind also reveals a corporate culture willing and often eager to use any methods to fatten the bottom line.

Weinberger and Lehman portrayed themselves as disciplined, market-oriented managers, bent on instilling a new ethic of efficiency and accountability in the Pentagon. In fact, what they oversaw was an age of lawlessness. "The reality they created was exactly the opposite" of what they professed, according to Senator Carl Levin, a liberal Democrat who opposed the buildup. Reagan's true believers "turned out to be pitifully poor managers," the Michigan lawmaker asserts, who left behind "a decade of real shame" that saddled the military with "more anticompetitive practices and sloppy management than any other time in the twentieth century."[59]

Beyond a doubt, Paisley, Galvin and the companies that relied on them inflicted worse pain on the Pentagon than the indictments and court transcripts reflect. They did more than corrupt specific contracts or give certain companies an unfair edge in bidding for business. The avarice that drove these men, combined with the breakdown of institutional controls and ethical standards in the Pentagon, helped sap public support for defense spending—perhaps for an entire generation. Looking back, Caspar Weinberger grudgingly sees the lasting nature of the damage. Voter approval for defense increases "is a very ephemeral thing," he notes, because "people in democracies don't like to spend money on the military." Paisley and his crew "obviously undermined some of the public support that was necessary," Weinberger now concedes.[60]

Many who had a ringside seat trace the mistakes to the top of Ronald Reagan's administration. By focusing so intently on a six-hundred-ship Navy and other doctrinaire goals, the president and Pentagon leaders neglected the details of how the money was being spent. "They lost sight of what was going on right under their own noses," Levin says.[61]

For the Navy, Lehman and Paisley ushered in one of the darkest periods since the bleak days following Pearl Harbor. Mismanagement, corruption and fundamental questions about its role in the post–Cold War world left the Navy adrift, suffering from a crisis of direction. Resentment that built up during the 1980s against what many considered Navy arrogance—both on Capitol Hill and inside the Pentagon—exploded with a vengeance. Not long after the Weinberger team bailed out, the service's top four aircraft programs were axed unceremoniously. Keeping the fleet from sinking below 350 ships became the measure of success. The sexual attack allegations stemming from the notorious "Tailhook" convention, followed by an internal probe that ended in a fiasco, further undercut public confidence in the caliber of the Navy's leadership. And overshadowing all these reverses was the shining promise of the Navy during the Reagan years, when it received more respect and support from Congress and the White House than any of the other armed forces.

Weinberger's departure from the Pentagon, a few months before Illwind became public, prompted a stream of flowery tributes. "I am confident that you will be remembered as the most distinguished and effective Secretary of Defense in our nation's history," President Reagan said in a flattering two-page personal letter accepting Weinberger's resignation "with the deepest regret." Your "incomparable service," Reagan wrote, "set an example in cracking down on waste and abuse" and reassured "American taxpayers that their hard-earned monies are being properly and efficiently utilized."

Today, given the details of what Paisley and his confederates did, the sentiments have a hollow, mocking ring.

The breakneck defense buildup of the early 1980s was supposed to usher in a marvelous golden age for the U.S. military, an epoch of unparalleled growth and respect. Ironically, the most enduring legacy of that period may be buried in stacks of wiretap transcripts heaped on the dusty shelves of FBI storage vaults. The chilling conversations captured on those pages—peppered with the funny and sometimes obscene boasts of insiders impudently breaking the law—reflect an utter disregard for the public and its tax dollars. Some of the investigation's targets ridiculed law enforcement. For "all the money I pay you," one industry official joked with his Pentagon contact, "I hope the FBI is listening."[62]

During one of the earliest exchanges, Marlowe and Sherman tried to negotiate a bribe for landing a Marine Corps contract. With agents hanging on every word, they pondered the risk they were running. The only way the government could stumble on the crime, they kidded each other, was if the FBI somehow managed to secretly record their discussions. Both men chuckled at the improbable notion. It was too far-fetched to worry about. Finally, Sherman jumped at the bait. His cocky response said it all: "We'll never get caught; we'll never get caught. I'm sure of it."[63]

Chapter II

THE SPOILS OF VICTORY

Well before Ronald Reagan locked up his party's presidential nomination in July 1980, the nation's defense contractors savored their impending good fortune. Among the industry's elite, Boeing had the most reason to celebrate. One of its top executives was busy helping Reagan campaign aides draw up huge Pentagon budget increases for the next administration. Boeing stood to reap untold billions of extra dollars in revenue. Indeed, like other weapons–makers, it already relished the prospect of having Reagan in the White House for a full eight years.

Benjamin T. Plymale, an immensely talented but eccentric engineer, was recruited by the Reagan camp to identify where the additional defense dollars should go. Revered as a founding father of Boeing's military operations, he was a pioneer in radar, missile guidance and multiple-warhead technology. With degrees in physics and mathematics from the University of Portland in Oregon, Plymale rose rapidly to become a vice-president responsible for the company's space programs. Later, he was put in charge of all of Boeing's nuclear missile work. As the venerable jet maker's business with the Pentagon grew over the years, Plymale also earned a reputation as an ingenious salesman and consummate power broker in Washington, D.C. He loved to hold court at his favorite hotel, the Colonial-style Georgetown Inn. Private meeting rooms were set aside, where he and other Boeing executives could work, gossip and catch up on industry news with Pentagon brass.

For nearly thirty years, Plymale developed complex theories of nuclear deterrence and bemoaned the government's lack of understanding and shortage of money to carry them out. Now, it was time to see if he could turn those dreams into reality. Not surprisingly, Reagan's advisers gave him the toughest job of all: proposing specific budget figures for every major weapon under production or consideration by the services.

A workaholic who in the past had not thought twice about dictating memos from a hospital bed, Plymale threw himself into his new task. He crammed large, three-ring white binders full of detailed program-by-program cost information. The budget documents filled a twenty-foot-long bookshelf, but Plymale demanded ever more data. He cajoled and browbeat assistants to crank out more and more analyses on selected weapons. Missiles, bombers, tanks, aircraft, submarines and surface ships—all of them would be neatly categorized and evaluated by the time election day came around. At the age of fifty-four and in spite of his poor health—he was suffering from cancer, had a badly damaged heart and had recently dropped more than sixty pounds off his five-foot-eleven-inch frame— Ben Plymale became Boeing's point man in the Reagan defense revolution.

Nobody could question his credentials as a nuclear-arms expert or as an astute observer of Pentagon politics. A president of Boeing's aerospace division considered him "a one-man think tank" on grave issues of nuclear vulnerability and survival. Fellow executives turned to him for advice on budgets and research, praising him as Boeing's resident "Buddha of strategic thinking."[1] They used to smile when Plymale, engaged in a heated debate about some obscure point, would use his pet phrase to clinch the argument: "Don't you see? It's intuitively obvious!"

Reagan's handlers were so confident of victory that they began preparations for an elaborate military buildup in the spring, while still in the middle of a hard-fought Republican primary race. Reagan titillated contractors with promises of the most sweeping defense hikes since the peak at the end of World War II. Even the Korean War spending increases paled by comparison. The upcoming election wasn't about minor policy adjustments or tinkering at the margins of Pentagon spending, the candidate told audiences everywhere he went. Voters faced a stark choice between weakness and strength, according to Reagan, because the Soviet Union was bent on establishing superiority in nuclear as well as conventional weapons. Without a crash effort to boost defense expenditures, he suggested, the survival of the United States could be in jeopardy. Speaking to the Chicago Council on Foreign Relations that March, Reagan was in especially fine form. "In military strength, we are already second to one: namely, the Soviet Union. And that is a very dangerous position in which to be."[2]

Such stump speeches pleased the defense community tremendously and generated great enthusiasm from crowds at campaign rallies. But they didn't reveal how much Reagan really wanted to spend on defense, or which companies would benefit the most. Behind the scenes, Plymale and a handful of senior advisers were supposed to answer precisely those questions. Amid all the uncertainty, one thing seemed clear: If Reagan captured the White House, the initial blueprint they presented to him was likely to determine the shape of America's defense industry for the foreseeable future. It would be the benchmark for decisions long after Inauguration Day.

The press knew almost nothing about the campaign's defense-related planning, let alone the extent of industry's involvement in it. Voters didn't really sense the scope of the increases that were in the offing. Plymale wanted to spend at least $200 billion more for defense by 1988. At the upper range of his projections, he fashioned plans exceeding Carter's defense outlays by a whopping $1 trillion over the same period. Plymale didn't want premature publicity. He moved carefully and methodically, relying on his instincts and broad experience to come up with numbers and arguments Reagan would find the most convincing.

The other pillar of Reagan's brain trust for defense was William Van Cleave, a forty-five-year-old former arms-control negotiator and a professor of international relations at the University of Southern California. His hard-line view of the Soviet Union, combined with a stubborn, abrasive manner, left little room for compromise. Before taking leave from his teaching post to join the Reagan team, Van Cleave had built much of his professional reputation pondering the unthinkable: He lectured and wrote extensively about the Soviet leadership's investment in super-accurate, long-range missiles supposedly designed to blackmail the United States in a crisis—and ultimately, he insisted, to prevail in a nuclear exchange between the superpowers. News stories described him as a lone wolf, living in the high California desert one hundred miles from his office, a man obsessed with doomsday scenarios and what he saw as the pervasive spinelessness of the civilians running the Pentagon.[3]

While still in his thirties, Van Cleave helped negotiate the original SALT pact during the Nixon years. But then he grew disenchanted with Henry Kissinger's overtures to the Kremlin and turned into one of the treaty's most ardent critics. His public unhappiness over the negotiations caused a flap. Before leaving his job at the Pentagon as a special assistant to Defense Secretary Melvin Laird, Van Cleave was suspected of leaking information to the press that was potentially damaging to the talks. He subsequently claimed that he took three separate FBI lie-detector tests and "came out absolutely clear."[4]

An ex-Marine grunt whose polyester suits and straightforward speaking style reflected his midwestern roots, Van Cleave ridiculed the "Gucci-loafer set" that he claimed dominated U.S. arms-control policies. There were too many self-important Ivy League graduates in high-level defense jobs, he angrily told friends and students after his experience in the Defense Department. The unrealistic, romanticized versions of Soviet society put forward by those appointees, Van Cleave complained, were as dangerous as they were mistaken.

Van Cleave hardly behaved like an intellectual firebrand. He wore bulky plaid pants and unfashionably wide ties. His hair was plastered on his head in a utilitarian cut. But in his businesslike, almost bland way, Van Cleave teamed with Plymale to propound frightening theories that shook up mainstream Washington. Soviet generals and admirals, according to their philosophy, didn't share Western-style principles of decency, logical limits and self-preservation. Van Cleave and Plymale saw the Kremlin's quest for military preeminence as relentless: Russian leaders were willing to pay any price and take any gamble to achieve it—including the awful risk of full-fledged nuclear war.

During the grueling months leading up to Reagan's November election, as well as the heady days right after it, Van Cleave and Plymale struggled to compile a defense plan to quell their fears. Old friends and philosophical soulmates, they had toiled together in the Pentagon during the Nixon administration and imagined ways to overhaul U.S. nuclear doctrine. Their assessment of Soviet intentions influenced Reagan's thinking not only on the campaign trail, but for much of his tenure in the White House.

From the beginning of the 1980 campaign, Reagan wholeheartedly embraced the notion that the Soviets were outspending the Pentagon on nuclear arms by almost a three-to-one margin. During an interview with editors and reporters of *The Washington Post* in mid-June, Reagan was explicit and adamant about the necessity for an arms race. It "would be of great benefit to the United States if we started a buildup" to eliminate the Soviets' advantage, he told the journalists.[5] Speeches and press conferences were tailored to drive home the same message—for both domestic and foreign audiences. "I deliberately set out to say some frank things about the Russians," Reagan wrote in his autobiography, to make sure they knew "there were some new fellows in Washington who had a realistic view of what they were up to and weren't going to let them" continue. "We were going to spend whatever it took to stay ahead of them in the arms race."[6]

The greatest impact on Reagan, though, may have come from three simple words: "window of vulnerability." Van Cleave takes credit for coining the phrase in 1976, when he helped out on Reagan's first, ill-fated run for the White House. Others claim they came up with the principle earlier. Regardless, Reagan adopted it and used it effectively throughout the next decade. Eventually, it merged into official Washington's vocabulary and became the foundation for conventional wisdom. The ominous phrase referred to a gap between the Soviets' rapidly improving nuclear arsenal and the less-potent, 1960s-vintage Minuteman missiles that were the mainstay of the Pentagon's land-based nuclear deterrence. Van Cleave maintained that the enemy's new generation of improved intercontinental ballistic missiles—equipped with more precise and dependable guidance systems than the West ever expected—made U.S. missile silos vulnerable to a surprise attack.

American submarines and bombers would be able to retaliate if fighting erupted. But Van Cleave, Plymale and other proponents of this theory sketched out a nightmarish spiral of events. Once most U.S. ICBMs were destroyed or put out of commission, they asserted, the Pentagon wouldn't have enough warheads left to wipe out all of the heavily protected Soviet missile silos, launching centers and underground command bunkers. America's submarine-launched missiles would not be accurate enough, and slower-moving bombers would take too long to deliver their payloads. Russian commanders, therefore, would threaten to use their remaining missiles for a direct attack on Washington, New York, Los

Angeles, Chicago and other metropolitan centers—putting 80 million or 100 million people in jeopardy. No American president would dare to call their bluff, and in the end, the Soviet Union would achieve domination around the globe.[7]

If this "window" wasn't closed quickly, Van Cleave and Plymale insisted, American forces and cities increasingly would be in danger of annihilation from a massive first strike by the Kremlin. They were convinced that the mere threat of such an attack could be enough to force any U.S. government to capitulate.[8] Unless the nation embarked on a dramatically different course, the two warned Reagan in a confidential report delivered shortly after the election, the world faced a perilous era of unfettered Soviet military adventurism: "The imminence and seriousness of this situation cannot be overstated."[9] The answer, they said, was to make immediate "fixes" to military hardware, and Van Cleave and Plymale were determined to be the tough, no-nonsense repairmen to get that done.

Many arms-control experts disputed their assumptions, dismissing Van Cleave and Plymale as leaders of an extremist faction of right-wing Reagan supporters—condescendingly dubbed "The California Primals."[10] The nuclear-tipped missiles on a *single* Poseidon submarine, President Jimmy Carter pointed out in his 1979 State of the Union Address, carried enough warheads "to destroy every large and medium-sized city in the Soviet Union." Moreover, submarines easily could avoid detection by Russian satellites. Inside the State Department and the Pentagon, Democrats scurried to find more evidence to rebut Reagan's alarmist judgments. Harold Brown, Carter's defense chief, decried the lunacy of matching the Soviets warhead for warhead and trying to quantify which side would emerge victorious from a nuclear war. In a personal note inserted in the Pentagon's closely watched "posture statement" in 1980, Brown said that threats of pulling the nuclear trigger "would constitute an unprecedented disaster" for both sides. He added that neither country, no matter what new weapons it possessed or what its politicians and generals argued, would be able to keep a limited nuclear confrontation "from escalating to a full-scale thermonuclear exchange."[11]

But for Reagan's aides and backers, the logic behind the "window of vulnerability" was irrefutable, and shutting the window became their supreme goal. The wealthy and elderly "Kitchen Cabinet"—an influential though unofficial group of advisers that included Colorado beer magnate Joseph Coors, Reagan's longtime Los Angeles attorney William French Smith and Nevada Senator Paul Laxalt—particularly shared the grim outlook. They saw Reagan's candidacy as a historic turning point for the country, and they expected him to step up Pentagon spending at the expense of domestic priorities. Even among Reagan's supporters, however, few people expressed their anti-Soviet sentiments quite as vehemently as Bill Van Cleave and his right-hand man, Plymale.

Before the July 1980 GOP convention in Detroit, Van Cleave and Dick

Allen, another trusted national security campaign aide, searched for ways to shore up their candidate's international-relations credentials. They assembled an advisory group of roughly one hundred defense and foreign-policy luminaries, including some of the most experienced executives from large defense firms, to help refine Reagan's positions. The sheer number and prominence of the names attracted media attention. Captains of the conservative movement rallied behind Reagan, notably at one of the early meetings held in the International Club on K Street in Washington, located a few blocks from the White House in the city's exclusive office district.

Van Cleave was one of three main coordinators for the five-hour event. Other featured slots went to well-known industry consultant John Lehman, already angling for a job in the Reagan transition; his hawkish and outspoken consulting partner Richard Perle, destined to become the Reagan crowd's arms-control chieftain; Fred Ikle, a former disarmament official and senior Rand analyst disgusted with Soviet belligerence; and Jeane Kirkpatrick, who went on to serve as Reagan's United Nations representative.

But inside the campaign, everyone knew who was calling the shots on Pentagon spending. Before Reagan flew off to Detroit, Van Cleave approached him with a novel and ambitious proposition, something no previous administration-in-waiting had ever attempted. He wanted to tap the expertise of the campaign advisory panels in order to draft a detailed blueprint for defense outlays through 1988. Top-notch industry executives, influential scientists and distinguished former government officials were members. "Why don't I put them to work; I mean, really put them to work?" Van Cleave asked Reagan during a private chat. "Not just for the campaign, but to come up with a real plan" for stepped-up weapons purchases that could be carried out by Reagan appointees immediately after election day.[12]

President Carter, by contrast, had hardly given a thought to defense budget decisions until two weeks before moving into the White House. Van Cleave and Plymale desperately wanted to avoid that. To pull off his bold idea, Van Cleave asked to be placed in charge of the transition team for the Pentagon after the election. His deputy would be Plymale. That would allow them to get an inside look at the military's most closely guarded financial secrets. With Reagan's imprimatur, nothing would be out of bounds; all of the Pentagon's highly classified budget data would be accessible.

Van Cleave's crew wanted to review and then incorporate internal Pentagon budget documents into its own spending road map. By comparing their projections with numbers developed by the Joint Chiefs of Staff, they hoped to paint a comprehensive, unvarnished picture of the advanced weapons best suited for the battlefield of the 1990s. Naturally, the team also would find out the research programs generals and admirals were content to see wither and die. For any secretary of defense—and surely for his largest contractors—identifying political losers was almost as important as supporting technological winners. Van Cleave had all this in mind when he broached the idea.

"I need to get into the building, to negotiate with the services about their needs," Van Cleave explained to Reagan.[13] By Inauguration Day, the transition team pledged to deliver a long-term spending package for approval by the president and whoever his defense secretary turned out to be. The preliminary spade work, Van Cleave explained later, was intended to get critical programs under way "without watching the Pentagon spin its wheels for a year" after the election.[14] What he didn't mention during the meeting, but clearly had in the back of his mind even then, was a strong desire to do more than simply write a report. Van Cleave, the loyal spear carrier, was counting on Reagan to nominate him for one of the top jobs in the Pentagon so he could personally implement the spending plans after January 20.

Ordering up a preelection defense budget caught Reagan's fancy. After a brief discussion, Van Cleave recalls, "I got the charter to do just that."[15] Within a few weeks, Reagan left for a tumultuous reception at the Detroit Civic Center, where he accepted the nomination and picked up momentum for his upcoming campaign against the Democrats. Van Cleave was also in the hall that sweltering week in July, joining Lehman and others to shepherd the platform through the convention. The rest of Reagan's coterie of defense advisers stayed behind in Washington, going to work in earnest with their briefing books and calculators.

☆

Based on his résumé and reputation, Ben Plymale seemed an ideal choice to craft Reagan's defense plans. He had cut his management teeth on Boeing's original Minuteman contract, which was an enormous technical success and one of the firm's cash cows. More than one thousand of the missiles were built, and in some years they accounted for the majority of the company's income. Boeing was still making big money producing updated versions nearly eighteen years after the first Minuteman was placed in the ground. Hidden in steel and concrete silos across the midwestern plains and designed to reach Russian targets at twenty times the speed of sound, the missiles were stark reminders of the life-and-death struggle Reagan and his advisers kept talking about. Boeing's official history book, published many years later, raved about the Minuteman as "a sword of Damocles poised over the Soviet Union during the most frigid years of the Cold War."[16] (Upgraded Minuteman III missiles still provide the core of America's nuclear forces. The forty-ton, solid-fuel missiles can deliver three nuclear warheads to targets more than six thousand miles away, and installation of new electronic components will extend their useful life beyond the year 2020.)

Inside Boeing, there was a definite mystique surrounding the project. It was a badge of honor to call yourself one of the early "Minutemaners," and people associated with the missile's growing pains climbed to high-level jobs at the company. Thornton Arnold Wilson, the sharp-tongued manager who was in charge of the Minuteman program at its inception, used it as a springboard to become Boeing's chairman. The trademark of "T" (as everybody called him) was a fearsome temper and an acute distaste for corporate regulations. Friends said he had a tough, blue-collar personality combined with a white-collar mentality that drove him to succeed.

As a young engineer, Wilson actually was a dedicated labor organizer. He was on the seven-member executive board of Boeing's in-house union, the Seattle Professional Engineering Employees Association, representing some twenty thousand engineers and technicians. Before joining management, the chairman-to-be left his mark by railing at those employees who chose not to join the union. Later in life, the same ornery independence served as his guide. Inside Boeing's boardroom, for instance, he was known for having a mesmerizing grasp of technical detail. Like other up-and-coming executives, he was sent by Boeing to MIT on a Sloan Fellowship. But his love of crude language never subsided. With a hawk nose and "eyes of feral acuity," according to one biographer's description, Wilson peppered every technical treatise with barnyard epithets "in his fruity native Missouri timbre."[17] Between the curses, Wilson routinely slipped off his shoes during important meetings, propped his stockinged feet on the nearest desk or conference table and silently challenged anyone in the room to complain.

No matter what the odds, Wilson was impulsive and intuitive. When the 747 jumbo jet development program was hemorrhaging, it was "T" who ordered draconian layoffs on the production line to control the losses—and then mercilessly pushed for further cutbacks in headquarters staff. "We can afford no more tolerance towards employees who do not produce or whose capabilities are marginal," he declared.[18] Despite his taunts, Wilson liked people who weren't afraid to talk back to him, which explains why he was drawn to maverick personalities such as Plymale. And he retained a soft spot in his heart for compatriots from the old days, giving them plenty of leeway to run other projects.

As chairman, Wilson fondly recalled Minuteman startup problems. He regaled his listeners with stories of test missiles exploding mysteriously in midair, and the tension of using the fledgling Minuteman to scare Fidel Castro during the 1962 Cuban Missile Crisis. Plymale felt close enough to the volatile Wilson to kid him about embellishing and repeating the same moldy anecdotes. "T," he chided one day, "you either gotta get some new stories or some new friends."[19]

Since the Minuteman's heyday, Plymale's stature and responsibilities had increased dramatically. From 1968 to 1972, he held a high-ranking research post in the Pentagon, advising the secretary of defense. As a matter of policy, Boeing liked to loan fast-rising executives to the government for a couple of years. It bred good will for the company and demonstrated the high caliber of its people. For Boeing, the practice also ensured a steady stream of up-to-the-minute intelligence about what was happening inside the services and the secretary's office. Armed with his fresh government contacts and insights about the status of nuclear-missile research, Plymale returned to Seattle and soon was assigned to head all new business development for Boeing Aerospace. The promotion seemed to be natural, combining his engineering strengths with his financial savvy.

Plymale's importance to Boeing, though, went beyond technical or manufacturing knowledge. Boeing used him to predict which programs were likely to fare best inside the Pentagon, and what research strategies the firm should pursue to maximize chances of winning those contracts. After Boeing's board of directors approved overall research budgets, Plymale was in charge of parceling out the money to defense projects he considered most promising. "Ben was a commonsense, down-to-earth genius," according to Van Cleave, because "he understood very well all the practical things" on top of the abstruse scientific questions affecting the arms race. "I've never seen anybody command the respect among top scientists that Ben did."[20] He could "cut through technical bullshit in a matter of seconds," says another admirer.

Plymale was part of a cadre of young, hard-charging engineers who hung on to T Wilson's coattails and capitalized on their Minuteman ties to take control of Boeing's entire defense operation by the 1970s. Their meteoric rise was envied and discussed inside the company. Oliver Boileau, Mark Miller, Bud Hebeler and their associates all belonged to the Minuteman clique—and each one was rewarded with a senior executive job. Mel Paisley, another principal member of the group, had the closest personal bond to Plymale. He was Plymale's favorite fishing partner and foil for off-color jokes. Paisley, who went to the same Portland high school as Plymale, was both a close friend and a protégé.

In a succession of marketing jobs, the affable, devil-may-care Paisley developed a reputation as a buccaneer. He stood out from Boeing's typically sedate management, racking up two-hundred-dollar-a-night hotel bills with abandon, using helicopters when limousines or even taxis would do just as well, and flaunting a succession of young girlfriends. Once he arranged to have a female Boeing employee fly from London to attend company meetings with him in a fancy Washington hotel when none of the other participants could figure out what official reason she had to be there. A second coworker, also young and female, accompanied him on foreign sales trips ranging from Australia to Germany.

While other Boeing executives attended Chamber of Commerce seminars and donated their time to help local charities through an organization called the Employees Good Neighbor Fund, the flamboyant Paisley went his own way. He partied ferociously, boasting to associates about hiring prostitutes while traveling on company business. The somber gray sameness of the "Seattle school of business and social intercourse," as one writer put it, never affected Paisley.[21] He certainly wasn't gracious, nor did he exhibit the earnestness that many of Boeing's technically rigorous executives seemed to exude. He didn't seem concerned about clambering up the corporate ladder, but the choice assignments and promotions kept coming. Plymale's prodigal friend seemed to be answerable to no one. In middle age, he tried to seduce the twentysomething daughter of his high-school sweetheart, according to a former top Boeing executive. "Mel is such a complex yet simple personality," one of his oldest friends marveled years later. "His penis has guided him most of his life."[22]

Some colleagues got a vicarious thrill from Paisley's exploits. Many more were offended by his behavior and language, every bit as vulgar as T Wilson's. But Plymale remained a solid friend through all the criticism, generally laughing off Paisley's escapades. He continued to loan Paisley tools, chainsaws and even a truck, and then ribbed him mercilessly for always returning the items in terrible condition. Other friends worried that Paisley's extracurricular activities could hurt his career, and they wondered how much of his personal entertainment wound up on expense reports billed to the government. Darrell Cole, one of his superiors, recalls fielding suspicious questions from Boeing accountants about Paisley's expenses in the early 1970s. "I just told him, you have to quit screwing around on these things."[23] Cole claims the reprimand succeeded in curbing Paisley's excesses, but others weren't convinced.

Insiders say Plymale and Wilson tended to disregard Paisley's antics partly because they enjoyed his macho, irrepressible personality. They never gave Paisley more than a slap on the wrist, considering him an effective salesman with wonderful connections overseas. Inevitably, the whispers spread around the company's Seattle headquarters: Mel and a few others got preferential treatment because they were part of T's crazy Minuteman brigade.

From a broader perspective, Minuteman was a pivotal factor in the company's evolution from a successful, albeit narrowly focused, airplane maker to a world-renowned industrial behemoth. Defense orders had been important to Boeing ever since its first few aircraft, made of wood and fabric, were sold as trainers for Navy seaplane pilots before World War I. Through the 1920s and 1930s, Boeing gained fame as a builder of agile single-seat fighters. When World War II erupted, it assembled the lumbering four-engine bombers, the B-17 Flying Fortresses, able to carry more than two tons of bombs at an altitude of thirty-six thousand feet to pound German cities into rubble. And the company built the *Enola Gay*, the B-29 Superfortress that dropped the first atomic bomb on Japan in August 1945.

When it came to the Minuteman program, Boeing actually manufactured a very small part of the missiles themselves. But it was hired to put everything together, to make sure that the sophisticated computers, solid-fuel propellant and guidance systems meshed properly. Boeing built the silos, tested the missiles, trained the crews and was responsible for maintaining all the equipment. The extraordinarily close ties that developed between the company and the Pentagon on Minuteman became a model for managing future weapons projects. Boeing and Air Force officials had such good rapport and understood each other's problems so well, Paisley liked to joke, that "pretty soon you couldn't see the difference between them." That symbiotic relationship paid off handsomely. Boeing ultimately collected nearly half of all Minuteman revenues, becoming the Air Force's favorite supplier in the process.

With the success of the missile, Boeing transformed itself from primarily an airframe builder to a high-tech aerospace giant ready to take on the challenges of space exploration. It was no surprise that Minuteman prompted Boeing to create a separate aerospace division. As the company's historian concluded: The missile proved that Boeing and its leaders were "capable of taking on any task as people began to look at the heavens in a new way."[24] By 1979, when Reagan launched his race for the White House, the world's most successful manufacturer of commercial jets had catapulted over other firms to grab the spot as the country's fourth-largest military contractor. Boeing was the unchallenged leader in supplying the Pentagon with nuclear hardware. T Wilson and Ben Plymale, a pair of aging warhorses, resolved to make it number one in all defense categories.

To a large extent, Boeing's concentration on defense business reflected economic pressures quite apart from its involvement in the Reagan campaign. A sluggish economy, high interest rates and soaring oil prices severely depressed orders for its new 757 and 767 airliners. During the early Carter years, commercial sales brought in four of every five dollars of corporate profit.[25] Suddenly, the numbers were flipping completely in the other direction. Pentagon contracts would have to provide the vast majority of earnings; it was the only way Boeing could weather the rough times ahead. Having recently lost a bid to build the Air Force's swing-wing B-1 bomber—one of the Pentagon's true megaprojects—the company was searching anxiously for sources of revenue to plug that gap.

Under President Reagan, Boeing shed its traditionally cautious bidding practices, lowballing defense contracts and thrusting itself into projects without getting a firm handle on the technical or financial variables.[26] The company assigned as many engineers to defense projects as it had working on commercial aircraft. Wilson accepted the risks because he understood, better than most of his employees, the indispensable contribution of military business to Boeing's continued vitality. A company director once asked him, "What percentage of military business would you like to have?" Without hesitation, Wilson replied: "All I can get."[27]

Plymale wasn't putting in his marathon weeks—commuting from Seattle to Washington several times a month—just to help Reagan. Early in the campaign, he and Van Cleave settled on proposals to boost the capability of U.S. nuclear forces—and also improve Boeing's own fortunes.

They analyzed the possibility of making existing Minuteman batteries mobile, by constructing some five thousand new silos and moving the missiles around to confuse the Russians. "The country has invested probably $20 billion or more in Minuteman," Plymale told an industry publication in one of his rare public statements. "We have to fix it so it isn't vulnerable."[28] The fix, costing as much as $15 billion, entailed restarting the Minuteman production line.

Another recommendation called for accelerated production of the Air Launched Cruise Missile, a state-of-the-art weapon built by Boeing and carried by the company's B-52 bombers. Boeing had just spent $50 million to erect a sparkling new, automated plant in suburban Seattle to manufacture the missiles using robots. Air Force orders for the ALCM program alone were expected to total as much as $3 billion. In addition, the Air Force was urged to increase purchases of AWACS radar surveillance planes also built by Boeing.

Van Cleave claimed the proposals transcended institutional rivalries and parochial budget disputes between Pentagon factions. Besides Boeing, other contractors were slated to receive hefty new orders, too. At the same time, the door was thrown wide open for top-ranking generals and admirals to promote alternate spending wish lists. "We are trying to stimulate the services to come up with their own programs," Van Cleave told the industry.[29]

Further down the road, Plymale and Van Cleave envisioned shuttling the Air Force's blockbuster MX missiles among hundreds, and perhaps thousands, of still-to-be-built shelters. Boeing anticipated landing some business to supply part of the MX's firing system, and it hoped to win major contracts building the vehicles and shelters that would transport and protect the missiles. All of the moves advocated by Van Cleave and Plymale were consistent with Reagan's oft-stated goal of providing a "quick fix" to close the "window of vulnerability." Many of the suggestions had been kicking around for years, supported by groups and individuals with absolutely no affiliation with Boeing. Some were advanced by the Pentagon before the 1980 campaign ever kicked off.

Still, Boeing was in perfect position to reap the benefits of any defense increases. Plymale was a master at acquiring data and massaging budgets. He knew what Boeing had to do to stay at the front of the pack. He also appreciated what it would take to sell the Pentagon and Congress—or the public, for that matter—on the panoply of expensive new weapon programs Ronald Reagan wanted. (As a matter of fact, the company's military sales more than doubled during the first two Reagan years.)

Though Plymale and Van Cleave were kindred spirits on professional issues, the Boeing engineer's personal life was an entirely different matter. Plymale was a true iconoclast, unwilling to live by the safe, middle-class norms of Seattle—a city dominated by "Mother Boeing," as some executives joked. He talked like a farmer and doted over an ancient, repeatedly wrecked Ford Mustang with more than two hundred thousand miles on the odometer, maintaining that nobody else could fix it. Brusque and profane, Plymale antagonized fellow employees with his mockery. At backyard parties and barbecues, he got a kick out of recounting how his kids poached salmon out of protected streams and sold the fish to unsuspecting customers. It grated on the respectful, industrious values of most Boeing executives. "Ben enjoyed tweaking the system, just to show he could beat it," says Seattle attorney Richard Brothers, a friend whose former wife worked as Plymale's secretary.[30]

In a conservative company that refused to serve alcoholic beverages on its property as late as the 1970s, the demeanor of men like Plymale and Paisley stuck out. Plymale, for one, drank gin heavily and did little to hide his alcohol habit. Darrell Cole, the executive who warned Paisley to be more precise on his expense reports, also socialized with Plymale during the same period. An avid fisherman, Plymale joined Cole and his wife one morning at four o'clock to take a motorboat out for a leisurely fishing excursion. Mrs. Cole offered the bleary-eyed sailors steaming mugs of coffee. Plymale asked if there was any booze on board. According to Cole, he proceeded to fill a glass full of gin and drink all of it down in a few quick swallows, without any ice.[31] Almost everyone who dealt with Plymale, friends and critics alike, recalls similar stories about his phenomenal alcohol consumption. Business guests were dumbstruck when Plymale invited them to what he called a "gin lunch." He downed four or five glasses of gin with the meal, and then went back to his Pentagon office hours later to work on a report or memo he had left half-finished.

After a particularly wild night of carousing when he was still a relatively low-level executive, Plymale found himself featured the next day in one of Seattle's newspapers. A traffic accident on Friday night, long after working hours, had left him and his beloved 1965 Mustang banged up. A car had stalled out in the middle of an expressway exit ramp, and Plymale's car pounded into its rear. His head went through the windshield. Unfortunately, his young girlfriend, who happened to be driving him home that evening, also was injured in the crash. She was hammered against the steering wheel. A picture of the accident scene, with the bleeding female victim slumped next to the wreck, made the Saturday morning editions. Plymale's wife was enraged. The messy divorce after twenty years of marriage shocked Boeing's staid management ranks, though it presented only a temporary setback to Plymale's career plans.

Plymale learned from his miserably bad luck with traffic infractions. He started carrying two spare tires in his car, so that when he smashed against median strips or other obstacles there would be a greater chance to keep the Mustang rolling. One night in Washington, three of his tires blew out when the car jumped a curb. He called a friend the next morning, laughing and yelling about what additional precautions he could take to avoid being stranded.

During his stint in the Pentagon, Plymale lived in Annapolis, on the shore of Maryland's Chesapeake Bay and a good hour's drive from the capital. No matter how late it was or how bad driving conditions were, he insisted on getting behind the wheel. Driving home intoxicated in the middle of a vicious thunderstorm, with Paisley sitting nervously next to him, Plymale had great difficulty seeing the winding country road. Paisley, who wasn't a heavy drinker, wanted to stop, but Plymale was adamant about pushing on. Chatting about his friend's poor hearing, suddenly Ben Plymale took off his glasses. The aged Mustang started swerving between lanes. No problem, Plymale reassured his passenger with the wave of a hand: "We'll make it. You can see for me, and I'll hear for you."[32]

The same mordant humor showed up at unexpected times. Plymale, who also drove an oversize Buick station wagon, used to tease his wife about the size of the burial plot reserved for the family. "Just put me in the Buick," he'd say. "Make sure the grave is big enough for both of us."[33] Plymale knew his lifestyle was slowly killing him, and he became fanatical about diet and exercise after suffering a life-threatening heart attack in his later years. At a dinner party hosted by the Paisleys, when he was recuperating from the heart problems and cancer already had taken one of his lungs, Plymale was asked why he stopped drinking but continued to smoke. "That's easy," he snapped. "A person starts out with two lungs, but you only have one liver."

In many respects, Plymale was a contradiction: a throwback to an earlier, more independent way of life. His father died when Plymale was a child, and friends sensed that he used sarcasm as a shield because he never completely recovered from the trauma of a lonely, difficult adolescence in Portland. The family was well off, though that didn't keep him from getting into scrapes with the law as a teenager. Later, he had plenty of expenses to worry about raising his own brood of ten children. Plymale was obsessively frugal in buying clothes, appliances and almost everything else for the family. But friends recall that he was obstinate about not allowing anyone else to pick up a bar tab or a check in a restaurant. "He never took anything from anybody; he was very strict about that," his good friend James Gaines recalls. Another thoroughly old-fashioned trait was his profound distrust of anything connected with Wall Street. Gaines says that Plymale's widow ended up with nine hundred thousand dollars stashed in ordinary savings accounts, since he refused to invest in stocks and bonds.[34]

Plymale thought of himself as a lady's man, even though his gruff style and sloppy dress upset the wives of most fellow executives. He wouldn't think twice about wearing sneakers or a ratty leather jacket, complete with oil stains, to some swanky corporate affair. The medicine he took to control his epilepsy turned his teeth a dark color and ultimately forced him to wear dentures. Other guests could never figure out whether he simply didn't pay attention to his appearance, or if his nonconformist getup was one more way to thumb his nose at Boeing's rules.

Plymale could be mulish, even hostile with friends. One year, he agreed to help edit a doctoral dissertation on arms control written by a company official who worked for him in Washington. Plymale returned the draft with no editing changes, merely tiny little checks placed in the corner of nearly each page. The author, who everybody thought was one of Plymale's favorite assistants, dared to ask what the checks meant. "You idiot," Plymale replied irritably. "Those are the pages that are all wrong." Thoroughly intimidated, the student nevertheless wanted a little more explanation about how to correct the mistakes. "You're the guy getting the Ph.D.," an exasperated Plymale finally barked at him. "And you're too dumb to know that?"[35]

Behind the rough exterior, Plymale was the ultimate professional. He had a knack for the kind of nuclear calculus the Reaganites put their faith in. Unlike Van Cleave, however, the chain-smoking Boeing executive also was a crafty marketeer. Plymale prodded Boeing to get serious about selling to the government. He set up thirteen marketing offices nationwide to get closer to military customers. He hired retired officers to collect budget documents from friends they left behind in the Pentagon, creating an information network that was the envy of the industry. Boeing's top decision-makers didn't ask many questions about how Plymale collected his nuggets, though they came to rely on the steady stream of inside information his troops supplied. "Program managers constantly would call demanding some document or other," says Charles Welling, who ran the marketing offices. "If they got a little bit, they always wanted more. It was indicative of a sickness that afflicted the whole industry."[36]

Much of the material shouldn't have left the Pentagon at all. Plymale's hand-picked assistants supervised a clandestine library back at headquarters—stocked by officials flying around the country to pick up sensitive documents—so Boeing managers would be confident of having the most up-to-date intelligence about internal Pentagon spending plans.

Through the fall and past election eve, Van Cleave and Plymale slogged on with their budget drills. Their exultation at Reagan's overwhelming victory was tempered only by concerns that the president-elect's transition team for the Pentagon would be expanded to include new faces, perhaps less committed than the two of them to across-the-board defense increases. They needn't have worried. In the end, Reagan appointed a thirteen-member team, formally headed by Van Cleave as expected, that mirrored the campaign's strident anti-Soviet theme. The new arrivals included Roland Herbst, a leading nuclear-weapons physicist who had worked closely with Plymale inside the Pentagon, and retired Air Force officer William Graham, another longtime proponent of Van Cleave's "window of vulnerability" argument. Herbst and Graham ran R&D Associates, a California-based think tank and consulting firm that serviced a glittering list of clients including the Pentagon, federal weapons laboratories running highly classified projects and some military contractors.

Other defense industry heavyweights also came to feast on the spoils of victory: Robert Silverstein, a brilliant, thirty-six-year-old aeronautical engineer, was a vice-president in Northrop's Washington, D.C., office and went on to be a prime strategist in marketing the firm's B-2 Stealth bomber to Congress. Before joining Northrop, he ran TRW's strategic studies operation in the capital. Silverstein had tremendous contacts in every corner of the intelligence community, his area of concentration during the transition. Richard Perle—John Lehman's partner in Abington Corporation, another politically well-connected consulting outfit—also moved into the transition team's office suite on the Pentagon's hushed E Ring, just a few doors down from the secretary's private conference room. As a former top aide to Democratic senator Henry Jackson of Washington, Perle's voice carried great weight with Boeing and other major industry players.

Much has been written about Ronald Reagan's ability, especially during his first few months in office, to translate vague conservative principles into concrete policies. Commentators have ascribed Reagan's success to several attributes: his immense popularity, a willingness to delegate authority and a shrewd sense of spending political capital only on one or two issues that really mattered. In the realm of defense, however, another reason was paramount: The core group of people advising Reagan knew each other and worked intimately on exactly the same issues for many years, often a decade or more. "We don't have an organizational chart," one transition aide quipped. "The unit is a team."[37]

Van Cleave was an active member of the Committee on the Present Danger, an ad hoc coalition of businessmen, labor leaders and former government officials formed in 1976 to promote increased defense expenditures. Reagan proudly counted himself a charter member, along with many of his senior advisers. Some members used to plot strategy in Abington's Washington offices. George Shultz, Richard Allen, Paul Nitze and William Casey belonged to the committee, as did Lehman, Ikle and Perle. All of them received weighty appointments in the administration. According to one account, fifty-one born-again Soviet foes who were part of the committee found government jobs under Reagan and firmly established control of nuclear policy.[38]

Indeed, Van Cleave's association with a number of these Cold War warriors had started years before the campaign, when they participated in a controversial gambit to second-guess the CIA's assessment of Soviet intentions. The potent language and sweeping assertions of the so-called "Team B" report—the most hotly debated intelligence estimate of the Iron Curtain era—created a bombshell at the time.[39] Even today, it has a horrific quality. Van Cleave and other conservatives were given unprecedented access to top-secret CIA archives while they prepared the study. They concluded that for the Soviets, détente and arms-control treaties were simply avenues to try to compete militarily with the West. The report's climax was stunning: "While hoping to crush [the U.S.] by other than military means," it concluded, Soviet Union leaders were "nevertheless preparing for a Third World War as if it were unavoidable."

Such extreme sentiments carried over to the Reagan campaign. Outsiders were struck by the frequent, almost nonchalant discussions of nuclear-war-fighting tactics. "The precise calculations and the cool, comfortable vocabulary" belied the ghastliness of a superpower clash, as one industry critic described it afterward.[40] The gap between computerized war games and blood-curdling reality distorted the judgment of Van Cleave and his supporters. When "the analysts bent over their computers," according to another observer, they were "transfixed by scenarios of a seemingly endless war; eighty million dead on either side, a government gradually crawling from the wreckage, a new series of nuclear salvos and counterstrikes."[41]

This was the mindset of the true believers helping Van Cleave and Plymale in 1980. T. K. Jones, another Boeing official close to the transition, showed how far the anti-Soviet dogma could be pushed. Jones had made his mark by computing that *only* ten million Soviet citizens were likely to be killed in a nuclear exchange, which he concluded was a small enough price to tempt the Kremlin to launch an attack against the United States. After getting a powerful job in the Reagan Pentagon, he made national headlines by declaring that Americans should know how to construct makeshift civil defense shelters. In the event of nuclear war, Jones urged families to "dig a hole, cover it with a couple of doors and then throw three feet of dirt of top . . . If there are enough shovels to go around, everybody's going to make it."[42]

In their own way, members of the transition group were just as fanatical. Morally certain that their mandate was nothing short of rescuing the country from a nuclear holocaust, they devised plans to spend and buy as much as possible. None of them worried about the dangers of duplication, production inefficiencies or possible price gouging by contractors. "We had gotten so far behind the Soviets, and we had so much to do to catch up," Van Cleave recalls, that there was scant interest in thinking about anything that could delay or distract the Pentagon from that goal.

More than a decade later, congressional auditors accused Van Cleave and the Reagan Pentagon of misleading and lying to lawmakers to justify the $350-billion nuclear-arms buildup. The General Accounting Office, in a classified, eight-volume report completed in June 1993, concluded that the military understated the cost of many big-ticket weapons. The GAO also determined that the Pentagon deliberately overstated the radar-evading capabilities of new U.S. bombers and exaggerated the threat posed by Soviet weapons and defenses.[43] Claiming that its study was the first top-to-bottom analysis of the 1980s buildup compiled by a federal agency independent of the Pentagon, the GAO blasted Reagan administration officials for creating a hyperbolic image of American vulnerability. According to the GAO's investigators, the Pentagon overstated

the necessity of the buildup, it relied on "unconvincing rationales" for development of nuclear arms in the first place and it often devised insuffi-
cient tests after weapons came off the assembly line.[44]

In 1980, however, fretting about acquisition rules and legal niceties was
anathema to the transition group; so were any concerns that certain contractors might gain an unfair advantage by obtaining preliminary budget
details. Compared to preventing nuclear Armageddon, protecting taxpayers' wallets seemed just a bit too mundane. "If some of the money is
wasted," Van Cleave admits thinking at the time, "let's go ahead anyway, if
that's necessary to get the important things done."[45]

☆

Plymale's transition role epitomized the Reagan administration's blindness to ethical problems. First, a handful of critics muttered about his ties
to Boeing. Reporters picked up and fleshed out those complaints. Predictably, editorial writers carped that defense executives—regardless of
whether they were on unpaid leave or remained on corporate payrolls—
shouldn't take part in transition activities. Incoming administrations in recent memory, according to these critics, had excluded industry officials
from important transition responsibilities to avoid the taint of conflict of
interest.

Just as predictably, Reagan aides became angry and defensive. Then
they went on the offensive, blasting Democratic activists and public interest groups for blowing the matter out of proportion. The president-elect
needs and deserves the best possible advice on rebuilding the military,
Reagan spokesman James Brady said. "You have to have people with
some experience and expertise" to do that.[46] If the criteria to serve on
transition teams are unduly restrictive, Brady wisecracked, "all we can
have is a 15-year-old nun."[47]

Charles Kupperman, a fellow member of the advance team at the Pentagon, also jumped to Plymale's defense. He called him a "good engineer"
with a keen understanding of defense strategy and production. "If we're
serious about" boosting defense, Kupperman told reporters, "that's the
kind of people we need."[48]

All around Washington, similar tugs-of-war played out at other agencies. The skirmishes between Carter's old guard and the advance parties of
the new regime not only were contentious, but they raised thorny legal
questions about conflicts between public and private interests during a
period of political musical chairs.[49] At the Energy Department, Carter appointees balked at turning over lists of prospective enforcement cases to a
transition team headed by an independent oil producer and his deputy, a
lawyer whose firm represented Standard Oil of California. At the Labor
Department, reports surfaced that Reagan's deputy team leader had filed a
friend-of-the-court brief with the Supreme Court challenging the de-

partment's enforcement of occupational safety laws. The most direct confrontation occurred at the Agriculture Department, where Assistant Secretary Carol Tucker Foreman refused to turn over option papers dealing with pending regulatory matters. Information about labeling of cured pork products had been requested by a transition team member. His real job was as a lobbyist for the National Pork Producers Council.[50]

From a partisan standpoint, the clashes were inevitable. There was an element of sour grapes on the part of the defeated party, and excessive exuberance by the victors as they rushed to grab the reins of power. Brady, Reagan's press spokesman, tried to cut through the din by announcing that transition officials would fill out conflict-of-interest forms and disqualify themselves in any conceivably questionable situation. Teams of volunteer Reagan attorneys fanned out to agencies to resolve questions. Arguing that Reagan loyalists were doing more than the law required, Brady insisted that "we have rejected having anyone serving" in any role "where they have a vested interest."

But questions about Plymale persisted. Reagan's advisers investigated his background in detail, Brady said, and found much ado about nothing. "He's near retirement age; and he's in the commercial plane program," the spokesman asserted.[51] The comment seemed straightforward enough.

In Ben Plymale's case, however, that was a less than forthright explanation of his checkered past. Less than two years earlier, he had been banished from Boeing's defense unit in disgrace and sent over to Boeing's commercial airplane division. The reason for the transfer was a criminal investigation of Plymale for illegally ferreting out top-secret Pentagon information about the MX missile.

Defense Department investigators pieced together an incredible story. Plymale, along with several Boeing officials working for him, managed to gain unauthorized access to a draft memo on the future of the MX prepared for President Carter. Disregarding the most basic security rules, they rushed to transmit the highly classified information to Boeing aerospace offices in Kent, Washington, by a telecopier over normal telephone lines—which the Pentagon believed routinely were monitored by Soviet intelligence agents.[52] Furthermore, once the misdeeds came under scrutiny, federal investigators accused the Boeing crew of engaging in a dogged coverup. According to a March 1979 report by the Defense Department's assistant general counsel, Plymale and a number of other employees conspired to try to hide their guilt by destroying evidence, fabricating documents and refusing to talk to investigators.[53]

It wasn't a coincidence that Plymale went to great lengths, and risked so much personally, to read that memo. Arguments about whether to deploy the new, nuclear-armed MX or upgrade Boeing's existing arsenal of smaller Minuteman missiles were at the top of the agenda for Carter and his top-level Pentagon appointees throughout 1978 and 1979. The decision, in effect, would lock in American arms-control concepts until the beginning of the next century. For Boeing, the outcome would determine whether the firm won or lost one of the prime chunks of Pentagon business.

The bizarre saga of the MX memo—a tortuous tale of deceit that attracted attention all the way up to Defense Secretary Brown and Boeing chairman Wilson—illustrated Plymale's cavalier view of the law. The episode revealed a great deal about the company's culture as well. Boeing's intense desire for inside information, whether it came from the Pentagon or other sources, was an integral part of its drive to succeed. It was one more way to get a jump on the competition. "The Country Boys from Behind the Cascades," as Boeing's executives were nicknamed by competitors, clearly were no rubes when it came to snaring industry or military secrets. Plymale, who ran the intelligence-gathering effort, was largely responsible for creating and satisfying that hunger at the highest levels of the corporation.

Ten years after the MX flap, when the Reagan buildup had taken place, Plymale's legacy came back to haunt the company. One of the little-known, midlevel employees he hired—a former Air Force budget analyst named Richard Fowler, whom the government quizzed about the MX memo—was prosecuted in a separate case for improperly obtaining more than a thousand other classified Pentagon documents through the mid-1980s. Fowler, who got his original marching orders straight from Plymale, was reputed to be the best in the business at cornering hot government memos. His conviction shook up Boeing's defense subsidiary and the tightly knit circle of marketing executives from other large contractors with whom he dealt. Boeing admitted its guilt in a document-swapping ring that focused on long-range military spending plans. In 1989, the company paid more than $5 million in criminal fines and penalties, with red-faced officials agreeing to tighten procedures for handling classified material.

Dan Pinick, head of Boeing's defense activities after the case was closed, didn't mince words about what happened. Lured by the promise of Pentagon largess, he told *The Wall Street Journal*, "We pushed too hard."[54]

The roots of that attitude can be traced back to a balmy spring day in March 1978, more than a decade earlier. Ben Plymale talked amiably with Seymour Zeiberg, one of Secretary Brown's deputies, amid the palm trees and ocean breezes at a defense conference in Santa Monica, California. Zeiberg was doing the same job for Carter that Plymale had done years before when Republicans controlled the White House. Plymale had supported his appointment, and the two men were friends. Before going to dinner, they went up to Plymale's hotel room for a private chat. Zeiberg said he wanted Boeing to know the administration's general thoughts about MX missiles. Always eager to impress his buddy in the Pentagon, Plymale cut him off. "My guys already told me, they got that information last week," he blurted out. "I'm way ahead of you." With gin glass firmly in hand, he reeled off in minute detail the Pentagon's options for deploying the MX.[55]

The longer they talked, the more visibly upset Zeiberg became. He was astounded that Plymale knew the intricate twists and turns of Pentagon deliberations, particularly since Carter hadn't yet seen the memo marked top secret, or made up his mind on the issue. Increasingly agitated, Zeiberg demanded to know how Plymale got hold of papers intended for the White House. Realizing the seriousness of his mistake, the Boeing executive ducked the question.

A furious Zeiberg flew back to Washington. He briefed Brown, who disliked Plymale from previous policy rifts. The secretary promptly ordered a top-priority probe of the leak. Carter's folks were upset, among other things, that the memo could have tipped off the Soviets to U.S. arms-control initiatives.

As the government discovered, Plymale actually had instructed one of his marketing assistants to round up the memo, titled "MX and Alternatives," as soon as he learned Zeiberg's office was writing it for the president. A Boeing official temporarily assigned to the Pentagon—another friend of Plymale's, naturally—obtained a bootleg copy of the draft and slipped it to the Air Force. A few days later, a sympathetic Air Force colonel allowed Plymale's assistant to read it and take notes. Within hours, a summary was on the way to Plymale's office in Washington state.

From the beginning, Boeing knew it was treading on dangerous turf. Charlie Welling, Plymale's corporate contact in the capital, gave him an immediate heads-up that the information coming on the telecopier "was extremely sensitive in my view, and they ought to treat it accordingly." The company's Washington, D.C., representative knew about handling Pentagon data acquired through illicit channels, but this was in a different league. "I don't usually call the vice president and tell him to be careful" before sending along the information, Welling acknowledged to investigators months later.[56]

Boeing and the Air Force were exceedingly eager to read Zeiberg's memo because one of the options called for placing Lockheed-built Trident missiles—designed for launch from submarines—in Minuteman silos. Such a Navy-inspired solution would have embarrassed the Air Force, while reducing Boeing's chances of winning future missile contracts.[57] "We were desperate to find out what was going to happen on the basing," Welling recalls.[58]

Company executives lied repeatedly to investigators in a vain bid to conceal their tracks. Initially, Welling swore that he knew nothing about the Zeiberg memo and got all of his information from "general observation and discussion among people interested in the MX."[59] As the Pentagon's inquiry heated up, Plymale, Welling and the others panicked. They concocted a ludicrous cover story. Plymale insisted that he had found a telecopied report containing the information on his desk early one morning, delivered in a plain brown, unmarked envelope by an unknown source. "That's what you will tell investigators," Plymale instructed Welling in emphatic tones, ordering him and everyone else to "tough out" the probe. "It was the dumbest thing I ever heard of," Welling now admits. But if "the boss man says do it, you tend to do it."[60]

When Russell Light, the head of Boeing's Washington office, learned how badly Plymale had screwed up, he was in shock. "Jesus Christ," he told Welling, "if you are interviewed again, for God's sake tell the truth."[61]

Ironically, Carter never actually got the notorious memo. But the escapade cost Plymale a fair amount of discomfort. In 1979, he and four others were disciplined for what Boeing diplomatically described as "handling classified information without appropriate safeguards." His secretary was threatened with summary firing. Other Plymale accomplices inside the company were demoted, shunted to dead-end jobs and had their salaries reduced. Some were forced to take early retirement. Two Pentagon officials were barred temporarily from working on missile programs.

Plymale's own security clearance was suspended, and his vice-presidential title was stripped away; the worst punishment, though, was reassignment to Boeing's commercial airplane division. Plymale complained about being exiled to "purgatory," and he never forgave Chairman Wilson, his old crony, for issuing the order. "Ben always was very critical of Wilson for doing it to him," says Plymale's friend Jim Gaines.

Chairman Wilson reacted quickly in other ways to protect the company. He assured the Pentagon that Boeing took the breach of security seriously, reminding employees that they shouldn't "solicit or accept classified matter" unless they had a legitimate need to know the information and would safeguard it. Boeing's public mea culpa got the government off its back in short order. The criminal investigation dragged on for a few more months, as prosecutors granted immunity to the assistant who snatched a look at the memo. But no charges were ever filed. Nobody above Plymale was punished, though Welling insists that higher-ranking executives "were intimately familiar with the memo's contents" and knew exactly how the information was gathered.[62]

Years later, critics said Boeing's actions amounted to a sham—a series of public relations moves calculated to convince the government that it had cleaned house so it wouldn't sacrifice any Pentagon contracts. The president of Boeing Aerospace determined that Welling had committed a "serious offense" by misleading Pentagon investigators. The punishment was laughable: Welling lost two weeks' pay. He also received an attractive severance package to encourage him to leave the company once the storm blew over.[63]

Plymale, for his part, was credited with doing an excellent job ironing out glitches in the navigation systems and cockpit instrumentation of Boeing's wide-bodied 757 and 767 airliners. By the spring of 1980, barely two years after the MX memo debacle, he was agitating to return to military pursuits. "I've been in the jail box long enough," he joked with his pals. "There's a time for forgiveness."[64] Chairman Wilson eventually obliged, though it isn't clear how much lost pay, bonuses and other perks Plymale was able to recover. Some of Plymale's superiors hinted that he never got back to his original salary level. But upon returning to the company's good graces, Plymale and his second wife maintained that the demotion and the transfers didn't cost them a penny of his benefits. Wilson backed their version of events to the hilt.

In any event, by the time Plymale joined the Reagan transition team, his security clearance had been restored. Reagan aides knew about his run-in with the law. Van Cleave was fully aware of the facts, having helped Plymale raise money to hire an attorney during the Justice Department investigation. Other Reagan intimates also knew about the MX memo, but it didn't make any difference. The president-elect's spokesmen admonished skeptical reporters that Plymale had been "fully exonerated." The rehabilitation was so complete that in late December 1980, barely three weeks from Ronald Reagan's swearing-in, news reports touted Plymale as the next head of research at the Pentagon. The cunning fox was back doing what he loved best—collecting intelligence for Boeing's defense business. Only this time, he was on the inside.

By any objective standard, Plymale's work for the transition should have been subject to tougher guidelines. He had unrestricted entree to the Pentagon's innermost secrets, from confidential budget projections to top-secret performance reports on specific weapons. Eager to please the new administration, the military opened up its information banks. Some of the material it turned over would have been extremely difficult, if not outright impossible, for an industry executive to see otherwise. Yet there were no clear-cut rules about the Reagan transition team's handling of the documents, or what information could be disseminated to other corporate officials.

Eight years later, President Bush imposed a blanket restriction on anyone using inside information acquired during the transition for personal gain. President Bill Clinton would go further, barring his aides for six months after the 1993 inauguration from lobbying federal agencies they had dealt with in the course of the transition. Clinton's guidelines also disqualified transition workers from activities or decisions that conflicted—or even appeared to conflict—with their family or business financial interests.

But in 1980, Reagan's aides were focused too much on the importance of the defense buildup to bother with such considerations. Contractor abuse of Pentagon information "wasn't anything I was worrying about," Van Cleave now explains. "It might have been careless of me, but it was not a major concern."[65] Plymale's ensuing behavior demonstrated how sizable a mistake that was.

Long after Reagan's permanent team had established control at the

Pentagon, Boeing continued to seek out documents at a furious pace. With or without Plymale's guidance, its executives had no illusions about what the company expected of them. Welling, Plymale's sidekick during the MX controversy, describes it best. "In over forty years in this business," he says, "I have never known a corporate management that desired or accepted the amount of raw intelligence that Boeing did."[66]

☆

The long flight from Washington to San Francisco in late December 1980 was nerve-wracking for Van Cleave and Plymale. Since it was the last Friday before Christmas, airports and planes were mobbed by holiday travelers. The harried crowds, mounds of luggage and hyperkinetic atmosphere made traveling difficult. But that wasn't the reason for the tense and worried look on the faces of the two transition officials. They hardly noticed the whirl of activity. Instead, they agonized over what Caspar Weinberger, President-elect Reagan's recently announced nominee for secretary of defense, would say when they briefed him on their work the next day.

In the race for the top spot at the Pentagon, Van Cleave and Plymale plainly had wagered everything on the wrong horse. Weinberger, a surprise entry, had come in first, and now the chits were coming due.

From the middle of the presidential campaign, Van Cleave had painstakingly kept Texas senator John Tower and former defense secretary Donald Rumsfeld informed about the budget package he and Plymale were assembling—confident that one of those two GOP stalwarts would be named Reagan's defense chief. Often, there were daily updates on progress. Van Cleave was close to both men, and felt he could work well with either one. Weinberger, on the other hand, was an unknown quantity. Van Cleave had butted heads with him or his stand-ins several times in the past few months, and the encounters left a bad taste in the transition team leader's mouth.

As early as September 1980, Van Cleave tussled with Reagan's handlers about defense-spending projections. Martin Anderson, the campaign's chief domestic-policy adviser, was among those questioning how politically smart—or economically feasible—Van Cleave's defense prescriptions were. Van Cleave wanted to maintain "complete flexibility" to avoid being pinned down to premature numbers that might act as a ceiling. "Let Reagan get elected without any commitments to specific dollar figures for defense," Van Cleave told Anderson hours before an important economic speech, then the administration "would be free to do whatever" it wanted.[67] Van Cleave lost that fight to the political pragmatists on the campaign plane, but the wrangling over the issue escalated.

During a staff meeting several weeks later, Weinberger told Reagan to use 5 percent as the likely annual increase in Pentagon spending. "Cap, you don't know anything about this," Van Cleave shot back, telling Reagan to "please stop using" the number.[68] Reagan's instincts said Van Cleave was right, though he tried to avoid a confrontation. Van Cleave got his revenge by publicly asserting that 5 percent was dangerously inadequate.

The sharpest disagreement of the campaign occurred shortly before election day. Holed up at a Virginia country estate formerly owned by Jacqueline Onassis, Reagan was preparing for his upcoming televised debate with Carter. Van Cleave, playing the role of a reporter, tossed the candidate a question about increasing the defense budget. Reagan used the 5 percent figure again. "No, no. That's wrong," Van Cleave interrupted, arguing that Reagan's best response would be to say, "We're going to increase enough to restore a margin of safety." Weinberger weighed in loudly on the other side. The rest of the advisers stood on the sidelines as the two men railed at each other. "That was a real clash," according to Van Cleave.[69]

If anything, the tension got worse after the election. Van Cleave and Weinberger knew the stakes suddenly had been raised; much more hung in the balance than pride. Reagan picked Weinberger partly because aides reminded him of the catchy moniker, "Cap the Knife," that the nominee had earned as Nixon's budget director, when he mercilessly slashed agency spending. The president-elect thought that the choice—and the cost-conscious attitude Weinberger's nickname symbolized—would be well received by the public. "Cap Weinberger is anything but a big spender," Reagan said. "I can assure you that Cap is going to do a lot of trimming over there."[70]

The nominee, in turn, demanded that Frank Carlucci, another Nixon budgeteer and one of Van Cleave's most bitter enemies, be named deputy secretary. Weinberger said he wouldn't accept the job otherwise. It was obvious that Weinberger and Carlucci had no room for Van Cleave or any of his spear carriers inside the Pentagon. "Why don't you wait until there is a sitting Secretary of Defense," a friend urged Van Cleave, "before you start picking people to work for him."[71]

The slight was too much for Van Cleave, who fancied the number-two or number-three spot at the Pentagon for himself. He went public with his venom, complaining to conservative columnists and longtime Reagan supporters that Weinberger was trashing the ideals that had brought the GOP to power. He felt betrayed as he was blackballed by Ed Meese and Reagan's other gatekeepers. "This is an outrage," Van Cleave told everyone who would listen. "You have a secretary who knows nothing about defense," and then he hires "a deputy who knows nothing about defense."[72]

As Van Cleave's distress grew more acute, he became increasingly quarrelsome and alienated a wider group of aides. After taking the oath of office, he suggested, the president should skip all the inaugural festivities and right away ask an emergency session of Congress to raise Pentagon spending. The proposal was rejected out of hand by the elder statesmen around Reagan. Van Cleave was slow to grasp how badly he was outmaneuvered in the internecine battles. His rough edges and inflexible style were no match for the intrigues and the bickering that pervaded the transition. Like jockeys maneuvering for the inside lane on the final turn, transition aides jostled each other to exert influence over Reagan—and Van Cleave was bringing up the rear.

To be sure, Washington had never seen a transition quite like the one that ushered in the Reagan era. For starters, it was significantly larger than any other. During the campaign, more than 450 policy advisers served up recommendations in every imaginable category. That number climbed to well above one thousand during the transition, with some agencies getting teams three or four times larger than those that helped ease Jimmy Carter's move into the Oval Office. Less than one-third of the people were paid with public funds. The rest served for token salaries or donated their time to the cause.[73] Hundreds of additional staffers labored around the clock to plan ten inaugural parties.

Ostentatious consumption was the order of the day. In addition to the formal inaugural balls, there were long waiting lists for innumerable breakfasts, lunches, teas, dinners and midnight dances hosted throughout the week by the First Couple's wealthy friends. Industrialist Armand Hammer used an inaugural reception at the Corcoran Gallery to unveil his latest Leonardo da Vinci acquisition. To impress the California crowd, chichi restaurants prepared gaudy and enormously expensive dishes with names like "Rodeo Drive Salad," "Shrimp 1600" and "Cabinet Pudding." The cost of hotel rooms and designer gowns determined one's place in the social pecking order. Such juicy morsels of news were gobbled up and evaluated breathlessly by the media. Day and night, Washington's glamour crowd was on the move. Limousines, for those lucky enough to find one available, cost as much as two thousand dollars per evening to rent. Invitations to the choice inaugural events, one society reporter huffed, "spelled the difference between lumpfish roe and triple 'O' beluga."[74]

Corporations were itching to participate in the glittering celebration, called "America—A New Beginning." Detroit's automakers donated five hundred cars and seventy limousines for inaugural events. California's Almaden winery donated cases of champagne. Leading defense contractors, including General Dynamics, Sperry and GTE, snapped up thousands of dollars worth of tickets to the balls. TRW loaned one of its Washington executives to assist the inaugural committee's executive director. The firms wanted to create goodwill in the new administration, but they also hoped to write off the contributions as business expenses. Privately, Reagan's team was totally sympathetic. Yet, for public consumption, the cochairman of the inaugural bash, Charles Wick, worried that talking honestly about tax breaks would make the administration appear too chummy with industry. "We should not be in a position," he warned an aide, "where it is inferred that we deal in this type of concern."[75]

John Lehman, who had started out as one of Van Cleave's assistants on naval issues, was among the transition leaders pulling the levers of power. He had ingratiated himself with every camp. Van Cleave and other arch-conservatives grudgingly accepted him. The more moderate, Kissinger wing of the GOP considered him sharp and competent. Lehman was promoted to oversee the entire national security transition apparatus, giving him an even more important post than Plymale or Van Cleave. In addition to the Pentagon, Lehman's domain took in the State Department, the CIA and the president's National Security Council. More polished and politically canny than Van Cleave, Lehman proved adept at skirting the rancor and ideological minefields that crippled his brethren. He had his eye firmly on one target and would talk openly about it: John Lehman had made up his mind a long time before that he would be the youngest secretary of the Navy in the nation's history.

His tenacity and strategically timed lobbying did the trick. George Bush and Tower were firmly in Lehman's corner. So was Senator Jackson of Washington, who years before had helped him land a lucrative consulting contract with Boeing. William Timmons, the man in charge of all seventy-three transition teams for Reagan, also gave Lehman's prospects a boost. Even Van Cleave, who accused Lehman of packing the transition with political hacks who didn't pretend to have the necessary professional qualifications, was impressed. "Johnny didn't overreach. He carefully marshaled all his support, and he went straight after the one job he wanted."[76]

Van Cleave and Plymale were less lucky. The morning they took off for the West Coast, the lead story in *The New York Times* disclosed that the transition team advocated an immediate $20-billion supplemental budget request for the Pentagon. The details were less significant than the article's prominence and tone. Van Cleave's picture was on the front page. The story suggested that he was trying an end run around Weinberger, to pressure the new secretary into embracing the numbers advanced by his transition panel. Van Cleave now claims it was a leak from one of his enemies. Nobody will ever know for sure. What was certain, even before the story appeared, was his proclivity for shooting himself in the foot. "Maybe I was too pushy," he explains today. "Maybe the political types and the White House types thought I was always getting in front of them."[77]

Van Cleave and Plymale were scheduled to spend most of Saturday, December 20, with Weinberger, meeting in his luxurious vice-president's office on the twenty-first floor of Bechtel Corporation's world headquarters overlooking San Francisco Bay. The agenda called for an in-depth, classified briefing on the Soviet threat, followed by a comprehensive report on budget options. Van Cleave surmised it would be a testy session. With a chuckle, he told one veteran Pentagon reporter the night before, "I'm making so many enemies around here, I'll probably end up at the Bureau of Indian Affairs."[78]

The reception was worse than Van Cleave imagined. Weinberger was ice cold during the first hour. He was seething but under control. Van Cleave began by explaining that the team wasn't trying to usurp the secretary's power. As the presentation got rolling and Van Cleave launched into his recommendations, Weinberger made up his mind. He abruptly halted the briefing: "I'm not interested," he interjected. "You are relieved. Your work is finished."[79]

Van Cleave was stunned. "But we're not finished with the work," he said, reminding Weinberger that he had been picked by the president-elect, and that Reagan had given him the green light to complete the report. The dispute, however, had more to do with personality clashes and slighted egos than with philosophical differences. Van Cleave's prickly disposition grated on Weinberger, who placed great emphasis on decorum. Van Cleave was loud and, in the heat of argument, often impolite, and he was unabashedly grabbing for attention. Far from looking or acting professorial, Van Cleave seemed to be telling the world he would deign to accept a Defense Department job in order to prevent the secretary's team from screwing things up too badly. The transition head couldn't modulate his approach, and the next defense chief wasn't about to let himself be pressured by someone he hadn't even picked to advise him.

"The result was like mixing oil and water," recalls Richard Armitage, who handled President Reagan's initial Pentagon appointments. Bill Van Cleave's basic approach, he explains, was akin to telling Weinberger, "I was gunning for your job, but now I'm prepared to be your deputy."[80] By all accounts, Weinberger, the prim lawyer who demanded gentility and proper etiquette from his staff, was outraged. He automatically looked down on anyone who stooped to sing his own praises. In Van Cleave's case, Weinberger considered it a case of unbridled presumption.

Weinberger now claims that the transition group he inherited "seemed to have taken on a totally independent life of its own," with members openly boasting that "they would stay on for a very long time."[81] During that fateful meeting in San Francisco, Van Cleave insolently said that the final version of the report would be finished "possibly by next June," Weinberger recalls.[82] That was the last straw. Tempers got hot, and both men raised their voices.

The secretary-designate wouldn't budge. "If you want to leave your report behind for the files, please do. But I don't need your team any longer," Weinberger snapped. Van Cleave said there was no way he would disband his transition operation right before Christmas. Weinberger gave him until January 1. In a last-ditch appeal, Van Cleave asked Plymale to step out of the room. "Cap, you can get rid of me, if you want to," he told Weinberger. "But I've got three or four people on the team who are really the top people in their field. You can't deny the Reagan administration the use of their talents."[83]

Van Cleave underestimated Weinberger's anger. The meeting was over. Shell-shocked, Van Cleave and Plymale stared at each other in the elevator going down to the lobby. "You know, I feel sorry for you," Plymale said, trying to break the tension. "This is the second time I've been fired this way; this is probably the first time you've ever been fired."[84]

Van Cleave didn't accept defeat graciously. He continued his hot-tempered assaults against Weinberger and peddled his version of the defense buildup to lawmakers and the Office of Management and Budget. According to Van Cleave, his firing was prompted by petty jealousy. He was the adviser most identified with Reagan's views on defense. He was the one who briefed industry leaders and members of Congress during the campaign and in the wake of the election. Weinberger couldn't tolerate his presence in the Pentagon, he claims, "because too many people would have continued to think of the Van Cleave plan rather than the Weinberger plan."[85]

With Plymale's help, Van Cleave took some of their budget books and set up shop in an office building in suburban Arlington. The space came free of charge, provided by a defense consulting firm run by an old friend of Plymale's. Van Cleave resumed teaching in Los Angeles, but he flew back to Washington nearly every weekend to work with Plymale. The report they promised Ronald Reagan was about 90 percent complete. Stubborn and proud despite their political downfall, the two friends were determined to finish every section and hand it over to the president as though nothing had interfered.

Van Cleave recalls leaving all classified material in the Pentagon. Lawrence Korb, one of the replacements Weinberger brought in to pick up the pieces, says just as emphatically that the new team found almost no files waiting for it in the Pentagon at the beginning of January. "There was nothing. We were starting from ground zero," Korb says. "We sat around the table and said, 'What do we do now?' "[86]

Whatever happened, Boeing's voracious appetite for Pentagon secrets didn't disappear when the first transition team was fired. From his early years, Ben Plymale was a strategic thinker, a big-picture guy able to see beyond narrow business interests and corporate pigeonholes. But in his heart, notwithstanding all the slights and disappointments he had suffered, Plymale was still a company man. Mother Boeing was in his blood, and her welfare remained his paramount concern.

It was crystal clear that neither he nor his boss, Van Cleave, would be rewarded with a prestigious Pentagon appointment. Weinberger would see to that. Van Cleave did get the nod for a second-tier, largely advisory job working on arms-control issues, but a lack of finesse precluded him from keeping even that after several months. Working for some other part of government on nondefense issues wasn't an option. So Ben Plymale shifted his sights to helping his company compete for a larger share of Reagan's defense budget.

The temporary quarters set up by Van Cleave and Plymale were only a block from Boeing's Northern Virginia offices. On quiet Sunday mornings when Van Cleave wasn't working, Boeing officials came by with the

combinations and opened the safes. They took documents back to their
building, photocopied them and returned the papers to Van Cleave's files
within a matter of hours, according to Dick Fowler, Boeing's ace budget
hound. The company obtained a virtual treasure trove of marketing intelligence. Drawers jammed with classified and unclassified program and
spending estimates from each of the services were culled for "stuff that
was of interest to Boeing," Fowler says. "I spent many Sundays from sunup
to sundown making the Xerox machine hum."[87]

Some documents were mailed to the company's headquarters. More
sensitive ones were hand-carried to Boeing's library in Seattle, according
to Fowler, to avoid entering them into normal security logs and thereby
disguise where they came from. Plymale didn't supervise the copying. But
in every instance, Fowler insists, he was told that Plymale had given his
blessing. "I wouldn't have known about the documents if they hadn't
asked me to help out," Fowler says. "I was told this was happening all over
the capital; transition teams were gobbling up stuff that would interest
companies."[88]

Van Cleave says he never heard about the secret photocopying. "If it
was done, it was done without my knowledge."[89]

But others who were part of Reagan's transition operation now aren't
so definite. They remember rumors about Pentagon documents somehow
finding their way to industry. Whenever a new administration takes over,
says Dick Armitage, who participated in three successive presidential tran-
sitions, "you get all kinds of characters throwing their weight around for
their own good." During the 1980–81 period, he says, there were persistent reports that some classified and even top-secret documents showed
up on Capitol Hill without the necessary Pentagon approvals. None of
those allegations were substantiated, but that doesn't keep Armitage from
believing the worst. "Since then, I've learned a lot more about the
propensity for greed" and deception when power changes hands in Washington, he says.[90]

By the end of March 1981, Van Cleave and Plymale had presented their
fifty-five-page report to the president. Weinberger also received a copy,
with a terse cover letter saying, "We hope that you will find this work
useful." From a strictly legal interpretation, the study no longer had any
official standing. But, in fact, large portions of it ended up in various
forms in Reagan's budgets and defense policy directives. To counter the
"global maritime challenge by the Soviets," the report emphasized the
importance of funding a six-hundred-ship, three-ocean Navy. "The de-
pendence of the West on imported fuel and raw materials, and on secure
sea lines of communication," Van Cleave and Plymale wrote, requires "a
major restructuring of our defense plans." There should be "no misunderstanding about the magnitude of the effort" or its cost, they concluded.
Under the most ambitious defense buildup, the report predicted it still
could take twenty-five years to catch up to the Soviets.

It all sounded like a vintage Weinberger speech. But if Weinberger concurred with the message, he challenged the honesty of the messengers. The members of the transition team, he claimed, were intent on pursuing more than the president's programs. Officers grumbled that the team had "seemed more interested in finding out details of existing highly classified military plans" than "helping to plan the transition," according to Weinberger.[91] Delving into the Pentagon's supersecret nuclear targeting procedures, for instance, didn't have "the slightest bearing on their transition work," the former defense secretary insists today. "I had a different view of their role."[92]

Weinberger acknowledges receiving more help from Harold Brown, the outgoing Democratic defense chief, than from industry officials who were supposed to be loyal Reaganites. The transition aides "assumed they were running the Defense Department," Weinberger recalls, so they "thought it was a nuisance to have other people around whom the President had designated" to be in charge full-time. "You can't have three or four separate Pentagon hierarchies."[93]

In a note to Ed Meese shortly after the inauguration, Weinberger bluntly said what many of Plymale's critics only whispered. The transition team wasn't helpful, he wrote, because "it had an agenda of its own."[94]

Chapter III

LEADER OF "THE BLACK GANG"

A weekend outing in the wilderness assured Melvyn Robert Paisley a job at the Navy's pinnacle of power.

The adventure began at a remote fishing camp in western British Columbia, almost three hundred miles north of the U.S. border, where Boeing frequently entertained customers and VIP guests. Surrounded by crystal clear lakes and the two-thousand-foot summits of the Pacific Ranges, Rivers Inlet was a spectacular spot to unwind from workaday pressures. The tip of rugged Vancouver Island was visible from a nearby sound, and an Indian reservation spread out in the opposite direction. The provisions were anything but spartan. A cluster of weatherbeaten but spotless cabins, well stocked with food and liquor, kept visitors dry and comfortable. With all the amenities, it was easy to forget that the idyllic hideaway was reachable only by amphibious airplanes, or that the nearest hospital was almost an hour's flight away.

The setting was stunning enough, by itself, to lure city dwellers on vacation. However, for serious fishermen it was difficult to conceive of a bigger thrill anywhere in the world. When the salmon were running down Canada's Pacific coast to spawn, the giant funnel of fish passed close to the camp. Anglers could hook fifty-pound giants in the surrounding wild rivers. Ben Plymale adored the place, using any excuse he could to entice friends to join him there. He enjoyed hunting and fishing almost as much as debating the strengths and weaknesses of nuclear weaponry. Plymale seemed happiest with a fishing pole in hand, sparring with an engineer or industry executive about the aerodynamic stability of some missile or airplane.

In August 1981, Plymale needed all the relaxation he could find. Recently reinstated as head of the company's advanced missile programs, he confided to a few close friends that his health was failing. The stress and long hours spent preparing the ill-fated defense budget recommendations for President Reagan had taken their toll. Once the report finally was put to bed, Bill Van Cleave remembers Plymale "hinting very strongly" that doctors didn't give him long to live.[1] An experimental drug, administered by an immunologist whose methods were ridiculed by the medical establishment, managed to halt the spread of the lung cancer that had ravaged Plymale's body years earlier. But the subsequent heart attack severely sapped his strength, and his circulatory system never recovered.

72

Watching his food and exercise couldn't compensate for his flagging condition. A strictly salt-free, reduced-protein diet imposed by his physicians, combined with a daily jogging regimen in which Plymale pushed himself mercilessly, made him gaunt and sickly looking. Plymale's sense of humor, though, didn't lose its sting. He liked to joke about where his connections to the president had landed him. Barely a few months before, he had been respected and feared by military and industry leaders as a linchpin of Reagan's "sub–Kitchen Cabinet." All of the Pentagon's doors, as well as its books, had been wide open for him. Seemingly everyone in the industry had sought his advice or pleaded for his support. After the election, Plymale felt strangely isolated. He didn't attend any of the glittering inaugural festivities. Suddenly, he was considered politically toothless, persona non grata among those closest to Weinberger. Associates detected a sardonic glint in his eyes and a resigned slump to his shoulders.

Reporters were told Plymale had pulled his name out of contention for a top Pentagon job for unspecified "personal reasons." His buddies knew better. He kidded with them about the possibility of being nominated ambassador to New Zealand, where the fishing would be stupendous.[2] The chuckles didn't last long, however. This was hardly the way his contributions to President Reagan's victory were supposed to be repaid, Plymale fumed.

Boeing still had a lot of clout inside the Pentagon. The firm boasted more than $2.6 billion worth of defense contracts, employing more than twenty-five thousand people. Nearly five hundred of them, in fact, had passed through the revolving door linking the company and the Defense Department during the late 1970s, more than at any other defense firm.[3] Quite apart from Plymale, Boeing had one of its former executives high up in the White House personnel operation from the start of the Reagan administration. Secretary Weinberger's animosity toward Plymale couldn't wipe out all those connections. Nonetheless, as Pentagon officials chewed over the spending decisions Plymale cared the most about, the Boeing executive's frustration reached new heights.

To forget about his troubles, Plymale organized an excursion to Rivers Inlet with a pair of longtime companions he trusted implicitly. John Lehman, the newly installed secretary of the Navy, left his pressure-cooker post that August for a few days of fishing and recreation. Mel Paisley, Plymale's protégé inside Boeing, also came to rendezvous at the camp, accompanied by his young bride, Vicki. From previous trips, Plymale knew how much both men shared his enjoyment of the experience. They wouldn't look askance at his problems or treat him like an outcast. He looked forward to reviving good memories while keeping himself plugged in to developments in Washington.

The trio of Plymale, Lehman and Paisley had spent a lot of time together on business over the past few years—and in the process made a lot of money for Boeing. Lehman was hired as a consultant by the company in 1977, primarily to advise it on broad nuclear modernization issues. Lehman's intellect and high-powered résumé—he was a senior staffer on the National Security Council in his mid-twenties and barely thirty-four when he left government as acting director of the Arms Control and Disarmament Agency—made him a valuable asset to any defense contractor. Lehman demanded to be paid about a quarter of a million dollars annually. Industry gossip held that the former Kissinger "whiz kid" approached a select group of contractors with a nervy, take-it-or-leave it offer: They could sign him up as a consultant at premium rates without prolonged discussion, or they could watch him march right over to the competition and wield his influence there. "I'm only going to work for three companies," Lehman told each potential client, according to Paisley. "You have the privilege of hiring me."[4]

At first, Plymale was put off by the steep fees and what he perceived to be Lehman's inflated opinion of his own value. "What the hell am I supposed to do with this guy" pressing to get three to four times what the average Boeing consultant received? Plymale angrily asked one member of his staff. But Boeing recognized that Lehman could be dangerous working for others. Higher-up executives wanted to strike a deal. "Maybe Paisley can use him," Plymale concluded. "I'll give him to Paisley."[5]

Lehman laughs off such stories, claiming that companies contacted him first because of his qualifications and knowledge of Capitol Hill. Whatever approach he used, it worked like a charm. Northrop and TRW snapped him up. Boeing also signed him as a consultant, three weeks after his firm, Abington Corporation, was incorporated. Lehman borrowed money to set up shop with one of his brothers and several other defense experts. Like all Boeing marketing consultants, the contract with Abington had to be approved by the chairman, T Wilson.

The Seattle airplane-maker, of course, was used to hiring technical consultants of every stripe to help with specific, clearly defined engineering or production questions. Sometimes, a world-renowned, Nobel prize–winning scientist or a former chairman of the White House Council of Economic Advisers would be flown in for an intense round of brainstorming about worldwide trends. Those engagements were highly paid, though generally they lasted only a week or two. "Johnny" Lehman, as some chums called him, was a different breed of consultant altogether. With his fiery ambition, flashy style and impressive Republican pedigree, he didn't fit the academic mold. He was more of a political operative, albeit a classy and erudite one. Lehman was on retainer for the long haul, and his role encompassed assisting several Boeing entities in a variety of ways.

By capitalizing on his overseas contacts, Lehman was supposed to help Paisley snare lucrative foreign military sales. As Boeing's management gained confidence in his abilities, that responsibility expanded to negotiating international joint ventures and guiding the company's leaders in pursuing trade sanctions against commercial jets sold by the European Airbus consortium. In one year, Lehman's consulting firm received close to $350,000 in fees from Boeing.[6] Based on his track record, many colleagues thought he was worth every penny.

In one of his biggest marketing triumphs, Lehman convinced Britain's Royal Air Force to buy a fleet of Boeing's Chinook helicopters—a first-of-its-kind deal that signaled the company's increased emphasis on defense business. But it was Lehman's dogged effort to sell AWACS radar-surveillance planes to NATO, another huge and highly prized contract, that really got him to know Paisley. The lengthy negotiations showcased their respective talents, and the close contact provided fresh insights for each one into the other man's frame of mind.

AWACS are specially rigged Boeing 707 jets, crammed with electronic gear and carrying a Frisbee-like, thirty-foot-wide rotating radar dome on top of the fuselage. The planes serve as "eyes in the sky" for the forces that fly them. Ground-based radar systems find it hard to lock on to low-flying planes, and they are notorious for scrambling moving targets with echoes produced by hills, trees or other stationary objects. Installing sophisticated radar in aircraft meant that AWACS was able to look down on targets, thereby giving it much longer detection range, wider coverage and unmatched accuracy in avoiding false images and other confusion. Without question, NATO commanders recognized the awesome advantage of using Boeing's system to keep track of enemy warplanes.

However, the members of NATO couldn't seem to get together on the fine points of equipping the AWACS jets. Closing the deal required agreement on a common configuration by high-ranking U.S. Air Force generals, the heads of several European governments and Boeing's own engineering hierarchy. Given the overwhelming military logic of purchasing AWACS, Lehman and Paisley ridiculed the petty delays. They pulled and prodded various decision-makers until contracts for eighteen of the planes were signed. Though many inside Boeing believed the sale was inevitable, Lehman and Paisley took full credit for the coup. "John is probably the smartest guy I've ever met," Paisley says. "He was head and shoulders above any consultant I ever dealt with."[7]

As a result of his success, Lehman ended up working for three different Boeing divisions, and his recommendations often went directly to Chairman Wilson. Lehman was no mere shill or door-opener for his clients. He was knowledgeable, thorough and fast on his feet during presentations, and his briefings and reports earned rave reviews at Boeing headquarters. His notions about successful consulting weren't hard to grasp: "Whatever you do as a consultant," Lehman confided to Paisley early on, "make sure that you're working for the boss."[8] Ironically, it was Paisley's decision to faithfully follow that advice many years later—after both men had worked in the Navy and returned to private life—that led to some of the most corrupting situations uncovered by Operation Illwind.

As Lehman's official ties to Boeing flourished, so did his personal relationship with the older Paisley. They visited and entertained each other every couple of months, forging a relaxed, solid friendship outside the office. During his trips to Seattle, Lehman liked to kick back his heels to philosophize about U.S.-Soviet relations and the intricacies of arms control. Many of Boeing's uptight executives found such conversations vague and pointless. Uninterested in international relations and bored by speculating about the state of the Kremlin, they wanted Lehman to keep his comments more focused. For these managers, the only important topics were revenues, business plans and specific contracts the company was competing to place on its books. "Most of the people he came to see weren't a damned bit interested in the big picture" Lehman liked to discuss, one associate recalls. "At the most, they wanted to talk about how Boeing's radar was better than Grumman's radar."[9]

Paisley, on the other hand, wasn't so rigid. He didn't find Lehman's lofty and rambling discussions the least bit unsettling. Indeed, he got a charge out of the talks. Paisley wasn't nearly as cerebral as Lehman, but he had the same expansive nature and fondness for repartee. Paisley was a great storyteller, but Lehman quickly recognized that his companion also was a very good listener. Despite a nearly twenty-year age difference and dramatically contrasting backgrounds, the two hit it off wonderfully. The camaraderie wasn't forced.

Frequently, Mel brought his newfound comrade home to dinner, treating him almost as if he were a trophy. After dessert, Paisley's wife and the rest of the guests would sit wide-eyed for hours as Lehman sipped the family's best port and spun out stories about the foreign capitals he had visited and the tuxedo-garbed royalty he had known. Lehman and Paisley turned out to genuinely enjoy each other's style and laughed uproariously at each other's jokes. They soon discovered they had a lot in common. Both men had the cocky strut and sharp wits of fighter pilots. Both delighted in the outdoors and loved skiing the deep powder of Idaho's slopes. They liked impromptu parties and were ferocious competitors, whether volleying on the tennis court or negotiating multibillion-dollar contracts. Though they never phrased it this way, Lehman and Paisley saw themselves as swashbucklers, eager to hack away at conventional ideas or bullheaded bureaucrats blocking their way. "Perhaps I over-romanticized him," Lehman now admits. "But everybody viewed Mel sort of as a buccaneer."[10]

On a deeper level, each seemed to have qualities the other most admired—and desired to emulate.

Lehman, for all his money and eye-catching accomplishments, was attracted to the earthy, rough-and-tumble disposition of his counterpart. Part of the allure, friends say, reflected the Lehman family's reverence for military service. Lehman's father won a Bronze Star as the captain of an amphibious landing craft in the Pacific against the Japanese. The younger

Lehman felt deprived of such heroic opportunities. An upper-class over-achiever who saw only a few weeks of limited combat in the Vietnam War as a pilot in the Navy reserves, he envied the chestful of medals Paisley had collected for aerial dogfights in World War II.

Lehman was convinced that the funny, rambunctious Boeing execu-tive—equally comfortable chatting with customers in Middle Eastern bazaars or recounting racy stories in midwestern office towers—had a core of steel. When Tom Wolfe released *The Right Stuff*, a popular paean to the personalities of heroic flyers, Lehman snapped up a copy of the book for his intrepid compatriot, Mel Paisley. The inscription was the highest form of flattery: "To someone who really has the right stuff," Lehman wrote.[11]

Paisley "was the kind of person you could give a task to, without hav-ing to call him every other day to find out whether he was doing it," Lehman recalls. "He would come back with a solution."[12] Paisley may have been a whiz at figuring out how to get things done, but he was hardly a stickler for rules. In an instant, he could switch from a charming, devil-may-care raconteur into an icy, calculating foe. "If Mel couldn't per-suade you in a debate or by a flurry of memos," says former Boeing exec-utive Darrell Cole, another admirer, then he would jump on any argument and rely on any trick to "get somebody with enough muscle in the organization to bludgeon you."[13]

Paisley, who grew up poor and lived in a one-room shack as a young-ster, was fascinated by his friend's polish. From the outset, Paisley was drawn to Lehman's family wealth, academic achievements and social graces. Lehman was a fervent Anglophile, who described his years in Great Britain as enchanting and contemplated settling there at one point. He took great pride in being the first American in nearly 146 years to be elected captain of a Cambridge rowing team. Rather small for the sport at five feet, nine inches, Lehman rhapsodized about using the "rhythm, bal-ance and finesse of bladework" to reach a state where "physical pain fades into an almost mystical satisfaction."[14] The Cambridge connection yielded long-term dividends Paisley could only marvel at. Lehman continued to hobnob with British royalty long after finishing school, and he jetted to reunions with upper-crust rowing pals all over the Continent.

In other ways, Lehman exhibited the trappings of a carefree, well-to-do upbringing. One of his great-uncles was a Pulitzer prize–winning play-wright and actor; another was a three-time Olympic gold medalist oars-man. Even as a youngster, Lehman attended elegant dinner parties arranged by Princess Grace of Monaco, another relative in his large and prominent Philadelphia family. Dancing in the private disco the princess and Prince Rainier set up on the ground floor of their royal palace, he would rub elbows with such political and cultural luminaries as Cary Grant, Frank Sinatra and Elizabeth Taylor.

The plush world John Lehman inhabited seemed wondrous to Paisley, a foul-mouthed former street kid who remembered picking crops and cleaning up chicken droppings with his mother from dawn to dusk to pay the rent. Paisley generally disliked upper-class families with refined accents and what he dismissed as snobby attitudes. But in Lehman's case, he didn't react that way at all. "John wasn't above mixing with the common people," Paisley noticed. "He struggled to keep in touch with average folks."[15]

Paisley came to respect Lehman as much as he respected Ben Plymale, the only other person he idolized as brilliant. He would do almost anything they asked. In early 1981, with Reagan appointees asserting authority over every cabinet agency, what the two of them wanted most was to land Mel Paisley an influential job in the Pentagon. Months before the August vacation, Plymale had recommended Paisley's appointment as an assistant secretary of the Navy. "You're going to have the best damn job in the Department of Defense," Plymale enthused, explaining that the office he had in mind was responsible for developing everything from fighter planes to tanks and artillery for the Marine Corps. "The Navy is going to build up," Plymale assured his buddy, adding that the transition team had recommended that in the strongest terms. "You need to learn about all of it. They're going to need a lot of help."[16]

Paisley was excited about the prospect of working in the Pentagon; he was stimulated by the idea of moving into rarefied circles of power he hadn't imagined were accessible to him. Still, he needed reassurance about the things he would leave behind. Paisley loved to watch the bulls and other animals that roamed his thirteen-acre farm in rural Kent, Washington. Located on an unpaved road about thirty miles from downtown Seattle, a large, western-style wooden arch served as the entrance to the main house's circular driveway. Inside the compound, highway noises and other urban sounds were replaced by the chirping of birds and the rustling of wildlife. Paisley wondered how different his days would be in densely populated Washington, D.C. In Kent, he had the chance to enjoy solitude as well as partake in the familiar rituals of middle-class life.

From the outside, Paisley's family life seemed above reproach. A basketball pole stood in one section of the yard. Handprints of his four children, reminders of a lighthearted family moment years before, were preserved in concrete near its base. The scene seemed to be an enduring emblem of Americana. Neighbors called Mel a "pickup truck kind of guy," who liked barbecuing ribs for visitors and raising pigs that one year were slaughtered for one of T Wilson's giant parties. His taste for gourmet food and vintage wines wasn't obvious until later. To celebrate the Bicentennial in 1976, for instance, the Paisleys roasted half a cow and invited two hundred guests to the festivities. For a masquerade party marking his fiftieth birthday, Mel entertained guests by dressing up in a King Kong outfit.

There were lots of projects at the ranch to keep Paisley happy. A crack mechanic, he bought a municipal bus with the guts torn out and spent

thousands of dollars to convert it by himself into a midengine touring vehicle for the family. A broken-down car usually was propped up on blocks
in the garage, waiting to be revived. During some of his trips to Europe,
he made sure to set aside time for the important task of scrounging for
auto parts. Paisley once got his hands on a hard-to-find transmission for
an ailing Triumph sports car, and he had the bellboy at a pricey London
hotel drag the crate up to his room to keep it safe. Paisley also got a kick
out of puttering over toy race cars he built for neighborhood kids. Such
sweet diversions, he knew, would end if he went to work in the Pentagon.

Paisley's supporters had their own worries. They feared that someone
with his makeup, and without any political experience, would be hopelessly out of his league in Washington. To begin with, there was the matter
of Paisley's manners. He didn't care about being rude, and his language
tended to be filthy. Mel Paisley talked like a construction worker trading
curses with the guys at the job site and making catcalls at every woman
who happened to pass by. He relaxed by telling raunchy jokes in a loud
voice and relished using four-letter words indiscriminately, regardless of
the company. The dark stubble and bushy moustache he sometimes had
could make him look downright menacing.

Paisley didn't moderate his behavior when it came to business settings.
Married for the fourth time, he had made a habit of flirting shamelessly
with women young enough to be his daughters and later bragging about
his conquests in the office. During an earlier marriage, he punctually
dropped off one of his sons at weekly Boy Scout troop meetings and then
just as dutifully drove to visit a female friend who lived in the neighborhood. Once his children became adults, Paisley surreptitiously bought
jewelry for and set up cozy lunches and dinner dates with a twentyish
woman who happened to be his son's girlfriend. He devised elaborate
ruses to spend time with a raft of other fetching young ladies. Arriving in
Brussels after a particularly eventful flight, he walked through customs in
his bare feet. Somehow, between the women he had been admiring and
the rush to exit the aircraft, Mel had lost his shoes. Plymale often teased
him about his romantic tastes. The parade of women seemed to be getting
younger year by year. "Mel, your next girlfriend hasn't even been born
yet," Plymale joked.[17]

Never lacking nerve, Paisley intimidated one of his wives into regularly
picking up his favorite paramour at the Seattle airport and driving her
home at odd hours of the day. The pattern didn't vary. The free shuttle
service was provided each time Vicki McKim—one of Paisley's youthful
associates at work—returned by herself from an extended business trip on
which she had accompanied him. Paisley's affair with the comely aide,
who started off as a glorified executive secretary but developed into his
closest assistant at Boeing, lasted well over a year. His officemates at Boeing knew all about the liaison. Paisley encouraged her to spend time with
his kids, and even wanted her to tag along during family trips to Europe

and summer vacations in Idaho. Barely half his age, Vicki McKim saw Paisley as a dashing figure who offered financial security and could help guide her budding career. At the age of twenty-five, she became the fourth Mrs. Paisley.[18] (One wife died and the other two filed for divorce, citing Paisley's extramarital affairs.)

In a meandering autobiography he wrote with Vicki's help—and paid to have published in 1992 under the simple title *Ace!*—Paisley devotes several long sections to reminiscing about initial sexual escapades. Some of his encounters went back to junior high school days. The book, among its many highlights, recounts "sharing spit" with one young enchantress and lusting after another's "pearly white thighs and dewy beaver." It describes a moment of passion in a steamy Belgian barn in the middle of World War II, when Paisley stood on top of an anvil behind a much taller woman. She begged for "pure, unadulterated animal sex," Paisley told his fellow pilots, until he obliged and his legs "turned to drifting columns of sand, slowly collapsing onto the frozen earth." Reacting to the breathless description, one of his buddies asked Mel mischievously, "Are you going to have to carry an anvil with you all the time?"[19] Paisley's hunger for excitement, and his love affair with planes and flying, comes through in the book. But so does his crude and selfish side.

"Amoral" was the adjective most people used to characterize Paisley. "He was a man absolutely living without rules," recalls a former head of Boeing's office in Brussels. "He had only one motto: If it feels good, do it."[20] Another old acquaintance summed it up this way: "Mel wasn't a guy you put on a pedestal."[21]

Despite Paisley's concerns about moving to Washington, the Plymales were pushing him hard to join Reagan's team. Ben's wife, Susan, especially, couldn't forgive Boeing for punishing and humiliating her husband in the MX document-swiping case years before. She complained about the unfairness of it nearly every night. Smarting from Boeing's treatment of him, Ben Plymale encouraged Paisley to make a radical change in his life by jumping at the Navy post Lehman proffered. Paisley had spent twenty-eight of his fifty-seven years working for Boeing. Bail out before the company turns on you too, he heard over and over. Vicki Paisley, who understood Plymale's reasoning, also thought it was time for her husband to do something different and more exciting. "Once you've been burned" like Plymale, she told friends, "you don't ever feel the same way about Mother Boeing."

Wilson, for his part, wasn't going to stand in Paisley's way. "I think it's a good idea for you to go," Boeing's chairman told him. "I would like you to take the job."[22]

Arriving at scenic Rivers Inlet that summer, Paisley still felt some ambivalence about the prospective move. He and Plymale weighed the pros and the cons, mulling over what his Pentagon routine would be like during the Reagan era. The fateful trip, however, brought matters to a head. It sealed the bond between Lehman and Paisley in a way neither man expected.

☆

The insistent knocking startled Vicki Paisley from a deep sleep after midnight on Saturday, August 8, 1981. As the rapping continued, she bolted upright in bed and jumped to yank open the door of her cabin. It was Plymale, looking ashen and weak and obviously having great difficulty breathing. "I'm dying," he said in a strained voice. "See if you can round up some help." While Vicki tried to soothe the afflicted man, her husband scurried to find assistance. Paisley shook Lehman out of his slumber by hissing the ominous phrase, "Ben's in trouble." Paisley also roused a nurse who happened to be at Rivers Inlet as a guest with another fishing party, and she ran to examine Plymale.[23]

He was conscious and understood what was happening. His heart was failing, and his single lung was filling with liquid. To improve circulation, the nurse instructed that Plymale's head be kept lower than his heart. She told him to stay on his hands and knees, so the fluid wouldn't choke him. The advice helped, and his breathing became less labored. But Paisley and the camp's proprietor, a grizzled bush pilot whose floatplane was moored at the dock, knew they had precious little time to whisk Plymale to a hospital.

With their adrenaline pumping, Paisley and the pilot took a cabin door off its hinges to make a primitive stretcher. They hurriedly stripped the seats out of the single-engine Cessna 182 to make room for the sick man. After the patient was on board and the party radioed ahead to alert a Royal Canadian Mounted Police aid station about the emergency, the pilot insisted it was too risky to allow any other passengers on the flight. There were no lights or navigation beacons, nothing to pinpoint the narrow pass between towering peaks that offered the only route to the rural hospital. If he made it, the pilot would have to make a landing in pitch-black water filled with floating logs and debris. "This is too dangerous. Nobody else can come," he said. Plymale's friend wouldn't listen. "I'm not letting this plane get out of here without me on it," Paisley yelled back.[24] The nurse also demanded to go.

She and Paisley were sprawled inside the tiny Cessna, hanging on for dear life, as it bobbed and weaved on the water. The plane skimmed the surface as it accelerated, before lurching into the air. "This is sporty stuff," Paisley muttered, as the vibrations became more violent. Using the pier lights as reference points, the pilot got the aircraft into as steep a climb as possible and banked sharply to avoid the closest mountains. He was navigating only by his ears, reacting to the drone of the single propeller and the sound of the engine echoing off the terrain he knew so well. Paisley and the pilot spotted the faint lights of a logging camp a few miles away, indicating the location of the pass.[25]

As the flight of mercy neared its destination, an ambulance drove down to the dock near the Indian reservation and trained its headlights on the inky waters. A red mooring light on a boat also served as a marker. The pilot prepared to make a low pass over the lake to get his bearings. The turn tightened, and Paisley could feel the plane begin to shudder, approaching a stall. The engine sputtered. Jesus Christ, he thought as he gritted his teeth, does this guy know what he's doing?[26] The next descent had to be perfect. With a quick thud, the plane splashed down and the pilot tugged at the switch to cut the motor. They barely avoided crashing into a row of submerged pilings.

Plymale was barely breathing when he reached the shore. Paisley kept up a flow of chatter to calm the wheezing man. "Ben, you're not going to have any trouble. We'll take care of you," Paisley repeated as a flashlight's beam lit up his face. The patient wasn't buying the pitch. "Take out my wallet," Plymale said in his weak voice, "and dig out a ten-dollar bill for yourself."[27] Paisley understood. The two of them had made a bet about who would catch the first fish of the trip, and Mel had won the wager the day before. Now, panting and choking in the middle of the harrowing darkness, the stricken man realized the trouble he was in. He was paying off his debt.

The nurse argued that putting someone in Plymale's condition in an ambulance, on his back, would kill him. The doctor disregarded her stern warning, maintaining that it would be less than a five-minute drive. They raced to the primitive hospital, frantically trying to keep Plymale alive when his lung stopped working. Sweating medics pounded on his chest and tried to revive him for almost an hour. After it was over, Paisley angrily recounted how his lifelong friend and benefactor died at the age of fifty-five on the hospital's front steps.

Skimming treetops in a tiny floatplane showed plenty of bravery. Lehman was stirred by Paisley's loyalty and selfless reaction in a crisis. The daring rescue convinced the Navy chief that Paisley possessed the character and the fortitude to take on bigger challenges. "His behavior with a friend in trouble impressed me," Lehman says. "I liked his personality; he was a pretty gutsy guy."[28]

But was it too late to ram Paisley's name through the administration's personnel screening system? Reagan aides began trolling for potential subcabinet nominees nine months before the election. By the late summer of 1981, about four hundred of the top one thousand or so jobs had been filled. At the Pentagon, most of the forty-odd jobs requiring Senate confirmation already were spoken for. Each remaining vacancy had four or five candidates waiting in the wings. By contrast, it would take Presidents Bush and Clinton well over a year to approach those figures.

Unlike the folks he was competing against, Paisley hadn't volunteered on the Reagan campaign; he didn't have a history of working diligently for conservative GOP causes. When his name first came up as a potential nominee, Paisley was told he had to get the support of a Seattle lawyer who was friendly with presidential counselor Edwin Meese and also was a leader of the conservative wing of the state GOP. Paisley didn't like the idea of going hat in hand to seek help from a stranger. But he did it, obtaining the necessary stamp of approval so his name could be formally submitted for White House action.

Paisley, though, had a more powerful ally than the local Republican party chieftain: The secretary of the Navy absolutely wanted him confirmed and was willing to fight to get it done. John Lehman, after all, had managed to beat out fourteen other candidates and outsmart some of Reagan's closest aides to become head of the Navy. He had known Vice-President Bush since the mid-1970s, regularly visiting the Bush summer estate in Kennebunkport, Maine, to give private seminars on arms control. In the same way, Lehman periodically briefed Senator Bob Dole of Kansas, the Republican leader, on defense matters over coffee and breakfast pastries. As a crafty Washington insider, Lehman appreciated the importance of having a strong right-hand man. He insisted on an assistant secretary who knew the industry well and would ride herd on the admirals. That required a gut fighter who was sufficiently tough and stubborn to help him grab control of the Navy. Lehman was so sure of his choice that he later acknowledged he had been poised to give Paisley a senior position, with or without the Senate's approval.

The Navy secretary took to heart the administration's oft-repeated dictum that "personnel is policy." Over the years, the shrewdest White House advisers learned that a president's ultimate success depends, to a large extent, on the effectiveness of appointees at Paisley's level. Reagan and his cabinet members could talk all day about their conservative revolution and the necessity of bringing about sweeping policy changes. But in almost every department, it was the assistant secretaries who actually had to carry out that mandate. They were the true agents of change, responsible for the nitty-gritty tasks of trying to steer a new course for the ship of state. Reagan's personnel czar Pendleton James expressed the principle best: "It is the sub-Cabinet that prepares the issue papers, frames the debates [and] sets the agenda" for highly publicized cabinet decisions, he said.[29] Though such nominations typically don't receive much press or congressional attention, some personnel experts describe them as the essential "factory floor of government."

Defense Secretary Weinberger didn't raise a fuss about Paisley because he believed in giving the service chiefs wide latitude to assemble their staffs and run their affairs. Anyway, Weinberger wasn't in a mood to belabor the point. He automatically preferred Lehman's choice—even though he knew virtually nothing about Paisley—to one of the political hacks he felt the Reagan campaign crowd always seemed to be trying to cram down his throat.

Inside the White House, an aloof and easily bored president didn't play

an active part in most appointments. Ronald Reagan plainly wasn't interested in determining who filled many of his high-visibility cabinet secretary posts, let alone the second- and third-tier jobs such as the one held
open for Paisley. The president, for instance, was content to follow the
lead of others in picking the secretaries of Interior, Commerce, Agriculture, Energy and Education.[30]

On those few occasions when Reagan did get personally engaged in
personnel decisions, his input tended to be unpredictable. Admiral
William J. Crowe was tapped to become chairman of the Joint Chiefs
partly because, during an earlier presidential briefing, he had spared Reagan from having to sit through a full-blown Pentagon show-and-tell on
the military balance in the Pacific. Crowe discarded his structured briefing notes and chucked his maps into a corner, launching instead into a
chatty, ninety-minute tutorial on China. Reagan remembered the folksy
anecdotes and down-to-earth approach when the time came to name a
new chairman.[31] By choosing Crowe over more logical candidates, the
president surprised many in the Pentagon and some of his own aides.
Reagan was known to get misty-eyed simply from watching the Joint
Chiefs march into the Oval Office in full dress uniform, and chances were
nil that he would interfere in the deliberations over Paisley.

Moreover, Paisley fit Reagan's rule of appointing people from outside
the Beltway to shake up federal agencies. The new administration chose
subcabinet appointees who were skeptical, if not outright contemptuous,
of the way government worked. According to Ed Meese, the basic approach was to come up with "people who did not want, or need, a job in
government" and had the "toughness to withstand the pressures and in-
ducements of the Washington establishment."[32]

Two months after the heroics in British Columbia, Paisley was nominated as assistant secretary in charge of research and engineering. He had
never supervised more than ten or fifteen employees at Boeing, or directly controlled a budget exceeding $2 million. Once the Senate agreed,
he would become the undisputed master of a nearly $40-billion-a-year
weapons development and acquisition budget affecting more than three
hundred thousand civilians and eight hundred thousand Navy and Marine Corps men and women in uniform.

Officially, Paisley was to be one of four equals grouped below the
Navy's undersecretary. In reality, he became the service's de facto number-
two official. As the Navy chief's most trusted adviser on almost every conceivable issue, he was undeniably one of the most powerful figures inside the
Pentagon. At the secretary's behest, he explained, "I find myself often
working procurement problems that are outside the research and development community."[33] In addition to procurement, many intelligence and
international programs also came under his authority. Lehman specifically organized it that way. Speaking of his boss, Paisley says the secretary "needed
somebody who was loyal. In my mind, I was the most loyal."[34]

The two families ended up living four houses apart in McLean, Virginia, an affluent, tree-shaded enclave of many million-dollar homes close by the Potomac's rapids. Nearby were splendid Colonial-era estates and well-groomed equestrian trails. The Kennedy clan's secluded Hickory Hill farm and the modern, palatial riverfront property of Prince Bandar bin Sultan, Saudi Arabia's ambassador, set the tone. The Paisleys' lifestyle matched the neighborhood. Mel and Vicki bought a spacious $435,000 house on a corner lot featuring an impressive six-sided dining room decorated with inlaid wood, with a Jacuzzi tucked next to the master bedroom. They frequented expense-account eateries on Washington's exclusive K Street. He zipped around town in a bottle-green, mint-condition Jaguar XKE. She wore stylish clothes and drove a matching, late-model Jaguar sedan.[35]

While his nomination was pending, Paisley became a consultant to the Navy, commuting back to Kent every second weekend. Paisley's youngest son, Beau, moved in with the Lehmans for a stretch, so he could start high school in Virginia in the fall. When the Lehmans broke a key in the front-door lock or one of their light switches had to be fixed, usually it was Paisley, the jocular and expert handyman, who offered neighborly aid. In short, Lehman came to rely on Mel Paisley much more than the typical second-in-command.

The nomination attracted scant notice on Capitol Hill, where busy lawmakers had to juggle hearings for scores of assistant secretaries. The Reagan political machine looked unstoppable in the wake of the 1980 GOP landslide. But Paisley's selection prompted disbelief among segments of the defense industry. People who knew his methods, including many who liked or were amused by him, couldn't fathom the choice. "I was simply amazed," says Charlie Welling, who worked with him at Boeing until 1979. "Mel was a fighter jock; a brawling, broad-chasing kind of a guy. He wasn't the assistant-secretary type."[36]

Most Reagan aides didn't have an inkling of who he was before the nomination. For many, though, the real-life impression didn't jibe with his official title. Rich Armitage, who handled personnel issues for Weinberger, remembers the shock upon meeting Paisley for the first time in a Pentagon waiting room. There was a bare-knuckle quality about the guy that seemed out of place, Armitage recalls: "He didn't look like a high-ranking government official. He looked almost like a prizefighter."[37]

Paisley's reputation as a ruthless operator prompted others to predict that he could not possibly survive a thorough FBI background investigation. Friends had a hazy recollection of a tawdry episode with a Boeing secretary in Washington, D.C., many years before. Police reportedly found the pair squirming in a car parked near the Mall in the wee hours of the morning, arousing immediate suspicion. Not even his best friends knew for sure what happened. Some said that the woman accused Paisley of trying to rape or sexually assault her. He denied doing anything wrong, but eventually admitted that he may have acted in a lewd manner. Paisley told a few friends he was taken to the station house and ended up being convicted of a misdemeanor. But there's no record of his being arrested or charged with any crime. His wife, meanwhile, believed that his Washington, D.C., court appearance involved testifying as a witness about a break-in at a hotel room where Paisley previously had been a guest.[38]

Paisley's superiors had different reasons to question his chances of moving into the Pentagon. They remembered how he used to boast of locking up international sales allegedly by paying off U.S. military advisers abroad. After years of listening to complaints about his boondoggles and wild soirees on the road, senior executives recognized the risks posed by Paisley's nomination. They hadn't reined him in, because Paisley always got the job done. Now, they held their breath, waiting for the whiff of scandal from some past business indiscretion to knock him out of contention. Inside Boeing, memos were distributed candidly expressing doubts about the likelihood of Paisley ever getting confirmed.

Lehman was so taken with his friend that he disregarded such naysayers. "I wanted him because he was a doer and an iconoclast," he recalls. "I fully expected that Mel would have enemies" trying to derail the nomination. "But I never had any reason to believe that he wasn't totally honest."[39]

As a courtesy, Lehman asked Boeing's acerbic chairman about tapping Paisley for the Navy post. Wilson's response, years before Illwind's prosecutions sullied the Pentagon, was a veiled warning that the selection could embarrass everyone involved. Boeing wasn't explicitly recommending him, the chairman said. "Mel is a terrific guy, he could do a great job for you," Wilson told the Navy secretary without hesitation. "But he's risky."[40]

Lehman didn't heed the advice. "I can handle him," came the response. He didn't ask exactly what Wilson meant by the warning: "You've got to keep an eye on him; you've got to supervise him."[41]

Today, John Lehman has a pat answer for the decision he made. Wilson's comments, he assumed, referred to Paisley's belligerence: a propensity to charge off single-mindedly toward a goal, without thinking of the impact on anyone else. With a cheeky retort, Lehman told Boeing's chairman he was determined to stand by his choice. According to Paisley, Lehman's explanation was classic: Given the Pentagon's cutthroat environment, the Navy chief cracked, "I could be at risk with my own mother."[42]

☆

Life was brutal in the logging camps and shantytowns of Oregon where Melvyn Paisley spent his childhood. Living close to nature can make a youngster grow up fast. For the kid with the flinty eyes and the pouting mouth, who didn't move into a city until he was eight, the Depression made those formative years extra hard. Mel's first memories were shaped by grinding poverty and the family's perpetual moves to stay ahead of bill collectors.[43]

His father, Frank, a rowdy, hard-drinking bear of a man, left Canada after World War I and snuck across the U.S. border looking for work. Clara, his mother, a plump, brown-haired young woman of Belgian descent, emigrated the same way a few months later. They ended up in Oregon, seeking their fortune in the dense forests along the Umpqua River. The region of fog-shrouded peaks and deep gorges was very different from the scrub grass and the dust-blown Canadian prairie where the couple had met and gotten married. The Northwest's lumberjacks were a churlish, brawling lot. And danger was their constant companion. In the camps, women and children lived in constant fear of hearing the snap of a safety rope or the sudden shrill whistle indicating that an accident had claimed another life. Mel was born in October 1924, when his parents toiled near the banks of the Umpqua. A train stacked with logs almost ran over the tyke one day, and only quick action by a friend of the family and an alert brakeman saved his life.[44]

Frank Paisley thrived on the thrill of logging, choosing to become one of the daring "high climbers" who shimmied up trees to chop off their top portions before the ancient giants were felled. He gambled and boozed ferociously, often losing the little income the family had for clothes and other essentials. His wife worked in the cookhouse while neighbors took care of Mel. When she cried and complained about their lack of money, the father would tell his son with a wink: "Don't you go listening to all that nonsense. I'm just an everyday working stiff, doin' what working stiffs do."[45]

The Paisleys moved 150 miles north to be closer to a center of civilization—namely, the metropolis of Portland—so Mel and his older brother, Gordon, could get decent schooling. Logging jobs were scarce, but the pull of the city's omnipresent card parlors was as powerful as ever on Frank. To escape his wife's harping about the sins of wagering and alcohol, the father would grab Mel by the arm and take him to gawk at the airplanes landing and taking off at the nearby Swan Island airport. Even then, the little boy with the unkempt hair and dirty overalls was mesmerized by flying machines. He peppered his father with questions about their size and speed. In his eagerness to see and touch one of the planes, the youngster almost ran into the whirling propellers of a Ford Tri-motor that was taxiing up to the terminal. A mechanic restrained him until the engines were shut down. Six decades later, Paisley still remembers standing next to the plane's wheels—which towered over his head like some magnificent alien contraption—and reflecting that nothing in the world could be more exciting.[46]

The elder Paisley scraped together fifteen hundred dollars from his inheritance for a down payment on a house in Portland, and he picked up regular work at the Bonneville dam west of the city. But soon after, tragedy struck. Mel's father and a fellow worker slipped off a scaffold at the top of the dam in a blustery wind. The other man died instantly.

Frank Paisley survived, but the fall injured his back and he had to wear an upper-body cast for nearly a year. It took twice that long to regain his vigor. Everybody else in the family, including twelve-year-old Mel, had to earn money by picking fruit. Crawling on hands and knees alongside migrant farmhands, Clara and her two children cleared strawberry plants and pushed through nettles and heavy vines to harvest blackberries. Paisley's autobiography paints a grim tableau of the family, after a day of such backbreaking labor, huddled on a straw mattress in a primitive shack. They silently wolfed down macaroni and cheese, as the foul odor of the nearby communal outhouse wafted overhead. The strain on Frank Paisley was enormous. He no longer felt like a proud logger, the king of the forest. He was ashamed of his surroundings. His waist got thicker, his hair got wispier and, most noticeably, his temper became much worse.

Mel Paisley inherited his father's thickset build and ribald humor. Nicknamed "Curly" or "Mophead" for his unruly mane, he lived to have fun. Long before puberty, Mel enjoyed fantasizing about girls and dreaming up wicked practical jokes. One Halloween eve, the gang he ran with poured concrete into some unfortunate homeowner's mail slot. Another late-night prank involved setting a smoldering bag of dog excrement on an unsuspecting family's front doorstep. The trick was to ring the doorbell, sprint to a safe hideaway and then watch the bleary-eyed man of the house stomp on the foul-smelling mess left on the doorstep with his bare feet or open-toed slippers.

But Mel's delinquent tendencies hid a burning desire. Like his guilt-ridden father, who prowled the campgrounds after sunset to try to ease his feelings of helplessness and inadequacy, the scrappy little boy desperately needed people to regard him as important. Frank Paisley's temperament always was "to seek the top of the pile," according to the son, but the older man's fate followed the opposite track.[47] Disenchanted and angry, the father became a seedy used-car salesman who didn't blink at making a fast buck off his own family. He had few nice things to say about his younger son. Before the father died, he gave Mel a diamond ring that was a prize from a long-forgotten streak of good luck at the gambling tables. The stones were huge and the setting was garish.

"You've never amounted to anything; you've got no goddamned class," Mel recalled his Dad telling him. The comments weren't designed to boost the son's sense of self-worth. "I'm giving this to you," Mel's father blurted out as he handed over the gift. It was a cruel jest. "Maybe this will help. You can call it your class ring."[48]

Long before receiving the present, young Melvyn was determined to make his mark. He promised himself that his life would be better than the lot of the downcast, intoxicated men he saw squatting in the camps. From his earliest recollections, Mel hated living next to migrant workers who were too depressed to act as advocates for themselves.[49] The youngster craved respect, no matter if it entailed shading the truth or skirting the rules. The deception started before he was out of his teens.

Mel was not quite fourteen when a friend's father offered to help him build a car to enter in the Soap Box Derby. Scrounging scraps from trash dumps, lumberyards and various backyards cut down the cost of building the racer, but the would-be driver still needed a few dollars to purchase metal wheels, axles and other standard hardware. Cutting lawns for twenty-five cents apiece provided the necessary funds. Mel worked hard to design a bullet-shaped, metallic gold body, patterned after the sleek chassis of the Pontiac touring cars he admired on the street. Firm but patient directions from his grown-up mentor taught the boy how to use a lathe and other tools to balance and refine the moving parts. After some suspenseful races, Mel won the regional competition by a mere six inches. An elated Clara Paisley placed the two-foot-high silver trophy in a place of honor in the household, where visitors couldn't help but marvel at its sheen. The victory propelled Mel to represent Portland at the national championships in Akron, Ohio.[50]

In those years, the derby billed itself as the Greatest Amateur Racing Event in the World. Perhaps it was an apt motto. In August 1938, racing fever seemed to grip the gray industrial city of Akron. More than one hundred finalists from across the land converged to test their mettle gliding down the half-mile course at Derby Downs. For Mel, the excitement was greater than he had expected. After the first train ride he had ever taken, the boy and the rest of the competitors were met by a motorcade. Limousines whisked them to a fancy hotel. No more of Mom's boiled cabbage and canned beets, the young Paisley thought. For once, he could have all the milkshakes and meat he desired. It was teenage ecstasy. A week of celebrations and room service caused Mel to gain eight pounds, nearly disqualifying him and his vehicle as overweight before the starter's flag dropped.

Race day was a glorious and sunny affair. More than one hundred thousand spectators jammed the bleachers flanking the three-lane strip. Military bands blared. Drums and tubas made an incredible racket. Red, white and blue streamers fluttered in the breeze, and a Goodyear blimp hovered overhead. Decked out in chrome helmets and new racing jackets bearing the derby's All-American logo, the awestruck contestants marched past the stands. Intoxicated by the cheers, Mel was barely able to keep in line. He won several preliminary heats, but his times overall weren't good enough to avoid elimination. Recounting his feelings at seeing the winner crowned, Paisley states in his autobiography that the experience taught him the ultimate meaning of sportsmanship. The derby, Paisley's autobiography concludes, showed him how to play by the rules and lose with grace.

That wasn't the entire story. The real lesson Paisley learned, it turns out, was dramatically different. Long afterward, Portland's standard bearer admitted that he scammed the judges to reach the finals in Akron. In a rare moment of introspection five decades after the event, Mel Paisley let his secret slip out. Ensconced in a gleaming Pentagon office suite—where clerks jumped at his every request and respectfully appended the word "Esquire" to his signature—Paisley described how he got away with cheating in the derby. He told Neel Patrick, a trusted Marine Corps aide, that portions of his racer's running gear had been modified contrary to contest rules.

Paisley didn't seem apologetic. He didn't pretend to have remorse, according to Patrick. If anything, the tone was a bit smug, as he smiled at outsmarting the rest of the field. Paisley was so competitive as a kid, Patrick now says, that he was determined to do anything "that would make him the fastest, the best of them all."[51] The trait didn't disappear after the stunt in Portland and Akron. Paisley's duplicity would resurface many times over the years.

His rebellious disposition came to the fore in high school. Instead of studying, Mel spent his energy chasing skirts and hot rods. Both pursuits ended badly.

Intent on impressing the girls with his rippling biceps, young Paisley went to the local YMCA and stacked all the weights he could find on one of the barbells. He told his buddies that he wasn't about to wait patiently for body-building results. Jerking the horrendously heavy load to shoulder level, Paisley lost his balance. He spun around like a punch-drunk boxer, groaning and struggling to keep the weight from crashing down on his feet. The mass was too heavy to control. "I slammed into the mat backwards," Paisley recalled matter-of-factly much later. He didn't release his grip. The crushing impact broke both wrists. "For six weeks I wasn't able to do so much as button my fly," he wrote.[52]

Paisley and his crew succeeded in wreaking havoc on the highway, too. He talked and dreamed about automobiles. Fixing and racing them became an obsession. His first car, a 1930 Model A Ford roadster purchased for sixty dollars, lasted only until he made the initial rounds of Portland's coolest drive-ins and meanest drag-racing joints. A souped-up coupe he worked on got banged up in a series of accidents. His father's jalopy was the next one to fall apart. Paisley describes the spectacular culmination of one late-night race, when he popped the clutch to burn rubber but instead wedged the tip of a broken gear in the transmission. The car's undercarriage exploded, splaying its broken innards on the asphalt "like a greasy gutted chicken."[53] Frank Paisley was too tired and hungover to sort out the details.

Crashes, speeding tickets and assorted traffic infractions soon earned Paisley the enmity of the police. They regarded him as a troublemaker. He tried to outrun them to avoid getting any more citations. In early 1942, when Paisley was not yet eighteen, a hair-raising chase by a squad car earned him a night in jail. His driver's license was canceled. The judge agreed to dismiss the charges only after he heard that Mel had dropped out of his senior year in high school to enlist in the Army Air Corps. The excitement of blasting through stop signs and fishtailing around winding roads would be replaced by the thrill and the camaraderie of flying P-47 Thunderbolts—the daredevils of the sky—against German aces throughout Europe. The new cadet thought of the slogan used by General Henry "Hap" Arnold to recruit pilots: "Send me the hot-rodders off the streets and I'll have an Air Corps that will bury the enemy."

By all accounts, Paisley was a gem in the cockpit. His academic skills were barely passable. But his confident attitude, good health, outstanding eyesight and excellent hand-eye coordination served him well at a succession of aviator training schools in California, Arizona and Louisiana. During the first few months, crammed with instruction in the air and in simulators, he was too busy for female high jinks. Fear of washing out of the program for pilots and ending up as a bombardier—or worse yet, an ordinary dog soldier toting a rifle—kept all the students on edge.

Paisley's introductory flight in the single-seat P-47 fighter, with its massive two-thousand-horsepower engine and a propeller taller than three men, was far from auspicious. The cockpit canopy, which hadn't been secured properly before takeoff, slammed into his forehead during the climbout from the field. Blood oozed down his face, and he barely avoided passing out while the plane circled the runway for an emergency landing. "Get your wheels down," the tower operator snapped as the woozy pilot's aircraft dove toward the tarmac.[54] In time, Paisley overcame many more mistakes caused by inexperience. He struggled through formation flying in near zero visibility. He understood how to put the rugged P-47 into a steep dive that would take it close to the speed of sound and how to ease it out of the dangerous maneuver when the g-force froze all but one of the warplane's control surfaces.

The nineteen-year-old warrior departed for overseas duty in the spring of 1944. He shipped out with four hundred hours at the controls of a Thunderbolt, a card certifying his proficiency at instrument flying and an unshakable conviction that nobody could beat him in the deadly game of stalking enemy bogies. All three would be essential to survive the violence and heart-pounding fear awaiting the new lieutenant, as the Allies launched the D-Day assault on Normandy's beaches.

Fast and agile, Thunderbolts were built to protect high-flying bombers from marauding "bandits," as Nazi fighters were called. That's what all the war-fighting manuals said, and that's how American pilots flew the P-47 for much of the war. But the invasion of France changed those calculations overnight. Led by the biggest armada in history, the Allies landed an astonishing 156,000 soldiers on enemy soil in a single day. The fighting was fierce and the casualties were heavy. High seas and well-defended German machine-gun nests pinned down some troops, while thick clouds forced paratroopers to miss their designated assembly areas. Bodies piled up in the shallow water amid wrenching pleas for medics. Along some sections of the coast, the British Army's daily advance was measured in yards rather than miles. But the beachhead held. Within a month, one million troops and half a million tons of supplies flooded the Continent. Once U.S. forces under Lieutenant General Omar Bradley surged inland and the Russian advance from the east began, it was only a matter of time until the Nazis surrendered.

The invading armies were moving fast to pierce the heart of the Third Reich, which left some of their divisions exposed to counterattacks. Supply lines were stretched to the maximum. General Dwight Eisenhower, the Allied supreme commander, knew the outcome would turn on logistics and reinforcements. The winning side would be the one most adept at hustling men and materiel around the battlefield. Allied ground troops needed air support to blast enemy armored columns, artillery, airfields, bridges, truck convoys and anything else that impeded the dash toward Berlin. In addition to providing air cover for strategic bombing raids, Paisley's squadron was assigned the role of tactical dive bombers. Strafing runs were the order of the day. If German flyboys were itching for a dogfight at low altitudes, the P-47 could handle that task equally well.

The expanded target list, Paisley noted later, included "anything on the ground that moved and anything in the air that interfered" with the Allied advance.[55] It was hazardous work, requiring low-level passes within range of enemy antiaircraft guns and even small arms fire. On a moment's notice, steel mesh runways were rolled up and relocated to keep up with the forward-deployed GIs. Paisley named his plane *La Mort*, which means death in French.

La Mort had a fair number of close calls. On Christmas Day in 1944, for example, Paisley's plane was limping back from a difficult mission, leaking fuel and losing power. He spotted four German Messerschmitt fighters cruising below at two thousand feet in an exposed formation. Paisley couldn't resist engaging them despite the damage to his aircraft. As he sprayed one adversary with bullets and gloated over the flaming cockpit, a pack of British Typhoons swooped out of the sun and blasted the crippled P-47 from behind. The Brits realized their mistake and retreated hastily. *La Mort* struggled on with a badly mangled aileron, which made it all but impossible to keep her wings level. She made it back home eventually, though Paisley's ground crew had sweaty palms about the possibility of his losing control at low altitude, imagining the right wingtip slamming into the ground and the seven-ton fighter cartwheeling down the runway in a ball of flame.

(Recounting the mixup to Prime Minister Margaret Thatcher during a 1984 visit to London on Defense Department business, Paisley let his impudence take over. Only half in jest, he demanded a written apology. He actually got one, albeit with the incomparable, stiff-upper-lip humor that exemplifies British civil servants. The manner in which the Typhoons launched their attack demonstrated "the quality of marksmanship and tactical percipience of the Royal Air Force," the letter opined. "The pilots' professionalism and enthusiasm were, in this instance, obviously misdirected." Noting that Paisley apparently "suffered neither a hard bump nor hard feelings," the letter concluded on a breezy note: "We hope to continue to have you in our sights for some time to come.")[56]

It was during the later stages of the bloody Battle of the Bulge, the Führer's futile, last-gasp offensive, that Paisley truly distinguished himself. On January 1, 1945, he led his squadron against a surprise, treetop-level raid launched by the Luftwaffe with the aim of catching Allied aircraft on the ground. A nearby cluster of British Spitfires was ambushed and destroyed before mechanics got the propellers cranking. But Paisley's squadron intercepted the much larger enemy force and made it turn away before reaching his airfield. Tenacity and sharp shooting helped decimate the attackers, including some of the most seasoned Nazi pilots. During the frenzied forty-five-minute aerial battle, Paisley bagged four of the bandits himself. Disregarding his own safety, he landed *La Mort* in the middle of explosions and fires to replenish her ammunition. "Load her up. I'm going back out," he screamed. The wild-eyed crew chief jumped on the wing, dragged Paisley out of the cockpit and flung him into a nearby protective ditch. Then the sergeant explained the lunacy of handling live ammunition with the field still under attack.[57]

Under Paisley's leadership, overall the squadron shot down twelve of the seventy Luftwaffe raiders that bitterly cold January morning—without losing a single American pilot. Paisley's exemplary heroism over the plains of Belgium, his commanding officer concluded, saved untold lives and helped defang the German Air Force. While taking the obligatory victory snapshot of Paisley crawling out of the cockpit, a senior officer handed him a cigar. The idea was to make the flier look older for the folks back home. The smoking habit stuck with him into middle age.

At a solemn ceremony in a Luxembourg stadium that spring, Melvyn Paisley received the Distinguished Service Cross, his country's second-highest medal for valor. A few days later, he found out he was about to be promoted to captain at the age of twenty.

Far from the front lines, Paisley sought out romantic interludes that befitted a pulp romance novel. He prowled the Pigalle district of Paris while on leave, carousing at bistros and cafés round the clock. His French vocabulary was rudimentary, but it didn't keep him from becoming infatuated with a member of the French underground. Seven years older and light-years more seasoned in love and war, Annie Simsen befriended the stocky young pilot with the crooked nose and ready smile. In her halting English, the Gallic beauty recounted chilling stories of blowing up bridges, sabotaging rail lines and avoiding the Gestapo along with the rest of her guerrilla band. She called him "my little Mop" and sent along a lock of her pubic hair when he went back to combat. Amazed by her grace and emotional strength, he dreamed about their life together. One poignant photograph in a nightclub shows Paisley, sporting a leather jacket and a macho expression, cuddled next to an alluring, dark-haired companion flashing a pixyish smile and clutching a wine glass.

Their affair of the heart was overtaken by affairs of the world. The conflict in Europe ended and Paisley, despite nearly two hundred sorties under his belt, yearned to be reassigned to a fighter group in the South Pacific. The wish didn't pan out. He boarded a plane to start his journey to the States clutching a swagger stick and claiming nine confirmed kills in air-to-air combat. The squadron's P-47s escorted the transport plane away from the airfield, bidding a fond farewell to their ace. His wingman in many of the battles, Sandy Ross, later extolled Paisley's take-charge manner and called him "a fearless, dynamic warrior" who was "the class of the squadron."[58]

But in the final analysis, Paisley's wartime exploits would be clouded by his predilection for embellishing the truth. The Pentagon gave him credit for downing four German fighters and sharing two half-kills with other U.S. pilots, not nine independent shoot-downs as he maintained. Critics cast doubt on Paisley's explanation that he had no incontrovertible proof because the gun camera jammed at critical moments. More important, some fellow aces bristled at his extravagant descriptions of aerial maneuvers, which they insisted didn't correspond with their recollections of the Thunderbolt's performance, range or shooting capabilities. Depending on whose version of history one accepted, Paisley received anywhere from sixteen to twenty-one decorations for his tour of duty in Europe.

The humdrum pace of Portland was torture for the hotshot captain. He was like a distraught diver locked in a decompression chamber: cut off from the pleasures and excitement that had been his sustenance and without money or a new job to replace them.

When the Armistice was signed by the Japanese, Paisley tried everything he could think of to remain in uniform. He hoped to become a military test pilot, but the results of his physical examination were crushing. A constant popping and audible ticking in his ears, which Paisley first noticed on the flight line in Belgium but tried to laugh off, hadn't gone away. Now, his hearing was no longer adequate to permit him to stay in the Air Force as a pilot. The flight surgeon said the most likely cause was months of extreme stress under fire, adding that nothing could be done to reverse the deterioration. Paisley kept looking for help at the Veterans Administration hospital, but the perplexed physicians didn't have a treatment for the condition either. Undaunted, Paisley tried to sign up with United Airlines. He was told not to worry about the physical. Before he left for training with the company, however, his ears did him in again.[59] The damage got him a partial disability pension from Uncle Sam and, in the end, would force him to wear a pair of hearing aids round the clock.

The next few years were filled with a string of aimless moves and dead-end jobs. In the beginning, booze and hot rods supplied the salve for his ego. Women and concerted partying also helped. Notwithstanding, the celebrated ace of the U.S. Ninth Air Force kept starting down paths and then abruptly changing direction. He enrolled in a business college on the GI Bill to become an accountant, though he concluded relatively early on that he had to do "something that moved a little faster."[60] Becoming a radio announcer was another hapless notion. Paisley's most stable occupation was owning a bar near Portland's waterfront, in the skid row district, where his main problem was keeping the loggers, sailors and international ruffians who were his customers from killing each other. According to community lore, it also was a convenient place to arrange for prostitutes. A 106-pound Great Dane named Ace was the watchdog and mascot of Curly's Roseway Tavern, named after Paisley's distinguishing hairstyle. The erstwhile proprietor drove around in a Cadillac convertible with imitation leopard-skin trim, and he kept a small plane for bouts of wild recreational flying.[61]

Increasingly restless tending bar, Paisley vowed to sail around the world with two friends. The plan was to outfit a fifty-five-foot ketch with provisions for four years and head for Alaska, Hawaii, Australia and then on to the Middle East. After several months of practice in calm waters, the vessel and her callow helmsmen ran into foul weather along the Oregon coast. She lost power, had to be towed into a harbor by the Coast Guard and broke her mast. Paisley's dream boat ended up as salvage bait for the lead in her keel, leaving him broke and once more without direction.

By this time, most of his chums had found jobs, started families and, in general, abandoned the reckless antics of their early twenties. Paisley simultaneously ran out of excuses and friends with whom to spend time. Nearly ten years after dropping out of school, he obtained a high-school equivalency diploma. Portland's Lothario got bitten by the matrimonial bug, too. His first wife, Genevieve, had grown up in Chicago and was anxious to return to be near her relatives. The newlyweds soon tossed their belongings into a trailer and headed for the Windy City, where Paisley attended the American Institute of Technology. His critics later dismissed it as a trade school for television repairmen, lacking full college accreditation. Nonetheless, Paisley earned his sheepskin and decided, at the age of twenty-nine, to enroll at the Massachusetts Institute of Technology for a master's degree in engineering. The quest for higher learning lasted one semester. "It just got damned tough," Paisley recalls, to keep up with the rest of the class. "I ran out of money and ran out of brain cells."[62] A recruiter from Boeing passed through the school, and he jumped at the chance to have a reputable job back on the West Coast.

Driven by his compulsive need to impress, Paisley couldn't admit that he was not able to succeed at MIT. Over the years, his cover story grew more elaborate. *Who's Who in America* listed him as being graduated from MIT with a master's degree in 1954. His official Navy biography indi-

cated that "Mr. Paisley . . . completed his graduate work at MIT." Those
who worked with him had no reason to think he was an impostor or
delve into his academic record. Paisley wore what appeared to be an authentic MIT class ring until he was in his fifties, when he had it melted
down to make a wedding band for Vicki.

Mel Paisley still doesn't understand all the fuss over the few months he
whiled away studying in Boston. Why is it his fault, Paisley demands, if
others misinterpreted or twisted around the things he did? The MIT ring,
he says, was handed out to foreign students and many others who didn't
receive a diploma. He can't explain how *Who's Who* published the false
information. And with a poker face, Paisley insists that he never tried to
deceive anyone by saying point-blank that he was an alumnus of the
school. "I used to tell everybody that I did my graduate work at MIT, and
that's all," Paisley explains, emphasizing the semantic distinction. "People
just assumed that I graduated."[63]

☆

The sign on the door said Boeing Applied Physics Laboratory. That's
where Paisley was hired as a junior engineer, barely a step above the
lowliest draftsman. Electronics was the up-and-coming segment of the industry. The company, in fact, had erected a separate building nearby to
handle the anticipated growth in business. Consequently, the lab's research
focused on microwave and guidance technology. It was the type of hands-
on work Paisley enjoyed. He designed and built equipment to check
manufacturing tolerances for radar domes used on early Cold War missiles. For someone like Paisley, enthralled since his hot-rod days by electronic gadgets, the place was a godsend.

But throughout the company, the physics lab gradually developed a
less-than-sterling reputation. Perhaps it was because few outsiders understood the classified and extremely technical work performed at the facility.
Maybe the close-knit style of the engineers and technicians, who tended to
spend their free time together and didn't fraternize much with employees
from other departments, prompted more than the usual amount of jealousy. Whatever the reason, many Boeing employees were convinced early
on that all kinds of weird—and, in all likelihood, nefarious—projects
were under way inside the lab. Paisley, and a few others who started there in
the mid-1950s and then faithfully followed him into marketing jobs, became known by more colorful names. Some called them misguided renegades. Others dubbed them, collectively, "The Black Gang."

The origin of the phrase was easy to comprehend. Long after leaving
the lab, Paisley and his cohorts continued to experiment with miniature
listening devices disguised as ordinary pens and tiny transmitters that
could be hidden easily in attaché cases. They also tinkered with larger and
more powerful electronic bugs, "capacitance mikes" in scientific lingo, ca-

pable of picking up conversations through thick walls and windows. After a while, their attention shifted to apparatus that attached to telephone jacks and could transmit intercepted conversations for greater distances. Paisley set up a system in his own house making it possible to eavesdrop on conversations in any room, until it was dismantled because of complaints from one of the children. Many of the tests were harmless pranks, spurred on by scientific curiosity and Paisley's exuberant, unpredictable personality. He was like a kid unwilling to let go of the latest toy. Other activities, though, took on a more ominous aspect.[64]

Much later, Paisley would claim that the experiments had a higher purpose, namely to protect Boeing from potential security breaches. But the bottom line, Paisley admitted, was that he had no corporate authorization to fool around with eavesdropping equipment. "I wasn't asked to look into it; I just did it on my own," he says, calling it "a counterespionage effort" to make sure Boeing's secrets didn't fall into hostile hands.[65] With Paisley, it was never clear whether the enemies he worried about most were the Russians or Boeing's competitors.

At one point, he devised a scheme to secretly record office conversations of top managers, such as Ollie Boileau, then president of Boeing Aerospace. Afterward, Paisley intended to stroll into Boileau's office and start complaining about the dangers of industrial espionage and how readily communist spies could bug company operations. To drive home the point, he envisioned brandishing the tape and then playing it back for the astounded executive. The result, Paisley figured, would be kudos for himself and installation of new equipment to improve security for all employees. He says the plan was never carried out. Some close to Paisley during those years, including his third wife, Millie, were convinced that the primary goal of the eavesdropping experiment was to outmaneuver and collect "dirt" on his rivals inside Boeing.[66]

When Boeing tried mightily to sell aircraft to Saudi Arabia in the 1970s, management instructed one of Paisley's colleagues to draw up a briefing to impress the royal family. Paisley resented that he wasn't the one assigned to assemble or deliver the presentation. One night, the papers were stolen out of a locked office drawer, according to the veteran company official who prepared them. The culprit wasn't found. "I can't prove who took it," the author of the draft document complained to friends. "But I know where it ended up."[67]

Paisley eventually succeeded in convincing his superiors to let him give the important briefing to the Saudis. His version shamelessly appropriated huge chunks of the stolen material that had been prepared for someone else, reportedly repeating many of the original portions word for word. Critics claim such trickery was one way Paisley succeeded in hoodwinking people he worked for with his uncanny salesmanship.

Another method was to keep his bosses entertained and off guard. Before the shah of Iran was deposed in 1979, one of his top defense officials agreed to buy up to twelve 747 jets from Trans World Airlines and pay Boeing's defense unit to convert them to haul military cargo. Paisley found out before word leaked to others. It was a glorious opportunity to upstage his haughty antagonists on the commercial side of the company, with whom he feuded constantly. In the middle of a management meeting, Paisley nonchalantly alluded to the TWA jumbos his department soon would modify for the shah's air force.

Bedlam erupted around the long wooden conference table. Executives guffawed and bellowed that it was impossible. They ridiculed Paisley's sources, insisting that Boeing's commercial sales force would be the first to hear of such a megadeal. Mel Paisley was in his element. He calmly ticked off the identifying tail numbers of each plane, watching his red-faced rivals fume and slump noticeably lower in their chairs.[68]

Around the same time, Chairman Wilson and Boileau, his top defense executive, flew to Teheran for a face-to-face session with the shah about a confidential oil-for-aircraft swap that was under consideration. Paisley and his compatriots were summarily told they weren't invited to the high-level confab. Boileau himself was chagrined at having to go. He hated travel and the unfamiliar customs of other countries so intensely that he once prowled Paris for a day seeking a self-service laundromat so his wife could do his shirts the way he liked them. Much to Boileau's displeasure, the long trek to Iran was a complete waste of time. At the last minute, the shah changed his mind and talked only to Wilson. Boileau jetted back to Seattle in a terrible mood.[69]

To prick his balloon further, Paisley and a buddy conceived what they thought was a brilliant practical joke. While attending the Farnborough Air Show in Britain, they took their wives to London's famous wax museum to see the shah's likeness. The couples snapped pictures of themselves mugging with the wax figure. They made obscene gestures and posed as if to throttle the shah. A copy of one outrageous shot was mailed to Boileau, with the briefest of notes: Sorry you didn't get to chat with the shah, it read. "We saw him, and he asked us to say 'Hello.' "[70]

The Black Gang's reputation for shady behavior also was fueled by a spate of allegations—frequently repeated but never proved conclusively—that earlier in the 1970s Paisley ordered the bugging of a competitor's office near Cape Canaveral, Florida. The allegations came from James Durst, a disgruntled former Boeing engineer who quit after a run-in with Paisley years later. Durst was a well-known malcontent, and people tended to dismiss his claims because he tried to make a profession out of nailing Paisley. Nevertheless, Durst offered some sobering information about the Florida incident to anyone willing to listen.

The yarn had the earmarks of a second-rate cinema thriller. As part of its diversification drive in the early part of the decade, Boeing was eager to grab maintenance work at nearby Patrick Air Force Base and NASA facilities away from Pan American World Airways. Both companies would

have to submit sealed bids for the the next contract, and Paisley supposedly wasn't taking any chances. The most expeditious solution, Durst
claims Paisley told him straight to his face, "was to bug the Pan Am guys
preparing their bid."[71] According to Durst, Paisley admitted sending one
of his henchmen to rent an office directly beneath the competition, drill
holes through the ceiling and slip an electronic listening device into
place. The assistant allegedly acknowledged the existence of the scheme
to Durst, as well. "The people who knew" about the episode "were ap-
palled by it," Durst recalled after the fact. "It was unbelievable that anybody would brag like this about federal felonies."[72]

Paisley subsequently denied bugging Pan Am's space, as did Boeing. He
did acknowledge sending an assistant to Florida "to scope out the people
and equipment they had." But the technician, he now claims, never passed
on the competing bid or indicated that listening equipment was used.[73]

In any case, Durst was riled up sufficiently to launch a one-man crusade. The former Boeing official wrote angry letters to the company's
management and its board denouncing Paisley. When that failed to produce results, he asked for a meeting with Paisley's boss. Durst and an associate came to the Hyatt House, overlooking Seattle's busy international
airport, armed with a typed, sixteen-page "white paper" laying out all of
Paisley's alleged misdeeds. Poor morale, loose organization and incompe-
tent management—Durst reeled off the introductory sections. Then he
got to the juicy part. Paisley's name was penciled in near a subhead that
read: "Deeply embedded corruption." These allegations were explosive:
"Prostitution on expense accounts," said one. "Snooping illegally on competitor's facilities," read another. Durst also mentioned bribes that reportedly went to land foreign weapons sales.[74]

Absorbing all this across the table was Benjamin T. Plymale, the last
man in the world who wanted to see Paisley punished.

Unfortunately, the whistleblower didn't know how close Plymale was
to Paisley. At the conclusion of the meeting, Plymale promised to ferret
out the truth. In the most heartfelt tone, he promised to take decisive action. "Ben looked at me and said: 'Every goddamn word of it is true,' " according to Durst. "And he said he would get back to us."[75]

He never did. Despite Paisley's flagrant disregard for the law, Durst
concluded, Boeing wouldn't budge. "The company covered him; I never
got over that."[76] Paisley carried on with his marketing responsibilities, un-
encumbered by any warning or retribution. But he would cross paths
with Durst again.

For the time being, Paisley's brashness added to his aura of invincibility.
He was self-confident and theatrical as hell. He claimed he wanted to be
a passenger on a jetliner hijacked by terrorists, just to have the chance to
become a hero. To show his affection for a brand-new secretary in the office, he pilfered her house key out of her desk drawer and had a copy
made. Then he told her about the duplicate key he had in his pocket

while asking for a date. The young lady demurred, saying she didn't know Paisley. "Some day," he confidently told the stranger, "you're going to love me so much your guts are going to ache."[77] More often than not, he was right. Women couldn't seem to resist his combination of impish charm and an undercurrent of danger.

By any measure, the most often cited example of Paisley's excesses dates back to his stint working on the nation's first wing of Minuteman missiles at an Air Force base in Great Falls, Montana. The story is part and parcel of his legend. Friends still grin when they recount how Paisley somehow convinced Boeing and the government to pay for the upkeep of his personal P-51 Mustang fighter, used to ferry assorted company and Air Force acquaintances around the West. The plane's care and feeding were included in overhead costs submitted to the Pentagon, according to friends. The arrangement was controversial, especially since Boeing had launched an internal investigation of expensive aircraft leased by other managers. "No more airplanes will be leased for work at Minuteman sites without the approval of T. Wilson" or his top deputy, a brusque memo told the staff.[78]

Paisley, though, had a knack for getting his way. He successfully argued that it was less costly to bill the Pentagon for the World War II antique—which reached 410 miles per hour and could pull six G's if Paisley was showing off for a guest sitting in the jump seat—than to have him buy commercial airplane tickets to and from Great Falls. The Mustang became his calling card. He once revved up its engine inside Boeing's hangar, and the prop wash damaged a bunch of planes.

Old friend Darrell Cole recalls his introduction to Paisley. A gleaming P-51 swooped down to the secluded field at Great Falls and screeched to a stop. The canopy was thrown open with a flourish. A beautiful young lady emerged, dressed in a revealing skirt and hugging a full-length mink coat around her shoulders to ward off the chill. The pilot scampered out next, wearing a leather jacket with a fringe. Laughing and strutting around like a conquering general, he presented an incongruous image next to the grim silhouettes of the half-finished silos and launch control centers dotting the flat vista. "Who the fuck is that?" Cole asked the gawking bystanders. The character couldn't possibly work for Boeing. "That's Mel Paisley, our engineering manager," came the reply.[79]

The curvaceous woman riding in the Mustang that morning was his second wife, Mary Lou. Several years later, she met a tragic and bizarre end. The circumstances surrounding her mysterious death, at the age of thirty, include allegations of a coverup and destruction of evidence.

☆

Paramedics found the body about 2:30 A.M., sprawled in a second-floor hallway of the Paisley home. The flesh on portions of the face and neck had been burned by a powerful caustic chemical. She couldn't be revived at the scene, and the family's doctor pronounced her dead in the ambulance on the way to the hospital.

At five feet, one inch and just over one hundred pounds, Mary Lou Paisley was a knockout. She had always prided herself on her saucy gray eyes, clear skin and trim figure. After six years of marriage to Mel, friends volunteered that she looked more stunning than ever. He bought her stylish clothes, gave her expensive jewelry and took her on jaunts to exotic destinations. At home, a studio was set up so she could pursue her hobby of painting. To please him, she cut her hair short and started dyeing it platinum blonde. She underwent surgery to get implants that made her breasts larger.

As part of the emphasis on her appearance, Paisley's wife also lived according to a jumble of homespun, often naive principles. Family members teased Lu—as almost everyone called her—about her never-ending health fads. She watched her diet, stayed away from alcohol and avoided sugar like the plague. She persuaded friends to stop serving Kool-Aid to their kids because of the artificial flavors and colors it contained. The most important rules could never be bent, let alone broken. Relatives used to smirk that Lu refused to take any drugs, even aspirin, claiming they were unhealthy.

In the predawn hours of May 8, 1968, it was difficult to grasp the extent of the damage to her pampered body. In addition to the burns that disfigured Mary Lou Paisley's features, her sternum was fractured and two ribs were cracked. There were ugly bruises on both forearms. Her liver was ruptured. Her lungs had filled with fluid, and her abdomen had filled with blood. The scene was all the more grisly because the couple's four-year-old son, Beau, was sleeping next door. Some of the injuries no doubt resulted from the desperate attempts to try to get her to breathe. But others didn't seem consistent with the sequence of events Mel Paisley laid out for the police.[80]

He said the two of them had been drinking champagne the previous evening and she swallowed two sleeping pills prescribed for him, before going to bed a little past 10:00 P.M. Upon waking four hours later, Paisley said, he found Lu crumpled on the floor of their son's bathroom, with her face buried in towels saturated with carbon tetrachloride, a dangerous industrial solvent. He assumed that she had become restless and decided to do a bit of painting and was overcome by the toxic fumes. The tiny room where she collapsed contained a large, open can of the chemical, which Paisley said his wife used to clean paintbrushes. The carbon tetrachloride must have been knocked over as she fell, he told the police, adding that he dragged her into the hall and tried mouth-to-mouth resuscitation before calling for emergency assistance.[81]

Two sheriff's deputies took a preliminary statement from him, but their questions were brief and perfunctory. Paisley looked appropriately bereaved. The house hadn't been ransacked, and none of the furniture or other belongings were broken to suggest foul play. The patrol officers accepted his explanation on the spot, without conducting a formal interview. They didn't take photographs of the bathroom or ensure that potential evidence wasn't disturbed. They never asked the detective squad to interrogate anyone. Perhaps the reasons were no more complicated than laziness. However, some of Lu's relatives and other critics later accused the sheriff's department of not wanting to appear overly aggressive in light of Paisley's ties to Boeing.

Admittedly, the neighborhood where she expired was an enclave of Boeing families. And the company dominated the area's business and cultural life to a degree unheard of outside Seattle. With more than one-third of all manufacturing jobs in the state dependent on Boeing, the peaks and valleys of the corporation's fortunes were as much a part of the regional landscape as the snow-capped Cascades. When the defense business all but evaporated right after World War II, nearly 80 percent of the company's workers were laid off in a single month. An upturn in commercial orders boosted Boeing's Seattle-area payroll to record levels around the time Mary Lou died, only to be followed by layoffs that left three out of every four of those workers unemployed in short order.[82] Turning to black humor to ease the economic pain, a local real estate firm put up a billboard near the airport with a taunting message: "Will the last person leaving SEATTLE—Turn off the lights."

Boeing's connections went straight into the coroner's office. King County's chief pathologist, who performed the autopsy on Paisley's wife, worked full-time for Boeing as a staff physician in addition to his job with the county. In the 1960s, at least, such dual loyalty didn't bother the people in charge. And friends of the pathologist insisted that his connections with the company wouldn't have affected his integrity by "one iota" in carrying out his official duties.

A few hours after Mary Lou Paisley's body was taken to the morgue, her death officially was ruled an accident. The original certificate listed two causes: "acute pulmonary edema," which is a catchall term for buildup of fluid in the lungs, and "drug hypersensitivity." The latter had a question mark typed next to it, suggesting that the examining pathologist himself didn't completely trust the conclusion. Much later, the coroner maintained that his staff physician never alerted him about nagging questions or doubts. "If it had been brought up, I would have done something about it," the coroner insisted.[83]

Discrepancies cropped up in Paisley's story almost immediately. His first comment to Lu's family was that she had tried to kill herself by mixing alcohol and drugs. Sitting on the steps of the grieving parents' house that morning, Mary Lou's sister flatly called that explanation nonsense. She told Paisley that Lu was too health-conscious to purposely hurt herself, and her devout religious upbringing made suicide unthinkable. "You will never, never make me believe that my sister put anything in her body that would kill her," Reba Klimas insisted. The sister grew more adamant when Paisley suggested the overdose could have been inadvertent. "She didn't take the liquor or the pills, Mel," Klimas repeated angrily. It also defied logic, she argued, that Lu opted to use the smallest and stuffiest room in the house for a midnight painting and cleanup session, when a large and airy downstairs patio had been converted for that purpose: "She had decent sense. She wasn't stupid," the sister said.[84]

Beyond that, Reba Klimas understood things about the victim's frame of mind that the police didn't. She knew that Lu, frantic about Mel's continuing affairs with women, had secretly hired a private eye months before to follow him and document his dalliances. Less than two days before her death, Lu told her sister that she had photographs of her husband's infidelities and finally was determined to confront him with the proof.[85]

With Lu's body still at the morgue, Reba broached the subject with her brother-in-law. She recalls Paisley admitting that his wife had been highly agitated the night before, and that the two of them had argued over his behavior. Lu took it as gospel that a married couple "should remain monogamous for the rest of their lives," Paisley said, pleading for sympathy. "Reba, you know that's unrealistic. People don't do that." The sister didn't mince words about how she believed the fight erupted. Both of you had very bad tempers, she snapped. "Both needed to be right and have the last word."[86]

For Klimas, the official findings did not make sense. She beseeched police to dig further. She pestered officials in the coroner's office with phone calls, asking them to do something more. Her refrain didn't change. "He didn't tell the truth about her death," she said over and over. "I never accused him or anyone else at the time. I just wanted better answers." But as a distraught, twenty-six-year-old single mother, without money or connections to hire a lawyer, her pleas were to no avail. Even her parents and deceased sister's friends urged her to drop the matter.[87]

That would have been the end, except for a pair of county homicide detectives who happened to be in the morgue when Lu's body arrived. The portions of her anatomy where blood had settled, they noticed, conflicted with how she supposedly died. Something was amiss. Dark patches on the shoulders and buttocks suggested that the victim had been lying on her back and not on her stomach as the officers reported from the scene. The burns on her face suggested she already was unconscious when her head hit the chemical-soaked towels. How could the condition of the corpse be reconciled with the husband's explanation of her last few hours? Based on a hunch, the two experienced detectives sought permission to investigate further. A supervisor told them to stop interfering.

Their suspicions multiplied when the toxicology lab results came back. No traces of sleeping pills or alcohol were found in Mary Lou Paisley's blood. Nor was there any indication that she had inhaled carbon tetrachloride fumes. The detectives made a second request to investigate the inconsistencies.

In retrospect, it's hard to pin down what the blood levels signified. The tests simply may not have been sensitive enough, or the alcohol and carbon tetrachloride could have reacted in her bloodstream to form some other chemical. One fact, though, was indisputable: The lab report didn't change the mind of the detectives' boss. "It's a done deal, leave it alone," he said. They were told there was no physical evidence to warrant opening a criminal inquiry, and more promising cases were stacked up waiting for action. The two senior investigators were ordered once more to stop poking around the Paisley death, or they would likely find themselves demoted to patrolling a beat in a squad car in the middle of the night.[88]

"I remember that I was hurt and shocked," says Dick Phillips, one of the detectives, who has since retired.[89] Phillips kept morgue photos of the body, he recalls, because "the facts of the autopsy disputed the facts of the case so strongly . . . In my mind, it was never justified that we never looked into it."[90] His fellow investigator reportedly threatened to quit or ask for a transfer over the incident, according to county police. Detectives later recalled that Paisley declined to take a polygraph test.

Eight months later, Paisley married for the third time. The lucky bride, a young Boeing secretary named Mildred McGetrick, was one of the women Mary Lou had received information about from the private eye. Some of Lu's friends ostracized the couple, but speculation about the tragedy faded.

The case stayed dormant for twenty years. Then, in the fall of 1988, Paisley's notoriety as a result of Operation Illwind prompted authorities to reopen the investigation. Police were determined to get some of the answers they should have demanded in the first place. Under the glare of national media attention, the King County sheriff's department pledged to make up for previous mistakes. "It doesn't appear as if this was a natural death or that it was accidental," the county's chief criminal investigator said. "It raises the possibility, at least, of a homicide."[91] The present-day coroner agreed that there were a lot of unanswered questions and inconclusive results. If Mary Lou's body had been found today, he said, "we would spend a great amount of time searching for information." Unlike the last investigation, this one would have many outsiders tracking the inquiry's progress as well.

To atone for sloppy police work in the past, local law-enforcement groups oversold what reasonably could be done in the present. Old records were retrieved and almost fifty people were interviewed. Still, investigators' frustration and their unanswered questions mounted. Finding solid evidence to back up suspicions about how Lu Paisley died proved to be nigh impossible.

After two decades, too many important witnesses had moved or passed away. The faint memories of those still around couldn't be trusted. Exhuming the body wouldn't help. And Mel Paisley made it clear, through his lawyers, that he wasn't willing to be interviewed. To this day, he disputes the recollections of key witnesses and insists that his story never deviated. His wife "was a flighty woman who had been boozing and was up to her eyes in sleeping pills," he maintains, adding that the allegations against him had been spread primarily by Lu's vindictive relatives.[92]

Larry Barcella, Paisley's lawyer, hired his own private detective to investigate Mary Lou's family. Barcella blasted the police for wasting valuable time and resources to conduct what he called a politically motivated homicide probe fueled by "garbage" allegations against his client. "It goes beyond dredging up the bottom of the barrel," he asserted.

In the end, the best that investigators found was a circumstantial trail that raised doubts about Paisley's basic veracity—and, by implication, his version of what transpired the morning Lu died. They determined that Paisley had actually told one acquaintance that he found her slumped over the bathroom sink, not facedown on the floor as the police were told. Records and interviews indicated that Paisley telephoned his lawyer and then talked to Ben Plymale, his best friend, before calling an ambulance for his unconscious wife. It also turned out that later that morning Plymale's wife, Susan, had cleaned up the house and almost certainly disturbed or threw out potentially significant evidence—including towels and other items in the bathroom—before the police had a chance to examine them.[93] Moreover, the 1988 investigation uncovered an ex-wife alleging that after the death, Paisley may have falsified insurance and other documents related to property owned by himself and his late wife.[94] This claim was never pursued by the police.

Finally, investigators kept gnawing on one jarring detail that didn't seem to make sense. At least two witnesses recalled that within a few minutes of Lu's death, a fire was blazing in the downstairs hearth of Paisley's house. Detectives pondered why a fire would be lit before dawn in the springtime. It was sheer speculation, definitely not admissible in court. Yet they persisted in going down this road. They couldn't help wondering what evidence, if any, was consumed by those flames.[95]

The homicide detective in charge thought he had gathered ample material to seriously consider seeking charges against Paisley. He made the recommendation twice, each time trying to convince the prosecuting attorney's office that the case would fly. The lawyers decided otherwise. They concluded that the evidence was too weak and the risk of looking foolish was too great to proceed with prosecution. Mary Lou Paisley's death remained classified as an accident.

Ironically, her demise helped educate a generation of King County police recruits. Starting in the 1970s, instructors at the sheriff's training academy used her story to demonstrate how inattention to details can botch a potentially promising homicide investigation. The case of Mary Lou and Melvyn Paisley was presented as a textbook example of what patrol officers should *not* do when responding to a fatality.

☆

Paisley's background check in 1981 should have set off alarm bells from one end of Pennsylvania Avenue to the other. Contrary to what many casual friends and journalists erroneously concluded after the fact, his life wasn't a classic American success story with disgrace in the final chapter. The few people who knew the real Mel Paisley had seen the signposts of his corruption long before. But, instead of being subjected to careful scrutiny by lawmakers, he breezed through his confirmation without being forced to answer a single accusation about his morals.

The Federal Bureau of Investigation received a number of allegations about his previous life. One letter, which got Paisley's prospective title wrong, nevertheless had a rather startling opening sentence. "Do you want an Undersecretary of the Navy," it asked, "who murdered his second wife?" The message came from Millie McGetrick, after she and Paisley went through a bitter divorce. The letter was intended for senators considering his nomination, but she apparently never mailed it to them. The draft copy obtained by the FBI accused him of lying, cheating, wiretapping and various other illegalities, posing a question at the end: "Is this the kind of person we want making decisions about war and peace?"[96]

During her interview by FBI agents, McGetrick also recounted free trips and merchandise as well as other favors Paisley allegedly accepted from companies doing business with Boeing. "I told them he was a dishonest person," McGetrick recalls.[97] The chairman of the Senate Armed Services Committee received separate written allegations from one of the nominee's former sisters-in-law. Paisley "is a man of such low morality," the letter said, that he "has been known to take bribes" from Boeing subcontractors.[98] The committee's staff disregarded the warning, sending back a drop-dead response indicating only that Paisley's name hadn't yet been formally presented "for nomination to any position." Republican John Tower of Texas, the chairman, later said Paisley "appeared to be well qualified" and "nothing out of the ordinary turned up" in the course of the background checks.[99]

The FBI's inquiry took three months, prompting Paisley to complain to the White House personnel office. He was told the delay probably stemmed from agents looking into his extensive work overseas. In the meantime, Lehman got wind of the unsavory attacks on Paisley and quietly raised the issue with the Navy's general counsel. Was there anything to indicate that Paisley wasn't fit for the job? Lehman asked. He was informed that the FBI had a collection of risqué allegations about the nominee's background, but that they didn't go beyond Paisley's private life. The secretary, who believed in Paisley and remained a steadfast supporter, didn't pursue the leads. Lehman accepted the notion that the assaults were unfounded, or were prompted by questions about his friend's colorful personality and lifestyle, not his fitness for office. Lehman didn't seek out Paisley to provide clarification. He didn't ask to see the FBI's documents. And certainly he never intimated to anyone in the Reagan administration that the nomination ought to be reassessed.[100]

Eventually, at the end of September 1981, the FBI hand-delivered a seven-page background report to the White House. Paisley needn't have fretted. While repeating some of the accusations about womanizing, the summary toned them down and stressed that the allegations were unsubstantiated. More important, the bureau didn't include any references to Paisley's allegedly illegal business activities.[101] The report also didn't dwell on other potential problems, including a stroke two years earlier that had nearly killed him. Paisley owed his survival to a quick-witted friend who connived to get a Boeing helicopter to pick him up at a company retreat and whisk him to a hospital. He was kept immobile for six weeks. (His girlfriend hid in the bathroom when his wife came to visit.) Despite early periods of confusion and irrationality, Paisley made a full recovery. All in all, the report's gaps and its low-key, skeptical treatment of allegations strongly suggested that the bureau didn't believe there was a smoking gun.

Inundated with requests for so-called Full Field Investigations of would-be appointees during Reagan's first year, local FBI offices sometimes cut corners. In this instance, the bureau was under pressure to complete its work because Paisley was the last of Reagan's top-echelon Pentagon nominees to go through the mandatory clearance process. Agents didn't contact any of Mary Lou's relatives, and they interviewed some of Paisley's acquaintances and friends quickly over the phone rather than in person. In general, some FBI supervisors figured, it was the White House's call to determine whether certain unsubstantiated claims deserved additional investigation.[102]

Like the FBI, the ethical watchdogs in the Reagan White House didn't feel the allegations against Paisley were credible. The counsel's office discounted the negative information, presumably because most of it was provided by vindictive ex-wives or their relatives, jealous coworkers and other people whose word the administration decided wasn't reliable. The ranking members of the Armed Services Committee didn't ask to see the FBI report. And White House aides never volunteered to provide summaries or excerpts. Based on the background investigation, Paisley received his top secret Defense Department clearance nearly two months *before* his confirmation hearing.

It wasn't until much later, when the Illwind scandal swirled around George Bush's 1988 presidential campaign, that the finger pointing began. The FBI claimed it did its job by compiling the allegations against Paisley in the first place. In later administrations, however, the bureau ordered agents to conduct much more thorough background checks of White House nominees. The guidelines required investigation of "lifestyle" or personal issues that could be used by someone to unduly influence or coerce any applicant. In addition, agents specifically were instructed to make certain that any "derogatory information" about a potential officeholder was "developed fully and resolved whenever possible."[103]

Embarrassed lawmakers, hard-pressed to explain why they never delved into Paisley's past, blamed the White House for failing to pass on at least the gist of the allegations against him. Belatedly, leaders of the Armed Services panel read the FBI's report on Paisley. Senators demanded greater access to raw background information on future nominees, and they vowed to review summaries supplied by the bureau with a more independent eye. Unable to justify picking Paisley for the plum job, George Bush's counsel grudgingly admitted that the original allegations "might conceivably have been pursued more thoroughly" before the name was sent up to Capitol Hill.[104]

In any event, Paisley's 1981 confirmation was assured in the Republican-controlled Senate. His hearing lasted all of ten minutes, with only two of the armed services panel's seventeen members present. Senator Henry Jackson, the senior lawmaker at the time from Paisley's home state of Washington, gave him a glowing endorsement. Listing years of military and industry accomplishments, Jackson at one point joked that the nominee was "a fast mover." The audience tittered.

Paisley's flair for the dramatic didn't forsake him. Asked why he wanted the Navy job, he puffed out his chest and quoted George Washington's maxim about patriotism: "Anybody who lives in a free democracy," he recited, "should be willing to give some part of his personal property and some part of his personal service to the defense of that society."

Chapter IV

TAKING THE CON

A ssistant Secretary Paisley's swearing-in celebration was the capital's version of an exclusive, long-awaited debutante ball. It gave him the first opportunity to mingle with some of the industry's most successful figures: the sought-after consultants and lobbyists who outlast the periodic turnover of political appointees to become permanent Washington power brokers. The guests, in turn, could size up and chat with the newcomer from Boeing, whose style would play such a big part in determining the fortunes of the giant defense firms for which they worked.

The actual ceremony was held in one of the dining rooms reserved for the Navy secretary and his top aides. Formality and decorum reigned in this wedge of the Pentagon. Wood trim, highly polished floors and starched linen harkened back to the resplendent days of Theodore Roosevelt and his cousin, Franklin Delano Roosevelt, the most famous assistant secretaries in Navy history. The ambience also raised faint echoes of the end of World War II, when Secretary James Forrestal commanded a triumphant fleet that had outfought Japanese and German warships in every ocean on the globe. Until 1950, the civilians who ran the U.S. Navy were full members of the president's cabinet. Portraits of those long-departed officeholders lined the corridors, bearing somber witness to the latest changing of the guard. Panoramic views of the museum buildings on the Mall, combined with the roar of commercial jets taking off and landing at nearby National Airport, added a touch of modern spectacle to the occasion. Paisley's relatives and friends were mighty impressed.

After Paisley recited the oath of office, the festivities perked up. Revelers moved to a private party room at the Crystal City Marriott hotel, in the same Northern Virginia complex that housed the largest concentration of the Navy's acquisition offices. The gathering swelled to nearly one hundred people, with Boeing and other contractors well represented. Paisley wasn't a completely unknown quantity inside the Beltway, having served on a Defense Department science advisory board a couple of years before. But since he didn't yet know many of the players, longtime friend Austen Watson served as the putative master of ceremonies at the reception that evening.

Watson probably had as broad a range of contacts in the defense establishment as anyone. A veteran marketing executive for Singer, which supplied guidance systems for a variety of aviation programs cutting across the services, Watson had worked closely with nearly every major aircraft and missile maker since the 1960s. He made friends with Paisley when they both were assigned to the Minuteman project in Seattle. The ties stayed intact after Watson moved back to the East Coast and rose steadily in Singer's hierarchy. In the summertime, they continued to go fishing together at a lakeside cabin in Idaho. Every time Watson paid a return visit to Seattle, he and Paisley would go out late, trade jokes and reminisce. As part of its industry-wide marketing campaign, Singer was known to rely on other friendly gestures. Watson's expense account seemed unlimited when it came to keeping big customers happy. To entertain executives from Boeing and other contractors, Watson sometimes rented out an entire French restaurant for the evening. One year, he had a Singer sewing machine delivered to the Paisley ranch in Kent as a surprise gift for Mel's wife at the time.

Subcontractors need considerable skill at swapping information to stay in business, and Singer was no exception. Making his rounds in Washington, Watson was regarded as one of the most discerning, best-connected corporate lobbyists around. Over the past few months, he had begun introducing Paisley to various industry acquaintances. The affair at the Marriott was supposed to cap that effort. If "Aut" vouched for Paisley as a good guy, that was as solid an endorsement as anyone could hope for.

After finishing dinner and drinks at the hotel, those hardy souls still in a partying mood were invited to stop off at a nearby condominium owned by another friend of Watson's. The two-story apartment was perched above the brightly lit Iwo Jima memorial and offered a breathtaking view of Washington's lights twinkling on the other side of the Potomac in the frosty December air. A Christmas tree–trimming party was under way, and the gracious host took pictures of everyone, including a beaming Paisley, placing ornaments on branches. A few days later, Paisley got a phone call from Watson's friend asking if he cared to have a copy of the snapshot. The heavyset, affable man who hustled into his Pentagon office introduced himself as William Galvin.

Following the usual pleasantries, Galvin recalls, Paisley "asked the magical question: 'What do you do for a living?' "[1] Coming from the Navy's newly installed procurement czar, it was an invitation that men like Galvin wait their whole lives to hear. He made sure to keep up the chitchat. As the conversation warmed up, Bill Galvin—industry lobbyist, consummate deal maker and self-promoter extraordinaire—saw his opening. He talked about his consulting work on behalf of Singer and Paisley's buddy, Austen Watson. Almost imperceptibly at first, Galvin steered the dialogue to other companies. He listed all the big contractors that supplied the Navy and also happened to use his consulting services.

Shrewd and aggressive, Galvin made his name snaring defense work for blue-chip clients. Before he established himself in Washington, however, his checkered career left a clutch of lawsuits, sour business deals and bad debts in its wake.

He grew up on Long Island amid comfortable circumstances, where his father, Jack, owned a fleet of trucks that carried cattle to a Brooklyn slaughterhouse. Galvin majored in political science at Hamilton College in upstate New York, later dropped out of St. John's University Law School and embarked on a variety of money-making ventures. Over the years, he sold industrial trailers, ran a hospital diagnostic center and operated a travel agency. The grandson of a rabbi, he struck up a friendship with "born-again" Christian entertainer Anita Bryant while living in Florida and booked medical visits to Miami for Latin American dignitaries, including the dictator of Bolivia.[2] Moving from state to state in the 1960s and 1970s, Galvin also marketed computer services and worked for a number of real estate concerns.[3]

From the early years, those who worked with Galvin were struck by his knack for putting people at ease. He was always "very good at the social-public relations-salesman-marketing end of things," one associate recalls.[4] While still in his early thirties, Galvin hooked up with the son of then-senator Dennis Chavez of New Mexico and learned the rituals of entertaining VIPs. If you wanted to find the best place to order a rare steak in New York or the hippest new French bistro in Washington's Georgetown district, friends would say, just ask Bill Galvin. Everywhere he appeared, acquaintances and coworkers remembered the engaging manner and salesman's glib tongue. "What did Bill Galvin sell?" says a defense executive who purchased one of Galvin's start-up companies. "He sold that he knew everybody."[5]

His first wife recalls Galvin's flamboyant style even when he was struggling financially. "It used to be a joke in my family . . . I never knew exactly what he did, except that we were wined and dined an awful lot," she says. "And we wined and dined a lot of contractors." His ex-wife, though, still considers him an "absolute charmer."[6] One retired Navy captain and former business associate describes him as "a wheeler and dealer of the first order."[7] Old salts have a nautical term for such a high-powered insider. With a combination of deference and distrust, they called him a "ringknocker."

Despite his adroitness as a promoter, Galvin had more than his share of embarrassing setbacks. His initial foray into Washington's culture of political deal making, alongside Dennis Chavez, Jr., ended badly in the early 1960s, when the lobbying firm closed under a cloud.[8] Galvin moved to California soon after that, relocated to South Florida and then returned to California a decade later. Lawsuits dogged his steps across the country. One disgruntled client sued him for allegedly refusing to return a mistaken payment from a New York avionics firm. In 1972, Galvin was fired as president of a publicly traded computer company in Miami. Local press reports said management accused him of collecting thousands of dollars in unjustified expense reimbursements. One former officer of the company, who won't let himself be identified, said he resigned from the firm's board of directors because "I didn't want my name in any way associated with Mr. Galvin."[9] Notwithstanding his interests in other businesses, Galvin never lost touch completely with the defense industry. His partner in a Florida travel agency in the mid-1970s wondered why Galvin kept receiving correspondence and invitations to air shows from major defense contractors.[10]

During the waning days of Jimmy Carter's presidency, when the Navy chafed under budget cuts that it claimed went deeper than those affecting the other services, Bill Galvin landed a job that finally got him back to Washington. He was hired as the marketing representative for a small Rochester, New York, contractor specializing in antisubmarine warfare equipment. "He told me he was quite wealthy when he came to work for me," recalls Edward McDonald, the firm's president at the time, "and that what I was paying him wouldn't pay his expenses." As part of his compensation package, Galvin was entitled to a company car. "He was mad because it was only a Buick," according to McDonald. "He was really peeved at me."[11] This job, too, fell apart, when it turned out that Galvin was entertaining Navy officers without paying heed to Pentagon restrictions on such contact. "He told me I was too straitlaced for insisting on rigorously following the rules," McDonald recalls. "He claimed that a company couldn't get business going down that road."[12] Galvin and McDonald parted company when Galvin was caught trying to obtain secrets about a competitor's sonar buoys by hiring a consultant who worked for the other contractor and pumping the fellow for information.[13]

It wasn't until 1981 that Bill Galvin found a vocation that truly matched his skills and his taste for excitement. Flush with ambition and money from mysterious sources, he hung out his shingle in Washington as an independent defense marketing expert. Galvin didn't have any engineering expertise, and therefore sometimes got tripped up by the technical wrinkles of the weapons he was hawking. Since he never worked his way up the ranks of a large military contractor, the manufacturing side of the business was equally unfamiliar to him. But somehow, his self-confident tone papered over any glaring misstatements. And Galvin's humor brightened any conversation.

Buttering up one Navy civilian who was feeding him prohibited bidding information, Galvin joked about calling to get "the word" about a project's status. "You're the source. You're the Oracle of Delphi," he quipped.[14]

If tension escalated during a meeting or telephone conference, Galvin's one-liners invariably brought out the smiles. "How's the never ending fight of man against sin," he would say with impeccable timing, to needle a friend. Or, with a twinkle in his eyes, he would try to soothe the nerves of a worried confederate in crime: "You're a great American," he told a jittery Pentagon aide who was struggling to steer a contract to one of Galvin's firms. There was a pregnant pause, and then the consultant added with a chuckle, "I'm not clear why."[15]

Discussing a rocket-motor plant he used to visit that overlooked Salt Lake City, Utah, Galvin sounded almost like a standup comic. "You make motors like you make a pound cake," he explained. "It's got to be smooth. I mean, you've got to put all those ingredients in there—a pound of eggs, a pound of butter and a pound of sugar." The residents around this plant all seemed to have two or three fingers on their hands, Galvin continued, winding up for the punchline. "The people down there pray a lot, because they know what's up on the mountain."[16]

As far as political leanings, over the years Galvin had been associated mostly with Democratic lawmakers. He claimed that his connections to the party went back to the difficult days of the Bobby Baker ethics investigation. One old friend recalls seeing him years later, pressing the flesh at a congressional barbecue featuring then–House Speaker Thomas O'Neill. "Galvin is very sharp. He was shaking hands with Tip O'Neill, and his wife was talking to people; she works a crowd just like he does." If there were important politicos or Pentagon types at a party, this friend says, "she would make sure Galvin met them all."[17]

After the Republicans' overwhelming victory in 1980, Bill Galvin switched allegiances. Acquaintances were only mildly surprised to see him attending some of the Reagan inaugural festivities. Access and gladhanding remained the gregarious consultant's trademark as the new administration's defense program took shape. He had connections at the working levels of the Pentagon, with congressional aides and among corporate marketing staffs. Tapping that network required perseverance and a talent for pleasuring sources. Galvin, for instance, loved to entertain military folks and industry executives at hockey games and racetracks. He bestowed favors large and small, providing free tires, clothes and other gifts to civil servants who could be helpful. He also gave away choice boxing and theater tickets with abandon—arranging for blocks of five or six seats at a time to several of the hottest Broadway plays to satisfy special requests.

Galvin's chauffeured Cadillac was available to transport government officials at a moment's notice. "I take Visa. Mastercard. American Express," Galvin kidded one civilian Navy official who called to confirm plans to be his guest for a French gourmet supper and springtime sojourn in the country. "We'll fatten up those girls," Galvin said, referring to their wives.[18]

Invariably, the overtures were light and friendly. Chatting about free ballet tickets he was providing to the same Navy official's family, Galvin joked: "Why would anybody pay money, and this looks like a lot of money . . . to the see the Pacific Northwest Ballet? I thought they'd give you those tickets for nothing."[19] Poking fun at another associate, he noted how easily the man accepted his generosity. "As Cleopatra said, 'I'm not prone to argue,' " Galvin told the recipient with a broad smile.[20] Under the surface, though, there was an implied admonition: Don't forget the source of all these goodies.

When one of Galvin's best contacts inside the military complained about being weary of government service, the consultant reacted quickly. For "a guy [who] lives a lifestyle like you live now . . . like I live," Galvin warned his fellow conspirator, it's not wise to make abrupt changes. By manipulating bids to help various Galvin clients, the Pentagon official already was well on track to becoming a millionaire. The riches in his grasp, he told Galvin gratefully, were possible "only because of you."[21]

And always, the consultant was quick to pick up checks for meals and drinks for his friends from the Pentagon. Six- or seven-hundred-dollar feasts at Lion D'Or or some other renowned Washington restaurant weren't unusual. "Your name will never appear on an expense account," Galvin reassured his government guests, so no outsiders could allege improper influence or trace acceptance of an illegal gratuity. "When you're with me," Galvin liked to tell officers and civilians alike, "you don't have to worry about being embarrassed."[22] The idea behind "rubbing" Pentagon decision-makers—as Galvin described his efforts to entertain and coopt those officials—was to make them "understand who I was and the things I was doing."[23]

What Galvin did best was forge relationships, then capitalize on them to benefit the companies that hired him. His attention wasn't restricted to the Navy. Galvin hobnobbed with Assistant Air Force Secretary Jack Welch, who was a guest at the high-school graduation party for one of the consultant's daughters. Galvin's other daughter worked as an aide to a Florida congressman. Galvin "was known as a deal-closer," says retired Marine Colonel Neel Patrick, who worked for both Galvin and Paisley.[24] In Galvin's own words, he was an industry "quarterback," a strategist able to bring together all the parties in a deal, make them feel comfortable and get things done. "That's what I do," the beefy consultant once explained. "I do it on the telephone. I do it in face-to-face visits, I do it with Congressional assistants."[25] In hindsight, Galvin says, he was "very, very good" at the social aspects of his job. Using friendship to corrupt the acquisition process to such an extent "could only happen in this town," he says. "I couldn't have [done that] anywhere else."[26]

Paisley liked the six-foot, barrel-chested wag with the gray hair and hearty laugh. Only a few years younger than the assistant Navy secretary, Galvin flaunted the identical macho image and wisecracking attitude. They were a pair of tough, street-smart battlers who had managed to overcome adversity. Like Paisley, Galvin also was prone to disregard the truth at times. Clients and fellow consultants respected his glibness. But behind his back, many said Galvin gave the word *duplicitous* a brand-new meaning. Darrell Cole, Paisley's trusted friend, called him "probably the fastest man in the world to spin a story."[27]

Galvin regaled Paisley with stories of his attachment to ice hockey, recounting how much he had enjoyed playing in college and dreamed about becoming a star in a semipro league. During a vacation in Idaho with their families one year, Paisley suggested, on the spur of the moment, that the group go ice skating. Inexplicably, his friend resisted the idea. After Galvin laced up his skates, the reason was obvious. He could barely stand up in the rink.[28]

The consultant also has been known to embellish a résumé. According to Galvin's vita, from 1974 to 1979 he was the president of a company responsible for the "design, installation and operations" of a diagnostic center at Miami's prestigious Cedars of Lebanon Hospital. In a sworn court deposition, Galvin later claimed he was retired during nearly that entire period. State and hospital files belie both stories. Florida's corporate records indicate that Galvin's firm was dissolved in 1976—two years after the diagnostic center opened its doors. Hospital personnel records, meanwhile, show that Galvin ran the center only from December 1975 to December 1976.[29]

Public personalities whom Galvin claimed he dealt with—from *The Tonight Show*'s Ed McMahon to former president Richard Nixon—couldn't remember ever meeting him. One former Navy official describes his astonishment at running into Galvin at a Capitol Hill function, where the consultant hailed him as a long-lost friend "even though I knew for sure that I had never met the guy in my life."[30]

Indeed, Bill Galvin was the first to admit that total honesty wasn't one of his virtues. If it was good for business, he didn't see anything wrong with fabricating a story. As an analogy, he explained, "I tell people their children are beautiful [and] they're not . . . It's not a lie."[31] Galvin has admitted that twenty years before meeting Paisley, he lied to a state grand jury investigating gambling in Florida.[32] In a 1984 civil case, he was accused of misrepresenting the financial condition of one of the handful of consulting firms he controlled, before selling it to San Diego investors. Talking with Paisley during the later stages of their friendship, Galvin once acknowledged the temptation to mislead clients. "I'm such a fucking liar," he blurted out.[33] The litmus test of friendship in Washington, he told Paisley before either of them knew about the Illwind investigation, "is whether you will stand up and lie for a friend, whether you will perjure yourself."[34]

Most telling, Galvin used flying as a bond with Paisley. Claiming that he saw action in the Korean War as a Marine Corps pilot, he recounted striking anecdotes about taking off from aircraft carriers and strafing targets in Korea's mountainous landscape. These anecdotes stirred fond memories in Paisley, the Navy's deskbound World War II ace. Galvin never admitted the truth to his friend, but he confided to others that he actually never saw combat in Korea because he arrived after the armistice had been signed.[35]

With so much in common, the two clicked with each other from the start. Soon after the chance encounter at the 1981 Christmas event, Galvin recalls, "we became very good friends." They enjoyed telling raunchy jokes, sharing meals and ruminating about how to boost the flow of funds to contractors. "Aviators have a lot of camaraderie," according to Galvin, and "our relationship developed from there . . . very quickly."[36] The families spent Thanksgiving and other holidays together. When the Paisleys bought new furniture, the Galvins got the used dining-room table and bedroom set to tide them over until they had time to furnish a new house.

In addition to the personal chemistry, Galvin says he never disguised his financial motives for striking up the friendship with Paisley. "He understood what my business was. He shared with me the direction in which the big boat called the Navy was going." Eventually, Galvin adds, "not a day went by when we didn't see each other and talk."[37]

A bitter Paisley recalls it differently. Trying hard to excuse his behavior by suggesting he was a gullible victim corrupted by big-city life, Paisley now claims Galvin tricked him. The wily consultant "moved with the speed of light," Paisley says, to ingratiate himself. "He cultivated me. I thought it was a real relationship, but it was all bullshit; I really got snookered."[38]

Each version is self-serving. But they agree on one important point. The tenor of Paisley's regime was set at the first get-together with Galvin. After that meeting, there is no disputing the fact that personal bonds drove Navy procurement decisions. Paisley was no innocent dupe of Galvin's. He grasped early on that the consultant was trading on his friendship. The assistant secretary's ego and greed overwhelmed ethical and legal constraints. The Pentagon and its biggest suppliers would never be the same.

Life also changed for Watson, who established the link between the two men. He gained double leverage to secure business for his company. The Singer subsidiary he worked for continued to rely on Galvin's assistance. But the company never again honored the invoices Galvin submitted demanding money. After the tree-trimming party, Galvin says, Watson "always reneged payment, acknowledging that something was due but never, never paying . . . He believed that introducing me to Paisley was payment enough."[39]

☆

The Reagan agenda for the Navy had been enunciated fully by the time Paisley was sworn in. Caspar Weinberger's decentralized management approach suddenly gave the civilian service secretaries real clout. In the past, they had been primarily administrative and honorific posts, with the services' uniformed brass and civilian bureaucracy making many important procurement choices, and the Defense secretary instructing the service chiefs on nearly all other weapons-buying decisions. Describing his immediate predecessor, Lehman snidely concluded: "The power of the office had atrophied from lack of exercise."[40] Secretary Lehman, by contrast, understood how the defense buildup altered that dynamic. Since Weinberger essentially was willing to support *everything* on a service's wish list, the fiefdoms inside the Pentagon could have free rein. In this vacuum of leadership at the very top, the premium was on speedy internal planning and good connections on Capitol Hill to make the increases a reality.

Lehman was the fastest, and by far the most adept, of the service secretaries at laying out his personal blueprint. It was written and ready for action practically the day he moved onto the Pentagon's fourth floor. While other appointees were cautiously feeling their way, he was already frenetically selling his plans on Capitol Hill. Lehman used to talk in terms of "saving" the Navy. "I feel very strongly that the Navy has to be fixed, and I know how to fix it," he would say.[41] Accordingly, it was important to stake out a well-defined course and not vacillate. In the past, he explained, there had been "far too much silliness and energy consumed on whether carriers should be big or small; whether we needed more single-screw small ships" or larger cruisers.[42]

If superiors in the Pentagon disagreed with his priorities, he covertly called on allies in the White House and Congress to stick up for him. When he was exposed for resorting to such alley-fighting tactics in Weinberger's staff meetings, Lehman argued down critics and grinned good-naturedly at the defense chief.[43] It took years for the rest of the services to catch on and longer for them to catch up.

The vaunted six-hundred-ship fleet, of course, was the heart and soul of the Navy secretary's grab for dollars. Shipbuilding was intended to be the largest single component of Reagan's procurement budget, swallowing one out of every four dollars. Though some of the vessels Lehman claimed credit for were funded and construction actually had begun under the previous administration, the six-hundred-ship concept made for great public relations. Lehman knew he had hit upon a simple yet politically sexy slogan: a rallying cry that could be embraced readily by everyone, from admirals to laymen.

Everything else flowed from that rationale. By sharply expanding the contingent of combat vessels, Lehman also provided justification for comparable increases in every nook and cranny of the Navy. Adding new carriers and reactivating mothballed battleships would require tens of thousands of additional sailors—along with more ships, planes, helicopters and missiles to protect them. That meant additional supplies, aircraft parts, radars and repair crews and more of just about everything else the Navy bought to keep its ships deployed. In barely a few years, the Navy's yearly budget would climb above $120 billion, from roughly $70 billion when Lehman came into office. The United States was the only country to revive giant, World War II–era battlewagons. Lehman's overall backlog of ship construction and conversion projects jumped above the $100-billion mark.

The pace of shipbuilding was slated to nearly double from previous years, and Lehman wanted to purchase at least twice as many planes as the average ordered annually by the Navy and the Marine Corps throughout the preceding decade. A network of new or upgraded Navy facilities was mapped out for a dozen cities around the United States. The official Navy explanation was that "strategic dispersal" of the fleet, called home-port-ing, would complicate Soviet nuclear targeting and make the Navy's prized carriers and "surface battle groups" less vulnerable to a surprise at-tack. It also was a legislative master stroke. Lehman realized that spreading money around states and congressional districts was a foolproof method to broaden geographical support for the buildup.

Politicians loved his plan because it created jobs. The Navy's leaders loved it too, because "they got a political base for a bigger fleet," one naval historian says. The concept, he explained, goes back "to the days when we began naming battleships for states and cruisers for cities, knowing every state and every city would want one of its own."[44]

Critics, who derided the notion as pure patronage and a crass political ploy, dubbed it "home-porking." They said the fleet would be no better protected from a barrage of thousands of Soviet warheads than if it stayed at existing ports. For instance, a new home port for the USS *Nimitz*, a carrier already based in Washington state, was projected to cost $272 mil-lion. The ship and her escorts were supposed to relocate a mere thirty-five miles up Puget Sound. Critics also pointed out an exquisite irony. One of the fixed-up battleships was to be based at an expensive new Hawaiian home—smack on Pearl Harbor's Battleship Row, precisely where the Japanese sank two of her sister ships on December 7, 1941.[45]

Nonetheless, just as Lehman predicted, lawmakers everywhere were in a lather to get the attendant jobs and construction money. When Lehman announced a decision to base seven ships on New York's Staten Island, a de-lighted Mayor Ed Koch likened it to "bringing the Brooklyn Dodgers back home."[46] The Navy secretary was expert at dangling other carrots in front of local politicians and members of Congress from both parties. Every time, he pounded home the point that the project hinged on attaining the all-consuming goal of six hundred vessels. Nothing less would suffice.

With his knowledge of Capitol Hill, Lehman never forgot how fickle its denizens could be. He was determined to squeeze every dollar out of Congress posthaste, including unprecedented approval to begin construc-tion of two mammoth *Nimitz*-class carriers at the same time. Without al-luding to it publicly, Lehman understood that the political climate could change quickly and end the Navy's time of milk and honey. This was his moment to shine. From the day John Lehman came into the Pentagon with grand political aspirations, "He exhibited the spirit of a man who

wanted later to be able to declare, 'I'm the one who built the real Navy,' "
says Admiral William Crowe, the retired chairman of the Joint Chiefs and
an ambassador to Great Britain.[47]

Trying to outdo Lehman, the Navy's champions on Capitol Hill were
pushing for an even larger fleet. By comparison, they made Secretary
Lehman appear almost conciliatory. Senator Tower of Texas—a former
master chief petty officer who retained a soft spot in his heart for the
Navy—led the fight as chairman of the Armed Services Committee. In
the spring of 1981, before Reagan's first budget had been approved, Tower
dispassionately told reporters that it would be "desirable to expand the
Navy to between 700 and 800 ships." Lehman's target, Tower said, was adequate "just to stay in the game" but not to guarantee U.S. naval superiority for the foreseeable future.[48]

Together, Lehman and Tower sketched out a vision markedly more of-
fensively oriented than the maritime doctrine the Pentagon had relied on
for the past thirty-five years. Citing U.S. intelligence reports, they reeled
off statistics about Soviet shipyards working at full capacity, construction
of Russia's first nuclear-powered supercarrier and two new Soviet classes
of superquiet submarines that were believed ready to go into production.
This hard-line view, formally adopted by Weinberger in late 1981, envisioned a bold U.S. response. "We had to regain the confidence of our allies," Weinberger recalls. The only sure way to do that, he adds, was "to
regain a great deal of military strength very quickly."[49]

Submarines remained integral to nuclear deterrence. The new vision of
the surface Navy, however, went far beyond ferrying troops, showing the
flag and keeping trade routes open. It centered on a dramatically enlarged
fleet ready to intervene anywhere in the world. The Navy was extolled as
the most flexible tool for projecting American power, able to wage long,
multiple wars against regional enemies or the combined forces of "the
Soviet military empire." Maritime supremacy over the Soviets replaced
earlier concepts of military balance.[50]

Many in the Pentagon resisted and tried to sabotage these arguments,
partly out of inertia and partly because the other services necessarily
would have to trim their budgets to accommodate the Navy's growth.
Detractors said that Lehman's priorities were skewed, and the result
would be a sadly unbalanced force. They argued that in the 1990s, aircraft
carriers and battleships could become sitting ducks for roving enemy submarines. Other doubters asserted that the greatest threat posed by the Soviet Union was a blitzkrieg-style ground war in Western Europe, in
which the U.S. Navy's participation most likely would be marginal. But
the Navy chief kept battling. He dismissed the opposing theories as "naive
and childlike." Command of the seas "allows you then to influence the
land battle" in a decisive manner, he countered.[51]

Lehman reserved his most inspired end runs for Pentagon higher-ups
who dared to block him. Early in his tenure, he prevailed on Reagan's se-

nior staff to craft a speech for the president that explicitly supported American "maritime superiority" and blasted the Soviets for assembling a "powerful blue ocean navy that cannot be justified by any legitimate defense need." Months later, when his sacrosanct fifteen carriers were under attack by Weinberger's deputy, the Navy chief persuaded allies in the west wing of the White House to perform a bit of trickery on his behalf. It certainly didn't hurt Lehman's cause that his younger brother, Christopher, worked for Reagan; or that Bud McFarlane, an ex-Marine, and John Poindexter, a rear admiral still on active duty at the time, were among the highest-ranking aides on the National Security Council. Lehman's network of supporters never ceased to amaze his enemies.

What Lehman's surrogates did was devilishly clever. They convinced the president, who was oblivious of the argument raging inside the Pentagon, to approve names for the two new aircraft carriers Lehman was struggling to keep in the budget. Weinberger and the rest of the Pentagon hierarchy weren't consulted. The press release was rushed out the same day. On the surface it seemed routine—an announcement of the names followed by two sentences of boilerplate indicating Reagan's support for building fifteen carriers to ensure "the requisite naval superiority we need." In the face of Reagan's personal endorsement, Lehman's critics inside the Pentagon were hogtied.[52] The Navy secretary was emboldened by this coup, and his diatribe against foes within the administration soon showed up on the front page of The Washington Post.

Weinberger rarely objected to such subterfuge. The Defense secretary didn't like in-house confrontations. And he was convinced that Lehman, with all his guile, was utterly loyal to the president. In his autobiography, Weinberger singled out the decision to recommission four mothballed battleships as the most striking symbol of the Navy's rebirth. Calling the World War II–era giants "mighty engines of deterrence," he said they added tremendously to "our ability to keep our peace and our freedom."[53]

Lehman's early success disheartened but didn't eliminate opposition. Critics groused that the fast-growing fleet would founder, due to the colossal operating costs looming down the road. Arming and provisioning all the vessels, to say nothing about manning them with top-notch crews, could become the Achilles heel of the Reagan defense revolution, these critics said. It cost upward of half a million dollars a day, for instance, to operate a single aircraft carrier even in the early 1980s. That covered food, fuel and pay for the crew, but not a penny for flying or maintaining the aircraft on board.[54]

Jimmy Carter's aides predicted that Lehman was building a huge modern armada that would be able to fight only for a brief period before running out of money and supplies. Other critics complained that the Reaganites were sowing the seeds for a more "hollow Navy"—deprived of adequate funds for manpower, training and maintenance—than the force John Lehman insisted suffered from such disrepair and low morale when he took it over. The multibillion-dollar new carriers, one House Democratic aide later snapped, only half in jest, "may end up becoming gigantic shuffleboard platforms for retired officers."[55]

Lehman was listening intently. He wanted to demonstrate his commitment to savings, though he absolutely refused to cut a single ship scheduled to be built. Rather, he discarded the best estimates of the Navy's budget professionals and knowingly replaced them with the "most optimistic estimate" of future construction costs. All of a sudden, the numbers looked noticeably better. The accounting sleight-of-hand infuriated critics.

For a longer-term fix, Lehman had other techniques in mind. In order to buy and operate all the hardware crammed into his budgets, he recognized, the Navy had to stretch its acquisition dollars. The old system "favored constant tinkering and design changes, with skyrocketing costs averaging 20 percent above inflation every year," Lehman noted.[56] That clearly wasn't acceptable. So he advocated a sea change in the rules for choosing suppliers and structuring contracts.[57] There was no alternative, if people were to take the six-hundred-ship goal seriously.

The lengthy list of policy changes was anathema to old Navy hands. The ideas were infused with a single principle: Lehman was convinced that enhanced competition among contractors was the answer. By relying on traditional market forces, he hoped to reduce costs, force defense firms to improve management and end chronic overruns that had plagued the Navy's programs for decades. Competition became akin to religious dogma in the service. For Secretary Lehman—who insisted that he was simply applying "logic and common sense" to reap the benefits of "true competition"—the key was making company and Navy decision-makers accountable for their performance.

"The thing that surprised me most about the procurement business at the Pentagon," he recalls, "was that there was no reward or punishment that was hooked to the actual cost" of any program. "No single human being had responsibility any more."[58] Sole-source contracts devised by the Pentagon's faceless and unbending "central planning" structure, according to Lehman, mirrored the failed, Big-Brother-knows-it-all ideology of the Soviets. The contractor producing one generation of weapon systems was the same one that huddled with Defense Department planners to map plans for the next round. Lehman said the arrangement made it easy for companies to monopolize programs, churn out shoddy equipment and jack up prices without impediment. He hated the loss of control.

The response was to demand competitive bidding in most instances. In the past, Lehman argued, the Navy had promoted "the mere appearance" of competition by "holding a beauty contest among competing designs" for a plane or a missile "and then awarding a monopoly to one company for decades of production."[59] His new approach was supposed to pit suppliers against each other in cutthroat struggles, repeated every year or two, to keep costs down. It yielded results in short order. Before Reagan's first term ended, the Navy awarded more than 44 percent of the dollar volume of its contracts competitively, up from 15 percent when Lehman arrived. Though estimates vary greatly, by the late 1980s some studies showed that share exceeding 80 percent.

Lehman dictated other changes, too. Instead of cost-plus contracts guaranteeing suppliers a hefty profit almost regardless of how high the price tag eventually climbed, the Navy shifted to fixed-price agreements for many big programs. These contracts set a firm limit on how much suppliers would be paid. Thus, weapons-makers were forced to assume a larger share of the financial risks. John Lehman didn't forget about the president's commitment to help contractors. He was hardly a rabid antibusiness activist. "We tried to force contractors to give us an honest price with a profit margin" that was reasonable, he recalls. "We wanted them to stay in business . . . not to lose money."[60] Companies nevertheless howled that earnings would plummet. But Lehman wouldn't be deterred. Fixed-price contracts became commonplace, even for risky development of prototypes. In fact, studies later showed that during the Reagan years, large contractors overall earned substantially higher profits on defense work than on their private-sector businesses.

Another favorite Lehman tactic was lining up two rival firms to manufacture the same weapon. Each was assured of getting a chunk of the orders, but head-to-head competitions were held regularly to determine their respective shares. Sometimes, a second company, or combination of companies, was invited to bid and brought on stream long after the primary supplier was producing. Price and quality were supposed to be the determining factors. "It makes sense in virtually all cases," Lehman insists to this day. Every area in which the approach was tried showed "dramatic reductions in price," he says. "It's just human nature; if you have to compete, you're going to control your costs."[61] The idea rapidly spread to the other services.

"We needed competition not only to get better prices, but to make sure we had more companies capable of doing effective defense work," Weinberger says. Lehman and especially Paisley, he adds, "made a big show" of how they were going after companies to "bang heads together and get all these low bids to save money."[62]

Quite apart from the criminality it spawned, this so-called "dual-sourcing" strategy became extremely controversial later on. It prompted critics to conclude that Lehman's score keeping was fatally flawed and many of his policy's ballyhooed savings were nonexistent.

For starters, the Navy often allowed the "lead" supplier to choose the company that was going to be installed as the second source. By picking a high-cost or less-experienced manufacturer for that role, the lead firm effectively was able to ensure that prices wouldn't drop appreciably. Further, it stood to gain a handsome fee for sharing technology enabling a second contractor to begin manufacturing the identical product.

Bill Galvin understood the subtleties exceptionally well. "When you pick a second source," he explained, "you pick a friendly, docile second source; you don't pick a tiger." This wasn't competition the way objective observers define the term. The aim, Galvin said, was to avoid an aggressive company that would snatch the technology but then "two years later puts you out of business . . . You wouldn't pick the Japanese as a second source."[63]

The Pentagon's inspector general concluded that the tendency to guarantee a large proportion of work to the higher bidder—sometimes up to 40 percent of the Navy's annual buy of a specific item—also negated any incentive for meaningful price competition. Both manufacturers could offer inflated bids, confident that no third party would undercut them. The result, according to the inspector general, was a system "conducive to price gaming" that often became a pernicious impediment to real competition. The benefits of dual-sourcing had been grossly overstated, and the Pentagon ended up wasting hundreds of millions of dollars in tooling and other costs to set up two separate production lines where it was pointless.[64]

Lawmakers and congressional auditors came to the same conclusion. They blamed Lehman for trying to dual-source everything, creating farcical screw-ups. Recognizing the gusher of contracts as a one-time bonanza, some shipyards submitted unrealistically low bids to get business while it was available. But the Navy's savings were short-lived. The all-out scramble to "lowball" contracts forced the same yards, a few years later, to seek hundreds of millions of extra dollars to cover escalating construction costs. The Navy drove "companies to do dumb things that are going to cost the taxpayer" in the final analysis, said industry representative John Stocker.[65]

Meanwhile, makers of missiles and other weapons were trying to outwit each other to come in with a slightly *higher* bid price—which would translate into lower production volumes but greater per-unit profit and consequently overall higher earnings. "The problem is simply one of too many programs" and manufacturers, the General Accounting Office said, with tremendous potential for waste and overlap. The GAO faulted Pentagon officials for allowing each command to sign dual-source contracts and build "its own program and budget based on how they define their needs."[66] Lehman's opponents went so far as to argue that a pattern of unwise second-source competition bloated manufacturing capacity and had the perverse effect of driving some midsize companies out of the industry forever when budgets got tight.[67]

But the initiatives served their immediate purpose. They enabled the mercurial Navy chief to systematically shut out the procurement overseers in Secretary Weinberger's office. A tight-knit group around Lehman made all the decisions, helping him score critical early victories against industry. During his initial months on the job, for example, Lehman jawboned General Dynamics to slash prices, drop huge claims pending against the

Navy and tighten manufacturing controls for nuclear submarines. He insisted that the company wouldn't be reimbursed for construction defects, including the use of improper steel and substandard welds.

This was perceived as a slap in the face to the whole industry. Lehman privately told the company that the Reagan team, more than anything else, needed quality and on-time performance from contractors in order to reach the six-hundred-ship fleet.[68] He said the Navy was willing to retool a second commercial yard to build ballistic-missile-firing Tridents, or even build them in government yards if that was what it took to reduce costs. If government facilities were used, Lehman declared in a huff, "We would save all the money and time we currently waste dealing with claims from private yards."[69]

David Lewis, the chairman of General Dynamics, fired back. "You don't need to go to the god-damned press and say those terrible things about us . . . That's just more blackmail."[70] Only Soviet shipyards had the wherewithal to build Trident subs, another senior company official told Lehman mockingly, and they weren't likely to provide the ironclad guarantees he wanted on price or delivery schedules.[71]

The nasty and very public squabble—including Lehman's angry televised outbursts and his withholding of contracts from the company for months—buttressed the secretary's basic point. The old-style contracting rules had been fundamentally rewritten. There would be no turning back. Lehman wasn't about to back down from the "pissing contest" with industry, as the General Dynamics chairman put it.[72] The Navy secretary and the company did work out a compromise in the end, but Lehman continued to make public pronouncements about how he had brought the nation's largest contractor to its knees.[73] When the Navy issued its solicitations for sealed bids, in theory there were no longer supposed to be sure-fire winners.

Lehman was equally high-handed with other contractors. He got interested in the powerful ground-targeting radars McDonnell Douglas installed in some supersonic F-15 fighters for the Air Force. The planes had uncanny precision in bad weather, zooming in on targets at altitudes as low as one hundred feet. Lehman wanted to see the system in action. McDonnell Douglas agreed to have a test pilot fly one of its most advanced F-15s from the St. Louis assembly plant to the Gulf Coast of Texas, where Lehman was on a working vacation. Paisley rode as copilot on the trip south. Without explanation or apology, the secretary kept the plane, its support crew and company executives waiting at a nearby naval air station for almost a day—while he and his hosts hunted, rode the range in four-wheel drive trucks and otherwise entertained themselves. "He expected us to bring a product like that fifteen hundred miles, totally at our expense, so he could take it for a spin" at his convenience, says a former McDonnell Douglas executive. "We weren't even selling the damn plane to the Navy."[74] Lehman claims that the demonstration flight was the company's idea.

Cost and performance weren't necessarily the driving forces behind all of Lehman's orders. Sometimes, he saw contractors as an adjunct to the Navy's hyperactive public affairs operation.

Lehman told the chairman of Tenneco, an old-line supplier with major shipbuilding contracts, that he needed the company's help to quiet protests in Puerto Rico about a giant bombing range. The Navy was eager to keep using the range at one end of Vieques Island. The other half of the dreary island, about twenty miles off Puerto Rico's eastern tip, was inhabited by several thousand unemployed natives in squalid villages. Puerto Rican politicians complained bitterly that the Navy wasn't doing enough to build up the local economy. John Lehman was tired of the bad press and threats by community groups to put an end to training flights using live munitions. His solution was to force Tenneco into investing nearly $3 million to launch a joint venture with the natives. The idea was to raise miniature vegetables. The fancy produce was to be air-freighted daily to high-priced restaurants in New York. "I made a commitment to get U.S. companies in there," Lehman told the contractor's top executives. "I expect you to do this."[75]

Some 150 workers were hired, a processing plant was built and the verbal attacks on the Navy halted—at least temporarily.

Tenneco's management saw the foray into agriculture as a white elephant from the word go. They argued that the project's underlying economics—a lack of skilled labor coupled with exorbitant shipping costs—made it a surefire money loser. But with billions of dollars in Navy contracts at stake, the firm decided it couldn't afford to alienate Lehman. Tenneco's chairman, James Ketelsen, personally approved the investment. "We're not doing this because it's a sound business decision," he reportedly told Lehman. "We're gonna lose our ass." In four years, the joint venture ran out of money and closed its doors.[76] According to Lehman, "There was no implied threat; I've been accused of many things, but not gross stupidity."

Even when companies did his bidding, Lehman could be arbitrary. Industry executives recall him strongly suggesting to bidders which subcontractors and law firms they ought to hire—and even the politicians they should support—in order to retain the Navy's confidence. Sometimes, contracts were handed out seemingly with scant relation to official selection criteria. In late 1984, around the time Tenneco was setting up its ill-starred Puerto Rican vegetable-ferrying operation, the company's Newport News Shipbuilding unit learned that it had submitted the low bid for all four nuclear-powered attack submarines the Navy put up for competition that year. The price tag totaled more than $1 billion.

Lehman decided to divvy up the work and award only three of the vessels to Newport News, with the fourth going to archrival General Dynamics. It was one more victory for dual-sourcing, though some of the issues were murky enough for Lehman to warn Newport News officials not to file a formal protest or repeat their conversations with him. The implication, these officials say, couldn't have been more clear. If Newport

News opted to challenge him publicly, the Navy chief was prepared to hold up future business for the firm.[77] "He tended to personalize every-thing," one senior industry figure says, requesting anonymity. "John could be ruthless and vindictive if he felt that you had crossed him."

Lehman and his lieutenants got a Raytheon vice-president fired for daring to publicly challenge the Navy's budget goals. "Nobody in the in-dustry wanted to have anything to do with me," recalls Lawrence Korb, who had clashed with Lehman previously as a Reagan appointee in the Pentagon. "It was like having leprosy." In private budget meetings, accord-ing to Korb, Lehman said he wasn't concerned about climbing mainte-nance and upkeep costs because the crunch wouldn't come until the Reagan administration had left office.[78]

Above all, the stubborn Navy chief was prone to substitute coercion for consensus. The A-12 Avenger, a cutting-edge, radar-evading bomber proposed for carrier missions, was the biggest aviation program taking shape during his watch. Down the road, the Navy wanted to buy more than five hundred of the exotic planes for perhaps $52 billion—a figure twice as large as the entire European community's annual weapons ex-penditures. Lehman kept rigid control of the project, running it in near-total secrecy under the most restrictive "Special Access" security designation. Even those with top-secret clearances couldn't get access to A-12 information without further security clearance. During all of his tenure, the Navy declassified only five sentences of meaningful explana-tion about the plane's likely cost and performance.

Behind the scenes, Lehman feuded incessantly with the contractors. He wouldn't approve certain design changes they maintained were essential. Over strenuous objections from engineers, he insisted on a side-by-side cockpit for the two-man crew as the optimum arrangement for a bomber. The companies told him it would mean a less stealthy and slower plane. They prepared lengthy briefings about weight and performance penalties. Still, the Navy chief persisted.

McDonnell Douglas and General Dynamics, the team developing the Avenger, finally resorted to an engineering scam. They came up with a modular concept for the cockpit, betting correctly that once Lehman left office they would be able to scrap the side-by-side design. It meant extra work and delays, but there simply was no other route to appease Lehman.[79]

Such tactics couldn't rescue the program, which became a focus of the Illwind probe and ultimately went into a death spiral as a result of stagger-ing cost overruns and manufacturing foulups. Too heavy to fly off a car-rier safely—it was estimated to be overweight by a whopping eight thousand pounds—the A-12 needed a last-minute wing redesign. Prob-lems also cropped up with its computer software, antennas and skin made out of high-tech composite materials. Nearly $3 billion was spent, with-out a single prototype ever being fully assembled.

Defense Secretary Dick Cheney pulled the plug on the Avenger after

Lehman's departure, complaining that he had been hoodwinked not only by the contractors but also by the Navy. "No one can tell me exactly how much more it will cost to keep this program going, and I do not believe a bailout is in the national interest," a livid Cheney announced, speaking for George Bush, another hawkish Republican president. "By the time Cheney found out" about the gross mismanagement, "he had egg all over his face," says Republican congressman John Kasich of Ohio.[80] Cancellation of the A-12—the largest U.S. weapons development program ever terminated by the Pentagon—set the stage for what is now shaping up as the costliest federal contracting dispute in history.[81] It could cost the Navy $2 billion or more to settle the litigation.

Moreover, the Avenger's death was a striking rebuke to Lehman and his policies. For many, the A-12 debacle displayed the Navy secretary at his most capricious. To some extent, the project was viewed by Lehman and his brain trust as a race with the Air Force. While mercilessly prodding Navy contractors to speed up design work and cut corners to beat the timelines and costs projected for the Air Force's next-generation aircraft, Lehman failed to provide Congress with reliable figures. Until his last day in the Pentagon, he insisted that a fixed-price development contract was adequate to protect the Navy against all contingencies. Every time A-12 contractors requested a change in specifications or schedule, Lehman's aides had a standard reply: "This is what the Secretary wants. This is the way we're going to do it. Period."[82] With Lehman, says one veteran McDonnell Douglas manager, "You never did get a reason; you only got a directive."

Simultaneously, the high-energy Navy secretary declared war on his own bureaucracy, especially the senior "blue-suiters" he loved to ridicule as panic-stricken by new ideas.

Even without Lehman's ambitious agenda, the Navy would have been the most cantankerous arm of the Defense Department for a new management team to tackle. President Franklin Roosevelt, recalling his clashes with the Navy, compared those fights to flailing away at a feather bed: "You punch it with your right hand and you punch it with your left," he said, "until you are finally exhausted and then you find the damn bed just as it was before you started punching." Lehman liked to use that quotation. He added that FDR, at least, didn't have to dismantle the cult of Admiral Hyman Rickover, who embodied the modern Navy's intransigence.[83]

A nonconformist who ran the nuclear side of the Navy for nearly three decades, Rickover personally interviewed every officer candidate hoping to serve under him. The four-star admiral's intellect and accomplishments were legendary, but so was his dislike for civilian interference. Rickover refused to exit by retiring gracefully when Lehman wanted to replace him at the age of eighty-two. During a hot-tempered exchange with the Navy secretary in the Oval Office, with Reagan trying to act as peacemaker, Rickover shouted that Lehman was "a piss-ant [who] knows nothing about the Navy."[84] In a tirade filled with expletives, Rickover then turned on the president, who had offered him a face-saving job as a White House adviser: "Aw, cut the crap," the admiral snapped. "Are you a man? Can't you make decisions yourself?" he yelled at the commander in chief. "They say that you are too old, and that you're not up to the job either."[85]

Lehman persevered and eventually pushed Rickover out of the Pentagon. But the admiral's animosity and disdain for his civilian bosses was shared, albeit to a lesser degree, by officers throughout the fleet.

One apocryphal story associated with former Navy secretary and revered arms-control negotiator Paul Nitze—and passed down from generation to generation inside The Building—highlights the armed services' contrasting reactions to strong-willed civilian leaders during the Cold War. The Army was so eager to please, according to this tale, that its generals almost tripped over each other rushing out the door to follow orders. Air Force generals only pretended to make mandated changes, betting that their high-tech wizardry would bamboozle outsiders. Lastly, the story describes the Navy's response: Without hesitation, top admirals told the upstart civilians to stick it in their ear. In a nutshell, the vignette captures the Navy's fierce independence. From Admiral Rickover to Lieutenant Colonel Oliver North of Iran-Contra fame, Navy and Marine Corps officers followed rules that didn't apply to others.

The service's temperament was shaped, in part, by the nature of command at sea. In the middle of the ocean, the captain of a warship is used to being in charge with comparatively little interference from higher-ups in Washington. His word is the law. Steeped in that tradition, the Navy's top brass over the years jealously guarded their authority in every forum, especially from the other services and congressional oversight panels. The prerogatives of the captain often bred arrogance. The essence of Navy leadership, one retired four-star admiral summed it up, "creates a mind set that wants to be apart."[86]

For Lehman, the admirals' mulish resistance to change equated to heresy. He started clipping their wings in purchasing, by ordering more programs to report to him or his hand-picked deputies. Old habits of doing business, which allowed the chief of naval operations and his large staff to make decisions and submit them for pro forma approval by the secretary, were history. Lehman demanded that his office be intimately involved in the procurement process, rather than rubber stamping the CNO's final recommendations, which left out all references to internal debates or dissenting views.

The Navy's Materiel Command was abolished—a practically unheard-of affront to the bureaucracy's typically nonconfrontational mode. Lehman set up a career track for officers specializing in procurement, which also shook up the old lines of authority in dealing with contractors. Development of some top-priority weapons was shifted to a fast-track approach, outside the bureaucracy's normal decision-making procedures altogether. And Lehman, along with his assistant secretaries, adopted a hands-on management style that didn't tolerate second guessing.

As his first few years as secretary drew to a close, Lehman figured out that those changes didn't hit the blue-suiters' most vulnerable pressure points. He shrewdly began asserting himself more forcefully in personnel issues. Control over promotions and assignments largely had been considered the bailiwick of the uniformed Navy—since those two things matter the most to career officers. Increasingly, Lehman took a role in deciding which officers moved into the choice jobs and higher ranks. Mucking around with buying practices and dual-sourcing regulations was one thing, admirals fumed. Inserting himself into the Navy's most sensitive, tradition-bound personnel decisions was another matter entirely.

Admittedly, for as long as anyone could remember naval promotion boards had been buffeted by intraservice politics and rivalries. The "nukes" and the "tailhookers"—as the submariners and aviators were called—constantly jockeyed for a larger share of promotions. The surface warfare contingent also stuck together, trying to push their buddies into major command jobs. Various quotas and benchmarks were used to divide up assignments and keep the three communities pacified. Attaining flag rank (rear admiral or above) often depended more on personalities and warfare specialties than an unbiased review of an officer's overall service record. "In the 1950s, the way to the top of the Navy was to be an aviator," one admiral explained. "In the 1960s and '70s, it was to be a nuclear submariner."[87] In the 1980s, the key was getting John Lehman in your corner.

The earlier tugs-of-war over promotions played out primarily inside the uniformed Navy. Outside pressure—either from the White House or from the Pentagon's civilian leadership—affected only the very highest jobs. Under Lehman's watch, that was no longer the case. Allegiance to the secretary and the changes he espoused seemed to take on paramount importance for lower-level promotions and transfers. Lehman prized initiative and loyalty above everything else. Disregarding the advice of the Navy's graybeards, in some instances the secretary passed over as many as two hundred more senior officers to reach into the ranks and promote a candidate whose spark and presence impressed him.

Lehman wasn't bashful about wielding such clout. The power that counts the most in the Pentagon's corridors, he sometimes argued, doesn't directly involve control of the purse strings. Budgets change frequently, as do the political appointees who sit in the defense secretary's suite of offices and draw them up. But according to Lehman, the head of one of the armed services "can really accomplish something . . . You have the power to make your actions stick because you control promotions."[88] As far as the admirals in charge were concerned, Lehman had done the unforgivable.

By the time Paisley's nameplate officially went up on an office five doors down the hall from Lehman's, the game plan was in place. The secretary would continue plugging his concepts to lawmakers and the media. Influential members of Congress were invited for cozy breakfasts whenever the "SecNav," as Lehman's staff referred to him in shorthand, was in town. Also, Lehman was acutely aware that congressmen, senators and their families thought that attending a ship christening was a lot more classy and fun than watching the roll-out of some new tank or armored utility vehicle. He spared no effort extending invitations for ship-launching ceremonies to anyone who could help him. No less assiduous in courting the press, aides recall, the indefatigable Navy secretary gave more than 150 interviews in a single year.

Meanwhile, Paisley and a handful of Lehman's other trusted aides were supposed to mind the store. Their instructions were to work diligently behind the scenes, grappling with obstinate admirals and browbeating stubborn industry executives. The task was to translate Lehman's broad pronouncements into concrete action. The secretary acknowledged that his dreams would come to naught "if we could not get the Navy bureaucracy on the one hand, and the contractors on the other, each to do their part of the job."[89]

Lehman was convinced that he had found the secret to getting that done. It didn't entail complex, multilayered organizational charts. Nor did it involve gradual adjustments to the Navy's weapons-buying structure. The true test of his policies, Lehman believed, was the caliber and gumption of the assistant secretaries working for him. He felt success would come from assembling a team of "really good people who were willing to accept the challenge and responsibility" of authority—and then giving them carte blanche to mercilessly attack the status quo.[90]

☆

Notwithstanding his impressive title, Mel Paisley was in dire need of help as soon as he was confirmed. He didn't know the most effective tack to try to sell the new policies to contractors or to obtain the corporate cooperation essential to carrying them out. He desperately needed to find an intermediary with industry.

Paisley's purview was immense. He was in charge of everything from developing cutting-edge stealth and radar technology to picking the engines that would propel jet fighters off carrier decks into the twenty-first century. His decisions also determined what kind of missiles, communications gear, satellite-reconnaissance projects, ultrasensitive submarine tracking devices and other equipment would go out to the fleet. Yet to accomplish all that, he had few people inside or outside the Pentagon to turn to for guidance.

To begin with, Paisley had left his trusted friends and supporters behind at Boeing. The admirals heading procurement certainly weren't sympathetic. Their top-level civilian staffers knew the system's faults and could have been enormously helpful, but they, too, were afraid of Lehman's take-no-prisoners attitude. The rest of the Pentagon wasn't likely to offer helpful suggestions either, since the Navy secretary was universally disliked by leaders of the other services. Lehman hardly ever passed up a chance to take a swipe at them. He scoffed at proposals to reduce the Navy's independence, claiming the result would "Prussianize" America's military. When he wasn't feuding with some Weinberger aide, he was raising hackles by mocking the Army and the Air Force as nothing more than "garrison" troops. Paisley saw how many folks in the Pentagon were rooting for Lehman's crew to fail.

To make his boss and himself look good, Paisley had to lean on someone with close ties to contractors, someone who could deal informally with executives, acting as both cheerleader and unofficial enforcer for the Lehman agenda. Bill Galvin was the natural choice. Paisley acknowledges that his smooth-talking compatriot provided an important boost when he most needed it: "Galvin knew more people on Capitol Hill and in industry that I did. He worked for so many companies; he helped me a lot."[91]

Indeed, at the outset Galvin provided substantially more assistance to Paisley than the reverse. Within weeks of taking office, Paisley was using him as a sounding board. The ill-fated A-12 was just a glimmer on the Navy's drawing boards at the time. The assistant secretary was toying with the idea of cutting costs by using a derivative of an Air Force–developed aircraft to replace the venerable, Grumman-built A-6 Intruders that were the mainstay of the fleet. Paisley wondered if Galvin knew anybody at Grumman, then the service's premier aircraft-maker, who could provide some informal counsel. One of the firm's vice-presidents was a Marine buddy, Galvin responded. In a matter of days, the three of them gathered in Paisley's kitchen over mugs of coffee to toss around ideas. Paisley's notions didn't pan out, and Grumman never got a contract out of the chat. But the session was a paradigm for handling his future relations with Galvin.

Walking out, the Grumman executive confided to the consultant: "You've got a good friend here in this Paisley. You get a guy to call you up and invite you to his kitchen to talk about things that would be of great value to companies." Looking back, Galvin acknowledges that the interchange "opened my eyes to a whole bunch of things."[92]

Galvin's connections were essential to feel out companies' willingness to become second-source suppliers to the Navy. Even if he had been determined to make such approaches by himself, Paisley still would have had to rely on Galvin to identify the best contacts at major contractors. As the collaboration developed, the consultant did much more than supply names. "It wasn't a question of just picking up the phone and calling someone" at a couple of companies to attend a formal Pentagon briefing, Galvin recalls. Paisley was used to operating in a more personal, spontaneous manner. In truth, he nodded off during many of the lengthy and dry slide presentations favored by the various purchasing offices. One-on-one exchanges had been his style at Boeing, and he didn't see any reason to change. "He wanted someone he could sit and talk to in his home in a relaxed environment," Galvin recalls, to sort out issues in a freewheeling atmosphere. "I provided that bridge for Paisley to a lot of people in industry."[93]

The travails of the Tomahawk cruise missile, the Navy's ultimate precision-guided weapon, reveal why Galvin's exertions many times proved invaluable. Fired from submarines and surface ships, the missiles are designed to skim over land or water to deliver everything from nuclear warheads to clusters of small antipersonnel munitions at a range of some two thousand miles. Tomahawks navigate by comparing images of the terrain they traverse with digitized maps stored in their computer brains. The missiles are capable of traveling hundreds of miles undetected by enemy radar—even sweeping around corners of city streets and penetrating windows and ventilation shafts of buildings with phenomenal accuracy, as they did in downtown Baghdad during the Persian Gulf War. If there are no glitches, Tomahawks can be depended on to strike within a few feet of their targets.

Lehman viewed that capability as an essential building block for his "forward-deployed" nautical doctrine, intended to bottle up the Soviet fleet in its home waters. Tomahawks would put Soviet ships, ports and other vital targets at increased risk, thereby allowing U.S. carriers to maneuver closer to the Soviet coastline than would have been deemed prudent otherwise. After a decade of development, Lehman decreed it was time finally to put the potent weapons on the decks of Navy vessels. It was one of the first big acquisition moves facing the Navy's new taskmaster. He crammed the idea down the throats of admirals, many of whom opposed the Tomahawk because it threatened to undercut the funding and rationale for their pet projects.

Manufacturing snafus, however, impeded the Tomahawk's progress. As General Dynamics ramped up to full-scale production, Lehman and Paisley realized the magnitude of the problem. Quality control was so lax that the Navy's program manager was removed, and Paisley threatened to stop accepting missiles until a solution was hammered out. Around that time, the Pentagon announced that the total projected price tag for the Tomahawk program had quadrupled in roughly twelve months. While a share of the increase was attributable to new features and additional quantities the Navy decided to buy, serious cost overruns at General Dynamics also were to blame. The escalating price sent Paisley into screaming fits.

Since the Navy planned to spend approximately $12 billion to acquire Tomahawks over the years, dual-sourcing loomed as an obvious choice. Under Lehman's market-oriented policies, competition was precisely the remedy General Dynamics needed. Pressure from a second supplier was supposed to improve the firm's efficiency, put a lid on costs and help clean up its troubled Tomahawk operations. Once again, Galvin was chosen as Paisley's emissary. "Why don't you find someone to become a second source on the cruise missile?" Paisley asked his friend one day. It was a request Galvin eagerly anticipated.[94]

Never one to minimize his stature, the consultant later portrayed himself as the Navy's semiofficial ambassador to the entire defense community. Galvin said he had been given a "portfolio" by Paisley "to talk to many of my friends in industry" and share Navy documents laying out Tomahawk manufacturing criteria. The first two companies he approached didn't bite. McDonnell Douglas, the next one on his list, sounded more enthusiastic. After consulting with headquarters, a senior executive told Galvin: "We might be interested. How can we do that?"[95]

Not long thereafter, Galvin escorted his McDonnell Douglas contact up to Paisley's office, where the assistant secretary spelled out exactly what he wanted. "Lo and behold," Galvin now cracks, "they were selected as the second source" for Tomahawks, built a plant in Titusville, Florida, and began manufacturing "a better missile than General Dynamics." Galvin pats himself on the back for doing "a very good thing for the United States Navy."[96]

Paisley also was extremely gratified with the outcome. Based on the dealings with Grumman and McDonnell Douglas, Paisley told his friend that they made a tremendous team and ought to continue working together. The possibilities for future cooperation were staggering. Galvin's assistance engendered excellent rapport with companies. "I knew who to call, and they would respond," Paisley explains. "In those days, that's how we did things."[97]

Likewise, McDonnell Douglas gave Galvin a sign of its appreciation. He landed a $180,000 consulting contract with the country's second-largest defense firm.[98] Rapidly, Galvin attained credibility inside the industry. With the early Tomahawk success under their belts, Mel and Bill were ready to set off on their marvelous adventure with nary a backward glance.

In social settings as well, Galvin quickly learned how to stroke Paisley's ego. When the Marine Corps honored the assistant secretary with one of its impressive ceremonies, called an "Evening Parade," Galvin hosted a reception in his apartment after the marching was over. Always solicitous about his friend's desires, Galvin arranged scores of get-togethers for Paisley through the years. There were dinners at pricey restaurants in Washington, San Francisco, the Caribbean and Europe; on a barge in New York's harbor; and in quaint country hideaways on both sides of the Atlantic. The consultant organized stays at Montauk, Long Island, and other popular resorts.

Galvin also invited his friend to relax by watching the Washington Redskins play and, as they got to know each other better, to be his guest at a closed-circuit telecast of a championship boxing match at the Capital Center in suburban Maryland. Galvin rented a private room at the arena and had a sumptuous buffet catered for the thirty or so people in his entourage. Unisys, one of his major clients, bankrolled the party. Paisley was indifferent to professional sports, but he liked the heady atmosphere and accompanying glitz. At the fight, he was joined by the assistant commandant of the Marine Corps and the general in charge of Marine aviation.[99] The hard-to-get tickets were prized by congressional aides, senior Pentagon officers and industry bigwigs, most of whom used them as a golden opportunity to greet and observe the capital's glamorous cast of characters.

Using Galvin as a guide, Paisley grew accustomed to traveling in a pretty fast crowd himself. His friends included a father-and-son duo of millionaire Israeli industrialists and international arms merchants, who in turn introduced Paisley to high-level Israeli embassy officials. There also was Nick Chorine, a mysterious Russian émigré, whose shaved head and mellifluous French accent intrigued women. He commuted from Brussels to provide Paisley information about developments at European weapons-makers. He also helped Galvin hide money in foreign bank accounts.[100] Still another acquaintance was a dashing British commando officer and mercenary named David Walker, reputed to have close ties to his country's spymasters, the U.S. Central Intelligence Agency and a bevy of African guerrilla groups. All these individuals would show up later on the periphery of Illwind. Until then, Mel Paisley loved the diversity plus the nonstop entertainment they offered, as did his wife, Vicki.

The couple traveled the world, ostensibly on Pentagon business. One taxpayer-financed excursion took them from Washington to Hawaii, the Philippines, Singapore, the island of Diego Garcia, the animal preserves of Kenya, Sicily, London and back home. In addition to the Paisleys, the party included two of the assistant secretary's military aides, a security officer, an executive from Hercules and James Gaines, the former Boeing official who followed Paisley to the Pentagon and remained his closest associate. As always, the living quarters were first rate. Commanders provided the most comfortable rooms at each stop and hosted dinners every night to honor the visiting dignitary. In London, for example, Paisley liked to stay at the elegant flat of the three-star U.S. admiral stationed there. To cater to the needs of the eight passengers on this particular trip, the modified Navy DC-9 jet carried a crew of nine.

Lasting nearly three weeks and racking up twenty-six thousand miles, the trip's purpose supposedly was collecting information for a study on defending the Navy's prepositioned supply ships. The participants made a breezy video of their globe-trotting, filled with shots of fishing, pleasure boating, partying and other tourist pursuits. A laid-back Paisley in a sport shirt described the interesting things they saw, singling out the excellent fishing. Gaines summed up the trip as the video's narrator. In London and elsewhere, he said, "We had good food and a lot of good sightseeing . . . with a little bit of business."[101]

As Mr. and Mrs. Paisley grew increasingly fond of Washington's social whirl, they appreciated Galvin's generosity. Mel urged some of his aides to partake in Galvin's largess, too. That was how Jim Gaines, the assistant secretary's loyal horseholder, was introduced to Bill Galvin. After breaking the ice by providing him theater tickets, meals, party invitations and numerous other tokens of appreciation, Galvin says, "I felt comfortable talking to Jim Gaines directly" about business matters.[102]

Paisley accepted Galvin's gifts and hospitality from the inception of their relationship, usually without making even a half-hearted gesture to pay his own way. "He just sat on his hands" when the checks came, Galvin says. Defense Department conflict-of-interest regulations prohibited Pentagon employees from accepting any gift or gratuity valued above five dollars "for themselves, members of their families or others" from any entity whose interests were "substantially affected" by the department. But the Navy's second-in-command knew how to protect himself. "He paid for the flagrant things, the things that would attract attention" from government auditors, according to Galvin.[103]

Paisley thought of many ways to try to beat the system. If air travel was involved, he might get a Navy plane to take him; or he would pay his host the cut-rate, round-trip tourist fare to their destination. That way, if anyone asked, Paisley could produce a receipt to legitimize the trip. At the same time, Galvin or one of his clients would foot the bill for lodging, food, drinks and incidental expenses. For special occasions Galvin preferred hiring an executive Lear jet stocked with champagne and lobster tail, Paisley's favorite treats. "The food cost more than Paisley's cost" of paying the cut-rate commercial air fare, Galvin explained. "It was that kind of relationship. That was one of my charms."[104]

Lehman wasn't impressed by Galvin's excessive spending. They first met in the summer of 1982, during a July Fourth party at the consultant's Northern Virginia condominium. Lehman dropped by briefly at Paisley's behest. Scanning the boisterous crowd of industry executives and lobbyists, Lehman spotted a large group gathered around his assistant secretary. Paisley, who had been on the job for barely half a year, thrived on the limelight. His boss, however, was perturbed. The spectacle created an appearance problem, if nothing else. Afterward, Lehman told Paisley that he "shouldn't be hanging around with all those influence peddlers." Lehman singled out Galvin for his displeasure.[105]

"He's a good guy," Paisley protested. "You're being paranoid." Lehman didn't let up, saying consultants of Galvin's ilk lived off favors and intimacy with senior officials. Wrapping up the discussion, Paisley said: "I understand; don't worry about it."[106] The secretary thought the issue was closed. He inferred that Paisley had gotten the message and wouldn't see any more of Galvin.

But over the next year or so, the consultant turned into a fixture in Room 4E732 in the Pentagon, the office of the assistant secretary of the Navy (Research, Engineering & Systems). "Everybody knew him," one impressed associate said after strolling with Galvin around the Navy's corridors in the Pentagon.[107] Paisley's receptionists and clerks gave Galvin the VIP treatment. They made small talk and laughed at Galvin's jokes, whenever he dropped by unannounced to chat with his friend in the inner office. If he happened to have a client in tow, the consultant poured on the charm to make sure that the office staff was especially friendly. When he phoned, Galvin didn't have to give a name. His cheery hello was instantly recognized by Paisley's secretaries.

At this point, neither man took great pains to hide the connection. The launch of Reagan's military buildup, along with those directing it, seemed unbeatable. The mood in Congress was one of accommodation and bending over backward to help the Navy, meaning that there were precious few critics eager to take potshots at the hard-charging procurement chief. Reveling in his power, Paisley had no time to worry about public perceptions. It wouldn't be right to throw a good friend overboard, he kept telling his other buddies, just to assuage Lehman's jitters.

The procompetition rhetoric provided perfect cover. It wasn't difficult, after all, to claim that contacts with Galvin were just another tactic to ensure that companies submitted bids on big Navy projects—purportedly saving taxpayers untold billions. Using this line of reasoning, Paisley was merely doing his job. "The companies were all hungry at the trough," he recalls. "Not a single one said it wasn't ready." Galvin was portrayed as a valuable source of industry intelligence for the Navy. While visiting contractors' facilities, the consultant sometimes made a big show of explaining that he was on "special assignment" or conducting "an unofficial audit" of certain technologies for the Pentagon.[108] Paisley "could not wait ten years for the bureaucracy to react," a senior admiral who worked closely with him rationalized. "His driving motivation was always . . . how do we get it to the fleet quicker and at the lowest cost."[109]

Still, complaints kept percolating up to Lehman. More than a year after the initial warning, he gave his assistant another dressing down. Lehman said he was concerned by reports that Paisley continued to consort with Galvin. The association not only is hurting you, Lehman cautioned Paisley, it's also hurting the image of the secretary's office. He demanded to know why the consultant still hung around the Pentagon. "That's bullshit," Paisley responded, lying that he had distanced himself from Galvin. "People are always trying to sow seeds of discontent," Paisley said, as cocky as ever. "I'm not seeing him."[110]

In all, Lehman raised the matter with his assistant three separate times in roughly as many years. Each time, he says, Paisley reassured him that the connection had been severed for good.[111] In industry circles, it was common knowledge that the friendship was as solid as ever. The rumor mill was working overtime: Middle-level managers, who had never laid eyes on either man and rarely set foot inside the Pentagon, discussed among themselves Galvin's special bond with Paisley. It was an open secret, which Lehman easily could have checked out. "If there was a marketer in the industry who didn't know that, he should have been fired," recalls one of Galvin's pals.

But the Navy chief seemed unable to acknowledge that the bureau-

cratic brawler he had recruited was a bad choice. Fundamentally, the secretary wanted to believe his friend and principal adviser. He never followed up his suspicions with action, relying instead on lame excuses for
Paisley's behavior. "I thought it was very insensitive of Mel" to hook up
with someone like Galvin, Lehman recalls. "But I ascribed it to the fact
that he was not a Washington person; he was just naive about how influence peddling worked."[112]

As the years passed, finding excuses for the Paisley-Galvin link grew
exceedingly difficult. In the fall of 1984, Paisley's wife planned to throw a
big bash on his sixtieth birthday. For Vicki Paisley, who was nearly thirty
years younger than her husband, the party had special significance. She resolved that it would be a memorable milestone in his life. Relatives, old
friends, former Boeing colleagues and a sprinkling of their new Washington acquaintances would assemble to pay respect to Mel's accomplishments. As soon as Galvin found out about her plans, he insisted on taking
charge. For him, the most important choices didn't revolve around food
or entertainment. They involved the guest list. To impress clients and business associates with his entrée to Paisley, Galvin invited dozens of them to
the birthday fete. The more who came, the easier it would be for him to
round up future consulting work. The timing was perfect, as Reagan's re-
election looked more and more likely. Galvin hoped to turn the affair
into a marketing tool for himself.[113]

Vicki Paisley was furious. She hadn't cared for the Galvins even before
the tiff over the party, privately referring to Bill as a loudmouth and a
bullshit artist. The two women were polar opposites. Vicki Paisley typified
the professional, career-driven wife who was knowledgeable about her
husband's official duties, whereas Evelyn Galvin belonged to an earlier
generation of stay-at-home wives and mothers who shunned the business
world. Galvin's matronly spouse reeked of perfume and insisted on treating Vicki Paisley as though she were a teenager, the slender and tomboy-
ish Vicki used to fume.

This time, Galvin's trickery really stuck in her craw. The conniving
SOB was horning in on the family celebration, she told her husband, because the only thing he cares about is cashing in on your name. Paisley
didn't get too worked up over the squabble, and the invitations went out
as Galvin wished.[114]

Others who saw the long list of industry representatives were outraged.
One officer who scanned the names went ballistic. He rushed to the
Navy's lawyers, complaining of blatant conflict-of-interest violations and demanding action. (The whistleblower was Admiral Frank Kelso, who
served as commander of the Sixth Fleet during Reagan's second term,
later was promoted to chief of naval operations under President George
Bush and retired in the aftermath of the Navy's "Tailhook" sexual-assault
scandal.) The general counsel's reaction to Kelso's alarm was swift. "Don't do
this," he told Paisley. "It's a problem."[115] The party was promptly canceled.

By now, Paisley had attracted the notice of the Navy's legal watchdogs. Several months later, the general counsel's office sent him another warning. "To avoid any appearance of a possible conflict of interest," Paisley was told he had to personally pay for the tickets of Austen Watson and certain other industry friends he invited to the black-tie Navy Ball.[116] Paisley finally sensed that he had to be more discreet. He gave his executive assistant strict instructions that Galvin was not to loiter around the office or sign the official visitor's log. Naturally, they continued to see each other regularly after work and on weekends. And the consultant could get Paisley on the phone any time he wanted.

Galvin demonstrated his prowess during one of the assistant secretary's meetings with Lockheed chairman Roy Anderson. A second company executive, who was a longtime Paisley cohort, also sat in on the session. Paisley's military aide came in and announced, "Galvin's on the line and insists that he interrupt." The office discussion ended in a flash, with Paisley putting his friend on the speakerphone. As usual, Galvin was calling about the prospects of a particular weapon he had been hired to promote. His favorite codewords were asking Paisley for "a little insight" or "some visibility" on a program. "Hey, is this really a serious program? Is the Navy really interested in this?" Galvin would demand to know, so he could relay the funding outlook to his client.[117]

When the Lockheed chief ducked into the bathroom, the other executive berated Paisley. Allowing Galvin to interrupt like that was "just about the most goddamned discourteous thing you could have done," he hissed at his buddy. "Somebody could knife you in the back," he told Paisley, for talking so freely to a consultant. There wasn't much of a response. "I hear what you're saying. But Christ, he's a friend," Paisley said with a grunt.[118]

In spite of all the admonitions, Mel Paisley didn't change. He continued meeting and talking extensively with Boeing officials, contrary to pledges he had made to avoid such contact and disqualify himself from decisions that could benefit his former employer. During Paisley's first few years in the Pentagon, Watson, the marketing specialist for Singer and his old friend, visited his office roughly fifty times.[119] The interactions with Galvin were more frequent and complicated.

Paisley agreed that upon retiring from the Navy, he would become a consultant and officially join forces with his talented sidekick, Bill Galvin. It was a pivotal decision. With his gift for gab, Galvin joked that they were primed "to march off into the moonlight together."[120] The pact was sealed not long after the botched birthday party, though it took two and a half years to turn it into reality. In the meantime, the two of them plotted to become very rich from their illicit partnership. With Paisley pulling strings on the inside and Galvin peddling his influence to industry, together they planned to amass at least an $18-million nest egg. Bribes and secret payments by contractors were to start flowing while Paisley still was in the Pentagon, with many more millions anticipated once he left government.

For all intents and purposes, the pals already were in business together.[121]

In this time frame, friends detected an undercurrent of unusual reck-lessness in Paisley. He seemed bent on proving something to himself, making a symbolic statement that only he could grasp fully. While he re-laxed with his wife and another couple in San Diego one evening, after a hectic round of meetings, Paisley's wilder side took over. Despite menac-ing "No Trespassing" signs, he wanted to scale a ten-foot-high chain-link fence in the darkness to reach another section of the beach. No amount of logical argument would dissuade him. "Listen, you crazy SOB," his friend exclaimed. "You're not only going to tear your suit, you will end up in jail." Paisley laughed and started to clamber up the fence, before the rest of the party somehow managed to drag him away.[122]

"Taking the conn" is a time-honored Navy idiom used when one offi-cer passes command of a vessel to another. Paisley heard it now and then, during visits to naval bases and on board ships. "Taking the con" might also be a fitting description of what happened to the Navy during the Reagan era.

Although President Reagan and his appointees talked endlessly about cracking down on waste and abuse, their promises lacked commitment. In his first speech to a joint session of Congress, Reagan called fraud in gov-ernment "an unrelenting national scandal, a scandal that we're bound and determined to do something about." But that was mostly palaver. The president's chief of staff acknowledged to one Reagan biographer that ethics in government was never "a big thing" to his boss. "I don't think it was something in the big picture," James Baker said.[123] Reagan spent prac-tically no time thinking about the topic, and he mistakenly believed that career civil servants were the crux of the problem. According to this au-thoritative biography, Reagan blindly "assumed that those who followed his banner necessarily had higher ethical standards than those who spent their lives in government service."[124]

For a long time, Paisley was good at conning Congress, the public, the press and many of his Pentagon brethren about the Navy's adherence to the highest ethical code. Like Reagan, he impressed lawmakers with vows to root out those who didn't share high moral principles. It was part of his disguise as a loyal apparatchik, reshaping the Navy to implement adminis-tration policies. Testifying before a congressional panel in the middle of his tenure, Paisley was asked what he would do with former military offi-cials who abused their connections to surreptitiously help defense con-tractors. The question was routine, but Paisley wanted his answer to attract notice. No matter what the setting, he always desired to be the center of attention; that was more important to him than substance.

"You can't have the kind of stuff you are talking about going on," the assistant secretary told lawmakers, raising his voice to stress disgust for in-fluence peddlers. He had an iron-fisted solution. "Hang them from a tree where everybody can see them," Paisley said.

Chapter V

MOON OVER SAPPHIRE BEACH

Strolling among the villas and flower-lined streets of St. Thomas, Mel Paisley and Bill Galvin enjoyed a respite from Washington's midwinter chill. The Pentagon's hectic pace seemed to have been left in another world as well. They admired the long swath of white sand at Sapphire Beach, sandwiched between the surf and the lush vegetation climbing the hillside. As they meandered around the sun-drenched Virgin Islands resort, the friends hatched a plot to rake millions of dollars for themselves off Navy contracts. Of all the schemes they had pulled off, this one was going to be the trickiest yet and, they hoped, the most lucrative.

The two men came to the Caribbean on a whim in December 1985, almost precisely four years after they met and started collaborating. The vacation, which included their wives, was a somewhat somber affair. Paisley recently had been diagnosed with prostate cancer. Military doctors who performed the biopsy leaked the results to Navy brass before they informed the patient. With gossip and speculation about his future rife in the corridors, Paisley felt a sudden need to get away from the Pentagon.[1]

At practically the last minute, Paisley thought about going to the islands for a week and proposed the trip to his compatriot. Galvin scampered to round up rooms and arrange for a Lear jet to get them there in time to celebrate Christmas in the tropics. "It was the only place we could find" on such short notice, Galvin recalls.[2] The chartered plane accumulated nearly nineteen thousand dollars' worth of flight time round trip, of which the Paisleys belatedly paid $902.[3]

The wives spent much of the time on their own, discussing Paisley's health and pondering the gloomy prognosis laid out by his doctors. Evelyn Galvin talked about the shock of losing her first husband to cancer.[4] The couples went back to Washington the day before New Year's Eve, earlier than planned.

By the time Paisley and Galvin boarded the return flight to Dulles Airport, however, details of their audacious plan were set. They agreed to form a consulting firm, aptly named Sapphire Systems, that would become a subcontractor on one of the Navy's supersecret missile defense projects. The program they chose was designed to better protect carrier battle groups from threats posed by the international proliferation of "smart" missiles. The initiative called for developing, testing and eventually outfitting the fleet with a new generation of shipboard sensors, computer software and perhaps electronic jammers to counter low-flying warheads. Taking place completely in the "black" world, the research was removed from competitive bidding and other normal procurement practices. The work was so highly classified that nobody was supposed to discuss it outside a secure "vault"—a specially constructed room-within-a-room insulated with heavy metal shielding to prevent electronic eavesdropping or tapping into computer signals.

Scientists laboring over the proposed antimissile system used the codewords "Maple Counter Stealth," a designation that still hasn't been declassified after all these years. "Moon" was how outsiders, including investigators who pursued the Paisley-Galvin partnership, referred to the project. Launched as a modest technical feasibility study, it had the potential to blossom into a $500-million to $1-billion-plus gravy train for those companies—and individuals—fortunate enough to get on board.

On January 3, 1986, the second business day after jetting home from the islands, Galvin incorporated Sapphire Systems in Virginia. He was the registered agent and one of the directors. Paisley's name never appeared on the papers, and Galvin pledged to keep others from finding out about his friend's stake. "I don't think I wanted that exposure, nor did he," Galvin explains. But from Sapphire's inception, the consultant insists, "Mel and I were owners fifty-fifty . . . He was a beneficial owner of half of whatever I had."[5]

In many ways, Project Moon was Paisley's brainchild. He helped create it and showed exceptional interest in the work's progress, well before deciding to tap it for his selfish reasons. The concept had its genesis in the 1982 Falklands war, when the Argentine navy shocked military analysts by sinking one of Great Britain's high-technology destroyers with a single Exocet missile. The performance of these small but elusive weapons—able to skim the waves at great speed and use radar to seek out targets—sent shudders through the U.S. Navy. The French-made Exocet and its cousins were available around the globe in scores of short-range and long-range models. Production of various derivatives was under way in Israel, Italy, Great Britain, the Soviet Union and such unlikely places as Norway and Brazil. Military magazines were filled with full-page advertisements hawking low-cost tactical missiles almost like new cars. Libya, Iraq, Iran, South Africa and a string of other second- and third-rate military powers were building arsenals bristling with such arms and the know-how to use them.[6]

One tiny, hard-to-spot missile carrying a few hundred pounds of conventional explosives could cripple or scuttle a billion-dollar vessel, if it hit just the right spot. The Falklands war highlighted the growing danger. "There is almost no such thing as a low-threat area of the world anymore," Secretary Lehman declared.[7]

Before the shelling stopped in the South Atlantic, the U.S. Navy stepped up the drive to upgrade missile defenses. In 1984, it began deploying a new class of Aegis missile cruisers, studded with sophisticated electronic-warfare devices and antimissile missiles. Costing about $1 billion apiece, the ship's barnlike superstructure houses extremely agile "illu-minating radars," programmed to track as many as two hundred incoming missiles at once. An array of high-capacity computers is designed to use the reflected radar beams to rapidly switch the ship's surface-to-air mis-siles from one target to the next, shooting at as many as eighteen at the same time if necessary. The radar's range is supposed to be two hundred miles. But as the first Aegis cruiser was in the midst of her sea trials, con-gressional investigators and some doubters inside the Navy raised serious questions. In early operational tests, the vessel missed all four low-altitude drones it tried to bring down.[8] Critics worried about the ability of Aegis to counter the ultimate threat: a flock of supersonic missiles fired from various directions and coming in barely over the wave tops.[9]

The potential damage from that type of attack became painfully evi-dent later in the Persian Gulf. Two low-flying missiles fired by an Iraqi Mirage jet tore through the hull of the USS *Stark*, devastating the four-thousand-ton frigate and killing thirty-seven U.S. servicemen. One of the warheads entered the area under the bridge, where sailors slumbered in their bunks. It detonated in a superheated explosion, sending flames spurting up through the decks and igniting the superstructure, until molten metal was dripping on those who survived the initial wallop. The ship, which had been on routine patrol, managed to limp to port in Bahrain with the fire still burning.

The *Stark* wasn't equipped with Aegis radar. Its Phalanx gun system, though, was described as a "last-ditch defense" against sea-skimming mis-siles. The Navy accelerated the Phalanx's installation as a result of lessons learned from the Falklands conflict. The computer-driven Phalanx is in-tended to smother approaching warheads with fire from a mammoth Gatling gun capable of shooting more than three thousand rounds a minute. The Navy subsequently admitted that it could be counted on to work no more than 71 percent of the time, and years later engineers still were searching for fixes. Official reports of the incident faulted the *Stark's* crew for failing to activate defensive equipment early enough. Three of the ship's officers insisted that the Phalanx radar had been turned on be-fore the Iraqi jet fired, but they claimed that the system never detected the missiles. Paisley said that without Moon, the rest of the fleet faced similar peril.

Before the visit to St. Thomas, the assistant secretary already had or-dered up a classified study and recommended accelerated procurement of hardware to put Moon into active duty as quickly as practicable. In grandiose terms, he compared it to erecting a protective radar dome over the fleet. Within a few months, Paisley got his wish. Lehman approved a prototype demonstration, yanking the program out of the bureaucracy, putting it on the fastest possible track and handing Mel Paisley direct control. It was basically a blank check for Paisley to determine Moon's destiny. For this program, unlike others, he was the sole person who could call policy meetings or allocate management responsibilities. That was un-usual enough, by itself. The first official moves Paisley made fenced off Moon from the uniformed Navy and extended his authority even fur-ther. He minimized oversight by the Navy's senior-level Special Programs Review Group, the panel that kept close tabs on other "black" programs. Over the objections of admirals, Paisley ordered award of sole-source contracts to companies of his choice.[10]

Initially, Paisley pushed hard to keep the Center for Naval Analysis, the Navy's primary outside think tank, in the driver's seat. It seemed the best way to protect and manipulate the program.[11] His good friend Thomas D. Bell, a Republican operative who had worked for Dan Quayle and was married to one of the vice-president's relatives, became chairman of CNA's board of overseers. Working closely with Bell and other influential Republicans, Paisley had fought successfully to move CNA away from the University of Rochester and place it under the auspices of the conserva-tive Hudson Institute, a pro-Reagan research outfit for which Bell also served as president. One key reason for the shift was Rochester's refusal to let Paisley choose CNA's leadership.[12] At the Hudson Institute, Paisley foresaw none of those problems.

Opponents claimed that Paisley's bid to establish control over CNA politicized what had been a nonpartisan study group. For public con-sumption, he liked to boast about the center's continuing independence and unbiased approach. "We don't always get the answers we are looking for" from CNA, Paisley testified before one House subcommittee. In confidence, however, he told friends that his longstanding ties to Bell and the revised institutional structure gave him greater sway over the center's activities than ever before.[13] The blue-suiters will have a mighty tough time now, Paisley thought, interfering with this CNA-run operation. The arrangement was ideal to keep Moon out of the public eye.

From Defense Secretary Weinberger down, everyone who counted in the Pentagon concurred that the program's objectives were vitally impor-tant. Weinberger and his staff also wanted to guard against leaks by sharply controlling the number of people cleared for access to the program. Nev-ertheless, Paisley's bid to shunt aside the admirals prompted a major blowup inside the Navy.

Putting a think tank in charge of a crucial prototype and potential fleetwide procurement effort was preposterous, the admirals insisted. Some CNA officials surprised Paisley by privately warning him that it wouldn't be proper or feasible for them to comply with his wishes. Paisley was livid. There was no other way, he yelled, to expedite development of the desperately needed technology. The bureaucracy was bound to screw things up by trying to jam Moon into a backwater under the Aegis um-brella, Paisley argued. Worse yet, he didn't want the uniformed Navy to reestablish control, delay decisions and raise a ruckus about this dark-horse company called Sapphire.[14]

So, Paisley and Galvin switched tactics by stressing the caliber of the companies slated to do the actual work. They tapped Martin Marietta, a diversified, Maryland-based defense firm consistently ranked among the Pentagon's largest suppliers, as the prime contractor for Moon. Martin Marietta had the lead on radar technology. BDM International, a powerhouse consulting firm with deep political roots, got a major role designing the project's communication links. The two companies didn't have to compete for the business and agreed, in turn, to bring in Sapphire as a junior member of the team. Initial funding for the sole-source contracts came from internal transfers among Navy accounts that didn't require congressional approval.

In November 1986, with Paisley and Galvin presiding, about $4 million for the program's first phase was allocated among the participants. The meeting took place in Galvin's office late in the evening, over a catered dinner. "We put the plan up on a blackboard" and proceeded to "cut up the pie," Galvin recalls.[15] Martin Marietta's share came to less than $1 million and Sapphire's was barely $300,000, but everyone had high hopes for more.[16] Tens of millions of additional dollars were supposed to start flowing soon.

To provide Sapphire at least the patina of legitimacy, the senior CNA scientist heading the Moon project was lured away to become its president. One of Paisley's military aides also went to work there, along with a veteran Navy engineer and a few other cronies of Paisley and Galvin. Nonetheless, with barely a handful of employees, inexperienced management and absolutely no track record, Sapphire hardly seemed in a position to help the Navy. Galvin put his wife, stepson and daughter on the payroll. "We set up a one-contract company," he once said, laughing, "and I hire the world." For a time, Martin Marietta had to advance funds to keep Sapphire going.[17]

As difficulties mounted, Sapphire's teammates hinted that Moon's technical guru, former Westinghouse engineer Joseph Yang, was a charlatan. Galvin himself admits that, at one point, "I got this cold chill" thinking "maybe this guy really is a technical fraud." Sapphire's staff was "churning a lot of paper," Galvin remembers thinking, giving the semblance of solid progress. But privately he wondered: "How is this going to happen?"[18]

None of the doubts mattered, as long as Mel Paisley was calling the shots. He made sure that Yang, the technical expert, received a prestigious civil-service award for outstanding performance. He also had an old acquaintance from Boeing installed as day-to-day program director, in violation of Navy regulations mandating that a commissioned officer fill that job. Under the top-secret alignment Paisley devised, Sapphire was supposed to get one-tenth of Moon's overall revenues. "Ten percent of the money you're talking about there," Galvin gleefully reminded associates, would make it "a very substantial little company."[19]

Already, Galvin was scheming how to parlay the subcontract into an even bigger windfall. He was hunting for a corporate buyer willing to pay a premium price for what was, in effect, a corporate shell. "The payoff for me and Paisley was the acquisition of Sapphire" by a third party, he recalls.[20] Galvin savored hammering out deals to spin off his consulting entities; he had struck pay dirt many times before. If this bid to market Sapphire succeeded, Galvin promised Paisley, they would "reap the benefit of that sale," retiring as truly wealthy men.[21]

☆

BDM and Martin Marietta were excellent examples of how Paisley's personal likes and dislikes dictated Navy weapons buying. The choice of the two firms to spearhead Moon was quite natural, considering the connection Paisley had with top officials at each one. Both companies were eager to use the Reagan buildup to increase significantly their share of Navy contracts, and they were certain they could depend on his support to accomplish exactly that.

BDM was one of the original so-called "Beltway Bandits," the gamut of consulting and "professional services" firms that sprouted around the capital offering advice to the Pentagon and its suppliers. Rising to prominence by helping structure U.S. nuclear arsenals during the early years of the Cold War, BDM grew to nearly four thousand employees, forty-seven offices worldwide and an immense backlog of military contracts. Its specialty was simulating performance of weapons on the battlefield, but it also was a dominant force in communications, computer design, laser development and space research. Paisley counted BDM's president, Earle Williams, and Dan McDonald, another one of it's founders and senior officers, among his friends. Moreover, from 1983 to 1986 Vicki Paisley worked at BDM as a marketing analyst, sometimes turning out projects for McDonald.[22] Later, she was hired as a consultant by the concern.

Before Paisley came on the scene, BDM hadn't been successful at snaring Navy business. During his tenure in the assistant secretary's seat, BDM's work for the service quadrupled to $6 million annually, growing twice as fast as its business with the other branches of the military. Revenue from the Navy continued to climb rapidly afterward. Regardless, Navy contracts still accounted for only a tiny fraction of the consulting giant's total income of more than $300 million in 1987. Company officials called the revenue "nickels and dimes stuff" compared to the rest of BDM's assignments, arguing that they didn't get preferential treatment from the Navy.[23]

Nevertheless, Paisley clearly was in BDM's corner, and it was easy for the rest of the industry to recognize the special affinity. Early on, he used his power to obtain a seat for BDM's president on an influential Navy advisory board. Because of his wife's job, Paisley had signed a letter promising to stay away from "any matters involving BDM" and the Navy. In defiance of that unequivocal pledge, he continued regular and extensive business contacts with the consulting company.

Mrs. Paisley's dealings with BDM also prompted many smirks and raised eyebrows within the Pentagon and around the Beltway. Some BDM employees whispered that hiring Vicki Paisley gave McDonald unmatched access to her husband. "No one ever talked openly about" her work for BDM, according to Jim Gaines, Paisley's confidant. "But no one denied it, either."[24] Galvin says "there were constant rumors about the relationship" of Paisley's wife to BDM and other contractors. "That issue ran through all of our relationships, from the time I met Mel Paisley."[25]

The discussions between McDonald and the Paisleys went beyond Moon. The wife of the assistant secretary set up meetings in the Pentagon for a BDM official on at least one unrelated program.[26] And McDonald used to call her husband, even after Paisley left his Navy post, to complain about what he perceived as Navy slights to BDM. Once, he fumed that his company unfairly was being squeezed out of a Marine Corps contract in Southern California. "We have to somehow or other beat the system," McDonald said. "Yeah, I think you can," Paisley replied, promising to "jam" one of his supporters into the deliberations. "You can beat it, if we just get the facts" to Navy decision-makers, Paisley said.[27]

In their zeal to corral Navy business, BDM's senior executives embraced Galvin without the slightest hesitation. They considered him one more avenue to ensure access to Paisley. As the early preparations for Moon played out, Galvin went to lunch with McDonald to talk about a consulting agreement. Paisley had paved the way admirably. "It was a done deal" before the appetizers were served, Galvin says. "I just presented myself and explained the mechanics" of getting paid. For a five-thousand-dollar monthly fee, Galvin's recalls, his task was simply "to bring BDM up to speed so that they would be in the catbird seat when the government went outside to let a contract for the Moon Program."[28]

At Martin Marietta, Paisley also had a high-level friend as his primary contact. Indeed, there was no one higher inside the company. Executives kidded Chairman Thomas Pownall, an Annapolis graduate, about his admiration of "silk scarf flyers." Mel Paisley was the most prominent illustration of his lifelong attraction to pilots.

Going back to a stint as head of its space unit during the 1970s, Pownall helped transform Martin Marietta from a second-tier aircraft-maker to one of the most forward-looking electronics and aerospace companies in the world. In the transition, the company shed such nondefense operations as cement, chemicals and aluminum. Once he took over as chairman, Pownall gained respect throughout the industry for his spirited though costly fight to fend off a hostile takeover bid by Bendix in the early 1980s. To remain independent, Martin Marietta devised the so-called Pacman defense, in which the takeover target tries to devour the would-be acquirer. With its development of the space shuttle's external fuel tank and various military rockets, satellites and civilian spacecraft, Martin Marietta established itself as a leading player in high-technology fields. Closer to earth, among other things it assembled the Patriot missile, night-vision targeting devices for pilots and other weapons that became famous in Operation Desert Storm against Iraq.

In the fall of 1994, after gobbling up General Electric's aerospace division, merging with Lockheed and changing its name to Lockheed Martin, it vaulted to become the nation's biggest defense contractor. The colossus has a combined workforce of 170,000 and controls as much as one-fifth of all Pentagon spending. It is double the size of its nearest defense competitor. With sales of about $23 billion annually, it nearly matches the clout of Boeing, America's largest aerospace exporter. Officials of the new firm called it "the forward look of two visionary companies."

Tom Pownall didn't foresee how far his strategy would lead Norman Augustine, his protégé and replacement. But in the 1980s, Martin Marietta already was poised for rapid growth. Despite his white hair and grandfatherly appearance, Tom Pownall was feared as a smart, aggressive chief executive. Boeing Chairman T Wilson had strongly urged Paisley to get to know Pownall as soon as he got settled in Washington. Eminently approachable, Martin Marietta's chief was one of the first CEOs the newly confirmed Navy official sought out.[29]

After contact was established, Pownall dropped by Paisley's house now and then for cocktails, a home-cooked spaghetti dinner and hours of informal conversation. "It's a big mistake," Paisley still insists, "to do away with that kind of social contact" between the industry and the Pentagon.[30] Pownall was about the same age as Paisley, and his winsome, down-to-earth manner was a hit with the Navy official. Pownall had served as the captain of a destroyer instead of pilot-in-command of an airplane, but he and Paisley had similar personalities. They partied together at foreign air shows. When Paisley brooded about his cancer and underwent grueling treatments, Pownall was there to lend a sympathetic ear. During the trip to Sapphire Beach, Galvin suspected that the case of fine champagne delivered to Paisley's cottage to toast the new year was a thoughtful present from Martin Marietta's top man.[31]

By the same token, Paisley was there when Pownall craved support during a rocky period in his marriage after some forty years. At an age when most men are focused solely on retirement, Galvin recounts, Martin Marietta's top executive was in the midst of a messy separation from his wife while he contined dating a younger woman. Paisley, who had gone down the same rough road a couple of times in his life, was totally empathetic.[32] The Pownalls eventually reconciled.

For such an understanding friend, Pownall was willing to be especially obliging. As Moon gained momentum in 1986, Paisley groused to Pownall about the difficulties and delays he faced selling his former residence near Seattle. He needed to unload the old farmhouse, yet it required paint and repairs to attract buyers. Paisley had toyed with the idea of a possible swap for a house in Virginia. Did Martin Marietta engage a real estate firm, he wondered, which helped employees trade homes when they re-located to a different state?[33] Pownall said no, but he grasped Paisley's de-sire for assistance.

Almost immediately, the chairman contacted his brother-in-law, who happened to be a developer, and arranged for the relative to deposit three thousand dollars in an escrow account to fix up Paisley's Washington state property so that it would be more marketable. The most pressing repairs were done in a few months. Pownall's brother-in-law declined to furnish additional funds for more work, when he received the request from the property's listing agent. Paisley then called to thank Pownall's relative for his help sprucing up the house to that point.[34]

To this day, Paisley says the transaction created "an appearance of im-propriety" but that he never talked to Pownall specifically about the money. Pownall maintains that the three thousand dollars was an arm's-length investment by his relative and wasn't solicited by Paisley. "Any sug-gestion to the contrary is false," he says through his attorney, adding that he had a "professional and cordial" association with Paisley "in order to enhance the service" his company could offer the government.[35] Pownall simply wanted to do a small favor for a friend battling to survive cancer, says one company manager, although "he felt sheepish about the whole thing afterward."

Notwithstanding these assertions, the relative's "investment" was never repaid. Martin Marietta's chairman kept the arrangement involving Pais-ley's house secret for more than five years and did not reveal it even to his own company's ethics watchdogs—until the final phase of Illwind made the circumstances public.[36] Pownall retired from the company's board of directors nearly a year after that, and Martin Marietta's internal investiga-tion concluded he had not acted improperly.

Around the time Paisley was fretting over hometown real estate values, Martin Marietta's chairman and CEO was mulling ways to get Navy con-tracts besides Moon. The executive was willing to offer a hand to Bill Galvin, too, if that was necessary to get results, though Pownall staunchly maintains that the consultant is "dead wrong" in asserting that the team of Galvin and Paisley obtained Navy business for the company improperly.

One morning in April 1986, defense industry leaders gathered in New York City for an annual event known as the Iron Gate weekend. The meeting derived its name from the imposing gates in front of the tony "21" Club off Fifth Avenue, whose owner always threw a bash for the military officers and corporate executives in attendance. This year, the brunch was on Saturday. Afterward, Paisley and Galvin took a break from the speeches and festivities. They strolled to the Helmsley Palace Hotel, a few blocks northeast of Times Square, and rode the elevator to Pownall's elegant suite. Looking over the skyline of midtown Manhattan, Galvin claims the three of them went down a list of Navy programs that quietly were going to be steered to the company. With Pownall joining in, "Paisley and I went through and established priorities on the shopping list," Galvin says. "Just the way you would make one out," he adds, if "you went to the supermarket."[37]

The discussion also touched on Galvin's attributes as a deal-maker. His friend, the assistant Navy secretary, got to the nub of what he wanted. "Paisley made a substantial pitch for me," the consultant recalls, urging Martin Marietta to put his friend on retainer "because Galvin understands many things." While skeptical at first about Galvin's continuing representation of one of his biggest competitors, Pownall didn't put up much resistance. Before the session broke up, Galvin says, the chairman "agreed to hire me to do Moon as well as several other projects."[38]

It didn't take long for the fast-talking consultant's star to shine, silencing the grumbles of suspicious lower-level managers. Armed with inside information supplied by Paisley, Galvin claimed credit for landing a string of contracts Pownall and Martin Marietta had hankered for over an extended period.

The firm won a second-source contract to produce a ship-launched antisubmarine rocket. It wasn't the lowest bidder initially. But Galvin persuaded the lead manufacturer to leak him the numbers, renew the bidding and subsequently agree that Martin Marietta was the best choice. The Navy liked to talk about "streamlining" acquisition decisions by delegating many of them to prime contractors. Galvin described the procedure more honestly. "Streamlining," he said, means "pick the one you want and give them a contract."[39]

Through the good offices of Galvin and Paisley, Martin Marietta scored more Navy business over the following months. It received a contract to supply sonar equipment for the advanced Seawolf attack submarine, after Paisley changed requirements at the last minute to give the company an advantage. It beat out the favorite to design supersonic drones used for target practice by the fleet. Martin Marietta wasn't the low bidder this time, either, but Paisley overruled some of his staff to slip it the contract.[40] (Much later, the Justice Department filed a civil suit accusing the company of using a ruse to cheat the Pentagon out of as much as $30 million for research related to the dummy missile.)

Pownall's firm also managed to gain a foothold in the highly competitive torpedo-making field—easily and at relatively little cost—thanks to the intercession of the two men. First, Paisley advised Pownall "to get into the torpedo business because it's very profitable," Galvin recalls. Next, the consultant scouted out a partner willing to help Martin Marietta, which, after all, had never built a torpedo. The team was awarded a second-source contract for the MK-50, a lightweight, long-range torpedo maneuverable enough to go after the latest Soviet submarines. Without a middleman to recruit a corporate partner and lock up the deal, the opportunity would have evaporated.[41]

Ironically, some Martin Marietta executives worried about an overflow of riches. When Galvin approached them with still another teaming proposal, this time to start building pilotless reconnaissance aircraft, he got an angry reception. "Enough already," he recalls the exasperated general manager of the company's Baltimore division saying. "My plate is so full, when am I ever going to get a chance to eat any of this stuff?" But Pownall and Paisley had decreed that the firm should get into the growing market for such drones, so the company eventually took up Galvin's offer.[42]

To compensate for all his efforts, Galvin decided to grab for the brass ring in late 1986. Arriving at Martin Marietta's airy, perfectly landscaped headquarters in Bethesda, Maryland, he marched into the second-floor office of Frank Menaker, the company's general counsel. Seated around a conference table flanking Menaker were Pownall and Caleb Hurtt, the firm's president. Galvin's proposal took them aback. He wanted to sell Sapphire in exchange for approximately $10 million worth of Martin Marietta stock, with the exact price to be determined when the deal closed in two or three years. Galvin said he was speaking for himself and a "friendly" investor, without mentioning Paisley by name.[43]

Pownall seemed agreeable. He talked about structuring a potentially tax-free transaction, according to Galvin, in which the price would be determined by Sapphire's future revenues and "everyone would walk happily into the sunset." Had the deal been consummated, Galvin said afterward, he would have been at Martin Marietta's beck and call. "They could make me a dollar-a-year man after that," he joked. "I'd be happy to do anything for them."[44]

The company's lawyer was less sanguine. How could Sapphire possibly be worth that much? Menaker kept pressing. In vague terms, Galvin mentioned a "genius" he had working for him on various contracts that he wouldn't identify. Sapphire has the technology and scientists to strike it big, Galvin kept repeating. "It will have a lot of value in the future," he tried to reassure Menaker. Martin Marietta already had been tapped as the lead contractor on Moon, although Menaker wasn't familiar with the project.[45]

The meeting adjourned after about thirty minutes, with Martin Marietta officials promising to get back to Galvin quickly. "I had a warm feeling about that," he says, suggesting it was tantamount to a handshake agreement. "It was a done deal," according to Galvin.[46] He was mistaken. Menaker and Hurtt shelved the idea, apparently concluding it was too risky financially and legally. They never started the paperwork to check Sapphire's credit or cash flow. "Pownall gave absolutely no instructions to proceed," Menaker recalls. "We never turned over a single a piece of paper. We never had any intention of buying that company." The contractor didn't take the bait, despite repeated calls and reminders from Galvin. Paisley later tried to help sell Sapphire to BDM for a substantially lower price, but that sale also failed to materialize.[47]

Menaker insists that he and Pownall had no knowledge of Paisley's financial interest in Sapphire. Pownall was not accused of any crime, after prosecutors tried but failed to find other witnesses to back up Galvin's allegations. Paisley and Galvin, for their part, felt that they deserved better treatment from Martin Marietta in the end. "All these programs that you're involved in," Galvin recalled telling one high-ranking company official late in the game, "somebody put you onto." In his raspy, rambling style, Paisley concurred. He recounted for Galvin a conversation he had with Tom Pownall along the same lines. Paisley wanted gratitude for securing Martin Marietta a share of Moon. "How in the Christ did you get that program" in the first place? Paisley said he pointedly demanded of his old buddy Pownall.[48]

☆

Touted as the implacable enemy of wasteful big government, Ronald Reagan's administration turned into a godsend for every conceivable kind of consultant and pseudoconsultant trying to peddle advice to the military or its suppliers. From sprawling international consulting establishments to small Beltway "boutiques," sometimes dubbed "rent-a-general" or "rent-an-admiral" firms, President Reagan's defense budgets provided a bonanza for them all. Many of the technical and scientific consulting arrangements were based on legitimate expertise. But "marketing consultants" often were shady figures, selling nothing but their shrewdness and connections. Business was so brisk that no public or private organization could get a handle on all the money spent for consultants—let alone supervise their work to ensure that the government wasn't cheated.

Civilian agencies, especially the Energy Department and the Environmental Protection Agency, also had huge budgets for consulting work. But the Pentagon was in a class by itself. At the peak of the buildup, congressional investigators estimated that the military was spending *somewhere* between $2.8 billion and $18.8 billion on consulting contracts annually. The projections varied, depending on whether services such as management reviews, technical assistance, special one-time studies and research support were included in the expenditures.[49]

Inside the Defense Department, consultants had important roles at every step in the weapons-buying chain. Sitting on the Defense Science Board and similar powerful advisory committees, they helped chart the future of weapons development in broad terms. They also helped contractors prepare, and promoted Pentagon enthusiasm for, specific proposals for new weaponry. Consultants then assisted the services in drafting specifications describing how the new hardware ought to perform; perhaps a different group of consultants helped evaluate the bids that came in; and in certain cases, still others supervised testing to determine if the military obtained all that it had paid for. Each time Congress ordered the Pentagon to prepare a batch of new studies on topics of special interest to lawmakers, much of the analysis was performed by outside hired hands. Lines of responsibility tended to blend. Consultants could work with military officials to shape a program one day and, within a few weeks or months, end up lobbying those same officials to make choices favoring contractors that were clients. "Cross-pollination is helpful," one former Pentagon aide explained, adding that "we've got to stop feeling that everybody is a crook."

Outside the Pentagon, the consultant's niche was equally significant. Major weapons-makers hired a platoon of consultants and paid them untold millions of dollars each year to supplement virtually every in-house corporate function. The vast majority of those costs, too, were passed on to taxpayers.[50] Consultants didn't have to register the way lobbyists were obligated to do, though frequently lobbying and public relations efforts were lumped in with their fees and improperly submitted to the Pentagon as part of normal overhead costs. By the mid-1980s, this culture was so deeply ingrained that some consultants earned enormous sums advising other consultants how to advise defense clients.[51]

The inherent conflict of interest was obvious, but before Illwind Congress adopted purely stopgap, watered-down legislation to deal with the issue. The Pentagon's own disclosure rules also proved ineffective, and contractors largely looked the other way when potential ethics infractions surfaced. In this environment—in which information was the coin of the realm and cagey consultants played both sides of the street—few people paid attention to the arcane, often confusing restrictions on consulting activities; fewer still ever got caught by understaffed Pentagon auditing teams for violating those restrictions.[52]

Bill Galvin rode the crest of this wave with aplomb, but even he could not claim credit for generating it. Part of the impetus behind the consultant boom came from salary caps and rigid manpower ceilings imposed on the civilian workforce of the Navy as well as the other services. While overall defense budgets increased rapidly, Reagan's policies emasculated the civil service. Personnel at some Navy procurement offices shrank dramatically. Many veteran civilian employees who managed to escape the cuts left for higher-paying industry jobs anyway. The consequences were predictable. Consultants recognized that the Navy, which traditionally relied most heavily on outsiders to draw up technical contract specifications, offered grand opportunities to twist programs to benefit one contractor or another.[53]

Emphasis on competition made the intelligence collected by Galvin and his fellow consultants more valuable than ever—and far more threatening to the integrity of the entire procurement machinery. The stakes became higher as many suppliers felt increasingly under price pressure. They were forced to spend hefty research dollars up front in the hopes of winning production contracts down the pike. This frantic race for proprietary defense data, without regard to its source, was comparable to the scandals that besmirched Wall Street's reputation at the end of the 1980s.

During Paisley's watch, the rubric of competitive bidding conveniently was used to camouflage the Navy's variation of insider trading. It was a prescription for corruption on a massive scale.

In practice, as Galvin's schemes demonstrated, second-source contracts were a fertile area for skulduggery. "If they don't have a competition," Galvin joked, "I don't have a reason for being." Unquestionably, he was a master of those tricks. Line procurement officers sensed when "the fix was in" from the front office to anoint a Galvin client as the number-two producer.[54] But incentives were great to find other ways to scam the system.

To try to drive down prices, Lehman and his assistants prolonged the bidding process by repeatedly demanding that suppliers come back with lower offers. Whenever the Navy was unhappy with a set of bids, or changed its requirements after reviewing them, contractors were told to prepare revised submissions. They were called "Best and Final Offers," or BAFOs, though the term itself soon became an oxymoron. Oftentimes, companies had to churn out two or three bids before the Navy finally picked a winner. The arm twisting was part and parcel of the competitive-bidding rituals during the Reagan era. The haggling could take months to play out.

Paisley says that repetitive BAFOs "were a good way to squeeze contractors," though he concedes that the procedure also offered great opportunities for dishonesty. Multiple bids, he says, created "a standing invitation to have marketeers scurrying around to find out competitors' numbers."[55] Hoping to get a better price, midlevel Navy officials sporadically gave bidders a rough sense of how their submissions stacked up. Once this door was cracked slightly, Galvin saw his chance to fling it wide open. He wasn't satisfied with informal guidance provided by bureaucrats with a wink and a nod. Galvin was after the full inside scoop from the Navy's most senior levels; he wanted to know everything about rival manufacturers' bids and how the purchasing commands intended to treat them.

With Paisley's connivance, the consultant came up with a foolproof method to rig bids almost at will. The Navy's procurement chief routinely passed him sensitive papers and slides, complete with a rundown of prices and company rankings. Some of the material originally was prepared for briefing Secretary Lehman. This was no longer a case of the Navy leaking selected tidbits to spice up a competition. Galvin was handed a road map of the service's procurement strategy for entire classes of weapons. "The only place I get those documents from is Paisley," Galvin said. Such detailed, up-to-the-minute bid summaries definitely were off-limits for contractors. The papers gave him instantaneous credibility in industry circles. Some clients thought he walked on water, Galvin chuckled, because he could flash copies of the confidential Navy documents. "I was in the communications business, you know," he boasted afterward. "It was my business to get those."[56]

If it suited his purposes, Galvin did more than snatch paperwork. He could prompt the Navy to rejigger engineering or performance standards to help particular clients. Better yet, he could get his friend to reopen the bidding on programs. "We can always cause a BAFO," a supremely confident Galvin told Paisley without equivocation.[57] "I would tell him what to do [and] he would go do it," Galvin boasted.

At the same time, the tight-knit nature of the group running the Navy convinced many contractors that they couldn't compete without hiring someone like Galvin. With fewer points of entry available to influence decisions, access became pivotal. "We had nobody knowledgeable to talk to" at lower levels, one defense executive complained. And catching the ear of higher-level Navy officials proved well-nigh impossible without an intermediary. "It got to the point," this executive said, "we had to hire consultants to get appointments with the people we should have been able to see on our own."[58] Complaining to the Navy's top brass typically didn't produce results, and the downside was that it would make Paisley furious.

Only after Illwind shone a spotlight on the murky world of consultants did the fault-finding commence. Consultants "who work both sides of the street . . . have gotten out of hand," the Pentagon's deputy inspector general declared sternly. Others decried the upsurge in industrial espionage, describing the result as "Silicon Valley come to Washington." Democratic senator David Pryor of Arkansas, a longtime foe of what he called the "invisible government" composed of consultants, blamed industry and the military for trying to keep the problem under wraps. "Who are these people? What services do they perform? Who monitors what they do?" Pryor asked on the Senate floor, complaining about "shadowy figures clinging to the Pentagon's coffers."[59]

To be sure, Galvin's wasn't the sole shadow hovering around the Navy. Lawyer S. Steven Karalekas called John Lehman "a best friend" and was the godfather for one of the Navy secretary's daughters. The two men kept each other company on Washington's black-tie party circuit, enjoyed weekend getaways together and served summer Naval Reserve duty in tandem. Starting in the early Reagan years, Karalekas used those connections to the utmost. Expanding a practice that had been focused heavily on government contract law, he signed consulting contracts with major weapons-makers such as McDonnell Douglas, General Electric and Unisys.

General Electric readily acknowledged that it "retained Mr. Karalekas to provide access to Secretary Lehman." One McDonnell Douglas vice-president was just as brutally frank. He said that Karalekas was recruited for a "door-opening job," primarily to furnish an "entrée" to Lehman. The consultant, whose name showed up more than one hundred times on the secretary's official logs over five and a half years, dealt with Lehman "on a very, very personal basis," this McDonnell Douglas man said. "He certainly didn't make any secret of that."[60] Looking back, Karalekas now maintains that he performed a variety of tasks for defense clients, adding that his ties to Lehman "weren't the sole and exclusive reason" he was hired.

"Spike" Karalekas, as nearly everyone called him, met Lehman when they worked together in the Nixon White House. During Reagan's administration, the social and business affairs of the two families were intertwined to an uncommon degree. Karalekas's wife, Christina, worked on the president's transition team and helped Lehman outmaneuver other job-seekers to get the Navy post. In one of his final official acts as secretary, Lehman gave her the honor of helping launch a new Navy minesweeper. In the intervening years, Spike Karalekas ushered a collection of defense executives into Lehman's spacious office to air their gripes and float their proposals. Critics murmured that Karalekas was Lehman's version of Paisley's Bill Galvin—but without the ostentatious gold chains and braggadocio.

When McDonnell Douglas hired Karalekas in 1982, the firm was in agony over cost overruns plaguing its F/A-18 Hornet jet fighter. Lehman, who had previously faced down General Dynamics over submarine price hikes, publicly threatened to stop buying the planes because they were getting too expensive. He put Paisley in charge of negotiating a firm price limit for F/A-18s. It's far from clear what role Karalekas had in ending the deadlock, though he acknowledges that relations between the firm and the Navy had reached rock bottom when he entered the picture. McDonnell Douglas executives "did have a problem with the Navy refusing to talk with them," Karalekas says. "They were looking to break the ice."[61]

Within a few months, they had done much more. Lehman and the chairman of McDonnell Douglas held a joint press conference in October 1982, announcing resumption of Hornet purchases for a fixed price, without any escalation clauses. Once again, Lehman got most of what he wanted. The contractor, on the other hand, was able to negotiate concessions protecting itself in the event of Navy-initiated design changes. Today, F/A-18s remain the backbone of U.S. naval aviation. In spite of their comparatively short range and relatively high price tag, the Navy continues to spend billions for updated models of the aircraft.

Admiral James Watkins, chief of naval operations during Reagan's first term, remembers Karalekas's name "floating around" the Pentagon and "within the secretariat circles" of the Navy. "People kept saying, 'Do you know him?'" Watkins recalls.[62] Many admirals knew Karalekas exclusively by reputation, but he frequently huddled with Paisley for help or advice. If anything, Karalekas's presence helped divert some of the sniping aimed at Paisley's affiliation with Galvin. With hindsight, Paisley says he "didn't see anything wrong if firms gravitated to Karalekas" to cash in on his obvious closeness to Lehman. "That's how contacts are formed in the business."[63]

At any rate, Karalekas was circumspect about the scope of his consulting agreements. He insisted that McDonnell Douglas also hire him to work on issues related to the Air Force and the Army. "I did not think it would be in [the company's] best interest or mine to be seen as someone who was strictly dealing with John," Karalekas explained. When Lehman left the Pentagon to return to private life, however, he temporarily shared office space in Washington with Karalekas's law firm.[64]

The consultant's activities came under intense scrutiny as part of the Illwind probe, but neither he nor Lehman was identified by prosecutors as a formal target or ended up charged with any wrongdoing. Karalekas says he was never interviewed by investigators.

Two characteristics set Bill Galvin apart from other prominent consultants. Flamboyance was part of his trademark, as was an apparent unwillingness to turn away any client ready to pay him top dollar. Struggling through a succession of business failures and near-misses during all those years away from Washington, Galvin had dreamed about climbing to the top rung of the consultant fraternity. Success turned out to be sweeter than his imaginings. Through Paisley, Galvin found much more than a dependable, six-figure meal ticket. With his buddy ensconced in the Pentagon, Galvin relished what amounted to a permanent seat at a fabulous banquet. There were bountiful tables everywhere he looked, and mouthwatering delights waiting to be devoured. Most of the time, he felt like the guest of honor for whom the thrills never stopped.

To stay on top, Galvin was brazen in invoking Paisley's name. Pushing the Navy to act is always difficult, he would say. "You need a special relationship to do it."[65] Talking with current or prospective clients, Galvin "practically declared that he had Mel in his hip pocket," recalls an industry executive who worked with both men.[66] Discussing vacation plans, the consultant would go out of his way to remind everyone that he had reservations to go skiing in the West with Paisley. By this time, Galvin was on good terms with a fair number of lower-ranking officials throughout the Pentagon. But in a crunch, they seemed irrelevant. If a deal got sticky, he had one irresistible ace in the hole: "Come to town, and I'll take you in to see Mel Paisley," Galvin promised clients.[67]

The fact that Galvin arranged for Vicki Paisley to form her own consulting firm, incorporated it under his name and then leased her some of Sapphire's office space only added to his reputation as Paisley's soulmate. VAMO, as the fledgling enterprise called itself, was set up as a surprise gift for her in 1986, not long after Moon got rolling. The acronym, which was Paisley's pet phrase for his wife, stood for the initials of her maiden name: Vicki Ann McKim. VAMO worked for BDM and tried to line up consulting work from a Textron unit, among others.[68]

Galvin's penchant for name-dropping, though, didn't stop with the Navy's procurement chief. If a company was smart enough to hire him, Galvin used to say, "I usually reported to the boss."[69] Frequently starting with Tom Pownall of Martin Marietta, he would reel off the names of chairmen and presidents of various Fortune 100 companies with whom he claimed to be on a first-name basis. "Every time I spent a few hours with Galvin," says one longtime associate, "almost every other word out of his mouth was about his buddy Bob Daniell," the chairman of United

Technologies.[70] Galvin was close enough to the chairman of the House defense appropriations subcommittee, historically one of the most powerful members of Congress, to invite him for dinner at his home along with Paisley and a top Unisys lobbyist.[71]

To get a feel for the names of senior military commanders Galvin trotted out to impress contractors, "All you had to do was thumb through a directory of active-duty officers," recalls one retired admiral. "Galvin pressed too hard . . . Anybody who had three or four stars, he invariably would end up using their name."[72]

As he prowled the halls of the Pentagon and nearby company offices, Galvin picked up a pair of nicknames. The first was "Santa Claus," a reference to his rollicking belly laugh and generosity in passing out gifts. The second was the one that stuck. In a tribute to his facile style—which raised the art of name-dropping to uncharted heights—the consultant was known simply as "Slam Dunk." Galvin "doesn't just drop a name," explained one former Defense Department official with awe, "he slam dunks it."[73]

Paisley did everything in his power to foster Galvin's meteoric career. The approach was anything but subtle. The Navy's acquisition czar would begin most meetings with contractors by posing the same question: "You fellows have Galvin as a consultant, don't you?" The opening remark set the tone for the rest of the session. Visiting executives usually bobbed their heads in unison, as they responded quickly, "Oh, yes, sir."[74]

Toward those companies that balked at hiring Galvin, Paisley's behavior tended to be outlandish. "I'm not liking what I'm hearing," he would snap, rudely interrupting conversations with anger boiling in his eyes. "He made it quite clear that if I hired that particular individual, it would help our case," says Charles Welling, a marketing man for Boeing and then for Bendix. Whether Galvin was sitting in the room or not during such exchanges, the implications were unmistakable. "Paisley didn't ask for anything directly for himself," according to Welling, but his closeness to Galvin implied that the consultant could "put something aside for him at a later period of time." Anybody who "understands the ways of Washington," Welling contends, "would understand that."[75]

Many executives dreaded face-to-face meetings with Paisley, partly, they complained, because he often came poorly prepared and didn't make even a pretense of listening to company arguments. A more telling gripe was widespread suspicion that Paisley seemed to be motivated by hidden agendas, which industry officials automatically assumed were linked in some fashion to his comrade's constantly shifting lineup of clients. Steering a single contract to a firm, as Galvin described it, could affect "all kinds of tentacles" stretching to related projects, several other companies and subcontract agreements among them. Some compared the interplay to a chain reaction. Others used the analogy of a three-ring circus. In this volatile arena, Galvin was the peerless ringmaster. "We are making deals based upon deals," he would say.[76]

Once, Paisley peremptorily ordered officials of Honeywell, an old-line Navy supplier based in Minneapolis, Minnesota, to the Pentagon for an emergency meeting. When the retinue of jet-lagged company executives trooped into his office early the next morning, Paisley announced he was tearing up the existing contract for a popular line of torpedoes. The Navy wanted a lower price as well as Honeywell's agreement to transfer certain technology to make dual-sourcing possible. Since Galvin didn't work for Honeywell, he stood to benefit from the changes. Surrounded by a gaggle of admirals who stayed silent, Paisley said the decision wasn't subject to discussion or negotiation.[77]

"Sign this document here and now!" one Honeywell manager recalls Paisley saying, as he threw down a thick file on the corner of his desk. "Do it, or there won't be any more business." Honeywell acquiesced, after executives concluded "that the admirals were scared to death of this guy. He was perfectly capable of terminating our part of the program, just to show how tough he was." Some of the participants still bristle at the heavy-handed treatment. "He was an arrogant jerk," Toby Warson, who took over the business after it was divested by Honeywell, has told associates.[78]

As time went on, Paisley's efforts to sing Galvin's praises grew increasingly outrageous. "Christ Almighty," Paisley told a BDM executive shortly after stepping down as assistant secretary, "the best guy in the world to help you on this thing is Galvin. There are things I can do. There are other things he can do."[79]

The queue of companies clamoring for Galvin's services became long, indeed. Between 1981 and 1988, he was hired by at least thirty-three companies, with some giving him separate monthly checks to represent individual units. In addition to early clients such as Martin Marietta, BDM, Sperry and McDonnell Douglas, the rest also were top-notch firms. United Technologies, General Motors, General Electric, Grumman, Northrop and Westinghouse all flocked to pay for his advice. A gang of smaller but well-established firms joined the lengthy list, including Loral, Litton, Teledyne, Whittaker and Hercules. From overseas, Rolls-Royce, Fiat and other world-class manufacturers looked to Galvin to safeguard their U.S. interests.[80]

To keep up with the workload, Galvin formed a string of companies to distribute and hide some of his wealth. He also kept adding employees, often based on Paisley's recommendations. "Mel was a personnel director for me in many senses," he recalls, "sending a lot of very, very interesting people" who were looking for work.[81] In exchange, Galvin taught Paisley how to launder money using secret Swiss accounts.

"Slam Dunk" was, proudly, a full-service crook. In the summer of 1986 he escorted one high-ranking Air Force civilian to a bank in Geneva, after supplying an airplane ticket with a phony name to disguise the man's identity. Galvin introduced the official to the bank's vice-president and gave his Air Force compatriot money to help him open a numbered bank account, on the spot, for stashing future payoffs.[82] To aid Paisley in bringing illicit profits back home from Switzerland, Galvin was ready to make all the arrangements on his own. "We talked about this stuff sometimes," Paisley told his friend, but "I don't understand how to do it." Galvin was accommodating as usual. "I would be happy to show you what I'm doing over there," Galvin explained patiently. "I just don't want anybody else to know about it."[83]

Galvin's international banking sources and his stable of blue-chip clients, however, weren't the best measure of his success. The consultant routinely was demanding—and getting—monthly retainers that would have been considered astronomical barely a few years before.

Sperry, for one, paid Galvin over $400,000 annually for consulting services before its merger with another company. The successor firm, Unisys, kept him on at almost the same pay. Loral and a unit of Goodyear it took over paid Galvin a total of almost $500,000 over a two-year stretch. He charged United Technologies nearly $200,000 during some years, which was the average fee for several of his larger clients. Even the Pentagon's coffers directly fed Galvin's flourishing empire. Upshur, one of his key consulting vehicles, received more than $280,000 during the early 1980s for "technical and analytic support" it provided to the Defense Department's Joint Cruise Missile Project. That office developed the Tomahawk missile, which Galvin subsequently helped McDonnell Douglas manufacture as a second source.

In 1986, when his influence reached its high-water mark, Galvin earned nearly $900,000 (though he reported only two-thirds of the total to the Internal Revenue Service).[84] At that rate, he was making more than many of the senior executives and heads of subsidiaries who depended on him. When he dunned an executive vice-president at Martin Marietta to up his fee to a quarter of a million dollars a year, Galvin was rebuffed. "That's more than I make," he was told. "Well, I'm worth more than that, you know," Galvin shot back.[85]

There were times Galvin pocketed huge sums without lifting a finger to help clients. The president of one United Technologies unit, for example, beseeched the consultant for assistance in convincing the Navy to buy his company's state-of-the-art radar for use on updated A-6 jets. "I really want to motivate you," the United Technologies executive told Galvin over a relaxed lunch at Manhattan's "21" Club, adding that the program "is very important to me . . . Your grandchildren will never have to worry about a thing."[86] Galvin's sarcasm came to the fore. "I have ten grandchildren," he said. "That's a good deal."[87]

In the end, the company needn't have paid a dime to win the contract. United Technologies' main rival discovered, well into the competition, that the radar equipment it proposed to install was larger than the space reserved for it on the aircraft. The United Technologies official was exuberant. "It was nice to know that he was going to appreciate it more," Galvin chuckled. "But I was going to win it anyway."[88] Such self-promotion was part of the essence of consulting. "When you talk to your contractors, you puff up and make them think you're doing more than you are," explained William Parkin, who had a senior post in the Joint Cruise Missile Office before hooking up with Galvin as a private consultant and becoming entangled in Illwind. "You tell them you went over and talked to this guy and that guy; a lot of things you are pulling out of your ass."[89]

At other times, Galvin's hardest task was keeping abreast of precisely which clients he was, in fact, representing. He calmly collected monthly checks for simultaneously helping archrivals—sometimes without informing the companies of his split allegiance. He claimed to avoid conflicts by selling his services on a project-by-project basis, rather than helping contractors across the board to sell their wares. It wasn't sheer coincidence, though, that the arrangement pumped up Galvin's overall income. Instead of a flat fee covering several projects, he could demand payment for each contract he attempted to land. "I was not hired as a utility infielder," Galvin explained. "If you want me to work on something else," he told contractors, "that's going to cost you additional money."[90]

In truth, nobody in the industry—including Galvin—could sort out his muddled web of clients. Loyalty meant assuring each one he was going all-out for its benefit, and then taking the most expeditious course to funnel Navy business to the firm that would profit him the most. Enraged executives were full of stories about how Galvin had double-crossed them. He worked on behalf of both Litton and Loral, selling their competing aircraft radar-warning devices. Both LTV and Teledyne Ryan paid him to try to get the same Navy drone project. Years earlier, Bendix had hired and then promptly fired Galvin, after finding out that he also represented Texas Instruments and Raytheon on proposals to build a high-speed air-to-surface missile the Navy wanted for attacking radar installations. The packets of confidential material Paisley gave him were promptly parceled out to clients. But occasionally, it was the information Galvin gleaned straight from one firm that made another of his clients happiest.

At one point, Austen Watson of Singer was sure that Galvin had leaked information and misrepresented himself to help a competitor win a contract to supply navigation equipment to the Norwegian Air Force. Watson was so disgusted, according to Paisley, that for a time the two men "likely would spit on one another if they were holed up in the same room." If they met by chance, Watson's wife insulted Galvin to his face.[91] Never one to lose sight of his long-term goal, Galvin took the attacks in stride. As he was fond of saying, "Money corrects embarrassment so fast you won't believe it."[92]

☆

The famous Watergate complex, a hulking gray landmark on the east bank of the Potomac, is one Washington's premier residential and business addresses. Adjacent to the Kennedy Center and across the street from the Saudi Arabian embassy, it has a hotel, stores, restaurants, gardens and its own security force. Strategically placed courtyards and balconies provide privacy for the diplomats, politicians, business leaders and assorted dignitaries who live there. Senator Robert Dole and his wife, one of the GOP's heralded "power couples" of the 1980s, had a penthouse apartment on one of the upper floors. Lawrence Walsh, the special prosecutor investigating the Iran-Contra scandal, stayed there and depended on room service when he was in town. Those attuned to symbols of Washington's pecking order knew that the location conferred immediate status on tenants.

Changes in Galvin's lifestyle indicated how much he took that notion to heart. As he and Paisley concocted increasingly ambitious schemes, the consultant traded nondescript, cramped office space near the Pentagon for a suite in the Watergate. One of the building's small, eight-hundred-square-foot offices, like the one Galvin first rented, cost about two thousand dollars a month. The more expensive quarters he leased on the sixth floor during Reagan's second term provided a better view and more space, including a distinguished-looking conference room.

Galvin's after-business surroundings also improved markedly. He and his wife moved into a condominium apartment in the Watergate and bought a seventeen-acre spread in rural Front Royal, Virginia, in the foothills of the Shenandoah Mountains. Featuring a swimming pool and tennis courts, the nearly $1-million property had a detached guest house perfect for discreet overnight stays by his Pentagon friends. The main, Colonial-style building protected by an electric gate was ideal for the elaborate parties for which the Galvins were known. In inimitable fashion, Galvin named his estate "Sans Façon," a French phrase meaning unpretentious.

In spite of his success and riches, Galvin's hunger to acquire things didn't abate. He purchased a 140-acre farm farther away from the city, excitedly describing to friends his concept for converting the ancient, half-collapsed barn into a first-class conference and proposal-drafting center. The Galvins owned a racehorse, which they proudly ran at the Pimlico racetrack one year. They talked about buying more horses.[93] For the hotshot salesman turned Pentagon fixer, raising thoroughbreds to compete against Virginia's blue-blooded racing clans was the epitome of the genteel country life he had always aspired to.

The summer of 1986 also was a high point for Mel Paisley. Doctors reported that his cancer seemed to be in remission. Plans to go into business with Galvin took on more distinct shape. Paisley was looking eagerly toward the future, gauging the opportune moment to leave government and plunge into the consulting game from the opposite side. He certainly didn't want to stay in the Pentagon after Secretary Lehman bailed out, and now that seemed a matter of only a few months.

For once, the White House had rebuffed Lehman. President Reagan picked Admiral Carlisle Trost, a Rickover disciple, to replace the retiring chief of naval operations. Reagan and his staff rejected Lehman's candidate, Admiral Frank Kelso, commander of the fleet in the Mediterranean and the architect of a successful nighttime bombing raid against Libya that April. Kelso also happened to be the officer who had raised a stink earlier about the invitations to Paisley's birthday party. The Navy secretary, who considered Kelso brilliant and loyal, wanted him to get the job as CNO very badly. Lehman staked his own reputation on the outcome. "I had gone very far in lobbying for Kelso's appointment—too far in the opinion of some of my close friends," he recalls.[94]

Before the choice was announced, Lehman expressed his extreme displeasure over breakfast in the White House with the vice-president. As a friend and mentor, George Bush advised him to face facts. "It's going the wrong way. You better get used to Trost," the vice-president counseled. Lehman took the blow very hard, threatening to resign if Kelso didn't get the nod. "Look, there's no way I can stay without a CNO that I have picked," the Navy chief responded. Bush tried to personally intercede with Reagan, but it was to no avail. "I'm sorry to tell you this," a downcast vice-president informed Lehman on the telephone that very afternoon. "The president reacted very badly. He reacted as though you were threatening him."[95]

Shortly thereafter, at a White House celebrity tennis tournament against drug abuse, Reagan walked over to Lehman and, in friendly tones, urged him to remain as secretary. Lehman's aides made the same argument. His wife—and his own instincts—strongly urged the opposite. Ultimately, Lehman did reconsider his position, agreeing to stay at the helm of the Navy for a short period to bring some pending issues to closure and arrange for an orderly transition. Bush and others succeeded in keeping the dispute from going public and saddling the president with one more vacancy to fill.

"I'll stay as long as John needs me," Paisley told acquaintances. But those closest to him knew the truth. Paisley's power would dissipate the instant Lehman left. Therefore, he wanted to beat his boss to the punch. In addition, Paisley was determined to return to private life before an impending deadline when somewhat tougher "revolving door" laws were slated to go into effect. If he stayed as assistant secretary past April 1987, there would be legal prohibitions against representing contractors on certain matters before the Navy. The restrictions could last up to two years. Consequently, Paisley was just marking time until he announced his resignation. He savored the prospect of relocating to a new consulting office in the Watergate—just three floors down from Galvin's bustling headquarters—with a shiny sign on the front door proclaiming that "Paisley and Associates" officially was open for business. He and Galvin had come a long way since the nights they spent talking as the moon rose over Sapphire Beach.

To celebrate the anticipated change, Galvin came up with a master stroke. In late August both he and Paisley planned to attend the Farnborough Air Show in Great Britain. Known as the Super Bowl of industry get-togethers, the biannual event gives companies a platform to show off their equipment and try to buy goodwill by plying guests with unlimited free liquor and food. Hordes of foreign buyers, especially from the Middle East, make the trek to the old Royal Air Force bomber field south of London to peruse the latest technology. The Pentagon and Congress send separate delegations. "There is a guise of selling aircraft and aircraft components," Galvin says. But the real business is entertainment. Companies set up chalets on the tarmac, offering free whiskey and buffets all day. At night, there are receptions, orchestras and ornate suppers galore. "Walk down the runway," Galvin says, and "you can see the entire aerospace industry. Everybody tries to outdo each other with parties."[96]

Always looking for a lark, the consultant suggested flying to Europe on the Concorde, taking in the festivities and sailing back to the United States on the stately *Queen Elizabeth II*. Since he represented Rolls-Royce, the maker of the Concorde's engines, Galvin liked to boast about flying the supersonic airliner "a lot of times for a lot of reasons" over the years. He couldn't help being a wiseacre. "I have to fly the Concorde," he used to say. "I mean, somebody's got to do that kind of stuff."[97] Paisley got caught up in the spirit, agreeing that the trip would be fun. So did Charles F. Gardner, a Unisys vice-president and mutual buddy, who said he would come along on part of the trip. Paisley's machinations were branching out to new territory.

In London, the trio cooked up a complicated plan to divide as much as $1 billion in future radar-warning contracts and other business between Unisys, Singer, Litton and Whittaker. In a suite at the Dorchester Hotel on Park Lane, one of the city's fanciest places to stay, Galvin and Gardner pored over confidential bidding documents brought to them by a Paisley assistant.[98] Once the arrangement was made to restructure the bidding criteria to favor Galvin's clients, the aide was dispatched back to the United States to explain the details to the companies. "Read from the big book," Galvin says Paisley instructed the official, "and tell them how it's ordained." The beauty of the scheme was that there was no paper trail: Only the three principals understood all of its twists and turns. "Our deals don't live and die on paper," Galvin explained. The potential profit for the consultant and his two compatriots was six hundred thousand dollars from this understanding alone.[99]

But Galvin wanted the Farnborough trip to be even more memorable. During the air show, Paisley put out the word to his broader industry contacts that he would be leaving the Navy in short order. As a gift for his friend, Galvin had silver Concorde luggage tags engraved with the inscription "Labor Day, 1986," to commemorate the day Paisley decided to leave government.[100]

Heading home across the Atlantic, Paisley and his wife delighted in their top-of-the-line accommodations on the ocean liner. They stayed in an "ultra deluxe" cabin, with three portholes, a queen-size bed, convertible sofa, video recorder and wet bar.[101] Photographs show the beaming couple sunning themselves on deck and posing arm in arm with Galvin. The voyage, however, also offered Paisley, Galvin and Gardner ample time to discuss business opportunities. "The three of us had a chance to drink our tea and our bouillon and discuss Paisley's future," Galvin recalls. Paisley contemplated consulting for three or four large contractors as soon as he submitted his resignation letter to the Navy, charging a quarter of a million dollars or so per client. Martin Marietta, United Technologies and McDonnell Douglas were logical candidates. Galvin claims that Gardner "chirped in and said, 'I'll give you a Unisys contract.'" Not to be outdone, Galvin pledged to provide Paisley seed money, which turned out to be ten thousand dollars a month, to launch his consulting career.[102]

Lounging in a stateroom or toasting each other in one of the ship's cozy bars, the three men exuded bravado; the heady attitude stemmed from more than bracing sea breezes. Paisley couldn't conceive that law enforcement would ever be able to pierce their intrigues. He had bested so many foes over the years. All those previous attacks and allegations— from his days at Boeing and his multiple marriages to the controversy he created in the Pentagon—had left him inured to danger. "He had gone through so damned much criticism and come through untouched," says friend Darrell Cole.[103]

The three conspirators had no inkling of what awaited them after the vessel docked. Within days, federal authorities were nosing around some lower-level consultants at the periphery of their schemes. Within a few weeks, Galvin popped up as a primary target of a growing task force of criminal investigators. Within a few months, all three of them were under virtual round-the-clock surveillance by a swarm of agents from the Federal Bureau of Investigation and the Naval Investigative Service. From then on, photographs and videotapes documented their movements. Investigators listened in on almost every conversation, secretly monitoring their business dealings, social calendars, medical appointments, even their love lives. The banter and off-color jokes that were part of their normal communication appeared crass and suspicious laid out in the daily transcript summaries. Teams of agents spent months replaying and analyzing their words, dissecting every nuance and stammer for possible indications of conspiracy, bribery, tax evasion and other crimes.

Chapter VI

INSIDE THE SHARK TANK

Federal agents tried not to use the whistleblower's real name, not even in conversations among themselves. He was called "Mr. X" or "The Tipster." His name didn't crop up in court files; nor was he one of those mentioned in government documents under the pseudonym "CI," law-enforcement shorthand for confidential informants. Investigators who knew him best coined their own poignant nickname: Out of respect, as well as the desire to protect him from industry retribution, they dubbed him "The Last Honest Man."

All the others who cooperated with the Illwind probe, agents pointed out, had legal guns at their heads. They snitched on friends and business associates to stay one step ahead of criminal charges, or to try to avoid incarceration. At the very least, the informers were motivated by the goal of reducing the time they would have to spend behind bars. Mr. X, on the other hand, was an entirely different character. He came forward from a burning sense of moral outrage. Pentagon corruption affronted his individual code of ethics, making him willing to take a huge risk to bring the felons to justice. "To have a contractor volunteer that someone was trying to shake him down really boggled our minds," recalls one senior investigator. "We suspected it was happening to a lot of them, but how in the hell did this guy get the nerve to speak up?"[1]

Only a handful of agents knew the man's identity to begin with, and they have protected the secret fiercely to this day. Not much else about the massive investigation has stayed so thoroughly hidden for so long. Despite an avalanche of court filings, depositions, testimony, interviews and legal memos—enough to keep throngs of government clerks and private paralegals busy for years cataloging and duplicating materials—the individual who started it all remains an abiding mystery. Almost as much as "Deep Throat" of Watergate fame, the most illustrious and inscrutable whistleblower of all, Mr. X has spawned a cottage industry made up of lawyers, journalists and Washington scandalmongers bent on identifying him. Conjecture and speculation about his personal history abound, as do far-fetched theories of his connection to John Marlowe, the defense industry consultant and convicted child molester responsible for helping launch Illwind.

In spite of all the effort, precious few verifiable details about Mr. X's life have been revealed. He worked for one of the Navy's procurement offices through the late 1970s and casually knew Major Marlowe, who was then still on active Marine Corps duty assigned to the Electronic Systems Engineering command. After leaving the service, Mr. X reportedly found a job as a marketing representative for Calculon, a small engineering and management firm specializing in designing telecommunications networks for the Pentagon. He moved on to do the same kind of work for another relatively obscure Northern Virginia contractor providing technical services to the Marine Corps. According to court records, his employer may have been called the Grim Company or an outfit known as Intercon. While sitting through Navy-sponsored briefings that urged corporate officials to be on the lookout for fraud, Mr. X clearly took to heart admonishments to turn in anyone who offered to break the law. From the inception of his role as an undercover operative, the only thing he demanded was anonymity. Without that, Mr. X insisted, there would be no cooperation; he would automatically take a hike. Federal agents solemnly promised such protection as soon as they received his fateful telephone call.[2]

The tip came out of the blue at the beginning of September 1986. Paisley, Galvin and Gardner were in the midst of partying on the high seas, enthralled by the casino, health spa and other luxuries aboard the thirteen-story *Queen Elizabeth II.* The cruise ship was several days from steaming back into New York Harbor. Meanwhile, in the Washington regional office of the Naval Investigative Service, agent Steven C. Fulmer happened to be doing paperwork that day. As he was one of the midlevel supervisors on the local fraud squad based at the Washington Navy Yard, the call was directed to him.

The voice on the line sounded really angry. Mr. X railed about the nerve of a fellow named Marlowe, a consultant he barely knew, who dared to solicit a bribe from him to land a roughly $3-million Marine Corps contract. "Buddy, I've got some information you can use," Marlowe had told Mr. X, indicating that the payoff for his contact inside the service would be no more than twenty thousand dollars. "If you want to win the contract, I could make that possible," Marlowe said.[3]

Mr. X never contemplated actually paying the money. But if he simply disregarded the offer, what would prevent Marlowe from approaching a competitor in the same brazen way and helping that firm snatch the business by illegal means? Mr. X had scruples, plus he figured it would be stupid to keep silent and thus become a patsy for Marlowe's corruption. His company yearned to stay in the running for the contract.

The first call was made to the NIS office in Quantico, Virginia, which routed it to Fulmer's unit and also routinely alerted the Federal Bureau of Investigation. Those passing on the message didn't see anything extraordinary in the complaint. The money involved was tiny, compared to the Navy's multibillion-dollar acquisition programs. Based on statistics, they knew that unsolicited calls inevitably turned out to be from quacks or disgruntled losers. The lead didn't appear terribly significant.

Fulmer, a lanky, born-again Christian with black-rimmed glasses and a thick South Carolina drawl, believed otherwise. An eager, thirty-five-year-old military history buff who had served as a captain in the Army Signal Corps before earning a master's degree in criminal justice, he had two consuming passions: reading about battlefield exploits and finding a place in law enforcement. Fulmer worked briefly as a stockbroker trainee in his hometown of Columbia, vainly trying to follow in his father's footsteps. He soon became fed up with business. With the Reagan buildup gaining steam, he joined the Naval Investigative Service as a civilian agent in the nearby port of Charleston. In the fall of 1986 he had barely five years of experience with the agency, having arrived in Washington about a year earlier. The most complex case he had ever handled involved inspectors taking old-fashioned kickbacks on shipbuilding contracts. But underneath his shy smile and awkward, Buddy Holly–like appearance, Steve Fulmer was famished for recognition. He knew precisely what it would take to satisfy that hunger.

Markedly more ambitious than the average agent, Fulmer longed to sink his teeth into one giant case that would seal his reputation as an outstanding white-collar crime fighter. For as long as his adult memory stretched, his dream had been to uncover big-league Pentagon corruption. Since the bulk of the Navy's procurement offices were located in a hive of offices in Northern Virginia, Fulmer specifically requested to be transferred to the region. His wife was less than thrilled. Living expenses were substantially higher than in sleepy South Carolina, and the move took her far away from friends and family. But the young agent was panting for a chance to show his abilities. "Naively, I thought Washington was the place to do more and bigger cases. Let others worry about prosecuting some machinist smoking pot on the job," Fulmer recalls thinking.[4]

The initiation period proved painful. Although he had changed locations, Fulmer found that many of his new coworkers exhibited the same short-sighted, lackadaisical attitude as the agents who had frustrated him in Charleston. He stopped trying to hide his anger. NIS was scarcely making headway by going after the small-time frauds that typically filled its caseload, Fulmer told a group of his supervisors only a few weeks before Mr. X appeared. There's a tremendous amount of crime out there and "we are making some cases," the disappointed agent complained, "but it's like licking the icing off a three-layer cake; we just can't seem to reach what's underneath."[5]

Fulmer claims that he had a premonition the second he picked up the receiver and heard Mr. X's story. "You might call it coincidence, but I call it providence," he says, reflecting the earnestness of his small-town upbringing. "I really did get a shiver, because I knew that somehow this tip was different."[6] First of all, the caller sounded intelligent and content to follow directions. Second, the lead was fresh. Unlike the vast majority of tips fielded by NIS agents, this was a report of an alleged crime in progress.

The focus was on current activities and pending contracting decisions, which could be tracked and presumably monitored in secret if Mr. X's information checked out as legitimate. Fulmer realized that he wasn't dealing with some murky, long-forgotten crime that would take forever to untangle—if the remnants of evidence could be deciphered at all.

Most important, the whistleblower had managed to keep his cool while talking to Marlowe. Fulmer's mind raced with recollections of honest, well-meaning company executives who had panicked when faced with exactly the same situation. Incensed at being accosted for a bribe, they let out a stream of curses and usually ordered the offending consultant out of their offices posthaste. At that juncture, even if company management decided to alert authorities, it was virtually impossible to reestablish communication with the criminals. By contrast, Mr. X's response had been tightly controlled. He said he would think about the proposition, resisting the temptation to tell Marlowe to get lost. "He said all the right things," Fulmer recalls, "leaving the door wide open for us to work with him."[7]

A few days later, Richard B. Wade, a special agent from the FBI's Alexandria office versed in white-collar crime inquiries, sat across Fulmer's desk reviewing Mr. X's tale and pondering the government's options. Several years older and more seasoned than Fulmer, Wade agreed that the case had great potential. If Marlowe had an accomplice inside the Marines slipping him bidding information, this truly could be an opportunity to get a worm's-eye view of a bribery scheme as it evolved. Chances were good that Mr. X and his small company weren't the only ones from whom the crooks hoped to score quick bucks. But let's not get swept away by the emotions of the moment, the FBI agent cautioned his excited partner. Wade knew that hot tips had a habit of not panning out. There were many possible booby traps and disappointments to overcome.

At the outset, investigators worried that Mr. X could be trying to suck them into some sort of weird scam. Next, they had to rule out the possibility that Marlowe was a smooth con artist, intent on extorting money from Mr. X's firm without tendering anything of value in return. Stranger twists had caused promising cases to crumble, Wade kept reminding himself. "This is what you do," the agents explained to Mr. X at the start. "Call back and tell Marlowe you need to meet with him and talk some more" about the competing bidders. In short order, Mr. X persuaded Marlowe to feed him his own company's secret bid numbers. It was striking proof that there was, indeed, a festering pocket of corruption inside the Marine Corps.[8]

Along with Fulmer, Rick Wade was regarded as a maverick. While he had the tenacity and discipline of a natural detective—strengths that served him well as a military policeman in the Army—a hot temper made him something of an outcast among fellow agents. Cerebral and low-key until he was riled, the six-foot attorney with the wispy brown hair loved jazz and had a brother who also worked for the FBI. A law degree from Florida State University and a taste for complicated financial transactions prompted Wade to gravitate toward white-collar cases soon after signing up with the bureau in 1975.

Moving from New Orleans to Savannah, New York City, Washington, D.C., and finally Alexandria, he sharpened his skill at digging up government corruption. He was considered aggressive and smart, even by detractors. Wade had the ability to think far down the road about an investigation, "to see the variety of directions it could go and plan for those contingencies," says an admiring FBI agent.[9] However, friends and associates recall there was a cloud over him. Warranted or not, Wade had a reputation of sometimes bucking the bureau's rigid hierarchy. A tough and canny advocate for his cases, he was inclined to speak his mind without being overly concerned for the bureaucratic toes that got stomped. The trait hardly endeared him to folks at the top. His transfer to Alexandria from the legal counsel's division at headquarters was, in some respects, a test to determine how he could fit into a smaller office, and to assess the quality of cases he could develop away from the close scrutiny of FBI chieftains.

Like his Navy counterpart, Rick Wade felt thwarted by the government's singularly unimpressive record detecting military fraud through the mid-1980s. Under Director William Webster, the FBI was outgrowing the late J. Edgar Hoover's emphasis on interstate car thefts and bank robberies. Narcotics and organized crime rated more attention, as did various "economic" crimes. But the Reagan defense buildup caught the bureau, like the rest of the Justice Department, absolutely flatfooted. In 1981, white-collar prosecutors at main Justice weren't pursuing a single major Pentagon fraud, and the FBI was loath to get involved in such cases. There was no formal liaison between the Justice and Defense departments, making it difficult for the armed services to refer allegations for in-depth investigation. In any event, government watchdogs were outmatched by high-priced and more experienced corporate defense counsel. "The industry was waiting for us to fail, which made us that much more cautious," according to one veteran agent.[10] The Pentagon's inspector general conceded that during those early years, his "auditors and procurement people didn't realize fraud when they fell over it."[11]

When investigators did attempt to take a swipe at large companies, their efforts tended to be slapdash and ineffective. Prosecutors generally looked for time-card tampering or sales of shoddy parts. Improper shifting of costs among accounts—and sometimes among private and public projects—were other frequent reasons for criminal charges. Hardly anybody focused on irregularities at earlier stages of the procurement process, when contracts were won and lost.

In 1984, prosecutors thought they had found the club to scare the industry. It was the first felony mischarging case brought against a prominent contractor. "We want to get corporate headquarters to pay more attention to what's happening on the shop floor," a Justice Department lawyer asserted. The outcome was pathetic. In Minneapolis, Sperry, which later became part of Unisys, pleaded guilty to overcharging the Pentagon on launch controllers for Minuteman missiles. The company's total penalty, including double damages and interest, was under $850,000—or less than one-third of its average daily revenue from the military. A federal judge berated the Justice Department, asserting that the fraud actually was ten times the amount Sperry had admitted. Demanding to know why no executives were prosecuted after a two-year probe, the judge complained that "there is little that I can do about it."[12] Adding insult to injury, taxpayers picked up most of the company's legal expenses for defending itself in the grand jury proceedings.

FBI and Justice officials kept trying. General Electric, after pleading guilty to 108 counts of felony fraud on a Minuteman missile contract, issued a new code of ethics and warned employees that "no corners will be cut, no rules will be bent and no ethical lapse will be tolerated." Over the next few years, GE would be convicted in three more criminal cases. TRW, United Technologies, Rockwell, Emerson Electric and Gould, among others, admitted criminal violations. They coughed up a few million dollars and pledged to shore up ethics programs—until the next time they were accused of basically the same fraudulent activities. One senator lambasted prosecutors for "skimming the cream to build up their statistics and run off press releases," rather than tackling the most difficult, precedent-setting cases to try to permanently change industry behavior.[13]

The blue-ribbon Packard Commission, named after industrialist David Packard, didn't help the Justice Department's predicament. The group stressed that "hordes of inspectors and auditors" were counterproductive. Instead of advocating additional prosecutors or tougher criminal sanctions, the presidential commission spent most of its ammunition attacking what it called "impossibly cumbersome" regulations, grossly overstaffed procurement offices and other "deep structural problems" afflicting the Pentagon. While asserting that poor management was having "a disastrous effect" on military purchasing, the Packard reports discounted criminality as the major contributor to overall Pentagon waste. The panel concluded that voluntary industry compliance was the best hope of catching cheaters.

By the time investigators stumbled on Mr. X, government statistics suggested a far different scenario. Nearly sixty of the military's top hundred suppliers were under active criminal investigation. "I keep turning over rocks, and each one I turn over, I keep finding things," the Pentagon's inspector general told reporters, adding that his office had opened seventeen thousand criminal and civil investigations in less than three years. In some busy U.S. attorneys' offices, almost one-third of the prosecutors handled Pentagon-related cases. Congress was vociferous in calling for faster results. The White House was busy assembling legislative packages. Suddenly, the attorney general considered defense cases a higher priority than insider stock trading or bank embezzlement. The FBI couldn't afford to be seen as out of step. Rick Wade's marching orders in Alexandria were to pursue high-impact defense fraud—even if his bosses had no clear concept of what that entailed.

Intuitively, Wade sensed there were splendid cases out there waiting to be made, prosecutions that needed only a lucky break or two to blossom into front-page news. Alert agents ran across hints and glimmers of them regularly. But on the whole, the bureau still was chasing stale leads when it came to the Pentagon. Most of the time, Wade complained to friends and colleagues, he was stuck with marginal cases that probably wouldn't amount to anything. He chafed at the plodding nature of the probes. Some of the transgressions were "garbage violations," he and other agents grumbled, involving free lunches or paltry gifts accepted by Pentagon employees that didn't merit felony sanctions.

The FBI suspected more serious wrongdoing, but all too often it failed to obtain indictments in those cases. Relying primarily on documentary proof—without the benefit of secret tape recordings or videotapes to get to the bottom of nefarious deals—the bureau regularly fell short of collecting the evidence necessary to file charges. Agents were confused by arcane procurement rules, or they were thrown off the scent by the acquiescence of military contracting officials in apparent infractions. Textron's Bell Helicopter subsidiary, for example, avoided criminal charges because the Army repeatedly gave its blessing to dubious billing practices. Before prosecutors could obtain an indictment, Army officials permitted the company to destroy accounting records that would have identified overcharges.[14] Such "historical" cases tended to be as ephemeral, and just about as hard to pin down, as smoke rings.

When he had pursued bank robbers early in his career, Wade recalled, it wasn't uncommon for them "to take off with the money and then brag about what they had done." To catch professional, educated crooks who snared a Pentagon contract illegally, he argued, law enforcement had to adopt a more proactive strategy. "If you and I meet in a garage and agree" to exchange a bribe, according to Wade, "how does the government investigate and prove that" if there aren't any documents or third-party witnesses? The FBI agent understood how easily corporate and Pentagon officials could agree on a clever cover story, sandbagging authorities and obfuscating events. Somehow, the FBI needed access to real-time intelligence about criminal schemes inside the industry, preferably *before* they were carried out. "You can attach different explanations to documents," Wade now says. "But you can't explain away motives if you're captured on tape. It was never any secret that a live case would be immeasurably better."[15]

That's why Mr. X's tip was so exciting. Three days after Wade and Fulmer's initial brainstorming session, the agents huddled with Mr. X in a shopping center parking lot. They fitted him with a concealed recording device and briefed him for a face-to-face meeting with Marlowe to go over the mechanics of passing bribes. The Friday afternoon get-together went smoothly, with the exhilarated agents hanging on to each phrase Marlowe uttered to incriminate himself more deeply. "There were indicators that this wasn't a one-shot, once-in-a-lifetime arrangement," Wade recalls. "Several statements indicated additional criminal activity beyond the bribe" that was broached with Mr. X.[16] John Marlowe appeared to aim toward larger game. The FBI agent took the tape home. He spent much of the weekend reviewing it and discussing the facts with higher-ups. Always double-checking his instincts, Wade sought reassurance that he wasn't going off half-cocked.

Shortly afterward, Wade and Fulmer sauntered into the U.S. attorney's offices in Alexandria and poked their heads inside prosecutor Clarence "Bud" Albright's cubicle. The duo looked unusually chipper. Grinning and waving the cassette with Marlowe's conversation above his head, Wade announced: "Here in my hand I have the case of a lifetime." Albright, who had an amiable relationship with the FBI agent from a previous case, snapped that he was too busy for practical jokes. "What kind of garbage are you guys hauling in here now?" he demanded, barely lifting his eyes from the stack of papers on his desk. "It must be a piece of junk, otherwise you wouldn't be so dramatic."[17]

The agents insisted on playing portions of the tape for Albright, and the trio made a couple of key decisions right away. In classic fashion, they planned to "roll" Marlow; that is, they would pressure the consultant to divulge his contacts and perhaps recruit him as a government informant. FBI psychologists were devising strategies that could be helpful in that attempt. Albright sensed the potential, but he was far from convinced that Marlowe would be as great a catch as the bureau predicted. Looking back, he uses drug busts as an analogy. "You take a dealer off the street and you confiscate a bag of cocaine," he says, "but many times the investigation never goes any further." Perhaps the street-level peddler "doesn't talk enough, or he leads you to somebody who doesn't know anything valuable," Albright explains. "So, you never get inside the ring. I figured this was going to be another instance where we got a nibble, and ended up with generally lower-level folks."[18] Setting aside such doubts, Albright concurred that it was worth at least making a run at Marlowe. He briefed head prosecutor Henry Hudson only in generic terms, vaguely mentioning the case at a staff meeting packed with details on other pending matters. The approach was chosen partly to minimize the visibility of Marlowe's investigation, while providing investigators utmost flexibility to follow their hunches.

Ordinarily, FBI and NIS agents were at each other's throats over significantly less important issues. Given its proud traditions and sheer size, the FBI had a habit of hogging the limelight. It was renowned for grabbing credit from sister agencies in joint investigations. "The bureau usually doesn't like to invest a year looking at documents," according to a grizzled NIS investigator. "It looks for the quick hit and maximum public relations impact. That's the way it has always operated."[19]

By contrast, naval agents felt jealous and generally insecure working with the FBI. They bridled at doing the grunt work for their higher-paid, more highly respected counterparts. "The bureau is so condescending, always trying to cut us out of the action," one of Fulmer's superiors muttered. NIS morale also suffered for other reasons. The agency had been roundly criticized by Congress and the media for its slipshod handling of espionage cases, including the John Walker family spy ring. Later, NIS was blamed for coercing testimony from Marine guards accused of fraternizing with Soviet spies at the American embassy in Moscow. As late as 1986, some admirals perversely wished to see NIS concentrate on investigating rapes, identifying homosexual sailors in the fleet and solving run-of-the-mill violent crimes. Cracking down on abuse of travel privileges by Navy personnel was considered a big deal by those running NIS. FBI teams, backed up by their vast jurisdiction and resources, ridiculed the Navy investigators' narrow charter.

Fulmer's tiny squad, for example, had only rudimentary computers and none of the high-powered cameras or other surveillance equipment commonly used by the bureau. "Steve was outgunned by the bureau's technical assets," according to one of his friends. Just before Marlowe surfaced, red-faced Navy agents had to swallow their pride and informally borrow a "body recorder" from Wade's office to apprehend a flasher exposing himself to women inside the Pentagon. FBI bigwigs wanted nothing to do with the "Weenie Waver" case, as wags at the bureau's headquarters condescendingly referred to it. "Don't you folks have any quality cases over there?" one of them asked. Wade and his boss had the opposite reaction. The case, by itself, was insignificant. But they were eager to help in order to persuade NIS of their good intentions and lay the groundwork for future cooperation. From his side, Fulmer also saw that the level of mistrust and animosity between the two agencies had to be lowered. His NIS comrades peppered him with suspicious questions from the commencement of Illwind: "Is Wade telling you everything? How can you work so closely with the bureau and not get burned? When is he going to try to screw you by taking over the case?" they kept asking.[20]

Fulmer and Wade avoided competition and acrimony thanks to a spectacularly lucky coincidence. They had joined forces on a daring, albeit unsuccessful, sting operation a couple of months before. Blessed by local supervisors, it was a rare FBI-NIS joint undertaking. Working closely together on the project, the two men picked up a few crumbs of information about the Navy's procurement system. In the process, they grew to trust each other. Quite apart from their southern roots and parallel professional yearnings, they discovered a lot of other common ground. Leisurely sharing confidences about family and office hassles, the pair forged a bond that transcended agency rivalries. "The timing was perfect," Fulmer recalls. "We respected each other; we knew the scene and had spent time together in the field."[21] That personal tie, established months before Marlowe's name meant anything to investigators, was one of the main reasons behind Illwind's ultimate triumph.

During the earlier, ill-conceived sting, agents attempted to lure marketing representatives away from defense contractors by offering them better-paying jobs with one of the FBI's phony firms. The bureau placed advertisements in newspapers, requesting résumés from applicants. Prospective employees were invited to Washington for interviews, wined and dined at government expense and then pumped for information about marketing secrets. It was a great idea that fell flat. The targets didn't suspect FBI involvement, but they still wouldn't loosen up to discuss illegal schemes. Their reticence should have been obvious. The agents posing as headhunters were utter strangers to the defense community. They didn't know the personalities who counted; they couldn't show mastery of the industry's vernacular. Without someone to vouch for them, such outsiders had no chance to penetrate the tight circle of corrupt contractors and consultants.

As a potential informant, of course, Marlowe didn't have any of those shortcomings. "He was knowledgeable and knew the players from the start," Fulmer recalls. "He was totally believable. He had a 100 percent pedigree."[22] Regardless of how much the government invested in future undercover efforts, Wade and Fulmer recognized it would be impossible to buy Marlowe's brand of instant credibility. But if he balked and refused to roll over, in a flash their carefully crafted plans would shatter.

☆

On September 24, 1986, barely three weeks after Mr. X placed his call to NIS, Rick Wade and Steve Fulmer trudged up to the second floor of a shabby Northern Virginia office building. Armed with a hastily signed search warrant and copies of secretly recorded tapes, they knocked on the door of Marlowe's company, Tri-Tech. Confronting him carried considerable risks. Investigators had plenty of incriminating conversations, but the consultant hadn't pocketed any money from Mr. X intended for bribes. Marlowe might give them a cold stare, summon an attorney and summarily reject government entreaties to cooperate.

From checking police and courthouse records, Wade knew all about Marlowe's disgraceful 1984 encounter with the two little girls at the Barcroft Apartments—only a short drive from Tri-Tech's location on Old Columbia Pike in Annandale. Distasteful as it was to contemplate, the sex conviction supplied the government with probably its most potent leverage. Fulmer, who had a toddler at home, couldn't bear to look through the court documents. He asked his partner how graphic the sexual abuse charges were. "You don't want to know," Wade had assured him.[23]

It was lunchtime, so Wade and Fulmer were betting that most of the employees would be out of the building. Marlowe and his wife, who doubled as his assistant, were alone. Flashing badges, investigators followed him into an inner office where they could talk uninterrupted. The agents wasted no time laying out their allegations. "We have information," Wade began in a nonthreatening tone, "that somebody is selling information about a contract." Marlowe replied that he had merely been approached by a contractor seeking information. The consultant became indignant ten or so minutes into the conversation, animatedly denying that he ever solicited a bribe. He claimed a competitor was trying to set him up. "It didn't happen," Marlowe asserted. "Oh, yes it did," the agents responded in tandem. Wade and Fulmer proceeded to recount, word for word, some of his juiciest exchanges with Mr. X. "My friend, do you want to listen to the tapes yourself?" Fulmer asked. Suddenly, Marlowe appeared less belligerent.[24]

Sensing an opening, investigators spelled out their proposal. By any standard, it was an enticing deal. If Marlowe agreed to cooperate and tape conversations at the government's behest, his maximum exposure would be a single mail fraud charge. Otherwise, he faced multiple felony counts and a lengthy prison sentence. Wade also explained that they were aware he was free on bail pending an appeal of his earlier conviction for aggravated sexual battery. The fifty-thousand-dollar bond had been approved by a judge in Arlington County only a month earlier. The investigators knew they didn't have to dwell on that topic. Their target already was fighting ferociously to remain out of the state penitentiary. He was sufficiently sharp to comprehend the implications if Virginia authorities were informed that he was in trouble with the law again. Yet Marlowe still wavered.

Scanning the decorations and Marine memorabilia on the walls, Fulmer tried a different tactic. "John, listen to me," he said. "If you work with us and do a really great job, you certainly will be helping your country. You will have earned another medal."[25]

Fulmer's words had impact. But not as much as the retired Marine officer's desperate financial condition. He had hefty unpaid bills from attorneys who had defended him in the state case, and the law firm was pestering him to settle the account. John Marlowe couldn't call the same lawyers for advice, and he couldn't borrow any more money from friends to hire new counsel. He had nowhere to turn for help. The agents didn't need the search warrant. After about forty minutes, Marlowe finally caved in. "All right, where do we go from here? What do you want me to do?" he asked. Wade and Fulmer glanced at each other, barely concealing their elation. This is awfully easy, Fulmer thought, impassively telling Marlowe, "Glad you feel that way."[26] Without any lawyers or paperwork, a handshake deal was struck. Marlowe agreed to sacrifice friends and associates to save his skin. Years later, he pared his reasoning to its essentials: "I got caught. I made the agreement because it was offered to me and it made sense."[27]

Wade seized the moment, taking out a tape recorder and laying it on Marlowe's desk. "Let's make some phone calls," the FBI agent said. It was more than a suggestion. "I didn't want to leave and have him change his mind," Wade recalls. "We were looking for something to cement the deal." The consultant complied immediately. Once he made the decision to go undercover, Marlowe sounded relieved, almost casual. "Okay, I'll call Jack," he replied. The agents knew that was his accomplice, though they still didn't have the man's last name. With the recorder on, Marlowe dialed the number of Jack Allan Sherman, a supervisory contracting officer at Marine Corps headquarters in Alexandria and the man who had furnished his alibi during the child molestation trial. They arranged a meeting for the next afternoon to talk about bribes. "It was like Christmas day," according to Fulmer. "All this wonderful stuff came rolling in; it was just amazing." As Marlowe chatted with Sherman, the NIS agent muttered under his breath, "God, don't stop now."[28]

John Marlowe was exceptional in his new role. A gifted actor who knew how to ingratiate himself with industry and Pentagon officials, he grew adept at shifting conversations to topics that most interested his handlers. Whether he wore a miniature recorder taped to his chest or conversed over telephone lines bugged by the government, Marlowe maintained his sangfroid. "I can do it for you," he reassured agents. "I can make it happen." As the probe progressed, he was proud of his skill at embellishing the ideas of investigators and posing leading questions to trap individuals. Friends and associates knew that Marlowe was in a jam for money, which made his approaches that much more believable.

Investigators found Marlowe agreeable and compliant. Before each of his biweekly get-togethers with Sherman—often spent driving around suburban neighborhoods to exchange information or envelopes stuffed with cash—Marlowe received a briefing about specific areas agents desired him to cover. The frequent meetings were designed to plumb Sherman's past and current activities. Marlowe stuck faithfully to the outline he was given. However, he could ad-lib nimbly and rewrite the script if circumstances dictated. Wade and Fulmer usually trailed after the two conspirators in an undercover car, taking in every word and furiously scribbling notes.

Admittedly, the government's mole did have a few peculiarities. He was a heavy drinker. Associates recall that when Marlowe was intoxicated, he sometimes resorted to weird behavior. His eyes focused on a face and then he would sit silently, seemingly transfixed, staring at that person for long stretches. Marlowe also loved to play music in the nude. "He was a very good piano player," Wade chuckles. But when it came to his undercover responsibilities, the man got the job done. Marlowe wheedled and prodded to get Sherman on tape talking at length about all of the contracting official's bribery plots. He also tricked Sherman into divulging other schemes, in which different companies and consultants were corrupting competition. Using inside bidding information obtained from Sherman as bait, Marlowe was able to record a couple of those consultants in further illegal activities. "I'm only doing this to get my butt out of a jam," a shaken Marlowe confided to Fulmer. "I'm betraying people who helped me." All the agent could say, in a sympathetic voice, was, "John, I know that."[29]

Jack Sherman was the first of Marlowe's victims whose life came unglued. A profane, middle-aged civil servant with a salary of roughly thirty thousand dollars a year, Sherman liberally supplemented that income by means of graft. He had been on the take for at least eleven of his fifteen years working as a buyer for the Marines, prompting one jokester to call him "as crooked as the Mississippi River." Initially, the bribes came directly from company executives. Sherman used to hide wads of bills, wrapped in aluminum foil, under trays of ice cubes in his home refrigerator. When friends or family members asked questions about his finances, Sherman lied that he won betting on the horses.[30]

In exchange for a total of eighty thousand dollars in illicit payments from Lee Telecommunications and its successor firm, California-based Whittaker Command & Control Systems, Sherman routinely violated acquisition rules, steered contracts to the companies and repeatedly promised to lobby inside the Pentagon on their behalf. He helped Lee avoid potential bankruptcy by giving it work and making sure that its invoices were paid expeditiously. Subsequently, Sherman personally authorized contract modifications guaranteeing Whittaker millions of dollars in extra revenue from development of the Marines Corps' battlefield air-traffic-control network. Normal competitive bidding and contracting safeguards were thrown out the window as he sought to aid Whittaker. "I'll always have something that they're going to need me [for]," Sherman boasted to Marlowe. "Don't worry about that."[31] Overall, Sherman didn't rise above relatively small-scale thievery. He helped secure approximately $6 million worth of business for the two companies, spread over six years. But the payoffs helped Sherman fix the roof on his house, build up his Individual Retirement Account, buy a truck for his wife and pay for Christmas presents.[32]

After a while, Whittaker executives devised a more sophisticated route to slip Sherman money to "do whatever was necessary" to "look out for the best interests of the company." Marlowe, one of the firm's consultants, served as a willing conduit. The money kept flowing even after Marlowe was cornered by the feds and enlisted to participate in the investigation. Over a nine-month stretch, he gave the unsuspecting Sherman more than forty-three thousand dollars in bribes, supposedly from Whittaker and at least one other contractor. In fact, the payments were part of an elaborate sting. All the bills were marked and supplied by the FBI, and the clandestine exchanges were captured on film.[33]

During the inquiry's early days, Wade and Fulmer had a lot to learn about proper eavesdropping procedures. For the first extensive dialogue between Marlowe and Sherman, agents picked a Marriott Hotel overlooking the Virginia end of two of the bridges spanning the Potomac. They painstakingly checked the layout and acoustics of the hotel's restaurant in advance of the meeting. The room was quiet and half empty in the afternoon. The tables had adequate space between them to filter out extraneous noise. Satisfied that everything was ready for the critical rendezvous, the pair congratulated each other for finding such a suitable spot.

Later in the week, when Marlowe and his partner in crime sat down together around noon, the choice no longer appeared ideal. The walls reverberated with the sound of rock music played extra loud to please the luncheon crowd. Alongside the blaring speakers, the crush of patrons waiting for tables added to the background noise. Recording the tête-à-tête proved excruciatingly difficult. Gritting their teeth, Wade and Fulmer could barely make out the muffled conversation as they hunched over listening equipment in the stakeout car downstairs. Their faces were taut with frustration. "We were straining on every word," Fulmer recalls. Such miscues were reduced as the investigative team expanded. The FBI flew in specialized surveillance crews from around the country, rotating them every month. Trained in hazardous counterintelligence and narcotics cases, these Special Operations Teams were expert at shadowing elusive lawbreakers. They had a multitude of disguises, vans and even helicopters at their disposal. Nonetheless, the roar of jet traffic around National Airport and the slurred, often disjointed speech of certain of the targets made it extremely difficult to fathom some of the conversations overheard during Illwind's covert phase.

Sherman and Marlowe, in turn, led investigators to consultant Thomas Muldoon, a longtime friend and business partner whom Sherman chided as "the biggest thief in the business."[34] With his white mane and garrulous manner, Muldoon sounded and acted like a masterful Irish ward heeler from Massachusetts. Graduating from Boston College with a law degree in 1957, he learned the rules of petty graft as a purchasing agent for the Army. After a brief fling in industry, he became a freelance consultant in the nation's capital. "It was the best job anybody could ever have," he says, with clients paying for drinks, lavish meals and other expenses. "I used to go the Jockey Club like most people go to McDonald's."[35]

Muldoon had been funneling bribes to Sherman from Whittaker for at least ten years. His dealings with Marlowe stretched back longer, to the days of the Vietnam War. Before a youthful, panicky Marlowe shipped out for a combat tour in Southeast Asia, he spent two weeks trying to drink himself into a coma and spilling his life's story to his warmhearted friend,

Tommy Muldoon. Marlowe repaid the favor by giving Muldoon contracting intelligence in later years about Marine Corps programs. Foul-
mouthed and lightning-fast with a quip, Muldoon went barhopping with
Marlowe and, less frequently, with Sherman. "Mully," as his confederates
called him, could be phenomenally masochistic. He downed thirteen
martinis at one sitting to try to impress another associate. While many
friends considered him a blowhard, he had played the consulting game
longer than Marlowe and had built up more contacts inside the industry
and the Pentagon. He even helped Marlowe get some consulting work.
Over twenty years, Muldoon counted Litton, United Technologies,
Unisys, Hazeltine, Honeywell, Emhart and Gould among his clients.[36]

Those firms weren't paying thousands of dollars a month for his understanding of the technical side of the business: That was plainly nonexistent. Muldoon's definition of a universal joint, friends used to laugh, was
"a really big nightclub open to everyone." Without a hint of parody, he
once admitted to a senior Litton manager: "I don't know fiber optics from
an ice cream cone."[37] Litton's worst crime, a company attorney observed
afterward, may have been hiring executives "who were stupid enough to
believe someone like Muldoon." Still, corporations hankered for his assistance. Living on the top floor of a condominium in the fashionable Kalo-
rama section of northwest Washington, Muldoon bragged that in an
outstanding year he earned a quarter of a million dollars.

Mysteriously, Muldoon constantly was strapped for cash. Inveterate
gambling kept him on the prowl for new and better ways to make money.
Years before, FBI agents had rousted him from bed as part of an investigation into a Washington bookmaking ring. No federal gambling charges
were ever filed against Muldoon. In the fall of 1986, when Wade and Fulmer began tracking his moves through the underworld of Pentagon contracting, they discovered a maze where the race for inside information was
as cutthroat as it was unrelenting. Agents observed Muldoon and his fellow
consultants peddling their hottest "numbers" from contractor to contractor
as calmly as door-to-door salesmen demonstrating the latest houseware
gadgets. "The entire industry worked this way," and only some "esoteric"
laws may have been broken, Muldoon says, trying to justify his actions in
retrospect. Claiming that companies didn't care how middlemen operated,
he asserts: "The hunt for inside information was universal."[38] That may be
hyperbole, but it is true that Muldoon hardly encountered a contractor
who was not interested in the marketing intelligence he was hawking.

With the help of Mark Saunders, a former Pentagon contracting official, and two corrupt civilians working for the Navy, Muldoon obtained
restricted bidding data for Litton on a trio of contracts valued at approximately $200 million.[39] The company's executives, who exhorted Mul-
doon to use his "channels" to find out the all-important numbers bid by
the competition, weren't newcomers to skirting the law. Some of Muldoon's tactics were comparable to "playing with fire," a Litton marketing

man acknowledged. Less than a year earlier, the Beverly Hills–based company had been forced to admit that it had methodically defrauded the Pentagon for almost a decade by inflating prices, charging twice for some raw materials and failing to disclose rebates from vendors on forty-five Navy electronics contracts. One of the tricks, dubbed "chicken fat" by insiders, consisted of obtaining blank price quotation forms from suppliers and filling them in with Litton's bogus figures. The inflated prices were submitted to the Pentagon for payment. Apologetic after being caught, Litton vowed publicly to mend its ways and tighten internal contracting procedures. Around the same time, though, it quietly hired Muldoon to do only one thing: secure procurement information that was deemed off-limits to contractors.

Despite his annual retainer of nearly one hundred thousand dollars from Litton, Muldoon wasn't inclined to strain himself chasing after the engineering wrinkles of competing bids. Such details were inconsequential, he confidently told a high-ranking Litton contact, unless a competitor happened to use some "hottsy tottsy design . . . that you might be able to steal."[40] Other times, Muldoon claimed his sources not only purveyed reliable information but could determine the outcome of contract awards. "Come up with the bread," he bluntly told a vice-president of one Litton unit, and the company would be assured of getting another shot at besting competitors' prices.[41] (Litton eventually pled guilty to Illwind-related charges, but that didn't end its troubles. Just last year, the company paid $82 million, one of the heftiest civil fraud settlements ever levied against a defense contractor, for systematically shifting data processing costs from commercial to Pentagon contracts.)

But Muldoon's bird-dogging didn't prevent Litton's elimination from contention for the largest of the contracts it had hoped to snare—a hotly contested, $100-million-plus program to produce high-technology, portable air-traffic-control centers for the Marine Corps. The Marines used the acronym ATACC, standing for Advanced Tactical Air Command Central. Undaunted, Muldoon set out to find an alternative buyer for his services. He knew how the remaining bidders stacked up pricewise, down to the last decimal point. In addition, he knew how each company was ranked on technical criteria. It's embarrassing if a government source delivers such exhaustive, hard-to-get data, Muldoon once confided to Saunders, and "he gives you information that you can't even make a dime on."[42] Muldoon wasn't going to let that happen with ATACC.

LTV was the next firm he approached with his illegal scheme to try to influence the contract. Sales executives there were intrigued by Muldoon's proposal and speedily arranged two meetings, perhaps because they already were paying another of his buddies for the same kind of work on a different project.[43] Muldoon demanded fifty thousand dollars up front plus five thousand dollars monthly. The early feedback was positive: "The guys are very much interested . . . and we would keep this mat-

ter very confidential," one LTV marketing man told Muldoon enthusiastically. "My golly, your credentials are impeccable . . . and you have repeat
customers." Muldoon suggested bypassing the company's attorneys. But
in the end, a higher-ranking executive got "cold feet" and vetoed hiring
Muldoon, the disheartened LTV official informed him. "He was afraid I'd
give him AIDS or something," Muldoon cracked.[44]

Within two weeks, Muldoon made the identical pitch to Norden Systems, a Connecticut-based subsidiary of United Technologies, the nation's
eighth-largest defense contractor at the time. Norden had a reputation for
exacting the utmost in bid-related intelligence. "You need a guy on the
inside, whether it's me or someone else," Muldoon argued.[45] This time, he
fared much better. A former senior vice-president of the unit, who was
advising the company, recommended hiring the consultant to procure
"the guidance" necessary to win. The vice-president of advanced programs agreed to the sixty-thousand-dollar annual retainer and decided
that Norden's "senior management should be advised that Muldoon
should be hired."[46] He earned every penny of that fee.

Before Muldoon got the job, Norden was ranked near the bottom of
ATACC bidders and its executives despaired of surviving the first competitive cut. Essentially, they had given up vying for the business. Relying
on luck and manipulation of bids by one of his crafty coconspirators inside the Marine Corps, Muldoon revived the company's prospects. The
firm was bumped up to a higher spot, thereby keeping it eligible for the
contract. "If it puts bread on the table," the corrupt Marine contracting
official said, "it ain't a waste of time."[47]

Muldoon crowed about squeezing Norden in as one of four finalists.
Corporate managers "certainly didn't do it by their own good fortune,"
he told his partner, Saunders. "They had nothing to do with it . . . Getting
the sixty K is light, you know, very light for what we did." When the
contractor was tardy issuing their consulting checks, Saunders exploded.
"We'll just go do business someplace else," he told Muldoon. Sometimes,
threatening to work *against* a contractor was the surest method to get its
attention. Norden's favorable ranking could be undone overnight, Saunders fumed. "Call them up and tell 'em it's fuckin' undone." Muldoon
stayed calm. "I can't afford to do that," came the reply. Saunders persisted.
"If I don't hear a fuckin' bonus in this son of a bitch, they ain't got a
chance," he snapped.[48] The United Technologies unit paid them some of
the money. But hedging his bets, Muldoon went ahead and shared his illicit information with at least two consultants representing other ATACC
bidders. If Norden lost, he still hoped to come out on top. The company
dropped out of the bidding the day the investigation went public, but not
before an executive hurriedly destroyed one of the incriminating documents supplied by Muldoon.

Throughout Illwind, Muldoon kidded with his accomplices about
phone lines that were tapped and law-enforcement officers who he sus-

pected secretly were recording his conversations. These asides were based wholly on bluster and a sarcastic sense of humor. Flip and uninhibited, Tom Muldoon was having a ball playing out his worst fantasies. He poked fun at the paranoia of associates, without ever suspecting how close to the mark his comments were. He also made investigators extremely jittery.

"This phone is tapped, so listen" carefully, Muldoon told Sherman in a conspiratorial tone early in their schemes. There was a pregnant pause. "Where's all the fucking stuff that I'm paying you for?" Muldoon yelled into the receiver, bursting into uproarious laughter as agents recorded every chortle. Sherman was silent. For another corrupt contracting official, Muldoon had a similarly mocking message: "When I told you I was going to take you off the payroll" during an earlier chat on the phone, he explained, "that was just in case the FBI was listening."[49]

Muldoon reserved his best barbs for Mark Saunders. "You noticed the phone [has] all that clicking," Saunders remarked at the conclusion of a telephonic brainstorming session on ATACC. "Yeah, I was gonna ask you about that . . . it's not normal. But it's your phone, right?" Muldoon asked. Saunders answered that he wasn't positive. "I've never had it before," Muldoon insisted, sounding increasingly concerned. Then he let the hammer drop. "They're probably taping you, you fuckin' crook. Ha, ha, ha."[50] The eerie jokes didn't deter either Muldoon or his henchmen from carrying out their dirty deeds. "One-half of their brains told them that their phones may be wired, but the other half blithely ignored the warning," Wade marvels.[51]

Investigators easily could have stopped as soon as they reached Sherman and Muldoon. Rarely did the government have such first-hand, unimpeachable evidence of bribery. The case would be a cinch to prosecute, while headquarters would be delighted with the agents' productivity. There was sentiment inside the FBI and the NIS to take that tack. "It would have been considered wildly successful," Fulmer says. But the agents in charge were resolute about following leads up the chain. "We were never willing to discuss stopping at Sherman. We knew he was small potatoes," according to Fulmer. Consistent with his military bent, Fulmer compares this stage of Illwind to General Douglas MacArthur's World War II island-hopping campaign in the Pacific: "MacArthur went around some islands instead of occupying them; they weren't worth messing with. We left Sherman alone for the time being and went on to investigate others."[52]

Sherman had direct responsibility for individual contracts worth only a few million dollars. Muldoon's tentacles didn't reach beyond the Navy's civil service ranks. The aim was to continue using John Marlowe—and anybody else willing to cooperate—to infiltrate higher-level criminality. "From the get-go, the idea was to go for the top; to keep rolling them and rolling them, until we reached as high as possible," recalls Joe Krahling, then head of the FBI's Alexandria office. The trail was confusing in the beginning, and investigators only guessed where Marlowe would lead them. They mostly reacted to the latest incriminating snippets of conversation captured on tape. Notwithstanding all the obstacles, the overriding goal never changed. "The whole strategy," Krahling says, was finally "to get beyond the garbage cases we had been working."[53]

Wade likened his role to that of a surgeon excising a malignant tumor. "He doesn't stop at the first site of cancer. Once you've taken the time and effort to get inside the body," Wade argued, "you've got to see if it has spread, if the cancer shows up elsewhere." The exploratory probes might be a bit gruesome and time consuming, he told friends, but they had to be done to "shine a light" on unacceptable behavior. "We had an obligation to take this as far as we possibly could." Above all, that principle drove Illwind. The key was always to move on. "Rick would keep reminding everybody, 'Let's focus on the next target,' " says a fellow agent. "He would ask, 'How do we get beyond the last one and move swiftly to the next one?' "[54]

Wade and Fulmer hit the jackpot less than two months into the investigation. Following their instructions, Marlowe had been pressing Sherman to link him with somebody who had access to higher-ranking industry figures. "Maybe I could become sort of an understudy to him," Marlowe explained. Sherman suggested a possible direction. "There's a guy named Bill Parkin," he volunteered. "I hear good things about him. He has a lot of good contacts."[55]

Marlowe and his handlers didn't wait long to strike. Marlowe called Parkin, introduced himself and came right to the point. "I've heard a lot about you. Mutual friends say you're a guy I need to meet," he said, deftly appealing to Parkin's delusions of self-importance. "We might be able to do some business together." Luck was on the government's side. Parkin, who liked the confident ring in Marlowe's voice and always stood ready to enlarge his information network, agreed to see him. "I have supposed smarts and know everybody," Parkin explained afterward, so he didn't think the call from a stranger was that unusual. The two consultants soon were hatching plans to share a windfall. They offered ORI Group, a midsize contractor in suburban Maryland, the inside "skinny" on an upcoming Marine Corps contract. Typically, Parkin told clients he could give them some "insight" or "analysis" to provide a competitive edge. Brusque and unsmiling, Marlowe didn't engage in such verbal foreplay. For ten thousand dollars down and two thousand dollars a month, "I can get you the numbers," he told the ORI contingent over lunch. "I nearly slid under the table" in the "little greasy spoon," Parkin recalls, and company officials all but "dropped their teeth" from shock. "We'll get back to you," they said, but the company didn't hire either man.[56]

Several rungs higher than Marlowe in the pecking order of consultants, Parkin turned out to be the perfect entrée to identifying corruption at the helm of the Navy. He knew Bill Galvin from the Joint Cruise Missile

Office and continued to do business with him, including supervising construction of the metal-shielded "vault" to shepherd classified documents for the Moon Project. Galvin was the one who filed incorporation papers for Bill Parkin's firm in the early 1980s. He helped Parkin get at least three consulting jobs and joined with him in the lease-purchase of a mobile home. Around the same time, Parkin was a passenger when Galvin crash-landed a rented twin-engine Beechcraft during a trip to inspect a condominium the two men were considering buying on Maryland's Eastern Shore. The plane's landing gear buckled from a hard landing. According to the Federal Aviation Administration, which fined Galvin for reckless flying, the logbook in the cockpit indicated that he hadn't piloted an aircraft since the 1950s. Never at a loss for excuses, Galvin claimed that he had misplaced his most recent logbooks.[57]

Bill Parkin also had ties to the Paisleys. He advised Vicki Paisley how to organize VAMO, her small consulting firm, and he claimed to be on excellent terms with her husband. Best of all, agents discovered that Parkin—who had sold aluminum siding and established beauty parlors, restaurants and beer halls before tackling the defense business—simply loved to talk. And Marlowe was a master at using flattery to draw him out. Parkin sat down one day and waxed philosophical about all the business he had steered to companies in his career, repeatedly daring Marlowe to "top this one." The tape "was absolutely incredible," one senior agent recalls, because of "the crimes they were openly admitting to each other." Among other things, Parkin described cruise missile contracts he had "thrown" to a Galvin client and what his "cut" of the transactions totaled.[58] When he wasn't boasting about his personal scams, Parkin relished gossiping about those pulled off by Paisley and other prominent industry characters he admired. The recordings were a treasure trove for investigators. "Our knowledge base grew exponentially," Fulmer recalls.[59]

Parkin's loquaciousness meant that investigators had little use for Marlowe any longer. They kept him busy recording conversations with marginal industry officials—he made 247 tapes in all—but that was partly to keep him in the dark about separate leads agents were pursuing related to Galvin, Paisley and the rest of the schemers in their orbit. Also, law-enforcement agencies wanted to avoid raising suspicions by having Marlowe drop out of sight for no apparent reason. Wade and Fulmer hoped to phase him out gradually. They racked their brains for a solution, but the Virginia Supreme Court beat them to the punch. Marlowe's appeal in the sexual assault case was thrown out and he was ordered to report to prison—abruptly ending nine months of undercover work. The industry contacts he had promised to help didn't suspect any ulterior motive for his disappearance.

Sherman, anxious to keep his spigot of bribes open while Marlowe was behind bars, looked to Muldoon to convey the money from Whittaker. Muldoon said no at first, arguing that Sherman was dangerously greedy and unpredictable. "He scares the shit out of me," Muldoon groused to a Whittaker executive, adding that the risks of acting as a bagman for Sherman were too great. "Business is business, you know . . . If I'm gonna be scared, I want to be remunerated for it."[60] Ultimately, Whittaker sweetened the pot and Muldoon agreed to be a stand-in for Marlowe.

While Marlowe was incarcerated, agents watched out for his welfare. Wade got permission to quietly pay Mrs. Marlowe ninety-five hundred dollars in several installments. The cash kept the family business solvent and staved off eviction from its offices. It was "proper for the government to compensate" the Marlowes, Wade said, in light of the "extremely large amount of time and effort" John had spent helping investigators to the detriment of his family's financial affairs.[61] Ironically, the FBI classified Marlowe as a "consultant," retroactively paying him fifty dollars an hour for his undercover activities. The FBI's rate didn't quite match the fat fees Muldoon, Parkin and Galvin pocketed. But then again, Marlowe didn't have to worry about being apprehended.

Moreover, as part of the original deal to gain Marlowe's cooperation, U.S. Attorney Henry Hudson wrote two glowing letters on his behalf to the Virginia Parole Board. Praising Marlowe as one of the individuals "principally responsible for the initiation" of Illwind, Hudson said his dogged undercover efforts "enabled federal investigators to make the vital contacts necessary" to ferret out corruption. "The assistance rendered by Mr. Marlowe," the letters concluded, "was both valuable and courageous." The straitlaced prosecutor seemingly had no qualms about urging the speedy release of a man convicted of molesting two girls under the age of eleven. Marlowe was paroled after serving one-third of his six-year sentence.

Upon returning to live in Northern Virginia, John Marlowe received a last gesture of gratitude from the federal government. He was never charged for the attempted bribery scheme involving Mr. X.

☆

Countless movies and television shows have glorified FBI agents as decisive leaders, willing to take enormous chances to carry out their mission. Since the 1960s, when Robert Stack portrayed iron-willed Eliott Ness in the popular series entitled *The Untouchables*, that grand image has dominated the screen and the country's psyche. In reality, as the rocky commencement of Illwind demonstrated, the bureau's leaders can be infuriatingly cautious. Layer upon layer of bureaucracy serves as a brake to innovation, and those calling the shots frequently are more concerned with potential public-relations problems than the needs or desires of street-level agents. Ostracized in the past for his individuality, Rick Wade had endured his share of scrapes to discern the organization's failings. FBI honchos were bound to recognize the explosive nature of the case he was trying to build.

As soon as he listened to Parkin's tapes, Wade's instincts said that an undercover operation was the most effective tool to penetrate the Pentagon's contracting network. Building on successful political corruption investigations such as Abscam, in which agents posing as representatives of a fictitious Arab businessman exposed greedy members of Congress, the FBI excelled at running stings. The technique was used to nab corrupt judges, mayors and county commissioners nationwide. Likewise, agents had relied on undercover informants to infiltrate bribery rings at two sprawling military purchasing centers in Philadelphia, where the services spent about $2 billion annually acquiring everything from screws and cables to sailor shirts and duffel bags. Wade felt comfortable relying on the same time-tested investigative formulas.

With the help of a sharp young assistant—assigned by the head of the Alexandria office "to cover Rick's ass in paper" by making sure all the necessary forms and procedures were followed—Wade spent several weeks drafting an undercover plan. The goal was to entice industry figures to proffer payoffs for bogus procurements. But Wade knew enough about the bureau's timid decision-makers to protect his back. In order to test the reaction "downtown," he informally circulated a preliminary copy of his proposal to a select group of officials at headquarters. The response was resoundingly negative. FBI interference inadvertently could cause some firms to lose legitimate Pentagon contracts, potentially costing hundreds of jobs and millions of dollars in revenue. The agency might be embarrassed, or worse yet, sued by a disgruntled contractor. In this instance, they decided, the undercover approach carried unacceptably high risks. "There's no way the bureau can get trapped in the middle," Wade was warned. "It's far too sensitive."[62]

His only other option was to seek court-authorized wiretaps, used over the years against drug kingpins and Mafia dons but never before applied extensively to uncover Pentagon fraud. Wade had used them in a gambling case once. Since defense consultants conducted much of their business over the phone, there was an inescapable logic to listening in on their daily conversations. But it definitely wasn't Wade's preference. Like many agents, he was leery of so-called Title III investigations for one basic reason: Wiretaps are incredibly time consuming and manpower intensive. In spite of all that has transpired, Wade acknowledges that "nobody really wants to get involved with" wiretaps except as a last resort. "They require an unbelievable amount of work."[63]

To establish taps in the first place, investigators must have reasonable cause to believe crimes are being committed, and they must convince a federal judge that there are no viable alternatives for gathering evidence. The legal threshold can be pretty high. However, that's only the first of many hurdles in Title III investigations. After court approval is obtained, each line needs to be manned practically around the clock. Judges demand monthly affidavits, often running sixty or seventy pages, justifying continuation of every single wiretap. They also want weekly updates summarizing the individuals and topics recorded on the lines. And, at each step, quick approvals by numerous prosecutors and senior Justice Department officials are essential. It's like jumping on a treadmill that's running at full tilt: There is no room for delays or slipups.

If he took this path, Wade knew that tremendous numbers of conversations would have to be sorted for relevance, and then transcribed precisely on unforgivingly tight timetables. Long-running wiretap cases carry a badge of honor among agents, since they are near the top of the law-enforcement pyramid. Except for counterintelligence work, nothing else the FBI does comes close to being as secretive or demanding. On the other hand, collecting, analyzing and systematically filing the recorded information entails an immense amount of drudgery. Neither Wade nor the youthful agents working under him had ever directed a full-fledged wiretap investigation. Nobody in the NIS hierarchy knew exactly how to run one. Considering the torrent of material they would handle, Fulmer compared it to "drinking from the nozzle of a firehose."[64]

Wade asked Debbie Pierce, his administrative case agent, to try her hand at drafting an affidavit requesting taps on Parkin's telephones. "I'm just wiped out" from grappling with higher-ups, he admitted. "I'm really frustrated. Give it a shot." Pierce had never tried writing such a document. "I was a gym teacher, you remember," she told Wade half in jest, referring to her job before taking the oath as an agent. "You're the attorney." Pierce cobbled together a rough version and, with the help of a sympathetic female lawyer at FBI headquarters, polished it so she was hopeful it could pass muster. Female agents were somewhat rare in high-profile bureau jobs, having been kept out of recruiting programs until the early 1970s. From that aspect, as well, Illwind was different. "Rick was surrounded by women throughout the investigation," Pierce recalls with a laugh. "He couldn't get away from us."[65] Around Thanksgiving of 1986, when the fate of the Parkin wiretap was uncertain, Wade was torn between excitement and foreboding. "If we can keep things together" and avoid leaks, Wade confided to his brother, "this is going to be a great case."[66]

By early January 1987, Hudson and the FBI's top brass had given their okay to "go up" on Parkin. Sign-off sheets at main Justice went all the way to the office of the assistant attorney general in charge of the criminal division. If the investigation collapsed, there would be plenty of spectators to assign blame. A federal judge signed the authorization several days later, and the bureau set up a van in the freezing weather to monitor Parkin's meandering chats with industry cohorts. Both his office and home phones were covered. To mark the achievement, Wade, Fulmer, Pierce and the others decided it was time to pick a name for their burgeoning investigation. One candidate was "Socrates," the Greek philosopher renowned for tirelessly hunting the countryside for an honest man. Agents submitted a handful of other suggestions. The FBI's repository for code names—indeed, the FBI does have a central office keeping track of such details—rejected them all as having been used in previous probes.

Leafing through military books and phrases copied from an encyclopedia, Pierce thought of a line of poetry that struck her fancy. " 'Tis an ill wind that blows no man good," she recited, glancing around the conference room to gauge the reaction. Wade and the rest of the crew liked the nautical flavor. Headquarters gave its stamp of approval, too.[67] Along with the name Illwind, agents crafted a logo: It depicted the head of a mythical character resembling Zeus, sketched with cheeks puffed out, blowing up a storm. Wade and his team got a rise years later, amid the media frenzy, when reporters mistakenly identified the investigation's code name as two separate words.

There was a raft of early rough spots. A probation officer rushing out of a judge's chambers unintentionally grabbed one of the Parkin affidavits with his bundle of papers. Pierce and prosecutor Bud Albright, waiting to see the judge next, were dumbstruck when their document couldn't be located on his desk. The very existence of Illwind was supposed to be one of the FBI's most closely held secrets, they thought, yet some outsider waltzed off with a litany of names and details about its future direction. The two investigators dashed after the unsuspecting man, cornering him on the sidewalk in the pouring rain and retrieving the file. As they nailed him with menacing stares, the frightened official could barely stutter his apologies. "You never saw this, understand," Albright said. "If you glanced at any names, forget them."[68]

FBI agents worried incessantly about other potential leaks, especially from the ranks of the NIS. Wade extracted a solemn promise from Fulmer that the Navy's uniformed officers wouldn't be briefed about Illwind at all. The pledge was a gutsy call by the agency's civilian managers, who technically worked for admirals and hadn't exhibited such independent spirit in the past. When activity on the "wires" heated up and naval investigators had no choice but to ask for additional personnel, the civilians kept their word. "My hat went off to them," one FBI man recalls. "They waited as long as they could, until they were on the brink of being out of money to operate."[69] Even then, specifics about the investigation weren't disclosed. The blue-suiters and the Navy secretary's office were given the barest of explanations about why NIS needed more funds. "It was the single most courageous decision during the course of Illwind," one veteran NIS agent insists.[70]

Wade happily repaid the favor. At one juncture, the civilians running NIS embraced the notion of shipping in reservists on temporary duty to help man the wires. Admittedly less expensive than assigning full-time agents, the concept petrified Fulmer. Reservists would have little training or motivation for the task, Fulmer complained, and they would be more likely to jeopardize the operation with a slip of the tongue. "We're playing in the damn Superbowl," the exasperated agent said, "and you want to

field a bunch of minor leaguers." Fulmer's pride also figured in the equa-
tion. "I didn't want to be embarrassed," he acknowledges. "I wanted us to
be every bit as professional as the bureau."[71]

When his bosses didn't listen, Fulmer fashioned a brilliant counterat-
tack. He made up a story that FBI managers, angered by the reservist proposal, were ready to bar NIS participation from the investigation. To help
his partner, Wade supported the pretense. "We had our first blowup with
the bureau," Fulmer reported to his boss, purposely painting a bleak picture. "I don't know if we can put this back together. They're really pissed
about the reservists." As a matter of fact, the FBI's hierarchy didn't care
whom the NIS assigned to monitor its share of wiretaps, and Wade had
no intention of proceeding on his own. But the two agents in charge surmised correctly that the mere threat by the bureau—which was supplying
the bulk of the equipment and expertise—would prompt the Navy to
jettison its cost-saving idea.[72]

Faced with chronic manpower shortages from the outset, FBI agents
tried subterfuges themselves. Joe Krahling, Wade's outspoken supervisor,
told superiors that his gang "had a tiger by the tail" as soon as investigators
focused on Parkin. He repeatedly asked for more agents, but the answer
was uniformly no. Krahling was only the acting head of the FBI's Alexandria office, so he didn't have the bureaucratic standing to get his way. "It
really stuck in my craw," he admits. Alexandria was slated to be merged
into the larger Washington field office anyway. Fed up with the road-
blocks, Krahling submitted his retirement papers to live on a fifty-foot
trawler and cruise the Intercoastal canal. That's when serendipity smiled
on him and all of the agents toiling away on Illwind.[73]

Krahling had impressed several high-ranking FBI officials during earlier assignments, which included head of the headquarters fraud unit and
a stint running the office responsible for background checks of judicial
nominees. Those supporters offered to do him a favor. His pension would
increase if he retired with the formal rank of special agent in charge of
the Alexandria office. Krahling's benefactors proposed naming him SAC
briefly, perhaps for no longer than a couple of months if he preferred, as a
symbolic reward for long years of loyal service. He pulled back his retirement papers, and the promotion whisked through the FBI's chain of
command.

After the official title was bestowed on him, Krahling's tenacity was
amazing. He didn't bow out as planned. Month after month, he badgered
his sponsors mercilessly for more resources. "You aren't giving us adequate manpower to do the things that we want to do and should be doing," Krahling insisted.[74] He stayed for more than a year. Unlike before,
the complaints couldn't be brushed aside. For once, the bureau's hierarchy
was hoisted on its own petard. "He finally had the authority that went
with the position," according to agent Debbie Pierce. "If it hadn't been
for Joe Krahling, the case never would have gotten off the ground."[75]

The value of the evidence collected by Parkin's wiretaps justified the extraordinary effort. Among the first people captured on tape was Bill Galvin, immediately prompting agents to begin preparations to tap his phones and place secret microphones in his office. Paisley's name also popped up during the initial thirty-day authorization period. Phyllis Sciacca, the curt, no-nonsense agent responsible for keeping wiretap records, was astonished at how rapidly the probe accelerated from Parkin. "This is better than anything I've ever worked," she confided to friends. "Not in my wildest dreams," she admits today, "did I think we would end up tapping twenty-four different lines" around Washington. Over eight thousand separate calls were considered incriminating. Agents literally couldn't wait to get to work to hear the latest outrages. "It was like turning on a soap opera," Sciacca recalls, "wondering what was going to happen in that day's episode."[76]

Over time, sixteen additional wiretaps were authorized in New York, California and other states. The NIS alone assigned 120 people to monitor the telephone intercepts. The FBI's manpower commitment was many times larger. For a while, graduates coming straight out of the bureau's training academy in Quantico, Virginia, were selected for Illwind duty. They were ordered to "sit on the wires" for a few months, before being sent to their first regular field assignment. Wade and Krahling wanted more experienced hands, though they made the best of the situation by subjecting the young agents to rigorous briefings before putting them to work. Investigators went so far as to consider installing miniature "bugs" directly in some Pentagon offices. But the presence of antieavesdropping safeguards on every floor of the building ruled that out.

The Illwind task force was quickly outgrowing its cramped conference room. With poor ventilation, elbow-to-elbow desks and frantic activity, it became known as "the Shark Tank." A strong bond of camaraderie made the backbreaking pace bearable for the core group of investigators. They were ferociously protective of the case. But agents who were there on temporary assignment, or anyone deemed to be a laggard, often felt psychologically mauled. "I wouldn't even walk into that place," Krahling says with a chuckle. "If you weren't totally devoted to their case, it was your ass." Following a peculiarly nasty tiff between one of Wade's assistants and a temporary supervisor who stormed out over a personality conflict, Krahling marched into the room. With a flourish, he took out a black magic marker and scrawled a giant numeral one on the wall: "Mark up another victim for the shark tank," he declared.[77] The designation stuck.

While listening posts were scattered around the region, raw tapes and transcripts were funneled to the "tank" for analysis. In one corner, agents huddled around cassette players and hurriedly printed out summaries of the most recent and pertinent conversations—called "pert sheets"—for daily review by prosecutors. Elsewhere in the room, supervisors labored over excerpts winnowed from longer recordings made days or weeks before. The youthful agents' work had to be checked constantly, not only for accuracy but to make certain that relevant portions of conversations weren't overlooked. Older tapes were meticulously reanalyzed based on newly acquired information, logs of intercepted phone calls needed hourly updating, and sudden schedule changes by subjects of the probe forced Wade and his assistants to make last-minute adjustments to the FBI's surveillance plans.

At first blush, some of the recordings didn't make sense. Tongue-twisting acronyms and ubiquitous code words sounded like gibberish at times to agents who lacked a guide or historical context. "The secret is assembling all those tidbits into a patchwork quilt that constitutes the conspiracy," according to Hudson. For fear of tipping off the culprits, investigators were prohibited from interviewing any company or Pentagon official to clarify what they overheard. For the same reason, no contract files were pulled and agents were instructed to refrain from making any overt moves to gather background information. "We didn't even run credit checks" on the individuals heard on the tapes, according to Wade. Thus, libraries and bookstores were the sole reference places left to try to fill the void. Investigators voraciously read industry newsletters, trade publications and other generally available materials. "We had to develop the capability to glean information from public sources," Wade recalls. "Some agents became really adept at doing that." Describing the Shark Tank as a "pressure cooker," he says their task resembled assembling a three-dimensional puzzle with most of the pieces missing.[78]

To relieve tension, photographs and cartoons of sharks were plastered all over the walls. Some Friday evenings, there were impromptu parties with chips and drinks. Would-be comedians among the agents found a better way to unwind. They wrote a promotional announcement for an imaginary movie about Illwind entitled "Watergate II: The Final Convict." Featuring make-believe raves from critics such as Rex Reed, who supposedly called it "bigger than *Dynasty*," the full-page flyer greatly amused fellow investigators.

The tongue-in-cheek cast was hilariously inspired. Clint Eastwood as Rick Wade and Jim Nabors as Steve Fulmer captured the spirit and contrast between the respective head agents. Robert De Niro was chosen to play Galvin, while Burgess Meredith got the role of Paisley. The witty list of bogus credits had other standouts, including Efrem Zimbalist, Jr., as Joe Krahling; Ned Beatty as the unctuous Jack Sherman; Foster Brooks as the greedy "gambler and man-about-town" Tommy Muldoon; Frank Sinatra as Charlie Gardner of Unisys; and fetching Molly Ringwald as Vicki Paisley, described as "young and looking toward her inheritance." Jim Bakker, the disgraced television preacher who had his own sexual hangups, was supposed to make the difficult role of John Marlowe come alive.

In the spring of 1987 the task force relocated to roomier quarters, occupying the ground floor of a steel-and-glass office building across the street from Alexandria's Colonial-style federal courthouse. The space had been an FBI recruiting center for years, so agents thought the flurry of activity wouldn't attract undue attention. The investigators were wrong. Tenants were suspicious about the unusual movement of people and equipment. Then they grew scared, worrying that a drug bust or violent raid was in store for the neighborhood. Building managers awaited an explanation. The FBI used the rather lame excuse that it was conducting a research project. Concern died down after agents scampered to reassure tenants that their safety wasn't in jeopardy.

By then, Krahling, who had worked so hard to generate support at headquarters, had decided to collect his retirement checks and enjoy the sailing life in South Florida. Not wanting to be undercut, Wade took charge of promoting the investigation internally. Contrary to his reputation, he assumed the mantle of the supremely patient team player, giving innumerable briefings to senior FBI and Justice Department officials. "We had to sell our product, and we always did it on the front end," Wade explains in retrospect, sounding almost like some of the marketing men he pursued. Budget problems never again disrupted the probe.[79]

As the wiretaps multiplied, investigators were divided into smaller groups to concentrate on specific targets. Some of the squads retreated to rented apartments to hold meetings or go over transcripts, because there weren't sufficient desks in the Shark Tank. NIS and the bureau needed still more apartments to house the listening apparatus and provide living space for out-of-town agents. FBI Director Webster started getting weekly status briefings, and he decided that Illwind was too sensitive to disclose to Congress. FBI technicians devised a computer program—which grew to include 540 subfiles—able to crossmatch names, phrases, contracts, surveillance reports and other bits of data from the jumble of thousands of phone conversations. The government was primed to handle the anticipated flood of information. In the meantime, agents assembled an airtight case against Bill Parkin, applauded on tape by one grateful client as the "magic swami" of Pentagon fraud.[80]

As an unscrupulous hustler, the sixty-two-year-old Parkin bartered and sold secrets to Galvin, Muldoon, Marlowe and a string of other consultants. Telephone intercepts indicated that he tried to collect inside information for no fewer than seventeen different firms, often handing contractors their own bid "numbers" as proof of his prowess. But that was just a fraction of his shameless repertoire. After a bitter divorce left him short of cash, Parkin seized on every conceivable trick to advance his illicit enterprise. At Galvin's urging, he had loaned money to an Air Force acquisition official whom he expected, in return, to steer business to selected contractors. To keep both the Navy and a corporate client happy, Parkin and Galvin joined forces to illegally lobby lawmakers to fund development of acoustic submarine sensors. Another arm of the Navy hired Parkin as a procurement adviser. He boasted that his ability to write con-

Flanked by Defense Secretary Caspar Weinberger (left) and Admiral William Crowe, chairman of the Joint Chiefs of Staff, Ronald Reagan envisioned a billion-dollar-a-day Pentagon budget as part of a military buildup he called the "most sacred, most important task of the presidency." *(Department of Defense)*

Prosecutor Henry Hudson, a courtroom bulldog renowned early on for pursuing drug and pornography cases, ultimately briefed two presidents about the bribery and rampant influence peddling that tainted his beloved Navy. *(Justice Department)*

Melvyn Paisley's official portrait as assistant Navy secretary, before he became the highest-ranking Navy official convicted of corruption charges since the Teapot Dome scandal of the 1920s. *(James P. Vineyard; Department of Defense)*

Secretary of the Navy John F. Lehman, Jr., who flew A-6 Intruder jets as a lieutenant commander in the reserves, failed to heed repeated warnings about Mel Paisley because he admired the fellow pilot's combat medals and considered him a "sort of buccaneer." *(Jane Kinney; U.S. Navy)*

FBI supervisory agent Richard Wade, who advocated the novel use of wiretaps to crack down on military fraud. "You can't explain away motivations if you're caught on tape," Wade used to say. *(Rob Crandall)*

Intransigent in fighting for huge budget hikes, Defense Secretary Caspar Weinberger was in awe of the president and served as the most fervent salesman of the Reagan-era defense buildup. *(Department of Defense)*

Joseph Aronica, the abrasive federal prosecutor derided as a
"control freak" by FBI agents, stubbornly maintained authority
over what turned out to be the most extensive and successful
probe of military corruption in U.S. history. *(Rob Crandall)*

Defense Secretary Frank Carlucci vowing, once the Illwind scandal
erupted, to take speedy and dramatic action. Later he reversed some
early decisions and, as a result, many of the Pentagon's responses
proved to be hollow. *(Scott Davis; Department of Defense)*

Secretary of the Navy John Lehman, a brash and savvy
Washington infighter, visiting the aircraft carrier USS *Kitty
Hawk* in Hawaii in 1981. Dogmatic and imperious, the
youngest Navy chief in history relished antagonizing his
admirals while championing the six-hundred-ship fleet.
(Ray Buley; U.S. Navy)

Convicted defense executive
Charles Gardner, a devoted
father and family man, masterminded a scheme to dole out at
least $17 million in bribes, illegal
campaign contributions and
sham consulting contracts.
(UPI/Bettmann)

The Navy's Aegis-class cruisers,
costing about $1 billion each
and equipped with radars capable of simultaneously defending
against two hundred incoming
missiles, became embroiled in an
influence-peddling scheme that
ultimately threatened to
bankrupt Unisys—one of the
Navy's largest contractors.
(Litton Industries)

Work on the Minuteman intercontinental missile, seen here in the final assembly process, transformed Boeing into a high-tech international aerospace giant and the Pentagon's largest supplier of nuclear hardware. *(Boeing Company)*

Before joining the Navy, John Lehman and Mel Paisley, his most trusted assistant, cemented their friendship by helping Boeing sell nearly two dozen such AWACS radar surveillance planes to NATO. *(Boeing Company)*

A pensive George Bush (right) watches Admiral James Watkins, assisted by Mrs. Watkins, take the oath of office as chief of naval operations in 1982. "Shocked and offended" by subsequent Pentagon corruption, President Bush nevertheless gave only lip service to improving the military's purchasing system. *(Helene Stikkel; Department of Defense)*

tracts and facilitate second-source production made him renowned as "the man with the golden pen." On the surface, the second Navy contract was legitimate. But Parkin corrupted it by skewing the conclusions of the report submitted to the Navy to benefit a small software firm with which he had a clandestine business relationship.[81]

There wasn't a ploy that Parkin considered beneath his dignity. He secretly gave one hundred dollars a month to a low-level contract negotiator in the cruise missile office where he used to work. As a precaution, his former secretary was the go-between and the checks were made out to "Smith's Maid Service." But the meager payments got Parkin what he needed. The female conspirator threatened to withhold lucrative missile business from a small contractor who was reluctant to pay Parkin's consulting fees. With regard to another project, she offered to pile pricing documents and contract information into the trunk of Parkin's car if he left it in her Pentagon parking spot.[82]

Parkin could be coy on the tapes, using veiled references such as distributing "a little green," or having to buy "a lot of spaghetti and meatballs to grease the skids."[83] At other times he was impetuously blunt. "We'd all go to jail" if the truth came out, he admitted, adding that companies "could guess from the things they were told" that bribes were exchanged. "You should have made more than enough" on one illegally acquired contract, Parkin told an executive he trusted, "to take care of our little pittance."[84] Fred Lackner, one of his partners in crime, gloated about their power. "You either want the business or you don't want the business," Lackner told one contractor's Washington representative. "Rest assured, if we don't do our thing, you guys ain't gonna get the business. Period . . . it's the end of the story."[85]

From the industry's vantage point, the mathematics of hiring Parkin were easy to comprehend. In 1987, for example, Unisys, Hazeltine and Teledyne agreed to pay the consultant two hundred thousand dollars combined. A chunk of the money was earmarked as bribes for a civilian Navy engineer in charge of writing technical specifications for electronics contracts. The rest was to be divided between Parkin and his non-Pentagon confederates. In exchange, the companies hoped to secure more than $300 million in Pentagon orders, some stretching into the twenty-first century. Such potentially hefty returns on their investment tempted executives to take equally big risks.

To assist Unisys, Parkin obtained all the bid numbers and the Pentagon's subsequent ranking of competitors for a large Marine Corps electronics program. Unisys ended up losing the contract anyway. For Hazeltine, a unit of Emerson Electric, Parkin did a lot more. He succeeded in actually influencing the Navy's selection criteria for a separate, larger contract for radar testing sets. With Parkin's help, Hazeltine also secured a draft of the government's acquisition plan spelling out how many of the devices the services projected buying over the next decade. The document was strictly off-limits for contractors. Hazeltine adjusted its bid accordingly, and it would have won the $170-million contract if Illwind hadn't interfered.[86]

But it was the tapes involving Teledyne—a freewheeling, 1960s-style conglomerate desperate for defense business to alleviate a cash crunch—that best illustrated Parkin's pervasive criminality. He took credit for landing a sole-source contract for the firm to manufacture portable test equipment for aircraft transponders. The specifications were tailored to fit Teledyne's product as closely as possible. To hide his tracks, Parkin said the Navy would run a phony technical evaluation "to make it look good." His accomplices "finessed this thing an awful long way," Parkin reminded Teledyne. "They have done their job and now they're entitled to their just reward." Afterward, he boasted in private about outsmarting Teledyne by collecting fees when it was obvious that no other firm could have met the specifications "within the time constraints" imposed by the Navy.[87] The contractor eventually pleaded guilty to conspiracy and filing false statements with the Pentagon, all the while maintaining it was more a victim than a beneficiary of Parkin's schemes.

(In fact, Parkin and Illwind were the least of Teledyne's problems. Headquartered in Beverly Hills but composed of scores of small, largely autonomous divisions operating around the country, the company soon became infamous in legal circles. Between 1989 and 1994, Teledyne and its units were the target of no fewer than sixteen separate criminal and civil investigations, including accusations that they sold material to help Iraq's dictator Saddam Hussein build cluster bombs. The allegations led to high-level executive firings and repeated suspensions from bidding on military contracts. The beleaguered firm paid in excess of $185 million in fines and penalties to try to put the heartaches behind it—pleading guilty to a spate of charges ranging from false testing to lying about overseas marketing commissions. Nevertheless, investigators kept opening more cases. As late as 1994 the FBI needed a special task force in Southern California to handle the deluge of whistleblower complaints against Teledyne and a few other contractors.)

In addition to corporate greed, Parkin had a disdain for all rules that made hard-boiled agents wince. He gleefully passed information to competitors on the same contract. He cheated the Navy official who was his pipeline to bidding secrets. Most of all, Parkin and his cronies seemed to get a charge out of bilking the U.S. Treasury. The instant Teledyne's competition for the transponder-testing devices was eliminated, Parkin ruminated about jacking up prices. Requests for a "Best and Final Offer" designed to save the government money, Parkin suggested, should be thrown back in the Navy's face. "They give you that option . . . fuck 'em," he told a senior Teledyne financial official. Laughing hard, the executive said the company easily could add 10 percent to its original bid "and say there it is . . . glad you asked."[88]

Another Parkin intimate ridiculed the public. "If the farmers in Indiana" ever found out how Pentagon funds were squandered in Washington, he said, "they'd come up there and kill everybody in that God damn town." Joining in the fun, Parkin agreed wholeheartedly. "You're right . . . it's pretty terrible," he guffawed, adding that he might don a straw hat so he could "be there to help them, too."[89]

☆

Fishtailing along icy roads in a four-wheel-drive pickup truck, the two female investigators raced against the clock to contact a federal judge. A vicious winter storm raged along the Eastern seaboard, clogging highways with snow drifts, shutting schools and forcing government workers to stay home. But the inexorable rhythm of monthly Title III reauthorizations had no respect for nature. The deadline was barely hours away, and a judge's signature was required to keep Galvin's wiretap in place. Next morning would be too late. With the courthouse in downtown Washington closed, the women drove through treacherous conditions to reach U.S. District Court Judge John Pratt's home in suburban Maryland.

There was an incongruous scene once they arrived. The elderly, silver-haired judge, a former Marine decorated for bravery in World War II, escorted FBI agent Debbie Pierce and prosecutor Pam Bethel into the house. The proud son of an admiral, he chatted about his father's medals and explained the naval pictures and mementos displayed in several rooms. While the visitors sat in the kitchen and warmed up with mugs of tea, Mrs. Pratt graciously served cookies. She arranged them on a fancy silver tray bearing the inscription "USS *Pratt*," the Navy ship named after the judge's father. "Do you believe this? Isn't it amazing?" the two investigators whispered to each other. How odd, they thought, that this scion of a venerable military family, with his intense love for the Navy and its trappings, was helping to topple Bill Galvin.[90]

Pierce, one of Wade's top assistants, remembered the first wiretap request she had submitted to Judge Pratt in the spring of 1987. The Marine Corps was very much in the news then. Court-martials were pending for former Marine guards at the Moscow embassy. Oliver North, another leatherneck, was on the congressional hot seat for shredding documents and misleading lawmakers as part of the Iran-Contra scandal. The judge carefully reviewed the material supplied to him about Galvin, including the consultant's background as a Marine Corps aviator. "It's a sad time for Marines. It's a sad day in our history," Pratt complained, though he quickly followed with words of encouragement for Pierce. "Go get 'em," he had told her that March morning. Now, many months later, Judge Pratt again signed the papers submitted by the Illwind task force. As they drove away, the two women reflected on the immense obstacles—ranging from personnel fights to turf battles inside the Justice Department—that investigators managed to overcome to close in on Galvin and Paisley.[91]

Clarence Albright, the assistant U.S. attorney who oversaw the early Parkin wire, left for a congressional staff job before Galvin's intercepts were approved. The lure of working for one of Virginia's senators was too powerful for him to resist. Also, the prosecutor appreciated the fact that Illwind was shaping up as a multiyear commitment. If he stayed to handle Galvin's wiretap, it would be that much more difficult to extricate himself for future job possibilities. Polished and savvy, Albright fostered political ambitions. He didn't have the disposition to grow old in law enforcement. "Remain in this job long enough," Albright said in jest, and "you start seeing every motorist who runs a red light as part of a conspiracy to undermine the nation's traffic laws."[92] Hudson transferred the case to two other lawyers. The briefings he received made it evident that adding manpower, and picking a lead prosecutor, would be necessary soon.

Simultaneously, members of the Illwind team were feuding with their counterparts in the office of the U.S. attorney for the District of Columbia. Since Galvin's business was located in the Watergate, federal prosecutors assigned to the district were the only ones who could ask the court for intercepts on his phones. Pierce and her colleagues in Alexandria drafted the necessary paperwork. The filings were reviewed by Hudson and his staff, then they were sent to the neighboring jurisdiction for formal submission to a judge. It was supposed to be a swift and painless handoff. But as the days turned to weeks, and then into months, there was no agreement on how Galvin's affidavit should read. D.C. prosecutors found an endless list of points to criticize. Some of their early suggestions were minor. When those were satisfied, they raised more substantial questions. The discussions dragged on interminably, enraging agents working for Wade and Fulmer. "This is bullshit," fumed Pierce, who was stuck doing most of the rewrites. "They simply want to keep us out of their court, out of their ballpark." Illwind agents also worried about possible leaks from the large number of draft documents that were circulated. Finally, Hudson went to the mat with D.C. prosecutors. The only solution, he insisted, was to deputize lawyers from his office so they could file papers directly with judges on the other side of the Potomac.[93]

To make the unusual arrangement work, Hudson needed to put a relentless prosecutor in charge. He was looking for someone experienced in using wiretaps and dealing with national security issues. The position called for a hard-nosed battler; somebody who wouldn't shrink from tackling the most powerful personalities in the defense establishment, or become bamboozled by jurisdictional squabbles. Joseph Aronica, the forty-two-year-old chief of Hudson's special prosecutions section, got the nod. The U.S. attorney had few misconceptions about the controversy the decision would spawn. "Certainly, there were lots of complaints about Joe's domineering style, that he pushed too hard," Hudson recalled years later. "Joe has quirks that people don't like. I knew he could be very tough to deal with."[94]

With the attorney general and the rest of the Justice Department's top echelon peering over his shoulder, Hudson was acutely aware that he couldn't afford any mistakes. The U.S. attorney wasn't a white-collar crime expert by any means, thus he acknowledged that the prosecutors previously assigned to Illwind required "the guiding hand of Joe Aronica to assist them." The choice was heavily influenced by self-preservation. "I needed someone able to maintain control," Hudson recalled, "a person who would have a complete grip" on an "extremely stressful, high-profile case" and "not give away the store." The pressures could get unbearable. "I called on Joe because I was sure he wouldn't fumble," Hudson explained. "That confidence was never betrayed."[95]

The move brought Wade's worst nightmare to life. Originally, he and Fulmer had fought mightily to try to block the prosecutor from meddling in Illwind. Wade maintained that the prospects for a big score were too promising to relinquish control of the investigation, especially since they had avoided the worst pitfalls.[96] If Joe Aronica wanted to get involved, agents had warned Bud Albright early on, the bureau would take the damn tapes across the river and let the U.S. attorney in Washington reap the benefits.

Hated and feared by numerous agents, Aronica was derided as an egomaniac and a "control freak." Lubricated by several rounds of off-duty drinks, FBI veterans called him much worse. They griped that Aronica was an obnoxious SOB who micromanaged every aspect of the inquiries he oversaw.

Wade's immediate boss had had a nasty run-in with the aggressive prosecutor in the past. Frequently instructing agents whom to interview, Aronica had also insisted on personally conducting interrogations of certain witnesses in earlier cases. The FBI complained bitterly to Hudson, arguing that the aide had blatantly overstepped his authority. "Henry, we simply can't let this go on," a senior bureau manager protested, adding that assistant U.S. attorneys weren't supposed to dictate investigative techniques or interview witnesses in their own offices. Not only was the behavior demeaning, Hudson was told privately, but it threatened to jeopardize pending cases. "My agents aren't going to be used as stenographers for a prosecutor who wants to act the part of a supercop," the FBI supervisor had vowed.[97] A compromise was reached well before Aronica was tapped for Illwind, but investigators remembered the clash. Wade was adamant about avoiding a replay.

Judged by his résumé, Aronica had the requisite seniority and breadth of experience. After all, he had a twelve-year record of successfully prosecuting murderers, communist spies, corrupt labor bosses and smugglers of contraband military goods to Iran.[98] He understood defense fraud, having recently nailed a small Northern Virginia defense supplier for relying on

false invoices to avoid competitive bidding. The Army paid eight times
what it was supposed to pay, getting mainframe computers instead of the
minicomputers spelled out in the original contract. Libertarian Lyndon
LaRouche, the perennial fringe political candidate accused of fraud and
campaign violations, was another one of Aronica's prominent courtroom
victims. Then there was Navy commander Richard Marcinko, a rogue
warrior sporting a Rasputinlike beard, who once headed the Pentagon's
supersecret counterterrorist squad known as SEAL Team Six. After years
of Navy inquiries and two bruising trials, Aronica convicted him of conspiring to overcharge the government and accept kickbacks from the
manufacturer of grenades used by the commandos.

In light of Aronica's accomplishments, Wade realized it would be futile
to raise a stink. Hudson already blamed the FBI for trying to ramrod the
investigation forward too rapidly, without giving prosecutors ample time
to digest wiretap evidence. Wade bit his tongue, conceding that additional
interference wouldn't be looked on kindly. No matter how vehemently
agents opposed Aronica, there was no chance of convincing Hudson to
reconsider. The selection was wholly within the U.S. attorney's purview,
and he would look impotent if he backed down. On top of everything
else, there was the danger of alienating one of the line prosecutors on the
case who liked Aronica and worked directly under him.

Short and trim, with aquiline features and a dark complexion, Joseph
John Aronica fits the archetype of the tough career prosecutor. He was
born in Brooklyn, and his nasal speech resonates with the earthy vocabulary of the working-class neighborhood on Long Island where he grew
up. He has the fluid, up-on-the-toes stride of a bantamweight boxer,
cocky and ready to pounce on an adversary. Aronica's self-assurance stems
from a close-knit Italian family that prized education and perseverance as
the highest virtues. His father stayed on the job as a butcher into his seventies. His mother raised four kids and worked as a jewelry saleswoman.
His sister is a nun with a doctorate in sociology, and one brother is a po-
diatrist.[99] An excellent student, Aronica earned his undergraduate and law
degrees at the University of Richmond, where he enrolled as a cadet in
the ROTC program.

As a young officer working for the Army's judge advocate general in
Thailand, Aronica revealed his independent bent. He roamed through
Asia on his own, visiting Nepal, the island of Macao and other sights off
the beaten tourist path. Back in the United States, he earned a master's
degree at Georgetown University at night and married a paralegal he met
while working as a labor lawyer at Justice headquarters. The department's
staid, regimented pace felt stifling to him after a short while. The same
was true of private practice, which he endured for a little more than a
year as an associate at a Baltimore law firm. Aronica joined the U.S. attorney's office in the Eastern District of Virginia to gain more independence. He got his wish, attaining the top civil service rank in his

profession: He was promoted to one of the Justice Department's two dozen senior litigation counsel slots. With Henry Hudson as his boss and an expanding band of investigators at his command, the prosecutor had greater authority and freedom than ever before to set his own course.

Stubbornness and volatility were the attributes most often mentioned when Joe Aronica was the topic of conversation. Supremely turf conscious, he refused to accept assistance from outside the district even when he badly needed manpower. "We'll take your help to this extent," he told officials at main Justice. "But we're controlling the investigation." Agents grumbled that he often appeared disengaged and didn't take notes during meetings, but Aronica persisted in doing things his way. He enjoyed getting under the skin of defense attorneys, sometimes by being rude and addressing them as "pal." If an assistant U.S. attorney "gets too many compliments from defense lawyers, he ought to be worried," the prosecutor maintained. "He might not be doing the right thing."[100]

Aronica, who rose to the rank of colonel in the reserves by the time Illwind was in full swing, cultivated his image as a coldblooded litigator. "I'm not a bluffer," he would tell opposing counsel. "This is the evidence we have. This is why your client is guilty. Now, what does he want to do?" As the defense lawyer was about to leave, Aronica would toss out his favorite parting shot: "Go chew on it."[101] The opposing side, he used to tell friends, had to see that it wasn't "dealing with some wimp who was going to fold."

Aronica eschewed the traditional give-and-take between prosecutors and defense lawyers, with each side probing and posturing until the last minute. He dismissed it as useless "jawing back and forth," adding that criminals "aren't going to tell you the truth unless you have something strong hanging over them." Convincing defendants to strike a deal, he snapped, requires one fundamental item: "evidence that you can push their noses into" to avoid protracted haggling. He did his level best to foreclose negotiation. "I give them the bottom line, right up front," he explained. "I want to bring things to a head. Take it or leave it." Aronica believed that nearly all white-collar criminals deserved "a taste of jail."[102] And pity the defense attorney who dared to disagree. "That's when he really got pissed and turned up the wick," according to Fulmer.[103] Wiretaps left the defense with the weak argument that "my client didn't really mean what he said," Aronica crowed. His response hardly ever changed: "Let the jury decide that." Hudson readily supported such tactics, further strengthening his assistant's position.

Joe Aronica's attitude wore down other prosecutors nearly as much as defense lawyers. His irritable personality scared away secretaries and would-be assistants, just as it aggravated even his most forbearing friends. He was impatient and prone to scream obscenities when mistakes were made. Agents complained that he discarded their recommendations without bothering to analyze them. Defendants hated his overweening manner. During the preliminary stages of Illwind, Aronica's wife gave birth to a baby girl. The experience softened him a bit, according to friends, who were astounded by the peaceful expression on his face when he chatted about child rearing. At work, however, he maintained his customary vehemence. Aronica lived and breathed the case for nearly seven years, insisting that practically every decision go through him and, in the final analysis, garnering most of the praise. Without pity, he pursued the strands that he believed were most important. By the same token, Aronica's unwillingness to cede a piece of the action delayed some prosecutions for years and may have helped some congressional targets escape punishment altogether.

To his credit, Aronica didn't let Illwind's emphasis on Paisley and the Navy blind him to high-level corruption inside the Air Force. Cubic Corporation, a leading supplier of electronic warfare devices, hired Galvin to illegally shut out competition for at least five Air Force contracts together worth roughly half a billion dollars. Since the 1970s, the San Diego firm had been the sole source for "Top Gun" air combat training systems used by U.S. fighter pilots. Cubic's technology allowed air crews to stage mock dogfights, complete with simulated missile firings, and then review their performance on videotape. The steady income stream had furnished the bedrock for the company's growth. But the Reagan administration's zeal for competition threatened to erode those revenues. Furthermore, rivals were chipping away at what had been another Cubic monopoly: making electronic instrument pods for Air Force jets. And the firm was looking to beat out Boeing and other competitors for a massive Air Force reconnaissance project.

Senior vice-president Colvin Clay Wellborn had his own vision of success. He hoped that Galvin would provide a springboard to Cubic's chairmanship. "Sam" Wellborn had sacrificed family life struggling up the corporation's executive ranks for three decades, working weekends and missing his only son's high school graduation.[104] His family worried about his alcohol consumption. Apparently to relieve stress, Wellborn would hide issues of *Penthouse* magazine in his office file cabinets.[105] By his mid-fifties, he had made it to the number-two spot. He was the heir apparent to Cubic's elderly chairman. The pending Air Force reconnaissance job, which Wellborn reverently called "the biggie," was the largest production contract Cubic ever tried to win. The driven executive pined to take credit for a victory. "With a little help, we can push this thing over," a revved-up Wellborn told Galvin. "Put me on the map, and I'll share with my friends."[106]

Cubic's secret weapon was Galvin's friend Victor Cohen, the deputy assistant secretary of the Air Force for tactical warfare. The long-winded title didn't do justice to the stature of Cohen, the second-highest-ranking Pentagon figure disgraced by the scandal. With a Ph.D. in mechanical engineering, the jowly official with the wire-rimmed glasses was widely respected for his common sense and technical acumen. More important, the balding New Yorker wielded a lot of power inside the Air Force. He also was the primary official on joint Air Force–Navy avionics procurements. Cohen's acerbic critiques, poking fun at ill-conceived or gold-plated designs, often forced generals to rethink acquisition plans. A notably negative reaction by him could kill a weapon system. Colleagues gushed about his intelligence, patting him on the back for saving tax dollars. Congressmen and their aides asked his advice, trusting the straightforward, down-to-earth explanations they received. Contractors treated Cohen with wary respect, considering him a formidable opponent whenever he opted to buck them.

Vic Cohen was a consultant's dream for other reasons, too. The programs that came under him—including radar jammers, pilot-training ranges and special operations forces—were the most stable parts of the Pentagon budget. Total defense dollars plummeted and new aircraft buys declined at the end of the Reagan era. Yet the radar-warning receivers and related electronic hardware built by Cubic and a handful of other firms stayed in high demand. The fewer planes the Air Force had, the more it was likely to spend outfitting each one with expensive "black boxes" to guarantee maximum protection against enemy radars. In that kind of fiscal environment, Cohen's influence was destined to grow. Of all the con men collared as a result of Illwind, he was the one who most shocked the Pentagon's acquisition corps.

Despite his professional accomplishments, Cohen came entirely under Galvin's spell. He accepted theater tickets and went to the racetrack as the consultant's guest. He let Galvin pick up the tab for meals and hotel rooms from San Francisco to Paris. A couple of times a week, the busy Air Force official would suspend his official schedule to visit Galvin's Watergate office and divulge upcoming procurement decisions. One of Galvin's associates gave him money to purchase a sporty Mercedes Benz touring car. When Cohen had trouble selling the vehicle a few years later, a second Galvin compatriot took it off his hands at an inflated price, constituting a $15,000 bribe. Fancying himself an international operator like Galvin, Cohen said his intention was to set up his own consulting firm because "we only come through this life but one time." So Galvin humored Cohen, agreeing to sell him Sapphire Systems and changing the firm's name to suit his friend's wishes.[107]

In return for illicit favors, Cohen proposed to run a "crooked competition" to ensure that Cubic would receive a small Air Force job. He was a virtual sieve of information on the huge reconnaissance contract, dutifully slipping Galvin and Wellborn internal Air Force rankings of all the competitors. Though Cubic's product was considered technically inferior, Cohen fought ferociously behind the scenes on the company's behalf. He prevailed to change certain requirements to give its bid a boost. At one point, Cohen coached Cubic in preparing written responses to questions posed by the Air Force acquisition board on which he sat. "He knows just what has to be done," Galvin boasted. "He delivers." Upon receiving assurances that Cohen was ready to do battle for Cubic, Wellborn was ec-static. "You don't know what this means to me, baby," he told Galvin.[108]

At the start, Galvin slipped small amounts of money to Cohen through a mutual friend. Then he set up a secret Swiss bank account for his compatriot. As Cohen's angry ex-wife continued dunning him for child support, the Air Force's procurement expert became less bashful about extorting direct payoffs from Cubic. Galvin whined that he had created a "mighty monster." There wouldn't be any more assistance, Cohen warned in August 1987, unless Wellborn began "acting like he talks" and handed over hard cash. Galvin passed on the message. "He wants some money," the consultant reported to Wellborn. "OK, how much," was the nonchalant reply. The Cubic executive explained that it would be a cinch "to move money from the company" to satisfy Cohen, but he would need Galvin's aid to launder the funds overseas. "I know enough not to do the dumb thing," Wellborn said, adding that he "could care less how it gets back" to the United States.[109]

In the end, Wellborn offered the impressive bounty of $1 million to the Galvin-Cohen duo if they captured the big Air Force contract. Cubic never landed the prize, and neither did Wellborn. "I'm going to hear about this for the rest of my fucking life," he complained.[110] After Illwind went public, Wellborn bailed out with a golden parachute amounting to nearly two years' salary. The company couldn't restrain itself from heaping accolades on him for "significant contributions to Cubic Corporation's growth and success."

Loral Corporation, another scrappy electronics manufacturer, also hired Galvin as a conduit to influence both Cohen and Paisley. Loral received preferential treatment from the Navy in a competition to build a proto-type blimp for radar surveillance. In the Air Force, among other things, Galvin helped the company win big orders to install radar warning de-vices on the Air Force's top-of-the-line F-15 and F-16 fighters.

Cohen secretly gave Galvin a full rundown on Loral's competition for the aircraft electronics gear, including proprietary data that were not per-mitted to leave the Air Force. Louis Oberndorf, the top marketing execu-tive for Loral's electronic systems division, promised to "put something" in Cohen's "back pocket" if the scheme worked. But Loral was no pushover. It expected quantifiable results for its bribes. "I got to tell you, Vic is not digging into this program and giving us any insight," Obern-dorf bitched to Galvin during a touchy period. "He isn't giving much. We're giving him an awful lot."[111]

As he did with most clients, Galvin submitted sham reports to Loral as a cover for his annual six-figure retainer. Sometimes, they were plagia-rized from magazines or other public sources. Companies dug up old re-ports on occasion and sent them to consultants, who conveniently mailed them back as justifications for enhanced fees. Galvin's buddy Bill Parkin used to tailor the size of the fee to the thickness of the report. Galvin had form letters prepared with a thumbnail summary of his recycled reports, sporting impressive titles such as "Outer Air Battle Study." When he got a new assignment, all he had to do was plug in the date and the name of the client—along with the agreed-on monthly fee—before attaching the letter to invoices.

The pretext worked until investigators heard the wiretaps. One of Galvin's form letters, for example, was so sloppy that it confused the Soviet Union's newest nuclear-powered cruisers with a class of ballistic-missile submarines. A senior Loral executive warned the consultant to scale back the amount he was demanding for a worthless report to $150,000, from the earlier $187,000 level. Alluding to the report, the company man acknowledged: "There isn't a whole lot of substance behind what we're trying to do."[112] To outsiders, "The materials in the contract files looked fine, they looked legitimate," according to Aronica. "But once we looked beneath the table, so to speak, you could see there was nothing holding it up; everything was broken and corrupt . . . The wiretaps showed what was really going on under the surface."[113]

For all these reasons, Oberndorf, a senior vice-president at Loral, was paranoid about being found out. Agents overheard him repeatedly discuss illicit activities, including personally photocopying briefing papers presented to the Air Force by a rival manufacturer. But to try to insulate himself from harm, Oberndorf beseeched Galvin to keep their arrangement "three arm lengths" away. "God damn it," he said, "keep it so . . . cut out" that the president of the Loral unit will be the only other person to "know about it."[114]

In sworn grand jury testimony after Illwind broke, Galvin claimed that Bernard Schwartz, Loral's flamboyant and autocratic chairman, "knew everything." Schwartz "knew how much I was being paid, understood the commitments, knew that I was taking care of Cohen and Paisley," the consultant asserted. "We have conversations that reflect that."[115]

Comments about Schwartz, one of the industry's highest-paid and most financially astute chief executives, also cropped up on some wiretaps. Loral stood out in the industry because it was based in New York City. One transcript prepared by prosecutors had Galvin referring to Schwartz as a "Jew from New York" with a fierce drive to succeed. The Loral chairman, Galvin told Paisley, was "one of these guys [for whom] you hit sixty home runs [and] he'll say, 'What are you going to do next year?' " Prosecutors sought but failed to find corroborating testimony about Schwartz's involvement with Galvin. Schwartz, who was never identified as a target and wasn't accused by the government of violating the law, calls Galvin's allegations "categorically not true." Loral's chairman goes on to say that he "was out of the loop completely" in the company's dealings with Galvin and Paisley, further asserting that Galvin's claims before the grand jury were "at variance with other testimony that he gave."

Rick Wade won't discuss Galvin's grand jury assertions about Schwartz.

Picking his words with exceptional care, the FBI agent declares that "as a general statement," Galvin's testimony and cooperation were determined to be truthful: "I think that he was pretty accurate, and I think that he was pretty honest." While the consultant may have forgotten some details, according to Wade, "I do not believe that he made up things."[116]

Unbeknownst to Wade and Aronica, another crew of federal agents was beginning to poke around Paisley's conduct while the wiretaps were still in place. The separate inquiry by the Defense Investigative Service, the guardian of military security clearances, touched on Boeing marketing officials who had illegally gained access to a cache of classified Pentagon budget documents. Since Paisley had once worked for the airplane-maker, he was quizzed about recent contact with Boeing. The interview didn't give him a clue about Illwind, and Paisley didn't appear to be implicated in the document-handling transgressions. The agents nevertheless remember the session vividly today, not for any useful information it yielded but because of the interviewee's insufferable arrogance. Even for Mel Paisley, it was a bravura performance.

To impress the two agents who came to see him, Paisley served up a grandiose story about why he took the Navy post. "He said he had been sitting on top of the world as Boeing's chief scientist, with an office ten times the size of his eventual office in the Pentagon," according to one of the investigators who recalls the conversation. "But he said he felt unfulfilled at Boeing; somehow he wasn't satisfied with his life." Paisley went on to recount that he and his wife agreed public service was the best way "to give something back to the people of America, to repay them for our good fortune."[117]

After listening to this monologue for half an hour, the agents were fed up. One of them made loud retching noises walking out of Paisley's office suite, pretending to race for the nearest wastepaper basket. Hunched over, he barely could contain his laughter. Paisley's aides, who were tagging behind, thought the man really was physically ill. "I have a stomach problem. All of a sudden, I thought I was going to throw up," the investigator mumbled, exchanging knowing glances with his partner. Paisley's story "was the biggest con job imaginable," the lead agent recalls, sparing no adjectives. "At that instant, I knew that he was slick as snot on a doorknob."[118]

Chapter VII

THE HARD CORE

Sporting well-worn baseball caps and windbreakers, the raucous group of middle-aged men came to fish and frolic in the brilliant sunshine of Cabo San Lucas, on the southern tip of Mexico's Baja Peninsula. When the sun went down, they drank and swapped stories in the hotel's dining room like long-lost schoolmates. It could have been a college reunion, or maybe a company-sponsored retreat. Most of the happy vacationers had the rough-hewn faces of outdoorsmen. However, their short hair and something in their bearing identified them as military.

They called themselves "the Hard Core": a cozy group of about twenty-five Pentagon officials and defense industry executives who hunted, fished and partied together regularly during the 1960s and 1970s. A similar outfit, called "Detachment 1," planned golf junkets for congressional aides, Air Force officers and industry bigwigs through the mid-1980s. The male-only organizations were bankrolled by contractors, and company planes often provided free transportation. Joining the groups was an essential rite of passage for the participants. They all knew that was what it took to get ahead in the industry. It was no secret that programs were plugged and friendships were cemented on these excursions. In fact, the close ties that were forged became the ultimate expression of the Pentagon's "revolving door" syndrome. The line between personal and professional relationships became so blurred that it lost all relevance.

The Hard Core had its own bylaws, arranged tours to exotic destinations each year and was extremely selective about who could come. To be invited, you had to be sponsored by a member. Ben Plymale of Boeing was active in the group until he died. So was Austen Watson of Singer, who sometimes invited Mel Paisley to join him on fishing trips and parties. General Dynamics, Thiokol and other major defense contractors were represented. Numerous active-duty officers and program managers from the Pentagon also came along on outings. If a newcomer was asked back a second time, he was duly initiated. Acceptance in the club translated into enhanced stature inside corporate suites. For officers and civilians working in the Pentagon, membership provided more than cachet. It all but guaranteed an industry job whenever they opted to leave government service.

This was the environment that Richard Lee Fowler, an obscure financial analyst for the Air Force, found on his introduction to the Hard Core around 1975. While fishing for marlin off the Baja coast, nobody pumped him for information or droned on about business. It was all quite casual. The social contacts, though, were only part of Fowler's motivation for going to Mexico. Already thinking of a second career once he retired from the Pentagon, he dropped hints about his hopes and plans to industry representatives. "The trip justified talking about future employment," Fowler recalls. "The group had to decide if somebody was compatible, if you were a guy who could fit in."[1]

A wiry, square-jawed civilian budget specialist, Fowler had spent the last eighteen years in the Pentagon crunching numbers and evaluating production schedules for Air Force weapons. He worked on the Minuteman missile and other nuclear weapons programs that were crucial to Boeing. Fowler wasn't flashy or senior enough to attract the attention of high-flying consultants. He didn't have any political connections, nor did he claim to have real authority within the Air Force. With his nasal voice, secretive nature and accountant's frame of mind, he seemed an unlikely person for Plymale and other industry leaders to cultivate. The founders of the Hard Core, on the other hand, knew that impressions could be misleading. Frequently, the worker bees in the bowels of the Pentagon—a sympathetic colonel or a cooperative civil servant like Fowler, with a loose tongue and easy access to sensitive information—could give the most assistance to contractors. Dick Fowler was invited on the first fishing trip because he was helpful and supportive of the industry. The following year, he went back with the guys to Mazatlán, Mexico. He was now a bona fide member of the Hard Core. The contractors were certain he could be trusted; they found that they could get along with him just fine.

Fowler's warm welcome was an affirmation of his lifelong fascination with and love for the armed forces. A Washington, D.C., native, Fowler was proud of the fact that his father was among the civil engineers who supervised construction of the Pentagon. With World War II raging, Fowler dropped out of high school in 1943 to take a job as a messenger for the War Department at the age of seventeen. After earning his diploma at night, he enlisted and became a gunner on Boeing B-29 bombers. Not even a terrible training accident in the Atlantic Ocean, which killed three of his fellow crew members and left him in a body cast for three months, cooled his ardor for the military.

The pilot of the stricken B-29 Superfortress was forced to ditch in heavy seas near Puerto Rico due to mechanical problems. None of the bomber's four engines was functioning as it smacked into the waves and broke apart. After struggling to the surface, Sergeant Fowler hung on to a jagged piece of the plane's fuselage. He gasped for air. The sharp edges of the metal cut deeply into Fowler's flesh, as he grappled to take off his sodden parachute and inflate his life-preserver. But the bloody, mangled hand, it turned out, wasn't the worst of his medical problems. Soon after

Fowler and the rest of the survivors were plucked from the water, he complained of a stiff neck. Since it was Sunday, and there were no physicians on duty at the base hospital, the technicians took some X-rays and calmly advised him to return to his duties. Monday morning, when the film was examined, the doctors were aghast: The impact of the crash had fractured the seventh vertebra in Fowler's neck. If the cracked edges of the bone snapped and broke apart completely, he could be paralyzed for life.

Oblivious of the danger, Fowler had been jumping on and off trucks and trotting up stairs to attend accident debriefing sessions. When the ambulance screeched to a halt outside the hangar and Fowler heard somebody frantically yelling his name, he was astonished. "Stay right there. Don't move an inch," the medic carrying a stretcher hollered up to the second floor. "You're going back to the hospital pronto. You have a broken neck." Fowler's contrarian nature was evident even then. Despite a cast from the waist to the top of his head, he insisted on being carried to simulators to complete gunnery training.[2]

Fowler served in the Pacific during the final months of the war, flying missions over Hiroshima and Nagasaki barely a few days after the nuclear bombs were dropped. He returned home to enjoy a suburbanite's passions: golf, gardening and spending time with his wife, Muriel, and their three children. The Air Force job provided stability and a sense of purpose, as did his leadership of an American Legion post in Northern Virginia. Commendations and promotions attested to his patriotic, hard-working lifestyle. Most of all, though, Fowler treasured his trips with the Hard Core.

One Saturday in February 1978, reading in his office on the fourth floor of the Pentagon, Fowler received another type of invitation from Boeing. Why didn't he join the company's Washington office, to collect and analyze the same budget and spending data he was wrestling with inside the Air Force? "When a prestigious company like Boeing says, 'We have a place for you,' it's extremely flattering," Fowler recalls. "I considered it the finest defense contractor" in the country.[3] He didn't need much time to decide. The deal was sealed later that day at the Georgetown Inn in northwest Washington, D.C., where Plymale met Fowler and slapped a completed hiring form into his hand.

Plymale complained that his current crop of employees wasn't any good at rounding up Pentagon documents. They didn't see the big budget picture and often duplicated each other's efforts. If they did succeed in getting their hands on something interesting, Plymale went on, none of them could make sense of it. Fowler was recruited to remedy those shortcomings. "My job was to collect any financial information that could be helpful to Boeing," according to Fowler, and to interpret it for management. "Classified or unclassified, it didn't matter; that's what they wanted."[4]

Fowler filled out more employment forms and, for a short period, attended Boeing briefings and learned about office procedures while still on the Air Force's payroll. From the moment he put on a Boeing employee badge, Fowler maintains, his instructions were unambiguous and never changed. Plymale told him not to worry about identifying people who supplied him information, or making sure that he had the required receipts before accepting classified material. "It's nobody's business where you got a document," Plymale insisted, telling Fowler to dissemble on the logs Boeing was obligated to keep. "Put down whatever makes you feel comfortable. All you're doing is filling in a square."[5] From then on, Boeing's new marketing analyst didn't bother listing the names of individuals who gave him classified data. "From the first document I entered into the system to the last, I followed instructions," Fowler recalls.[6] He used the initials "AFRD" to identify the source of all his documents—regardless of where they originated. The abbreviation stood for Fowler's former employer, the Air Force's office of research and development.

His salary was minuscule compared to the billions of dollars Boeing stood to gain from Pentagon contracts. Fowler sheepishly asked for $25,000 a year. He was ecstatic when Boeing offered him $29,500 as a starting salary. Plymale's assistant also put him on Boeing's payroll a week early, so Fowler could draw an advance to pay for a previously scheduled golfing trip with his Pentagon chums to Myrtle Beach, South Carolina. The expenses totaled a piddling four hundred dollars, but the message to Fowler was unmistakable. From disbursing petty cash to obtaining classified papers, he saw that Boeing was willing to stretch the rules.

Fowler's pay doubled over the next eight years, but that first check and the ones that followed may have been among the best investments Boeing ever made. He was the perfect company man, bent on currying favor with his bosses and proving his value to a firm he admired. Dick Fowler was a human dynamo when it came to corralling classified documents from friends still in uniform or working for other companies. His Air Force sources were incomparable, slipping him documents even members of Congress weren't entitled to see. In addition, he found and nurtured excellent industry contacts. To expand Boeing's information net, Fowler secretly bartered documents with General Dynamics, Grumman, Honeywell, IBM, LTV, RCA, Singer and other companies. Some of the material made its way to Raytheon, Hughes Aircraft, Martin Marietta, Ford Motor's aerospace unit and a number of additional recipients.

Defense firms legally are entitled to accumulate a vast array of classified materials, from technical research papers to production forecasts and financial breakdowns of specific contracts. Such documents can be obtained in a completely aboveboard manner, becoming part of the lifeblood of every contractor. Industry couldn't function without access to this kind of information. Exchanges of these documents were and continue to be commonplace, helping foster a spirit of teamwork between contractors and the services. Given the extent of sharing and cooperation sanctioned by the Pentagon, it's no wonder that companies often consider their interests to be complementary to those of the military.

However, in Fowler's time there was a second category of classified information generated by the Pentagon. This group of documents was intended to remain, from its inception, strictly off-limits to industry. Companies weren't supposed to see the Pentagon's internal planning and decision memos. Industry wasn't authorized to get the multitude of budget projections spelling out which programs the military had resolved to pursue, and which were likely to be axed since there would be no funding requests in coming years. These documents—dealing with the thought processes and deliberations of decision-makers on critical funding issues—were required to be handled altogether differently from the first category.

All classified documents were supposed to be kept in locked safes, with receipts showing how they got to each of the firms, who read them and how outdated files were destroyed. Companies generally weren't allowed to make copies without prior government approval. Document-control records were inspected twice a year by the Pentagon, and violators were subject to severe penalties. On paper, at least, that was the way classified information was protected. Every single government and company official with a security clearance signed forms pledging to abide by the rules.

In practice, their promises meant little. And the perfunctory government inspections meant even less. Dick Fowler was part of an underground network that broke or skirted the laws and regulations every day. Members trafficked in classified documents they weren't permitted to have, obtaining and passing them out without attempting to verify who had a legitimate "need to know" the information. Pentagon officials supplied a steady stream of illicit material. Their counterparts in industry quietly distributed copies of the documents without any qualms—and right under the noses of poorly trained government inspectors who didn't fully understand the rules and failed to grasp the severity of the violations.

The Justice Department eventually identified Fowler as one of the undisputed leaders of a nationwide information-gathering ring, dubbed "the Clique," composed of executives from Boeing and nearly a dozen other large defense firms. Fowler and his cohorts routinely intercepted internal reports and budget documents before they reached their destinations within the Pentagon. The Clique's biggest challenge was to see how soon after the official sign-off on a document it could come up with a bootlegged copy. The lag was seldom more than a couple of days. Exchanging such data was little different from exchanging business cards, Fowler recalls. Industry marketing officials, he says, considered it "as common as kids swapping baseball cards" on street corners or in playgrounds.[7] The former teenage messenger, who once dutifully delivered classified memos around the musty corridors of the War Department, had grown up to be a master at gleaning the secrets of Reagan's arms buildup forty years later.

Fowler was, by far, the most prolific of Boeing's employees at securing information, bringing in more than thirteen hundred documents over an eight-year stretch. Management invariably sought his help when the chips were down; some officials placed orders with Fowler for documents, and the company applauded his success. As competition turned more fierce, headquarters clamored for "more data, better data, more intelligence, harder intelligence and better analysis" of plans formulated by the government and Boeing's rivals, recalls Charlie Welling, Fowler's first supervisor.[8] Executives wanted documents to reassure themselves. They wanted documents to help reassure their superiors. The company's appetite for data became so pronounced that marketing managers felt their very jobs were in jeopardy. The race was on to round up documents, often simply for the sake of satisfying the boss. Verbal reports weren't as impressive. "Boeing had to see hard copy," Welling says. The standing order from Seattle was: "Let me see paper!"[9]

On April 24, 1985, President Reagan's national security adviser, Robert McFarlane, wrote a highly classified memo on proposed space-based missile defenses, known as "Star Wars." The draft of the so-called National Security Decision Directive was addressed to just three senior officials: Defense Secretary Caspar Weinberger, Secretary of State George Shultz and General John Vessey, chairman of the Joint Chiefs of Staff. In a blatant breach of security rules, Fowler landed a copy of the memo with the help of his buddies, including a former Boeing executive who had a high-level Pentagon job. Fowler sent it off to Boeing's headquarters several weeks after it was prepared.

Fowler's nose for lower-level documents was equally keen. One Air Force lieutenant colonel assigned to the Pentagon, who was unusually fond of Fowler, would slide the in-basket on his desk over to the Boeing analyst during office chats. "See if there's anything you want in there," the colonel used to say matter-of-factly. "Just put it in a stack and I'll make copies for you."[10]

Sometimes, Pentagon pals used Fowler as an unofficial messenger, asking him to transport Air Force files back and forth between the Pentagon and meetings at Andrews Air Force Base in suburban Maryland. He was happy to oblige, since it could mean an early look at some documents. At any rate, his friends in uniform knew how to repay such favors. One grateful Air Force major, for instance, faithfully alerted Fowler with a telephone call almost every time the officer was designated as the courier to take important budget-related memos out to Andrews. Boeing's man immediately drove to the Pentagon's south parking lot, where the major met him with bulging boxes of documents. "Take a copy out of the box," Fowler was told. "That's yours."[11] Before the shuttle bus carrying the courier drove twenty miles to the air base and the contents of the boxes were distributed to the generals there, Fowler would be comfortably back at his desk underlining the memos. "No one got material quicker than I did," Fowler proudly recalls.[12]

Inside the Pentagon, many abandoned the principle of keeping contractors at a respectful distance. Since Boeing and other companies got so much information anyway, through legitimate means, officials turned their backs on the concept that certain documents had to stay out of bounds for industry. It didn't matter how secret the information was. Boeing's central role in nuclear programs, for example, made it essential for the company to gain access to the Strategic Air Command's daily reports covering missiles and bombers on alert. Few officers outside SAC ever saw the status sheets, which were considered exceedingly sensitive. But Boeing didn't rest until it got an Air Force source to provide the reports promptly the same day, according to a former industry official who dealt with Fowler.[13]

One year, a veteran civil servant affiliated with the Air Force's Space Command asked Fowler to carry an attaché case filled with government documents from Los Angeles to Washington. The Air Force official had decided to tour the West Coast on a brief vacation, and he didn't want to lug the heavy stack of papers around with him on the family outing. There was no discussion of signing for the material. According to Fowler, his buddy's instructions were explicit: "Xerox what you want; I will call you when I get back to Washington, and then you can bring them over to me." Fowler drove straight to Boeing's Los Angeles office to review the information with local corporate managers. He made copies of everything, including classified data, and then flew the Air Force files back to the East Coast as requested.[14]

Boeing and the other contractors basically didn't seem to care how or where the information was obtained. Years later, when Boeing faced legal trouble, its lawyers tried to portray Fowler as a renegade tiptoeing around company regulations. But Boeing's own records revealed that in addition to Fowler, at least fifteen other of its executives acquired classified papers without the necessary authorization. One of them snared the Army's "acquisition plan" for special operations helicopters two days after it was typed. Another marketing official snatched the Navy's comparison of Boeing's E6 communications plane with archrival Lockheed's EC-130 aircraft. Five company-run libraries were used to store all of the documents, and the list of executives who perused the material included at least one president of Boeing's aerospace division, the head of the company's military airplane unit and several division vice-presidents. Overall, nearly three hundred company officials handled or read versions of the ill-gotten files.[15] The director of the Defense Investigative Service indicated that top industry officials must have condoned the improper behavior. "It seems inconceivable," he concluded in a memo, that senior management at Boeing and other companies "did not look the other way in some instances."[16]

Some friends referred enviously to Fowler as "the mother lode" for confidential Pentagon budget numbers. His documents tended to be particularly valuable because of their timeliness. Proud of how much his sources trusted him, he developed his own unique set of rules. Fowler never paid anybody for information, and he didn't try to sell any secrets for personal profit. That would be enough to keep him out of trouble, he believed. "I didn't steal, blackmail or coerce anyone to give me documents. If these government officials thought it was criminal, they wouldn't have given them to me."[17] Fowler and his associates actually felt they had more scruples than the rest of the industry. They looked down on Bill Galvin and consultants of his ilk, who earned big bucks by peddling information to the highest bidder.

Such distinctions didn't deter prosecutor Henry Hudson from pursuing the Clique. But the case was more subtle than Illwind. Neither Hudson nor any other U.S. attorney had experience prosecuting information-swapping schemes where no bribes or patently illegal gratuities changed hands. The hemorrhage of classified information decidedly was serious, violating national security laws and the Pentagon's own regulations. There seemed little doubt about that. But the dozen or so Defense Department officials who supplied Fowler with classified documents over the years didn't do it for the money. There was no readily identifiable quid pro quo for their illegal acts. Pentagon insiders could claim, as Fowler did, that they merely were helping out a friend. And unlike Illwind, in which defendants rolled over and cooperated with the government, in this case Hudson didn't have any damning wiretapped conversations to penetrate the heart of Fowler's intrigues.

Nonetheless, the document-swapping ring led by Fowler was every bit as pernicious as the criminality exposed by Illwind. Illegal document swapping compromised the integrity of the military's procurement system as much as did the payoffs and tainted contracts Galvin, Paisley, Gardner and Muldoon were overheard discussing. By disregarding fundamental security precepts, Boeing and the rest of the Clique got an indispensable peek at the Pentagon's long-range spending priorities. As prosecutor Hudson put it: "The illegally obtained documents certainly cost taxpayers a great deal of money."[18] He compared it to stealing the opposing team's playbook before a football game.

Recipients all held the requisite clearances, so the concern wasn't over military secrets falling into unfriendly hands. Rather, as investigators and lawmakers delved into the details, they became incensed by the widespread nature of the security breaches. Democratic senator William Proxmire of Wisconsin, a prominent Pentagon basher, denounced the "black market" in classified documents as "one of the most reprehensible practices in the procurement of weapons." Trafficking in information by Boeing and other firms, he said, inevitably "leads to collusive bidding" that cheats taxpayers.[19]

Other critics saw the result as a prostitution of the relationship between industry and government. Michael Costello, the senior Pentagon criminal investigator who pursued Fowler, says the Clique "completely subverted government contracting procedures." The Pentagon lost all control of the documents, many of which were copied and circulated at will among contractors. "They corrupted the system across the board," Costello says, not just on individual contracts. "And the people who did it knew they were doing the wrong thing."[20]

Some of the planning documents Fowler acquired illegitimately were clearly stamped, on the front cover, SECRET and NOT RELEASABLE TO CONTRACTORS/CONSULTANTS. Many more documents were stapled to cover letters warning that the information couldn't be "furnished to anyone outside the Executive Branch without the expressed written consent" of the Defense Department's comptroller. Fowler realized he was at risk, especially after the government launched an industrywide probe of how classified documents were distributed. Still, he continued to tell friends he felt safe because Boeing's management was aware of his activities. "I was doing exactly what I was hired to do," Fowler maintains to this day. "I didn't try to hide it. I wouldn't have done anything to jeopardize my job."[21]

Fowler's career was changed forever in September 1985. It happened unexpectedly over lunch at the Tivoli, an upscale Italian restaurant located on the mezzanine level of the suburban Virginia complex where Boeing had moved its offices from downtown Washington. A Lockheed marketing representative, who had known Fowler years before in the Air Force, pulled him aside to tell him that the Justice Department was cracking down on contractors' use of classified materials. If Boeing didn't want to be caught with suspicious Pentagon documents stashed in its safes, the friend urged, get rid of them. Do it quickly, Fowler was told, before surprise government inspections begin.[22]

Barely two weeks earlier, a prominent consultant named Bernie Zettl had been indicted for illegally providing GTE Corporation classified documents dealing with electronic-warfare programs and then trying to disguise the true nature of his services. GTE, among the top twenty U.S. defense contractors, admitted its guilt the same day the charges against Zettl were announced. Perhaps that was because prosecutors dug up the following internal memos written by the company's marketing managers: "We do not want to list on paper the work" Zettl was hired to do for the firm, one note acknowledged. A second memo praised him for providing "advanced marketing and planning information which isn't available through" normal corporate channels.[23] GTE's penalty was scarcely more than half a million dollars. Nevertheless, the whole industry was stunned, as it struggled to understand the ramifications of the case.

For Fowler, Zettl's indictment was the beginning of the end. The whispered admonition at noontime shocked him into action. Fowler rushed back to his office on the twentieth floor of the Rosslyn Center and ordered the security clerk to start purging files. He passed along the message to Seattle and to Wichita, Kansas, where Boeing also had major defense facilities. It took weeks to ship out and shred the large volume of classified material, and some Boeing loyalists carped about discarding such valuable information. Fowler's documents, nearly all without the required receipts, alone filled five drawers in the company's main aerospace offices in Kent, Washington. In the meantime, he became much more wary about receiving documents.

Even at this late date, Dick Fowler believed he could avoid Zettl's misfortune.

After years of sacrifice for his country, he didn't understand how investigators could possibly question his motives. Fowler was convinced he could still evade the wrath of the Justice Department's dogged band of prosecutors. Always the optimist, he thought it was inconceivable that he and other members of the Hard Core were the primary targets of a federal grand jury. "He was a patriot, for heaven's sake, not a subversive," says an industry pal.[24]

☆

In the shadowy realm of electronic warfare, where "black boxes" and radar-jamming devices can render jet planes and nine-thousand-ton submarines virtually invisible to the enemy, Bernie Zettl was a star. The gregarious former Air Force major learned the secrets of his trade before signing retirement papers in the early 1960s. After setting up shop as a consultant, he earned a six-figure income by attracting an assortment of blue-chip corporate clients. At one time or another, Zettl worked for more than ten giant military contractors, including GTE, TRW, Northrop and Sanders Associates. His name meant nothing to the uninitiated. But spanning more than two decades, he collected authorized as well as illicit Pentagon documents. When it came to purveying information about the Pentagon's latest submarine-surveillance capabilities, new infrared tracking devices and improved radar-evading missiles, Bernie Zettl ruled the roost.

His prominence stemmed from more than his connections throughout the Pentagon. Zettl helped create and then served as president of the Association of Old Crows, an influential fraternity of electronic-warfare experts that spanned the globe. The name came from the code word "Raven" or "Crow," which was used to identify Allied aircraft that jammed German signals during bombing raids in World War II. Originally, the group consisted of a small band of intelligence and electronics officers eager to knock back a few beers and retell stories of those glory days on the battlefield. The Old Crows, however, soon became much more than a social club.[25]

By the mid-1980s, the organization had grown in size and importance.

Boasting more than twenty thousand corporate executives and current and former military brass as members—the majority carrying top-secret clearances—the Old Crows matured into a powerhouse in the weapons industry. There were chapters, or "roosts," from Australia and Japan to the Middle East and Europe. They offered a remarkably efficient way to share early tipoffs on Pentagon plans.[26] Members conducted technical seminars and advised the military on complex scientific issues, while the Pentagon happily sponsored their meetings, provided space for annual conventions and approved the presentation of classified papers there. Lynwood Cosby, another of the association's founders and a former senior manager at the prestigious Naval Research Laboratory, explained that the Old Crows weren't interested in impeding or criticizing their benefactors in the Pentagon. What they wanted, he said, was to "create the environment where exchange of information between the military and contractors can flourish."[27]

Zettl and some of the industry chieftains he dealt with took that philosophy one step further. Contemplating future business opportunities instead of old flying exploits, they formed a conduit for the surreptitious flow of information out of the Pentagon. Zettl had to know that the documents he snared could be a gold mine for contractors. So, he quietly fed certain clients classified budget summaries the military didn't want released. The documents laid out Navy and Air Force acquisition plans for communication and intelligence-gathering equipment, along with various other spending projections. In three years, Zettl earned $120,000 from GTE alone for his cunning. The Old Crows' motto was as pertinent to his flouting of the law as it was to the memory of the World War II aviators it was intended to honor: "The Old Crow didn't get old by being the fastest of the birds, or the strongest, or the bravest. He got old by being wily."[28]

Two seemingly insignificant slipups, which occurred two thousand miles apart, spoiled Zettl's game plan. In Mountain View, California, the home office of GTE's Government Systems unit, agents of the Defense Investigative Service were plodding through a standard security inspection in 1983. Randomly selected employees had to pass lie-detector tests to have their clearances revalidated. A midlevel GTE marketing official seemed to be acting weird. He said he simply couldn't take the test. "Why not?" puzzled agents demanded. Upset and tongue-tied, the employee finally blurted out his fear: The polygraph would reveal that he knew GTE frequently received classified Pentagon documents, outside of authorized channels, from a source in Washington. The DIS team looked through the company's files, found the offending material and traced it back to Zettl—GTE's well-paid consultant on the banks of the Potomac.

Around the same time, federal agents in Ohio were chasing separate allegations that some firms garnered inside information from NASA's Lewis Research Center in Cleveland and the giant Wright-Patterson Air Force Base outside Dayton. Several high-ranking Pentagon and NASA officials were implicated. During the investigation, agents scoured government travel records for possible leads. They got lucky. The director of NASA's research facility had submitted sixty-eight hundred dollars of false vouchers covering trips to Washington over a two-year period. Who was he visiting so frequently in the capital, and why?

The person who helped the NASA official prepare the phony bills, investigators discovered, was his good friend Bernie Zettl. GTE also showed up in the Cleveland probe as one of the firms paying to obtain classified documents. Prompted by this fortuitous turn of events, Pentagon investigators cast a wider net. They confronted a veteran GTE marketing executive, who acknowledged that he had never tried to clamp down on Zettl's unauthorized activities. Why hadn't he tried to stop the flow of unauthorized documents? "If you already have your feet in the mud, why take a shower?" he told agents. "You still can't get rid of past dirt."

Branching out from GTE and Zettl, agents asked a lot of questions and came up with some disturbing answers: There appeared to be a prevalent industry practice of using bootlegged documents to help contractors flesh out military spending priorities. A heretofore unknown web of consultants and company officials seemed to be living off this illegal trade. The full extent of the trafficking was difficult to determine. But by the fall of 1985, Pentagon investigators identified twenty-five companies—many of them household names—suspected of participating in the "indiscriminate distribution of both proprietary and highly classified government documents."[29]

Joseph Sherick, the Defense Department's inspector general at the time, acknowledged that unlawful "peddling" of classified documents was more common and harmful to competition than previously imagined. "This clandestine traffic in documents" by consultants "acting as information brokers," he wrote to Defense Secretary Weinberger, puts Pentagon negotiators "at a disadvantage." Contractors and consultants "who profit from this activity," the inspector general warned, "can only do so by coopting and corrupting government officials."[30] Armed with names, flow charts and an overarching conspiracy theory—which presumed that all of the companies and executives somehow belonged to one huge cabal—Sherick and his excited assistants demanded a full-court press by prosecutors.

The response, as a matter of fact, was nothing but acrimony, foot dragging and bureaucratic snafus. The evidence initially was presented to Richard Sauber, who headed the Justice Department's Defense Procurement Fraud Unit. The young prosecutor had barely a few years' experience in the white-collar crime area, and most of that had been spent pursuing commodity scams or arcane violations of energy price controls. The small group he headed was just as green. Cobbled together in a hurry, the outfit partly relied on outcasts—Pentagon agents who had been written off by the military as ineffective or otherwise undesirable before being transferred.

Sauber's ragtag band of investigators was busy tracking down all sorts of leads—they disparagingly called them "cat and dog cases"—that U.S. attorneys throughout the nation judged were too risky or marginal to chase. But since he was strong-willed and ambitious, Sauber pined to make a big splash. He knew that a high-profile corporate plea would give his fledgling organization instant credibility: One flashy case, wrapped up cleanly with a big criminal fine and lots of complimentary news stories, instantly would put him in the big leagues of Pentagon procurement prosecutors. "We need something quick to put us on the map and change people's thinking about these issues," the prosecutor said.[31]

Sauber looked at the document-swapping investigation as the path to respectability for his untested outfit. But from the outset, he clashed with Pentagon agents over how to proceed. Prosecutors had qualms about the military's recommendations to rely primarily on espionage laws to go after the wrongdoers. More important, Sauber thought it was hilarious that agents hoped to tie all the suspected culprits into a single information-swapping ring. Such grandiose "conspiracy theories are bullshit," Sauber snapped during one heated strategy session. It would be practically impossible to fit so many major contractors and more than forty individuals into a massive criminal conspiracy, he argued, and tougher yet to keep defense lawyers from shooting gaping holes in the prosecution's case.[32]

The arguments, which started over factual and legal questions, degenerated into personal diatribes. Pentagon investigators griped that their partners at Justice were overly timid. They grumbled that prosecutors were unwilling to take risks to establish new legal precedents and seemed determined to end scrutiny of many large firms prematurely—before solid evidence could be assembled. Sauber, by contrast, denounced Defense Department investigators for overreaching. He made fun of their gullibility, chortling that many of the agents didn't realize the targets they were after tended to be "bullshit artists claiming that what they had was more important than it really was." Some agents were so naive, he fumed, that they irresponsibly advocated "criminal theories that were both inappropriate and not based on any evidence."[33] The bad blood caused additional delays in putting together a viable prosecution.

Over the objections of the Pentagon, Justice opted to focus entirely on GTE and Zettl. That would be the test case, intended to send a signal to industry to stop squirreling away documents. When an agent approached one of Zettl's GTE contacts for questioning, the reply was instantaneous. "You don't have to explain. I know why you are here," the GTE executive said, volunteering to talk about the flow of secret data he saw.[34] Defense lawyers managed to delay an indictment for six months by threatening to take their complaints all the way to Attorney General Ed Meese.[35] But in the end, Zettl was charged with conspiracy, fraud and unauthorized conversion of documents. He faced twenty-five years in jail. Two of his associates inside the company also were charged in the indictment.

The prosecution got off to an inauspicious start, and it went downhill steadily from the first day. All along, Bernie Zettl maintained that he was unfairly singled out for punishment. "I wasn't the only person in the loop," he said, claiming that his actions were identical to what "was done by many other people" in the field.[36] His sole crime, Zettl argued, was being the scapegoat when the government suddenly decided to try to score public relations points.

Supporters chimed in, arguing that the government wasn't a victim. Zettl's information sharing actually was beneficial, they said, since it provided suppliers and all segments of the military critical "guidance and direction" for future weapons requirements. Norman Augustine, a former undersecretary of the Army and the chairman of Martin Marietta, ended up framing the issue in its starkest terms: "The government is the only customer," he wrote snidely, "that asks for help and then passes a law against telling what the customer needs. It is a bit like going to a doctor and refusing to tell where it hurts."[37]

Other industry executives sounded a slightly different refrain. Security restrictions, to be sure, were important, these spokesmen conceded. But they weren't *that* important, compared to the corporate bottom line. With tens of billions of dollars in contracts at stake, "players in the Washington defense game" understandably "find it hard to take such restrictions seriously," one veteran industry observer opined. "They know that some third-level bureaucrat may have ordered a document classified out of rote."[38] At the most, Zettl and his attorney asserted, he had unwittingly committed "technical violations" of national securities laws. If it was common industry practice, how could the government claim the consequences were so terrible? And how could any jury vote for conviction?

Zettl's lawyers adopted scorched-earth tactics, making prosecutors' headaches grow worse. The defense vowed to drag scores of corporate and Pentagon heavyweights into court as witnesses, in the process pointing a finger at other leading contractors for keeping their own illicit cache of documents. Drawn-out arguments over protecting military secrets and declassifying information further delayed a trial. The prosecution of Zettl floundered and then began unraveling totally.

Snarled by technicalities, the case bounced back and forth between federal district court and appeals court. The judicial limbo lasted until 1986, when the government reluctantly dropped all charges against the pair of GTE executives. The accusations against Zettl himself were whittled down to a solitary charge of unauthorized possession of a Navy report. Investigators grasped, once they attempted to prove their theories in court, how difficult it was to win convictions. "It was all new territory, and we just stumbled along to a certain degree," one senior Pentagon investigator admits. "Justice was fighting us, too, and we sure didn't need that."[39]

Despite the setback in the courtroom, the Reagan administration continued to rail against leaks of classified information to the Soviet Union. The Navy was reeling from spectacular spy charges brought against retired warrant officer John Walker and his son, Michael. The Walkers were accused of slipping top-secret codes and other intelligence secrets to Moscow. Justice and Pentagon policymakers pressed for expanded use of lie-detector tests and tough new sanctions—including immediate suspension of clearances—aimed at government officials who violated security rules to help journalists. For instance, Samuel L. Morison, a former Navy intelligence analyst, was charged with sending classified satellite photographs of a Soviet military base to a British magazine. Morison gained the dubious distinction of becoming the first person ever convicted under American espionage laws for leaking information to the press.[40]

Security problems cropped up at more and more companies. In July 1986, Lockheed conceded that controls at its Burbank, California, plant were so lax that it couldn't account for fourteen hundred classified military documents stored there.[41] The plant—famous throughout the industry as the "Skunk Works"—worked on supersecret "black" projects the Pentagon deemed too sensitive to identify publicly. Lockheed's chairman told Congress the mistakes were "inexcusable." A few months earlier, Pentagon inspectors found what they described as "major" security lapses at ten out of fifty General Dynamics facilities they visited. At Northrop, officials couldn't account for more than one thousand documents connected with development of the B-2 Stealth bomber. Other companies supplied false certificates stating that classified materials were shredded, when in reality the documents had been either lost or stolen.[42]

Even retired admiral Thomas Hayward, President Reagan's initial chief of naval operations, was caught passing classified U.S. intelligence reports about South Korea's shipbuilding plans to his corporate consulting clients. Hayward's defense was that he was trying to help U.S. firms compete more effectively with foreign contractors for that business. As a director of Litton Industries, a six-figure consultant to other defense contractors and a board member of several other big firms, the admiral was an inviting target for prosecution. Nonetheless, his case attracted only lukewarm interest inside the Justice Department and received scant press attention. Hayward was never punished, partly because he relied on personal relationships with officers of the Pacific Fleet, not cold cash, to secure the information.[43]

Similar loopholes bedeviled leads growing out of the original GTE investigation. The Justice Department developed cold feet about bringing additional cases. With the roller-coaster litigation over Zettl still pending, prosecutors at headquarters refused to file charges against any new targets. Transcripts of incriminating grand jury testimony gathered dust in file cabinets. Boeing and Fowler were depicted in some of the testimony as masterminds of a broader document-swapping ring—far above Zettl or

GTE. One of the consultants who exchanged documents with Zettl also admitted doing the same thing with Fowler. The government was handed what amounted to a smoking gun. Incredibly, prosecutors failed to make the link. They stopped interviewing witnesses and put all investigative efforts on hold. Justice wouldn't budge until the courts disposed of Zettl's appeals. As a result, tips grew cold and promising avenues of inquiry were allowed to languish for more than two years.[44]

Once on the cutting edge of law enforcement, Bernie Zettl's case had turned into a legal and public-affairs disaster for the Justice Department. The charges against Zettl disclosed "only the tip of the iceberg," Senator Proxmire said during his final congressional hearing before retiring in 1988. Since troubles with the case had surfaced, Proxmire added tongue in cheek, the Justice Department "thinks the iceberg is a mirage or will melt away."[45]

The ominous warnings seemed to be well-founded. Time was running out for the government to prosecute Fowler and his buddies. Unless the remaining cases were investigated aggressively and criminal charges were filed rapidly, the statute of limitations would run out. That would preclude any more prosecutions. Fowler's legal difficulties suddenly would become moot. The industry, convinced the worst was behind it, breathed a collective sigh of relief.

It shouldn't have. Mike Costello, one of the Pentagon's most experienced criminal investigators, was not going to stand by meekly and let the Clique get away. Costello was a stubborn, hard-boiled New Yorker, and his inclination was to go straight for the jugular in white-collar crime probes. He had spent more than sixteen years climbing up the Drug Enforcement Administration's hierarchy, before switching his sights to Pentagon fraud. As the special agent in charge of the Defense Criminal Investigative Service's Northern Virginia field office, Costello couldn't bear to see years of laborious legwork go down the drain. One of his agents, for instance, devoted three months one summer to perusing fifty-five thousand receipts in the Air Force's research and development office. All the tedious checking was done by hand. Fowler claimed that he had acquired his information legally, so the files should have indicated when he signed for classified documents. Dick Fowler's name didn't show up on a single slip of paper.[46]

Costello was in a rage about Justice's refusal to go after Fowler, Boeing and others. He stormed into prosecutors' offices one day, berating them for inaction. "Shit or get off the pot," Costello demanded. "Do something, or let me take them over to the eastern district of Virginia," where the leads will be pursued.[47] He cursed and yelled some more. It was unheard-of behavior; investigators didn't talk to prosecutors this harshly. "I pushed them to the wall," Costello recalls. But the outburst had the desired effect. Costello walked out that afternoon with a portion of the files under his arm, and within days every one of the document-swapping cases was transferred to Henry Hudson's jurisdiction in Alexandria. They were assigned to Joe Aronica, the senior Pentagon fraud prosecutor on the staff.

Recognizing the potential of their investigation, Costello and his agents kept plugging away. But they continued to be dismayed by the lack of progress. Because he had his hands full with Illwind, Aronica gave the document-swapping cases short shrift as well. No other prosecutors were available to pick up the slack. The FBI said it wasn't interested in Costello's cases, declining flatly to supply manpower. Boeing and the rest of the companies predictably did their utmost to avoid prosecution by stretching out the investigation. The years dragged by, and Hudson's office resorted to fresh excuses about why it wasn't ready to focus on Fowler.

Eventually, it took an entirely new cast of prosecutors and a revised theory of the crime to satisfy Costello. In August 1990, nearly five years after he was indicted, Zettl pleaded guilty to one felony count. For what had become the oldest pending criminal case in the Eastern District of Virginia, the resolution was closer to a whimper than a bang. In a whopping anticlimax, he paid a ten-thousand-dollar fine, and the judge sentenced him to 150 hours of community service. Investigators had figured out that Bernie Zettl—in spite of his insider's reputation and boasts that he "knew virtually everyone in the business"—was close to the end of the information chain. He was, in fact, a relatively minor player in the document-swapping game. By then, the government was locked on much juicier targets. The Clique, which prospered for twenty years with the acquiescence and support of Pentagon and industry leaders, was under direct attack.

☆

The first day Randy Bellows came to work for Henry Hudson at the U.S. attorney's office in Alexandria, he was looking for a place to lick his psychological wounds. The date was March 15, 1989, and the thirty-seven-year-old lawyer had been hired as a senior fraud prosecutor to pursue the Clique. Hudson was convinced that Bellows had the skills for the assignment. But in his heart, Bellows was despondent and lacked confidence. No matter what anybody said, he felt that he had a lot to prove—especially to himself.

Brought up in a close, devoutly Jewish family that moved to South Florida from Long Island when he was a teenager, Bellows excelled at an early age. He majored in journalism at the University of Florida, won a batch of national writing awards and became editor in chief of the campus paper at the age of twenty. Bellows never imagined becoming a lawyer, until he got embroiled in a nasty, public battle to stop the school's president from shutting down the *Daily Alligator*. The student-run tabloid—proud of its twenty-five thousand daily circulation and national

reputation for editorial independence—enraged the university's conservative leadership by printing the names of local abortion counseling centers. The previous editor had been criminally prosecuted for the offense,
and the university was after Bellows's head, too. The school wanted to
muzzle the paper, or destroy it by withdrawing all subsidies. Bellows
fought back savagely. He crisscrossed the state to drum up support for the
paper, and hired a law firm to file suit if the university ousted him.

The aspiring investigative reporter spent long weeks and weekends in the
law library, deciphering the legal jargon the university tried to confuse
him with. Gradually, his interest in the law broadened. For the first time in
his life, Randy Bellows considered that journalism was not the only honest,
worthy profession under the sun. The realization hit him hard, forever
changing his view of the world. "The legal process," he concluded, "gives you
options to accomplish things that journalism doesn't."[48]

The campaign to save the paper succeeded, and Bellows continued to
be enthralled with the law. As an exchange student for a semester at predominately black Florida State University, he cajoled a warmhearted law
school professor to let him take a third-year course in constitutional law.
Bellows was enthralled by the class and the heartfelt respect for the Constitution expressed by fellow students; he still beams about those months
as an inspirational experience. After getting his undergraduate diploma,
Bellows attended Harvard Law School and then blossomed into a wun-
derkind of federal financial-crime prosecutors.

The one-time journalist seemingly had punched all the right tickets
for a stellar legal career. He started out working as a public defender in
Washington's black ghetto for a couple of years. In that role, he told
friends, "You never win unless you're extraordinarily aggressive." Bellows
compiled his bittersweet experiences afterward into an eloquent essay on
youthful criminals, their victims and the value of compassion. His spirited, often perversely uncompromising defense of rapists and murderers
put him at odds with his wife, planting the seeds of their later divorce. But
the young public defender adored his job. He described feeling transfixed
and almost breaking into tears at sentencing hearings, "as if it were my
life and liberty hanging in the balance." To conscientiously defend the
poor and downtrodden, Bellows wrote, "You have to be able not only to
advocate, but to advocate passionately." If judges or juries sense that "you
do not like your client, that you just do not care if he goes down the
drain, sure as anything they will flush him."[49]

He carried this dedication and high-minded resolve into government
service. As a hotshot Justice Department prosecutor, Bellows exulted in
old-fashioned values: "I get paid to do what I believe is right; to do the
public good."[50] He uncovered and convicted an international ring that
tried to pull off the largest maritime fraud in history. The $56-million
scheme involved scuttling the *Salem*, a 214,000-ton, Liberian-flag super-
tanker, and collecting insurance for her nonexistent cargo of oil. The scam

also involved efforts to circumvent the international embargo against oil sales to South Africa. It would have worked, except for one glaring slip. Before sending out the first distress signal, crew members took time to carefully pack their suitcases, change into clean street clothes and cram lifeboats with tens of thousands of cigarettes. Sailors on a passing British merchant ship, which picked up the Salem's survivors, became dubious and alerted authorities.

From disappearing tankers and mysterious signs of oil smuggled to South Africa, Bellows graduated to big-time Pentagon fraud cases. By the end of 1985, five years after the Salem sank, he was the lead prosecutor for the most formidable—and probably the most publicized—defense over-charge case filed by the Justice Department at the time. General Dynamics and four of its executives were accused of bilking the government of $7.5 million by using fraudulent bills to hide cost overruns on the Army's Divad antiaircraft gun.

Production of the tank-mounted weapon, designed to counter Soviet helicopters and warplanes, had been terminated earlier by Secretary Weinberger. Critics accused the Pentagon, among other things, of faking videotape tests showing the Divad in action and warming the gun for six hours with a heating device before testing its cold-weather capabilities. In spite of such shenanigans, the ill-fated cannon could not effectively per-form its mission of protecting U.S. tank columns by being able to hit fast-moving enemy choppers at a range of three or four miles.

General Dynamics had built some of the prototypes, and investigators smelled an easy victory. They argued that the Divad's collapse was a text-book case of a contractor supplying shoddy equipment and padding its costs. The firestorm forced James Beggs, the company's former executive vice-president and one of the men charged with the alleged conspiracy, to step down as head of the National Aeronautics and Space Administration. Bellows, who pushed his team of agents to analyze one million time cards and collect millions of pages of other documents during the exhaustive investigation, was outraged by what he found. Amid the fanfare and press interviews, prosecutors called it a classic example of a contractor "pillag-ing the U.S. Treasury."

Bellows soon left Justice, moving on to work for Lawrence Walsh, the independent prosecutor investigating the Iran-Contra scandal. He switched to private practice after that, winning a spot at Covington and Burling, one of Washington's preeminent law firms. His rumpled suits and easygoing style didn't fit well with the firm's starchy, dignified charac-ter. Bellows felt forlorn, adrift among the polished mahogany desks and tastefully muted designer coats hanging in the closet. His mind also tended to wander. The civil cases he handled were a far cry from the rough-and-tumble world of criminal prosecutions, although the financial rewards were grand. The single father reveled in having more time to spend with two young daughters. Taking advantage of his newfound prosperity, he bought expensive camping equipment, fancy touring bicycles and other playthings he had never been able to afford before.

Randy Bellows's good fortune ran out with a note pinned to a bulletin board at the federal courthouse in downtown Los Angeles. At 4:30 on a drowsy Friday afternoon in the summer of 1987, when the clerk's office was closing and reporters on the East Coast were engrossed in making weekend plans, the Justice Department announced that it was abandoning prosecution of "U.S. versus General Dynamics Corp." The department hoped to bury its mistake with as little notice as possible. No press release was issued to notify the Washington press corps. Government lawyers admitted, out of the blue, that they had botched the Divad case, which had rocketed Bellows into national headlines. The U.S. attorney in Los Angeles took the highly unusual step of asking a judge to dismiss the indictment without delay.

Demoralized Justice Department officials conceded that the charges involving Beggs and the Divad were a horrible misunderstanding. Prosecutors didn't comprehend fully the intricacies of the procurement system and had failed to conduct key interviews. Belatedly, Pentagon officials came forward to vouch for the company's billing practices on the prototype of the tank-mounted antiaircraft gun. Eighty-two boxes of documents, dug up a year and a half after the indictment, were the last straw: They fatally undercut the government's case. An assistant attorney general told a press conference after the story broke that General Dynamics adhered to "perfectly permissible" billing methods and, in fact, had cleared its charges with the Pentagon. "The government is standing up and saying, 'We were wrong.' Nobody is happy about this," the mortified official said.[51] Beggs demanded a public apology and sought to have all references to the case expunged from court records. "If the Justice Department is going to bring fraud cases against contractors," he said, "they ought to get some expertise in government contracting. In this case, they didn't have any, obviously."[52] At Bellows's expense, editorial writers nationwide excoriated the scoundrels responsible for assassinating a decent man's character.

Distraught and unable to defend himself because he no longer had anything to do with the General Dynamics case, Bellows brooded for a long time. Doubt and anger tore at him, as he second-guessed why things fell apart. Hudson's job offer in March 1989, two years after the General Dynamics prosecution disintegrated, was the chance of a lifetime. It was a tempting escape from the stifling routine of corporate law and a rare opportunity to redeem his reputation. Bellows was convinced that he would regain his composure and build up his self-confidence gradually, by prosecuting a string of mundane felonies. "I had no expectation or desire to get a big case out of the gate."[53]

However, that wasn't what Hudson had in mind. The morning Bellows arrived at the U.S. attorney's office to claim his desk, he received a huge surprise: "I have a case for you," Bellows's immediate supervisor said, his voice cracking with excitement: "an investigation of the Boeing Company." In his consternation, Bellows says, "I kind of gulped."[54] The newcomer was assigned to an immensely complicated, highly visible defense probe. After Illwind, it was potentially the biggest and most far-reaching Pentagon fraud inquiry Justice had under way. After pondering a bit, "I still had mixed feelings," Bellows recalls. On one level, it galvanized his thoughts and made him determined to live up to Hudson's vote of confidence. But, on a different level, Bellows feared making another bad mistake. He was jittery about rushing headlong into a sprawling investigation filled with unknown hazards. "I wasn't eager to get involved, right away, in another complex procurement case."[55]

As Bellows immersed himself in the task, Boeing's security logs were uppermost in his mind. The company had acquired untold numbers of documents improperly since the late 1970s. But once the material was in hand, Boeing followed the letter of the law in keeping track of classified items. Since the flap over the top-secret MX memo that embarrassed Ben Plymale and the company, Boeing had placed great store in neat and up-to-date paperwork. The trait also reflected the obsessive nature of the engineers who were in charge and the firm's emphasis on rigid quality control. Whatever the motivation, the logs kept by Fowler and his colleagues—tracking the daily movement of classified papers within the company—unquestionably were the most complete and accurate records found by investigators. Bellows sensed that the logs were the key to cracking the case. He just didn't see how to make the best use of them yet.

At some contractors, the government learned that executives tried to cover their trail by maintaining shoddy, half-completed logs, or by claiming they couldn't locate security records for certain documents at all. Other firms kept a double set of books, investigators found: one for internal use and a second one, mostly for show, that was useful when Pentagon inspectors knocked on the door. Over the years, industry officials devised increasingly elaborate tricks. To hide suspect documents at Honeywell, for example, officials put them in envelopes marked "working papers" or periodically moved them into a vault designed to store the most secret information on "black" programs. Government inspectors never discovered the subterfuge, since they didn't have the top-secret clearances required to enter the vault.[56]

In San Diego, General Dynamics executives came up with similar ruses to make sure that inspectors never asked messy questions or stumbled on anything untoward. To begin with, a post office box was set up to receive classified documents. When Pentagon security agents informed General Dynamics about an upcoming visit, suspect files were tossed into a grocery cart and stored in a less conspicuous part of the plant. At the company's Washington-area office, wheels were installed on safes holding illicit copies of Pentagon documents. Just before inspections, the papers were deftly rolled out the door and trundled up to the roof.[57]

By contrast, the logs retrieved from Boeing's Rosslyn office were amazingly thorough. Large, rectangular ledgers covered with brown leather, they were filled with uniformly precise handwritten entries. Page after page recorded the date and classification of every sensitive document Fowler brought in. There was a column for reference numbers, and another column containing the titles of the reports and memos. Boeing's security clerks didn't doctor or disguise titles. All of it was orderly, legible and meticulously preserved. The ledgers were turned over to investigators before Bellows appeared on the scene. The notations, on their face, didn't divulge whether documents were obtained wrongfully. Pentagon agents, however, years afterward were able to reconstruct the sequence of events based on Boeing's logs.

Above all, Bellows set out to build a simple, easily provable case. He wanted to avoid the pitfalls he had encountered with Beggs and the Army's Divad project. That prosecution had self-destructed as a result of unclear procurement rules—the kind of contract language subject to wildly differing interpretations. Bellows still recoiled at the phrase Justice lawyers reserve for such a calamity. They refer to it as "road kill," a courtroom analogy to a speeding tractor trailer disposing of a raccoon or other wildlife unfortunate enough to stray under its wheels.

In Bernie Zettl's case, the government got sucked into endless squabbles over the subject matter of classified documents, and whether their contents could or should be made public for a trial. Bellows needed a short cut around such unproductive arguments. He set a grueling pace—working fifty-four consecutive days in one stretch, including Thanksgiving—searching for a pared-down, manageable strategy. Forget about past mistakes, Bellows kept telling the fatigued agents helping him. This time, prosecutors weren't going to be outgunned. They weren't going to be caught flat-footed by defense witnesses who had greater expertise in the Pentagon's procurement maze.

From the start, Bellows's team assumed that Fowler and Boeing would rely on the most obvious defense: They would claim that every big company in the industry obtained the same type of classified documents. The argument had a certain amount of jury appeal. But it wouldn't fly if the government was able to show—beyond a reasonable doubt—that Fowler sidestepped or habitually disregarded commonly accepted security rules. Then it would be irrelevant to consider what information other companies secured. Fowler's attempts to hide his violations would be enough to demonstrate criminal intent. And, by inference, his actions would indicate Boeing's culpability.

Bellows hit upon a surprisingly powerful notion. He wasn't concerned in the least about the substance of the documents, or trying to unravel circumstances surrounding the award of specific contracts. Those issues would unduly complicate his job. He also didn't want to get bogged down using espionage laws. Instead, Bellows told agents to begin assembling evidence to prove a single point: that Fowler and Boeing acquired and maneuvered classified documents contrary to lawful procedures. He would go after them for failing to have mandatory receipts, for trading classified documents on street corners and out of car trunks. Using Boeing's detailed logs, combined with evidence already cataloged by the Pentagon, Bellows assured Hudson and the Defense Department's Costello that a bare-bones case would be ready to go in short order.

☆

Pentagon investigator Mathew Walinski, a burly former police lieutenant in Washington, D.C., badly needed the morale boost. He had spent the last three years dogging Fowler's footsteps, without seeing his quarry brought to justice. The Justice Department's on-again, off-again investigation frustrated Walinski, and the lackadaisical attitude of previous prosecutors infuriated him before Costello jumped into the fray. On bad days, Walinski felt he was becoming a laughingstock in the law-enforcement community. For the tough-talking ex-cop, who inherited the muscles and the pride of his ironworker father while growing up in rural northern Michigan, that was not a comfortable feeling.

Fellow agents told him to forget the blasted document-swapping ring and get on with his life. "You're the only person in the Pentagon or the Justice Department convinced that what they're doing is a crime," he kept hearing.[58] Refusing to concede defeat, Walinski tried vainly to convince higher-ups to proceed with prosecutions. "Thievery is thievery," the obstinate investigator told skeptics long before Bellows ever took over. "They're stealing stuff from the government, and they know it's a violation. Let's get them for that."[59]

Walinski's perseverance sent shock waves through the "good old boy" network shielding Fowler. Frank Lozito of Honeywell, one of Fowler's closest associates, tried to be calm and noncommittal when poker-faced Pentagon agents showed up at his desk early one morning, without warning. Lozito already had chronic headaches from the stress of participating in the black market for Pentagon information. The agents peppered him with questions about document exchanges, but he pretended ignorance and denied supplying anyone with documents.[60]

Minutes after the interview ended, Lozito called Fowler in a near panic. "I've got to come talk to you, right now," Lozito said. They met around 9:45 A.M. on a busy street corner in Rosslyn, half a block from Boeing's high-rise offices. The discussion was apprehensive and rushed. Lozito said the network "was in a lot of trouble" because investigators were pushing hard, fishing for connections to Zettl and other industry figures. He was mighty worried, repeatedly warning his friend to be extra careful.[61]

Despite the snooping by government agents, Fowler seemed strangely unperturbed. "He was quiet. He stood there; I did all the talking," according to Lozito.[62] Fowler hadn't yet gotten his hush-hush warning, in the middle of the Tivoli restaurant, to start purging documents. Boeing's document wizard made it clear to Lozito that he had no intention of changing his mode of operation, because he didn't do business with Bernie Zettl or other consultants who traded information for a profit. Fowler still felt confident that Justice wouldn't prosecute anyone for document swapping unless money changed hands: "If a guy was dumb enough to buy or sell information," he said with a shrug, "the SOB *should* be prosecuted."[63]

The pressure on Fowler truly heated up after agents spotted one of his budget documents, sitting out in plain sight, at Boeing's Huntsville, Alabama, facility. Bearing the deceptively bland title "Program Element Description," the classified report was quite a catch. Exceeding one thousand pages in the full version, it summarized the status of every research and acquisition program funded by the Air Force. The document had been left carelessly on a desk, unattended and without proper security safeguards. The inspectors noticed it through sheer coincidence, as they passed through the complex to do a seasonal audit. Once they examined the pages, agents demanded an explanation of how it was acquired in the first place. Walinski was itching to grill Fowler face to face. But his lawyers said their client wanted protection from prosecution. Fowler, in effect, was asking for a blanket grant of immunity covering all the documents he had bagged before agreeing to sit down for any interviews.

"He wanted to walk away without any liability; he was looking for a hundred percent free ride," Walinski recalls.[64] The government summarily rejected that idea. So, Walinski did the next best thing to confronting Fowler: He ratcheted up pressure on Fowler's employer.

For the first time, outsiders were able to see the full gamut of Boeing's information system. The company was forced to turn over the weekly "Activity Reports" Fowler supplied to his superiors. The reports consisted of long, verbatim excerpts of classified material Fowler got his hands on, but with all security markings and official stamps removed. Many of the reports were sent to the Seattle area without the minimal precaution of using registered mail. Others were transmitted by telecopiers, using regular commercial phone lines that were vulnerable to eavesdropping. Such blatant security violations enraged Walinski and the other agents. They concluded that Dick Fowler, without the government's knowledge or approval, had taken it upon himself to declassify virtually truckloads of budget and program information. He was accused of disseminating the data throughout the company, as though it was his own analysis.

Fowler had a rather convoluted response, one that even Boeing couldn't endorse wholeheartedly. He claimed that most of the suspect material was classified for political reasons, not out of legitimate national security concerns. In any event, he argued, classifying a document didn't automatically make every line on every single page classified. According to Fowler's explanations, the "Activity Reports" he prepared didn't compromise Pentagon security one whit because he left out those paragraphs or phrases that he knew were sensitive and therefore deserved to be classified.[65]

Fowler also kept asserting that high-ranking Boeing managers, who read his summaries voraciously year after year, never raised a red flag or asked him to justify his conduct because the rules were fuzzy. They saw nothing wrong, he said, since Boeing and the Pentagon "were out to achieve the same goals" of protecting national security.[66]

Starting with Ben Plymale, Fowler reminded friends, company executives had assured him that the government didn't care much about proper receipts. Furthermore, Fowler maintained that the company's top security watchdogs years ago informed him that the government specifically wanted contractors to have the documents: "Boeing officials knew what I was doing; I didn't try to hide it. Hell, I briefed many of them myself."[67] The bottom line, Fowler insisted, was simple. "There wasn't anyone I dealt with who didn't know what I was doing. Period."[68]

The security clerk who logged in most of the documents later corroborated the gist of his story. Debra Null said she couldn't fathom why prosecutors were after her former boss. She insisted that the activities in the Rosslyn office had been sanctioned by company and Pentagon security officials. "Boeing was supposed to have the documents," she recalled being told by her superiors, "and Fowler's job was to bring them in." Null also told investigators that Pentagon inspectors understood there were no receipts in the files for much of the material, yet they implicitly approved the practice by not prohibiting her from receiving any more.[69]

But Walinski and his teammates wouldn't be sidetracked. They were convinced that such explanations were phony, dreamed up after the fact to confuse prosecutors. With moral indignation swelling, the investigators remained certain that Fowler was the best wedge to crack open the Clique's mysteries.

Recognizing the gravity of the allegations involving Fowler, Boeing's lawyers and security experts meanwhile had completed their own inquiry. Fowler had no choice but to talk to them. He provided the name of one of his suppliers of information, a civilian working in the Air Force's research shop who had passed him the document that raised the ruckus in Huntsville. The individual no longer worked for the government. Boeing's security chief assured Fowler that naming the person wouldn't harm anyone, though it might get the government off the company's back. "All the feds want to do is plug the leak," Fowler was told. "If the guy is retired, that's perfect. The case is closed."[70]

That's not exactly how it wound up. Bob Green, the source Fowler grudgingly identified, was flabbergasted at being fingered by a former Air Force colleague. The day Fowler broke the news to him over lunch, Green went into a funk: He would have to hire an attorney; his name would be dragged through the mud; prosecutors could come down hard on him. Fowler gasped at the hurt and disappointment he glimpsed in his old friend's eyes. A solid, although unspoken, promise had been broken. "I watched the devastated look on his face, and I thought: Jesus Christ, I'm responsible."[71] At that instant, Fowler made a solemn pledge to himself. None of his other sources would ever be subjected to such agony if he could prevent it. Green avoided any punishment, according to Pentagon records. But Fowler, adamant about protecting his friends, vowed to withhold the names of all the others who supplied him with information stretching back to the 1970s. If keeping silent meant bucking investigators and going to jail, he was ready for anything the government threw at him.

The crackdown turned Fowler's world upside down. As the investigation dragged on, he became preoccupied and withdrawn. He lost weight and developed a painful skin condition from the tension. Friends and family harangued him to cooperate with investigators and divulge the names of his sources, though it was to no avail. The scars of the ordeal, like those cut into his palms when he clung to the wreckage of the B-29 in wartime, never left him. "It was like a low rumble," says Tony Asterita, a longtime friend.[72]

Investigators got into the habit of making unannounced visits to Boeing's Rosslyn office. Boeing called in first-rate legal talent for advice, and that was what really convinced Walinski he was getting close to pay dirt. Top-notch agents have an intuitive feel for hints dropped by defense counsel, and Matt Walinski was no exception. His antennas were twitching feverishly.

Typically, disputes over a company's handling of classified documents are relegated to junior attorneys; the cases are viewed as humdrum, and almost without fail they tend to be resolved administratively. That definitely wasn't Boeing's approach. The first time Walinski and a fellow agent visited the firm's Virginia offices, a trio of high-priced criminal defense lawyers rushed to meet with them. "We hadn't even gotten our coffee, and three lawyers from downtown Washington popped in the door," Walinski recalls. They were falling over each other to make employees available, to set up interviews. Long-winded explanations were offered before questions were asked. Walinski grew increasingly suspicious. "I said to myself: Wait just a minute. How did they get here so fast? If the company hasn't done anything out of the ordinary, why are these guys, wearing two-thousand-dollar suits and each making half a million bucks a year, telling me there's absolutely nothing wrong?"[73]

The Air Force also reacted in uncharacteristic fashion. When Walinski briefed Air Force brass about Fowler, he didn't pull any punches. The agent laid out how Fowler prowled the Pentagon's fourth floor, ducking into Air Force offices uninvited, conversing with friends and often leafing through classified documents on a whim. Walinski returned for followup interviews a few days later. Miraculously, that whole section of the Pentagon had become extremely security conscious. Overnight, conspicuous signs appeared on the floor occupied by the Air Force's research organization. Hand-lettered warnings facing the corridor, taped on the door of every office in a variety of colors and sizes, declared the same thing: "No Contractors Allowed Inside." Air Force personnel started checking the passes of outsiders, requiring them for the first time to sign visitors' logs. Hundreds of industry marketing representatives lost easy access to Air Force research offices when their building passes were revoked.[74]

In June 1986, nine months after Zettl's indictment rocked the Clique and put Boeing on notice about potential criminal charges, Fowler's security clearance was suspended. Desperate to impress Boeing's management that he could still do great things, he kept seeking hot data.[75] Fowler had faith that Boeing would stand by him, too. Several weeks after the suspension, the company flew Fowler back to Seattle for a banquet honoring him as "Marketing Employee of the Quarter" for the aerospace unit. The letter accompanying the award trumpeted: "Your contributions are appreciated." Fowler's boss, Paul Demetriades, added plaudits of his own. Don't fret about the investigation, he reassured the veteran analyst in a telephone call before the ceremony. "You will be just as valuable to Boeing without a security clearance as with one."[76]

Fowler didn't realize it, but his days at Boeing were practically over. Boeing didn't realize it either, but its ballyhooed corporate image—a reputation for integrity combined with technical excellence envied by the rest of the industry—was about to take a hit. The company had managed to evade punishment for Plymale's boneheaded coverup of the MX affair, and it wasn't charged for questionable severance packages provided to retiring executives going into the government. Ultimately, Boeing also would escape largely unscathed from its involvement with Mel Paisley and the sordid deals brought to light by Illwind.

However, the contractor wouldn't be that fortunate this time. Prosecutors and agents pursuing Boeing's handling of classified documents weren't relying on circumstantial evidence or second-hand witnesses. They had the firm's own logs to buttress their case. They had Fowler's buddies prepped to expose violations under oath. Undeniably, Walinski and Bellows were trying harder. They were committed to getting maximum mileage out of their evidence and legal theories, as a way to compensate for earlier government inquiries that didn't pan out. Significantly, the two bullheaded, relentless investigators had a very personal stake in destroying the Clique. The pair meshed so well partly because they viewed their undertaking as more than a criminal investigation: It became an emotional cause for both of them. Each man, to some degree, longed for vindication. Going after a target such as Boeing would help make up for the mistakes and the ridicule they had endured in the past.

Fowler's fate was sealed during the very first briefing Bellows received from his team of agents. The day happened to be Walinski's thirty-ninth birthday. The investigator was so eager to convince a prosecutor to run with the case that he brought along his own set of flip charts. The visual aids and the rest of the presentation, which lasted several hours, urged prosecution of both Boeing and Fowler. The enthusiasm rubbed off on Bellows. He gave Walinski the best birthday present imaginable: After listening intently to the evidence, the prosecutor leaned back in his chair with a triumphant gleam in his eye. He was almost licking his lips. "Yeah, this is a great case," Bellows declared. "Why wasn't it filed before?"[77]

Five of the nation's top ten contractors eventually confirmed that assessment by pleading guilty to charges of illegally amassing Pentagon secrets.

Chapter VIII

OPERATION UNCOVER

Richard Lee Fowler's last day at Boeing was a peculiar, almost sur-realistic affair. Returning to work from a two-week vacation in the fall of 1986, Fowler was sipping his Monday-morning coffee and still trying to clear his head when the phone rang. Marshall Heard, his boss and the senior Boeing aerospace official in the Rosslyn office, wanted to discuss something immediately. Fowler got along well with Heard, appreciating his encouragement over the rough stretch of the past few months. Fowler recalls Heard, a cynical old Washington hand, predict-ing that the document-swapping controversy would blow over soon. The company's harshest punishment, he surmised, was likely to be suspending Fowler for a couple of weeks without pay. After all, Heard reminded his subordinate, wasn't that how Boeing had treated most of those responsible for the 1978 MX missile caper? Surely, he kept saying, Fowler's behavior didn't merit worse punishment.[1]

Fowler didn't mind walking down the hall to see Heard; he could use an-other upbeat chat. But his mood changed as soon as he noticed the sour look on the boss's face. "It's much worse than I thought," Heard muttered, turning the meeting over to a personnel manager who had flown in to take care of the matter. The visitor unceremoniously laid down the edict from headquarters: For refusing to divulge his sources and transmitting classified information in unclassified reports, Fowler had to go. "We don't want you on the premises," the emissary from Seattle said. Fowler was given until 5:00 P.M. to clean out his drawers, pack up his personal be-longings and clear out of his corner office overlooking the Potomac.[2]

The tension was eased by Marsh Heard's sympathetic comments. He commended Fowler for his past performance, adding that others in the company "share my opinion and respect for your work."[3] Two days later, Fowler received a telegram at his house signed by Heard and eight other former coworkers in Rosslyn. "Dick, we will always remember you," it said, "as a dedicated employee and a trusted friend. We will arrange for lunch with you ASAP." Shortly thereafter, the group pre-sented Fowler with a silver mug, inscribed with his name and dates of employment. Retirees received the same gift when they left Boeing. It hardly seemed like the sendoff for someone accused of lying and violat-ing the company's trust. Fowler's response was just as incongruous. On his dismissal form, he put down only one sentence: In neat, crisp letters, he declared, "It has been a great 8.5 years working for this fine company."[4]

Expressions of mutual high esteem, however, couldn't disguise the reality of what had occurred: Boeing had summarily fired one of its most experienced and popular marketing officials—a model employee, according to many who worked with him—to try to defuse a looming corporate scandal. Walinski and other federal agents were hot on Dick Fowler's heels, and Boeing desperately wanted to distance itself from him.

Barely a few months earlier, company officials had written letters to the Department of Defense strenuously defending Fowler's pursuits. At that time, Boeing made it seem as though *it* was the aggrieved party, rather than the government. John Clark, Boeing's security chief, indignantly told Pentagon officials that the contractor had a "legitimate need" to know future funding and weapons requirements. He offered no regrets or apologies. Corporate access to the long-range, classified budget documents Fowler obtained, Clark asserted at that point, was "in the government's interest" because it ensured that industry would be "prepared technologically to meet DOD needs in a timely manner."[5] The company also had claimed that Pentagon officials "soundly exercised" their judgment by releasing the information.

The feisty words didn't last long. Boeing's tone changed dramatically as the investigation gained momentum and Pentagon agents continued digging for names. Boeing executives prodded Fowler to talk, suggesting that cooperation was the best way to protect himself and the company. He gave a stock answer to all such entreaties: "If you're in trouble, why pull someone else in with you?"[6] Fowler insisted that he wasn't willing to turn his back on "the good, loyal, patriotic government officials who assisted me in doing the job I was hired to do."[7]

The situation made Boeing's lawyers nervous, especially since some congressional committees were monitoring the case with great interest. Eventually, Fowler's intransigence made the company's lawyers and officers furious. It was time to cut him loose, or risk losing Pentagon business. So Boeing decided to appease investigators. It would try to portray Fowler as a pariah and attempt to place the blame for the entire mess on his head.

Management worried sufficiently about Fowler's reaction to his firing to post a security guard in a nearby office, in case he became agitated. Though amazed by the sudden dismissal, Fowler stayed calm. He didn't waver in his allegiance to Boeing, understanding from the beginning that employees were expendable and that the company's paramount concern was protecting its bottom line. There were no recriminations or outbursts. He shook hands amicably with Heard and a group of others. A janitor agreed to pack up the collection of industry coffee mugs that lined his shelves. A little after 2:00 P.M. on September 8, 1986, Dick Fowler walked out of Boeing's office on Wilson Boulevard, in the midst of suburban

Rosslyn's high-rise bustle, for the final time. He drove home to tell his wife the news.

Fowler holed up in his house for months, trying to cope with the aftershocks of his firing. After working thirty-plus years in the military and another eight for Boeing, he waited for Pentagon and industry associates to rally around him. The support never came. What Fowler sensed, instead, was that government investigators were bearing down as never before. They combed through records at his golf club, hoping to find the names of sources buried in a receipt for some long-forgotten foursome.

When that drew a blank, the government switched to more aggressive techniques. For months, agents surreptitiously recorded every phone number Fowler dialed from his home. There weren't any wiretaps on Fowler's telephone lines, such as those approved by federal judges in Illwind. Prosecutors didn't capture his actual phone conversations on tape. By using a so-called pen register on his receiver, however, the government hoped to find a pattern of calls that would point to Fowler's sources in the Pentagon. Investigators thought he would be scared and upset enough to try to contact some of those individuals, or that they might call him. Then the Justice Department would be able to trace the phone numbers and break the case wide open.[8]

That tactic, too, failed to pierce Fowler's wall of silence. He was nothing if not stubborn, and already the Clique had withstood a barrage of government moves to infiltrate it. Years before, investigators had persuaded a veteran consultant—who dealt with Fowler and Bernie Zettl, among many others—to go undercover. William Kasper, the well-connected industry figure, was enlisted to eavesdrop on the Clique around the time Zettl's prosecution was on the front burner. The government had high expectations for his assistance.

Kasper appeared to be tailor-made for the role of informer. A retired Army officer who counted General Dynamics, IBM, Honeywell, Sanders and several more companies among his clients, he was one of the defense community's most active and sly information gatherers. During twenty years in the business, he perfected an assortment of tricks to keep documents in circulation. But, as a born-again Christian determined to stay out of jail at any cost, Kasper evolved into a compliant witness. He didn't clam up or try to bluff his way out of trouble. When investigators demanded to know how he got hold of classified documents, Bill Kasper readily acknowledged violating security rules. He reeled off the names of people he dealt with, including Fowler. "Like most of the rest of us," he told investigators, "Dick did a lot of leg work" to round up information.[9] According to Kasper, the market for contraband documents thrived for one basic reason: Boeing and the other companies were impatient. They expected instant access to the latest budget details. "You don't stay in business very long without timely information," he cracked.[10]

Kasper wasn't part of the Clique's inner circle because he was an independent agent peddling his wares to anyone willing to pay the price. Also, he really couldn't claim any valuable sources inside the Pentagon. His documents came primarily from contacts at defense firms. In spite of his shortcomings, Kasper was outrageously successful. He built a lucrative consulting practice, pocketing thirty thousand or forty thousand dollars annually from some clients for serving as a repository for bootlegged Pentagon data.

Bill Kasper procured and sold an "astounding volume" of information, seemingly without pause, according to one of his clients. He trafficked in documents from all of the services "without fancy DOD packaging and without restrictive markings," this satisfied customer told prosecutors.[11] Moreover, Kasper didn't blink at using secrets obtained from one firm to land a consulting contract with the firm's archrival. As a matter of fact, usually he tried peddling the same piece of information to several contractors simultaneously. That was the answer, after all, to every consultant's dream: minimizing effort while maximizing profit.

Through Kasper, investigators began to fathom the breadth and duplicity of the information-sharing network. As a consultant to IBM's defense operations, for instance, Kasper was hired to provide "unclassified briefings" on budget issues. That was what his contract called for, and that was the language IBM officials could point to if Walinski or other investigators decided to start snooping around. IBM was "protective of its squeaky clean public image," one former marketing man recalls. Company executives, he says, feigned horror at breaking security rules. Therefore, Kasper and others were "strongly discouraged from bringing unauthorized documents" into the company's facilities.[12]

As with many aspects of the defense industry, though, Kasper's work for IBM and other firms wasn't nearly that straightforward. The consultant rented a high-rise apartment in Crystal City, virtually around the corner from the offices of IBM's Federal Systems Division. He stashed illicit Pentagon documents there. IBM marketing managers didn't want to risk storing such classified papers in their offices, but they still desired easy access to the information. If an internal report or memo needed to be completed quickly, prosecutors were told, IBM's crew would stroll over to Kasper's apartment. The reference material they needed was removed from one of the safes. And within a few minutes, IBM officials would be taking copious notes from Kasper's illegitimate stockpile of Pentagon secrets.[13]

IBM learned other lessons from the slippery Kasper. One of the company's senior marketing executives used to call on various large contractors once or twice a year, seeking permission to read and take notes from their store of classified documents. IBM thereby got the benefit of the Clique's information flow, without any of the attendant dangers. Why did his hosts almost always comply? Each firm received a copy of a position paper, written and elaborately researched by IBM's own staff, evaluating the latest wrinkles in Pentagon planning procedures. That was the compensation for opening their files. In industry circles, these periodic IBM updates were regarded as *the* authoritative explanation of changes in military budgeting, explains one former IBM official.[14]

When Kasper wanted to retire, he offered to turn over his consulting firm to Fowler. "I know you could take care of the business," Kasper told him, "as long as my seven current customers stay under contract."[15] In exchange for transforming Fowler into an entrepreneur, Kasper reportedly wanted a 10 percent cut of all future revenue. The proposal got a glacial reception, and the deal never went anywhere. Later, as the investigation expanded, Kasper tried to ingratiate himself again with Fowler's brotherhood of marketing officials. Only this time, he was being coached by federal agents. With investigators planning to tape his conversations, Kasper was told to chat up his contacts and solicit business as usual.

The maneuver came too late. Amid all the publicity prompted by the government's crackdown on insider information, the industry grew paranoid. Rumors about undercover operatives and federal "moles" were rife. Potential snitches were seen everywhere. The word had gone out to members of the Clique: "Whatever you're doing with Kasper, stop," an associate remembers being told. "Don't deal with him."[16]

Bill Kasper's chameleonlike personality added to the government's problems. Unbeknownst to prosecutors, he shamelessly tipped off some industry pals, warning them that discussions with him were being preserved for posterity. Paul Blumhardt of Martin Marietta, for one, recalls a parking lot get-together as early as the spring of 1984, at which Kasper revealed his dual role and the focus of the continuing federal investigation.[17] Prosecutors still ended up getting a few leads from the tape Kasper made, though the conversation was less illuminating than expected.

Unperturbed, prosecutor Bellows had more weapons in his arsenal. In addition to Kasper, dozens of officials from other firms were hoping to escape prosecution by lining up to help investigators. For the same self-serving reason, many current and former Boeing employees tried to elbow each other aside to sit down for interviews with investigators. In return for grants of immunity from prosecution, the witnesses promised to supply a gusher of evidence against Fowler.

The decision to rely first on Kasper, and then on statements of other cooperating witnesses, was influenced heavily by two factors: Illwind's extraordinary success going up the chain to penetrate corporate misdeeds and Randy Bellows's friendship with Joe Aronica, the assistant U.S. attorney who fine-tuned those tactics. Even the most rudimentary description of Illwind demonstrated, beyond a shadow of doubt, the importance of devising a strategy to use lower-tier figures to trap primary conspirators.

Based on appearance and conduct, the prosecutors were the unlikeliest of confidants. Bellows was the chubby and introverted one. Self-conscious and unfailingly courteous, he rarely let his anger show, frequently masking his intensity with self-deprecating humor. Aronica displayed the opposite traits. Lean, mean and extroverted, his hair-trigger temper was feared throughout the Justice Department. So was his huge ego, which wasn't tempered by jokes or social polish. Each man was too proud, and too in-dependent, to collaborate comfortably on cases. Their vanity wouldn't al-low it. "We both want to be the chief, not the one following somebody else's orders," Bellows admits.[18]

Nevertheless, the pair overcame differences to build a solid friendship. Both worked crazy hours, staying late into the night and studying endless stacks of grand jury transcripts on weekends. Since they had offices next door to each other, the prosecutors often tried to unwind by sinking into the nearest chairs and engaging in legal small talk. In hindsight, Randy Bellows plays down that cross-fertilization. The two investigations, in fact, didn't overlap; there were no common targets. But at the same time, with the less experienced Bellows trying to kick-start an investigation botched by those who had preceded him, Aronica's track record was self-evident. Ill-wind proved the value of avoiding trials, if possible, and ensuring the co-operation of prospective defendants.

By this time, Dick Fowler had become an outcast in the industry he idolized. Sixty-one years old and without a college education, Fowler had no job or career prospects. Somehow he could rationalize being aban-doned by Boeing, but it was harder to swallow rejection by friends. After the farewell gift from his office, the anticipated messages of solidarity didn't materialize. Except for one or two individuals, the members of the fraternity ostracized him. They didn't even call to invite him out for an occasional lunch or other innocent social event. Out of fear and self-preservation, his sources decided it was extremely dangerous to keep in touch with Fowler. They were "smart enough to just stay away," he said years later. "They didn't know what to say."[19]

The fact that he had sacrificed so much to protect his friends made their silence doubly painful. "I never got a thank-you card or a telephone call, not a single one," Fowler recalls, from the people he shielded during all those months. "Nobody wanted to be guilty by association."[20]

Boeing continued to pay Fowler's sixty-dollar-a-week pension and agreed to cover his legal fees, though that hardly eased the emotional trauma. Meanwhile, the financial burden of being unemployed eroded Fowler's loyalty to Boeing. He was obsessed with the same set of ques-tions, throwing them at family and friends whenever they happened to be within earshot: Why was he the lone company official fired? If Boeing really wanted to go after employees who had participated in gathering documents, he insisted, there were plenty of others who deserved punish-ment. In his fulminations, Fowler went so far as to assert that fairness required management "to fire every marketing representative in the country, from Albuquerque to Boston."[21]

A former Air Force buddy finally came to the rescue, seeking out Fowler for a marketing job with a computer rental company in Virginia.

The pay was good, Fowler could set his own schedule and sales were climbing, despite his scant contribution to the firm. Fowler stuck with it for roughly a year, but then he could no longer stomach the idea of living off a friend's pity. After resigning, he went to work as the head cashier at a men's discount clothing store. The manager took a fancy to the taciturn former aviator, and Fowler felt less out of place. The cashier's job gave Fowler a steady paycheck and a welcome sense of belonging, while behind the scenes investigators pressured one former associate after another to turn against him.

Witnesses kept coming forward with stories of shadowy documents and sub rosa libraries used by the Clique. They talked about frantically covering the windows and fumbling to lock the doors of corporate copying rooms to prevent detection by unsuspecting employees or security guards. In a pinch, armloads of classified papers plainly stamped SECRET were taken to commercial copying centers in spite of the risks; anxious executives paid with wads of cash to avoid leaving a trail. Sometimes, special courier passes were used to avoid inspection of packages by corporate security guards.

Getting rid of incriminating files frequently was the most difficult hurdle of all. At Martin Marietta, legitimate and "black market" documents were bundled together for shredding to mislead security personnel.[22] One veteran Hughes official nearly gave in to hysteria when his automobile—in reality, a portable classified library for which he certainly had no authority or conceivable justification—was involved in a traffic accident near Los Angeles. (He was lucky that a curious police officer didn't sneak a look in the trunk.) Another Hughes marketing analyst tossed batches of classified papers into a giant vat of swirling acid to make sure they were destroyed.[23]

Boeing's transgressions were equally serious. Little by little, as Fowler's one-time conspirators recounted these and other anecdotes, the truth about the company emerged: Its hunger for inside Pentagon information was unrestrained. Bellows and Walinski, for their part, began to sketch a portrait of the renowned airplane-maker no outsider had ever glimpsed. What they saw contradicted the law-abiding, model-citizen image the company's executives assiduously tried to project. Breaking security rules, the government discovered, had been ingrained in Boeing's leadership for as long as almost anyone could remember. The skeletons in its closet turned out to be legion.

☆

Gloria Mahaffey and her shoebox stuffed with names made a big contribution to Boeing's eventual undoing. Bellows and his team barely could contain their glee as they followed the twists and turns of her amazing tale.

A faithful employee whose tenure with the company stretched back nearly to World War II, Mahaffey personified Boeing's implacable drive to collect information—even if it meant violating the law. Twenty-six when she joined Boeing, she toiled away at a succession of secretarial jobs until the early 1970s. At that point, Mahaffey told investigators, she was recruited to help set up the company's illicit library. That was the era when Ben Plymale was riding high as marketing manager for the company's aerospace unit. Two of his assistants helped secure the initial documents and organized the storage system.[24] They patronizingly told Mahaffey the Pentagon passed out the material "to give certain companies an edge in gaining contracts."[25]

Located on the second floor of a steel-and-glass building in Boeing's sprawling administration and research complex in Kent, Washington, the marketing library looked as bland as the surrounding office suites. It was in a bay separated from the larger, legitimate Boeing Technical Library and an adjacent congressional reference room. No special entrance, guards, or other telltale security devices hinted at what went on inside. The "Classified Reading Room," as Boeing insiders referred to Mahaffey's operation, was furnished sparsely. It contained a nondescript table and several chairs. From the outside, it seemed perfectly routine.

Five or six roomy file cabinets with built-in combination locks made up Gloria Mahaffey's domain, and she periodically went through the drawers to weed out old or no longer relevant files. She had an access list of executives who could drop by to read documents. The library's users, in Mahaffey's view, knew the origin of the information she supplied. The "appearance and content" of the materials, she acknowledged in retrospect, should have alerted everybody "that Boeing was not supposed to have them."[26] Even so, slapdash Pentagon inspectors never took the time to set foot in her territory to peruse the classified papers.

The reading room catered to what Mahaffey called "a very select group of marketing managers" and their top assistants, perhaps thirty executives altogether, who demanded the most up-to-date intelligence on Pentagon budgets.[27] She would alert them when documents came in. If her customers wished to take some of the documents back to their own offices, Mahaffey was eager to please. She obliged such requests by obliterating the SECRET markings stamped on the top and the bottom of each page—either by cutting them off or by covering them with strips of paper before making copies. "If a decision was being made" to fund or kill a multibillion-dollar program, she calmly explained much later, "you don't want yesterday's news" cluttering the files.[28]

Sometimes, Mahaffey's duties required extraordinary ingenuity. During her first years running the library, not all the material was entered into Boeing's logs. That created complications when the time came to make room for new documents. She had to spend tedious days burning tens of thousands of pages of outdated documents in the two fireplaces at her house. It was painstaking work, dropping the ill-gotten papers into the flames page by page as she had been instructed to do. Mahaffey repeatedly asked for help, imploring her boss, one of Plymale's intimates, to "take on some of the burden" because the effort was overwhelming her. She got a temporary respite, "but pretty soon I was back doing it all again."[29] The strain didn't ease until Boeing made the decision to log in everything as though it had been obtained properly. At that juncture, commercial destruction outfits took over the onerous task of disposing of unwanted documents.

Fowler would arrive at the Kent library every few months, often without warning, carrying two large briefcases crammed with classified papers, Mahaffey recalled.[30] He would help sort the documents that should be tossed out and replaced by the next batch. As the volume increased and the controversy over the bootlegged MX-basing memo flared up, Boeing's management became scared. She was told to close the library immediately and destroy everything. But Mahaffey, ever the resourceful guardian of Boeing's classified treasures, came up with a better plan. Rather than waste hard-to-replace information, she volunteered to pack up the files and take them home with her in a van.[31] For two weeks, she stayed out of the office. The four large crates sat in her recreation room out of harm's way, guarded by her dog. Then, without any explanation, Mahaffey's boss gave her the word that the danger had passed. "I was called and told to come back to work and open up shop again."[32] Boeing's pursuit of documents became more feverish after her return.

Mahaffey retired in 1983, but she didn't leave empty-handed. Guessing that Fowler's activities eventually could get her and the company into hot water, she took with her a fairly inclusive list of the executives who had used the library. "I just knew somebody was going to get into trouble" over Boeing's document practices, she confided to investigators years later. "I knew the records for all the Fowler stuff would prove to be important."[33] The evidence she squirreled away was intended to be her legal lifeline: It would provide her surefire protection from prosecution. Mahaffey stuck the records in a shoebox and left them on a back shelf of her garage for six years. But she remembered to pull out her trump card when Bellows and Walinski came calling.

"She was a smart lady; she had the valid books," Walinski notes. Mahaffey's intuition proved astute in another respect. She bet correctly that the government would jump at the opportunity to cut a deal with her to get the list of names. Whatever happened, Walinski says almost admiringly, "She knew she wasn't going to take the fall" for Boeing's criminal behavior.[34]

Fowler had assured Boeing that few, if any, of the classified documents he acquired ended up in the possession of other companies. As Bellows and Walinski interviewed officials from other contractors, they quickly realized that wasn't accurate. There were a number of "good old boy" networks, instead of a single, all-powerful ring. The groups had overlapping members, and many times they hunted for the same documents. The information sharing was truly national in scope. Documents traveled quickly from the East Coast to the West Coast, passing through a variety of intermediaries and companies—frequently without the first person ever knowing the identity of individuals at the opposite end.

For example, Fowler claims he shared information with Austen Watson of Singer, Paisley's close friend, on the lush greens of Bethesda's Congressional Country Club, northwest of the capital. As a subcontractor with a stake in many programs, Singer could use all the documents it could get. "He was a super guy. If Austen asked me for something and I had it," Fowler recalls, the answer invariably was," 'Sure, I'll get that for you.' "[35] Besides Singer, many other companies shared in Fowler's generosity. Some of them, in turn, passed along chunks of their ill-gotten data to independent consultants. If Kasper or other freelancers got copies of a document, there was no telling how many more firms they would sell it to.

Traveling across the continent with freshly acquired documents in his bag, one Hughes executive contemplated the weird circumstances of his job. "I wonder where the stuff came from? And I wonder where it's finally going to end up," Max Franklin pondered one night, staring out the plane's windows.[36] The question tugged at him, though he knew the answer was out of his reach, like the twinkling lights of cities and highways passing far below the jet.

The glue binding the participants, though, tended to be the same at every location: an affinity among those doing the sharing. Frank Lozito, a retired Air Force lieutenant colonel who met Fowler some twenty-five years before the two of them became entangled in the criminal probe, illustrates how crucial friendships were in this subculture. When Lozito started working for Honeywell in the 1970s, intense pressure was put on him to round up classified material. In his periodic evaluations, he was ordered "to establish meaningful contacts with the Air Force."

Lozito knew that meant getting his hands on bootlegged memos and reports. He withstood the exhortations for a few years, until they became unbearable and the company threatened to withhold raises and promotions. The Reagan buildup prompted contractors to increase their intelligence gathering, and Honeywell coveted being in the forefront of that trend. Mulling over his plight, Lozito decided to approach his old chum, Dick Fowler, who had shared an office with him when they worked in the Pentagon. "I had to come up with something," Lozito recalled, so "I contacted Mr. Fowler and told him that I was desperately trying to get some budgetary data."[37]

The appeal worked like a charm. In less than a month, Fowler called back with good news. "I have something for you," he told his distressed friend.[38] Lozito drove to the street in front of Boeing's offices and parked at the curb. There was a bus stop nearby, and pedestrians were milling around. But the presence of strangers didn't stop Fowler from handing over a hefty Air Force document, which featured "descriptive summaries" of weapons programs. It was exactly what Lozito's bosses desired. The two men would use the same curbside procedure, in the heart of downtown Rosslyn during the day, to swap classified papers nearly once a month for the next few years.

"There were no formal ground rules," Lozito said later.[39] There weren't any logs to maintain, and the documents weren't enclosed in two sets of protective wrappings as required by law. "He was letting me have a document that I could make a copy from," and return it to Boeing as soon as possible, Lozito explained.[40] A grateful Honeywell secretary earned a tidy bunch of overtime checks duplicating the material late at night. Fowler himself didn't know, until years later, that some of the copies popped up throughout the industry.

Prosecutors uncovered additional clandestine exchanges between Fowler and his associates at other contractors. Like most large defense firms, Boeing swapped documents with its competitors out of necessity. Quite simply, there was no other method to ensure getting the most complete, up-to-the-minute set of Pentagon budget numbers. The documents had mind-numbing acronyms, foreign to all but the most knowledgeable military aficionados. Fowler and his cronies, by contrast, considered the papers a wellspring of critical information: PEDS stood for Program Element Descriptive Summaries; PDMs were Program Decision Memoranda, often signed directly by the secretary of defense, spelling out policy and allocation of funds; FYDP was the abbreviation for the all-important Five-Year Defense Program, issued three times annually, which summarized the overall resources budgeted by the Pentagon; and POM was shorthand for Program Objective Memorandum, which laid out the spending priorities for individual services. The secretary of defense and the service chiefs churned out several versions of these and related planning documents each year. The blizzard of papers didn't stop. New drafts replaced out-of-date drafts, and the budget projections changed from month to month.

No contractor, by itself, could possibly accumulate all of the permutations and backup documents for each of the services, no matter how hard it tried or how good its sources were. Boeing had the inside track for Air Force documents. Honeywell had the reputation of being closest to the Army. And General Dynamics was respected as the most dependable collector of Navy documents. Trading with fellow industry representatives, therefore, was the logical solution to fill gaps in a company's database.

Frank Caso of Hughes, regarded as one of the ablest at such trades, says that the information provided a semblance of continuity amid the ever-changing winds of Pentagon policy. "It was part of the psychology of the time," he asserts. "If a program wasn't included in the FYDP, it wasn't considered a solid program."[41] Another of Fowler's cohorts recalls, "You never had all the pieces. You constantly needed to keep fleshing out the picture."[42] Boeing thus gave up copies of classified material it already had in its grasp—though Fowler was reluctant to part with his most sensitive and current documents—for helpful bits of information the competition had managed to gather.

Phil Jackson of RCA, for instance, was intimately familiar with regulations to safeguard classified information. He had twenty-four years of service in the Air Force under his belt, followed by a three-year stint working at the secretive Arms Control and Disarmament Agency. As an intelligence analyst, he held the highest security clearance while in the government: He was cleared for "special compartment" programs, which required a codeword for access and were more restrictive than the average top-secret clearances. Bellows asked Jackson to explain why, soon after joining RCA in the late 1970s, he succumbed to the temptation of trading documents with Fowler. Jackson's response was unequivocal: RCA couldn't afford to stay out of the loop.

The seemingly endless hunt for better data had an exasperating side: It resembled a frenzied race to piece together a giant jigsaw puzzle, but one that shifted and changed shape unpredictably. A single Pentagon document, even if it happened to be extremely recent and detailed, wasn't a reliable basis for making management decisions. By matching pieces that were acquired from different sources and reflected varying stages of the budget cycle, Jackson and others tried to decipher the Pentagon's authentic commitment to any given project. They took soundings every few months. Each new analysis depended on having the full gamut of Pentagon budget numbers. The documents indicated "new opportunities" RCA might pursue by better targeting its research money or massaging its customers, Jackson told investigators. By the same token, he added, classified budget memos were essential to reveal "a weak program" that the company should abandon since it "might not survive in the government's decision process" anyway.[43]

Jackson, who had retired as a full colonel, wasn't picky about how he arrived at such insights. He knew full well that the Clique lived on the fringes of the law, recounting to prosecutors how Fowler consistently encouraged associates "to seek, acquire and develop their own, independent sources."[44] Boeing didn't insist on one-for-one document swaps, nor did other members of the Clique. Sharing documents with colleagues was a way of life, not a contest that needed to be scored week by week. Nonetheless, everyone had to contribute in order to enjoy the fruits of the arrangement. Every member was expected to serve up fresh information at some juncture.

There were times, Jackson said, when Fowler asked him to come to Boeing's offices but to use a side entrance, apparently to get around signing the visitors' log.[45] On other days, Boeing's man set up a rendezvous at a parking garage. The two would meet in the basement of Boeing's office building, where Fowler's full-size, maroon 1979 Chevrolet Caprice was parked. Fowler would reach into the trunk, Jackson recalled, take out a document and pass it over without a word. Jackson spotted additional copies of documents tossed into the car's spacious trunk, ready for distribution to officials from other companies.[46]

Investigators delved into one episode that epitomized Fowler's mastery at scooping up classified information. Jackson and Max Franklin, an industry friend who worked for Hughes and later for Martin Marietta, managed to snatch a hard-to-get portion of a classified Army spending plan. They had the section pertaining to research and development projects, and they were eager to show off their trophy to Fowler.[47] Franklin, especially, was enthusiastic about forging a closer alliance with Boeing. Inside Fowler's office, he took the fifty-page document out of his briefcase. This was a big deal, Franklin's smug smile broadcast. He proudly handed it to Fowler.

"That's very good," Fowler said, seemingly impressed by what he was reading. "I am glad you were able to get that," he told the two men. "Now, look what I have."[48] Reaching into a drawer, Dick Fowler pulled out his own copy of the same section of the document. A few seconds later, he gingerly stacked several other sections of the report on top of his desk. He had a copy of the entire Army Program Objective memo, not just the small slice of it Jackson and Franklin had brought to him. The five or six volumes of classified papers Fowler gestured toward were piled two feet high. "I was astounded," Franklin later admitted.[49]

Fowler, Jackson and others talked quite openly about sharing information, alerting compatriots over the phone immediately after landing a particularly useful document. The discussions were casual, with little emotion or suspense in the air. No one felt the need to resort to any codes or mysterious vocabulary. However, asking about the original source was strictly taboo. The fraternity had a novel code of ethics, and such questions were deemed totally out of line. That was one of the reasons the Clique endured for so many years. "We did not nose into sources for other people," Jackson explained later. "It was not the gentlemanly thing to do."[50] Also, the credentials of the folks doing the swapping kept junior members of the Clique from raising many questions. Curiosity could prove embarrassing, and it could get someone into dreadful legal trouble. As a coconspirator from LTV put it, the hub of the network was made up of "West Point graduates, colonels in the Air Force, people who had been in Vietnam. I didn't question any of their integrity."[51]

In this stealthy world, Fowler took secrecy to the limit. Much of his work was done during leisurely lunches with Pentagon pals at Trader Vic's, Michelangelo, the Watergate Terrace and other posh Washington-area restaurants. In filling out his expense reports, though, he was adept at sidestepping the names of the guests. At most, he would identify them only as "industry officials" or mysterious representatives of the "executive branch." No matter how prosecutors pried, the expense vouchers yielded no clues about Fowler's sources.

The same innate caution marked the rest of his actions. Bellows suspected that right before routine document inspections were due to take place, Fowler conveniently arranged to have many of his files trucked away for destruction. Boeing insisted that the timing of the cleanups was utter coincidence, though precisely the same pattern was repeated nearly every six months. If questionable papers happened to be on the premises when Pentagon inspectors arrived at Boeing's front door, Fowler didn't worry. He knew from experience that the inspectors would be too trusting or harried to bother opening boxes slated to go to the shredder.[52]

Like clockwork, Fowler drove to Andrews Air Force Base and other defense facilities in the Virginia or Maryland suburbs every few days, submitting mileage reimbursement forms to the company. But always, he was careful not to let his guard down. To protect the identity of his sources, Fowler never jotted down the names of the officers or civilians he visited, not even as passing references in his personal notebooks. If Boeing officials inquired good-naturedly about the source of some unusually hot tip, Fowler bristled. With a withering glance, he would snap back: "That's none of your business." The company got only cryptic descriptions of the reasons for his local trips. Conscientious as always, Dick Fowler told his bosses the purpose was "data pickup" or "data delivery." For other drives, he put down "data review" or "data return."[53]

The notes tantalized investigators, without offering a shred of hard proof about the makeup of Dick Fowler's pipeline within the Air Force. As the months went by and a parade of witnesses testified in front of the grand jury, Bellows and Walinski felt stymied. They had more than ample evidence pinpointing the Clique's wrongdoing. Yet they had nothing but hunches and vague theories about the identity of Fowler's accomplices. Building a solid case against the leakers inside the Pentagon appeared awfully elusive.

Borrowing a phrase from the war against drugs, investigators stressed the importance of going after big-time suppliers rather than "the guys dealing on the street corner."[54] In line with this dictum, Bellows thought he could squeeze Fowler to cough up the names. The proposition was eminently logical, and investigators carried it out with exemplary dedication. By all accounts, it should have succeeded.

☆

The summer of 1989 was showdown time for Bellows and Fowler. After years of false starts and dead ends, the prosecutor recognized that the cat-and-mouse games had to stop. In the same way, Fowler realized that the time for posturing was over. For outsiders, though, there weren't any signs that the document-swapping investigation had reached a climax.

It was a typically hot summer. Haze shrouded the dome of the Capitol, and its cavernous hearing rooms remained dark and unused. Flotillas of pleasure craft puttered past the gray spires of Georgetown University and the Kennedy Center's festive promenade above the Potomac. The boats drifted downriver, toward the rich fishing areas and crabbing nooks of the Chesapeake Bay. As they did every August, Washington's prominent decision-makers fled the city for cooler vacation spots. Their subordinates from various government agencies weren't far behind. The summer doldrums enveloped the Pentagon as well. The collapse of the Berlin Wall prompted calls to slash U.S. defense spending. Illwind was chugging along at the same time, as investigators closed in on Bill Galvin and Mel Paisley. Notwithstanding such weighty concerns, the Pentagon stayed unusually tranquil. Its corridors were quiet, and the tempo inside many offices slowed noticeably. A generally relaxed atmosphere settled over the building.

Before vacation fever struck, Defense Secretary Dick Cheney had launched his long-delayed campaign to revamp weapons procurement. He wanted to create a leaner and more professional arms-buying organization. The much-ballyhooed effort—described by Cheney as "front and center on" President Bush's "list of priorities"—got off to a rocky start when it was unveiled in June. The "reforms" Cheney ended up announcing were notable mostly for their modesty. Put together partly by a team of advisers who had no intention of staying to carry them out, his game plan was fatally flawed.

Cheney's approach lacked urgency and focus. John Betti, the top acquisition official working for the secretary, blithely assumed that he would have up to a year to learn the ropes and get accustomed to the issues before having to make hard choices. That was wishful thinking. At the last moment, Cheney pulled back from ordering wholesale organizational changes or making deep personnel cutbacks. Carping that the defense chief was overly diffident toward the bureaucracy, critics demanded that he go further. Hobbled by opposition from military brass and miscalculations by his own management team, Cheney's "blueprint for cultural change" appeared to be stalled.[55]

But the turmoil facing the military somehow seemed to fade into the background, compared to the scenes of Washingtonians at play. August is the city's traditional season to rest and regroup, to take a welcome break from the feverish tempo of briefings, "talking points" and endless budget deliberations. As a former Republican congressman from Wyoming, Cheney was attuned to the rhythms of Washington's officialdom. True to his circumspect style, the secretary intended to use the month to weigh his options. He wanted to tinker with his reorganization plans. He planned to seek advice from management experts and rethink his next steps, before the hubbub of congressional debate resumed in the fall. Public opinion assumed that little Pentagon business was likely to get done in the interim.

Yet the mood in the U.S. attorney's office in Alexandria, less than a ten-minute drive from the Pentagon's massive riverfront entrances, couldn't have been more different. There was no hint of listlessness there, in spite of the steamy, ninety-degree days. It was all excitement and anticipation. Located on the fifth floor of a modern, red-brick office building in downtown Alexandria—where trendy stores, outdoor cafés and art galleries flank Revolutionary War houses along cobblestone streets—the place rippled with energy. Bellows and his team huddled in the conference room to plot strategy. Running out of time as well as patience, prosecutors and agents weren't holding anything back. Recreation was the last thing on their minds.

The urgency was almost palpable inside 1101 King Street. Apprehensive, Bellows munched on crackers, wolfed down candy bars and ate nearly anything else he could pop into his mouth. When a case reached a high level of intensity, Bellows literally locked himself in the office for days and had meals delivered to sustain him. His favorites weren't pizza or takeout Chinese food. Coworkers were taken aback by the packages of Kool-Aid and bags of prepared foods stacked next to Bellows's desk. The stash included Chef Boyardee spaghetti and tomato sauce, which the prosecutor fancied in a crunch. He devoured the pasta cold, straight out of the can. His office resembled a combination locker room and oversized pantry.

Behind his back, defense lawyers made fun of Bellows's indifference to routine grooming. They turned up their noses at his slept-in-looking shirts, which he often kept stacked on his bookshelves. They ridiculed his personal hygiene. "He was simply horrible," according to one lawyer. "He was a physically dirty person and absolutely unpleasant" to face across a negotiating table.[56] But, more than appearances, the nasty criticism really was a reaction to the strength of Bellows's convictions and his workaholic habits.

Walinski, meanwhile, hovered over computer printouts of document logs, nervously double- and triple-checking them for accuracy. He was available to respond in an instant, whenever Bellows raised a question or wondered aloud about some technicality. The anxiety reflected the difficult decisions ahead. There would be no room for slipups. The government had to file initial charges quickly, and do it with utmost precision, in order to demonstrate its resolve. Otherwise, there wouldn't be any followup cases. Bellows would throw away any chance of prosecuting Boeing or other major targets down the road.

The lead prosecutor was painfully aware that some who deserved punishment probably would escape anyway, no matter how well things jelled. Bellows knew that he lacked the manpower to take on every company and official at once. At Boeing alone, subpoenas had gone out seeking records from a dozen current and former executives. Simultaneously, prosecutors were sparring with defense lawyers from roughly forty other firms, many boasting more seasoned litigators and deeper pockets than the U.S. attorney's office. With investigative work in midstream, even one or two long trials could stretch the office's resources past the breaking point. If most of the contractors implicated in the probe chose to fight it out in the courtroom, government lawyers would get hopelessly bogged down. At the same time, Bellows didn't have the luxury of delaying his first prosecution until all of the grand jury testimony was finished and he had more ammunition. By then, the five-year statute of limitations would run out. "We had to do legal triage," he says. "We could have spent the whole time investigating Boeing, without getting to any of the other companies."[57]

The only sensible alternative was to begin with Fowler but keep chasing evidence against additional individuals and their employers. If the government assembled a convincing enough case against Fowler, Bellows predicted, then probably there would be a guilty plea. Hopefully, that would prompt others to start thinking in earnest about settlement negotiations. The prosecutor and his tireless sidekick, Matt Walinski, opted for one final gamble: a calculated, all-out push to try to threaten the Clique's kingpin into submission.

Fowler was presented with a stark choice indeed. If he admitted his transgressions and gave the grand jurors an unvarnished description of his criminal activities, he would face a maximum of fifteen years in prison. At sentencing, the court undoubtedly would give a great deal of weight to his cooperation. Most likely, he would receive substantially less than a year behind bars, with the rest of his sentence to be served in a halfway house or performing community work. The carrot dangled in front of Fowler was tempting. But if he refused to plead guilty and continued to shield his sources, investigators had a big stick in reserve. Bellows vowed to seek an indictment carrying penalties vastly more severe.

It didn't take long for the government's proposal to be rejected. Dick Fowler prided himself on never waffling on matters of principle. When an automobile dealer once refused to fix a problem on his teenage son's new car, Fowler took two days off work to picket the dealership. He called off a fancy, country-club wedding for one of his daughters at the last instant, after all the preparations had been made and the invitations had been mailed, because the groom dared to raise the subject of a prenuptial agreement. The offended father of the bride personally wrote to each disinvited guest, explaining why the celebration was canceled.[58] When it came to the Justice Department's offer of a plea agreement, the reaction again was vintage Fowler. He declared there would be no negotiations, period. He wouldn't listen to his friends or lawyers, who urged him at least to consider the idea.

"I know I make you mad," Fowler blurted out to a friend one day. "A lot of people don't understand, and I'm not asking that people understand. But if I talked, I wouldn't be able to face myself in the mirror."[59] Not even his wife of thirty-five years could sway him. "You got screwed" by Boeing and the government, Muriel Fowler told her husband afterward, blaming him for putting the family through hell. "And you didn't even get a kiss."[60]

Dick Fowler didn't flinch. On August 15, 1989, he was indicted on thirty-nine counts of conspiracy, fraud and illegal conversion of government property.

Bellows structured the indictment for maximum impact. It alleged improper handling of more than a hundred documents and accused Fowler of committing 380 distinct felonies in the process. There were juicy details of clandestine document drops; abuses of top-secret memos prepared by the White House; classified files turned to ashes in home fireplaces; and phantom logs maintained by some of the conspirators. Fowler faced at least three separate charges for handling the same piece of paper: obtaining it in the first place, using the mail or a courier to transport it to Boeing's headquarters on the West Coast and then illegally destroying it. The prosecutors' triple play would result in exponentially harsher punishment in the event of a guilty verdict. In the lingo of defense counsel, Fowler's exposure had rocketed to the stratosphere. Conviction on every charge meant up to 310 years in jail, plus the possibility of a $225,000 fine. Fowler was being squeezed by a master.

Mike Costello, the Pentagon investigator responsible for keeping the case alive, found other means to stoke public interest. He insisted on describing Fowler and his cohorts derisively as "the Gang of Twelve," referring to the number of big firms the government believed were in the loop. Later, Costello went even further. Without conferring with prosecutors, he dreamed up a catchy code name for the inquiry: "Operation Uncover." Bellows laughed out loud when he read the phrase for the first time in a newspaper article. He asked Pentagon agents why they wanted to use it. If the FBI has codewords for its most important operations, Defense Criminal Investigative Service agents replied in a huff, their probe of the Clique deserved the same respect. The publicity and the magnitude of the charges, Bellows reassured his team, were bound to cause Fowler to have second thoughts.

Dick Fowler still didn't fold. He told his lawyers to prepare for trial. Investigators underestimated Fowler's fidelity to those who had spurned him. They also guessed dead wrong about his response to escalating threats.

Once more, Bellows was forced to shift gears. Now, he hoped to use the pretrial preparations to scare other potential defendants. Using a portable computer on trips and working through weekends, he wrote legal briefs filled with evidence of Boeing's misdeeds. The most detailed filing was drafted during a nonstop week of effort on the Harvard campus. Bellows was a guest lecturer at the law school during the day, but after dealing with the students he retired to his room to toil over Fowler's case until dawn. "I was trying to educate the judge about the case" and the complexities of handling classified documents, Bellows says.[61] But the briefs also had a more subtle purpose. The information Bellows was able to place in the court record—more extensive than the typical filings before a trial—had two salient goals: It was designed to lay out the prosecution's case for the benefit of Fowler's attorneys, while impressing the legal team advising Boeing with the strength of the evidence gathered by the government.

Robert S. Bennett, Boeing's main outside counsel, tracked the prosecutor's feints with a wary eye. He and Bellows held preliminary discussions before Fowler's indictment, but both sides agreed to put the talks on hold pending the outcome of the pretrial maneuvers. Bennett could have insisted that the U.S. attorney's office make a quick decision about whether to charge the company. The posture would have been consistent with his reputation as one of Washington's sharpest and most pugnacious defense lawyers. Known for his booming baritone, Brooklyn accent and substantial girth, Bennett was a fierce battler whenever the facts or the law dictated. His youthful experiences as a boxing champion of the Flatbush Boys Club stood him in good stead. He excelled at legal counterpunching. If Bob Bennett accepted a case, regardless of how arduous or complicated it was, clients could depend on one thing: He would throw everything he had into the fight.

Famous for intimidating lawyers and even judges, Bennett earned the warmest praise from fellow practitioners. "If I were in trouble, I would like to have Bob represent me," confided John Dowd, a prominent defense attorney in his own right.[62] In fact, Bennett's record was nothing short of amazing: After handling hundreds of high-profile criminal cases, he had lost only two at trial. Countless other clients escaped criminal charges entirely, thanks to his advice. "You've got to stop indictments—that's the key," Bennett says, explaining why it's not always smart to antagonize the opposition. "You've got to remember the interest is the client. It's not for the world to say you're a great trial lawyer."[63]

By the late 1980s, "Bullet Bob"—a nickname Bennett picked up for bowling over players while huffing down the baseline in softball games—was near the top of a very short list of Washington's best white-collar defense lawyers. People called him "a lawyer's lawyer." He had the moves and the moxie to be recognized, perhaps in time, as indisputably *the* top defense attorney in town.[64] It wasn't just his legal skills clients wanted. "What I really enjoy is the application of law to a fast-moving situation. Law and politics. Law and public relations," he says.[65]

In addition to representing Boeing, Northrop, BDM and other defense firms, Bennett went on to investigate the "Keating Five" as a special counsel for the Senate Ethics Committee. He grilled five sitting senators accused of accepting contributions from convicted financier Charles H. Keating and protecting Keating's corrupt Lincoln Savings & Loan from federal regulators. The national television exposure further boosted his stature. On a flight back to Washington in the midst of the hearings, another passenger in the plane's first-class section greeted him effusively, calling him "Senator Bennett."[66]

Sterling political connections gave him extra firepower, in or out of the courtroom. To unwind, Bennett played poker with a gang of Washington luminaries including Supreme Court Justice Antonin Scalia and Chief Justice William Rehnquist. The fact that his politically conservative younger brother, Bill, had served as President Reagan's education secretary and President Bush's antidrug "czar" made him an even bigger force to reckon with. When attorney Robert Altman and former defense secretary Clark Clifford needed legal representation in the BCCI bank scandal, Bob Bennett got the call. Marge Schott, the owner of the Cincinnati Reds, looked to him to rescue her from a legal and public relations nightmare for making racist remarks. He also orchestrated Caspar Weinberger's hotly debated pardon for charges of lying to Congress and withholding evidence about the Iran-Contra affair. Leonard Garment, President Nixon's counsel, believes that in "a high-profile, rock-'em, sock-'em defense, there is nobody better to represent a public figure than Bob Bennett."[67]

Bennett's prowess hasn't been constrained by partisan labels. He was at the side of White House aide Harold Ickes, a member of the Clinton administration's brain trust, during the early stages of the Whitewater criminal probe. As the special prosecutor's investigation picked up steam, Bennett became a leader of the White House's outside defense strike force. Bill Clinton, for example, looked to Bennett to defend him in a lurid sexual harassment case filed in Little Rock, Arkansas, by a former state employee. In addition to Bennett's knowledge of criminal law, the president knew he would receive sage political and media relations advice.

During the same period, Bennett's firm also defended veteran Democratic representative Dan Rostenkowski, accused of kickbacks, embezzlement and bilking taxpayers of hundreds of thousands of dollars over a quarter of a century. The veteran Illinois lawmaker rejected his lawyer's advice to strike a plea bargain with prosecutors. Bennett warned it was a huge misstep and the two men parted company. Days after turning down a deal, Rostenkowski was hit with a broader-than-expected set of charges. He was indicted on seventeen felony counts for allegedly padding his congressional staff with phantom workers; pocketing tens of thousands of dollars intended to buy office stamps; obstructing justice; and misusing public funds to obtain cars, home repairs and merchandise while serving as chairman of the House Ways and Means Committee.

Renowned for his intellectual preparation, Bennett could be equally formidable making an emotional, gut-wrenching argument in the heat of a trial. He was never a natty dresser, preening in front of a jury like many of his brethren. For a gag at his fiftieth birthday party, his law partners dressed up as Bennett lookalikes—with shirttails out and food stains on their ties.[68] A few years later, one bemused writer described how his "blocky, laundry-bag appearance" is able to disarm judges and juries by producing "warm resonances" of the TV detective Columbo.[69] Still, Bennett's presence set him apart from would-be imitators. He came to be respected as the consummate legal warrior, cerebral and visceral by turns. Those who know him best swear that Bennett possesses an unerring instinct—a born gambler's intuition, they say—telling him when to negotiate instead of fight. Admirers call this gift his secret weapon. "When you do what I do," he says, "you are a kind of orchestra leader, bringing all the instruments together."

For most defense contractors, Bennett knew that battling in court was a no-win situation. "There is more incentive to plead guilty than to fight [an indictment] and win," he likes to say. "It's usually a better business decision. You must rise above principle."[70]

In the summer of 1989, Boeing's hired gun perceived that a conciliatory approach was best. Patience seemed to be the smartest course against Bellows and Walinski, Bennett deduced. If the Justice Department stumbled, for whatever reason, in prosecuting Fowler, the case against Boeing would come apart, too. Bennett proposed to postpone a resolution for three or four months. Bellows jumped at the delay. To indict Boeing while his prosecuting team was preparing for Fowler's trial would have been a horror show. So each side concentrated on figuring out its adversary's weaknesses.

Early on, Bennett decided to be cagey rather than ferocious. He toyed with the prosecution, pretending to be overwhelmed by the intricacies of the laws controlling classified documents. "Explain this to me again," he would say quietly to Bellows, playing the naive outsider. "I don't know exactly what we're doing here."[71] In short order, investigators saw through his act. They would receive tons of unimportant documents from Boeing, without ever hearing a peep from Bennett. But when an especially damaging memo had to be turned over to the government because it was covered by outstanding subpoenas, Boeing's lawyer was on the phone in an instant. "Well, Randy, we better talk about this," he offered.[72]

By the fall, Bennett was convinced that a corporate guilty plea was the optimum outcome. He persuaded Boeing's management to adopt his view. The evidence against Fowler, coupled with the likelihood that Gloria Mahaffey and others would take the stand to implicate higher-ranking company officials, made Bennett leery of going to trial. The risks of fighting Bellows were extraordinarily high, Bennett informed his client. There was a good chance the government would try to hit the firm with sweeping fraud and conspiracy allegations. He urged speedy action to try to narrow the scope of any charges, even before Fowler's case went before a jury. Boeing's in-house lawyers concurred, and settlement terms began taking shape.

Randy Bellows was sitting on a one-of-a-kind case, so he could afford to hang tough on some demands. At a minimum, the company had to admit that some of Fowler's past supervisors were aware that documents had been acquired and disseminated illegally. Bellows was determined to nail the parent Boeing Company, not one of its lesser-known units. And the prosecutor insisted that the firm make restitution for its misdeeds.

Even so, Bellows had supreme esteem for his antagonist. When word leaked out one weekend about the impending plea, the prosecutor and the defense lawyer worked the phones in tandem to squelch exaggerated rumors that might depress Boeing's stock the next Monday. The company's lawyer invited Bellows and Walinski to his office to work out settlement language. Bennett said he was too busy with another case to meet elsewhere. That was the first and only time in his career, Bellows recalled, that he didn't insist on defense counsel coming to Justice Department offices for such talks.[73]

Boeing had plenty of pragmatic reasons to shy away from a trial. First, if it managed to steer clear of an indictment, the company effectively could guarantee that none of its other current or former officials would be prosecuted. Second, by acknowledging its mistakes and helping the government convict Fowler, Boeing would alleviate its public relations problems. A guilty plea naturally would make a big splash in the newspapers the day it was announced. But after that, Boeing hoped its involvement in the scandal would drop off the media's radar scope. If the company came across as apologetic and cooperative, Bennett predicted, the press and prosecutors mercifully would move on to other targets.

Most important of all, simple economics dictated a settlement. Boeing would be in a much stronger position to remain eligible for government contracts. Bellows couldn't promise that the company's defense unit wouldn't be suspended at all from receiving new Pentagon work, or how quickly it would be reinstated. Those decisions were in the military's purview. But if there was a plea, Bellows pledged to inform the Pentagon that the firm was cooperating fully with prosecutors and had, indeed, taken good-faith steps to clean its own house. A prolonged court battle, on the other hand, meant that the Justice Department wouldn't offer those assurances. Even if Boeing emerged victorious at trial, the Pentagon would have no choice but to bar portions of the company from competing for business during all the months leading up to an acquittal. That scenario sent shivers down the spines of Boeing's directors.

Once company officials crossed the threshold of accepting criminal responsibility, the negotiations were far from over. In truth, that was when the serious horse trading began. Bellows and Bennett had to agree on an appropriate penalty. It was like pulling numbers out of thin air. Placing an accurate dollar value on the suspect documents was next to impossible, and there were precious few precedents to help guide the negotiations. Bellows insisted the size of the payment had to reflect the seriousness of the charges, as well as the government's intention to seek millions of dollars from other firms. Boeing maintained, no less vehemently, that it wasn't about to pay an exorbitant fine simply to satisfy the prosecutors' swagger.

Through all this, Walinski fumed on the sidelines. He railed at "the paper pushers at main Justice," complaining they had a wretched habit of letting contractors off the hook.

At the end of the day, the company pleaded guilty to obtaining two secret documents in 1984 "without legal authority." Of all the hundreds of classified documents Dick Fowler had gotten his hands on, Boeing admitted receiving a five-year defense plan and a Program Decision Memorandum addressed to the secretary of the Navy. Bellows had set $10 million as the upper range for any settlement. Boeing agreed to pay $5.2 million to the U.S. Treasury—a nice, round sum that sounded good on the evening news. Four million dollars was restitution, another million dollars was intended to reimburse the cost of the investigation, and the company was ordered to remove $200,000 from overhead charges previously submitted to the government. Only $20,000 was to be paid as a criminal fine.

The denouement came in mid-November, shortly before Fowler's trial was scheduled to commence. Court approval was necessary to make the settlement binding, so Bellows and Bennett showed up in the packed courtroom of Judge Thomas Ellis III. The government's lawyer calmly laid out the evidence against the company. Bennett assured the court, in his confident and dulcet tones, that Boeing considered the violations "a very sad day in its history." Management was determined to punish anyone still on its payroll who was "culpable in any way," Bennett stressed, adding with a flourish, "Your honor can rest assured that this is a very serious matter for us."

Guilty pleas entail a lot of explanations, but they seldom produce legal fireworks. Everyone took it for granted that the hearing would be relatively brief and largely pro forma.

Half an hour into the explanations, the proceedings threatened to veer out of control. Judge Ellis, a courtly southern gentleman accustomed to receiving more of a heads-up in complicated cases, wasn't sticking to the script envisioned by the lawyers. He seemed to sweep aside Bennett's protestations. The judge demanded to know why no other corporate officials were being charged, when the documents obviously "circulated around" the firm and "a sizable group of people within Boeing had access" to them. He asked why only two bootlegged documents were listed in the three-page criminal information, and how the penalty was calculated. Describing the corporation's persistent hunting for documents as "a very serious breach" of discipline, Judge Ellis questioned whether Boeing's senior management exhibited legitimate remorse. "For a group to know they have these documents and take no action" to plug the leaks for more than a decade, he concluded, "is fairly arresting." Staring sternly down at both lawyers, the judge declared: "It caught my attention." Given the incontrovertible nature of the evidence, he wondered if Boeing's management was resisting "the typical contrition that any defendant would express."

Bob Bennett tried his utmost to deflect the judge's anger. Boeing had beefed up its ethics rules and trebled the number of corporate security supervisors to enhance its self-inspection program, the company's counsel pointed out. It had "purged the system of this problem" long ago, Bennett argued. Quickly, he also apologized that Chairman Frank Shrontz wasn't in attendance to personally accept responsibility and express the company's regret. A pinstriped lawyer from Boeing headquarters, looking properly solemn and crestfallen, added his profuse apologies on behalf of Mr. Shrontz.

The thrust and parry went on for ninety tense minutes. Then the judge relented. He gave his consent to the plea agreement, curtly saying he was convinced "it's an appropriate disposition."

Surrounded by reporters and well-wishers, Bellows fielded questions on the steps of the Alexandria courthouse, under the same white Colonial steeple and ornate clock that later would serve as the backdrop for many of the television shots of individuals convicted in Illwind. Bellows savored his moment of triumph, deftly talking about the implications of the plea and explaining why it was an important victory for the government. All of his answers pointed to one conclusion: Mighty Boeing finally had been humbled. Amid the jostling crowd and the camera crews brandishing their bright lights, the most pertinent question wasn't asked: How did Boeing and its champion, Bob Bennett, manage to walk away with a settlement that was such a fabulous deal?

Chapter IX

CANOGA PARK MYSTERIES

Almost before the ink was dry on Boeing's guilty plea, company leaders were hard at work rewriting history. The public relations drive, like those launched in the wake of earlier criminal cases that also embarrassed the firm, had one overriding goal: to find a way, no matter how strained or far-fetched, to somehow disguise the full significance of Boeing's courtroom admissions.

The company had plenty of experience at such rationalizations. Going back nearly two decades, the brilliant engineers from Seattle had demonstrated their proficiency at after-the-fact rehabilitation. They knew just when to admit wrongdoing. Boeing's management had shown a willingness to accept a black eye in order to avoid worse legal bloodshed down the road. But over the years, executives became ever more discerning. They grew adept at explaining away criminal missteps, especially right after prosecutors filed legal charges against the company. Increasingly, Boeing became a master at turning what ordinarily would be bad news into a public relations campaign demonstrating it was an outstanding corporate citizen.

In the mid-1970s, with Congress, the Justice Department, the Internal Revenue Service, the Securities and Exchange Commission and other federal agencies cracking down on corporate payoffs abroad, Boeing found itself under intense scrutiny. Dozens of other multinational corporations also were investigated. Politicians in Japan, Italy and Holland were toppled for taking money from Lockheed, and the company's two top officials resigned in disgrace. Northrop and its chairman, Thomas V. Jones, admitted making unlawful campaign contributions to President Richard Nixon. Northrop also was exposed as having controlled a slush fund for marketing agents that it used to entertain and influence generals and politicians in the United States and overseas. State Department officials were embarrassed for having looked the other way.

But Boeing's illicit foreign payments were among the most striking. One internal U.S. government document, for example, alleged a series of "bribes" paid by Boeing to middlemen and officials of foreign airlines to win commercial aircraft orders. From Kuwait and Egypt to Honduras and tiny Royal Air Nepal, the pattern was identical: Boeing allegedly funneled money to fictitious offshore companies, secret consultants and sometimes directly to relatives of those it was trying to influence.[1]

In South Korea, $3.5 million went to officers of that country's airline, allegedly to clear the path for Boeing 747 and 727 passenger jet orders. In Spain, $3.4 million secretly was paid to a consulting outfit after the company explicitly assured the country's flag-carrier, Iberia, that there were no commissions in conjunction with the sale of twenty-nine of Boeing's latest 727 models. And the general manager of Lebanon's Middle East Airlines—which acquired three jumbo jets for more than $100 million—got Boeing to deposit $3.5 million in "undisclosed and irregular commissions" into an escrow account in Switzerland for the benefit of a mysterious Liechtenstein company.[2] This was the same territory—indeed, these were some of the very countries and the kind of shady middlemen—around which Mel Paisley navigated with such aplomb before moving into the Pentagon.

Overall, the SEC charged that Boeing made $52 million in questionable payments in at least eighteen countries. Saudi Arabia, Iran and Egypt accounted for the largest share of the money.[3] The Defense Department weighed in with its own allegations, arguing that the stakes were too high and the temptations to pay off foreign officials were too great without added antibribery rules. Chairman Wilson fumed about the various probes, claiming that his people didn't do anything wrong and wouldn't admit to any violations, period. He cursed the government's holier-than-thou attitude. Even his friends couldn't calm him down, despite the obviously increasing public clamor against such foreign business practices. The standoff continued for years, while McDonnell Douglas, Westinghouse and many other firms admitted overseas payment violations.

Eventually, cooler heads prevailed. Edward Bennett Williams, one of the most respected criminal lawyers in the nation's capital at the time, negotiated a relatively painless plea agreement for Boeing. In mid-1982, as the Reagan team consolidated control at the Pentagon and the friendship between Paisley and Bill Galvin blossomed into business ties, T Wilson walked into court to do what he had vowed wouldn't happen on his watch: Boeing paid four hundred thousand dollars and pleaded guilty to filing false statements with the Export-Import Bank. It was a sweet deal for Boeing. The criminal charges didn't include bribery, and no executives were prosecuted. Instead, the company admitted that forty invoices it submitted to the Ex-Im Bank, which financed some of the commercial sales, concealed questionable payments abroad. The papers had failed to mention the use of consultants, as the bank's rules required. The criminal plea covered only four countries and less than 15 percent of the questionable payments identified previously by the SEC. The entire court hearing took fifteen minutes.

Prompted by these and other suspect payments by U.S. industrial powerhouses, Congress took action. The Foreign Corrupt Practices Act specifically outlawed payoffs to foreign officials and gave prosecutors an important new enforcement club. For the first time, the law mandated hefty corporate fines and lengthy prison sentences for individual offenders. Meanwhile, Wilson put his own spin on the violations, assuring the world that "tightened company policies" and tougher internal controls would prevent a repetition of the problem.

To this day, however, many at Boeing maintain the government's response was unwise and overblown. An in-depth review of 162 separate foreign sales agreements by the company's board convinced directors that Boeing "never knowingly made a payoff to anybody" during all of the 1960s and 1970s.[4] Privately, Wilson remained unrepentant to the end. He continued to bellyache to friends about the heavyhanded federal investigation and how objectionable he found it that Boeing's own lawyers seemed eager to sign a guilty plea in order to end the long-running investigation. "I've never felt like such a liar in my whole life," Wilson told one associate, "the day I had to stand up in court and say I was guilty."[5] Some of the acknowledged illegal payments amounted to nothing more than a slight "technical violation," according to this line of argument. They represented only a "termination of service fee" for a consultant Boeing had been told to drop by one of its customers.[6]

Other probes provoked similar retroactive explanations and tortured logic from top managers in Seattle. When Boeing was caught improperly billing the Pentagon for contributions to a variety of state and local political causes in the early 1980s, the response was familiar. The company claimed that including the contributions in its overhead was an honest mistake, which happened to be blown out of proportion by headline-hungry reporters. The same explanation covered unauthorized public relations costs Boeing tried to pass on to the government.

No matter how small the amount or questionable the purpose, Boeing was determined to have its bills covered by the Pentagon. One year it sought to recoup fifty-four thousand dollars in travel expenses for the wives of executives, arguing that the trips were legitimate reimbursable items since the presence of the ladies helped "meet business objectives." Golf fees, banquet costs and bar tabs at executive retreats also should be reimbursed by the Pentagon, the company said, because such perks improved the morale of managers "while at the meeting and upon return to their daily work environment." Eleven thousand dollars for the company-sponsored "World Paper Airplane Championship" was a perfectly reasonable federal expense, in Boeing's view, because it was an "appropriate community relations activity" benefiting the Boys and Girls Clubs of America. Even a $105 traffic ticket issued to a company limousine in downtown Washington, D.C., was submitted as part of Boeing's normal overhead costs. Defending its claim, company auditors said the driver decided "it would be less expensive" for the government to pay the fine "than to inconvenience the executives . . . by causing them to be late for appointments."[7]

Then in 1985, long before the public ever heard of the Clique, Boeing became embroiled in a bidding dispute with eerie parallels to the case later brought against Fowler. Federal auditors accused Boeing's computer services unit of cheating and capitalizing on inside information to win a $6-million civilian contract from an arm of the Interior Department. The size of the contract may have been insignificant for the company, but the allegations surely weren't. One of the subsidiary's executives helped the National Park Service draft specifications for the computer contract. Boeing managers also obtained a version of the competition's bid and went so far as to draft agency responses to a potential competitor. When the irregularities were uncovered, Boeing hastily withdrew its winning bid.[8]

Facing a criminal inquiry and a possible limited ban on bidding for new contracts, corporate response teams jumped into overdrive. As usual, the aim was obfuscating the severity of the violations. Boeing launched an in-house investigation and took swift disciplinary action against seventeen individuals. Some employees were let go, while others were reprimanded or had their paychecks docked. The methods were ruthless. A pair of fired executives was warned not to cooperate with government probes or Boeing would stop paying their legal bills. "It was a matter of protecting the company, and someone had to be blamed," one of the executives recalls. Higherups knew about the irregularities beforehand, he says, but there was "a general attempt to cover up a lot of things that were happening."[9] Boeing's hardball tactics succeeded. The suspension was lifted in a matter of weeks, with government investigators gushing about Boeing's ability to handle the crisis quickly and effectively. Still, accusations of waste, fraud and abuse against leading defense contractors refused to fade away, and the escalating complaints threatened to tarnish Boeing's image.

Management hit upon something it believed was a guaranteed winner: The company promised to reimburse the Air Force and take back certain Boeing-manufactured parts, no questions asked, that were deemed unsatisfactory for whatever reason. The company found one more trick to turn criticism to its advantage. If the Pentagon decided that prices for some parts were unreasonable, there was a simple way to rectify the problem. This "money-back guarantee" eventually applied to all military parts sold by the company to any of the services, so long as the original price was under one hundred thousand dollars. The idea generated a burst of goodwill on Capitol Hill and in the Pentagon. Boeing appeared more cooperative than other weapons-makers, prompting praise from Defense Secretary Weinberger himself.

Behind closed doors, company officials expressed quite different sentiments. They couldn't hide their bitterness about what they called prosecutorial overkill. Every time some Pentagon honcho thinks he has discovered some malfeasance, complained Henry Tucker, director of operations for Boeing's aerospace office in the capital, "the solution is to hire more auditors." Since "those people have the assignment to find something wrong," he added, it's "kind of a self-fulfilling business."[10] Dean Thornton, who headed Boeing's commercial aircraft division from 1985 through his retirement in 1994, reflected the firm's abiding animosity toward federal watchdogs. The adversarial relationship between the company and government investigators, he said, had degenerated to the point that Boeing's defense executives worried about "whether it's illegal to buy somebody a cup of coffee." Thornton didn't hold back his anger. "I don't need that," he snapped.[11]

This was the corporate history against which Boeing's November 1989 document-swapping plea had to be measured. Once again, Chairman Frank Shrontz and his spokesmen were whittling away at the government's contention that Boeing had knowingly violated the law. In a letter to Judge Ellis immediately following the hearing at which Boeing admitted illegally acquiring Pentagon data, the chairman was abjectly remorseful: "I assure you," he wrote, that Boeing is "deeply distressed over this episode" because "it challenges the company's reputation and integrity." The conduct "to which we pleaded guilty," the chairman stressed, "is completely inconsistent with the ideals that I want all of our employees to strive for and attain." To others, Boeing's chief pledged to "turn over every rock in this company" if that was what it took to root out corruption.[12] T Wilson, the man Shrontz replaced, privately apologized to Boeing's board for failing to prevent the legal problems.

But the remorse was considerably less pronounced, and Shrontz appeared much more spontaneous, during subsequent interviews with hometown reporters. "Certainly by today's standards, that conduct was not something we're proud of," the chairman told the *Seattle Times*.[13] Full of excuses, Shrontz seemed more compassionate than irate about Fowler's activities. "I feel a little sorry for him, to be honest with you," he admitted to the local newspaper.[14] The chairman also dredged up the old bromide that document swapping used to be common industry practice. "As time passed, ethics changed [and] legal requirements changed," Shrontz explained to a company historian, but Fowler didn't adjust and simply "got caught up in this mentality."[15]

Trying to minimize the damage, other senior Boeing executives appeared more sympathetic toward those who trafficked in Pentagon secrets. "People acquired documents from the government, and the government knew it," argued Dan Pinick, president of Boeing's Defense and Space Group at the time. "They weren't sneaking around at night stealing documents."[16]

The Pentagon pretended to get tough after the guilty plea. Boeing's Rosslyn office was suspended temporarily from having any contact with government agencies on procurement matters, and there was muttering that the ban could be imposed for a longer period. Likewise, the office's employees were barred for the time being from conducting business with the Defense Department, whether they stayed with Boeing or got a job elsewhere. "Seventy percent of the people" working in Rosslyn "never knew Fowler," grumbled Boris Mishel, who was in charge of the office. "They couldn't do their job and they couldn't work for anyone else."[17]

Though highly unusual, the punishment was almost entirely symbolic. Fewer than one hundred employees in Rosslyn were covered by the suspension. Thousands of Boeing officials at other locations—at manufacturing plants, design centers, laboratories and, of course, executive suites back at headquarters—weren't affected at all. Everyday work on military programs proceeded apace. The previous year, Boeing's defense contracts had accounted for $4.8 billion in revenue. Suspending a single office, even if contact with the Pentagon was prohibited for a year or more, was just about the most lenient thing the government could do.

From a financial standpoint, the plea was tantamount to a disconcerting but minor inconvenience for Boeing. Neither Bellows nor Walinski ever deceived themselves into thinking they would seriously squeeze the company's revenues. Realistically, the settlement hardly put a crimp in the giant contractor's cash flow. For starters, defending itself in a trial would have cost a sizable portion of the $5.2 million it ended up paying to the U.S. Treasury. A glance at Boeing's balance sheet told the rest of the story: Profits for the year, after taxes and other charges, amounted to nearly $3 million a *day*.

If anything, the contractor's fortunes in the defense arena improved during the suspension, which lasted from November 19, 1989, to February 23, 1990. On November 20, the day after the suspension went into effect, Boeing and its partner in a joint venture received a $167.6-million contract from the Army to develop a new attack helicopter. Several other major Army and Air Force contracts followed over the next fourteen weeks. By the time the suspension was lifted, the Pentagon had awarded Boeing new business worth an additional $443.6 million, and that total didn't include work the company obtained from other federal departments.

A few weeks before the document-swapping plea, Boeing asked three of its outside directors to determine if other company officials deserved punishment. The committee and its lawyers interviewed Fowler, questioned his associates and pored over company records. The probe continued for well over a year, long after reporters and prosecutors stopped paying attention. (Bellows, for example, moved on to prosecute a Virginia gynecologist who hoodwinked couples by faking fertility tests and secretly using his own semen to artificially inseminate female patients. Television networks covered the doctor's trial for weeks, and reporters beseeched Bellows for interviews. None of them seemed to care about his old Pentagon cases.)

The findings of Boeing's internal investigation were utterly predictable. Not a single soul besides Fowler was publicly identified as being complicit in the gross violations of law. In spite of the company's unflagging efforts to make amends, nobody else was demoted—let alone fired. "No current employees were culpable or responsible" for the misconduct, Boeing told the Air Force Debarment and Suspension Review Board in January 1993. The language was bland and impersonal, giving few clues about the extent of concern among Boeing directors. "Accordingly," the company's update concluded, "no [additional] disciplinary action was taken."[18]

What was the upshot of years of ethics seminars, corporate soul search-ing, internal investigations and company pledges to "turn over every stone" to get at the truth? Except for Fowler's situation, it was hard to sort out the punishment. Eight employees in all "received letters of admonish-ment," Boeing reported to the Air Force, without identifying who they were or what the letters said. The Pentagon decided it wasn't necessary for Boeing to make public any more information, and the company still re-fuses to provide details.[19] An Air Force bureaucrat who saw the discipli-nary letters said they ranged from a mild warning about management responsibilities to "dismay over one employee's lack of forthrightness" with company investigators.[20]

Insiders tried to dismiss the investigation as "an anomaly in Boeing's morally antiseptic world." No sinning preacher, they said, "ever fell from grace with a louder crash."[21] A company spokesman added: "I would hope that people would not be so short-sighted to let almost seventy-five years of good work be affected by the recent incidents."[22] Boeing's vice-chair-man was even more emphatic, claiming that the firm had a "moral imper-ative" to be above reproach. "If that takes forever," he said, "then we will work at it forever." Carefully calibrated to swing public opinion toward the company's side, such self-righteous claims provoked precious little re-action from government agencies or other official quarters.

A tiny group of independent critics continued to howl about Boeing's evasive and closemouthed policies. One editorial in the *Seattle Times* urged the company to "try to set the same high standard for ethics as it does for airplanes."[23] Years later, a House Energy and Commerce subcom-mittee computed that Boeing had been forced to pay the government a total of $161 million in criminal, civil and administrative penalties pri-marily growing out of defense fraud investigations. Reputations of many other contractors had been shattered by much less. Yet the National Aero-nautics and Space Administration still selected Boeing as the prime con-tractor to build the space station, though the company failed the agency's own cost-control reviews. "If Boeing will diddle the Department of De-fense, why won't they diddle NASA?" demanded Congressman John Dingell, the Michigan Democrat who chaired the House panel. "You ap-pear to have a wonderful, trusting relationship with Boeing," he told NASA administrators.[24]

But the criticism didn't make any difference. Like its earnings, the company's standing with the public and the government seems immune to lasting damage. The Seattle aerospace giant remains the darling of regu-lators. When Federal Aviation Administration officials debated new air-traffic-control rules to prevent accidents caused by potentially deadly turbulence from Boeing's 757 models, for instance, concern about the company's economic well-being was high on their priority list. Despite several fatal crashes of smaller planes attributable to so-called wake turbulence from 757 twin jets—and stern warnings from experts that more deaths could result—the FAA delayed action for years to avoid antagonizing Boeing.[25]

These days, a Boeing jetliner takes off from some airport in the world every two seconds. The latest Air Force One, a customized Boeing jumbo jet with offices and sleeping quarters for eighty passengers and twenty-three crew members, has become synonymous with the pomp and pageantry of presidential visits. With the American flag on its tail and the world's most sophisticated communications gear in its belly, the White House's sparkling 747 proudly carries Boeing's logo around the globe. Back home, the company's executives are lionized as superior managers and America's preeminent exporters.[26]

In annual surveys conducted by *Fortune* magazine, Boeing consistently ranks among the country's most respected corporations. *Fortune's* February 1993 issue, published almost three years after Operation Uncover disappeared from the headlines, showed the firm's resilience. Boeing made the list of the ten "most admired" companies, alongside phenomenally successful consumer-goods marketers such as Procter & Gamble, Wal-Mart Stores and Coca-Cola. In the defense industry, Boeing easily outpolled other concerns to claim the top spot as the most highly acclaimed aerospace outfit in the United States.

Notwithstanding its frequent brushes with the law, Boeing is a peerless "symbol of American technological excellence, establishing standards by which others are judged," according to one corporate profile. "The simple sentence 'I work for Boeing,' " this company-supported history concludes, remains "a declaration of pride" for everyone affiliated with the firm since the first Boeing airplanes were produced in 1916.

☆

For Fowler, Boeing's 1989 guilty plea was a heart-stopping surprise that added to his misery. It undercut his legal defenses and left him more vulnerable to attacks by the company and prosecutors. Boeing executives, by now claiming that Fowler was a "lone wolf" who shamelessly corrupted the firm's legitimate security system, professed to be shocked by the volume of documents he had acquired. Walinski and his boss, Mike Costello, recognized the unfairness of singling out Fowler, though the dynamics of the investigation left them no choice. "Our feeling was it went way up the company's organization," Costello recalls.[27] The government had piles of "circumstantial evidence to implicate" higher-level Boeing officials, he says, but it needed Fowler to supply the missing links. Bitter and somewhat defensive, today Costello ponders the possibilities that eluded him: "Nobody wants to go to trial with purely circumstantial evidence." Wistfully, he adds, investigators "tried to move the case up as high as we could."[28]

Fowler's trial began in early December 1989, and it lasted four days. The prosecution relied on the testimony of federal dignitaries and military brass to highlight the sensitivity of the documents Fowler traded and copied at will. From the beginning, Judge Albert Bryan seemed sympathetic to their arguments and sharply restricted the defense's maneuvering room. "This 'everybody does it' business is not a defense," the judge warned Fowler's attorneys from the start, swatting down their objections one after another. His comments and glowering looks indicated the odds were stacked in favor of Bellows. The government "doesn't excuse speeding," Judge Bryan snapped, just "because everybody speeds."

Many defense lawyers hated to practice before the judges in Alexandria, privately criticizing them for tending to favor the U.S. attorney's office. Some in the defense bar rolled their eyes and derided those sitting on the bench as "Neanderthals," preoccupied with disposing of cases as rapidly as possible. Hiding behind anonymity, others threw worse personal epithets at the judges. Reflecting the speedy trials, the district court was dubbed "the Rocket Docket." Delays and continuances were frowned on. Novel or imaginative defense theories, for the most part, were a waste of time; they probably would be shot down by procedural rulings before ever getting in front of a jury. Fowler's attorneys struggled gamely to show that their client was a creature of his environment. They tried, but ultimately failed, to introduce evidence that an assistant secretary of defense allegedly gave another company's marketing officials some of the same documents that got Fowler indicted. Judge Bryan wouldn't allow the testimony, ruling it was irrelevant.

Knowing that he no longer had to contend with defense attorney Bob Bennett in the courtroom also increased Bellows's confidence. Boeing's erstwhile document wizard "was the common thread running through" various branches of the Clique, the prosecutor told the jury in a powerful summation. "Mr. Fowler played a unique role in the conspiracy: he was the supplier."[29]

The jury took less than two hours to reach a verdict. Jurors saw that Fowler wasn't alone in what he did. "I sympathized with him," one female juror acknowledged afterward, openly wondering if Fowler wasn't a scapegoat. "I think everybody felt badly ... Everyone [on the jury] saw he was a basically good man."[30] Other jurors chafed under the judge's instructions, too. However reluctant they were, the members of the jury did their duty. Fowler was found guilty on all thirty-nine counts.

When the foreman announced the verdict, Fowler's wife, Muriel, collapsed in tears and had to be escorted out of the courtroom. "The government lied," his sobbing daughter blurted out. "We'll get even," she said. "Just keep quiet," Fowler reprimanded her, as he was led away.[31]

A shudder went through the rest of the spectators, too. Many who sat through the trial were defense lawyers, representing other companies and individuals caught in Bellows's sights. They were stunned by the prosecution's victory. It was a sobering jolt of reality for anyone thinking of challenging Bellows. Boeing and Bennett, with all their clout and acumen, didn't dare risk a trial. Hard-headed Fowler, who took the chance and fought the government tooth and nail, lost resoundingly. The lesson couldn't have been any more transparent. The smartest course, chastened defense lawyers concluded, was to sign a bunch of plea agreements and try to put Uncover behind the industry.

During the trial, Bellows bet his cocounsel ten bucks that Fowler would take the stand at the eleventh hour. "He knows what we have in store for him" if he doesn't testify, Bellows bragged.[32] For the final time, Dick Fowler took the contrary tack. He never testified in his own defense, preferring to risk conviction rather than subject himself to cross-examination that might force him to identify his sources. In early January 1990, a month after the verdict, Fowler was summoned to appear before a grand jury in Alexandria. Since he had been found guilty, there was no possibility any longer of invoking his Fifth Amendment right against self-incrimination to avoid answering Bellows's questions. Fowler stayed in the grand jury room for hours. He did provide some answers, identifying a few of the industry officials with whom he had dealt. But he wouldn't divulge what Bellows wanted above everything else: the names of his contacts in the Pentagon.

Annoyed, Fowler's legal team had warned him to stop acting foolishly. The sources he was protecting no longer were in jeopardy, the lawyers maintained. "It is unlikely that your testimony could be the predicate for prosecution of any of these individuals," attorney Cary Feldman bluntly told Fowler in a confidential letter before his client marched into the grand jury room. The government "has a very good idea of who these people are," anyway, Feldman continued, but prosecutors won't have enough time to charge any of them before the statute of limitations runs out. The bottom line, Feldman wrote, was that truthful and complete grand jury testimony by Fowler would "at best only minimally advance" Bellows's investigation. But refusing to name sources, he warned, "will greatly advance the possibility of your spending more time incarcerated than you otherwise would."

The attorney was absolutely correct. New Year's festivities were barely over when Fowler was held in contempt of court and whisked to jail. He was handcuffed and shackled in leg irons, then placed in a holding cell with violent criminals. "We'll see how long he can sit in jail" before talking, one of the agents said.[33] Fowler's reason for keeping silent didn't waver: "I would never subject anyone else to the things I have gone through," he told friends. Nine months of his life was spent behind bars for lack of responsiveness in the grand jury room.

On the heels of that sentence, Dick Fowler was staring at a second prison term—this time for his conviction on the underlying thirty-nine felony counts. Appealing for clemency, Fowler claimed that he hadn't coerced or bribed anyone, nor did he ever intend to harm the Pentagon or show disdain for the law by swapping documents. His arguments to the court were nothing if not consistent: "I was not aware it was a crime," he kept insisting, "and the government was not aware it was a crime."[34] Those assertions fell flat, when the judge sternly declared Fowler was "too smart a person not to know" how serious his transgressions were. A federal appeals court concurred, ruling that the government's "misplaced belief that contractors would not betray the trust reposed in them could not justify Fowler's role in this betrayal." The sentence was two more years in a cell at the federal prison camp in Petersburg, Virginia.

As hard as he tried to hide it, life as an inmate was extremely tough on Fowler. He maintained that the inner peace he gained was well worth the price. "My head is held high. I sleep well at night," he proudly asserted.[35] Reading World War II novels and walking several miles a day on the penitentiary's exercise trail kept up his spirits, Fowler reassured visitors. "If I had to do it over again—go to jail or maintain my integrity—I would make the same decision," he insisted. "I have to live with myself."[36] In the meantime, the company was confident that Dick Fowler wouldn't break his silence about old activities.

Photographs from those years show a gaunt, hollow-eyed man, wearing an ill-fitting khaki uniform and dragging on a cigarette in the foreboding shadow of a prison-yard gun turret. There is a pervasive sense of loss in the pictures. Hauntingly sad eyes and furrows around the corners of his mouth dominate Fowler's sallow face. His tone generally stayed defiant. However, a hint of self-pity started to creep into his speech. For the first time, Fowler referred to himself as a "fall guy." He called himself a "sacrificial lamb," thrown to the wolves by Boeing. He immersed himself in preparing rambling memos—which relatives dutifully typed up and then distributed to interested reporters—summarizing past events and labeling some of the material "smoking gun" evidence of his superiors' criminality.

Among the things that sustained Fowler were signs that, in a roundabout way, he was turning into a budding folk hero. Praise for his strength and his beliefs sprang from out-of-the-way places, and clearly Fowler liked the notoriety. A Boeing assembly-line worker who had never met Fowler composed reams of poetry about his life. Aptly entitled "Please, No Names," the collection of typewritten pages glorified Fowler's silence and suffering. Boeing "fired me quicker that I could stop to think," Fowler is quoted as saying in one of the poems. "No hearing, no questions, just get out the door." Another poem, glorifying news reports about Fowler's travails, stressed the skills he had exhibited: "My talent was to gather information. They hired me to do just that sort of thing . . . So many did the same many times before." The poem ended with a plaintive cry. "Am I the victim of a corporate sting?"

The men inside Petersburg's walls also gave him the deference he craved. They understood, better than anyone else, the price he was paying for his perseverance. Inmates joked that half of them were snitches, and the rest were the victims they had snitched on. The punch line was always the same: "Then there was Fowler."[37]

Belatedly, the skeptics in his family joined in the chorus of hosannas. One of Fowler's daughters, Robyn Ann, admitted that her initial reaction was wrong. She had urged cooperation with Bellows, ridiculing her father's cantankerous nature. But now, she told him with a big hug, she realized that his principles elevated him far above detractors. "I'd rather have a jailbird for a father than a snitch," she said.[38]

Long before Fowler settled into his prison routine, Bellows was on a roll. Boeing's previous plea and the light punishment meted out to the firm, combined with the surprising ease of Fowler's conviction, afforded cover for other companies that were itching to settle. "They fell like dominoes," Bellows explains. "Management saw that they could plead guilty and survive."[39]

Barely a few weeks after Fowler was incarcerated, several of those contractors admitted their guilt. In early February 1990, General Electric paid $2.5 million to settle its part of the investigation. But since GE had merely inherited the problems when it acquired RCA Corporation years earlier, that was a relatively easy score for Bellows. By late March, Grumman and Raytheon also signed comparable guilty pleas. The whirl of settlements forced Bellows's team to work harder than ever, completing agreements late at night and then rushing them to the courthouse the very next morning. Sometimes there was only a day's pause between court appearances.

Envious veterans at main Justice, try as they might to denigrate the work of their Alexandria counterparts, couldn't recall another string of major Pentagon-related convictions coming so quickly on each other's heels. As Bellows picked off his targets—each one a multibillion-dollar company with international prestige and a great deal at stake—the rest of the industry was flabbergasted. Companies weren't the only ones at risk. In addition to Fowler, five other midlevel executives from other firms were convicted as the inquiry wound down. Some of the marketing people Bellows caught knew Dick Fowler well, while others dealt only with intermediaries and didn't ever lay eyes on him.

Despite the government's victories, huge chunks of the case remained half-finished. Through all the courtroom maneuvers and pressure tactics, Fowler's Pentagon suppliers stayed out of the prosecution's reach. Thanks to a quirk in the law and the Justice Department's aversion to turning over investigative files to the Pentagon, his best sources managed to avoid even an administrative slap on the wrist.

In the same fashion, many prominent industry players evaded punishment. From the start, Bellows saw his job as getting the most convictions in the limited time available. By going after the easiest targets, that's exactly what he did. But in the process, a number of large firms and big-name executives under investigation escaped unscathed. When pressed by associates, Bellows acknowledged that he walked into the case too late to focus much attention on senior management. Perhaps the biggest name implicated in Uncover was Malcolm Currie, the polished, silver-haired chairman of Hughes Aircraft and a pillar of the defense establishment since the beginning of the 1960s.

☆

Inside Hughes, Frank Caso's claim to fame was getting a personal Xerox machine and having it installed in a locked room to which he had the only key. As Caso confided to a few trusted coworkers, there was no other option if he wanted to do his job. And, beyond a doubt, he was a loyal, gung-ho member of the Hughes family.

Copying speed and quality were important to Caso, who became an authority at evaluating different brands of high-volume duplicating machines. He soon picked up the technical lingo and came to appreciate the little-known mechanical quirks that were so crucial in a jam. He would experiment to find out the maximum number of copies a new model could run in a fifteen- or twenty-minute stretch going full tilt. But, for the kind of work he had to do, privacy was the essential ingredient. Having an intruder burst in the door and start nosing around "when you're knocking out some thousand-page document" at the last minute, Caso recalled from painful experience, "was really panicksville."[40]

The hard-working Mr. Caso wasn't some overambitious clerk or conscientious copying-room supervisor. His job was in marketing: He was responsible for identifying new business opportunities for the company. Caso's official title was marketing analyst for a portion of Hughes's giant defense operations. One of a handful of such analysts scattered throughout the company, he was barely an asterisk on formal organization charts. Assuredly, he was not well-known enough to fuel the gossip mills that tittered over the gaffes of Hughes's leading executives and handicapped the ups and downs of their careers. Though he boasted decades of seniority, Caso's salary never came close to six figures. His staff consisted of a sole assistant and a secretary. Nonetheless, those familiar with Caso's work knew that the modest pay and lack of executive perks belied his usefulness to senior management. He was supposed to divine the specifics of Pentagon budgets and contracts coming down the pike.

Starting with his first few years at Hughes—when he blithely exchanged classified budget materials sitting at restaurant booths with fellow industry marketers—Frank Caso didn't ever lose sight of his goal. There was only one job description that mattered: He was the company's designated document hound.

Each of the Pentagon and industry officials he dealt with "knew that I didn't sit at a very high position in the company," Caso says. Yet they continued feeding him information, because the assumption was that he worked for those at the top. "Every marketing director, every division manager within our group, [and] every senior executive," Caso claims, "knew what I was doing."[41] The excitable Caso was prone to hyperbole and inflating his role. But, in light of his twenty-eight-year track record at the company, a string of high-ranking executives must have given him at least tacit approval for those activities.

Early on, Caso's contacts included Ben Plymale and other associates of Mel Paisley at Boeing. As the Reagan defense buildup peaked, he furiously exchanged documents with members of the Clique and other information-swapping networks. Frank Caso, though, wasn't one of those gradually swept along by the document-sharing tide. With his extensive list of industry contacts, top-of-the-line copying machines and the acquiescence of his bosses, Caso became the quintessential disseminator of Pentagon budget secrets in the 1980s. A Hughes executive referred to him as "a collection agency" for such information. If a worthwhile document was floating around, it was bound to land at Caso's doorstep. His nickname added to his persona: Friends and supervisors delighted in calling him "Mr. Document."

Dick Fowler may have been unequaled at prying classified documents from government sources, but Caso, in fact, turned out to be the most successful at duplicating and distributing them. Generally, he was able to do so in record time. Whether it required personally delivering documents during innocent-sounding trade association seminars or submitting phony petty cash vouchers for material surreptitiously mailed to his buddies at other firms, Caso kept the copies moving nationwide. "Frank was the guy who put the packages together, he was the ultimate middleman," a former assistant recalls.[42]

Stretching back to the early 1970s, Caso was a fixture at the Hughes missile systems division in Canoga Park, California, a placid, tree-lined suburb in the heart of the San Fernando Valley, less than thirty miles from downtown Los Angeles. Sprawled between the imposing crests of the Santa Susana Mountains to the north and Malibu's exclusive beaches and whitewater views to the south, the complex accounted for nearly one-fifth of the company's revenues. More broadly, it exemplified the ebullience of Southern California's defense community under Reagan and Weinberger.

Few residents could remember the future looking so bright. College graduates, weeks after getting their diplomas, frequently had to choose among concurrent job offers from three or four defense concerns. In the rush to find the bodies they needed, some contractors were eager to hire candidates even before conducting full-fledged interviews. Generous pay and steady overtime gave tens of thousands of blue-collar workers instant access to middle-class dreams of buying a home. From the bustling San Fernando Valley to the arid plains of Palmdale, where assembly buildings for both the B-1 and B-2 bombers loomed over the Mojave Desert, local economies were growing at unheard-of rates. Suppliers and small businesses catering to the industry, from eateries to mom-and-pop machine shops, couldn't expand fast enough to keep up with orders. Hughes benefited from the giddy era as handsomely as any firm. From its vantage point in Canoga Park, the business landscape looked as rosy as the sunsets that painted nearby mountain passes with breathtaking hues in the evenings.

Tracing its humble beginning to a rented hangar, where the young Howard Hughes tinkered with innovative planes before World War II, the company boasted a host of ground-breaking achievements. In the 1940s, it built the *Spruce Goose*, the mammoth, eight-engine wooden flying boat that President Franklin Roosevelt hoped would stem shipping losses from Nazi submarines. With its 218-foot-long body and 160-foot wing span, the HK-1 Hercules, as it was officially called, achieved distinction as the largest airplane ever built. To accommodate its tremendous bulk, Hughes had to build a plant unlike any before: The cavernous, six-story assembly hangar, covering the area of two baseball fields, was heralded as the largest wooden structure erected at the time. More than twenty other buildings eventually were put up at the site.

The company's ostentatious headquarters, including mahogany-trimmed walls and a private apartment for Howard Hughes, added to its founder's bigger-than-life reputation. He also laid out the world's longest private runway, stretching nearly two miles along a bluff overlooking the Pacific Ocean. The eccentric Mr. Hughes was at the controls when one of his experimental craft lifted off the strip and crashed in Beverly Hills, nearly killing the industrialist. The *Spruce Goose* didn't fare much better. The star-crossed behemoth flew only once over Los Angeles Harbor, and the Allies never used it in the war. But the engineering relic helped advance the firm's standing as one of the military's most imaginative suppliers. The characterization stuck. Hughes grew to be the largest industrial employer in all of California. At the height of Reagan's Pentagon spending increases, it had well over eighty-two thousand employees on its worldwide payroll.

Hughes's Southern California facilities also shed light on the disposition of the technocrats riding the crest of the aerospace industry's unparalleled expansion. Canoga Park, El Segundo, Fullerton and other Hughes locations evoked previous glories, while offering a haven for many of the most intense personalities among the new crop of scientists and engineers. They came from all over the country to work on cutting-edge projects, the latest in radar development, guidance technology and ultrasecret satellite weaponry.

Past accomplishments were part of the draw. To begin with, the world's first laser had been created at the company's legendary research laboratory in Malibu. Hughes scientists went on to do pioneering work in infrared imaging systems, high-frequency transistors, superconducting ceramic circuits and fiber-optic networks. They built the first sophisticated commercial satellite, developed the lunar lander for NASA and were trend-setters in space-based communications. The defense boom added to that luster. Once the early Reagan budgets were locked in place, Hughes became a leader in a wide range of Pentagon programs: It manufactured the Army's much-praised TOW tank-killer weapons; produced a variety of air-to-air missiles and satellites for the Air Force; supplied the radars used in all B-2 bombers; and won several competitions to design small, antimissile interceptors commonly known as "Brilliant Pebbles." The company evolved into the Air Force's de facto primary research laboratory.

Acquired by General Motors in 1985 for $5 billion, Hughes also became deeply involved in communications ventures with broad commercial appeal, such as direct satellite-to-home television broadcasting and advanced mobile-phone services. While the company's impact on California's economy was obvious and immense, its influence extended far beyond those borders. In certain respects, Hughes became the crown jewel of Southern California's high-tech revolution. Scientists and managers who left the company often started their own firms. Eventually regarded as a beacon for converting military technology to civilian applications, Hughes was considered by many observers the closest thing the United States had to a technological hothouse for the twenty-first century.

But the region's patchwork of defense companies included other gems. Lockheed's fabled "Skunk Works"—the top-secret design and manufacturing center where radar-evading "stealth" aircraft became a reality—prospered in Burbank, just on the other side of Hollywood from Canoga Park. The Air Force's weird-looking F-117 Stealth fighter took shape there, with its peaked cockpit and boxy body suited to absorb radar signals. It was the birthplace of the SR-71 Blackbird, the world's hottest spy plane, and of the infamous U-2, the world's highest-flying single-engine aircraft. Officially designated as Lockheed's center for Advanced Development Projects, the Skunk Works also gave birth to a fantastic array of other experimental craft the public never guessed existed. With nearly eight thousand people sworn to protect its secrets, the complex was more of a think tank than a manufacturing plant. Designers were encouraged to let their imaginations soar. Bureaucratic fences separating scientific disciplines were eschewed in favor of cohesive teams combining engineers and other specialists with various types of expertise. Creativity and new problem-solving approaches were rewarded. Individual craftsmanship and hand tooling reigned supreme in those buildings, not the faceless, predictable rhythm of assembly-line production.

In tiny El Segundo, nearly one hundred thousand workers streamed in every day to the plants and offices belonging to Northrop, TRW, Rockwell, Hughes and other contractors. The mob of aerospace workers quadrupled the city's daytime population, clogging streets and giving a boost to local merchants. Many of the workers settled down in El Segundo, making it the self-proclaimed "aerospace capital of the world." Prosperity, combined with a sense of community, made the city "a fine place to raise children and a fine place to be old," in the words of one civic leader.[43]

Elsewhere along the coast, next to busy factories in blue-collar neighborhoods, was the historic Santa Monica plant where Douglas Aircraft Company had built thousands of its DC-3 turboprop workhorses in the early years of commercial aviation. A few miles to the south, in fast-growing Long Beach, stood modern plants where the firm's new incarnation, McDonnell Douglas, turned out jets and military transport planes. Aviation's ghosts also could be felt further away from the ocean. With President Reagan solidly behind the long-range B-1B bomber, Rockwell alone had a small army working in the Antelope Valley around Palmdale. At the height of production, four B-1s rolled out every month from the giant, seven-story desert plant forty miles northeast of Los Angeles. Described by critics as goldplated and unable to penetrate Soviet airspace as promised, Rockwell's bomber nevertheless accomplished two crucial goals: It brought back good times to the Antelope Valley and served as a dramatic illustration of the Air Force's ethos of the dominance of air power.[44]

Still deeper in the desert, secret aircraft performed loops and dives under the blistering sun at renowned Edwards Air Force Base. With the temperature reaching 120 degrees, the planes landed on a huge dried-up lake that formed a natural airfield of gigantic proportions. Edwards provided an eerie habitat for the men and machines that shaped the industry from the beginning. It was a cinch to identify true airplane buffs, one observer wrote, by checking their reaction to the isolated desert site. Those who fit in best were the ones who loved "the challenge of the climate and the camaraderie of the cut-off community" that distinguished Edwards.[45] The tasks and the dangers of perfecting military airplanes remained undisturbed by outside influences. The hectic flight-test schedules reminded old-timers of the stubby Bell XP-59A, which made history at the base in 1942 as the nation's first jet-powered plane. Edwards was the place where Chuck Yeager first broke the sound barrier in "Glamorous Glennis," his X-1 jet. It was where test pilot Neil Armstrong, before becoming the first astronaut to step onto the moon, restarted the engines on a flamed-out X-15 jet barely seconds before it would have pancaked into the ground.[46] In the 1980s, Southern California's residents hoped that the activity at Edwards marked the end of the boom-and-bust cycles that had plagued aerospace companies in the past.

As the Reagan agenda came to fruition, similar expectations were rising in industry circles. Given the Pentagon's wholehearted support and financial commitment, nothing seemed out of the question for the largest contractors. Ambitious dreams and grand ideas that had been dormant for years suddenly appeared to resonate among the world-class defense firms that had sunk roots in the state. Seemingly in every corner of the Los Angeles basin, companies were bent on reaping big profits by extending the frontiers of aeronautical and space flight.

On top of the professional challenges, Hughes was a magnet for top-notch talent partly because of its location. For many transplanted easterners, the lure of Southern California's natural wonders proved irresistible. So did the recreational outlets. A short drive from densely populated cities, the Angeles National Forest beckoned hikers and other lovers of the outdoors with its rugged arroyos and canyons. Barely half an hour longer by car, you could reach ski areas that stayed open into the springtime. Those interested in a different kind of splendor could stare at the mansions along the infamous hairpin turns of Mulholland Drive, not too far from Hughes's offices. A jaunt in another direction took the curious past estates ringed by high fences, guardhouses and patrol dogs. Movie moguls, stars and would-be stars mingled until the early morning hours at screenings or elegant swimming pool parties inside those secluded hideaways, which still give the Hollywood Hills their exotic flavor and aura of risqué glamor.

At first glance, Frank Caso didn't look as if he belonged in this world. He wasn't in tune with the fashionable or scientific side of Los Angeles. He was a chunky Italian from New York City with an overbearing attitude, and his effusive, sometimes combative manner tended to turn people off. He worked briefly for a mail-order advertising firm and knocked around the aerospace industry for a few years before arriving at Hughes. With a master's degree in business administration and the gladhanding personality of a natural salesman, Caso was in his element on the marketing side. A born kibitzer, he enjoyed the give-and-take over cocktails and drawn-out lunches he had with compatriots from other firms. He traveled frequently, joining them at industry-sponsored events that resembled the convivial atmosphere of earlier sessions sponsored by the Hard Core. But compared to those who depended on the fruits of his labor, Caso had neither technical nor manufacturing expertise.

Likewise, he didn't have the intellectual rigor that allowed others to dissect Pentagon documents until they yielded unexpected insights. In truth, Caso was an analyst only in the broadest definition of that term. The most analysis he did, one friend recalls, was instructing his secretary to remove SECRET markings from papers he had just acquired. Once the official stamps were obliterated with tape or correcting fluid, Caso went to work. Frequently, he took the main body of the document, put his name at the top, perhaps added an introductory paragraph or two to make it seem more like a Hughes-generated analysis, and then rushed to deliver photocopies of the memo to superiors. The cosmetic changes took as little as five minutes, and the final product sometimes went all the way up the chain to senior executives in the missile unit.[47]

On a day-to-day basis, dealing with Caso could be problematic. Prickly, jealous of colleagues and quick to claim he had been slighted, Caso craved attention from higher-ups. He pined to be seen as indispensable. A secretive nature, on the other hand, kept him isolated from many of his peers. All in all, despite his top-secret clearance and good performance ratings, Caso hardly fit the mold of the cerebral engineers and standoffish numbers-crunchers Hughes management typically favored.

Somehow, the differences didn't seem to matter. The quality that made Caso so valuable to Hughes, and the reason the company lobbied hard to keep him from jumping ship, was his intuitive appreciation of how a steady stream of secret Pentagon documents could help contractors. Caso realized, long before many others in his line of work, the importance of following closely the iterations of the budget numbers within the military departments. If he obtained the documents, others at Hughes would be able to analyze their contents in painstaking detail. There was no better insight into the Pentagon or the ever-shifting lineup of factions feuding over weapons expenditures.

Armed with such knowledge, Hughes could prepare more cogent budget justifications for weapons. Indeed, it would be able to assist the services in presenting more persuasive arguments to lawmakers and the secretary of defense. The seller, in effect, would help the buyer figure out why the purchase was absolutely necessary. To Caso and his supporters at the company, the logic was irrefutable.

In order to reach that level of detail, Hughes and other contractors needed a reliable supply of information. Instead of poring over smudged, incomplete copies of Pentagon documents—some of which had been passed around so long that even a magnifying glass couldn't make the figures legible—Caso set his sights higher. He needed volume and certainty. There was no substitute, he decided, for the timely, predictable flow of clean documents. "You have to understand the cycle" to get the most benefit from the paperwork, Caso now explains.[48] And that was precisely where he excelled.

According to Hughes's personnel records, "The duties performed by Mr. Caso" included maintaining "contact with financial and planning segments of customer organizations" and assembling "a central market intelligence file" to help management forecast five- and ten-year sales trends. In his earthy Brooklyn accent, Caso cut through the corporate gobbledygook. "In this business, you have to know when to massage the customer," he told a young assistant. "Get whatever documents you can. That's what your meal ticket is going to be."[49]

Caso embraced this lifestyle with little trepidation. His participation in document gathering "was not passive or hesitant," one prosecutor recalled. "It gave him status . . . [and] a sense that he was immune from being laid off."[50] Nevertheless, he still could be petty. Feeling betrayed by an aide who left Canoga Park to accept a promotion at another part of Hughes,

Caso blackballed him from receiving any more classified packages. Similarly, Caso had no qualms about calling his counterpart at General Dynamics in San Diego, simply to rebuke him for thinking about dealing with any-body else at Hughes when it came to Pentagon documents.

To ensure an orderly flow of bootlegged data, every avenue was pursued. Nothing was left to chance. The Electronics Industries Association, for instance, scheduled two major conventions each year to share ideas and contemplate the general state of the defense business. Since it was among the industry's most influential and politically plugged-in trade groups, the EIA meetings were well attended. Caso and his confederates naturally jumped at the occasion to trade with one another during, in be-tween and after the formal program. Over the years, the after-hours hud-dles became the centerpiece of the week's activities.

Each fall, EIA also issued something called the "Gold Book," a hefty publication jammed with projections and trend lines for future military orders. If those estimates were helpful, Caso and others decided, why not go a step further. The EIA committee responsible for compiling the data—called the Requirements Council, appropriately enough—included Caso, one of Bernie Zettl's associates at GTE and nearly a dozen other marketing executives. They specialized in sub rosa document handling. The panel set up interviews with senior Defense Department officials, os-tensibly to get information to prepare the "Gold Book." The ground rules were that none of the government officials would be quoted by name in the report, which helped loosen their tongues. Indisputably, EIA leaders gleaned more from the private get-togethers than their public prognosti-cations indicated.

For all intents and purposes, those interviews provided a pipeline into the Pentagon's long-range planning process. Everybody in EIA wanted to sit in on the closed-door briefings. "Really great stuff came from those interviews," says Max Franklin, who worked for Hughes and later for two other contractors. "There was prolonged, persistent and pervasive involve-ment in document swapping," he insists, "at the highest levels" of the EIA.[51]

Another active and official-sounding outfit, called the Aerospace Plan-ners Discussion Group, included many of the same individuals. Meetings were rotated among host companies every few months. Those sessions, too, became prime opportunities to swap industry gossip—and more sig-nificantly, to exchange illicit documents—among some members.

Caso later argued, with some validity, that many in government were aware of such activities but failed to halt them. In retrospect, glaring warning signs were overlooked. In the late 1970s, federal officials ordered an unannounced, one-day security crackdown at Pentagon entrances. As part of the experiment, all documents and other items were inspected on the way out. Bags and belongings were carefully searched, regardless of whom they belonged to. The guards were amazed at the mounds of illicit items they recovered, including so-called "unreceipted" classified papers of the type in which Caso trafficked.

The results still weren't enough to prompt decisive action by the government. The enforcement machinery didn't lurch into action to stop, once and for all, unauthorized document exchanges. For a while, there was talk of change. The Pentagon's security bureaucracy urged adoption of new rules requiring registered mail receipts for classified material furnished to consultants or company executives. But the industry complained vociferously until such talk faded away. The "good old boy" connections held fast. The bonds didn't fray. No action was taken, and the enforcement idea was "rejected as being unfeasible."[52]

Perhaps Caso's most devious trick was ensuring that his ill-gotten papers didn't meet the same fate as the original versions from which they were copied. He was worried that fellow Hughes officials, once they recognized the quality of the files he brought into the company's classified library, would haphazardly try to duplicate them. Frank Caso didn't want anyone else peddling or taking credit for his hard-earned documents. Nobody was going to grab a free ride on his coattails. He finally devised an apparently foolproof solution. First, he meticulously removed government warnings that the documents were out of bounds for contractors. Then, he replaced them with bogus, though equally stern, warning messages of his own. "In light of retention authority requirements," the replacement stamps admonished in perfect legalese, "this document shall not be reproduced without the permission of F. J. Caso." It was the ultimate perversion of classification rules.

No wonder Caso bragged about being a "marketable commodity" who had to fend off job offers. From the East Coast to the Pacific Northwest, industry insiders yearned for a peek at his latest treasures. The cramped office at Canoga Park became known as a convenient clearinghouse for information defense firms desperately wanted—but knew they legally couldn't have.

Caso was just as shrewd at marketing himself to top management. In the summer of 1977, the whole company was buzzing about the new president of missile systems. Malcolm Currie, a senior, well-respected Pentagon official under President Gerald Ford, had been recruited to return to Hughes as head of the Canoga Park division. More than anything else, Caso was aching for recognition. Hoping to impress the incoming boss, he began putting together a special briefing about the marketing department's intelligence-gathering efforts. The two men knew each other from Currie's earlier days at the company, which helped Caso line up a few minutes on the newly arrived executive's packed calendar.

By any measure, Malcolm Roderick Currie wasn't likely to be easily impressed, let alone hoodwinked, by his staff. A dapper engineer with a patrician bearing and a Ph.D. from the University of California at Berkeley, he came with a long list of awards under his belt. As early as 1960, when Currie was in charge of the company's famous Malibu physics laboratory at the age of thirty-three, he had been honored as the "Nation's Outstanding Young Electrical Engineer" and one of five "Outstanding Young Men of California." Currie rose to corporate vice-president within two years, responsible for running several research labs. Before his fortieth birthday, he had climbed to engineering manager for all Hughes aerospace projects, supervising development of the first infrared and laser devices capable of producing images. There was never any question about Currie's scientific brilliance, including twenty-four patents under his name. With his poise and management skills, Hughes veterans tagged him as an ideal candidate for bigger jobs.

Taking a break from corporate life to learn the political byways of Washington, Currie served four years as director of research at the Pentagon. The job was a killer, requiring grueling workweeks and putting him at the center of the most hotly contested defense issues. Other industry leaders had wilted under such pressure, or became fed up with the endless carping by critics in the press and on Capitol Hill. Currie, the Pentagon's fourth-highest-ranking civilian, for the most part avoided those pitfalls. Comfortable in the spotlight, he used his technical credentials and political instincts to appease lawmakers and keep the generals in line. His candid style appealed to contractors. Many of the capital's pundits buzzed about his courteous but no-nonsense demeanor. Such straightforward answers, they remarked, seldom came from defense figures at his level.

But the praise wasn't unanimous, and it didn't last through the end of his tenure. During his final year at the Pentagon, the public glimpsed another side of the ambitious Dr. Currie. There was a flap over a Labor Day weekend trip to a fishing lodge on tropical Bimini, paid for by Rockwell International, one of the biggest Pentagon contractors in the mid-1970s. A Rockwell jet flew Currie, his daughter and a friend to a company-owned lodge on the Bahamian island, where they joined Rockwell's chairman and his family. The jet took Currie's party back to Miami two days later, also at no charge.

Currie and Rockwell spokesmen insisted that no business was discussed during the trip. It still raised a stink in Congress, where critics accused Currie of creating a conflict of interest by continuing to make decisions affecting Rockwell projects such as the B-1 bomber and a Navy air-to-surface missile called the Condor. They clamored for his removal. Defense Secretary Donald Rumsfeld was acutely embarrassed, since the incident came to light immediately after the Ford administration issued new ethics rules barring Pentagon officials from accepting complimentary trips to hunting lodges and fishing resorts, or any other free entertainment from contractors. Rockwell acknowledged hosting more than forty other civilians and officers at company hideaways, but Currie's slipup provoked the most controversy.[53]

Rumsfeld had vowed to "land all over individuals" in the Pentagon who dared to take freebies from defense firms. The secretary considered all his options, presumably including firing Currie, but ended up slapping him with a "severe reprimand" and ordering him to forfeit about three thousand dollars in pay. Currie repaid the cost of the excursion, recused himself from taking part in Condor production decisions, and acknowledged that he had "exercised bad judgment at the time, and I sincerely regret it." The congressional flak was heavy for a couple of months. One lawmaker demanded Currie's suspension for operating under "a dark cloud of suspicion" and denounced his punishment as a "whitewash."[54]

Currie was also criticized years later for his involvement in a second big-ticket missile—this one called the AMRAAM and manufactured by Hughes—that was plagued by loose screws, improperly soldered wiring and other examples of substandard workmanship. AMRAAM production costs were running three times above budget, and Pentagon inspectors found that only six out of ten circuit boards met quality control standards. The assembly-line "instructions didn't follow the designs, and the workers didn't follow the instructions," as one Air Force analyst summed it up. The quality-control snafus induced Congress temporarily to stop accepting the missiles.

Though the criticism of the Rockwell trip was intense, the research chief survived and kept his influence. He stayed until President Jimmy Carter's Georgia Mafia began political housecleaning at the Pentagon after the 1976 election. At that point, Currie opted to go home to Southern California's sunshine and the familiar Hughes hierarchy that had supported him in the past. Democratic senator William Proxmire of Wisconsin, the nemesis of defense contractors, attacked Currie's movement between the Pentagon and Hughes as "a devastating example of the pitiful weakness" of conflict of interest laws.[55]

As Currie settled in at Canoga Park, Caso was wrapping up preparations for the briefing. The idea, as Caso enthusiastically explained to Max Franklin, his assistant at the time, was to lay out "what we do, and how we do it." Preparing flashy charts, summaries and even excerpts of some classified Pentagon documents, Caso intended to present a thorough explanation of his contributions. As always, the intent was to demonstrate how vital his work was to Hughes. Caso "really wanted to impress the hell out of the guy," says Franklin.[56]

But Franklin grew increasingly dubious about the whole notion. It seemed unnecessarily risky, he muttered to himself, and truly dumb. Dr. Currie, after all, recently had been one of the Pentagon bigshots responsible for preparing the documents Caso managed to snare outside regular channels. "He signed some of these things," Franklin worried out loud, getting more and more agitated. "Isn't that going to be a bit awkward?" he asked Caso. Hughes's marketing specialist remained unperturbed, pledging to go ahead with his full presentation as planned.[57]

On briefing day, Franklin stayed behind in the office, sweating to "find out if Frank had been fired." Caso came back beaming. Currie "was very, very impressed" with the quality of the budget information and "wants to see more of it," Caso reassured the anxious assistant. "He wanted to know how I'd gotten that stuff. I told him I had industry contacts."[58]

Describing Currie's return to the company, Caso elaborated years later on what happened. Currie "thoroughly supported" gathering Pentagon documents, Caso claimed under oath, alleging that the missile division chief told him the intelligence was "something that we need" to compete. "In his very nice charming way," Caso claimed, "he put his arm around me and said, 'I've known you a long time, Frank. I am looking forward to working with you a long time.' "[59]

☆

Francis J. Caso realized the government was gunning for him when a federal agent unexpectedly showed up at his office building with a subpoena. Startled by the phone call from the security desk, Caso told the guard to stall. Breathing hard and pacing frantically, he needed time to think. What did it mean? What kind of trouble was he in? Where should he turn?

The time was June 1989, and Bellows was cranking up his probe. Caso knew beforehand that both he and Hughes were under criminal scrutiny. Three months earlier, over his vehement objections, the company had abruptly reassigned him after getting wind of the Justice Department investigation. He no longer had any role in handling classified documents or identifying new Pentagon business. But this sudden activity by prosecutors made Caso's heart race. He called his lawyer, excitedly telling him "the guy is waiting downstairs in the lobby, right now." His voice raspy and low, Caso sounded hysterical. "What should I do?" he kept asking.[60]

The plan Caso came up with was elementary. Caso rushed down the stairs and ran out the back door. After driving home at breakneck speed, he hid out for two days. Caso's attorney accepted the subpoena for testimony before the grand jury, responding that his client opted to take the Fifth Amendment. Soon afterward, Caso plotted his next move to try to outsmart prosecutors. Despite promising to share information with Hughes and fight the government in tandem with company attorneys, he was drawn to a completely different strategy. Instead of fighting Randy Bellows, he pondered, why not cooperate with him? Caso hoped to save himself by implicating Mal Currie, who was now the chairman and chief executive officer of Hughes.

The new title gave Currie instant celebrity status. Though he had been one of the defense industry's leading lights before the promotion, the average person wouldn't have recognized him. That wasn't true any longer. As chairman, Currie was the featured spokesman in the company's national advertising campaigns. His carefully coiffed countenance, with the high cheekbones and penetrating eyes, appeared in prime-time television spots. His smiling face peered out from full-page color ads in national news magazines. Dignified yet seemingly unpretentious, Currie's image transcended the defense arena. He wasn't in the same league as Chrysler's chairman, Lee Iacocca, the flashy and irascible darling of the news media. But Hughes's advertising consultants saw parallels between the two executives. In the nation's psyche, Currie also came to symbolize the comforting, human face of Big Business. Caso figured the public attention had to work in his favor. No aggressive young prosecutor, he concluded, would resist such a prominent target.

Two weeks after Caso's midday sprint to avoid the law, Dean Francis Pace, his defense counsel, made an initial pitch to the government. The approach wasn't subtle. Was the U.S. attorney's office "interested in getting a CEO?" Pace asked Bellows. There was a pregnant pause, as the prosecutor waited for elaboration. Caso was prepared to cooperate fully with investigators and make sure they grasped the intricacies of the industry's marketing structure, the lawyer explained over the phone. He finally came to the nub of the issue. In exchange for blanket protection from prosecution, Caso "would give the government the CEO of Hughes Aircraft on a silver platter."[61]

Bellows already had circumstantial evidence to make him suspicious of Hughes's top management, and more would be dug up as the investigation proceeded. It turned out that Caso and his associates had written several memos to Currie plainly referring by name to classified budget material contractors weren't supposed to have. Exactly the same kind of memos went to executives right under Currie. In these instances, there was no subterfuge employed. The opening paragraph of one memo Caso wrote on which Currie was copied, for example, explicitly mentioned that information dealing with the MX missile was extracted from the Pentagon's "Consolidated Guidance" document, well known to be classified. The guidance was intended only for the eyes of high-level Pentagon decision-makers.

A lengthy March 1983 memo, following up on a specific Currie request, declared point-blank in the introduction that Caso had "reviewed" the Pentagon's Program Objective Memorandum on certain advanced missile programs. Never bashful about touting the service he provided, Caso quoted numbers in the text taken straight from the Pentagon's Five-Year Defense Program. Although some of the information inevitably was available to the defense community, so-called POMs and FYDPs were supposed to be closely held within the Pentagon and were not authorized to be distributed even to representatives of contractors carrying top-secret clearances.

Still another memo that went to Currie had the unmistakable heading, in bold capital letters, "SUBJECT: POM 84." A few months later, Caso's office advised some of Currie's most trusted subordinates that it had a copy of one of the volumes of the latest FYDP. "If you would like any additional programs tracked," the memo helpfully offered, "please notify this office."

Caso's suspect memos were not the only evidence that could be interpreted to implicate Currie. Sharyn Pinkstaff, Caso's executive assistant, later swore that she actually delivered some of the bootlegged documents—not just summaries of them—directly to Currie's office. Sometimes, Caso contends, terse instructions would come back from Currie's office. "I would highlight some portions," Caso alleges, adding that he would get back a note saying, 'Follow this or that program,' "[62] With high-ranking Hughes executives receiving unauthorized information, there was little concern at lower levels about potential criminal violations. At most, Pinkstaff claims, she believed the potential sanctions were akin to risking "a traffic ticket." If Currie "didn't know the rules and security didn't know the rules," she asks, "who was I to know? I had to rely on them."[63]

Currie strongly denies even receiving copies of Pentagon documents that contractors weren't supposed to have. He maintains that he never approved illegal document gathering, adding that assertions to the contrary were merely ploys by Caso to try and save himself. Moreover, Bellows was not convinced by such evidence. He made up his mind early on that he wasn't interested in prosecuting Currie or anyone else who had possibly illicit budget information in his in-basket. A higher standard of proof was required, the prosecutor concluded. Nevertheless, investigators questioned Currie as a witness.

Bellows laughed at Caso's bid for immunity. He was bemused by Pace's pompous, condescending delivery. The defense lawyer from Los Angeles fancied himself a gourmet, regaling everyone he met with stories about rare wines and outlandish dishes. Pace's high opinion of his own skills was exceeded only by the number of times he steered the conversation back to himself in a ten-minute chat, according to Bellows. Dealing with hard-nosed prosecutors requires another mindset altogether. This guy is a piece of work, Bellows decided. He may understand civil law or tax cases, the prosecutor thought, but he is naive in criminal matters. "It was an amazing experience," Bellows chuckles to this day, noting that Pace "insisted on talking about himself in the third person, using all three names."

There were more telling reasons Caso's gambit to avoid prosecution was bound to fail. Investigators felt insulted by suggestions that, after breaking their backs to unravel the industry's information network, they couldn't make sense of the case without Caso's explanations. From the beginning, Randy Bellows also had a visceral distrust of the man's truthfulness. Criminals will say anything to avoid serving time, the prosecutor used to remind his alter ego, Matt Walinski. Bellows swore by an axiom he had picked up around the Harvard quadrangle. Too often, he used to say, prosecutors delude themselves into believing they are getting the complete story from cooperating witnesses. "But when you get inside the grand jury room," he lectured Walinski repeatedly, "they'll probably tell you 80 percent. When you go trial, they're going to tell you only 50 percent."[64] Bellows wasn't about to step into that trap.

On top of everything else, the prosecutor was incensed that Caso had persisted in trading documents—continuing to rely on a separate log with a secret code—long after some industry chums had dropped out and warned him to do the same. Caso and his accomplices "ignored the stop signs," Bellows liked to say. "They ignored the red lights . . . [and] virtually every aspect of their obligations" to the government.[65]

Caso eventually hired counsel more experienced in representing white-collar criminal defendants. The lawyers accused Bellows of "missing the boat" by not paying more heed to Currie and other high-ranking Hughes officials. "Why pin the little guy," defense attorney Marcus Topel complained angrily to Bellows, while allowing "upper-level participants to skate" away. "I just thought it was unconscionable, and I told him that," the feisty Topel recalls.[66] But the die was cast. Bellows had declared, flat out, there would be no immunity for Caso. Had Caso agreed to plead guilty and face a prison sentence, his allegations would have been taken more seriously. "The government wasn't going to let him walk, under any circumstances," according to the prosecutor.[67]

At the same time, attorneys representing Hughes were acting macho as well. Crowing about what a strong case they had, the attorneys said the company was adamant about going to trial if it was charged. They reassured Caso he could depend on their help. The rhetoric boosted Caso's spirits, convincing him that the joint defense agreement he had signed with Hughes was a lifeline. In fact, the combative talk was nothing but a ruse. Unbeknownst to Frank Caso or his lawyers, Hughes was posturing to cop a plea.

The contractor had other legal headaches driving it toward Bellows's grasp. An unrelated Justice Department investigation of bribery involving commercial satellite contracts was creating a great deal of anxiety inside Hughes. Already, the probe had forced out Albert Wheelon, Currie's predecessor in the chairman's office. Wheelon wasn't charged with any crime, but he stepped down two weeks after the government subpoenaed his records. A pair of senior officials at Intelsat, an international telecommunications consortium based in Washington, D.C., became implicated in kickbacks. The scandal threatened to spread.[68] Currie's elevation to chairman in May 1988 was intended, in part, to ease the turmoil and distance the company from past mistakes. Two years later, Bellows was making that job a lot harder.

Hughes couldn't take the chance of being indicted on document-swapping charges in Alexandria, while the second criminal probe was still chugging along across the Potomac. The board of directors of General Motors, the parent company, saw only one safe path. As embarrassing as it would be, common sense dictated a plea bargain. Once Hughes started negotiating, it took only a few days to seal the deal.

On Friday, March 9, 1990, Hughes Aircraft Company agreed to pay $3.6 million to the government, admitting that it illegally acquired two classified Pentagon budget documents. The bare-bones felony charges, less than three pages long, left out details of how the scheme operated. "Based on evidence developed to date," prosecutors told the court that they didn't "presently intend" to file charges against any current or former Hughes officials except Caso. Magnanimous in victory, the Justice Department went out of its way to cushion the impact on Hughes. Prosecutors vouched that the contractor had cooperated fully with them over the course of the investigation.

Based on the felony conviction, the Air Force threatened to bar the Canoga Park operation from bidding on military contracts for three years. Newspaper articles speculated about one of the most draconian penalties ever imposed on a major defense firm. Company spokesmen moaned that government retribution could be "fatal" for the missile group. But the punishment quickly was revealed to be a sham. In spite of the government's saber rattling and a temporary suspension meted out to the missile group, other Hughes subsidiaries had no trouble picking up over $620 million in new Pentagon business during the ensuing months. By mid-June the missile unit was reinstated as a "responsible contractor," making it eligible again to take on fresh business.

The company's decision to throw in the towel was devastating for Caso. "Getting Hughes to plead was a big deal," so Bellows "figured anything after that was icing on the cake," contends Topel, the defense lawyer. Whatever interest the government may have had "in using Caso to get Currie or other higher-ups at Hughes," Topel claims, evaporated at that point. The facts of the case "justified activity in that direction," he says. "But I sure didn't see any."[69]

Chairman Currie was a model of rectitude throughout the episode. In a letter circulated to employees the afternoon of the plea, he declared that "acquisition and possession of such documents was wrong and cannot be justified. We have learned from this incident, and we should all renew our personal commitment to the standards of business conduct and integrity we have set for ourselves." But such comments didn't keep questions from being raised about Currie's involvement.

Ten days after nabbing Hughes, Bellows got the shock of his life. Wrapping up loose ends in the case he was preparing against Caso, Bellows was in the midst of interviewing a former Hughes security officer. So far, the session was unremarkable; the questions and answers were traipsing over old ground. Out of the blue, Jim Calder, the former security man, blurted out that high-ranking executives had approved Caso's document-identification system. The prosecutor's mind sprang to attention. "It's all in the memo," Calder insisted. Bellows was positive the government had never obtained such a memo. "So, you have it here with you?" the prosecutor asked, holding his breath. Calder calmly handed over four neat, single-spaced memos, all written by him in the late 1970s, touching on Currie's alleged dealings with Caso.[70]

The papers told a story investigators hadn't heard before. In the spring of 1978, Hughes security cited Caso for bringing in classified documents without receipts and destroying them via back-door arrangements. Caso was outraged. "I have done everything you guys told me to do," he said, protesting that the violation could jeopardize his "Top Secret" security clearance. "Why do I have to take the fall?"[71] He allegedly appealed to Currie for help, according to his testimony and one of the memos, and claimed that new procedures were authorized to ensure that the flow of illicit information would continue.

Calder spelled it out, point by point, in a memo to the file dated July 10, 1978, apparently written months later. Caso and the head of marketing "described their meeting with M. R. Currie," the memo indicated, "in which Currie was made aware of both the current and previous system that Caso has maintained for sensitive information gathering." Calder went on to write that both marketing men "stated that Currie supports the continuation of information gathering." The last line of the memo was the most titillating: "Allegedly, Currie told Caso to be extremely careful in his involvement with this matter."

Caso testified much later that Currie was sympathetic, cordial and eager to solve the problem. "As I walked out" of his office, Caso recounted, "he again shook my hand and said, 'No, don't worry; things will work out fine.' "[72]

During the next seven years, Caso essentially was able to bring any papers he wished into Hughes's classified library without company security officers scrutinizing their contents. Eventually the rules were loosened even more for Caso, making him the only executive at Canoga Park authorized to log in classified material merely by making a phone call to a Hughes clerk.[73] The head of corporate security memorialized the procedure in a written directive, even though it circumvented government requirements.[74] Another Calder memo indicated how advantageous the marketing intelligence was for Hughes. "Caso may not be the only person in the company doing what he considers to be important for our business," the memo stressed, "but he is the only one I know of with an identifiable charter."

The existence of Calder's stash, which he took with him when he left the company, created pandemonium in the U.S. attorney's office more than a decade later. Bellows gulped for air; he didn't know what to say. It was a prosecutor's nightmare. "You could have peeled me off the ceiling," Bellows recalls.[75] In all his years chasing crooks, he couldn't remember such intriguing evidence showing up *after* a guilty plea.

The attorneys for Hughes were no less dumbfounded. They buzzed about the rest of the paper trail Caso had left behind. In agitated tones, they swore to Bellows that none of Calder's memos had turned up when they combed through files to compile documents demanded by federal subpoenas. Stepping into a nearby room for a minute, Bellows heard the company's lawyer shrieking at Calder for withholding information from Hughes.

Calder's memos clearly were new information, meaning that technically Bellows could have reopened the probe and gone after additional targets. But the evidence was old, and Calder's memory seemed spotty. More important, there still was no corroboration of what, if anything, had transpired between Currie and Caso out of other people's earshot. Indeed, Currie contended he was out of the country during the period of the alleged initial meeting. It would come down to one man's word against the other's, and the prosecutor had written off Frank Caso's veracity some time ago.[76]

The bottom line, Bellows felt, was that it would be inappropriate to prosecute individuals who merely read snippets of illicit files, or failed to curb the flow of unauthorized information. Those who actively gathered and circulated the documents, he decided, were the most culpable and deserving of punishment. Calder's memos, as fascinating as they were, by themselves "weren't enough to convince me that any other people were guilty," Bellows says in hindsight.[77] One former associate of Calder and Caso recalls that investigators never asked her about Currie.

In any event, the prosecutor didn't have the luxury of agonizing over what to do. If he didn't seek an indictment against Caso immediately, the statute would expire and the Hughes marketing analyst would slip away for good. Two days after the memos surfaced, Bellows persuaded the federal grand jury to act. Caso was indicted for conspiring to defraud the United States over a fifteen-year period.

In court, the defense played its Currie card to the hilt. Caso was portrayed as a humble "salaried Joe," a dutiful "little guy" performing his assigned tasks in blissful ignorance of federal laws. Caso alleged, in his testimony, that Currie's intervention was the catalyst that helped him funnel hundreds of documents into Hughes. "If anybody would know whether there was anything illegal or criminal," Caso told the jury, Currie "certainly would." When he had a job offer from another contractor, Caso testified, it was Currie he sought out for advice. "Hughes wants you to stay here," Caso recalled the boss saying.[78]

The defense strategy hinged on having the Hughes chairman testify. Topel was convinced that getting Currie to take the stand would raise questions in the minds of the jurors about the government's case, giving Caso "very, very powerful equity in the courtroom." The theory, however, was never tested. Attempts to serve Currie with a subpoena summoning him to appear as a witness were unsuccessful. Currie's lawyer declined to accept the subpoena. By the time a livid Topel demanded a hearing to compel testimony, the Hughes chief had left for South America on a previously scheduled trip as part of a trade delegation led by Commerce Secretary Robert Mosbacher. "I considered that highly improper," Topel recalls. "I'm a big boy. I know how the game is played. But that was pretty rough."[79]

The defense wasn't able to salvage much from the clash. Currie never testified, nor did two other high-ranking Hughes executives Caso's lawyers wanted to question. Currie's lawyer insists that his client "did nothing to make it difficult to get his testimony introduced at the trial." As a sop to Caso, the judge agreed to instruct the jury that the executives weren't available "despite the best efforts of the defense."

Bellows tried to play down Currie's possible role during the trial. How handy, he told the jury, for Caso to "trot out" the names of high-ranking Hughes executives to defend his behavior. "These men are Mr. Caso's cover story," Bellows snapped, nothing more. They never authorized or instructed Caso to break the law, the prosecutor said. Bellows pushed this argument to the limit in his summation. Even the improbable notion that some of Caso's bosses knew about or condoned illegal conduct, he argued, doesn't absolve the defendant of guilt. "Mr. Caso is no less guilty because Mr. Currie may be guilty, too . . . or anyone else at Hughes," Bellows told the jury.[80]

Sarcastic and indignant by turns, the prosecutor engaged in some hyperbole of his own. In the event Caso is acquitted, "You had better batten down the hatches because the law doesn't mean anything any more," Bellows breathlessly warned jurors. The rhetoric got superheated after that. "You can throw out the way we function as a society," Bellows declared, if Caso can ignore the rules simply "because he says I decided to ignore them."[81]

Caso was found guilty and sentenced to six months in a halfway house. His wife, Nanette, also was pushed off the Hughes payroll. Speaking of Caso, Jim Calder now maintains, "I knew that same day this particular loose cannon would end up hurting the company." The conviction was appealed unsuccessfully all the way to the Supreme Court. Caso enjoyed a modicum of revenge by filing a civil action accusing the contractor of reneging on the joint defense agreement. The suit alleged that Hughes should have alerted Caso about its intention to plead guilty. But by this time, Caso was too worn down, psychologically and financially, to be a credible adversary. To help pay for huge psychiatric bills, he worked for a time in a Roundtable Pizza parlor. Frank Caso finally accepted a face-saving settlement with Hughes that basically covered the legal fees in the civil case but nothing else. The final act of Operation Uncover was over.

The way the curtain came down still galls Mike Costello, the senior Pentagon agent who participated in the investigation. He can't hide his disdain for executives who encouraged the black market in documents but conveniently insulated themselves from its consequences. One senior Democratic senator terms it the industry's "Wild West mentality of grabbing what it can" while mouthing patriotic platitudes.[82] Costello puts it another way. "The ones that got away, got away by the skin of their teeth," he says.[83] By 1990, the Justice Department and the media had shifted their focus back to Operation Illwind, the other Pentagon fraud case, trying to unravel the Reagan era's excesses. The government was closing in on Mel Paisley, the flamboyant former Boeing and Navy official who knew casually some of the defendants prosecuted by Bellows.

☆

Mal Currie, meanwhile, conducted a quiet campaign to undermine the credibility of his critics. At the time of Caso's trial, all he said publicly was that the allegations against him were based on "innuendo and hearsay." He steadfastly maintained that he "did not know or approve of the unlawful activities." Since then, the explanation has expanded. His lawyer says that Dr. Currie "had little contact" with Caso, attended "few, if any" one-on-one briefings with the marketing analyst and "absolutely didn't know about the Caso scheme." If Currie received information from illicit Pentagon documents, the lawyer asserts, he "did not know the source" and assumed that the budget data came from newspapers or industry publications that frequently published excerpts from classified reports. "It doesn't mean that the underlying document had been made available" to Currie, says attorney Herbert J. Miller, dismissing such allegations as sheer "nonsense." Still bitter about anyone daring to question his integrity, Currie, through his lawyer, insists that he "never approved a system to make it easier for Mr. Caso to bring Pentagon documents into the company."[84]

Currie's supporters also point to congressional reports stressing chronic Pentagon confusion over which documents contractors were entitled to review. The month before Hughes's guilty plea, for instance, a Senate Governmental Affairs subcommittee concluded that the military was relying on rules that were "highly complex, confusing, unclear, and occasionally misunderstood even by the officials responsible for administering them." The panel found 336 separate guidelines and regulations, with senators complaining that disclosure rules among the services were inconsistent.[85] The legal issues were clarified by the early 1990s, when Congress demanded full public disclosure of many of the long-term budgeting and planning documents Caso and Hughes had taken such great risks to obtain.

Currie retired from Hughes on schedule in early 1992, upon turning sixty-five. Before stepping down, however, he vented his spleen at a procurement system he claimed was out of control. Criminal investigations and litigation "have become a way of life" for contractors, he complained, and almost every decision mistakenly is based on "the inference that everything is fraudulent." The result, Currie asserted, is horrendous delay, extra cost and a paucity of top-notch executives willing to accept jobs in the Pentagon. "We're being managed by lawyers and accountants, rather than real leaders," he railed. Federal investigators have "gone way too far" worrying about fraud and abuse, Currie told his hushed audience. "One hundred times too far."[86]

Upon leaving Hughes, he made the transition to eminent industry consultant and sought-after civic booster without missing a stride. As a University of Southern California trustee and an advisory board member for the University of California at Berkeley and UCLA, his academic ties remained intact. He also served on the board of Unocal Corporation, an oil giant with headquarters in downtown Los Angeles. Joining forces with Roy Anderson, the chairman emeritus of Lockheed, Currie headed a blue-ribbon commission set up to create jobs and attract industry to California to compensate for defense cutbacks.

Today, the stature of the former Hughes chief seems undiminished, and he is as much in demand as ever. An endless string of business and philanthropic groups vie for his endorsement. He holds press conferences with California's governor and state legislative leaders. He travels around the country assessing defense conversion projects, and his testimony is solicited by public and private organizations. Currie is widely quoted on the issues of American competitiveness overseas and high-speed rail and alternative-fuel vehicles back home.

Federal and state agencies eagerly heed his policy prescriptions. Electric-powered cars are "a blueprint for the environmental and economic revitalization of California," he confidently told one air-pollution public hearing in the spring of 1994. While dozens of other witnesses cooled their heels, Currie was lauded profusely and allowed to speak first. To widespread applause, he described California as "an invaluable laboratory of the future," where government and industry cooperation has "stimulated a tremendous surge of entrepreneurial activity."

As the invitations and speaking engagements keep rolling in, friends say Currie feels vindicated. His creative juices are flowing. The retiree's latest venture is a startup firm producing tiny, environmentally benign engines able to be installed on everyday bicycles but supposedly powerful enough to make them cruise at twenty miles per hour. Current admirers couldn't care less about the Canoga Park mysteries once evoked by Jim Calder's faded memos. They have no time to ponder the allegations made by Frank Caso and others, which are filed away in the Justice Department's yellowing cardboard storage boxes.

The investigators who packed up those files also fared pretty well. Bellows received a letter of commendation from Attorney General Richard Thornburgh, praising him for collecting $15 million from the defense industry. The prosecutor was pleased, framing it and hanging it in a prominent place on his office wall, next to his daughters' finger paintings.

Matt Walinski grabbed his share of the limelight in the end. He received a big promotion and a plaque from fellow agents expressing admiration for his accomplishments. "I never worked on anything that hard in my life," he recalls with satisfaction. With his new job and public acclaim,

Walinski still harbors bittersweet emotions. Intellectually, he understands he was lucky to jump on the case of a lifetime. But in his gut, he feels the natural letdown after an epic struggle. No matter how long he stays in law enforcement, Walinski realizes, in all probability he will never again savor quite the same rush of adrenaline. The words come haltingly. But the apprehension is heartfelt. "It was my opportunity," Walinski says. "I'll never get back to that; I'll never be named fraud investigator of the year again."[87]

In the face of Operation Uncover's success, Hughes Aircraft now acts as though it was untouched by the faintest whiff of criminality. Boeing's charmed public image also survived the investigation, as well as an unrelated $75-million settlement of government overcharge allegations in May 1994, intact. Depicting some of Boeing's accounting tricks in the subsequent case as "particularly egregious," federal investigators said that the company had padded thousands of Pentagon accounts with research and hazardous-waste-disposal costs that should have been covered entirely by corporate funds. The Justice Department characterized the bills as part of a "complex and deeply rooted" pattern of mischarges spanning the 1980s. The U.S. attorney in Seattle alleged that the company lied to investigators to try to cover up the phony billing system.

Regardless of what Boeing is caught doing or failing to do, however, it always seems able to ride out the controversy with minimal setbacks. Unfazed by the government's contentions in 1994, Boeing's legal department was busy spinning a different story. The firm's press release announcing the settlement never used the word "mischarging" or admitted violating any laws. According to Boeing, the tens of millions of dollars in dispute stemmed from minor misinterpretations of federal procurement rules. The company said the issues were nothing more than "unintended cost classification errors"—just good-faith differences of opinion over hard-to-grasp accounting details, if you will—that should have been resolved in a less adversarial manner. Coming long after Uncover and Illwind, the airplane-maker felt that the civil settlement was just another irritant it had to shake off to claim its rightful place in the pantheon of American industry.

In Springfield, Virginia, Dick Fowler's saga finished on a more somber note. His wife, children and grandchildren were overjoyed when he returned home after serving a total of twenty-seven months in prison, but Boeing alumnus Charlie Welling described Fowler's situation in gripping terms. He said that Boeing's managers, who instigated and rewarded criminal activity, ultimately "hung Dick out to dry." They could have protected him "as well as they protected all their vice-presidents, their senior program managers, all the guys who profited from Dick's work," Welling said.[88] He likened the company's performance to "bluefish in a feeding frenzy: the more they eat, the more they want until the water is nothing but a bloody froth ... Then the school moves on, leaving the mess behind."[89]

Another former colleague of Fowler's, retired Air Force colonel

Richard Coupland, put it this way: Boeing's criminal fine "was a bargain" that gave high-ranking executives "total immunity," while it "appears to have sacrificed a single participant."[90] Even Walinski grudgingly admits that Fowler is "a stand-up guy." His superiors "knew he wasn't going to give them up," the agent says, "and he still hasn't."[91]

The ignominious finale was a message from Boeing's legal department. The company had paid in excess of $780,000 to cover Fowler's legal fees over more than seven years, including the unsuccessful appeal. A first-class Washington firm represented him during the entire ordeal. It didn't spare any expense, and Fowler hardly ever perused the bills. Suddenly, Boeing determined that he had to repay the full amount. Conviction by a jury, the icy letter from company counsel Nancy Higgins declared, necessarily meant that Fowler "had reasonable cause to believe that his conduct was unlawful." Under those circumstances, she said, the company wouldn't be responsible any longer for the bills.

Fowler smiled when he opened the letter. He and his wife live in a rented townhouse, in a decidedly modest section of Northern Virginia. A financial statement provided to Boeing shows that he isn't employed and has no savings accounts or stocks and bonds to fall back on. His federal pension amounts to less than thirty-five thousand dollars a year. Boeing could repossess his fourteen-year-old Oldsmobile, or it could grab the twenty-five dollars he sends the government each month as an installment to pay off his criminal fine. "If Boeing can find a way to get blood out of a turnip," he cracks, "they can stop making airplanes." Rubbing his stubbly chin and breaking into a lopsided grin, he says: "I'm not too worried about it."[92]

Chapter X

FINDING AN ALTER EGO

Cruising above Lebanon's arid hills and the teeming refugee camps of the Israeli-occupied West Bank, Caspar Weinberger didn't suspect that he and his aircraft would be employed as props to demonstrate Israel's military wizardry.

The defense secretary was touring the region early in his tenure, sent by the White House to promote President Reagan's cease-fire proposals. At a stop in war-ravaged Beirut, Weinberger mingled with a contingent of U.S. Marines serving as part of an international peacekeeping force. Setting out from Israeli soil early the next morning, the secretary and his entourage crisscrossed the desert in a flock of helicopters. They flew over terrorist training areas and swooped down for brief inspections of destitute Arab villages, before completing an aerial survey of Israeli settlements. Israeli defense minister Ariel Sharon explained that his countrymen chose to live on higher ground, perched on promontories with a view of surrounding communities, to assure themselves "the maximum military advantage."[1] At the end of the bone-jarring ride, Weinberger's hosts invited him to partake in some refreshments and relax by watching a short movie.

The secretary was amazed at what he saw. It was a videotape of his recent travels, including the previous day's morale-boosting visit with American troops. The film had been shot from a high-altitude, Israeli-built drone that neither Weinberger nor his bodyguards had noticed circling overhead. The images were uncannily sharp. The pilotless aircraft's sophisticated camera was stabilized to remain in focus, and its relatively slow speed provided excellent picture quality. Impressed by the performance of the remotely controlled planes—whose small size made them hard to spot and fairly inexpensive to build—Weinberger subsequently instructed the Joint Chiefs of Staff to provide comparable equipment for American servicemen.

Later in the Reagan era, during one of John Lehman's trips to the Middle East, the Israelis repeated the dramatic show. By this time, the Navy chief had heard about the drones and their outstanding capabilities. He was surprised nevertheless when, after landing at what looked like a sleepy outpost with a few deserted vehicles alongside the tarmac, he was escorted into a van and shown closeup films of his aircraft touching down barely a few minutes earlier. "I saw the results. I saw how well it worked,"

Lehman recalled.[2] "It knocked his socks off," according to an Israeli official.[3] Tel Aviv had won another convert for its technology. In the same stroke, the stage was set for Mel Paisley to ram through one more contract to benefit himself and his associates in crime.

Paisley's portfolio in the Navy included international research efforts, of which collaborative endeavors with Israel were among the most secretive and important. As he had done with other classified projects, Paisley convinced Lehman to give him carte blanche to oversee spending in this arena. "We've got to get these programs under the same discipline" as the rest of the Navy's research agenda, Paisley emphatically told his boss. "All of them . . . should be put under my supervision."[4] Since Israel received nearly two billion dollars in U.S. military assistance each year, its willingness to cooperate on a wide range of sensitive weapons experiments was hardly surprising. Paisley, for example, was put in charge of a joint effort to develop miniature night-vision scopes for Navy helicopter pilots. He was responsible for work on so-called "bunker buster" bombs, designed to penetrate fortified underground command shelters. Israeli scientists also were on the cutting edge of missile development, so they participated in research on one aspect of Reagan's futuristic antimissile shield concept, popularly known as "Star Wars."

Paisley established strong unofficial ties to Israel as well, as his private life intersected with his official duties. Shlomo Zabludowicz, a friend of former prime minister Golda Meir and one of Israel's richest arms dealers and manufacturers, had spent the better part of a decade cultivating both Paisley and Lehman. The patriarch of the Zabludowicz clan controlled a sprawling financial empire of munitions factories, real estate holdings, offshore companies and international investments conservatively estimated as worth hundreds of millions of dollars.[5] One of his U.S. subsidiaries won a share of a hotly contested Army mortar contract after building a manufacturing plant near Scranton, Pennsylvania: The factory's managers also wanted to sell the weapon to the Marines and turn out training ammunition. As a token of respect, Zabludowicz once sent a working model of the weapon to Paisley's office through the mail. Pentagon security guards didn't bother to check the contents. When the crate was opened, Paisley wisecracked, "I could point it out the window and lob shells right into the Rose Garden."[6] Some of the other Zabludowicz enterprises were looking for possible Navy work down the road. When Paisley left the Pentagon, the family hired him as a consultant in what one of the old man's lawyers acknowledged amounted to an "insurance policy" for future business.

Meanwhile, younger members of the family had befriended the Navy's assistant secretary. Zabludowicz's son-in-law, an acclaimed medical researcher working in the United States, advised Paisley on various treatments for his diagnosed prostate cancer. Zabludowicz's playboy son, nicknamed Pujo, had a mansion in suburban Virginia and partied with the fun-loving crowd of influential Pentagon appointees and congressional staffers that included Paisley and Lehman. Once Pujo decided to settle down, Mel and Vicki Paisley were invited to his ornate wedding.

Unmanned Air Vehicles, as drones are called in military parlance, were prime examples of the benefits of U.S.-Israeli cooperation. The two governments had talked for a long time about pooling resources, and a substantial volume of technical data had been exchanged. The subject gained urgency in late 1983, when a U.S. armada, led by the newly recommissioned USS *New Jersey*, was dispatched for action off the Lebanese coast. The vessels were sent to retaliate for continued shelling of the Marine Corps compound at the Beirut airport, and they were supposed to punish militant Arab forces fighting in the Shouf mountains farther inland. Shortly thereafter, terror gripped the Marine detachment. A suicide bomber driving a yellow Mercedes truck loaded with an estimated nine tons of TNT crashed into its headquarters building. The explosion lifted the four-story structure off its foundation, killing 241 Marines and wounding 100 others in the rubble.

With their awesome firepower, Lehman's World War II–era battleships seemed ideal for coping with the chaos in Lebanon. Heavy armor made the *New Jersey* and her sister ships practically invulnerable to enemy missiles or artillery. Floating safely offshore, their sixteen-inch guns could hurl eight hundred tons of shells in thirty minutes at targets that were twenty miles away. But as the Navy secretary learned, much to his chagrin, this type of long-distance bombardment wasn't effective without spotters, hovering overhead, to direct fire to selected points. The Joint Chiefs complained about the lack of accuracy.[7] Saturation shelling was the only way a battleship could knock out certain missile emplacements, for instance. Worse yet, commanders were reluctant to use the big guns if they couldn't be certain of not hitting innocent civilians. Sending pilots in as spotters was dangerous, as the downing of two jets by Syrian antiaircraft batteries amply demonstrated. The Navy chief came away from the deadly Lebanese encounter convinced that the fleet badly needed UAVs, not only to help naval gunners but also to assess damage from bombing raids.

Usually insistent on competition, in this case Secretary Lehman wasn't willing to wait three to five years to go through the normal development phase and competitive bidding process. "I'm tired of hearing all this bullshit about a joint program," he snapped. "We need something now. Do it."[8] In 1984, over the vehement objections of several American manufacturers, he ordered the purchase of a handful of land-based drones straight from the Israelis.

About a year later, in what the program officer described as an "extraordinary" departure from the Navy's procurement rules, Lehman "dictated" the purchase of as much as $100 million worth of additional drones.[9] These had to be rocket-assisted versions, capable of being launched from and recovered on the decks of battleships. Secretary

Lehman decreed that a fast-track competition would be held, bypassing normal purchasing safeguards and slashing perhaps 80 percent off the typical decision time for such a new and complicated program. The drones had to be deployed before their in-use performance was verified. Proponents argued that the extremely unusual, "buy-before-you-fly" approach was the sole way to satisfy the Navy's urgent needs. Lehman considered it a commonsense antidote to the "red tape and twenty-year development cycles that had become the norm in the Pentagon."[10] What the secretary envisioned, according to one veteran officer, "was like turning on a light switch."

On the other hand, critics claimed that the novel acquisition procedure, dubbed a "Quick Go" program, was geared toward Israel from the beginning. To start with, the Navy said it would accept only off-the-shelf equipment. Moreover, the performance parameters seemed tailored to fit the Israeli-designed Pioneer, a single-engine, four-hundred-pound craft able to fly for three hours and transmit video images up to one hundred miles. The Navy also sought a remote-receiver station, portable controls and a backup communication channel—all of which were considered unique to the foreign system.[11] Wags said the Navy's biggest headache was finding someone to translate the glossy Hebrew brochures outlining the Pioneer's specifications into English in time to issue the request for bids.

Mostly, competitors howled that the rushed timetable put them at an immense disadvantage, making the outcome a foregone conclusion. "We really felt that the Navy secretary was very thick with the Israelis," a California contractor recalls.[12] Richard Armitage, a top Weinberger deputy who dealt extensively with the Middle East, agrees that Israeli representatives "were flogging [the drones] around Washington . . . They came in to lobby all of us, all the time."[13] The Israelis hooked up with an American partner, suburban Baltimore–based AAI Corporation, to seal the victory. For a variety of reasons—including the Navy's stubborn refusal to relent even slightly on the schedule—no other domestic drone-maker took part in the planned flyoff.

In short order, the Navy signed a contract to buy the Pioneer, along with an array of communication and flight control components. The price tag totaled more than a quarter of a million dollars per copy. Admirals soon complained about crashes, poor quality and inadequate logistics. Navy auditors recommended holding up funding for the drones, plus withholding any follow-on contracts, until obvious shortcomings were resolved. Their warnings, though, were to no avail. Paisley kept pushing for increased reliance on hardware manufactured by Mazlat Limited, the Israeli firm that created the Pioneer. In-depth operational tests could be conducted down the line, he argued, reminding critics at every juncture that the streamlined procurement steps had been reviewed and affirmed repeatedly by Lehman. Those wishing to slow or stop the top-priority program, Paisley wrote the vice-chief of naval operations, were engaged in "unacceptable" behavior. The Pioneer's foes, Paisley's memo concluded, were ignoring the secretary's explicit guidance by trying "to force the UAV program back into the conventional business as usual approach."[14]

What Paisley didn't disclose was that Mazlat early on had retained Bill Galvin as a consultant to help land Navy business. According to the plan the two buddies hatched, the initial Pioneer buy would become the key to Mazlat's participation in longer-range, more powerful spy-in-the-sky drones the Pentagon was contemplating purchasing. Demand for remotely controlled aircraft was poised to rise dramatically. Some estimates pegged the overall market in the billions of dollars by the end of the decade. Dazzled by the possibilities, Paisley, Galvin and two more compatriots secretly agreed to split roughly six million dollars—to be siphoned off illegally from Mazlat with the help of Israeli accomplices—as the firm received more and more U.S. orders.[15]

Ground control stations were especially profitable. In one wiretapped conversation, Paisley boasted that the Mazlat-manufactured apparatus was "going to make money ... forever."[16] While Galvin privately mocked the Israeli company's performance as a "fucking joke" and dismissed its ground station as "a piece of shit" that wasn't engineered to U.S. standards, the devices became the centerpiece of the scam.[17] Navy officers craved more advanced digital models. Nonetheless, in May 1986 Paisley signed a directive essentially requiring bidders to incorporate Mazlat's old-fashioned, analog control equipment in every future UAV proposal. Within a week, the first installment of his payoff was deposited in a numbered Swiss bank account. Mandating a common ground station "was such a tough one to work" into the Navy's acquisition profile, Paisley said at the time.[18] Trying to justify his actions, Paisley now claims that in the long run he always intended to open the ground station contract to competition. Notwithstanding his own courtroom admissions and reams of documents attesting to his guilt, Paisley vainly maintains that investigators misunderstood his role and wrongly assumed that he was fully cognizant of Galvin's financial arrangements overseas.[19]

Over time, the conspirators' original dream of a six-million-dollar windfall was whittled down to a potential kitty of approximately two million. That still offered plenty of incentive, however, to corrupt Navy decision-making. "It would be great to pull all this off" for Mazlat, Paisley told Galvin at one point, because "they're the only guys over there we seem to be able to do anything with that makes sense dollar wise." A pair of Israeli accomplices was equally upbeat. "In two years," one of them enthused, "each of us [can] take half a million dollars or more to the bank ... That's a lot of money. We have to protect it." Galvin's reply was unequivocal: "That was the plan ... of course."[20] For such stakes, the consultant was willing to do the most reprehensible things. When his trusted Swiss attorney, Max Moser, died suddenly, Galvin forged the deceased man's signature so payments from Mazlat would continue to flow into the secret bank account in Geneva. "They don't know he's dead," Galvin cracked. "For this purpose, we'll still use Max."[21]

Pioneer was no mere sideshow for Israel's defense establishment. Its very existence, in fact, was prompted by decisions at the highest levels of that country's government. One-half of Mazlat was owned by Israeli Aircraft Industries, the premier state-owned defense contractor aggressively seeking foreign customers. IAI's exports climbed more than tenfold during the Reagan years, accounting for nearly one-tenth of Israel's overall export earnings. Drones were among the products IAI hoped to capitalize on for continued hefty growth. The other half of the Mazlat venture was Tadiran, a giant Israeli conglomerate with close ties to labor unions and broad experience in telecommunications, defense electronics and remotely piloted aircraft. Until 1984, Tadiran and IAI had waged a fierce battle over drone contracts on every part of the globe. By pressuring the rivals to sign a truce and join forces to form Mazlat, Israel's defense minister and cabinet hoped to alleviate that bloodletting.

A secondary aim was to more effectively promote Israeli-made weaponry worldwide—a trend that culminated in shipments of missiles to despotic regimes from China to South Africa, accompanied by sales of cluster bombs and radar jammers to Ethiopia, Chile and other nations. Access to the Pentagon, with its panoply of classified research programs, was crucial in this regard. Frequently, Israeli firms acquired high-tech U.S. components, installed them in their weapon designs and then indiscriminately sold the finished systems to third countries willing to pay the price.[22] In 1987, Israel formally gained the status of a full ally—equal to any member of the North Atlantic Treaty Organization—for sharing in high-level U.S. military research contracts and scientific exchanges. Ultimately, the country's thirst for foreign military orders put it at loggerheads with State Department concern over proliferation of U.S. classified technology. In late 1994, to the consternation of American officials, Israeli Aircraft Industries helped Beijing build a prototype jet fighter that is expected to give the Chinese Air Force a quantum leap forward in capability. The issue has created friction between the United States and Israel.[23]

While Paisley was calling the shots in the Navy, though, Mazlat succeeded in recruiting top-notch talent for what looked like a booming niche market. Zvika Schiller, a retired general and a former senior intelligence officer in the Israeli army, was the company's president. He had pioneered the use of drones. On top of those credentials, Schiller was familiar with the United States from a stint in the early 1980s as deputy military attaché in the Israeli embassy in Washington. Uri Simhony, another decorated and retired Israeli army general, worked as a marketing consultant for Mazlat. From 1983 to 1986, the rough-hewn Simhony had served as his country's defense attaché in the United States—perhaps the most important overseas posting an Israeli career soldier could attain.

Both men were friendly with Galvin and Paisley from those earlier times, so it was natural for them to renew the relationship on a different plane. Wiretaps revealed that Schiller browbeat Mazlat's comptroller into transferring large chunks of company cash to Switzerland. All told, roughly three hundred thousand dollars was sent there. Not only did the schemers defraud Mazlat, but Zvi Schiller even tried to steal from Simhony, his good friend and comrade in arms, when he needed extra money. "Uri's not my partner," Galvin said, happy to oblige when it came to cheating someone. "Uri's your partner," he reminded Schiller.[24]

The two former Israeli military figures were indicted in absentia during the last portion of the Illwind investigation. The pair never stood trial. The charges were largely symbolic, since Washington and Tel Aviv don't have an extradition treaty. For lead prosecutor Joe Aronica, reeling under a torrent of information from the wiretaps, the indictment was almost an afterthought, one final maneuver to wrap up his work on Mazlat in a neat legal package, regardless of whether prosecution was remotely possible.

Yet the eminent backgrounds of the accused conspirators—coupled with their involvement in clandestine intelligence-gathering operations over the years—left a sour aftertaste in the mouths of many of Aronica's investigators. The indictment laid out a kickback case and nothing else. Prosecutors and agents suspected but weren't able to substantiate that the Israeli government may have turned a blind eye to some of Mazlat's dealings with Paisley and his accomplice Galvin. Court documents, among other things, indicated that Schiller obtained approval from Mazlat's executive committee for one of the payments that went to Galvin's Panama-registered shell company.[25] The size and timing of the illegal fund transfers raised questions about why IAI's management wasn't more vigilant. In addition, court papers alleged that Schiller introduced Galvin to an unidentified "high-ranking official of Tadiran" during a trip to New York.[26]

Since then, outsiders have speculated that the Pentagon may have been eager to do business with the Israeli outfit partly in exchange for intelligence information about American hostages held in the Middle East. Each side bristles at the mention of such links, vehemently denying any suggestion of government impropriety. Israeli spokesmen assert that Schiller and Simhony were renegades, acting entirely on their own. American participants in the Mazlat transactions share that view. "Nobody told me to do business with the Israelis," according to Paisley.[27] Similarly, Lehman maintains that the Navy bought the Pioneer and a decoy called the Samson in what he believed were transparent, totally above-board business deals. "There was no quid pro quo needed," he says. "We bought for cash."[28]

The Reagan administration made half-hearted attempts to secure cooperation from Israeli law-enforcement agencies. There were preliminary discussions of possibly granting some Israelis immunity from prosecution, but the notion fizzled before the talks reached a serious stage. Aronica and his boss, Henry Hudson, were savvy enough to realize the futility of heading down that route. They knew the odds were against them. In legal circles, Israel is renowned for stonewalling U.S. criminal investigations that threaten to embarrass its ruling parties. As late as the summer of 1992, the Israeli government impeded a much-publicized Justice Department inquiry of an Israeli air force general who skimmed tens of millions of dollars in U.S. aid involving military sales by General Electric, United Technologies and General Motors. Tel Aviv officials refused to permit crucial interviews for reasons of "sovereignty, national security and the public interest."[29] The snubs continued, even after Washington threatened to cut off some aid monies. Aronica didn't deceive himself into thinking that he could singlehandedly reverse Israel's tradition of stiff-arming foreign probes. "It's unlikely that we will ever get [Schiller and Simhony] here for trial," he acknowledged. Confrontation would force the Israelis to balk that much more.

On both continents, the Schiller-Simhony affair faded away without announcement of a definitive resolution. Given Israel's reputation for being less than forthcoming, says Pam Bethel, one of Aronica's team of prosecutors, "we never asked them for much help" of any kind. "We weren't stupid . . . Their society and culture are very closed. I'm not sure we would have gotten much if we really tried."[30] Cloaked in anonymity, another young, gung-ho prosecutor puts it more bluntly: "If we investigated for a million years, nobody would ever get to the bottom of official Israeli complicity. Why pursue it, when it's a dead end and the culprits are going to stay in Israel forever?"

☆

As the Shark Tank's inhabitants dug into the intrigues of Paisley, Galvin and the rest of the criminal band, Aronica discovered a trail of old investigations that had been aborted, or simply had petered out, for lack of clear-cut evidence. The overlaps were uncanny.

The string of unsuccessful federal cases—stretching back to the 1970s and encompassing much more than the Navy—was painfully long. And the names they bore were all too familiar. The principal cast of characters was practically identical to the targets at the center of Operation Illwind. The laundry list of suspected improprieties in the distant past resembled more recent transgressions under scrutiny by Aronica's crew. The resemblances were startling and, for the investigators, downright disturbing. Sifting through the closed cases did yield one bright note, however: It made Illwind's promise seem that much sweeter.

Galvin had been investigated by FBI and Pentagon criminal agents at least five years earlier, along with Bill Parkin, his associate in the Joint Cruise Missile Office. Parkin allegedly had accepted meals, free trips, gambling money and other favors from consultants and contractors, and then steered business to them. Galvin's name surfaced as the supposed conduit. Justice Department lawyers tried but failed to develop hard evidence showing that the Galvin-Parkin connection went beyond the customary give-and-take binding industry marketers and government buyers. Prosecutors were stymied. "We tracked down a host of people who worked at the cruise missile office and hauled them in front of a grand jury," one of the government lawyers recalls. "We yelled and screamed at them . . . we pursued every wacky lead."[31] Galvin's lucrative consulting work for the cruise missile program was perused at length. Paisley told friends that his name also came up tangentially in the investigation, provoking Lehman's ire. But without wiretaps, it was impossible to prove what truly had transpired. "Agents suspected that there was a bigger conspiracy out there," according to one senior NIS supervisor, "but they couldn't devise a means of cracking it."[32] In the final analysis, it was Parkin's word against that of others.

Aronica's assistants stumbled on the files of a separate Parkin investigation involving potential income tax violations and suspicious real estate transactions. That one, too, had resulted in no charges being filed. And years before that, Parkin had been formally reprimanded by the Navy for disregarding procedures by failing to report that he had been offered a bribe by a contractor. (Navy officials never claimed that he actually took the money.)

Veteran Air Force acquisition official Victor Cohen, an intimate of both Galvin and Parkin, was questioned in the tax case as well. A year later, Cohen became the target of prosecutors for allegedly accepting free entertainment, a box of French wine and assorted gratuities from a Southern California contractor that he later helped snare a multimillion-dollar cluster-bomb manufacturing contract. Galvin's name cropped up again, only this time Cohen warned him of the danger before the FBI got too close.[33] The Cohen-related leads eventually were folded into Aronica's Illwind database.

The government's aging criminal case records held still more surprises. Mark Saunders, consultant Tom Muldoon's partner in crime, had been charged with insider trading in 1982 while working as a civilian for the Navy's space and surface warfare command. Saunders bought the stock of a military supplier on the basis of confidential information he gleaned about an upcoming contract award. To try to ward off suspicion, he put the shares in his daughter's name. In a plea bargain, Hudson's predecessor allowed Saunders to plead guilty to a misdemeanor—rather than the felony charges that could have been sought—on the condition that he would resign from the service and sever contact with his former associates. "If this guy is as bad as you suspect," Saunders's defense lawyer told prosecutors during the negotiations, "he will be back in your sights."[34] In the course of Illwind, of course, Saunders was shown to have maintained extensive and illicit dealings with his former Navy office.

But it was Paisley who had survived the closest brushes with the law.

As a prelude to Illwind, he went through two full-fledged criminal probes—launched barely a year apart by different prosecutors—without receiving a proverbial scratch.

The first one was touched off by James Durst, Paisley's nemesis from Boeing days, who had tried so hard to get his nomination killed. Shortly after Paisley moved into the Pentagon's E Ring, Durst went back on the warpath. He wrote lengthy, vituperative letters attacking Paisley's criminal tendencies and "unsavory character." The diatribes found their way to Nevada's senator Paul Laxalt, President Reagan's number-one political operative on Capitol Hill. Durst ticked off allegations of overseas bribes, bugging domestic competitors, hiring prostitutes and other aberrant activities while Paisley worked at Boeing—in short, the full array of complaints critics had aired before the confirmation without eliciting much reaction. "Every major company has one guy who does the dirty business," Durst said. For Boeing, he insisted, Mel Paisley "was that guy." According to Durst, Paisley had been so blatant in offering payoffs to sell Boeing jets in Australia that he was declared persona non grata in that country.[35]

Durst expanded on his allegations in six interview sessions with FBI agents, who presented the information to the U.S. attorney's office in Alexandria. Prosecutors didn't see a compelling case. They concluded that some of the allegations were too old to pursue, whereas others related to overseas marketing violations for which Boeing already had been punished. The decision to decline prosecution was made by Elsie Munsell, who had been the U.S. attorney before Hudson got the job.

Laxalt's office initially passed Durst's allegations to the Pentagon in April 1982, calling them "most serious" and assuring third parties that they would "likely be checked" by Weinberger's aides. Simultaneously, the senator's office started collecting newspaper clippings and other background information on Paisley. About a year later, at Durst's urging, Laxalt's staff again alerted senior Pentagon officials about the matter and handed over the complete file.

Weinberger's deputies basically sat on the allegations. They had no intention of trying to oust Paisley from the Navy. But the juicy morsels of intelligence were kept in reserve, ready for use when he tried to get a higher-ranking post in the Pentagon. One former Weinberger aide, who declines to be identified, recalls that the potentially damaging information was kept by William H. Taft IV, the Defense Department's general counsel and later deputy secretary. "It was good leverage, if we ever needed it," according to this person. The Navy secretary and his top aides also were aware of the file. Lehman remembers Taft objecting to a possible promotion for Paisley by arguing that there was "too much controversy over his background."[36] According to Paisley, Lehman told him directly not to be concerned that Durst's letters had reached the upper stratum of the Pentagon. "Don't worry about it," Lehman supposedly said. "They're not doing anything with them."[37]

By 1984, the FBI felt it finally had pinpointed Paisley's Achilles heel. Under Boeing's longstanding practice of giving extra severance payments to executives who landed high-level government jobs, Paisley received a $183,000 "golden handshake" upon leaving the company. Originally, Vicki Paisley had drafted a request for a tidy $800,000, based on calculations of her husband's prospective salary loss, forgone stock options and other financial sacrifices. Four other Boeing executives concurrently requested sweetened severance packages to join the Reagan administration, though Paisley was the only one who made a personal appeal to Boeing's chairman, T Wilson.[38] "It's outlandish," Wilson snapped. "He has lost his mind; I'm not going to do it." Despite the struggle, Paisley ended up pocketing more money than three of those colleagues combined.

Agents jumped on the arrangement, considering it a classic conflict-of-interest violation. Under their interpretation of the law, Boeing, in effect, was improperly supplementing Paisley's salary as a public official. Not only had he received money over and above his vested retirement benefits, but the amount seemed to be pegged to how much Boeing believed he could help the firm from his Navy post. Internal company documents confirmed that such severance packages explicitly were based, in part, on which departing Boeing executives would be able to exert the "greater influence" once they entered government. One memo recommended a generous payment to a Paisley cohort based on the fact that he "will hold a *key* job" at the Pentagon. A second memo, dealing with another former Boeing executive, predicted that he "will be helpful to us *while* he is in Washington." Incredibly, the emphasis on the operative words was part of the original memos. A third departing Boeing man, slated for a job with a NATO air command team, was baldly described as "an asset to Boeing in the NATO arena."[39]

Boeing sensed that Paisley would be in a position to provide maximum help. But top officials, who knew Paisley's ruthless methods and personal history, wanted reassurance that he wouldn't grab the money and then be rejected by the Senate. One Boeing senior vice-president warned that not a penny should be disbursed unless "Paisley ends up as a government official or as a consultant" for the Navy. On his federal financial disclosure forms, Paisley listed the severance payment as "compensation for services." By seemingly thumbing its nose at the government, Boeing had buried Paisley's severance costs as part of the overhead charges submitted to the Pentagon.

For all these reasons, a grand jury was convened and a furious Vicki Paisley, among many other witnesses, was summoned to testify. The probe lasted two years. The FBI's primary agent happened to be Phyllis Sciacca, the flinty, hard-charging investigator who later was put in charge of Ill-wind's wiretap records. Sciacca and her team recommended seeking criminal charges against Paisley in the severance case. They were overruled by lawyers from the Justice Department's public integrity section, partly on the grounds that there was no "apparent corruption [by the] government officials" involved.[40] The department filed a civil suit instead. Litigation dragged on for years, until the Supreme Court ruled in Boeing's favor on a technicality. When the justices heard the case, they also pointed out that they weren't aware of misconduct by any of the former Boeing employees who had received severance payments.

Nevertheless, Boeing's behavior prompted Congress to tighten conflict-of-interest laws. Among attorneys and Capitol Hill staffers, the new statute was mischievously called the "Paisley law." When Illwind became hot and Paisley's name circulated throughout the Justice Department, one of the line prosecutors who had suffered through the ill-fated severance probe called to rejoice with Sciacca. The message was short and triumphant: "You got him anyway," she crowed.[41]

☆

Melvyn R. Paisley's first day as a private consultant was hectic, jammed with appointments and profitable. Even by his high-flying standards, it was extremely profitable.

When he walked out of the Pentagon at the end of March 1987, carrying nothing but a jar of jellybeans and a shoeshine kit in his attaché case, Paisley didn't have an office yet. He didn't have a secretary, to say nothing of telephones, stationery and other necessary business supplies. Half a dozen boxes of files and mementos from the Navy—including his beloved airplane models—would be packed by dutiful aides and sent along in due course. For the time being, Paisley didn't need any of those trappings. As usual, he could count on his friendship with Bill Galvin to tide him over.

On April 1, ensconced at a spare desk in Galvin's sixth-floor Watergate office suite, the freshly retired Navy procurement czar started calling contractors around eight o'clock in the morning. He set up a lunch with one of the founders of BDM, a sizable Pentagon contractor, for that very day. Next, he scheduled future dates to meet with the chairmen of Martin Marietta and United Technologies. At two o'clock in the afternoon, Paisley called his wife happily to report that he had cinched deals with all three of those firms for six-figure annual consulting contracts.[42] Two of the contracts had a three-year duration. McDonnell Douglas also agreed to retain Paisley, who spent hours talking with its chairman that summer "about a lot of things" and afterward said he "felt very good" that he had "cultivated a friend."[43]

When Martin Marietta had second thoughts about following through with its promise to hire him because of potentially negative public perception, Paisley was incensed. "I didn't worry about it when I was in the government," he fumed to top company executives. Galvin coached his friend how to fight back, urging him to tell Chairman Thomas Pownall: "I took chances for you and [now] you're showing me that you won't take a chance for me."[44] Pownall's brain trust opposed hiring Paisley, warning that the company could be embarrassed or, in the worst-case scenario, face legal broadsides from Paisley's multitudinous enemies. The behind-the-scenes debate raged for months. Ultimately, Paisley triumphed by tweaking the chairman's pride. "I know as much about my business as Henry Kissinger knows about diplomacy," he bragged. "If you're willing to let underlings run the company and make the decision for you," Paisley claimed he told Pownall, "that's okay with me."[45] The chairman put his foot down, insisting, "I'll take Mel." He personally signed the two-hundred-thousand-dollar-a-year agreement, which specified that "the primary contact under this agreement shall be Mr. Thomas G. Pownall."[46]

April 1 was a day that Hudson, Aronica and their harried band of investigators also had anticipated for a long time. After months of agonizing delays, the first court-authorized wiretap on Galvin was ready to begin operation. Illwind agents had wanted to "go up" on the consultant much earlier, only to be blocked by bickering and second-guessing by Justice Department headquarters. Ideally, the FBI had hoped to start listening in on Galvin's conversations long before Paisley left the Navy, but bureaucratic squabbling and nagging manpower shortages precluded that. Taps on Paisley's phones were even further behind schedule. They wouldn't be activated for two more months, partly due to disagreements with main Justice and partly because the young agent drafting the affidavit was inexperienced and overworked. Still, approval for the Galvin "wire" was a huge step forward. With hundreds of telephone calls coming into his office on a busy day—and assorted industry figures dropping by to chat, unwind in the conference room and enjoy his well-stocked liquor cabinet—investigators were confident that the tapes would provide a gold mine of information. Each of Galvin's four incoming phone lines was tapped. To capture the rest of the conversations in the office, a pair of tiny microphones were secretly installed on the premises.

Agents could hardly believe their good fortune when, during the first few hours, they picked up Paisley's distinctively gravelly voice on tape. It was no April Fool's joke. His discussions were studded with references to bribes and personal relationships with senior corporate officials. There was candid talk of fortunes hidden overseas and Navy program managers who could be threatened or who were worth "rubbing a little bit" to ensure their cooperation.[47] As Aronica's team listened intently, Paisley exposed the underbelly of industry and Pentagon corruption that investigators always had assumed existed. "It was like manna from heaven," Steve Fulmer, the lead Navy investigator, recalls. "We were scooping it up."[48] Within a few weeks, Paisley had revealed plans to continue wielding influence inside the Pentagon. The recordings spelled out for prosecutors, in excruciating and undeniable detail, how he intended to perpetuate his scams by relying on loyal surrogates working for the government.

Leaving nothing to luck, Paisley had carefully laid the groundwork for his exit from the Navy. He recalled a skiing trip with Lehman to Idaho earlier in the year, when the secretary acted distant and preoccupied. Mel and Vicki found out by watching news reports that evening on CNN that Lehman had formally submitted his resignation to Weinberger and the White House. Instantly, Paisley recognized that his larks at the Pentagon were drawing to a close. He began dialogues with a few prospective consulting clients. He received what he said were "unsolicited offers" from many others, insisting that no substantive negotiations occurred while he was still on the Navy's payroll. Paisley spent extra time with Galvin, reaffirming their private financial arrangements involving Mazlat and Project Moon, the Navy's supersecret missile defense system from which they also hoped to rake in millions.[49]

Lehman, whose black-tie farewell party was boycotted by the uniformed brass he loved to deride, became a prosperous New York investment banker. He wrote a self-congratulatory book about his Navy experiences and accepted prestigious fellowships from Yale University and the Johns Hopkins School of Advanced International Studies. He grew to enjoy living in Manhattan, while shuttling frequently to Washington and renewing bonds with government and business dignitaries on both sides of the Atlantic. Lehman agreed to sit on the boards of two second-tier defense contractors, including a British helicopter manufacturer. He kept in touch with Paisley, sometimes talking with him several times a month. Paisley, in turn, referred possible clients to Lehman, claiming that his former boss had "the only real defense analyst capability on Wall Street." Generally, Lehman tried to establish PaineWebber, the brokerage firm with which he was affiliated, as a major deal-maker in the defense area.

Paisley's leavetaking, too, was marked by fanfare. Weinberger wrote a glowing letter of appreciation, praising his "dedication to restoring a competitive environment" that saved untold billions of dollars in acquisition costs. "You can certainly be very proud," Weinberger concluded, "and I congratulate you on your accomplishments." Lawmakers chimed in with similar praise. Upon Paisley's departure, Congressman William Chappell, the powerful chairman of a House defense appropriations panel, called him a "great American" who "made an unusual contribution to the Navy and to our country."[50] A year later, Chappell himself was disgraced by the revelations of Illwind. In all likelihood, the veteran Florida Democrat would have been indicted for his contacts with some of Paisley's associates if he hadn't died before prosecutors presented the matter to a grand jury.[51] According to one irreverent Navy investigator, "We had the tapes. We had other evidence. We just didn't have the body."

In his consultant role, Paisley kept his attention squarely on the Navy. Like Lehman, he was legally barred from participating in or lobbying the service on certain programs he had personally supervised. The consulting agreements themselves highlighted the restrictions. But they were hardly impediments. James Gaines, his stalwart former deputy in the Pentagon and a crony from the "Black Gang" era at Boeing, was instructed to watch out for those companies and funding decisions in which Paisley had a special interest. "Jim's the guy who's going to keep all this junk flowing," Paisley confidently told one contractor two days after his resignation went into effect.[52] When a Martin Marietta executive questioned whether Paisley's friend was motivated enough to look out for his company's interests, Galvin responded immediately. "Absolutely," he shot back, noting that Gaines had clear orders to act as the "alter ego for Mel." The man "has his instructions," Galvin explained. "We're approved all the way up the line."[53]

A short, chain-smoking former high-school English teacher with bad teeth and a pockmarked complexion, Gaines had risen through Boeing's ranks by hitching his fate to Paisley's star. During that whole period in Seattle, he was more of a follower than an independent actor. Before he passed away, Ben Plymale, Boeing's notorious marketer, counted Gaines among his close friends, as did a couple of other company old-timers. Behind his back, however, younger colleagues hissed that Gaines was a shameless sycophant. Early in his career, he had been in charge of preparing audiovisual displays for the company's marketing efforts. He also helped write proposals, served as a financial analyst and did odd jobs for the international group headed by Paisley. Gaines's last year or two at Boeing had been filled with tension, because Vicki gradually replaced him as her husband's primary sounding board and jack-of-all-trades adviser. Consequently, Gaines was excited about changing jobs and locales when Paisley offered to bring him into the Reagan administration.

In Washington, the assistant secretary had the Navy create a new slot for his servile chum. The official title was director of acquisition management, international programs and congressional support. Gaines "knew nothing about any of the three subjects," Galvin said years later, condescendingly calling him "Paisley's go-fer" and a "pipeline" for information out of the Navy.[54] To his newfound friends, Paisley branded Gaines as faithful and willing, but someone who was "not that good" at manipulating the system. Once his protector left, Gaines's main task continued to be to intervene in issues at Paisley's behest. In this way, Paisley obtained a gusher of material that wasn't supposed to leave the Pentagon—from classified research studies and sensitive procurement information to confidential correspondence with senior representatives of foreign governments about sales of McDonnell Douglas F/A-18 fighter jets.[55]

"Get on top of it and push it," Paisley would urge Gaines when an important project appeared to be stalled. At other times, he ordered Gaines to fetch him a copy of a restricted report from a Pentagon vault, or prodded him to get a data "dump" from some fellow Navy official. Routinely, Gaines was the person Paisley enlisted to lobby admirals and lawmakers on specific acquisition decisions. Paisley the consultant kept his hand in many other projects besides Moon and Mazlat. As a favor, for instance, he asked his stand-in to give him inside bidding information about the

Navy's next-generation bomber. Similarly, Paisley sought assistance on other multibillion-dollar projects, including Tacit Rainbow, a radar-seeking missile shrouded in secrecy; the Advanced Cruise Missile; simulators for antisubmarine warfare training; and a proposed airborne early warning system for the fleet. Galvin also used the compliant Gaines to gather marketing intelligence and try to steer contracts. Mrs. Paisley asked Gaines for a tipoff about proprietary computer software used by certain companies, but he drew the line there. He respectfully declined to assist her.[56]

If a Pentagon official refused to be helpful, Paisley would jest with his former staffer: "Put the grip on him . . . put his head in a vise [and] give him a kick in the crotch."[57] Paisley and Galvin knew that their compatriot needed constant encouragement. "Goddammit, Jim," Paisley counseled his friend at one point, "speak up and pretty soon people [will] say, 'This guy's our goddamn leader.' " The exasperated Paisley doled out more advice: "Act like an asshole like I did occasionally, so they'll know who you are."[58]

Gaines was looking for something beyond the satisfaction of pleasing a buddy of more than twenty years. He and his family accepted theater tickets, meals and other tokens of gratitude from Galvin, and sometimes they used Galvin's car and driver. Galvin persuaded Goodyear, a good client, to give free automobile tires to one of Gaines's daughters. Another free set of tires was supposed to be delivered for the late-model Chrysler driven by Gaines and his wife. After a while, such generosity was wearing thin. Feeling isolated inside the Navy and homesick for the Pacific Northwest, where his house overlooked a scenic marina, Jim Gaines perceived that he was being taken for granted. Paisley "just assumed that I was going to be there for as long as he wanted me to be there," he recalls.[59]

"You didn't train [Gaines] well," Galvin kidded Paisley one day. "He's not a bad crook," Paisley responded, alluding to the dozens of free tickets Gaines and his relatives had accepted from Galvin over the years for performances at Washington's Kennedy Center for the performing arts.[60] When Gaines talked about quitting the Navy, his mentors nearly fainted. "Oh ye of little faith, hang in," Galvin urged. Paisley admonished Gaines to stay in the strongest terms. "Just settle down," Paisley advised. "I worked hard to get you into the government. So think a lot before you think of leaving."[61]

To soothe Gaines, Galvin and Paisley switched to a different incentive: a dependable flow of hard cash. They searched for a way to slip him a five-hundred-dollar monthly stipend to cement "a nice working arrangement," without drawing attention to the payments.[62] Gaines's son Sean, a budding artist attending college, was asked to design business cards for Paisley, provide him with stationery and perform other unspecified "creative" work. Inflated bills would serve as a convenient pass-through to his father.[63] Galvin predicted that it would be a "piece of cake" to carry out the idea. After all, he asked Paisley snidely, "how much fucking stationery" can a one-man office justify buying? Conversely, Galvin noted, "I don't need to know how many hours" young Gaines worked on certain "creative ideas" to add those charges to the regular printing costs.[64]

The elder Gaines mistakenly submitted the first bill in his son's name, infuriating Galvin and Paisley. "Nobody listens," Galvin complained. "First of all, I said [to Gaines], is your name gonna appear? He says, no, they got a name of a company." Paisley concurred that the payments had to be disguised. "Let's change it," Paisley offered, and "have him send me this bill" on behalf of a graphics company formed by Sean Gaines.[65] Galvin's secretary retyped the invoice several days later, inserting the corporate identification. Investigators didn't find any other source of income for the brand-new company.

An aide to Aronica summed up the transaction by noting that "Galvin had only business interests in mind." Gaines knew full well that the benefits his family enjoyed "weren't based on any friendship," according to this prosecutor. Rather, he went on, they were given "as a thank you for things [done] in the past" and for business favors anticipated in the future.[66] Today, despite being convicted of accepting gratuities and other felony charges, Gaines maintains that he "never took a bribe or was offered one, at least that I recognized as an offer."[67] Gaines says that prosecutors were gunning for him unfairly, just so they could use him to nail Paisley. And he never imagined, Gaines asserts, that the wealth of classified documents shared with Paisley would be distributed with such abandon by his friend to corporate clients. Gaines nonetheless refused to cooperate with the government, even when Aronica threatened to file charges against his son.

At any rate, while the cash and the value of the gifts Gaines received was relatively modest, the manner in which they were treated indicates that everyone involved was acutely aware of skirting the law. As a present for Gaines one year, Paisley purchased "The Lonesome Whistle," a limited-edition lithograph of a cowboy riding the range with a steam-powered train chugging in the background. It was worth about fourteen hundred dollars. Paisley told associates that his friend was "enthralled" with the scene, which was reminiscent of the farmland and rural train siding where Gaines grew up. When the time came to deliver the print, a Paisley associates warned against using a commercial courier to take it into the Pentagon. Vicki Paisley agreed, remarking that the frame was fragile and easily could be broken. "I was being even more cautious than that," came the reply. "My courier might [have to] log that in," the confederate explained, exposing both donor and recipient to potential legal liabilities.[68] Paisley personally handed over the lithograph a few weeks later.

For his part, Gaines was flippant about the dangers he confronted. As they sat side by side one winter afternoon leafing through documents spirited out of the Pentagon, he and Paisley ruminated about the vagaries of the laws governing release of classified papers. "I wonder if this is secret at all," Paisley blurted out, complaining about the Pentagon's tendency to overly protect documents. "They overclassify shit . . . so nobody can get hold of it."[69] Gaines warned that the information they had was highly sensitive. Don't mail it to any companies, he explained, "just talk it." When his wife entered the room, Paisley asked her for secretarial help. "Hey, Vicki . . . run a copy of this for me," he said. Watching her approach the copying machine, Gaines couldn't resist making a joke. "Nobody would put a nice girl like you in jail," Gaines observed. Paisley said nothing, except to tell his wife: "Thanks, darling."[70]

It may have been hidden underneath his bravado, but Mel Paisley was guided by a streak of caution. From the start, he made it clear to corporate bigwigs that the information he provided had to be treated with extraordinary care. As an example, he asked the vice-president of aerospace business development for McDonnell Douglas to designate a permanent confidential contact within the firm to receive classified research material. The phone call was made the same day Paisley got his hands on a batch of especially closely held documents. "I'll contact him and he needs to know . . . I'm only gonna deal with him . . . because of the nature of the whole thing," Paisley explained. He said he wanted somebody the senior executive felt "pretty comfortable about," who could then "pass it throughout the corporation."[71] As a result, McDonnell Douglas got the benefit of seeing classified reports that ordinarily were out of bounds for industry, including a study on antisubmarine warfare under the ice. Paisley gave five other companies a chance to read the same documents.

For Martin Marietta, less explanation was necessary. Paisley informed the head of the company's electronics and missiles group that he had the charts used in the latest classified briefing on the submarine issue. "I need to sit and have somebody go through those with me . . . On this subject, I need to only deal with one guy," Paisley emphasized. Once the choice was made, he asked to have a meeting quickly because the illicit material had to be returned to Gaines. "The window . . . is this week," Paisley reminded his liaison.[72] But Paisley desired an additional layer of deception. He told a higher-ranking sponsor, who was promoted later to the presidency of Martin Marietta, that there was bound to be "stuff that occasionally comes up that I probably should deal with you [about] . . . and not deal with anybody else." The answer was positive. "Okay" was the only word the senior Martin Marietta man uttered.[73]

Executives at United Technologies Corporation—a $16-billion-a-year international behemoth manufacturing everything from combat helicopters to commercial products such as Otis elevators—were just as content to honor the former Navy appointee's wishes. Paisley knew Robert F. Daniell, the firm's chairman and chief executive, well enough to buy him a personalized Christmas gift and arrange social get-togethers. Nearly a decade younger than Paisley, Daniell had clambered up the management ladder by making the Sikorsky helicopter unit profitable in the early 1980s. After that, he served as senior vice-president overseeing all of the defense businesses of United Technologies, and then as president of the parent company. UTC's boardroom was famous for its strong-willed personalities and bizarre intrigues. Daniell's predecessor as president had been forced out amid public accusations of mysterious buggings and break-ins of his home and office.

It had taken Daniell twenty-nine years to reach the top perch. With three honorary university degrees and a seat on the boards of Shell Oil and the Travelers group of insurance companies, Bob Daniell was the epitome of the seasoned captain of industry Paisley aspired to deal with. "When I wanted to get something done at UTC, I always went straight to him," Paisley recalls.[74] The two men chatted frequently over the phone, and Paisley claimed that he interceded with Daniell on behalf of numerous friends and former Navy officials looking for work. "I've done some greasing with Bob," Paisley reassured one apprehensive job seeker.[75]

When it came to winning defense contracts, United Technologies likewise was satisfied to follow the consultant's lead. As testimony to that trust, the company had agreed to pay Paisley and Galvin combined fees of $390,000 annually. Daniell himself worried out loud that no UTC consultant had ever earned as much as Paisley demanded. He reportedly told Paisley that the deal would have to be okayed by the rest of the company's directors. "They'll go along," Paisley predicted, adding his trademark rejoinder: "I've got other companies waiting in the wings to take me on."[76] UTC was nervous enough to request a formal legal opinion from the Navy.

As a matter of fact, Paisley started helping United Technologies before his consulting contract had completely cleared the legal hoops. On April 30, 1987, barely a month after Paisley left the Navy, the Washington-based vice-president of the conglomerate's Pratt & Whitney subsidiary got a startling invitation. "If you can get over here, I'll make you happy," Paisley told Eugene Tallia, urging him to bring along a pad and a pencil. "I'll give you some numbers." The executive didn't equivocate or waste a second debating the propriety of what he was about to receive. "Oh, wonderful," Tallia replied, as he waited for Galvin's chauffeur to whisk him across the city to the Watergate.[77]

Around the same time, Pratt & Whitney was locked in a ferocious battle with archrival General Electric to divvy up billions of dollars worth of military jet engine orders into the twenty-first century. Dubbed the "Great Engine War," the competition was sparked by Reagan administration efforts to end monopoly purchases of big-ticket defense items. General Electric traditionally had enjoyed a lock on providing larger engines for military aircraft, while UTC's subsidiary had been the sole supplier of generally lighter, smaller models. Pratt & Whitney's F-100 high-thrust turbofan engine, equipped with afterburners capable of roaring from idle to maximum power in four seconds, was supposed to be the hotrod of the world's aircraft powerplants. Two of them could rocket a twenty-ton F-15

fighter up to thirty-nine thousand feet in less than a minute and accelerate it through high-G maneuvers even if the pilot had the jet's nose
pointed directly toward the sky.

But performance and reliability problems had dogged the F-100 series
since the 1970s. Past complaints of poor quality control, including substandard and unsafe turbine blades that had to be scrapped in large quantities, damaged Pratt & Whitney's reputation with the Air Force. The
F-100's durability also remained a question mark, as a result of its high
operating temperatures, exotic metallurgy and other unprecedented features. If mechanics tuned the engines to run cooler and thereby prolonged their useful lives, Air Force pilots squawked about a noticeable loss
of power and acceleration in their F-15s. At high altitudes, maximum
thrust could drop as much as 20 percent below the manufacturer's specifications, allowing 1950s vintage fighters to outrace F-15s. Plus, the Pratt &
Whitney engines were prone to spew out large volumes of smoke—a potentially fatal flaw in aerial combat, where stealth and the element of surprise mean survival.

General Electric had been favored heavily by the Navy's uniformed
leaders. Pratt & Whitney engines had been used exclusively on the Air
Force's most advanced fighters. Those once-sacrosanct preferences, however, were breaking down by the spring of 1987, creating havoc among
executives at both firms. Under the watchful eyes of Lehman and Paisley,
the Pentagon had agreed to invest a bundle setting up Pratt & Whitney as
a second source for the Navy's dual-engine, F/A-18 Hornets and upgraded A-6 aircraft. Lehman had signed the directive years earlier, and
Paisley had fleshed out the timetable with Daniell and other UTC executives while he was in the Navy. As one of his last official duties, Paisley attended a meeting at which the Navy's top civilians reiterated the
"fundamental policy of establishing dual-source procurement and competition" for this family of engines. UTC spent $130 million up front to
stay in the game.

As soon as Paisley became a consultant, Pratt & Whitney received
nothing but bad news from the Navy. Stung by complaints from the
Naval Air Systems Command that its prices were unreasonable, the en-
gine-maker found itself at a crossroads. It was worried about being shut
out of naval engine work for the foreseeable future. General Electric had
offered tempting, long-term discounts if the Navy abandoned second-
sourcing plans for engines powering F/A-18s, A-6s and the next generation of attack planes. Itching to return to their previous sole-source
relationship with General Electric, many admirals mercilessly demanded
deeper price cuts from United Technologies. Gene Tallia complained that
"things were falling apart" because Pratt & Whitney's higher overhead
costs were "killing" his prospects with the Navy.[78] He called Galvin for
advice. Galvin in turn enlisted his newly arrived consulting partner for assistance.

That was the reason Paisley rushed to the rescue, providing a break-down of the competition's cost projections, its overseas sales and other sensitive marketing data submitted to the Pentagon. Navy officials had only hinted at the price bogeys the two companies needed to hit. Overnight, Galvin and Paisley showed UTC executives precisely what to bid. "You pulled [the] chips out of the fire," Tallia gratefully acknowledged. Chairman Daniell was "pleased with the numbers," the executive said, noting that Pratt & Whitney wouldn't make any new offers without first hud-dling with Paisley.[79] Paisley's telephone logs listed three calls to Daniell during the critical period when the engine contract was in dispute.[80]

Recognizing the sensitivity of the material Tallia managed to corral, lower-level company officials went out of their way to disguise where it had originated. When Tallia called to thank Paisley profusely a day later, the reaction was telling: "We're not through yet," Paisley promised. Pratt & Whitney submitted a revised price, exactly matching General Electric's offer. The victory took only two weeks. Pratt & Whitney snared 30 per-cent of the F/A-18 engine orders for the first year of the contest, produc-ing $111 million in revenue.[81]

Paisley and Galvin were caught on tape gloating about their coup. They talked about going "above and beyond the call of duty" to rescue Pratt & Whitney from what had seemed to be a hopeless bind. The engine contract "fell out twice" before they and company executives could "make it stick," Paisley recalled. The price data "saved that program, by the way," Paisley proudly told Galvin, by enabling the company to convince the Navy that it could "bring the price down as well" as its rival.[82]

Galvin laughed that executives were so appreciative that "now they want to do something for us in addition to the money they pay us." He men-tioned the possibility of buying an airplane and getting the engines free of charge.[83] A few months later, Pratt & Whitney officials strongly urged con-tinued use of Galvin's "expertise," telling corporate headquarters that his mar-keting intelligence "has always been 100 percent accurate."[84]

How did Paisley get his hands on the crucial documents? "I stole the whole package before I left the building," he told Galvin matter-of-factly.[85] The comment turned out to be the single most damaging nugget of evidence the government collected against Paisley. "The FBI salivates when they hear that sort of thing," he acknowledges in hindsight.[86]

During the intervening years, Paisley has cobbled together a lame justi-fication for his behavior—one that even he concedes doesn't absolve him of guilt. He claims that the Defense Department allowed him to depart with several packing cases jammed with files and even forwarded his cor-respondence months after he had given up the Navy job. "I had cost data for every ongoing aircraft program," he says, jumbled up with classified notes, unclassified documents and personal papers tossed into the pile by his former staff. Paisley asserts that he didn't tell Galvin the truth, because his partner "would have been down there in a minute, pawing through all the boxes."[87] Eventually, federal agents found the suspect General Electric numbers in Tallia's attaché case. "It shocked everybody and set off alarm bells," according to Robert Powers, a senior Navy investigator.[88] Lawyers told Paisley that he could spend $1 million or more defending himself against Illwind charges, but no expense could counteract the words that had come from his lips. "I knew I shouldn't have given [General Electric's prices] to anybody," Paisley admits today. "That's the truth of the matter."[89] If the case ever went to a jury, Paisley's defense attorneys insisted, there was no credible argument they could propound that would alleviate the remark's sleaziness. "From a jury's perspective, it would have polluted the whole case," recalls one of his lawyers. "It sounded so ugly. It was the classic turd in the punchbowl."

Meanwhile, United Technologies also offered some elaborate explanations. Tallia had no idea that the documents had been stolen, the company asserted. Its string of other justifications seemed endless: The Navy wanted industry to have the documents to begin with; comments on the tapes were ambiguous and confusing; Daniell never saw the illicit data and didn't delve into the details of Pratt & Whitney's operations; and taxpayers weren't victimized in any way. The company's triumph was short-lived anyway, because shrinking budgets and changing policies eliminated its share of the Navy engine work two years after the original contract award. To cap its defense, the contractor argued vehemently that it could have obtained the same pricing information through legitimate channels under the Freedom of Information Act.

A phalanx of corporate attorneys ridiculed Aronica, insisting that UTC had never been convicted in a defense fraud probe and was absolutely determined to fight the allegations in this instance, too. Investigators maintained that the evidence against the company constituted one of the strongest Illwind cases. Legal arguments raged for more than four years. Despite its posturing, United Technologies, high on the list of the world's fifty largest industrial concerns, caved in at the end. The firm, among other admissions, pleaded guilty to charges that it had illegally acquired the engine-price data from Paisley. It agreed to pay the government a total of $6 million. As part of the plea bargain, neither Daniell nor Tallia was accused of wrongdoing.[90]

Daniell, who had been one of Paisley's staunchest supporters, embarked on a campaign to lecture his roughly 180,000 employees about the rewards of ethical conduct. On the heels of Illwind, Howard Baker, a former Republican senator and White House chief of staff, was hired to help draft a more comprehensive, companywide code of ethics. Critics detected a whiff of cynical excess in the chairman's eloquent and repeated sermons about avoiding questionable behavior at all cost. "Government procurement laws may be complex," Daniell declared solemnly, "but they must be obeyed in every particular . . . [and] almost isn't good enough. Where ethical matters are concerned, there must be no exceptions."[91]

Common sense and caution were to be the company's new guideposts. Executives were ordered to ask questions if they felt the least bit "uncomfortable" receiving marketing information. Even minor lapses caused by poor judgment were decreed totally unacceptable. "We will not allow the desire to win—or the fear of a loss—to compromise our standards," Daniell chided the rest of the company.[92]

Barely nineteen months later, United Technologies paid $150 million as part of the largest-ever civil settlement of a whistleblower suit, though it didn't admit violating the law. The government claimed that the company had inflated billings and prematurely sought payment for manufacturing certain military helicopters, receiving what amounted to interest-free loans from the Pentagon through most of the 1980s. Then in the spring of 1995, the Justice Department filed an unrelated civil suit accusing Pratt & Whitney of conspiring to divert $10 million of U.S. military aid as a "bank" or "play money" for the Israeli air force.

☆

The FBI's own focus on winning ironically came close to derailing Illwind midway through its covert phase. A comedy of errors almost blew up in the government's face, threatening to destroy everything that Hudson, Aronica and Rick Wade, the FBI's point man, had struggled to assemble over so many backbreaking months.

In order to properly maintain its eavesdropping equipment and assure round-the-clock surveillance of the offices used by Paisley and Galvin, the FBI had rented a tiny office in the Watergate under a phony company name. It was on the same floor as Galvin's suite. Building security was so tight, according to Joe Krahling, Wade's first supervisor, that there was no other way to shuttle agents into the Watergate compound or keep them there after working hours. The undercover location had other notable benefits. Agents with concealed cameras snapped pictures of unsuspecting visitors who strolled down the hallway or emerged from meetings with Galvin. The photographs allowed the FBI to match identities and faces with the disembodied voices heard on the tapes.[93]

The strategy worked without a hitch until Galvin decided to replace the telephone system for Athena Associates, his primary consulting firm. The FBI overheard him scheduling an appointment to have the work done. An alert phone company installer could spot the bureau's listening devices, possibly tipping off the occupants. Krahling wasn't willing to run such a risk. Relying on court authorization, he ordered bureau technicians to break into Galvin's suite. Their orders were to remove the telltale electronic paraphernalia before the phones were slated to be swapped. In the predawn stillness of the following day, the FBI was supposed to sneak back to replace the bugs. Not one hour of taping was to be sacrificed. The entire operation was expected to take roughly half an hour.

Wade, whose nickname of "Ranger Rick" suggested a steady temperament, had no justifiable reason to participate personally in the cloak-and-
dagger escapade, except that he simply couldn't resist joining in the
action. His motivation may have been the historic nature of the site, con-
juring up memories of the botched 1972 Watergate burglary that toppled a
sitting president and transformed the country's ethical outlook and political vocabulary. Or perhaps, saddled with the lonely task of deciphering
countless recordings made within those walls, Wade succumbed to an
overwhelming urge to see the layout of Galvin's lair for himself. In any
event, there was a sense of unusual urgency and anticipation while he
watched the squad prepare its tools. The experts said little, but their darting
eyes and rapid breathing displayed excitement. Rick Wade tagged along as
the bureau's experienced "sound men"—dressed in the dark overalls and
heavy work clothes of their trade—tiptoed into the pitch-black office.[94]

Around two o'clock in the morning, the FBI crew was shocked to hear
rustling in the corridor. Watergate security guards were walking around
the sixth floor, flashlight beams heralding their footsteps. There was a
commotion outside, followed by loud voices arguing on the telephone.
The entrance to a nearby office had been found unlocked. When guards
discovered the open door almost directly across the hall from Galvin's
suite, they assumed there had been some kind of burglary. Within earshot
of the nervous intruders, there was a prolonged discussion about conducting an emergency room-to-room search. Feeling tremendous pressure, the FBI specialists hid behind furniture and barely dared to breathe.
Wade crouched under a desk, sweat running down his back.[95] He won't
talk about the incident. But in general, Wade now concedes that any premature publicity "would have been catastrophic for us."[96]

Joe Krahling, his boss, was pacing by the telephone in an apartment a
few miles away, waiting to hear that all had gone well. The senior FBI
agent planned to leave for a family vacation later that morning. But he
couldn't go to sleep until the team was safely back in the bureau's space.
Krahling kept calling the undercover office, without getting an answer.
Usually unflappable, he had visions of front-page headlines attacking the
bureau for reenacting a poor-man's version of the scandalous break-in
that brought down Richard Nixon. The wait was excruciating. As the
minutes dragged on, Krahling envisioned FBI leaders fumbling to explain
his case agent's presence in the building. The bureau would be terribly
embarrassed. The fate of Illwind hung in the balance. He couldn't shake
the dreadful images. Still, there was no word from the Watergate.

Finally, nearly ninety minutes later than expected, Krahling got the all-
clear signal. He learned that building personnel had called off the proposed search at the last moment, after tracking down an employee who
remembered leaving the door unlocked. Paisley and Galvin never realized
how close they came to evading the FBI's net.[97]

Wade was responsible for another careless blunder. Hurrying to call one of the apartments converted into a government listening post, Wade absentmindedly dialed a number he had scribbled down from a document in the Shark Tank. "Is this Oakwood?" he snapped. The man on the other end was one of Illwind's identified targets. Startled by the question, he demanded to know who was calling. Wade slammed down the receiver. FBI agents could barely contain their sarcasm when they called Wade to report that he had just been picked up on one of the active wiretap lines.[98]

Coincidentally, around the same time a Naval Investigative Service agent began dating Galvin's older daughter. Fortunately for the government, the agent wasn't part of the Illwind team and didn't know any of its secrets. The relationship never became serious.

Other missteps also could have exposed the existence of the probe before federal authorities were ready to take it overt. On Long Island, where Unisys had one of its main plants, an FBI technician tried to bluff his way in disguised as a telephone repairman. The facility had a self-contained, independent telephone switching system, making it impossible to establish wiretaps exclusively through external switching stations. Someone had to physically do the work on site, where the trunk line was located. The undercover FBI operative showed up with a phony work order, asking to be escorted to the main wire room. His manner made a veteran company switchboard operator suspicious, and the elderly woman demanded to speak to the workman's supervisor. The phone company number she was told to call for an explanation was, in reality, manned by bureau agents who supported the cover story. After the crisis passed, the mollified Unisys employee handed the receiver back to the would-be repairman. "Get your ass out of there," his FBI supervisor barked. NIS then proposed installing wiretaps while pretending to sweep the firm's offices for signs of electronic "bugs" planted by foreign spies. The idea was rejected as too risky.[99] Agents never did set up a "wire" inside the Unisys complex.

While these slipups were nerve-wracking, none of them created lasting damage. But as the probe expanded, Aronica became increasingly anxious about the sheer number of agents, prosecutors and office support staff brought into the loop. Literally hundreds of people knew details of the case, from Justice Department functionaries to typists who were struggling vainly to churn out transcripts in spite of the government's rapidly growing backlog of raw tapes. In late 1987, an unusually large group of law-enforcement officials gathered in a basement conference room at FBI headquarters. The core of Aronica's supervisory team was there. So were dozens of new agents, who needed to be briefed about what they should listen for when they started monitoring the wiretaps. Senior Justice and FBI officials also attended, eager to be kept up to date on developments. Winter coats were heaped in a corner to free space for those who wanted to hear. Roughly one hundred people crowded into the auditorium-style room, filling every seat, lining the walls and even spilling outside. When Aronica marched through the door, he couldn't believe the turnout. "Oh, shit," he muttered, eyes flashing and jaw muscles twitching. Keeping his voice low, the lead prosecutor dressed down aides for inviting so many people.[100]

Aronica understood, all too well, that Illwind's fascinating characters and anecdotes would make perfect fodder for Washington's cocktail parties—where guests often make a sport out of impressing each other by leaking, or pretending to leak, secrets about the government. FBI and NIS agents had strict instructions to tell no one. Their superiors presumably knew better than to talk about a nationwide criminal probe in midstream. Intellectually, Aronica recognized the safety precautions that were in place. Yet he couldn't stop fretting about the impact of a stray comment whispered to a spouse or a friend, or an indiscreet slip of the tongue by some inexperienced agent. Given the right circumstances, Aronica warned, such tiny mistakes could spread through Washington's press corps like a brush fire and end up on the defense industry's grapevine. "We were very lucky to keep it secret for so long," he acknowledges.

Illwind was still roughly eight months from becoming public. But already, its chief prosecutor was plotting the end game. "I was anxious to bring it down," Aronica recalls, partly because he knew that the wiretaps wouldn't stay secret indefinitely. He was toying with ideas about the best way, and the most opportune time, to let the world see the strength of the evidence the task force had amassed.[101]

The investigation's reach also surprised those running the Justice Department. Attorney General Edwin Meese knew about Illwind in broad strokes, though he was distracted by an independent counsel's inquiry into his own ethical fumbles. The pudgy former Southern California defense executive—nicknamed "No Problems Ed" for his reluctance to deliver bad news to his close friend Ronald Reagan—barely avoided indictment for helping a minority-owned New York City contractor receive Pentagon work and for allowing a longtime friend to benefit from access to him. In the face of such personal attacks, it was unthinkable that Meese would risk further criticism by interfering with the work of the department's professionals. The attorney general was kept informed about Illwind largely as a courtesy. He didn't receive any wiretap transcripts. He didn't make prosecutorial decisions. Once allegations against the industry burst into public view, Meese recused himself from involvement in the case altogether. The Washington law firm defending him in the independent counsel matter also represented potential targets of Illwind, creating a blatant conflict of interest for Meese and the firm's partners.

Assistant Attorney General William Weld, on the other hand, was kept abreast of Illwind's progress. Aronica and Wade knew the importance of shoring up bureaucratic support. "You can't just tell management, 'Trust me. Give me fifty more agents and fifty more computers,' " Wade explained. "We had to tell the people in charge what was going on, almost step by step."[102] As head of the Justice Department's criminal division, Weld did more than sit through the briefings. A Boston Brahmin who had served as a U.S. attorney and would go on to become the most popular Republican governor of overwhelmingly Democratic Massachusetts in a generation, Bill Weld quickly realized the legal and political wallop of the facts he heard.

Investigators reeled off some impressive statistics for him: In addition to the wiretap request covering Paisley, many more affidavits were in the mill. In the end, more than fifteen hundred individuals could be classified as subjects of the probe. Sixteen of the nation's top twenty defense contractors were under varying degrees of scrutiny. Seeking clarification, Weld posed some questions. "Do you mean to tell me," he probed with a deadpan expression, "if we blackball all these companies at the same time, the government would hardly have any contractors" left to deal with?[103] The room fell silent. Certainly, investigators didn't expect to prosecute all of the firms. They didn't dream of trying to nab every individual who made a suspicious comment on tape. No U.S. attorney's office could handle the volume of cases such action would spawn. Aronica and Wade merely had intended to drive home the scope of their undertaking.

Weld's reaction showed how well they delivered that message. If prosecutions resulted in wholesale exclusion of contractors from Pentagon business, Weld said, the rest of the industry couldn't possibly pick up the slack. "We're going to have to keep that in mind," he told the group.[104] Although it hardly changed their game plan, the exchange had a sobering effect on Aronica and Wade. Their fondest wish had been fulfilled. The investigation was duly recognized as the most significant legal threat ever to hammer the nation's leading weapons-makers. The firms in their crosshairs were the same ones that had shrugged off previous Justice Department probes. Operation Illwind was racing headlong into uncharted waters.

Chapter XI

REAPING THE WHIRLWIND

A devout churchgoer and devoted father of nine, Charles F. Gardner seemed to embody the qualities Pentagon contractors wanted outsiders to admire the most. He projected a patriotic and energetic professional ethic, coupled with a personal lifestyle that appeared to place his family paramount. Friends and neighbors had nothing but praise for the crewcut, ramrod-straight defense executive, who was respected as a leader of Long Island's business and social community.

As early as the 1960s, while he was still in his thirties, Gardner began negotiating big-ticket contracts with the military on behalf of New York–based Sperry Corporation. Although his early training concentrated on accounting and contract administration, Gardner's innate shrewdness and excellent communications skills soon made him the company's top salesman to the armed services. He established an outstanding Washington presence for Sperry, setting up its first consolidated government affairs office in the 1970s. Many industry observers ranked it as one of the most politically plugged-in and aggressive marketing operations in the capital. Bill Galvin, certainly no laggard in performing such tasks, looked to Gardner for pointers on how to manipulate congressional committees and shoehorn tens of millions of dollars into spending bills to resuscitate specific programs.[1]

More than anyone else in his company, Charlie Gardner had the independence to sign up a large group of lobbyists and consultants, including retired Sperry officials and former House staffers. The stable of helpers reported directly and solely to him. Gardner, in the meantime, was a regular at certain fashionable Capitol Hill watering holes and in the waiting rooms of influential lawmakers, gaining recognition as Sperry's ultimate political fixer. "Charlie had great access both to the Pentagon and Congress," recalls one federal investigator, "because he spent as much time around Washington as the folks hired to work for him . . . He didn't just sell Sperry products; he used his connections and reputation to make sure the right people were absolutely committed to keeping Sperry programs alive."[2]

Gardner remained the spark plug of this formidable Washington network, even as he took on additional responsibilities at headquarters. He rose to general manager of the company's Surveillance and Fire Control Division in Great Neck, barely fifteen miles outside New York City on

Long Island's densely populated northern shore. Then in 1986, Sperry was swept up in Wall Street's merger mania. It joined forces with Burroughs Corporation, a Detroit-based maker of commercial mainframes, to form what was supposed to be the primary challenger to IBM's dominance among computer makers. The combined entity, which became Unisys Corporation, had a management style and culture different from those of the conglomeration of autonomous Sperry units. But for the fifty-five-year-old Gardner, who continued to head marketing for the entire Great Neck division and also kept his vice-president's title, the job essentially was unchanged.

Unisys was a $10-billion-a-year firm bent on becoming a $20-billion-a-year firm as quickly as possible. Led by senior managers from the Burroughs side who were preoccupied with the goal of rapid expansion, revenues and profit margins in every part of the company came under intense examination.[3] Gardner's new bosses had relatively little experience in the defense arena. Nevertheless, military businesses on Long Island, in northern Florida and near Minneapolis, Minnesota—all of which relied heavily on his marketing knowhow and irreplaceable Capitol Hill ties—were slated to be among the corporation's engines of growth. With overall Pentagon budgets no longer climbing and more than ten thousand Unisys defense workers trusting him to safeguard their jobs, Gardner redoubled his efforts. If anything, the changes in control at the top made him more determined to prove his clout by landing contracts.

While the military accounted for only about one-quarter of the merged company's annual sales, Unisys had a pivotal role in several huge weapon programs that were part of the foundation of U.S. national security. As its biggest defense customer, the Navy depended on Unisys, among other things, to provide navigation equipment for the latest generation Trident II ballistic-missile submarines. The Marines needed the company to supply portable air-traffic-control consoles rugged enough to be deployed wherever leathernecks set up bivouac. For the Army, Unisys built a wide range of computers and information-handling systems designed for offices as well as the battlefield. And the Air Force, historically one of Sperry's least important customers, counted on Unisys as a major participant in a supersecret radar program. The North Warning project, consisting of a net of air-defense installations across the Alaskan and Canadian wilderness, was intended to track incoming Soviet missiles if the Cold War suddenly turned violent and nuclear. By some yardsticks, Unisys already was one of the top three contractors supplying computers and communications gear to the Pentagon.[4]

A cluster of other potential big orders was on the horizon at the time of the merger. Officials at the Great Neck complex, in particular, were searching for ways to sell the Navy upgraded fire-control systems for missiles installed on so-called Aegis cruisers. They also aspired to win a share of contracts for similar Aegis radars and state-of-the-art combat electronics considered crucial to the success of the Navy's newest and costliest ship, the Arleigh Burke–class guided missile destroyer. Between the two types of warships, Secretary John Lehman's plans envisioned nearly sixty vessels commissioned through the late 1990s. Unisys's slice of those contracts easily could exceed one billion dollars.[5] Some optimistic estimates pegged the total several times higher. All this was on Gardner's plate, and he knew he had to come up with some ingenious solutions to satisfy his superiors.

Gardner stood out from rivals for other reasons, too. In contrast to many of his macho contemporaries, Gardner didn't pick up women during his frequent trips around the United States and overseas. Nobody would ever think of accusing him (unlike Mel Paisley) of padding his expense accounts to arrange parties with prostitutes. Gardner took time off one busy summer to take his wife and a teenage son on a two-thousand-mile drive to savor the grandeur of the Canadian Rockies. If stormy weather or late meetings stranded him in Washington on a Friday evening after the last shuttle flight to New York's LaGuardia Airport had departed, Gardner didn't rent a hotel room. He rented a car instead, gladly making the five-hour drive to Long Island without sleep to get home in time to attend one of his children's Saturday high-school basketball games. His focus didn't shift even after Illwind made him an outcast to many friends and colleagues. "Above all," a remorseful Gardner told the federal judge at his sentencing hearing, "I would like to apologize . . . especially to my wife, for the hardship and the hurt that has been caused."[6]

But like the industry he represented, Gardner had a nefarious side. The doting parent and enthusiastic booster of local school athletics was bursting with contradictions. He adopted altogether different values in his business life, a sphere in which only vanquishing the competition seemed to count. As part of this strangely schizoid view of the world, Gardner was driven to win, no matter what that entailed. He pushed the pendulum further than his predecessors. Associates used to chuckle during discussions of what they called "Charlie's Capers," marveling at his outrageous schemes to snare Pentagon business through illegal means.

Notwithstanding his family-oriented philosophy, the Unisys executive masterminded the most elaborate influence-peddling ring ever exposed in the defense community. He secretly controlled a "slush fund" of at least $17 million, using it to bankroll bribes, clandestine campaign contributions and other crimes through the 1980s. Gardner's "marketing" techniques featured phony consulting payments and widespread bid-rigging. He tried to bill the Pentagon for nearly all the trickery and sham consulting deals. Some investigators believe that the full amount was closer to $32 million, including illicit activities stretching across Gardner's earlier Sperry career, though they never traced his steps back quite that far.[7]

He specialized in slipping bribes to high-ranking Pentagon players, passing payoffs to lower-level procurement officials and directing assorted conspiracies to boost Unisys's defense sales. No plot appeared too scandalous for Gardner and his cohorts. One associate quietly doled out college scholarships to children of members of Congress.[8] Others provided free airplane transportation and vacations to lawmakers, and they gave various Gardner cronies choice seats to cultural and athletic events, including the finals of the NCAA college basketball championship tournament, without asking for payment.[9] Tenacious in his thievery, Gardner later estimated that the government paid a big chunk of the nearly one million dollars' worth of tickets his network distributed over the years. Still others doing Gardner's bidding tried to improperly sway Air Force decisions by renting, furnishing and maintaining a Florida condominium for a mid-level Air Force research official over a five-year period. The funds were funneled through shell companies approved by Gardner.[10]

From his earliest years in Washington, cultivating Congress was another integral part of Gardner's modus operandi. He made it a point, for instance, to link up with lawmakers and aides when they went on junkets to Paris, Venice and other foreign pleasure spots. Gardner also arranged plant tours and weekend outings for members of Congress, always playing the gracious host and sometimes picking up bills for hotel rooms, meals and theater tickets. As a parting gesture of appreciation, he would add an "honorarium" of two thousand dollars or so to sweeten memories of the trip. The money came out of bogus "technical service agreements" Gardner authorized for his accomplices.[11]

His forte was stroking and humoring lawmakers to get action on Pentagon spending bills. "Members only move if you're doing something for them," Gardner told one of his consultants, not because someone gives them a "great idea" to improve government. "I understand what they want," he boasted.[12]

The herd of "consultants" at Gardner's disposal helped fill the campaign coffers of sympathetic congressmen. Individual consultants and their relatives were instructed to make political contributions in violation of federal campaign laws and the rules of the Federal Election Commission. Usually, Gardner's assistants collected the undated checks, bundled them together and palmed them off on campaign committees as if they were all legitimate maximum personal donations of one thousand dollars apiece. Corporations were barred from contributing more than two thousand dollars to a single race. However, using corporate funds Gardner earmarked for this purpose, individual donors were reimbursed liberally for their contributions. Many made a hefty profit in the process, while Sperry and subsequently Unisys far exceeded allowable campaign spending limits. Some of the donations were folded right into company budgets. The benefits for lawmakers were immense. Two lucky recipients received a total of $118,000 through the cunning maneuvers, with smaller amounts going to many more lawmakers over the years. Gardner's tactics went so far as to include one political donation in the name of a three-year-old child.[13]

Under his tutelage, Sperry and then Unisys grew ever more audacious at using corrupt consulting arrangements to create a vast pool of dollars available for making payments under the table. The tricks became increasingly convoluted. To execute the subterfuge, Gardner and his corporate assistants fabricated documents that were later used by consultants to justify their fees. Dummy companies sprouted and disappeared at Gardner's whim. In all, he laundered funds through at least thirty-eight separate consultant outfits, sporting exotic names such as Anchorage International, Coastal Energy Enterprises, Polaris Tech and Tactical Warfare Analysis Group. Ordnance S.A. and Electromech were other mysterious names for front companies, organized in part to circulate money between the United States and offshore banking havens ranging from the sun-baked Cayman Islands in the Caribbean to the fog-shrouded Guernsey Islands and the Isle of Man in the North Atlantic. Some $1.7 million went to a Virginia firm owned by Gardner himself.[14] "It's always good to have an extra company around," Gardner admonished one underling in a wiretapped conversation.[15]

At least a few upper-level executives were aware of some of the underhanded moves, though they may not have known details and perhaps didn't appreciate the extent of the misdeeds. Gardner, after all, hadn't changed his methods simply because there was a new emblem on the corporate letterhead. "They saw my expense accounts," he argues. "What did they think I spent the money on?"[16] The managers in whom Gardner confided were holdovers from the Sperry era, and they generally understood the thrust of Gardner's Washington activities.[17] Like many contractors, Unisys "hired consultants and then wound them up and turned them loose," according to U.S. attorney Henry Hudson. Orders from the executive suite, he claims, left no fingerprints. But they had one unmistakable message: "Do whatever you have to do, and don't tell me about it."[18]

When he dealt with newly installed Unisys managers, Gardner spared no effort to show his independence. He didn't mince words in stressing the importance of his Capitol Hill connections. "If you want to play in the big leagues," he would say, "this is how it works; this is what it takes to win."[19]

Investigators coined a phrase to describe the phenomenon: They dubbed it "willful blindness" on the part of high-level management.[20] If the requisite paperwork was filled out—purportedly supporting invoices for reports or "technical services"—Gardner's superiors signed approval forms by rote. The executives felt no obligation to satisfy their suspicions by prying below the surface or going beyond what one investigator calls the "four corners" of the bland cover memos. "They ought to have been looking carefully at the papers, or reviewing the budgets," asserts FBI agent Dan Larkin.[21]

By the same token, the existence of what Gardner called "window-dressing" in the files made it difficult for prosecutors to bring criminal charges against anybody higher in the company's chain of command.[22] "By itself, the paperwork told you nothing," he says.[23] But "the multiplicity of consulting contracts was well known" inside Unisys, he says today. "The large number of contracts going to a single person was equally well known."[24] Looking back, Gardner admits that his crimes were motivated by what he calls "the pushcart way of doing business . . . If I didn't do it, someone else was going to do it to win the contracts." Wiretap transcripts and court files eventually were studded with references to the culpability of those working for Gardner. In the end, more than two dozen of his consultants, buddies and coworkers were convicted.

Self-protection was the key to hiring some consultants, Gardner maintains, because "you knew damn well they were working for three other companies at the same time."[25] Still, he was careful in carrying out his deceptions. Initially, he had authority to okay fees of up to one million dollars, without obtaining sign-offs from superiors. But Gardner tended to keep individual consulting contracts smaller, typically under one hundred thousand dollars annually, to avoid attracting undue attention from above, or by outside auditors, to his money shuffling.[26]

Nonetheless, there were some prominent exceptions to that rule. Graft flowed so easily that one relatively low-ranking Navy civilian engineer, who was taking home less than fifty thousand dollars a year in legal salary, ended up with more than four hundred thousand dollars in bribes sitting in a Bahamian bank account after less than two years. The civil servant, who appeared to be a tangential figure from a distance, was important in shaping a multibillion-dollar, automated electronic maintenance program for Navy weaponry. A Gardner assistant hand-delivered the last five monthly payoff checks. When the aide wondered why the contractor was being so generous, Gardner replied that the company badly wanted the official's assistance and the Navy man, in turn, "wanted the money" for a retirement "nest egg." Despite the exertion, Gardner lost the contract.[27]

That didn't deter him from embarking on similar forays with others. From 1979 to 1988, four Gardner associates and a former technical expert from an Air Force base in upstate New York split more than $720,000 in illicit payments. A portion of the money was set aside explicitly to entertain and otherwise "influence" Air Force procurement officials. Company files were stuffed with useless engineering reports, often plagiarized from military magazines, in order to confuse auditors. Wads of cash, adding up to fifteen thousand dollars or twenty thousand dollars each, frequently were exchanged inside airport terminals.[28]

In return, Gardner obtained technical rankings and bid-related information for pending Air Force electronic projects. In one instance, his sources actually handed over the original Air Force document spelling out the competitive lineup of bidders for the North Warning missile defense net. Besides methodically passing on such payments as valid costs, he helped hide some of the transactions from the Internal Revenue Service.[29]

As Illwind unfolded, the scope and complexity of the fraud surprised Joe Aronica and his fellow investigators. "With all the consultants and congressional types under his wing, Charlie was slipping money to everybody who could conceivably help him," recalls former federal agent Mike Cox.[30] The FBI suspected that Gardner's skulduggery might have tainted as many as forty distinct Pentagon programs, everything from work on advanced fiber-optic cables to the commonplace office computers used by Navy sailors and warehouse clerks fleetwide.[31] None of those endeavors, though, promised as large a payoff, or required as much finesse, as Gardner's web of illegal ventures with Bill Galvin and Mel Paisley.

As long as the trio managed to squeeze contracts out of the Navy, Unisys could breathe easier. Galvin boasted a great track record aiding one of Gardner's longtime bosses, so the consultant was hired to take on extra work. "What other good things can you do?" Galvin remembers being asked. The rest of the conversation, he recalls in his typically sarcastic manner, involved questions such as "Can you turn lead into gold, you know, that kind of stuff?" The things the company needed most, Galvin replied, were precisely the strengths he brought to the table: "I represented . . . a cozy relationship, a relaxed technical dialogue, with the policymakers of the Air Force and the Navy."[32]

Gardner could decipher that code in a heartbeat. His assignment was to use Galvin to get close to Paisley, who at that point still occupied the assistant secretary's chair. "I let them communicate," Bill Galvin explained much later. "It wasn't necessary for me to have my hands on the throttle [involving] everything that went down."[33] After a while, Gardner and Paisley felt comfortable dealing one-on-one. They talked frequently on the phone. If they saw each other on business trips, they chatted about family and other personal topics. Meeting after work at a high-priced hotel on San Francisco's Nob Hill one weekend, Paisley agreed to steer radar-warning business to Gardner's company. Afterward, joined by Galvin and a few others, the two men enjoyed a festive dinner at Ernie's, one of the city's priciest and best-known restaurants.[34]

Characterizing his links with Paisley, Gardner now says simply: "We were too close." The relationship "became cozier and cozier," he explains, admitting that their social chitchat and get-togethers rapidly shifted into an area that he fancifully describes as "bribesville."[35] Indeed, the two men finally were so tight that the Navy appointee seemed to be an extension of the Unisys sales staff.

At the start of 1987, Gardner complained to Paisley that he needed to unload $116 million worth of shipboard radar upgrade kits to meet corporate sales projections, in spite of opposition from the White House and the Navy's uniformed leadership. Admirals ridiculed the equipment as unnecessary and obsolete. President Reagan's proposed fiscal 1987 budget sought to ax the program entirely. But Paisley embraced the company's goal as his own. He rattled the bureaucracy and pushed the paperwork through the system. Working in tandem with Gardner, Paisley prodded Congress and especially the House appropriations committee to move quickly to maintain funding. Barely three weeks after the vote, the Navy signed a contract for expedited purchases of six radar kits from Unisys for the whole $116 million—exactly on time for Gardner's internal reporting deadline.[36]

When it was a matter of asserting his authority to assist Sperry/Unisys on other projects, Paisley could be even more forceful. For example, he intervened at the last minute to block one of Gardner's rivals from winning a $100-million order from the Marines for air-traffic-control equipment. Paisley sprang into action the day the decision by another Navy appointee was slated to become final. He ordered the files transferred immediately to his office and demanded a personal briefing that very afternoon, effectively halting the procurement.[37]

Paisley's delay evolved into a veto. He hounded program managers to give Gardner's team a second chance. Over the objections of Pentagon officials and a member of his own staff, who complained that Paisley's intransigence would end up costing the government tens of millions of dollars unnecessarily, the Navy abruptly threw out all the bids. It drafted new bidding rules skewed to favor Gardner's firm. Leaving nothing to chance, Paisley helped Gardner figure out precisely what numbers to use in the revised submission.[38] The pressure worked like a charm. Capping two months of hectic phone conferences and strategy sessions, Gardner proudly informed his management that he had landed the hotly contested Marine Corps contract. The Air Force's Victor Cohen, another Galvin intimate, agreed to pocket bribes to help Gardner peddle the same hardware to the Air Force.[39]

Designating Unisys a second-source supplier of Aegis missile-defense systems—one of the Navy's plum electronics-integration tasks—took extreme patience and resourcefulness. Named after the mythical shield that protected the Greek gods, Aegis SPY-1 radars give a continuous and instantaneous picture of the bowl of sky around a ship—providing much more comprehensive and rapid coverage than conventional, rotating-basket radars, which can take as long as six seconds to complete a sweep of the horizon.[40] The system also includes signal processors and fire controllers to intercept incoming missiles. RCA Corporation, which later merged into General Electric, had a monopoly on the technology from its inception in the 1970s, although both Congress and the Naval Sea Systems Command had talked for years about injecting competition into the mix. Secretary Lehman weighed in simultaneously, ordering development of second sources for Aegis components. Paisley and Gardner were more than a match for that test. They seized the opportunity to take control of the decision-making machinery.

The Paisleys' stylish, two-story house in McLean, Virginia, with shade trees and a screened porch overlooking the spacious yard, served as a makeshift command post for the conspirators. One Saturday afternoon in the spring of 1986, Gardner and Galvin joined their jovial host to hammer out a foolproof plan. Competition to supply the building blocks of Aegis was fierce, and Gardner appeared headed for defeat unless something dramatic happened. Instead of competing for the antenna, radar transmitter and other elements of the Aegis system separately, they concluded, why not establish Unisys as the leader of a team and force a winner-take-all competition for second-sourcing? The sudden change gave Paisley direct control over each phase of the procurement.[41] His support guaranteed that there wouldn't be any objections from others at the helm of the Navy. And undoubtedly, he could browbeat lower-ranking Navy officials into accepting the concept.

Furthermore, Paisley's pledge to accelerate the bidding timetable assured Unisys an edge by making it infeasible for contractors left out of the loop to submit realistic proposals. The following week, Paisley told a senior Westinghouse official that he had no alternative but to join the Aegis "B Team." The company readily agreed.[42] Competitors howled. Navy lawyers complained that the bid solicitation was issued in a "noncompetitive environment." But the complaints fell on deaf ears. The scam was firmly in motion, and the results would endure for four years. Now, all Gardner and Galvin had left to do was to devise a novel payoff to thank their benefactor.

Within days, the pair hit upon the ideal answer. They alluded to it cryptically as their "potato project."[43]

Paisley had casually mentioned that he owned a condominium on the ski slopes of Sun Valley, Idaho, which was proving mighty difficult to sell. The area's real estate prices were depressed, Paisley complained to Galvin, adding that there were "probably fifty ski condominiums" listed in close proximity. In addition, there was a balloon mortgage on the property, requiring Paisley to come up with a large amount of cash if he didn't find a buyer.[44] "Can we do something to help?" Galvin asked Gardner on the spur of the moment. "I've got a guy who can do that," Gardner responded, hardly giving it a second thought.[45] Using corporate funds laundered through a series of paper companies and offshore accounts, Gardner moved quickly to take the unit off Paisley's hands. The terms were favorable, indeed. Gardner agreed to pay the full asking price of $149,000, roughly 50 percent over what investigators maintained the condo's value was in a slumping market. When an associate advised him that the price was too steep, Gardner answered there was no need for negotiation.[46]

Gardner didn't directly broach the issue of the real estate transaction with Paisley. However, investigators determined that the Navy official had learned the purchaser's true identity from Galvin. Not only did Vicki Paisley tell her realtor that she and her husband knew who the real buyer was, but her attempt to change sales agents threatened to jettison the deal and prompted a rebuke from Galvin. Galvin warned Paisley that her interference was hampering Gardner's bid to close the all-cash purchase at the agreed price.[47]

To this day, Vicki Paisley desperately clings to the rationalization that she didn't know who was behind the purchase offer. But through her actions, she made it impossible for her spouse to argue convincingly that it was an arm's-length arrangement.[48]

Mel Paisley, for his part, seems oblivious to what he did. Though he has admitted committing various felonies—including taking bribes—from his jail cell he continued to strenuously deny that there was any quid pro quo in the case of the condominium. The Aegis teaming idea was supported by other Navy officials, he insisted, and his Idaho condo actually sold below fair market value.[49] "If Gardner wanted to buy it, what would have been wrong with that anyway?" Paisley asked, seemingly blind to the ethical lines that were violated. He couldn't admit, even in a jailhouse interview, that greed drove him to desecrate his oath of office. Prosecutors "took something that was a legitimate deal," he claimed, "and made it stink."[50]

But in Gardner's mind, the motivation was never in doubt. Paisley "knew that Galvin was arranging the purchase" through Unisys, he says flatly. "It was wrong to begin with. It was a bum decision."[51] Shortly after the Unisys/Westinghouse team submitted the sole bid to become the second source for the Navy's Aegis weapon systems, Gardner got rid of the unit in Idaho for one hundred thousand dollars. Buying it from Paisley "was the dumbest thing I ever did . . . The condo [was] the top of bribesville," he concluded.[52]

☆

Congressman William V. Chappell, Jr., a cigar-chomping Democrat with a passion for travel, plush women and shady backroom deals, was a staunch Gardner ally. Other contractors prowling the Capitol's corridors for votes envied the strength of that bond. Whenever Sperry or Unisys got into a pinch, competitors watched the lawmaker from northern Florida rush to the rescue. Chappell prodded the Navy mercilessly to speed up contracts for Aegis systems as well as the smaller radar upgrade kits Gardner wanted credit for selling. "We are going to rely on Chappell not to give an inch to the Navy," Gardner vowed to one associate.[53] And, when it came to defense spending in the House of Representatives, Bill Chappell wielded the biggest stick of all.

A white-maned former Speaker of the Florida House of Representatives and onetime county prosecutor, sixty-six-year-old Bill Chappell was serving his twentieth year on Capitol Hill. A former aviator and captain in the Naval Reserve, he invariably ranked near the top of the list of legislators receiving political contributions and speech fees. Chappell was the last in a long line of iron-fisted, truly dominant chairmen of the House defense appropriations subcommittee. The powerful panel, numbering eleven legislators, controlled most of the Pentagon's purse strings. Their technical and political judgments—filtered through the prism of pet peeves, biases and self-serving agendas of some members—determined which programs would thrive and which would collapse. Often, no justifications were given for picking the winners. And there was no recourse for the losers.

"We fund weapons systems, we don't fund companies," Chappell liked to say.[54] But buried in the fine print of appropriations measures he shepherded through the House, the chairman was renowned for helping his corporate favorites and delivering congressional pork to friends and constituents alike. He became, as journalist Walter Lippmann aptly put it a generation earlier, "public official and private promoter inhabiting the same body." Chappell remained unrepentant after the scandal erupted, declaring that allegations against him were "just a lot of bunk." He told reporters: "I am what I am, and I have no apologies."[55]

The House Armed Services Committee, which shares jurisdiction over the Pentagon, was too large and diverse for a single company or lobbyist to control easily. The Senate, with its arcane procedural rules and unanimous consent motions, could be quirky. The compact House appropriations subcommittee, on the other hand, was a predictable, known quantity. In 1987 alone, Chappell's panel approved nearly $11 billion *more* in military expenditures than either the House or Senate armed services committees. Many of the extra items the military itself didn't want.[56] One Navy wag described the congressional bullying and micromanagement in the following terms: "When I get a critical message from the fleet saying they want vanilla ice cream, I'm doing well if I can get Congress to send fudge ripple."[57]

The chairman, who bragged about meeting with as many as one hundred defense industry officials a day, held the reins tightly on his members. He didn't allow the Senate to grab the initiative. And Chappell certainly wasn't bashful in acknowledging where he got his guidance "A lot of times, [we] learn more about systems from contractors than we do from the Pentagon," he opined as Operation Illwind hurtled toward its climax.[58] "We get some of our best information out of industry on [acquiring] our weapons systems more efficiently."[59]

With Chappell's backing, contractors could outflank Pentagon officials—or figuratively bowl them over, if that seemed more appropriate—to cram money into the budget for their highest-priority projects. The very first week one of Paisley's aides arrived for work in the Pentagon, the assistant secretary told him flatly that Gardner's crew "had the best connections . . . to get anything they wanted" through Chappell, "and nobody would vote against them on the subcommittee."[60] Unisys agreed to draft a white paper for the chairman's use to "whack [critics] over the head with" and try to convince the chief of naval operations to support one of the company's programs.[61] As Gardner reminisces about those years, he dwells on the same point: "Whatever you wanted to do" to influence Pentagon budgets, he says, "the chairman of the appropriations subcommittee could do."[62]

Gardner was far from a newcomer to this venue. Years earlier, he had carried campaign posters and pounded the pavement in heavily black neighborhoods to get out the vote for the panel's previous chairman, Congressman Joseph Addabbo, whose district included a portion of New York City's borough of Queens. Following Addabbo's death in 1986, the gavel and Gardner's allegiance both passed to Chappell. Immensely popular in his sprawling Florida district—which extended from booming Jacksonville and the seaside residential enclaves north of Cape Kennedy to the rural hills and thoroughbred farms on the outskirts of Ocala—Chappell was regarded as a major force in the House until Illwind unseated him.

Gardner's political outlook was dispassionately bipartisan. He also sidled up to Republican congressman Joseph McDade of Pennsylvania, another longtime member of the panel, who was in line to assume the chairmanship of the full Appropriations Committee once the Republicans won control of the House. Unfortunately for McDade, the 1994 GOP landslide found him under indictment on racketeering charges and for grabbing nearly $100,000 in alleged bribes and favors from Gardner and representatives of three other firms.[63] The allegations against McDade included illegally accepting free air travel, a free vacation at a Long Island resort and "sham" campaign contributions—furnished partly at Gardner's direction. Speaker of the House Newt Gingrich and his Republican confidants skipped over McDade to pick a less controversial head of the committee. The veteran congressman, who handily won reelection twice while under indictment, continues to deny all the charges. "When the dust settles," he has predicted, "my conduct will be vindicated, my integrity will have been upheld and I will be found not guilty."[64]

With Chappell, Gardner's bearing was that of a pal more than a supplicant. In the midst of generating a whirlwind of political donations, he still had time one summer to keep close tabs on the chairman's goal of collecting half a million dollars to discourage any potential primary challengers.[65] As part of his all-purpose advisory role, Gardner also went to great lengths to polish the congressman's public image. He helped organize a charity golf tournament in Florida that same year, ostensibly to raise money for a community college in the lawmaker's district. In reality, the political and media benefits were foremost in Gardner's deliberations. Chappell was the honorary chairman, and defense contractors were asked to ante up five thousand dollars apiece.

Using the term politicos use for contributions that don't go directly to pay campaign expenses, Gardner assured Chappell in one wiretapped conversation: "Good soft money, I look at it. Good publicity." The "advertising looks great," Gardner exclaimed at another fork in the discussion. "You can't see Daytona Beach College. You only see 'Congressman Chappell, Honorary Chairman.' "[66]

To prod the dubious general manager of one Westinghouse division to participate, Gardner argued, "This is really for Bill . . . so that he gets the [campaign] workers . . . the [news]papers and everything for his, you know, publicity."[67] The executive continued to balk, complaining that "this kind of stuff is out of control." Gardner was persistent, zeroing in on Chappell's clout. "You got the Aegis program," Gardner reminded his counterpart at Westinghouse. "Put [the contribution] in, and we get the $100 million [first chunk of funding] and get the goddamned program going."[68] Westinghouse was one of nearly twenty firms that sponsored the tournament. Grumman and others flew in senior executives just for the event.

More roundabout methods also assisted in demonstrating Chappell's value to his district's voters. At Gardner's behest, Unisys guaranteed to give subcontracts to a new firm set up in the chairman's bailiwick. One of Gardner's confederates teamed with Galvin to open Armtec Incorporated, producing electrical wire harnesses for military projects. Starting with less than one hundred thousand dollars of capital and fewer than twenty employees in a tiny building in an industrial park, Armtec soon blossomed into a major employer in Palatka, Florida. There were no other defense firms in the economically reeling community, hunkered amid the scrub pines and the tributaries of the St. Johns River. Palatka was far removed from the state's bustling resort areas and affluent coastal developments. The city didn't have a pool of skilled workers, nor did it have any local job-training programs to speak of for its ten thousand residents.

Why pick such a desolate, out-of-the-way site for a manufacturing plant employing some one hundred workers? one consultant wondered. The reason was rudimentary: "It's like the old real estate guy says: Location. Location. Location," came the reply from a Gardner crony.[69] Bill Chappell, who championed the plant, was hailed as a hero for bringing hope and a payroll of nearly $1.5 million to a struggling corner of his district.

Unisys was hardly the only contractor relying on such stunts to curry favor with legislators. Charlie Gardner and his accomplices, however, tended to be more adept at pulling them off. And they understood, perhaps more acutely than the competition, the fickle rules of the game. When Gardner tried to argue good-naturedly with Chappell regarding the itinerary for one of their overseas trips, the congressman slapped him down. The vehemence of the reaction was revealing: "I haven't marked up [the appropriations bill] yet," Chappell snapped, ending the exchange.[70]

Meanwhile, representatives of other arms producers frenetically cultivated the same lawmakers. Martin Marietta's vice-president for government relations, for one, took part in a private business transaction that relieved Chappell and his companies of more than a quarter of a million dollars in unpaid debts.[71] The complicated chain of events in 1984 involved an Ocala health club that went into foreclosure and could have required the lawmaker, who was then the second-ranking Democrat on the subcommittee, to personally repay part of a substantial loan. A Martin Marietta subsidiary acquired the failed business a little more than a year after Chappell was able to bow out of the debt-ridden enterprise, though the company described that as an arm's-length business decision.[72]

An official of Avco Corporation, another large defense firm with hundreds of millions of dollars in revenue hanging on the subcommittee's decisions, allowed Chappell to live at his house rent free for several months. The Avco executive happened to be a former aide to the congressman. House rules prohibited members from accepting a gift worth one hundred dollars or more from any source "having a direct interest in legislation," but Chappell insisted he had not done anything wrong.[73] The jostling among competitors trying to get his attention grew more intense over the years. "Chappell doesn't have enough assholes for the noses that are there now," cracked consultant Tom Muldoon, one of Gardner's buddies, shortly before Illwind went overt.[74]

The Unisys congressional steamroller tapped the power of other relentless infighters. New York's fiery GOP senator Alfonse D'Amato received what the contractor later admitted were illegal campaign contributions, as did Senator John Warner of Virginia, another influential Republican. Neither lawmaker was accused of complicity.[75]

Armand D'Amato, the senator's younger brother, was paid $120,000 to represent the company in Washington. "It was a job that I enjoyed immensely," he recalled, extolling the "fine relationship" with what he called "my best client." During more than three years as a Unisys consultant, Armand D'Amato contacted only one other congressional office in addition to his brother's. Company officials testified under oath that they hired the Long Island attorney solely to gain access to the senator, and that he basically did no work for Unisys other than to pass on its requests to him.[76] He billed thousands of dollars per month for scanty reports regurgitating newspaper stories. Some reports actually were written by company officials. "He traded not on his skill or knowledge," according to one federal prosecutor. "The only thing he traded on was the familial relationship he had with his brother."[77]

The younger D'Amato first denied the allegations by asserting that "I didn't discuss clients with my brother." Later, to dispute government claims that his fees defrauded Unisys, the consultant switched gears and asserted with equal fervor that he deserved the money because he had, in fact, successfully lobbied the senator.[78]

Both versions had a common thread. Armand D'Amato acknowledged using his brother's office and stationery to lobby the military. He took draft letters prepared by Unisys urging the Navy to allocate funds for certain company programs, and then had the senator's office send them out on official letterhead over his brother's signature. According to both

D'Amato brothers, the letters were no more than everyday constituent service. Armand D'Amato was convicted of seven counts of mail fraud after a lengthy 1993 trial, but an appeals court threw out the conviction for lack of evidence proving his criminal intent. The Justice Department never filed charges against Alfonse D'Amato, who insisted he wasn't aware of the letters signed by an aide on his behalf. He still contends that his family was the victim of vindictive prosecution.

But the junior senator from New York—who proudly bills himself as "Senator Pothole," for bringing home the legislative bacon—didn't escape blame completely for his brother's behavior. While declining to formally censure or otherwise punish the bombastic GOP legislator, the Senate Ethics Committee sharply criticized him at the conclusion of a two-year inquiry. The committee called him "negligent" for conducting "the business of his office in an improper and inappropriate manner." Interpreting those findings as an "exoneration," Senator D'Amato choked back tears at a news conference. "Momma's prayers have been answered," he sighed.[79]

Gardner's fundraising for Congressman Roy Dyson, a hawkish, four-term Democrat from Maryland's conservative eastern shore, had a tragically grotesque ending. Dyson was a natural supporter of Unisys, since defense jobs provided the lifeblood of his district. Sperry had operated a research center in the area for decades. The tidal floodlands and bird sanctuaries on the shores of the Chesapeake Bay provided the backdrop for one of the Navy's elite aircraft-testing centers, the Naval Air Station at Patuxent River. Away from the water, the Army conducted chemical-warfare experiments and other classified tests at the Aberdeen Proving Grounds, another leading employer in the region.

At the end of April 1988, the thirty-nine-year-old lawmaker and two of his aides accepted an invitation from Unisys for two days of work and recreation in New York. Charlie Gardner arranged for a Saturday briefing and a tour of the Great Neck facility, confiding to one of his helpers: "These guys don't even want to see the plant ... They really want a weekend in New York."[80] Gardner and his visitors shared a meal in Manhattan's picturesque Little Italy, after which the congressional delegation went to see *The Phantom of the Opera* on Broadway as guests of Unisys. Part of Gardner's hospitality called for presenting Dyson with twenty thousand dollars in contributions, the same amount he had received during a similar excursion the year before. "The Dyson/Chappell team seems to be working out well," Gardner told friends.[81]

FBI agents were following and photographing the group on Saturday. Yet they couldn't prevent the lamentable train of events that occurred the next day.

A little after noon on Sunday, Thomas "Tony" Pappas, Dyson's chief aide and campaign adviser, jumped out of a twenty-fourth-floor window at the posh midtown Manhattan hotel where Unisys was paying the tab.

Police concluded that Pappas killed himself because he was despondent over a front-page story in *The Washington Post* that morning, criticizing his autocratic control of Dyson's office and suggesting that he was gay. The lengthy article said Pappas was under investigation by the Federal Election Commission. Staff members were quoted alleging that he had pressed coworkers to socialize with him, and they recounted an episode at an office party when Pappas supposedly asked a male aide to do a striptease.

Dyson was apprised of the suicide upon finishing a lighthearted breakfast with Gardner at the hotel. A brief altercation ensued over Unisys's decision not to pick up the bill as planned, in light of the questions that were sure to come.[82] Afterward, the company "provided a plane expeditiously" to rush the congressman away from reporters and back to Washington, according to Gardner.[83]

When detectives scoured Pappas's room for clues, they found a handwritten note on the unmade bed. The free-verse poem had a weird twist. "Ill winds that taunt us through peace and understanding will not cause us to have a crash landing," the end of one stanza read.[84]

Joe Aronica and his investigators discount theories linking the phrase in the note with Operation Illwind, calling it sheer coincidence. "There was no indication that [Pappas] felt distressed because he knew about our probe," declares one FBI agent.[85] Pappas would have been a central witness, as he was Dyson's intermediary with Unisys and other contributors. Without the trusted aide's testimony, many angles couldn't be pursued fully. Roy Dyson fought gamely to control the damage, admitting that he made "mistakes of judgment . . . mistakes of the head, [but] not of the heart."[86] He wasn't prosecuted, but he lost his seat as a result of the scandal.

For public consumption, Unisys pretended there were no problems. "I am satisfied that all activities associated with the official portion of the congressman's visit [were] in conformance with congressional and Unisys ethics guidelines," Frederick Jenny, the president of the company's defense operations, assured his managers a few days after the incident. "All expenses not associated with the official portion of the visit [were] borne by the congressman," the memo said, adding that "commitment to the highest standards of ethics and integrity remains our number one objective."[87]

But inside Unisys's boardroom, the macabre publicity surrounding the suicide sparked renewed worries over Gardner's affairs. In truth, the tragedy only heightened top management's nervousness. The seeds of concern had been sown almost immediately after the company was formed.

At the outset, when Unisys auditors and lawyers were trying to impose more centralized controls, they found what seemed to be trifling expense account violations in another defense unit. Barely a few thousand dollars were at stake, although the pattern was disturbing. There were indications of deceptive travel and entertainment bills, compounded by suspicious political contributions. Gardner's Great Neck operation wasn't part of that in-house probe. But through a fluke, it was highlighted as a ripe target. "If you think this is bad," one frightened marketing man under scrutiny volunteered, "you should see what Gardner's division is doing."[88]

Then the dam burst. Senior executives and the board of directors ordered a full-scale internal inquiry. Outside counsel was hired. The company's ethics ombudsman was called in. Voluminous records were reviewed, consulting contracts were analyzed and interviews were conducted. The Pentagon's inspector general was alerted about the details of the initial irregularities uncovered outside Great Neck, though the government wasn't given information revealing Gardner's suspected transgressions.[89] The wily manipulator felt the pressure building, and so did his friends. The FBI's daily wiretap transcripts were filled with their grousing about Unisys's stepped-up examination of "purchase orders" for consultants. One perturbed buddy described Gardner's predicament succinctly: "I never thought anybody could bring him down."[90]

Ironically, that was not at all what Unisys intended. Gardner's pluck, combined with the company's reluctance to scrap his supremely successful lobbying network, earned him kid-glove treatment. Gardner was pushed into early retirement. But he pocketed a comfortable bonus not long before he left, and the company signed him up on the spot as a consultant to continue tilling the fertile congressional fields he knew so well. "He was the only link we had to the House appropriations committee," recalls one former high-ranking executive. "The idea was to get him off the payroll, without forsaking our marketing edge."[91]

Unisys management talked a great deal about newly drafted ethics codes. The phrase "Performance with Integrity" was bandied about in employee communications. The internal investigation also prompted a spate of memos cautioning employees to exercise restraint in dealing with Congress. On the surface, the message seemed stern. "No corporate funds, products, services, or other corporate resources can be contributed" to political candidates, one memo concluded. "Engagement of lobbyists or consultants cannot be used as an indirect vehicle for making campaign contributions."[92]

At the same time, top executives recognized that encouraging workers to make political contributions, arranging congressional fact-finding visits and paying honoraria were important tools to keep Unisys programs alive. "I want us to continue these activities," Fred Jenny told managers after Pappas's death, warning them to be more careful paying for food, hotels and gifts for lawmakers. Frequently, the directives seemed to concentrate not so much on eliminating improper lobbying as on improving coordination among company units. "I am extremely concerned," Jenny said in another of his memos seemingly aimed at Gardner, that certain Unisys lobbyists are "working their own parochial programs" to try to "unduly influence the normal procurement process." If Pentagon officials feel antagonized by excessive pressure from members of Congress, the memo concluded, other company programs could be jeopardized. Unisys threatened disciplinary action against anyone who skirted its main congressional liaison office.[93]

According to Gardner, the changes were primarily cosmetic and aimed at reducing Unisys's legal exposure. He claims that the programs he was responsible for tracking didn't change and neither did his routine. Gardner is adamant that nobody ever told him to stop using his old coterie of consultants. "Management didn't want to annihilate the Washington operation," he asserts. "Unisys wanted to continue it and make it more effective."[94]

Aronica's band of agents adopted much the same view. They saw the contractor resist firing Gardner, who could have wounded it badly by opting to go to work for a rival, and then equivocate at surrendering damaging information to authorities. "He was a big rainmaker for Unisys," according to Fulmer, the senior Navy investigator. "They gave him a lot of rope."[95]

Bringing Gardner back as a hired gun was approved at the highest levels of the company—all the way up to the board's audit committee and Charles Ruff, the former Watergate prosecutor hired as its chief outside compliance watchdog.[96] Once the decision became public, red-faced executives stretched for a justification. They said there was no other way at the time to ensure Gardner's cooperation with internal probes. To demonstrate its newfound sensitivity to ethical issues, Unisys pledged to investigate its own investigators. Not surprisingly, many federal agents and critics scoffed. They pointed out that in the end, the contractor failed to turn over to the government all of its internal reports on Gardner's transgressions on the grounds that Illwind went public before the documents were completed.[97]

(On top of the criminality at Great Neck, Unisys inherited three more Sperry divisions where accounting shenanigans cost it dearly down the road. In New Mexico, the company paid $12 million to settle claims that it had padded bills by improperly passing on state taxes to the Pentagon. In Arizona, Unisys pleaded guilty to inflating charges for Army computer work. And, in a 1991 case that investigators contend reached a peak of corporate arrogance, Unisys was convicted of systematically overcharging the military on flight-trainer contracts. When the Navy requested fixed-price proposals including the "best estimate" for future labor costs, the firm secretly added a cushion for extra profit. Lawyers for Unisys later argued that it was a good-faith error, pretending that the company simply had assumed the Navy wanted it to submit "the estimate that was best for us.")[98]

As Unisys struggled to insulate itself from Gardner, Mel Paisley and Bill Galvin wrestled with their own severe problems: They confronted a mutiny throughout the Navy against virtually everything connected with them or programs they had championed. Emboldened by the confirmation of Navy Secretary James Webb—an Annapolis graduate and decorated Vietnam veteran who tended to support the uniformed leadership—senior admirals were bent on "dismantling every Paisley/Lehman initiative they can," Galvin grumbled.[99] The bureaucratic housecleaning was revving up barely a couple of months after Paisley's resignation.

The plot to sell Mazlat ground stations to the Navy, which once looked so promising, was disintegrating from one week to the next. "We bet the wrong horse," one of Galvin's Israeli accomplices bellyached. Paisley marched out of the Pentagon with "so many things hanging" fire, Galvin responded, that he and the rest of the conspirators "let a beautiful deal slip away."[100]

The closely held Moon Project, calling for Martin Marietta to share the spoils by channeling subcontracts to Galvin and Paisley, no longer was the "big plum" they had envisioned either. Lamenting their travails, Paisley admitted to his partner that "this thing has backfired on us" and suggested that a "recovery plan" probably was too late. He kicked himself for not staying in office longer to enable them to wrap up the details and complete the scam. "We would have been home free," Paisley acknowledged in frustration. "It would have been bed[ded] down ... where [they] couldn't do anything" to disrupt it.[101]

His partner was just as downcast. Opposition from Congress and the hated "blue-suiters" meant that the "wheels came off the wagon on this thing," Galvin noted, complaining bitterly that he would be forced to swallow a four-hundred-thousand-dollar investment without landing a single Moon subcontract.[102] Clinching a lucrative deal to sell Sapphire Systems, the Galvin-created company that was supposed to get the classified work, likewise turned out to be a pipe dream. Shortly after Paisley became a private consultant, Galvin fumed that the Navy was moving to squeeze out Martin Marietta and eliminate the project altogether. "The Navy closed the door behind [Paisley], and [Moon] never came to fruition," he explained.[103] The admirals "didn't give it to somebody else," Galvin said in disbelief. "They canceled it."[104]

For Paisley, whose egotistical disposition had lapped up the pomp associated with his Pentagon post, the personal slights were as traumatic as the financial losses. Before Lehman left, he helped Paisley wangle a job consulting for the chief of naval research. The intercession permitted Paisley to keep his "Top Secret" security clearance, as well as the more restricted "Sensitive Compartmented Information" clearance needed for work on so-called "black" programs.[105] Paisley never conceived anyone would challenge his access. But that's exactly what he faced, and the blow-up was acutely embarrassing.

It took Webb less than two weeks to veto the arrangement. "Don't do anything for Mr. Paisley," the recently sworn-in secretary ordered an assistant, immediately after hearing of the former Navy official's plans. "I want him cut off from all security [clearances]."[106] "It just didn't look right" to keep Paisley on as a consultant to the service, Webb explained later, because it appeared to be a conflict of interest. "It would have given him the ability to come in and get updated on all the major programs."[107] Paisley blustered, threatening to appeal the decision to the secretary of defense, but Webb's order stood. When Paisley tried to get highly classified information on the next-generation Navy bomber—one of his key consulting assignments for McDonnell Douglas—even his good friend Jim Gaines muttered that it might not be wise. "The admirals are asking, have you got tickets?" Gaines said, using military lingo for security clearances. "Now, you don't have tickets."[108]

Other defeats followed. Admiral James "Ace" Lyons, commander of the Pacific fleet and a favorite of Lehman and Paisley, was pushed into retirement by Webb and the chairman of the Joint Chiefs of Staff. Lyons landed a cushy consulting job with McDonnell Douglas, but Paisley lost one more defender inside the service. From his vantage point on Wall Street, Lehman called it "the revenge of the nerds."[109] Roughly at the same time, Paisley's hand-picked replacement for the assistant secretary slot ignominiously was forced to withdraw his name after he had already settled into a temporary office on the Pentagon's E Ring. John Brett, the would-be nominee, had worked with Ben Plymale and was a good buddy of Gaines and Austen Watson, another of Paisley's longtime friends. Paisley assured the Pentagon's personnel office that he considered Brett an outstanding choice, persuading Lehman also to express support.

One huge blunder sank the appointment. The would-be nominee, who hadn't been graduated from college, had previously submitted a résumé to the Navy listing a baccalaureate degree. Brett and his supporters claimed it was an oversight.[110] Once Paisley's foes latched on to the issue, however, there was no chance to make amends. No stranger to such academic amnesia himself, Paisley couldn't bluff his way out of this scrape. Thus, he lost what he perceived to be the last chance to try to carry on with his schemes.

To top it off, Secretary Webb, as part of the general retribution engineered by flag officers, ordered wholesale investigation of programs that had been advocated by Lehman and Paisley. Predominately, it was a fishing expedition, with the Naval Investigative Service and the Navy's inspector general poking around areas at the whim of superiors. The new secretary, among other things, was livid that Lehman's team had pushed through a flurry of last-minute promotions for officers and commitments to dignitaries for future ship commissioning ceremonies. "As soon as I get done with one probe, they give me another one to do," the inspector general joked. Webb referred so many requests for audits that frazzled agents hung up a large blackboard devoted solely to tracking Lehman/Paisley inquiries.[111] Tips from Paisley's enemies kept lengthening the list. Some of the suspicion concerned Sapphire and Galvin, so Navy agents had no choice but to brief their new chief in broad brushstrokes about their larger investigation. Webb was informed that it involved Paisley and wiretaps, but he wasn't told much more than that.[112]

As a former House staffer and assistant secretary of defense for veterans' affairs, Webb knew enough to be cautious. He didn't press for elaboration and avoided telling the defense secretary's office what he had found out. "I had a duty to keep my own counsel," Webb later explained. "I [did] not want to get tangled up in this thing."[113] The unexpected turn didn't interfere with Illwind, though there was a great deal of scuttlebutt about Paisley being under scrutiny.

Suddenly, firms that had been loyal to him and Galvin sensed the drastic shift in the climate inside the Navy. Many bailed out of consulting agreements with them in a hurry. "They look upon us as the enemy now," Galvin said of one former client.[114] Disputes over money led to hard feelings between the two men, prompting them to split up on terms that weren't amicable. Galvin joked that if he was asked, "Where is your friend Mel Paisley?" his retort usually was, "Mel who?"

Galvin was looking to build a new business by linking with Charlie Gardner instead, hoping to concentrate on massaging congressional psyches. "I've got a big financial problem . . . I'm really taking gas right across the board," he told Paisley at one point, complaining that his former compatriot wasn't sympathetic enough. "Partners have to take the short end . . . as well as the good news."[115]

Looking back at their heyday, the two former standouts sounded worn out. "We had a deal going . . . you and I were able to work something," Paisley said. But given the Navy's new lineup, he added, "I don't know who to go talk to . . . We have no influence . . . we don't have the ability to make things happen."[116]

The comeback was quintessential Galvin. He complained that Webb didn't like meeting with contractors and kept out of procurement details. Claiming that he recently had a chance to meet the new secretary, Galvin said with disgust: "He didn't even know what the fuck I do . . . Even if you sat in his back pocket, he wouldn't know what to do."[117]

☆

The faces of the FBI agents seemed too serious, and the classified papers they were examining looked too authentic, to be part of any practice drill. Under the solemn gaze of leader Rick Wade, squads of agents conducted interviews and diligently picked through filing cabinets and desk drawers in what appeared to be the offices of a good-size defense contractor. Supervisors barked orders about how to rummage through files for relevant documents and the proper way to log materials into portable computers. In another room, agents posing questions had to put up with uncooperative receptionists and obstreperous subjects. It all looked believable, down to the indignant defense attorneys racing to the scene after search warrants had been served.

But the ferocious activity that day in the spring of 1988 was merely a rehearsal for the real—and wholly unprecedented—FBI moves that soon were to come. Wade's crew acted out roles. Classified "files" supposedly purloined by a corporate consultant had been planted beforehand as training devices. The sessions, held at the bureau's sprawling training academy in Quantico, Virginia, were foreplay for the nationwide raids that would trumpet the arrival of Operation Illwind to the public. "In the movies," Wade says with a grin, "police just pick up the evidence, stick it in their pocket and walk out with it." His agents would do nothing of the kind. They had thick briefing books, reams of memos and bundles of triplicate inventory forms spelling out, step by excruciating step, the procedures that had to be followed.[118]

In its inimitable style, the FBI settled on a name for the remarkable operation long before it picked the precise date: Henceforth, the largest coordinated search in the history of government fraud investigations was to be known as "Operation Whirlwind."

The bureau spent three nonstop months preparing, treating the raids like a fine-tuned military campaign. Agents were flown to Washington for lengthy briefings and pep talks. Team leaders were designated, followed by assignment of interrogators, document gatherers, inventory agents and "computer entry" personnel. Photographers were instructed to take snapshots and make sketches. Some squads were assigned their own legal adviser, in case unforeseen complications arose. As the deadline approached, Wade's assistants sent out customized packages that included laptop computers, search warrants and scripted interview questions. Also enclosed were thick affidavits, carefully kept under court seal, laying out the gist of the criminal schemes under investigation.[119]

Quite apart from ego gratification, Wade and Aronica consciously designed Operation Whirlwind to make a big splash. Surprise and maximum deterrent effect were cardinal considerations. For both psychological and tactical advantage, they intended to grab the industry's attention as never before. The "shock value" of pouncing on contractors without warning, Aronica stressed, would graphically illustrate the gravity of the violations and the government's determination to punish those responsible. As a bonus, documents would be protected from possible destruction. And targets would be forced to choose between instant cooperation and the prospect of prosecution for lying during initial interviews. "You either want them to confess," the prosecutor put it bluntly, "or you want them to lie their brains out."

Aronica maintained that the lesson for industry would be stark: "The government is determined to investigate this kind of behavior, and people will go to jail. So, you better be careful and, better yet, not get involved in similar crimes."[120] Henry Hudson, the man ultimately responsible for deciding how to unveil the probe, agreed that surprise raids were likely to scare witnesses into cooperating. "It was an attempt to show the strength and the breadth of the government's case," he recalls.[121]

For some grizzled agents, accustomed to seeing contractors elude punishment for felonies, revenge was a bracing tonic. How will it feel, they wondered gleefully, when agents wearing weapons begin carting away mountains of evidence from corporate headquarters as if they were making a drug bust or arresting some underworld kingpin? The industry will be so dumbstruck, chuckled Joe Krahling, the former Alexandria FBI chief, that "some contractors may be eating their bananas sideways for fear of being accused of homosexual tendencies."[122]

Operation Whirlwind also was primed to go for more pragmatic and selfish reasons. Eighteen months of wiretaps needed to be transcribed and digested, then followed up with nearly a thousand interviews. If the "wires" stayed up longer, inundating investigators with more tapes and then truckloads of still more subpoenaed documents, many worried that the task force literally would collapse.

Already, fourteen-hour days and six- and seven-day workweeks were taking their toll. Those manning and analyzing the wires were burning out rapidly. Wade, for example, arrived at the "Shark Tank" by 4:30 A.M. most days to get a head start on his paperwork. Debbie Pierce, his stalwart aide, remembers working seventy-two days in a row during one stretch.[123] Agents were obsessed with not missing a stint at their desks. One young woman ran five miles through a blizzard to reach the deserted office, on a morning when no vehicles were able to move on area highways. Getting ready for the raids, over and above the daily grind, hiked stress levels still higher. The troops were itching for relief from the unrelenting pace. "It needed to stop," says Phyllis Sciacca, who oversaw the wiretaps. "Every case has several phases [and] we needed to move on . . . You can't keep one phase going forever."[124]

Moreover, federal judges weren't inclined to keep signing wiretap approvals for the same phones unless they saw that the investigation was continuing to expand by exposing brand-new conspirators or deceptions. Judged by that standard, some existing lines were prime candidates for shutdown. Preliminary plans to pull the plug on all the wiretaps months earlier had been shelved, after supervisors succumbed to the temptation of trying to pick up additional evidence. Wade and others did their best to boost agent morale. "You folks are like miners digging up nuggets in the jungle," Fulmer told his fatigued NIS crews. "We're not going to have any beautiful jewelry unless you gather up all the nuggets we need."[125]

As the summer of 1988 drew near, agents dreaded another round of "re-ups," as the monthly court authorizations were called. The strain on everybody was enormous. Above all, fear of leaks—which had resembled a low-grade fever before—reached new heights. Every suspicious comment overheard on the telephone lines exponentially increased the anxiety of Wade, Aronica and their aides.

On one occasion, Lehman was captured on tape giving Paisley a heads-up about pending investigative efforts. The former secretary, who had gotten a whiff of the Webb-inspired flurry of internal Navy probes, confirmed that Paisley appeared to be their main target. "Now what have you done?" he asked his onetime sidekick, half in jest. "There's another investigation of you."[126] At first, agents were terrified that the words on the tape referred to Illwind. But they never came across any other evidence substantiating that theory. The comments themselves, short and oblique, were open to various interpretations. Significantly, the task force didn't detect changes in Paisley's subsequent behavior or come across any phone conversations suggesting that he knew the FBI was eavesdropping.

Lehman steadfastly maintains that he made an innocent remark in a kidding fashion. The former secretary's enemies floated rumors based on various versions of the taped exchange, always insinuating that somehow he had allegedly tried to obstruct justice. Nevertheless, agents eventually accepted Lehman's own explanation. The hotly debated snippet of conversation, they concluded, amounted to idle gossip.[127]

By May 1988, FBI and NIS headquarters were clamoring to see a public relations payback from Illwind, which had been a steady drain on resources since late 1986. Bureaucratic pressure and the risk of unauthorized exposure, balanced against the likelihood of diminishing returns from the wiretaps, convinced Wade and Aronica to set a firm cutoff date. Nervous and exultant at once, they ordered all preparations to be completed by mid-June. Mostly, subordinates could hardly wait to get the searches behind them at long last.

However, a tiny minority of investigators delving into Unisys's machinations on Long Island was livid. The stubborn cadre of agents demanded more time to unravel what they argued was potentially the biggest political corruption case in their lifetimes. On some tapes, defense industry officials plotted to funnel illegal campaign contributions to House and Senate leaders, including House Majority Leader Jim Wright and Speaker Thomas (Tip) O'Neill. Other conversations had industry insiders scheming to secretly pump money into the campaign of Democratic presidential candidate Michael Dukakis, who publicly eschewed defense contributions. Excited agents, relying on wishful thinking and sketchy evidence, spun theories implicating as many as twenty incumbent lawmakers.[128] Any role of the prospective recipients was far from clear, and establishing the facts would require months of additional wiretaps. But beyond a doubt, it was the most auspicious entrée yet to the well-hidden secrets of Capitol Hill. "It's our best opportunity to penetrate the political arena," one senior FBI man reported up to the bureau hierarchy without self-promotion. "It looks very good."[129]

Andrew Maloney, the Brooklyn U.S. attorney who specialized in such investigations, supported the position of the agents working with his office. Like them, he believed that given adequate time to develop, this offshoot of Illwind held tremendous promise. Who cares if Hudson and Aronica control the Pentagon bribery and bid-rigging side of the case, Maloney told associates, as long as Brooklyn gets its chance to pursue the more provocative Capitol Hill angles. "If everything pans out," he told his staff with enthusiasm bordering on hype, the case could make previous congressional prosecutions "look like pimples on an elephant's ass."[130] To protect his prerogatives, Maloney was willing to go to the mat to try to convince Justice Department headquarters to delay the raids.

Gardner led Maloney's agents to Grumman Corporation, Long Island's biggest aerospace concern, and John O'Brien, its combative chairman. "I know O'Brien from the island," Gardner boasted to friends. "He's done me favors . . . That is not bullshit."[131] The tentacles extended to a political action committee run by James Kane—a phenomenally prolific fundraiser and lobbyist who was exceptionally close to O'Brien—and then straight to the nodes of power in Congress. Although the wiretap on Kane's office had been active only for six weeks, it yielded intriguing tidbits of his influence with lawmakers. For instance, Kane seemed to be able to produce Speaker O'Neill almost at will to visit Long Island and meet with Grumman officials.[132]

For sixty years, Grumman had been synonymous with the best of U.S. naval aviation. Bearing menacing names such as Wildcat, Hellcat and Avenger, sturdy Grumman-built planes helped turned the tide in the Pacific during World War II, with a young pilot named George Bush playing his part. In Korea, Vietnam and elsewhere, Grumman jets roared off carriers to defend the fleet and scare the enemy. By the mid-1980s, though, the company and its thirty thousand employees were in a nasty political dogfight to keep production lines open.[133] The design of its planes was getting long in the tooth, while deficit-conscious lawmakers were upset by the steep price tag. Grumman contemplated hiring Gardner, two of whose children worked for the company, as a special consultant.

O'Brien also relied increasingly on Kane, a political junkie and weekly golfing partner. Kane owned packaging companies that sold paper, cardboard and plastic to Grumman and other Long Island aerospace firms. Plus, he leased two warehouses to Grumman. But the supplier wasn't content to invest his profits and dabble in lobbying. An abrasive, self-made millionaire who habitually wore sneakers with business suits, Kane devised a powerful fundraising tool that gave him disproportionate political muscle. The crux of it was squeezing Grumman vendors for campaign donations. Naturally, Kane and his buddies decided which lawmakers received the funds.

With O'Brien's unflagging encouragement and advocacy, Kane's umbrella organization, called the Long Island Aerospace PAC, raised more than $1.2 million in just a few years. He created it and ran it like one of his family companies. Kane employees provided clerical support. Committee records were stored in his office. The listed accountant was his personal accountant.[134] Supposedly, Kane headed a voluntary association of business people promoting civic pride and investment in local industry. In actuality, investigators determined that the organization was a coercive instrument of Grumman's political agenda, and some of its methods were branded as a sophisticated form of corporate extortion.[135]

Subcontractors that valued Grumman as a customer knew they had better give Kane the contributions he was constantly dunning them to make. Those who refused to donate, or withdrew as dues-paying members of Kane's committee, risked being cut off from a share of Grumman's two billion dollars a year in purchases. Company officials didn't have to spell out an ultimatum to get results. "People don't do business that way," according to Gardner. "If they do, they are clowns." Vendors learned soon enough that Grumman's implied threats could have real bite. Smaller suppliers were intimidated the most. They were caught in the middle, since many were dependent on the aircraft-maker's business to stay afloat.

Grumman purchasing officials were in charge of collecting campaign donations, and O'Brien's assistants sometimes imposed quotas for the amount of money that had to be raised for particular candidates. By 1988, Grumman suppliers and landlords nationwide were being solicited and forced to participate. "It became a frenzy ... like feeding the sharks," one high-ranking company official remembers. "We went crazy."[136]

The impetus came from the top. Employees who aggressively raised campaign loot were rewarded with promotions and bonuses. Conversely, O'Brien threatened to fire or demote workers who were less than wholehearted in aiding Kane. The chairman's reaction could be explosive. "He made it clear to me ... that the procurement department had to become politically active ... working with Long Island Aeropac," one of his victims recalls. "He was pounding the desk ... [and] screaming at me ... I thought my job was in jeopardy." Another time, the irate chairman ordered Grumman's vice-president of procurement to stop buying from a valued but politically recalcitrant supplier called Monitor Aerospace. The subcontractor quickly toed the line and rejoined Kane's lobbying association. "Not to do business with Monitor because [it wasn't] a member ... was insanity," the shocked executive told prosecutors afterward.[137]

Kane's economic interests meshed perfectly with his politics. He shared private business deals with two sons of now-deceased Speaker O'Neill, as well as trying to drum up Grumman business for one of them. He quietly gave O'Brien six hundred thousand dollars in real estate and other loans, which Grumman's chairman then repeatedly lied about to his own board of directors. In fact, agents discovered that Kane showered gifts on virtually every Grumman employee with whom he had contact. Gratuities included cases of liquor, college scholarships and free vacations at two luxury Florida condominiums and a Vermont ski chalet he owned. Sometimes, the present was a monthly payment of one thousand dollars.[138]

There was a striking symmetry to these arrangements. On the opposite side of the ledger, Kane Paper Company received roughly $17 million in favorable or no-bid contracts from Grumman over the same period. Sole-source jobs were made to look like competitive awards. Grumman even paid Kane for "no ship" contracts involving fictitious supplies, for which the bills were passed on to the Pentagon as part of normal overhead costs. Kane had no official position with the contractor. He wasn't formally a consultant. Executives smirked when they used his nickname: Grumman's "unofficial executive vice-president." But when Kane marched into a company office, boasting of his friendship with the chairman and pointedly referring to him as "John," the man almost always got his way. "Who the hell is running this place?" one of O'Brien's senior managers demanded one day, prompting a shouting match with the chairman.[139]

The head of Grumman's shipping department may have summed it up best. "I did check with my superiors" about paying Kane, he testified years later, "and was told to do whatever he wants done."[140]

The deeper investigators probed the bonds between Kane, O'Brien and members of Congress, the more disenchanted Navy agents became with what they considered lack of support from superiors in Washington. Chronically short of manpower and filled with inexperienced personnel, the NIS team working on Long Island barely could keep up with the information cascading off the wires. "Those kids were working weekends and really humping," according to Jimmy Whitener, the lead agent at the time. But supervisors in the capital wouldn't approve a dollar of overtime pay. The squads also were expected to pursue dozens of other, less important investigations, and new cases still had to be opened and documented at the normal clip. Worse yet, increasing friction over the rules for recording conversations created bad blood between street agents and some of their bosses in Washington.[141]

Trouble was evident from the opening. The prosecutor assigned to supervise the Gardner and Kane lines was more conservative than the Navy agents in interpreting when the law required taping to be suspended. Except for the handful of congressmen specifically mentioned in sealed affidavits filed with the court, Whitener's crews basically were instructed not to tape phone calls involving other lawmakers or their staffers. Such calls were supposed to be monitored for the first two minutes only, and then largely left alone unless obvious criminal discussion had been overheard.[142]

Either out of an abundance of caution, or for more conspiratorial reasons nobody will ever be able to pin down, a tiny group of NIS supervisors wanted to take those restrictions a giant step further. They argued that their agency's legal charter didn't cover investigating congressional corruption, so that aspect of Illwind should be left primarily to others in law enforcement. Some NIS veterans also fretted over possible negative

impact on Navy budgets as fallout from the inquiry. Whitener was ap-
palled, complaining to friends that many of the signals he was getting
from the higher ranks threatened to impede his work.[143]

"We are not going to target congressmen," Whitener recalls one high-
level supervisor telling him point-blank. If NIS agents happened to "flip
the switch" to immediately turn off the tape machines when a congressman came on the line, Whitener was told, the FBI would never find out.
He chafed at the suggestions and objected to the limits officially imposed
on his agents by the Justice Department, as did a number of managers
above him. "The real question," one longtime NIS investigator liked to
say, "is whether we lack the charter or the balls to go after lawmakers?"
The dispute split the organization badly, and the Long Island probe never
regained momentum.[144]

NIS agents quietly took their concerns to Maloney and his assistants,
who assured them that the U.S. attorney's office was four-square behind chasing all leads. But by then, the subject was moot. Whitener was abruptly
demoted and transferred, for reasons that NIS insisted had no connection to
Illwind. Meanwhile, 250 miles to the south, the tag-team of Hudson and
Aronica had managed to outmaneuver Maloney in the turf battle over the
anticipated raids. Senior Justice Department officials decreed that Alexandria,
not Brooklyn, was in charge of determining timing. Furious at being relegated to a secondary role, Maloney and his staff gradually lost interest. He
would fight and lose a number of other internecine battles with Hudson,
while the few criminal cases left under his jurisdiction languished.

In fairness to Hudson, the dispute went beyond oneupmanship. There
was widespread professional disagreement over the strength of the wiretaps and their ability to tie lawmakers directly to illegal activities. Congressmen could assert constitutional immunity, claiming that their
statements, votes and other acts were off-limits for prosecution. Legislative
staffs typically insulated them from fundraising details. Furthermore, there
was no Title III wiretap approved for Kane's home telephones, leaving
substantial gaps in the government's evidence.

The wires, by themselves, did not ipso facto prove criminal intent on
the part of lawmakers. A senior investigator who listened to the tapes offers the following analogy: "Presidents do things all the time for people
who donated money to their party. It looks bad. It may smell bad. But unless there is a hard link between the money and the decision, there's no
crime." Waiting to see how the Long Island inquiry progressed was too
dangerous, Hudson and his supporters argued. The task force had reached
its saturation point for information. Delay would mean that cases teed up
against Paisley, Galvin and their accomplices would lose their edge.

Having bested Maloney in the bureaucratic wars, Hudson and Aronica
told the FBI to move posthaste to commence the action. Four days before
"D-Day," as most agents called it, there was a conclave of more than 150
people back at Quantico. Assembled in the auditorium were the most ex-

perienced FBI and NIS agents, who would quarterback the searches simultaneously in eleven states and the District of Columbia. Wade's briefers outlined the history of the case and reiterated the rules, from safeguarding documents to how materials should be identified and transported. Maps were distributed, along with procedures for gaining speedy access to classified areas. The requirements were comprehensive and strict. "We want your [laptop] computer diskettes seventy-two hours after the searches wrap up," Wade's majordomo for administration told the crowd.[145] The meeting broke up Friday afternoon. Getting targets to cooperate "is going to be as easy as smacking a cue ball into a tight rack," Fulmer predicted in his folksy drawl, trying to soothe the nerves of the participants.[146] That weekend seemed like an eternity to many of them. Operation Whirlwind was scheduled to start swirling early the next week.

On Monday, June 13, 1988, prosecutors dropped their bombshell in the lap of Defense Secretary Frank Carlucci, Caspar Weinberger's replacement. As a courtesy and to make sure that Pentagon officials wouldn't inadvertently hamper the execution of search warrants, Hudson and Aronica decided to advise him of the upcoming raids. The meeting didn't play out as expected. A military driver assigned to pick up the pair couldn't find the U.S. attorney's office, although it is only five subway stops from the Pentagon. By the time they hustled into the secretary's wood-paneled meeting room late in the afternoon, Carlucci was rushed and distracted. He kept glancing out the windows, toward the racket made by an honor guard preparing to welcome a visiting foreign dignitary. Carlucci had to be downstairs in a few minutes to preside at the ceremony.

The two prosecutors hastily laid out the sweep of the operation planned for the next day, withholding some names but disclosing that rooms in the Pentagon would be among those sealed and searched. A small band of the defense chief's aides listened intently, betraying no emotion. Previously, Hudson and Attorney General Ed Meese had told Carlucci in vague terms that a round of searches was coming.[147] In the crush of other business, the secretary hadn't focused on the public uproar that was bound to result. Upon hearing some of the specifics, he was quite perturbed. "Well, what should I do?" Carlucci asked at the session's conclusion. "Should I suspend some people? Should I do something else?" Hudson's reply was emphatic: Don't take any precipitous step that might tip the government's hand.[148]

The secretaries of the Air Force and the Navy received more thorough briefings the same day, without being given details of all the targets and locations either. The Defense Department's inspector general was notified in a telephone call. Senior officers at NIS and other military investigative agencies also were told about the plan. The Pentagon's public affairs mill quietly started drafting statements that would be used to answer press queries once the investigation became public. With so much activity under way, Hudson and the FBI suspected that the media would be alerted. Miraculously, despite the buzz throughout the building that some major move was imminent, there were no big leaks. Hudson remembers a call from a national television correspondent in the evening, demanding to know what was afoot. Her tone was unnerving. "When this thing happens," the reporter asked coyly, "where should we be to make sure we don't miss it?" His noncommittal answers helped keep a lid on the story.[149]

As the sun rose on Flag Day, June 14, hundreds of agents fanned out to prearranged positions at forty-four sites across the country. Military facilities, companies and private homes were all part of the plan. The list stretched from trendy Southern California suburbs to corporate marketing offices a few blocks from the White House, encompassing big cities and small towns in the Northeast, South and Midwest. The teams had orders to be at the staging areas and ready to roll before 9:00 A.M., but to wait for a radio signal before proceeding. There were hints that maybe some spots weren't going to be hit. "The searches will be conducted once the main interview target has been located," the three-page, single-spaced instruction memo from headquarters reiterated. Resigning themselves to a long wait, leaders at each location made certain that their agents stayed loose and didn't attract unnecessary attention.

There was plenty of nailbiting by those directing the operation, too. Aronica took his place at a large horseshoe-shaped table in the command post, inside the FBI's Washington field office. The building was in a rundown section of the capital, called Buzzard's Point, close to the Potomac and surrounded by junkyards and crack houses. But inside the converted conference room, everything hummed and glistened. Prosecutors and agents leaned against the back wall. Aronica and the rest of the Whirlwind supervisors sat in the middle of the room, flanked by phone consoles and teletype machines. On a wall in front of them was a giant map of the United States, with blinking lights and slips of paper indicating the location and status of search teams. A bank of television monitors flickered in one corner.[150] The scene resembled some futuristic, remote-controlled police chase in a science-fiction movie. But human emotions, not technology, would determine the outcome of this adventure.

Driving to his first appointment that Tuesday, Charlie Gardner had no clue that he was "the main interview target." Nor did he have any inkling that a small army of federal agents would spring into action—or abort part of their mission and retreat in silence—based on his reactions over the next few hours.

The FBI had used a ruse to get Gardner to voluntarily visit its Long Island office early that morning. Appealing to his patriotism, the bureau pretended that it wanted Gardner to come for a chat about whether he might have crossed paths with Soviet intelligence operatives during his international business travels. The approach seemed far-fetched, but it worked better than anticipated. Since the agent offering the invitation sounded friendly and shared his Irish wit, Gardner had said yes. Arriving half an hour later than expected, he was quickly ushered in to meet his contact. Gardner also was introduced to Rick Wade. Then he glanced around the room.[151]

Gardner's shock was instantaneous. Posted on a blackboard were rows of blown-up pictures of himself, meeting with Illwind targets in various cities, airports and other locales. Excerpts of his wiretapped conversations were cued up and ready to be played on tape machines. Wade calmly described the extent of the investigation, emphasizing that the FBI was aware of Gardner's gamut of crimes and had roomfuls of evidence to back up charges for each one in court. After thirty minutes of verbal jabbing, the agent circled for the knockout. The government wants your cooperation, he told Gardner, handing over a draft agreement. The proposed plea bargain, Wade stressed, left out some of the most serious violations. Gardner's maximum exposure would be less than twenty years in jail and not more than a hundred-thousand-dollar fine, with excellent chances for a significantly more lenient sentence.

There was a kicker in the proposal, however. Gardner had to become a government informant, secretly taping conversations with his industry and congressional buddies for at least one year, maybe two. "We want you wired," Wade emphasized, explaining that the FBI would coach him extensively on how to extract information in his undercover role. "We will give you the questions." Instead of court-ordered wiretaps, Gardner would serve as the prosecution team's listening post for wayward corporate and Capitol Hill figures. "And we will tell the judge that you cooperated," Wade promised.[152]

In devising the strategy to confront Gardner, agents remembered how smoothly a similar pitch had worked to "roll" John Marlowe and launch the initial investigation. Admittedly, Gardner's response was a crap shoot. This time the target was more sophisticated and had a great deal more to lose. Wade's hunch was that Gardner, a religious Irish Catholic who believed in redemption, would try to atone for his guilt and protect his family from embarrassment as much as possible. Aronica and the FBI had agreed to hold off the searches to see if he caved in. If that happened, perhaps Whirlwind would be pared down and some targets, especially those connected with Gardner and his lobbying network, would be left alone to further incriminate themselves.[153]

Gardner didn't storm out and he didn't ask to call an attorney. At first, he insisted that he hadn't done anything wrong. "What you're saying is ridiculous," Wade replied. "We know different." After a brief period, it became obvious that Gardner was willing to acknowledge at least part of his guilt and consent to be debriefed by investigators. "Let's get it over with. I want to end it today," he kept telling Wade. "You guys are good. I know it's over. I can't fight the FBI." Gardner gave a brief but formal statement regarding his activities. "He answered questions somewhat truthfully," according to Wade. "He made some admissions."[154]

Still, there was no deal. The former Unisys executive absolutely balked at doing what Wade and Aronica demanded most vociferously: He wasn't willing to record discussions with other people. "I'm not going to get taped," Gardner repeated angrily. "I don't think that's right." He said he wouldn't think about it for a "millisecond." Investigators didn't really have a fallback position. "No way," Wade responded. "Thank you very much, we'll talk to you later." Taping had to be part of the deal, the agent said, "or we will continue blasting forward."[155]

Hours went by, with an increasingly jumpy Wade threatening and cajoling by turns. He sweetened the offer by reducing the penalty range, but that made no difference. Periodically, Wade cut off the discussion out of exasperation, ordering Gardner to leave. Each time, Gardner retreated to the waiting room. Agents conferred with an agitated Aronica by telephone. The FBI receptionist would walk back to Wade after a few minutes, informing him that Mr. Gardner still hadn't left the building and wished to resume talking. "What was the point of leaving?" Gardner asks rhetorically. "I couldn't just go back to work. It wasn't something you could write off as a bad day, and say tomorrow will be better."[156]

Neither Rick Wade nor Joe Aronica are willing to admit it, but the architects of Whirlwind fundamentally misjudged Charlie Gardner's character. Like Richard Fowler, Boeing's ace document collector, Gardner stiffened under pressure. He became more resistant and irrational the harder the government pushed him. "I was willing to tell them everything, right there," Gardner recounts. "They never understood that. I wanted to get down to the bottom line immediately. They wanted to get to the bottom line two years later."[157] Neither side budged.

As the sessions dragged on, the dynamics tilted subtly in Gardner's favor. Wade seemed to be the one wilting under the strain. The searches couldn't be held in abeyance much longer. A decision had to be made. One man's stubbornness was sabotaging a nationwide, carefully synchronized operational timetable. "You've got twenty minutes," Wade snapped. "The answer is still no," Gardner said, secretly enjoying the notion that the FBI agent was getting visibly distraught. This guy is a blooming idiot, Gardner chuckled to himself. He's jumping all over the place like a yo-yo, grabbing the phone to get advice and shouting at me that my time is running out. Even now, Gardner can't fathom why Wade and Aronica refused to accept his answer. "They had no depth in their approach," he maintains. "They had tunnel vision; they wouldn't move to the next step."[158]

Around noon, Aronica ended the standoff. If Gardner wasn't willing to accept the government's latest proposal, he told Wade, "tough shit, that's it." The radio signal went out to the search teams. "OK, let's do it," Aronica told the FBI contingent on Long Island, slamming down the phone.[159]

Gardner stayed at the bureau's offices several hours longer, vainly trying to cut the deal he desired. "Christ, I'll take you to the house," he said, insisting that he didn't keep any business records there. "You don't have to raid it." Finally, Wade became disgusted with the repetitive arguments. "Charlie, we're going to conduct a search," the agent said in midafternoon. "Your family is there. I really think you ought to be there." Gardner was allowed to call his wife to tell her that agents staked out nearby were going to enter the home. By the time Gardner's car pulled into the driveway, more than a dozen FBI agents were rooting through files, personal papers and even his trash.[160]

In Washington, a television crew showed up at the offices of United Technologies shortly before the searches began. Spooked agents called Buzzard's Point to describe the situation. "Has the FBI been here yet?" a cameraman asked a dazed company secretary, who tracked down the office's press spokesman having lunch at a restaurant. He was astonished by the question. Frantic calls went out to the firm's executives, startling one senior attorney who was about to fall asleep in his London hotel. Outside defense counsel were contacted right away, but they also were in the dark about the Justice Department's plans. Once the signal to carry out the raids was sent, agents coming into the United Technologies suite were greeted by whirring cameras. "Oh, you must be here for the searches," one of the television technicians said, shifting the minicam on his shoulder for a better shot.[161]

A few blocks away, a larger FBI and NIS contingent arrived at the Watergate to search the offices of Galvin and Paisley. Nearly twenty agents milled around the building's front door. A few were dressed in business suits and carried attaché cases. The rest, wearing blue jeans and windbreakers, carried file boxes, folded-up packing cartons and dollies to move heavy files or pieces of furniture. Confused and scared, the doorman swiftly lowered several nearly floor-length security panels to keep the team from entering. Gesticulating and holding the search warrants against the locked glass, agents demanded to be let in. "I have to check with my boss," the doorman said, reaching for the telephone.[162]

Team leaders had instructions to surprise subjects of the searches. It was imperative to get inside rapidly. Several agents distracted the doorman, allowing a petite female agent to sneak away and wriggle through a gap between the floor and the lower edge of the glass partitions. Inside the lobby, she threw open the front door and summoned two elevators. Her teammates surged through the entrance and raced for the open elevators, while the befuddled doorman waited for his call to be connected. Galvin and Paisley weren't in their offices. A slightly tipsy Evelyn Galvin, nursing an injured leg and entertaining friends at her condominium in the same building, was in shock when agents announced their presence.[163] The searchers took everything from personal calendars and bank statements to computer disks and scrap papers. At Paisley's house, they even combed through his sock drawer looking for contracts.

There were some unexpected glitches at the Pentagon, too. Television cameras captured the dour faces of agents standing guard outside the Air Force office of Victor Cohen, one of Galvin's main coconspirators. Inside, the phones rang incessantly. Reporters and congressional aides had received sketchy reports of the raids, and they desperately wanted to know the latest developments. One Democratic House staffer who knew Cohen relatively well wouldn't give up. He kept dialing. Eventually, someone in Cohen's office picked up the receiver. "I'm trying to get hold of Vic to find out what the hell is going on," the congressional aide blurted out. "Has the FBI visited your office?" After a lengthy pause came the reply: "This is the FBI."[164]

Prominent white-collar defense lawyers were deluged with requests for help from contractors and individuals embroiled in Whirlwind. The panicked calls came ten or fifteen minutes apart, often from different states, but they recounted a nearly identical sequence of searches and interviews. Veteran industry executives were aghast. If nothing else, Whirlwind had the gut-wrenching impact on most targets that Wade and Aronica had envisioned.

The extreme example was Bill Parkin, Galvin's accomplice dating back to their work on the cruise missile. Parkin came home from a shopping trip to find a platoon of agents swarming over his Northern Virginia home, searching it from attic to basement. Rooms were plastered with small pieces of sticky paper, left behind to show where materials had been seized.[165] "We have all this evidence," agents warned him. "You better come clean." As it did with Gardner and a group of other targets, the FBI tried but failed to prod Parkin into wearing a "body mike" to tape conversations with associates.[166] His assertions of innocence hid feelings of pervasive despair. In the wake of the searches and months of relentless pressure from investigators, the sixty-five-year-old Parkin tried to commit suicide by overdosing on sleeping pills. "I've paid the price" for years of illegitimate deals, he told one reporter after being discharged from the hospital and pleading guilty. "Life isn't worth living."[167]

James Gaines, Paisley's alter ego in the Navy, was no less shellshocked by the first FBI interview in his Pentagon office. Even partially filled-out personal tax forms in his briefcase were numbered, cataloged and carted away by the bureau. With his privacy shattered, every sentence Gaines uttered on the tapes became a potential dagger to his self-respect and freedom. Newspaper stories were filled with inaccurate reports that he had agreed to become a government witness. He couldn't sleep for three days after the raids. Vicki Paisley, a slender woman with a history of depression, looked ashen. She complained of agonizing headaches. In the immediate aftermath of D-Day, she confided to one friend, her digestive system stopped functioning and she began losing weight.[168]

Others somehow found the strength to be cavalier about the investigation, at least in its early stages. Galvin and Gardner went to the racetrack together the day after Whirlwind, talking almost as much about horses as about finding a good lawyer. Mel Paisley also tried to laugh off the probe at first. He hosted a backyard barbecue featuring a pig on a spit that he facetiously named "Henry"—in honor of Henry Hudson. "I've fought against the Gestapo and stood up to the Russians in my lifetime," he told friends, "but I never felt as violated" as during the course of Illwind.

Consultant Tom Muldoon, the irrepressible jokester who had needled drinking buddies with references to make-believe wiretaps, outdid himself on D-Day. He and his girlfriend were on a ferry from Long Island to his hometown of Bridgeport, Connecticut, after attending a wedding. A clutch of investigators armed with a subpoena had waited near the dock since dawn, to guarantee that they wouldn't miss him. As the unsuspecting couple ambled off the gangplank shortly after noon, an FBI agent rushed forward. "Mr. Muldoon, Mr. Muldoon," the youthful agent said breathlessly, introducing himself and explaining that the consultant's Washington apartment was being searched as part of the nationwide raids. "This is the biggest operation in the history of the FBI," the agent proudly informed him. Muldoon pondered the statement for a few seconds. "You mean bigger than Dillinger or Al Capone," he shot back with a smirk. Almost reeling from the remark, the insulted FBI man warned that Muldoon wasn't taking his predicament seriously enough. "Of course I am," said the consultant, "but not as seriously as you."[169]

Investigators kept a handful of wiretaps in place past June 14, hoping to lull some targets into making comments that would land them in deeper trouble. In law-enforcement circles, the term of art is "jiggling the wires." Right after the raids, Muldoon's accomplices kept reminding him that some of their chats might still be wiretapped. Bill Parkin said he was sure a mutual friend was recording conversations. That very friend told Muldoon that he was certain Parkin was working undercover for the government. "Enough already," Muldoon snapped. "Between the two of you, I'm likely to be electrocuted." James Kane's phones, for instance, remained under electronic surveillance, and his company wasn't searched for another week. Agents raided the Baldwin, Long Island, premises only after overhearing discussions about tossing records into a dumpster.[170] Four additional searches occurred around the same time.

Probably the most exciting pyrotechnics, though, came early in the morning of Wednesday, June 15. After Tuesday's searches were finished and weary agents straggled into the command post around eight in the evening, a remaining wire picked up snatches of highly suspicious dialogue. John Roberts III, one of Gardner's minions whose home hadn't been searched, received a call from an associate recapping the day's unforgettably scary twists and turns. With the FBI listening, Roberts indicated his determination to destroy evidence before investigators got around to visiting him. "I don't have a fireplace," he told his buddy, "but I've still got a trash can."[171]

Roberts's wife, Robbie, proceeded to "straighten out things" in their house's second-floor office, as she slyly put it, by ripping up incriminating documents dealing with Unisys campaign contributions. She stuffed the pieces into paper bags. To help dispose of the remnants, John Roberts pleaded with a family friend to come right over because it was "real, real important." He didn't want to go into details, Roberts said anxiously over the phone, because outsiders were listening "in one way or the other."[172] By this time, the FBI had surrounded the property. The orders were to let nobody in or out. But it was close to midnight, and the bureau needed a search warrant to get inside.

Groggy from exhaustion and the tension of an incredibly hectic day, Debbie Pierce, Wade's administrative wizard, slumped at a computer terminal to draft an emergency request to search Roberts's dwelling. She scrawled the last few sentences of the affidavit by flashlight, bouncing in the front seat of a Jeep speeding to reach a federal magistrate. It was about two o'clock in the morning when the bedraggled agents stood on the doorstep of the magistrate's home, imploring her to sign. A stickler for protocol, the woman roused Aronica from bed. "Why aren't you here with these agents?" she demanded to know over the phone. "I have just been handed the messiest affidavit I have ever had to look at in my entire life."[173]

The next hurdle was making copies of the signed warrant, as the law required. Racing the clock and their own dwindling energy, Pierce and a fellow agent opted to use the Xerox machine at the nearest municipal jail. As their brakes screeched to a halt at Roberts's house with the finished paperwork, the agents saw members of the search squad pacing impatiently next to the driveway. "Good luck," Pierce said, handing over the package. "We're going to bed."[174]

The agents who executed the warrant were flabbergasted by what they discovered. When the couple heard the FBI demanding entry, there was no time to ditch the bags filled with telltale scraps. Mrs. Roberts sat silently as the search began, doggedly chewing what agents later insisted was a golf-ball-size wad of paper.[175]

☆

Two days after the searches, Hudson strode into the Oval Office to brief President Reagan. The nine o'clock morning meeting also was attended by Ed Meese, Vice-President George Bush, General Colin Powell, the president's national security adviser, and others. Hudson's placid demeanor betrayed none of the thrill that he felt. How often does a U.S. attorney get the chance, Hudson reminded himself, to discuss cases in this setting? He brought no charts or documents to distribute during the presentation. In a steady monotone, the prosecutor spent half an hour describing the raids, explaining the suspected violations and laying out his next moves.[176]

The subtleties of criminal law weren't uppermost in the minds of those listening. The battle-tested politicians gathered around the mahogany conference table, including the president's chief of staff and top Capitol Hill lobbyist, didn't care about the fine points of military procurement rules. They were focused on one central issue: the investigation's impact on the November presidential elections, looming less than five months away. Reagan's initial public comments stressed that he was "disappointed and upset" by the allegations of criminality, while noting that it was "understandable how such things can happen" in a bureaucracy as massive as the Pentagon. "I'm not taking this lightly at all," the testy president assured reporters, adding that his administration deserved credit for ferreting out wrongdoers.[177] But defense fraud is unavoidable, Reagan insisted, "because you can't be down there watching several million people . . . every day."

Bush, whose aides already had decided that John Lehman was too big a liability to remain as an adviser traveling on his presidential campaign plane, took other preemptive steps to distance himself from Illwind. Saying that he was "shocked and offended, like all Americans, at the abuse of public trust," Bush suggested that he wouldn't let such slipups occur on his watch.[178] As a presidential candidate, he promised, "I will not tolerate lawlessness in the Pentagon, in the streets or in the Congress."

Other Reagan intimates tried just as hard to spread the blame for the scandal, which spawned the inevitable label "Pentagate." Defense Secretary Carlucci, who inherited the mess, said it was impossible to make the Pentagon "greed-proof." Acknowledging that there were "defects in how America equips its forces," Carlucci asserted: "Some can be traced to the Defense Department, some to Congress and some to industry."[179] His predecessor, Caspar Weinberger, expressed no second thoughts regarding his stewardship of the department. "I certainly don't feel culpable," Weinberger maintained, though he went out of his way to remind everyone that Lehman had been a "great friend" of Paisley's and had "praised him highly and quoted him frequently" when the pair worked together in the Pentagon.[180]

The media weren't the only places where the administration was getting pummeled. Lawmakers couldn't wait to jump into the fray, wringing their hands and scheduling a raft of hearings. There was no downside to looking tough. Senator John Warner of Virginia, a former Navy secretary and a ranking GOP member of the Armed Services Committee, called the influence-peddling investigation "the most serious case in the history of the Department of Defense . . . It is widespread and it is deep."[181] The sentiments weren't merely public relations ploys. Mistakenly believing that his microphone was turned off during one nationally televised hearing, Warner expressed his private misgivings to a colleague. "There are fifteen companies involved," he said in a plaintive whisper. "Rampant bribery in the government."

The debate fueled a surging partisan backlash. Without lifting a finger, Democrats had been given a perfect vehicle to attack the president and his appointees for being asleep at the switch. Senator Sam Nunn, the studious chairman of the armed services panel, who was not prone to lambasting the Pentagon, said the probe would show whether there were "a few rotten apples" or basic flaws in the country's weapons-buying machinery. The Georgia Democrat, who had raised no fuss when Paisley was confirmed years earlier, belatedly complained that Reagan's appointees had been "selected for their ideological beliefs [and] for their salesmanship, but not for sound management."[182] The rhetoric became more incendiary daily. Veteran representative Jack Brooks, a curmudgeon from Texas, reflected the animosity of many Democrats. The euphoria of the Reagan buildup had worn off, Brooks argued, "and we are staring at the cold reality" that "much of the money invested was squandered . . . [by] 'see-no-evil' officials who mindlessly defend the Pentagon's purchasing system."[183]

With a potent threat to the GOP brewing, Reagan asked Hudson at the end of the White House briefing how quickly there would be action to muffle critics. Choosing his words as carefully as if he were addressing a jury, the prosecutor replied: "Mr. President, based upon the strength of the wiretap evidence and the interviews the FBI has conducted, I feel reasonably confident that I will have some pleas of guilty in this case within ninety days."[184]

After the meeting broke up, a swarm of reporters peppered Meese and Hudson with questions as they stood on the White House lawn. The attorney general's answers were rambling and imprecise. Meese indicated that sweeping grand jury indictments, rather than pleas, would be forthcoming between thirty and ninety days. Hudson cringed. He couldn't contradict his boss. But those confident predictions of how rapidly grand jurors would act—coupled with the Justice Department's refrain that there would be a total of one hundred prosecutions—rebounded to haunt Illwind. On the ninety-first day following the raids, according to Hudson, his office switchboard "lit up like a Christmas tree" with reporters asking about the lack of indictments and the investigation's overall slow progress.[185]

The arbitrary timetable made Joe Aronica nearly apoplectic. "I don't know where Henry came up with those numbers," he told associates in a frenzy. "I have no idea . . . they never came from me."[186] Aronica and his agents did have a game plan, but it was overly optimistic and soon overwhelmed by events. They expected Gardner to plead guilty in roughly two months, becoming the linchpin of prosecutions practically from the beginning of Illwind's overt phase. It took almost a year for Gardner to sign a plea bargain. He agreed to be a government witness but never taped conversations with industry pals. Originally, Aronica expected to wrap up cases against the rest of the top-tier targets approximately a year after the raids. Getting close to that goal actually took closer to six years, while some prominent individuals and big firms wriggled off the hook.[187]

Some of the difficulties stemmed from the inherent dynamics of Illwind. Investigators had to master an awesome volume of documents, and they interviewed well over two thousand witnesses. The top-notch caliber of the opposing lawyers also tended to drag out resolution of cases. In the aggregate, contractors and executives under scrutiny spent untold tens of millions of dollars on mock trials, futile efforts to quash subpoenas, dilatory procedural challenges to throw out wiretaps and other defense tactics. Within a month of the raids, for example, sixteen well-known Washington defense lawyers wrote an irate letter demanding an internal Justice Department probe of what they contended was a "virtual flood of leaks" and blatant "sensationalization" of Illwind by law-enforcement agencies.

During contemplative moments, Aronica and Wade theorized that the very nature of white-collar criminals frequently precluded speedy admissions of guilt. Many months or even years had to pass, according to investigators, before Paisley, Galvin and others of their ilk could admit to themselves the crimes they had committed. Rationalizations were embedded too deeply in their minds; there was simply no way to fast-forward the process. As shrewd and proud as these men were, Wade surmised, they would not be ready to stand before the bar of justice until they reached a psychological turning point and shed their self-deception. "They set up so many protective barriers over the years," the FBI agent explained. "The seduction was powerful. They were able to pretend, 'I'm doing business like everybody else.' If everyone does it, then it must not be a crime."[188]

Beyond such hurdles, Aronica's caustic personality was a leading cause of delays. His fanatical need to assert control enraged agents and obstructed assistant prosecutors from making progress independently. Unwilling to delegate decisions but unable to attend to the multitude of details himself, the chief prosecutor became the chief bottleneck. One agent likened Aronica to a harried train conductor with too many boxcars lined up on a siding but no orderly plan to move them to the main line. "Joe is not a juggler, he was not comfortable proceeding down several avenues at once," according to another former senior Pentagon investigator who knew Aronica well. "He lined everything up in a queue and concentrated on one item at a time. Agents felt they lost twelve, eighteen, even twenty-four months of precious time."[189] One high-ranking FBI manager suggested farming out cases to other U.S. attorneys to break the logjam. "Hudson and Aronica looked at me like I was crazy," he recalls.[190]

In the meantime, the prosecution's style stretched out cases for different reasons. Aronica would invite targets and defense lawyers to what he called his "dog and pony shows," at which they were confronted with wiretap recordings. The taped excerpts were selected for maximum effect, and sound bites sometimes were accompanied by copies of draft charges. Aronica was expert at pinpointing an opponent's vulnerabilities. To increase his leverage, he threatened to seek felony charges against wives, adult offspring and other relatives. For example, Gardner complained that his married daughter, Barbara, was pestered by agents during the last months of her pregnancy.

Aronica's maneuvers generally proved effective, but they ate up the calendar. Defense lawyers and their clients would be overwhelmed with batches of tapes and transcripts provided by the government, then left alone for months to fret over their exposure and ponder what the prosecution team's next steps might be. "If some of them needed more time" to decide whether to plead, Aronica says, "that was fine; we had plenty of targets." Mostly, he was willing to follow the path of least resistance. "You look at what you can prove, that's the bottom line," he says. "I'm not going to go out on a limb and insist that someone plead to something [for which] there isn't any basis." Unquestionably, one man was in charge of all the negotiations. Agents fumed that junior prosecutors had no power, and that Aronica's superiors wouldn't listen to complaints by the FBI or NIS. "After sweating for a year and a half, it was incredibly frustrating," Fulmer recalls. "We wanted to enjoy the payoff." Defendants soon realized that they, too, had no chance of circumventing Aronica by appealing directly to Hudson or Meese.[191]

Federal courts became just another element of Aronica's drawn-out rituals. In the weeks following Whirlwind, he fought hard to keep judges from unsealing search warrant affidavits on the grounds that the contents would prematurely disclose the heart of the prosecution's theories. Later, when it suited his purposes, Aronica went back to the same judges and urged them to make the information public at once. The prosecutor cleverly also made a habit of slipping damaging information about targets into public court filings. He managed to avoid trials in almost every instance, partly due to his aggressive stance and partly because contractors knew that the Pentagon reserved its stiffest punishment for those firms that fought and lost.

Regardless, protracted delays diminished the ultimate deterrent value of Illwind's convictions. Leads became stale, and memories of witnesses faded. Agents felt betrayed. "Every one of them had some angle that he or she felt really should have gone the distance, but it just didn't work out," recalls one FBI supervisor ruefully.[192] As Justice Department priorities shifted, many of the most knowledgeable and dedicated investigators were transferred to work on unrelated cases. Another experienced agent puts the onus squarely on Aronica. "Paisley and others sat around for years, waiting for the prosecution to move and using the time to concoct stories" for their defense, he says.[193] Speedier justice would have prevented some of this excessive posturing.

The inquiry's slow pace also gave those running the Pentagon plenty of opportunities to temporize. In grand bureaucratic fashion, Secretary Carlucci set up a task force to study the matter and give him regular updates. With much fanfare, he vowed to take action straightaway once the Pentagon received specific evidence of corruption. "We do not need to await convictions," he told a hastily called press briefing after the first few portions of affidavits were released. The Navy, in particular, pledged to scour contracts for any scintilla of wrongdoing. "Every program that is in any way implicated will be reviewed in its entirety," promised Lawrence Garrett, who had replaced Jim Webb as Navy secretary.[194]

The tough talk produced minimal results. Not a single major Navy contract was scrapped or handed to a rival firm. Carlucci suspended a few Pentagon officials and temporarily barred a small number of companies from competing for orders. He halted progress payments on a scant nine contracts—and then reversed his decision in a matter of days. Other Pentagon responses were equally hollow. The pattern of multiple "best and final offers" was ended, supposedly to block eleventh-hour scrambles for inside information. Before receiving new business, a handful of firms was required to certify that they had not used fraud, collusion, or other illegal activity to win bids. The Navy dreamed up that policy and sold it to Carlucci. The Pentagon's general counsel, among others, considered the idea "silly," practically useless and "no more than a Band-Aid."[195] Despite the special procedures, loopholes kept business flowing to nearly every arms-maker tarred by Illwind. Units of larger contractors were reinstated in the Defense Department's good graces relatively swiftly and painlessly.

Companies reacted appreciably faster to the crisis than the government, severing ties with Galvin, Paisley and dozens of additional consultants within hours of the raids. Some firms stopped payment on checks already mailed out. Tom Muldoon joked that one company was so nervous it fired him twice. To head off federally imposed ethics rules, corporate America counterpunched by singing the praises of voluntary compliance. If codes of conduct are mandated by Washington and "shaped by a government checklist mentality," one industry lawyer argued, they are bound to fail. Don Fuqua, the aerospace industry's top lobbyist, decried what he called the "lynch mob" mentality of investigators and the media. Attacking the press, he said he was outraged by reports suggesting "that fraud is rampant and widespread . . . That is most definitely not the case."[196]

Aronica's breakthrough came in March 1989, nine months after Operation Whirlwind. Looking emaciated and dejected after his recent suicide attempt, Bill Parkin pleaded guilty to bribery, conspiracy and other charges. A broken man, with his eyes downcast and head bowed, he agreed to cooperate with prosecutors. A federal judge berated Parkin as "scum" and "a dog" for defrauding the military by scheming to snare contracts illegally for Teledyne and other corporations.[197] Pentagon purchasing rules were an "outrage," the judge said.

From the start, Parkin's was supposed to be the first major plea. The denizens of the Shark Tank celebrated. To mark the accomplishment, Wade, Pierce and their fellow FBI agents gathered around a hundred-dollar bottle of Dom Perignon champagne. The bottle had occupied a conspicuous spot on top of Wade's desk from the investigation's fledgling days. As a gag, usually it was adorned with signs and ribbons. At Christmas time, the bottle was festooned with decorations. "It's finally time to pop the

cork," Wade declared with a grin. Time and temperature fluctuations had
turned the fine champagne flat, almost tasteless. "We have destroyed it,"
Wade told the laughing crowd, as he triumphantly took a sip from a paper
cup and passed the champagne to others.[198] The evidence provided by
Parkin more than made up for the poor quality of the bubbly.

More significant cooperation was in the offing. Charlie Gardner's long-
awaited guilty plea, which came about the same period, boosted the investigation to a higher level. "He made a decision to make a clean breast
of everything," according to his lawyer, and "never held anything back"
from the government afterward.[199] The first topic of Gardner's FBI interrogation was his relationship with former Texas senator John Tower, President Bush's ill-fated choice for secretary of defense. Tower's nomination
already was running into serious opposition on Capitol Hill over accusations of drunkenness, womanizing and other excesses. Agents conducting
the nominee's background check also gathered various unsubstantiated
allegations that Tower had accepted illegal campaign contributions and
free transportation from individuals associated with Gardner or Unisys.
Once Gardner began cooperating, the FBI redoubled its efforts to pin
down the facts.[200] Rick Wade was the bureau's point man.

Gardner admitted paying his associate, Muldoon, twenty thousand dollars for a copy of a confidential letter written by then-senator Tower urging the Navy to fund Unisys programs. Muldoon acknowledged that he,
in turn, had passed money along to a former Tower legislative assistant
who helped obtain the document. Wade and the rest of the agents grilled
the participants to ascertain the truth. When senior FBI officials inspected
the Illwind task force in spring of 1989, they were advised that agents
were building a strong criminal case against Tower himself.[201]

That turned out to be a wild exaggeration. The incident had happened
years earlier, and neither Muldoon nor Gardner claimed to have firsthand
knowledge of any money going to Tower. Muldoon insisted he had given
Tower's onetime aide a forty-thousand-dollar loan to help buy a house.
The former legislative staffer backed up that version, denying that he had
done anything improper. After months of inconclusive answers, the issue was
dropped by investigators.[202] In an extraordinary piece of political theater,
Tower publicly swore never to drink alcoholic beverages as the Pentagon's
chief. "I'm going all the way," Tower vowed. The vote was postponed repeatedly. President Bush claimed that Tower was the subject of "very unfair
treatment," buffeted by rumors and innuendo that had "no facts to back
them up." The Senate nevertheless narrowly rejected the nomination on a
party-line vote, humbling Bush and highlighting flaws in his White
House political team.

Tower never recovered from the controversy. In a vituperative autobiography, the diminutive former senator complained about the FBI's willingness to grant Muldoon and others limited immunity from prosecution.
The Justice Department, Tower claimed, had been bent on carrying out

what he called an "open-ended investigation-allegation-investigation cycle" to tear apart his private life. Agents responded that they had an obligation to follow the trail. In his book, Tower wrote that he was the victim of unethical plea-bargaining maneuvers by his accusers. The process besmirched his reputation to such an extent, he added bitterly, that "it would be impossible to scrape [the mud] off in a month or a year or a lifetime." He did not have much time to clean up his place in history. John Tower died in a commuter plane crash during the Bush administration.

Bill Galvin was the next formidable Illwind target to fold. He maintained an ironlike facade to the bitter end. "My life has been one of service to my church, my family and my country," he told the court after admitting his wrongdoing. It almost had the ring of a military eulogy. "I have never done anything to jeopardize the wellbeing of the United States," Galvin said.[203] Sentenced to thirty-two months behind bars, Galvin was ordered to pay back taxes and interest totaling more than $647,000. His stepson, who participated in some of the scams, also was convicted of federal tax evasion.

The U.S. attorney's office had Galvin testify in front of federal grand juries on nine occasions, for a total of thirty hours. Some agents remained dubious about the consultant's veracity. "The guy would give up his own mother if he thought it would do him some good," asserted one veteran naval investigator.[204] But Aronica and Wade came to be less suspicious, relying extensively on his testimony to advance the prosecution. By the summer of 1991, Galvin's admissions sounded the death knell for Paisley's defense.

It took marathon negotiations, and the imminent threat of indictment, to finally persuade Mel Paisley to consider pleading guilty. He made the initial decision at a Northern Virginia barbecue restaurant called The Three Pigs, sitting with his tearful wife and a friend from Pentagon days. Vicki Paisley had cried hysterically throughout the previous night.[205] Her husband said he would plead to save the Navy the embarrassment of a trial. Later, he claimed it was to shield Vicki from further pain. The real reasons were more complex and less altruistic: Money and health problems drove the former Navy official to lean toward admitting his guilt. His legal fees had climbed close to a quarter of a million dollars. A lengthy trial would cost at least that much again, with no likelihood of acquittal. Medical conditions afflicting the couple, including his prostate cancer and her chronic depression, only figured to get worse with the constant stress. Paisley's lawyer, former prosecutor Larry Barcella, hammered out a potential agreement that deleted all references to Vicki Paisley. Under the deal, his client could take issue with some of the specifics laid out in the prosecution's factual summary. But would that be enough to make Paisley sign?

Three years of investigation had exacted a heavy toll on the couple, sapping their energy and turning them into virtual hermits. Nearly every friend and acquaintance they had was deemed a potential suspect or witness, which meant that such individuals were off-limits for any social contact. Vicki Paisley, a voracious collector of newspaper stories about Ill-wind, sometimes compared reading the stash of articles to reading her own obituary. She desperately wanted the torture to end.

Barcella was just as eager to reach a resolution. Without a negotiated plea, he foresaw a series of indictments against Paisley. During the last flurry of negotiations, Barcella pleaded and yelled. "You can say you don't agree with everything" the prosecution crammed into the plea documents, he told his client. "Just sign them." The pressure tactics worked. Paisley and his wife skimmed through the final court papers early one morning in the U.S. attorney's office before marching into court a few minutes later to seal the bargain.

Even so, the defense lawyer was utterly realistic about the limited co-operation the government was likely to get from Paisley. "Aronica had this abiding belief," Barcella recalls, that Paisley would experience a sudden conversion and provide "the key to unlock the secrets of various corporate boardrooms." Once the emotional shock was behind Paisley, prosecutors expected that he would undergo a catharsis and emerge much more docile and cooperative. Those expectations were largely wishful thinking, based on Aronica's earlier experiences with Gardner and Galvin. With those defendants, the prosecutor saw a physical and emotional transformation after the men acknowledged their guilt. "I kept telling prosecutors they were barking up the wrong tree" as far as Paisley's orientation went, Barcella recalls. In the end, Paisley never got the opportunity to fully air his disagreements with the prosecution before a judge.

Investigators were eager to use Paisley to try to go after John Lehman, or in Aronica's words, to "move laterally over to pursue CEOs" of some top contractors.[206] More than anything else, the debriefing sessions resembled a prizefight. The antagonists shook hands at the beginning and then proceeded to pummel each other without mercy. Four or five days a week for several months, Paisley bobbed and weaved as he was bombarded with questions. Agents slouched in chairs or paced the perimeter of the bare conference room, scribbling on notepads as Paisley talked. Periodically, they would leaf through stacks of thick, three-ring binders containing debriefing materials.

Although the former Navy official vividly recalled some events that occurred as long as twenty years before, his memory was extremely fuzzy about the participation of senior executives in the Illwind scandal. Paisley resorted to delay and obfuscation. He claimed to have almost no recollection of the events agents were most interested in pursuing. Incidents and activities that took place barely three of four years earlier remained shrouded in mystery. Paisley admitted almost nothing. Belatedly, he even challenged the accuracy of the papers filed as part of his guilty plea. "I could have told a good story on Lehman and the others," Paisley says today. "I could have made it stick; that's what Galvin did. However, it wouldn't have been true."[207]

"Uncle Mel," as agents came to call him, often would show up wearing a tie with an American flag motif. He munched on peanut-butter-and-jelly sandwiches on home-baked bread prepared by his wife. Agents would start each day's questioning in soothing, friendly tones. Frequently, they would be shouting and nervously shaking their pencils at his unresponsive answers after a few hours. But such signs of anger were to no avail. When he was asked about dealings with Thomas Pownall, the chairman of Martin Marietta, Paisley called him a "true patriot" and cut off further discussion. The same pattern was true for other executives under scrutiny.

Paisley would have been "a congenital idiot," as his lawyer put it, not to understand what the government wanted to hear. Prosecutors provided "the chapter, verse, stanza and sentence" in their court filings, according to Barcella. Still, Paisley stuck to his denials. Through sheer force of personality, he believed he could win prosecutors and agents over to his side. "I have a bad memory," Paisley told the judge after frustrated prosecutors halted the interrogation sessions. "He has misled agents repeatedly," Aronica countered. "He has a selective memory." The prosecutor added that Paisley had flunked a lie-detector test "across the board."[208]

Considering his age and questionable health, Paisley was convinced that home detention was a strong possibility. "I didn't think I was headed for jail," he now claims. "I never conceived it could happen."[209] In seeking a light sentence, Paisley told the court: "I have been a patriot all my life . . . I don't think I will say any more."[210] His wife described "the shining light" in their lives as joint volunteer work at a school for severely handicapped children. In private, she bitterly attacked prosecutors for believing Galvin. Judge Claude Hilton, Henry Hudson's old friend from the county prosecutor's office, didn't buy Paisley's arguments. The judge listened intently as Hudson and Aronica asserted that Paisley didn't deserve any breaks. The sentence was four years in a federal prison camp outside Las Vegas, Nevada.

The prosecution similarly was stymied by Unisys. Initially, agents threatened the company with potential fines in excess of $400 million and charges that would brand it as a "racketeering enterprise." Three of its units had been suspended from receiving new Pentagon business, and Joe Aronica opposed reinstating them until a comprehensive settlement was reached. Howling that the giant firm could be forced into bankruptcy, Chairman Michael Blumenthal personally appealed to the Pentagon for help. He maintained that he was "appalled and dismayed" by the revelations of improper activities, and then tried to pin the blame on the previous Sperry organization. As a former secretary of the treasury, Blumenthal insisted that a guilty plea for the firm was out of the question. His pleas for support were answered promptly.

The Navy's leadership didn't want to be used as leverage to extract a criminal plea. So the suspensions were lifted in less than three months, in spite of Aronica's strenuous objections. To show its good faith, Unisys's defense division fired all of its domestic political and marketing consultants; and it put a host of new ethics guidelines in place. Under the new rules, most consulting agreements had to be approved by corporate headquarters, while more than forty employees received some form of punishment.

The legal tug-of-war with prosecutors lasted two more years, ending with a landmark agreement following Blumenthal's retirement. Resolving civil and criminal investigations in four separate jurisdictions in the fall of 1990, Unisys signed the most expensive "global" Pentagon fraud settlement in history: It amounted to $190 million in fines, penalties and foregone profits. By then, the Navy had eliminated Unisys as a controversial second-source supplier of radars for its Aegis fleet. But since the settlement payments were pegged to the company's future earnings and spread over a long period, the Bush administration essentially had acceded to Unisys's wishes. In the spring of 1995, overcoming years of frustration, Unisys finally joined the defense industry's consolidation trend by selling its lagging defense and aerospace operations to Loral for more than $850 million.

Tossed back and forth between Alexandria, Brooklyn and the public integrity section at main Justice, the congressional leads withered. Partly because of the bureaucratic squabbles, not a single lawmaker or top congressional staffer was hit with parallel criminal charges. James Kane died of cancer after the scandal hit the headlines. John O'Brien hired Brendan Sullivan, Oliver North's firebrand lawyer, to represent him as the stop-and-go Grumman inquiry dragged on. More than two years after being forced out as chairman, O'Brien threw in the towel. He pleaded guilty to two counts of filing false personal-loan applications, becoming the highest-ranking industry executive convicted as part of Illwind. He received no prison sentence and paid only a ten-thousand-dollar fine.

Grumman's long fight to avoid criminal prosecution proved equally anticlimactic. The company paid twenty million dollars and escaped with a civil settlement. It wasn't barred from Pentagon contracts, though one prosecutor described the outside ethics controls imposed under the agreement as "the closest thing the government can do to putting a corporation on probation."[211]

☆

Illwind's echoes continue to resonate in the current political landscape, as Republicans control Capitol Hill and again favor defense spending over social programs. The reprehensible abuses of the 1980s—when a few strong-willed individuals dominated public debate with rigid ideology and partisan fervor—left a profound legacy for the post–Cold War military. We ignore its teachings at the peril of inviting an encore performance.

Ronald Reagan's buildup should have debunked the notion, once and for all, that more dollars automatically translate into better defense programs. The combination of immense budgets and inadequate controls was a prescription for criminality inside the Pentagon during that period. The dynamics haven't changed that much a decade later. Interplay of those factors poses an equally grave hazard today as Congress and the White House clash over how to reshape the military for the twenty-first century. Nonetheless, the country seems bent on lumbering down the same dangerous road. Many of the costly mistakes that marred Reagan's vision are all too familiar. Now, they threaten to undermine realistic cutbacks while making meaningful reforms a nearly impossible goal.

Admittedly, Defense Department budgets have been shrinking. Some procurement accounts are half of what they were barely a few years ago. Lehman's beloved armada of World War II battleships sits decommissioned, and the number of supercarriers patrolling the world's oceans has been slashed. Instead of six hundred vessels, the Navy is fighting to keep half that number on the high seas. With fewer dollars to spend, military planners view the earlier emphasis on competitive dual-source contracts as a misguided and expensive vestige of a bygone era. These days, Navy brass unilaterally allocate ship and submarine construction contracts to try to keep existing shipyards open.

The changes impact every region of the United States. Bases are closing at the fastest clip in forty years. Congressionally imposed cuts and relentless industry consolidation have eliminated 1.1 million private-sector jobs since 1987, and the toll is expected to reach 1.8 million jobs by 1997. At least another half million direct military jobs have been put on the chopping block. California, for instance, could end up with only one-third of the defense-related workers the state had at the peak of the Reagan years.

Not so gradually, however, the pendulum is starting to swing in the opposite direction. There is immense pressure to slow down the reductions under way and halt further defense budget declines. A former Marine Corps commandant warns of an impending "train wreck" in training and preparedness unless huge chunks of new money are found. Some expenditures already are climbing faster than ever. For the acquisition of transport planes and spy satellites to routine maintenance work that used to be handled strictly by Defense Department depots, the Clinton administration anticipates giving contractors tens of billions of extra dollars over the next few years. Indeed, a resurgence of prodefense sentiments already has GOP legislative leaders cramming billions more into spending bills than the Pentagon requested. And Republicans are boasting about overall Pentagon spending increases by the end of the 1990s.

Meanwhile, surveys show that marketplace pressures increasingly are driving American workers, including many on the payrolls of military suppliers, to consider cutting ethical corners or avoid blowing the whistle on colleagues who do. Job-loss worries and overly aggressive business goals, among other things, have been blamed for this trend. In such an environment, incentives for employees of defense firms to step over the line probably have never been greater. Henry Hudson and other prosecutors argue that passing tougher laws is not going to alleviate the problem. One former Pentagon inspector general contends that many executives still cling to a catch-us-if-you-can philosophy. "At a time of tighter budgets, we expect to see more violations," she says. "All of us need to be that much more vigilant."[212]

While contractors watch their orders erode, there also are signs of a corresponding upturn in fraud cases. In 1994, criminal fines and civil recoveries from the industry by government reached a record $1.2 billion, eleven times the annual rate during the mid-1980s. Nearly seventy of the top one hundred Pentagon suppliers are under active investigation by the inspector general's staff, a larger percentage than ever before. In a single nine-month period, suppliers returned some $1.4 billion in overpayments to the Pentagon. (To put that amount into perspective, the entire federal budget for child protective services is $4 billion a year, according to the Child Welfare League of America.) As a prescient journalist has written: "Nowadays, the public hardly notices when even a record criminal fine is assessed against a defense firm," apparently reflecting voters' "ennui with military issues and a jaded acceptance of defense fraud."[213] The U.S. attorney for Los Angeles counters that the Justice Department cannot afford to set its priorities based on "what causes the public jaw to drop."[214]

Unquestionably, Illwind set the standard by which law enforcement agencies henceforth will gauge the relative success of criminal probes. If more stringent laws, tighter regulations and continual audits fail to produce successful programs, one industry analyst complains, then the government's attitude seems to be "to throw the rascals in jail or cow them with a grand jury."[215]

On a mundane level, Illwind was a fabulous success. There was a flood of guilty pleas and hardly any trials. The twenty million or so dollars spent to carry out the investigation eventually was returned more than tenfold to taxpayers. But the most important lessons of the 1980s go beyond such cost-benefit analyses, beyond identifying the tactics best suited to finding and prosecuting wrongdoers. Hudson believes that Illwind helped create "a level playing field for all bidders," particularly small and midsize companies that had despaired of getting fair treatment but can now compete "without having to manipulate the system."[216]

Notwithstanding his assertions, the investigation markedly fell short in another arena: It failed to produce lasting, deep-seated cultural change throughout the Pentagon, as many critics had hoped. Although the opportunity to lock in authentic "reforms" may have been at an all-time high, both Republican and Democratic administrations dropped the ball. Management overhaul initiatives mostly degenerated into short-term budget-cutting exercises or quick-fix accounting gimmicks. As a result of the men chosen to run the Pentagon—and the lack of personal commitment by George Bush and Bill Clinton to fundamentally revamp acquisition rules—the status quo remains largely intact.

Optimists can point to some modest improvements. The Pentagon's "revolving door" has been slowed, and legislation is in place to clamp down on illicit dissemination of classified documents. Officials in charge of the biggest, most complex weapons programs have to wrestle with somewhat fewer levels of bureaucracy. More and more, prime contractors are required to build and test prototypes before getting the green light for production. And, thanks to Defense Secretary William Perry's urging, commercial products are more readily available for military applications.

Still, the changes essentially are incremental. It is generally accepted that weapons continue to cost too much, and the rules under which they are built continue to be overly cumbersome. Even after Operation Whirlwind rocked the defense establishment, the old ways of doing business survived. Stockpiles of excess or unusable spare parts, ranging from jet-engine components to truck tires, hit a whopping $29 billion. The services also managed to squirrel away nearly twice that much in unspent funds accumulated from previous years, with billions more earmarked for what was simply called "unanticipated requirements."[217]

More recently, Congress managed to limit some of these excesses. But the culture's antipathy to change persists. Just a few months ago, congressional investigators found that "very little has changed" to improve day-to-day accountability of the troubled fund that pays for the military's network of commissaries, spare-parts centers and repair facilities. In another example of terrible management, auditors concluded that the four-billion-dollar effort to build a dependable reconnaissance drone—once Mel Paisley's pet project—produced an unmanned aircraft that was "logistically unsupportable" and "unsuitable for use" on the battlefield.[218]

The collapse of the Soviet Union has not prompted admirals or generals to abandon their rationale for pushing technology to the extreme: The services still want to rush weapons through the development phase as rapidly as possible, and they remain wary of decision-making outside the uniformed chain of command. At this late date, far too many high-ranking officers and civilians evidently still see themselves as salesmen—rather than managers—for the programs they are running.

Representing a new generation of hawks, House Speaker Newt Gingrich concedes that all the talk about changing the Pentagon has yielded scant benefits over the years. "Don't try to reform the current system," he fumes. "It is hopeless. It is impossible."

Despite Illwind's missteps and blemishes, its symbolic impact should not be underestimated. Referring to the whistleblower who initially fingered John Marlowe and set the stage for the wiretaps, Aronica trumpets the fact that "one person does count" and sometimes is able to change the course of history.[219]

Above all, Illwind is a landmark in the annals of law enforcement. The guilty pleas and corporate mea culpas undoubtedly served to prevent some further misdeeds. Once corruption is discovered inside the Pentagon, though, there is only one sure antidote. An FBI agent sums it up categorically: "What we need most is another Operation Illwind."

EPILOGUE

MELVYN PAISLEY—Seemingly in robust health and as feisty as ever, the Navy's former procurement chief spent his period of incarceration as a leader among fellow inmates. Paisley helped run the prison camp's library, participated in ethics seminars sponsored by Pepperdine University and organized the local chapter of the Toastmaster's International Society. Some of his activities in the Pentagon still can't be discussed in detail, he argues, because that would divulge military secrets and endanger national security. His wife, Vicki, says that Paisley's fondest wish while he was locked up was once again to flex a fishing pole in his hands and wade through his beloved trout streams in Idaho or Montana. Behind bars, he wrote an unpublished novel about the excesses of federal law enforcement titled *Losing Truth*.

WILLIAM GALVIN—After serving time behind bars and cooperating with the Justice Department, he retired to South Florida and relative obscurity. Galvin refuses to discuss anything related to Operation Illwind with journalists, though his assistance to prosecutors was substantial enough to allow him to spend part of his sentence at home instead of in a halfway house. In a perversely fitting turnabout, Galvin himself was the victim of a shrewd con man. The trustee of his retirement fund was convicted years later of bilking the family out of $1 million.

CHARLES GARDNER—Sentenced to thirty-two months in prison, he was released early and became a model government witness. His defense lawyer claims that in twenty years of practice representing white-collar criminals, "I can't remember anyone who has ever cooperated [with prosecutors] the way Mr. Gardner has" or exhibited more repentance. "I am sorry, no doubt about that," Gardner says, calling his years of crime "a waste." Through a friend, the former Unisys executive briefly landed a job selling used cars at a Cadillac dealership on Long Island.

HENRY HUDSON—Illwind's top law-enforcement figure never realized his dream of running for Congress, and Hudson was passed over for a federal judgeship he had badly wanted. Following a stint as head of the U. S. Marshal's Service at the end of the Bush administration, he left government service, joined a small law firm in Northern Virginia and hosted a local radio talk show.

JOSEPH ARONICA—After years of false starts searching for a job in private practice, the abrasive prosecutor finally got an attractive offer and resigned from the Justice Department. His decision was prompted in part by the fact that President Bill Clinton's personnel aides did not recommend him for nomination to be the U.S. attorney in Alexandria, Virginia. Aronica joined the Washington, D.C., office of Mudge Rose Guthrie Alexander & Ferdon, a blue-chip corporate law firm with strong Republican connections, where Richard M. Nixon and former Attorney General John Mitchell once worked as partners. In response to allegations by the Paisleys, the government investigated and exonerated Aronica of improperly pressuring defendants to obtain guilty pleas.

RICHARD WADE—Promoted a number of times in the wake of Illwind's success, he is considered a rising star in the FBI's hierarchy. Wade won a job as the number two agent in the bureau's Los Angeles office, which focuses heavily on investigating defense fraud.

STEVE FULMER—He resigned from the Naval Investigative Service before Illwind was wrapped up, complaining about disrespectful treatment and lack of leadership. Fulmer, among other things, says he was disillusioned by revised NIS procedures that stripped agents of authority to launch any wiretap investigations without explicit, up-front approval from senior admirals. He returned to his hometown of Columbia, South Carolina, to work as a criminal investigator for the federal Veterans Administration.

RANDY BELLOWS—The workaholic assistant U.S. attorney who nailed Boeing and "the Clique" continued to pursue high-profile targets in later years. In 1995, he successfully prosecuted William Aramony, formerly the top national executive of United Way, for defrauding the charity and diverting its funds to finance a sexual affair with a teenager. Worn out and desiring less-stressful cases, Bellows eventually asked to be reassigned to handle run-of-the-mill bank robbery and homicide trials in the Alexandria federal prosecutor's office.

JOHN MARLOWE—The consultant who touched off the biggest Pentagon scandal ever was released from state prison and returned without fanfare to his wife and home in Annandale, Virginia, a short ride from the basement where he had been arrested for molesting two little girls. He has shunned all media interviews, refusing to discuss his conviction on the sexual battery charges or his undercover work for the government afterward.

NOTES

Chapter I

1. Details of Marlowe's actions come from his trial transcripts, from appeals filed by his lawyers and from interviews with prosecutors.
2. Testimony of McCrocklin and the girls in Arlington County Circuit Court, October 1984.
3. Testimony of the two girls.
4. Testimony of Marlowe and Officer Pope.
5. Interview with George Varoutsos, June 1988.
6. Interview with Henry Hudson, February 1992.
7. Interview with Henry Hudson, October 1992.
8. Robert F. Howe, "Henry Hudson: No Breaks, No Regrets," *Washington Post* (May 27, 1991), p. B1.
9. *Arlington Journal* (July 27, 1989), editorial page.
10. Interviews with Henry Hudson.
11. Walker's summation to the jury.
12. Sherman's testimony.
13. Sher's closing argument to the jury.
14. Edwin Meese III, *With Reagan* (Washington, D.C.: Regnery Gateway, 1992), p. 176.
15. Lou Cannon, *President Reagan: The Role of a Lifetime* (New York: Simon & Schuster, 1991), p. 26.
16. Ronald Reagan, *An American Life* (New York: Simon & Schuster, 1991), p. 294.
17. Meese, *With Reagan*, p. 178.
18. Walter S. Mossberg, "U.S., in Defense-Strategy Switch, Plans Power to Fight 2 Big Wars Simultaneously," *Wall Street Journal* (June 15, 1981), p. 12.
19. Walter S. Mossberg, "Problems With the Reagan Defense Budget," *Wall Street Journal* (March 2, 1982), p. 30.
20. Caspar Weinberger, *Fighting for Peace: Seven Critical Years in the Pentagon* (New York: Warner Books, 1990), p. 10.
21. Ibid., p. 32.
22. Cannon, *President Reagan*, p. 162.
23. Nicholas Lemann, "The Peacetime War; Caspar Weinberger in Reagan's Pentagon," *Atlantic Monthly* (October 1984).
24. Tim Carrington, "Weinberger Finds His Well-Worn Strategies Always Succeed in Blunting Defense Budget Ax," *Wall Street Journal* (March 1, 1985), p. 48.
25. Ibid.
26. Tim Weiner, *Blank Check* (New York: Warner Books, 1990), p. 17.
27. Rick Atkinson and Fred Hiatt, "Contracting Conducted Over Golden Safety Net," *Washington Post* (March 31, 1985), p. A1.
28. Hedrick Smith, *The Power Game: How Washington Works* (New York: Random House, 1988), p. 189.

29. Lemann, "The Peacetime War," *Atlantic Monthly* (October 1984).
30. Smith, *The Power Game*, p. 187.
31. John F. Lehman, Jr., *Command of the Seas* (New York: Charles Scribner's Sons, 1988), p. 163.
32. Ibid., p. 99.
33. Ibid., p. 100.
34. Ibid., p. 153.
35. Wayne Biddle, "John F. Lehman Jr.; Giving New Meaning to the Word 'Shipshape,' " *New York Times* (September 13, 1984), p. 18.
36. Lehman made his comments during a September 23, 1992, public ceremony in Washington, D.C., honoring Weinberger.
37. *Hearings Before the Subcommittee on Strategic and Theater Nuclear Forces of the Committee on Armed Services, United States Senate*, 97th Cong., 1st Ses. (Washington, D.C.: Government Printing Office), p. 89.
→ 38. J. Ronald Fox with James L. Field, *The Defense Management Challenge* (Boston: Harvard Business School Press, 1988), p. 331.
39. Hearing of the Investigations Subcommittee of the House Energy and Commerce Committee, April 30, 1985, as reported by *The Wall Street Journal* and *The New York Times*.
40. Interview with Senator David Pryor, November 1993.
41. Tim Carrington, "Support in Congress for Larger Military Budget Fades Amid Weinberger's Credibility Problems," *Wall Street Journal* (May 24, 1985), p. 50.
42. Interview with Caspar Weinberger, April 1993.
43. Ibid.
44. Carrington, "Support in Congress for Larger Military Budget Fades," p. 50.
45. Marlowe's testimony during the trial of Thomas Muldoon in Alexandria, Virginia, federal district court, December 12, 1989.
46. Interview with Steve Fulmer, May 1992.
47. Transcript of William Galvin's testimony before a federal grand jury in Alexandria, Virginia, August 1990.
48. Lehman, *Command of the Seas*, p. 232.
49. Interview with John Lehman, December 1992.
50. Ibid.
51. Interview with Melvyn Paisley, March 1993.
52. Ibid.
53. Court documents filed by prosecutors in connection with guilty pleas by Melvyn Paisley and William Galvin.
54. Court documents filed with Paisley's guilty plea.
55. Ibid.
56. Art Pine, "Defense Giant Litton Pleads Guilty to Fraud," *Los Angeles Times* (January 15, 1994), p. 1.
57. Interview with Don Fuqua, December 1992.
58. Rick Wartzman, "Anders Is Set to Pilot General Dynamics," *Wall Street Journal* (October 3, 1989), p. B12.
59. Interview with Senator Carl Levin, May 1993.
60. Interview with Caspar Weinberger, April 1993.
61. Interview with Senator Carl Levin, May 1993.
62. Brian Duffy and Paul Glastris, "The Enemy Within," *U.S. News & World Report* (July 4, 1988), p. 16.
63. Interview with FBI Supervisory agent Rick Wade, August 1992.

Chapter II

1. Interviews with James Gaines, Darrell Cole and other former Boeing officials.
2. George C. Wilson, "A Buildup in U.S. Forces, Reagan Advisers Urge More for Defense," *Washington Post* (June 16, 1980), p. 1.
3. Nicholas Lemann, "The Peacetime War: Caspar Weinberger in Reagan's Pentagon," *Atlantic Monthly* (October 1984), p. 74.
4. Michael Getler, "Defense Policy: The Reagan Approach," *Washington Post* (October 24, 1980), p. 1.
5. Lou Cannon, *President Reagan: The Role of a Lifetime* (New York: Simon & Schuster, 1991), p. 297.
6. Ronald Reagan, *An American Life* (New York: Simon & Schuster, 1991), p. 267.
7. James Fallows, *National Defense* (New York: Random House, 1981), p. 145.
8. Ibid.
9. A confidential report by Van Cleave and Plymale to Reagan and Weinberger on March 25, 1981, urging dramatic Pentagon spending increases.
10. Clarence A. Robinson, Jr., "Rancor Erupts Within Transition Team," *Aviation Week* (November 17, 1980), p. 21.
11. Fred Kaplan, *The Wizards of Armageddon* (New York: Simon and Schuster, 1983), p. 386.
12. Based on interview with William Van Cleave, November 1992.
13. Ibid.
14. Deborah M. Kyle and Benjamin F. Schemmer, "Reagan's Defense Transition Team: A Dramatic Contrast to Four Years Ago," *Armed Forces Journal International* (December 1980), p. 24.
15. Interview with William Van Cleave, November 1992.
16. Robert J. Serling, *Legend & Legacy: The Story of Boeing and Its People* (New York: St. Martin's Press, 1992), p. 176.
17. Clive Irving, *Wide-Body: The Triumph of the 747* (New York: William Morrow and Co., 1993), p. 228.
18. Ibid., p. 338.
19. Serling, *Legend & Legacy*, p. 331.
20. Interview with William Van Cleave, November 1992.
21. Irving, *Wide-Body*, p. 227.
22. Interview with James Gaines, August 1992.
23. Interview with Darrell Cole, October 1992.
24. Serling, *Legend & Legacy*, p. 177.
25. Rick Wartzman and David J. Jefferson, "Boeing Tries to Vector Its Defense Operations out of Recent Clouds," *Wall Street Journal* (July 30, 1991), p. 1.
26. Ibid.
27. Serling, *Legend & Legacy*, p. 178.
28. Clarence A. Robinson, Jr., "Reagan Team Asks Capabilities, Priorities of Services," *Aviation Week* (December 8, 1980), p. 16.
29. Ibid.
30. Interview with Richard Brothers, September 1992.
31. Interview with Darrell Cole, November 1992.
32. Interview with Melvyn Paisley, April 1993.
33. Ibid.
34. Interview with James Gaines, November 1992.
35. Interview with William Van Cleave, November 1992.
36. Interview with Charles Welling, February 1993.
37. "Reagan's Defense Transition Team," *Armed Forces Journal International* (December 1980).

38. Tim Weiner, *Blank Check* (New York: Warner Books, 1990), p. 43.
39. Don Oberdorfer, "Report Saw Soviet Buildup for War," *Washington Post* (October 12, 1992), p. 11.
40. Kaplan, *The Wizards of Armageddon*, p. 390.
41. Weiner, *Blank Check*, p. 44.
42. Kaplan, *The Wizards of Armageddon*, p. 388.
43. Tim Weiner, "Military Accused of Lies over Arms," *New York Times* (June 28, 1993), p. 10.
44. Ibid.
45. Interview with William Van Cleave, November 1992.
46. Steven Rattner, "Conflict Questions Raised in Transition," *New York Times* (December 4, 1990), p. 27.
47. George Lardner, Jr., "Conflict Questions Raised for Some Transition Aides," *Washington Post* (December 11, 1980), p. 11.
48. Associated Press report on November 26, 1980.
49. Dick Kirschten, "Spinning the Revolving Door," *National Journal* (December 13, 1980), p. 2128.
50. Ibid.
51. Lardner, "Conflict Questions Raised for Some Transition Aides," p. 11.
52. Kenneth H. Bacon, "Pentagon Studies How Boeing Got Secret Information," *Wall Street Journal* (March 1, 1979), p. 1.
53. Richard Burt, "Boeing Aides Mishandled Secrets and Tried Cover-Up, Inquiry Finds," *New York Times* (March 2, 1979), p. 1.
54. Wartzman and Jefferson, "Boeing Tries to Vector Its Defense Operations," p. 1.
55. Based on interview with Charles Welling in February 1993 and the transcript of Welling's sworn deposition to Pentagon investigators in February 1979.
56. Welling's deposition to Pentagon investigators.
57. Bacon, "Pentagon Studies How Boeing Got Secret Information," p. 1.
58. Interview with Charles Welling, February 1993; and with John Brett, one of Plymale's associates, in 1995.
59. Welling's deposition to investigators.
60. Interview with Charles Welling, February 1993.
61. Ibid.
62. Ibid.
63. Based on an interview with Charles Welling and a March 19, 1979, letter to him from Oliver Boileau, then president of Boeing Aerospace Company.
64. Interview with former Boeing executive Henry Hebeler, November 1992.
65. Interview with William Van Cleave, November 1992.
66. Andy Pasztor and Rick Wartzman, "How a Spy for Boeing and His Pals Gleaned Data on Defense Plans," *Wall Street Journal* (January 15, 1990), p. 1.
67. Martin Anderson, *Revolution* (New York: Harcourt Brace Jovanovich, 1985), p. 133.
68. Interview with William Van Cleave, November 1992.
69. Ibid.
70. Lemann, "The Peacetime War," p. 34.
71. Interview with Lawrence Korb, November 1992.
72. Interview with William Van Cleave, November 1992.
73. Edwin Meese III, *With Reagan* (Washington, D.C.: Regnery Gateway, 1992), p. 58.
74. Enid Nemy, "New Yorkers Gear Up for the Inaugural Whirl," *New York Times* (January 16, 1981), p. D15.
75. Memo from Charles Z. Wick to Barry Zorthian, December 31, 1980.
76. Interview with William Van Cleave, November 1992.
77. Ibid.

78. George C. Wilson, "Few Immediate Major Changes Planned by Reagan Pentagon Team," *Washington Post* (December 20, 1980), p. 3.
79. The dialogue between Van Cleave and Weinberger is based on an interview with Van Cleave and several newspaper columns written by Rowland Evans and Robert Novak recounting the incident.
80. Interview with Richard Armitage, December 1993.
81. Interview with Caspar Weinberger, April 1993.
82. Caspar Weinberger, *Fighting for Peace: Seven Critical Years in the Pentagon* (New York: Warner Books, 1990), p. 41.
83. Interview with William Van Cleave, November 1992.
84. Ibid.
85. Ibid.
86. Interview with Lawrence Korb, November 1992.
87. Based on interviews with Richard Fowler, October and November 1992.
88. Ibid.
89. Interview with William Van Cleave, November 1992.
90. Interview with Richard Armitage, December 1993.
91. Weinberger, *Fighting for Peace*, p. 41.
92. Interview with Caspar Weinberger, April 1993.
93. Ibid.
94. Weinberger, *Fighting for Peace*, p. 41.

Chapter III

1. Interview with William Van Cleave, November 1992.
2. Interview with Charles Welling, February 1993.
3. Kenneth A. Bertsch and Linda S. Shaw, *The Nuclear Weapons Industry* (Washington, D.C.; The Investor Responsibility Research Center, 1984), p. 146.
4. Interview with Melvyn Paisley, April 1993.
5. Interviews with James Gaines, August and November 1992.
6. Paisley and several other former Lehman associates confirm the amount. Boeing disputes the figure and company spokesmen decline to provide specific numbers.
7. Interview with Melvyn Paisley, April 1993.
8. Ibid.
9. Interview with James Gaines, August 1992.
10. Interview with John Lehman, December 1992.
11. Interview with Melvyn Paisley, April 1993.
12. Interview with John Lehman, December 1992.
13. Interview with Darrell Cole, November 1992.
14. John F. Lehman, Jr., *Command of the Seas* (New York: Charles Scribner's Sons, 1988), p. 55.
15. Interview with Melvyn Paisley, April 1993.
16. Ibid.
17. Based on interviews with one of Paisley's former wives and with Reba Klimas, a former sister-in-law.
18. Ibid.
19. Melvyn Paisley with Vicki Paisley, *ACE!* (Boston: Branden Publishing Co., 1992), p. 192.
20. Interview with Joe Johnson, a former Boeing official, in November 1992.
21. William C. Rempel and Douglas Jehl, "Scandal Figure Had Right Stuff," *Los Angeles Times* (June 27, 1988), p. 1.
22. Interview with Melvyn Paisley, April 1993.
23. Descriptions of Plymale's medical emergency and evacuation are based on inter-

views with John Lehman, Melvyn Paisley, James Gaines and others familiar with the events.

24. Ibid.
25. Ibid.
26. Interview with Melvyn Paisley, April 1993.
27. Ibid.
28. Interview with John Lehman, December 1992.
29. Stephen Barr and Al Kamen, "Transition Momentum Bogs Down at Sub-Cabinet Level," *Washington Post* (January 11, 1993), p. 4.
30. Lou Cannon, *President Reagan: The Role of a Lifetime* (New York: Simon & Schuster, 1991), p. 85.
31. William J. Crowe, Jr., *The Line of Fire* (New York: Simon & Schuster, 1993), p. 118.
32. Edwin Meese III, *With Reagan* (Washington, D.C.: Regnery Gateway, 1992), p. 63.
33. Melvyn Paisley's comments on a videotape of one of his official trips, May 1986.
34. Interview with Melvyn Paisley, April 1993.
35. Michael Satchell, Robert Kaylor, Peter Dworkin and Marianna I. Knight, "The Private Life of Melvyn Paisley," *U.S. News & World Report* (July 4, 1988), p. 23.
36. Interview with Charles Welling, February 1993.
37. Interview with Richard Armitage, December 1993.
38. Interviews with James Gaines, in August and November 1992; with Joe Johnson in November 1992; and with others who talked with Paisley about the episode at the time. Today, Paisley declines to discuss the matter.
39. Interview with John Lehman, December 1992. (T Wilson declined to be interviewed.)
40. Based on interviews with John Lehman, Melvyn Paisley and T Wilson.
41. Interviews with John Lehman, December 1992, and with T Wilson in January 1995.
42. Interview with Melvyn Paisley, April 1993.
43. Descriptions of the family's early years are based on Melvyn Paisley's autobiography and interviews with him, two of his wives and several of his old friends.
44. Paisley, *ACE!*, p. 17.
45. Ibid., p. 27.
46. Ibid.
47. Ibid., p. 47.
48. Based on interview with Joe Johnson, a former Paisley colleague, in November 1992.
49. Paisley, *ACE!*, p. 47.
50. Descriptions of the Soap Box Derby events are based on Paisley's autobiography and comments he made to friends over the years.
51. Interview with Neel Patrick in 1993. Paisley disputes the anecdote.
52. Paisley, *ACE!*, p. 71.
53. Ibid., p. 76.
54. Ibid., p. 128.
55. Ibid., p. 149.
56. Ibid., p. 304.
57. Ibid., p. 201.
58. Letter from Sandy Ross to Judge Claude Hilton, July 19, 1991, regarding Paisley's sentencing.
59. Paisley, *ACE!*, p. 258.
60. Ibid.
61. Ibid., p. 262.
62. Interview with Melvyn Paisley, April 1993.
63. Ibid.
64. Based on interviews with friends and a relative of Melvyn Paisley.

65. Interview with Melvyn Paisley, April 1993.
66. Oliver Boileau has consistently refused to talk about his dealings with Paisley.
67. Interview with Don Hillman, former Boeing executive, November 1992.
68. Interview with James Gaines, November 1992.
69. Interviews with James Gaines.
70. Interviews with James Gaines and Merrill Grant.
71. Christopher Drew and Elaine S. Povich, "Defense Probe Targets a Corrupted System," *Chicago Tribune* (July 3, 1988), p. 1.
72. Susan Smith, "The Man Who Always Knew How to Get the Right Information," *Seattle Post-Intelligencer* (June 15, 1991), p. 4
73. Interview with Melvyn Paisley, April 1993.
74. Bob Drogin and Glenn F. Bunting, "Earlier Allegations About Paisley Told," *Los Angeles Times* (June 26, 1988), p. 1.
75. Ibid.
76. James E. Lalonde, "Paisley Bribes Told to Laxalt, Durst Says; Ex-Nevada Senator Reportedly Informed Weinberger, Lehman," *Seattle Times* (June 27, 1988), p. 1.
77. Based on interviews with a relative of Melvyn Paisley. Paisley denies the incident.
78. Robert J. Serling, *Legend & Legacy: The Story of Boeing and Its People* (New York: St. Martin's Press, 1992), p. 170.
79. Interview with Darrell Cole, November 1992.
80. Based on King County, Washington, police records and interviews with current and former county police officials.
81. Descriptions of Mary Lou Paisley's death based on Department of Public Safety and Coroner's Office records from King County, Washington, as well as interviews with Mary Lou Paisley's sister, Melvyn Paisley and others familiar with the events.
82. Jeff Cole, "Boeing's Bid to Avoid Swings in Its Business Falls Short of Hopes," *Wall Street Journal* (February 16, 1993), p. 1.
83. James Lalonde, "New Twist in Paisley's Death—Pathologist Who Performed 1968 Autopsy Worked at Boeing, Too," *Seattle Times* (July 21, 1988), p. 1. (Both the pathologist and the police official who resisted opening a full-blown investigation have since passed away.)
84. Interview with Reba Klimas, March 1993.
85. Ibid.
86. Ibid.
87. Various news stories in 1988 and interview with Reba Klimas, March 1993.
88. Based on King County police records and interviews with investigators.
89. Louis T. Corsaletti and James E. Lalonde, "1968 Death of Paisley's Wife to Be Probed," *Seattle Times* (July 6, 1988), p. 1.
90. "Police Find No Evidence of Foul Play in 1968 Death of Wife of Melvyn Paisley," Associated Press (July 17, 1988).
91. "New Probe into Paisley's Wife's Death; Incident 20 Years Ago Involved Key Figure in Defense-Fraud Case," *Orange County Register* (July 7, 1988), p. 1. Story distributed by Knight-Ridder Newspapers.
92. Interview with Melvyn Paisley, April 1993.
93. Based on King County police records and interviews with investigators.
94. Ibid.
95. Ibid.
96. Based on copy of the draft letter obtained later by King County police.
97. Jack Broom and James E. Lalonde, "Paisley Got a Boost from Scoop—in '81, Sen. Jackson Praised Navy Nominee as 'A Fast Mover,' " *Seattle Times* (July 28, 1988), p. 1.
98. Letter from Mikey Pierson to Senator John Tower, dated May 29, 1981.

99. John G. Tower, *Consequences: A Personal and Political Memoir* (Boston: Little, Brown and Company, 1991), p. 99.
100. Interview with John Lehman, February 1993.
101. Based on letter from Presidential Counsel C. Boyden Gray to Senator Carl Levin, dated February 1, 1989.
102. Based on interviews with Paisley's friends and FBI agents, including Supervisory Agent Dan Larkin.
103. Bob Woodward, "Background Checks Spur FBI Complaint," *Washington Post* (January 5, 1993), p. A7.
104. Boyden Gray's letter to Senator Carl Levin, dated February 1, 1989.

Chapter IV

1. William Galvin's grand jury testimony, August 1990. Despite repeated requests, Galvin declined to be interviewed for this book.
2. Jim Schachter, "Consummate Deal Maker Focus of Pentagon Probe," *Los Angeles Times* (July 24, 1988), p. 1.
3. Michael Wines, "Lively Days of a Military Consultant," *New York Times* (August 2, 1988), p. 1.
4. Ibid.
5. Ibid.
6. Ibid.
7. Ibid.
8. Based on interviews with William Parkin, a friend and associate of Galvin's, August 1988, by Edward T. Pound.
9. Schachter, "Consummate Deal Maker Focus of Pentagon Probe," p. 1.
10. Wines, "Lively Days of a Military Consultant," p. 1.
11. Ibid.
12. Interview with James McDonald, August 1994.
13. Wines, "Lively Days of a Military Consultant," p. 1.
14. Transcript of wiretapped conversation, April 29, 1987.
15. Transcript of wiretapped conversation, April 9, 1987.
16. William Galvin's federal grand jury testimony, September 1990.
17. Based on interviews with William Parkin, a friend and associate of Galvin's, August 1988, by Edward T. Pound.
18. Transcript of wiretapped conversation, April 30, 1987.
19. Transcript of wiretapped conversation, April 9, 1987.
20. Transcript of wiretapped conversation, April 30, 1987.
21. Federal court documents filed along with William Galvin's guilty plea.
22. William Galvin's grand jury testimony, August 1990.
23. Testimony of William Galvin during the federal trial of James Gaines, March 3, 1992.
24. Edward T. Pound, "Weapons Inquiry Soon Will Provide a Look at Consultants' Role," *Wall Street Journal* (July 19, 1988), p. 1.
25. Schachter, "Consummate Deal Maker Focus of Pentagon Probe," p. 1.
26. Testimony of William Galvin during the federal trial of James Gaines, March 3, 1992.
27. Interview with Darrell Cole, November 1992.
28. Interview with Melvyn Paisley, April 1993.
29. Schachter, "Consummate Deal Maker Focus of Pentagon Probe," p. 1.
30. Wines, "Lively Days of a Military Consultant," p. 1.
31. Testimony of William Galvin during the federal trial of James Gaines, March 3, 1992.
32. Ibid.

33. Transcript of wiretapped conversation, July 22, 1987.

34. Transcript of wiretapped conversation, June 22, 1987.

35. Interview with William Parkin, August 1988, by Edward T. Pound.

36. William Galvin's grand jury testimony, August 1990.

37. Ibid.

38. Interview with Melvyn Paisley, April 1993.

39. William Galvin's grand jury testimony, September 1990.

40. John F. Lehman, Jr., *Command of the Seas* (New York: Charles Scribner's Sons, 1988), p. 116.

41. Interview with John Lehman, December 1992.

42. Wayne Biddle, "John F. Lehman Jr.; Giving New Meaning to the Word 'Shipshape,' " *New York Times* (September 13, 1984), p. 18.

43. Hedrick Smith, *The Power Game: How Washington Works* (New York: Random House, 1988), p. 188.

44. James M. Perry, "Budget Deficit or No, Navy Builds a Port for Every Battleship," *Wall Street Journal* (June 15, 1989), p. 1.

45. Ibid.

46. Smith, *The Power Game*, p. 192.

47. William J. Crowe, Jr., *The Line of Fire* (New York: Simon & Schuster, 1993), p. 240.

48. Walter S. Mossberg, "Reagan Bid for More Defense Funds Cut by Senate Unit; Tower Backs Big Navy," *Wall Street Journal* (April 2, 1981), p. 7.

49. Interview with Caspar Weinberger, April 1993.

50. Walter S. Mossberg, "Reagan Five-Year Program Stresses More Offensive Stance, Larger Navy," *Wall Street Journal* (February 8, 1982), p. 6.

51. Michael R. Gordon, "Lehman's Navy Riding High, But Critics Question Its Strategy and Rapid Growth," *National Journal* (September 21, 1985), p. 2125.

52. Based on an interview with John Lehman, December 1992, and details recounted in Smith, *The Power Game*, p. 193.

53. Caspar Weinberger, *Fighting for Peace: Seven Critical Years in the Pentagon* (New York: Warner Books, 1990), p. 59.

54. Tim Carrington, "Expanding Navy Is on a Collision Course with Budget Politics," *Wall Street Journal* (August 29, 1985), p. 1.

55. Tim Carrington, "Navy Frets That Its Growing Fleet May Founder for Lack of Sailors in Climate of Budget Cutting," *Wall Street Journal* (March 1, 1987), p. 64.

56. Interview with John Lehman, December 1992.

57. John Cushman, "Navy Has Made Dramatic Shifts in Procurement," *New York Times* (June 24, 1989), p. A11.

58. Interview with John Lehman, December 1992.

59. Lehman, *Command of the Seas*, p. 243.

60. Interview with John Lehman, December 1992.

61. Ibid.

62. Interview with Caspar Weinberger, April 1993.

63. William Galvin's grand jury testimony, September 1990.

64. Testimony and reports presented by Derek Vander Schaaf, deputy inspector general DOD, before the Congressional Military Reform Caucus, November 2, 1989.

65. Tim Carrington, "Navy May Have Pressed Too Hard on Shipyards," *Wall Street Journal* (May 29, 1987), p. 54.

66. "Defense Budget Increases: How Well Are They Planned And Spent?" General Accounting Office report (April 13, 1982).

67. Ralph Vartabedian, "At the Pentagon, Competition Is No Panacea," *Los Angeles Times* (May 13, 1990), p. D1.

68. Patrick Tyler, *Running Critical* (New York: Harper & Row, 1986), p. 285.
69. Walter S. Mossberg, "Navy Says General Dynamics Must Settle Its Claims to Get More Trident Contracts," *Wall Street Journal* (September 16, 1981), p. 5.
70. Tyler, *Running Critical*, p. 306.
71. Ibid., p. 301.
72. Lehman, *Command of the Seas*, p. 221.
73. Tyler, *Running Critical*, p. 311.
74. Interview with a former McDonnell Douglas executive.
75. Based on interviews with industry officials, who insist on remaining anonymous but are familiar with the discussions.
76. Ibid.
77. Ibid.
78. Interview with Lawrence Korb, November 1992.
79. Based on interviews with industry officials who insist on remaining anonymous.
80. Interview with Congressman John Kasich, March 1991.
81. Andy Pasztor, "Dispute over A-12 Navy Bomber May Be Costliest Federal Suit Ever," *Wall Street Journal* (July 27, 1994), p. B2.
82. Based on interviews with industry officials who insist on remaining anonymous.
83. Lehman, *Command of the Seas*, p. 36.
84. Ibid., p. 1.
85. Ibid., p. 4.
86. Carrington, "Expanding Navy Is on a Collision Course With Budget Politics," p. 1.
87. Bob Woodward, "The Admiral of Washington," *Washington Post Magazine* (September 24, 1989), p. 44.
88. Interview with John Lehman, December 1992.
89. Lehman, *Command of the Seas*, p. 196.
90. Ibid., p. 265.
91. Interview with Melvyn Paisley, April 1993.
92. William Galvin's grand jury testimony, August 1990.
93. Ibid.
94. Ibid.
95. Ibid.
96. Ibid.
97. Interview with Melvyn Paisley, April 1993.
98. William Galvin's grand jury testimony, August 1990.
99. Based on diaries prepared by Melvyn Paisley and his assistant, James Gaines.
100. Court papers filed along with the guilty plea of William Galvin.
101. Videotape of trip made by Paisley and Gaines, May 1986.
102. Testimony of William Galvin during the federal trial of James Gaines, March 3, 1992.
103. William Galvin's grand jury testimony, August 1990.
104. Ibid.
105. Interview with John Lehman, December 1992.
106. Interviews with John Lehman, December 1992 and January 1993.
107. Schachter, "Consummate Deal Maker Focus of Pentagon Probe," p. 1.
108. William Galvin's grand jury testimony, August 1990.
109. Letter about Melvyn Paisley from retired admiral James Lyons to U.S. District Court Judge Claude Hilton, August 16, 1991.
110. Interview with John Lehman, January 1993.
111. Interview with John Lehman, December 1992.
112. Ibid.
113. Interview with Melvyn Paisley, April 1993.

114. Ibid.

115. Ibid.

116. Excerpt from Melvyn Paisley's computerized diary, prepared for his lawyers.

117. Interview with Darrell Cole, November 1992.

118. Ibid.

119. Based on Melvyn Paisley's diary.

120. William Galvin's grand jury testimony, September 1990.

121. Based on court documents and William Galvin's grand jury testimony.

122. Interview with Darrell Cole, November 1992.

123. Lou Cannon, *President Reagan: The Role of a Lifetime* (New York: Simon & Schuster, 1991), p. 795.

124. Ibid., p. 794.

Chapter V

1. Letter from Vicki Paisley to U.S. Judge Claude Hilton, September 1991.

2. William Galvin's federal grand jury testimony, August 1990.

3. Robert Gillette and Gregory Crouch, "Paisley Took Luxury Trips with Defense Consultant," *Los Angeles Times* (July 23, 1988), p. 1.

4. Based on Melvyn Paisley's calendar and diaries, which were compiled and edited by Vicki Paisley.

5. William Galvin's federal grand jury testimony, August 1990. After pleading guilty and admitting his ownership stake in Sapphire, Melvyn Paisley reversed himself and claimed that he was not a silent partner and didn't own any portion of the firm.

6. Walter S. Mossberg and Felix Kessler, "Power of Small Missiles in Falklands Leads U.S. to Mull New Defenses," *Wall Street Journal* (June 4, 1982), p. 1.

7. Ibid.

8. John J. Fialka, "Two Tests of Navy's Aegis Cruiser Give Widely Disparate Marks to Ship's Abilities," *Wall Street Journal* (November 4, 1983), p. 37.

9. John J. Fialka, "New Antimissile Ship Faces Further Storms as Costs, Doubts Grow," *Wall Street Journal* (June 30, 1983), p. 1.

10. Based on Melvyn Paisley's calendar and diaries, as well as documents filed in federal district court in Alexandria, Virginia, in connection with Paisley's guilty plea.

11. Documents filed in federal district court in Alexandria, Virginia, in connection with Paisley's guilty plea.

12. Michael R. Gordon, "Navy Secretary Moves to Take Control of Independent Consulting Center," *National Journal* (April 2, 1983), p. 693.

13. Interview with Darrell Cole, November 1992. (Bell says such claims "couldn't be further from the truth," but he declines other comment.)

14. Based on Melvyn Paisley's calendars and diaries.

15. William Galvin's federal grand jury testimony, August 1990.

16. Documents filed by the government in Alexandria, Virginia, federal district court in conjunction with Paisley's guilty plea.

17. Based on wiretap transcripts (September 21, 1987) and interview with Neel Patrick, 1993.

18. William Galvin's federal grand jury testimony, August 1990. Yang declined to comment for this book.

19. William Galvin's federal grand jury testimony, September 1990.

20. Ibid.

21. William Galvin's federal grand jury testimony, August 1990.

22. Interviews of James Gaines and chronologies he prepared for his defense lawyers.

23. Douglas Jehl and William C. Rempel, "Firm Flourished After Employing Paisley's Wife," *Los Angeles Times* (July 10, 1988), p. 30.
24. Based on chronologies prepared by James Gaines for his defense lawyers.
25. Testimony of William Galvin during the federal trial of James Gaines, March 3, 1992.
26. Based on Melvyn Paisley's calendars and diaries.
27. Transcript of wiretapped conversation, November 9, 1987.
28. William Galvin's federal grand jury testimony, August 1990.
29. Interview with Melvyn Paisley, April 1993.
30. Ibid.
31. William Galvin's federal grand jury testimony, August 1990. (Paisley disputes the testimony.)
32. Ibid.
33. Based on an interview with Melvyn Paisley, and on documents his lawyers submitted to the court in October 1991, before his sentencing.
34. Based on documents filed with Melvyn Paisley's guilty plea, and on excerpts of a draft indictment prepared by prosecutors but never returned by a federal grand jury.
35. Letter from Earl Silbert, dated June 27, 1994, regarding Thomas Pownall's dealings with Melvyn Paisley. Pownall declined to be interviewed for this book.
36. Based on interviews with Martin Marietta officials, who refuse to be identified, who are familiar with the matter.
37. William Galvin's federal grand jury testimony, September 1990.
38. William Galvin's federal grand jury testimony, August 1990. Martin Marietta officials dispute the story, indicating that Galvin had been retained by one of the company's units a year earlier.
39. William Galvin's grand jury testimony, September 1990.
40. Ibid.
41. Ibid.
42. Ibid.
43. Based on William Galvin's grand jury testimony, August and September 1990, and on interviews with Martin Marietta and industry officials, who refuse to be identified.
44. Ibid.
45. Based on interviews with Martin Marietta and industry officials, who refuse to be identified.
46. William Galvin's grand jury testimony, August 1990, and Melvyn Paisley's chronology.
47. Court documents submitted by Melvyn Paisley's lawyers in connection with his sentencing, October 1991, and interviews with Frank Menaker.
48. Excerpts of wiretap transcripts included in documents filed by prosecutors along with Melvyn Paisley's guilty plea.
49. Helen Dewar and Molly Moore, "Consultant Fees Called Understated," *Washington Post* (June 22, 1988), p. 1.
50. Based on testimony presented by William H. Reed, director of the Defense Contract Audit Agency, to the Senate Governmental Affairs Committee's Federal Services, Post Office and Civil Service Subcommittee, December 13, 1988.
51. Edward T. Pound, "Weapons Inquiry Soon Will Provide a Look at Consultants' Role," *Wall Street Journal* (July 19, 1988), p. 1.
52. Tim Carrington and Edward T. Pound, "Pushing Defense Firms to Compete, Pentagon Harms Buying System," *Wall Street Journal* (June 27, 1988), p. 1.
53. Ibid.
54. William Galvin's grand jury testimony, September 1990.
55. Interview with Melvyn Paisley, April 1993.

56. William Galvin's grand jury testimony, September 1990.

57. Excerpt of wiretapped conversation, May 1, 1987.

58. George C. Wilson, "Navy Chief Filled Vacuum at Pentagon," *Washington Post* (June 19, 1988), p. 1.

59. Pound, "Weapons Inquiry Soon Will Provide a Look at Consultants' Role," p. 1.

60. Glenn F. Bunting, "Old Friend Gave Companies Entree to Lehman," *Los Angeles Times* (July 21, 1988), p. 24.

61. Ibid.

62. Walter Pincus, "Lawyer Allegedly Claimed 'Entree' to Lehman," *Washington Post* (June 24, 1988), p. 1.

63. Interview with Melvyn Paisley, April 1993.

64. Glenn F. Bunting, "Old Friend Gave Companies Entree to Lehman," p. 24.

65. Transcript of wiretapped conversation, September 21, 1987.

66. Interview with Darrell Cole, November 1992.

67. Michael Wines, "Lively Days of a Military Consultant," *New York Times* (August 2, 1988), p. 1.

68. Based on Melvyn Paisley's calendar and diary.

69. William Galvin's grand jury testimony, August 1990.

70. Interview with Darrell Cole, November 1992.

71. Interview with Melvyn Paisley, April 1993.

72. Interview with a retired Navy admiral, July 1988, who refuses to be identified.

73. Pound, "Weapons Inquiry Soon Will Provide a Look at Consultants' Role," p. 1.

74. William Galvin's grand jury testimony, September 1990.

75. Interview with Charles Welling, February 1993.

76. William Galvin's grand jury testimony, September 1990.

77. Based on interviews in 1991 with former Honeywell executives, who decline to be identified.

78. Ibid.

79. Excerpt of wiretapped conversation, April 30, 1987.

80. Based on documents prepared by Illwind case agents but never made public.

81. William Galvin's grand jury testimony, August 1990.

82. Court documents filed with the guilty plea of Victor D. Cohen.

83. Excerpt of a wiretapped conversation included in court documents filed with the guilty plea of Melvyn Paisley.

84. Court documents filed with the guilty plea of William Galvin.

85. William Galvin's grand jury testimony, September 1990.

86. Ibid.

87. Ibid.

88. Ibid.

89. Interview with William Parkin, August 1988, by Edward T. Pound.

90. William Galvin's grand jury testimony, August and September 1990.

91. Melvyn Paisley's calendar and diaries.

92. William Galvin's grand jury testimony, September 1990.

93. Based on chronologies and diaries prepared by James Gaines for his defense lawyers.

94. Lehman, *Command of the Seas*, p. 418.

95. Interview with John Lehman, February 1993.

96. William Galvin's grand jury testimony, September 1990.

97. William Galvin's grand jury testimony, August 1990.

98. Based on William Galvin's grand jury testimony and court documents filed by prosecutors along with the guilty plea of James Gaines.

99. William Galvin's grand jury testimony, September 1990.

100. William Galvin's grand jury testimony, August 1990.
101. Gillette and Crouch, "Paisley Took Luxury Trips with Defense Consultant," p. 1.
102. William Galvin's grand jury testimony, August 1990. In court documents filed by his lawyers, Paisley claims he has "no recollection of any such promise by Mr. Gardner."
103. Interview with Darrell Cole, November 1992.

Chapter VI

1. Interview with former FBI senior agent Joseph Krahling, April 1993.
2. Based on interviews with investigators and industry officials, as well as on testimony in Thomas Muldoon's December 1989 trial in Alexandria, Virginia, federal district court.
3. Interview with Steve Fulmer, May 1992.
4. Ibid.
5. Ibid.
6. Ibid.
7. Ibid.
8. Ibid.
9. Interview with FBI special agent Debbie Pierce, January 1993.
10. Interview with William Dupree of the Pentagon Inspector General's office, April 1992.
11. John Koten and Tim Carrington, "Beating the Rap: For General Dynamics, Scandal Over Billing Hasn't Hurt Business," *Wall Street Journal* (April 29, 1986), p. 1.
12. "Judge Accepts Guilty Plea From Sperry in MX Contract Case," Associated Press story with no byline, May 23, 1984.
13. Howard Kurtz, "Defense Unit Said to Lag in Prosecutions," *Washington Post* (March 24, 1985), p. 8.
14. Tim Carrington and Andy Pasztor, "Textron, Motorola to Settle With U.S. in Pentagon Cases," *Wall Street Journal* (March 11, 1988), p. 30.
15. Interview with Richard Wade, August 1992.
16. Ibid.
17. Interview with Bud Albright, November 1992.
18. Ibid.
19. Interview with NIS agent Jimmy Whitener, June 1992.
20. Interview with Steve Fulmer, May 1992.
21. Ibid.
22. Ibid.
23. Ibid.
24. Based on interviews with Richard Wade, Steve Fulmer and others familiar with the incident.
25. Interview with Steve Fulmer, May 1992.
26. Ibid.
27. John Marlowe's testimony in Alexandria, Virginia, federal district court during the trial of consultant Thomas Muldoon, December 1989. Despite repeated requests from the author, Marlowe refused to be interviewed for this book.
28. Interviews with Steve Fulmer and Richard Wade.
29. Ibid.
30. Jack Sherman's testimony in Alexandria, Virginia, federal district court during the trial of consultant Thomas Muldoon, December 1989.
31. Transcript of conversation recorded by agents; date is not public.
32. Based on documents filed along with Jack Sherman's guilty plea in January 1989, and Sherman's subsequent testimony at Muldoon's trial in December 1989.
33. Ibid.

34. Affidavit for wiretap authorization submitted by prosecutors to federal court in early 1987.
35. Interview with Thomas Muldoon, October 1992.
36. Ibid.
37. Wiretapped conversation between Thomas Muldoon and Chris Pafort, January 1987.
38. Interview with Thomas Muldoon, October 1992.
39. Based on court documents filed by the government in the prosecutions of Thomas Muldoon, George Stone, Jerry Manning and Mark Saunders.
40. Transcript of wiretapped conversation between Thomas Muldoon and Christopher Pafort, August 1987.
41. Transcript of wiretapped conversation between Thomas Muldoon and Thomas McAusland, July 1987.
42. Transcript of wiretapped conversation between Thomas Muldoon and Mark Saunders, January 1988.
43. Court documents filed by prosecutors in connection with LTV's guilty plea.
44. Transcripts of wiretapped conversations between Thomas Muldoon and Eugene Streips, October and November 1987.
45. Transcript of wiretapped conversation between Thomas Muldoon and Jack Richardson, December 1987.
46. Court documents filed by prosecutors in connection with the guilty pleas of Roger Engel and Thomas Muldoon, and the transcript of a wiretapped conversation between Muldoon and James Rapinac, November 1987.
47. Transcript of wiretapped conversation between Mark Saunders and George Stone, February 1988.
48. Transcript of wiretapped conversation between Thomas Muldoon and Mark Saunders, March 1988.
49. Transcript of wiretapped conversation between Thomas Muldoon and Jack Sherman, October 1987, and court documents filed by prosecutors in connection with the guilty plea of Jerry Manning.
50. Transcript of wiretapped conversation between Thomas Muldoon and Mark Saunders, January 1988.
51. Interview with Richard Wade, December 1992.
52. Interview with Steve Fulmer, May 1992.
53. Interview with former FBI senior agent Joseph Krahling, April 1993.
54. Interview with FBI special agent Debbie Pierce, January 1993.
55. Interview with Steve Fulmer, May 1992.
56. Interviews with William Parkin, August 1988, by Edward T. Pound.
57. Dana Priest and Caryle Murphy, "Portrait of a Deal-Maker," *Washington Post* (July 11, 1988), p. 1.
58. Interview with former FBI senior agent Joseph Krahling, April 1993.
59. Interview with Steve Fulmer, May 1992.
60. Transcript of wiretapped conversation between Thomas Muldoon and John F. Van Tassel, August 1987.
61. Testimony of Richard Wade in Thomas Muldoon's December 1989 trial in Alexandria, Virginia, federal district court.
62. Interview with FBI special agent Debbie Pierce, January 1993.
63. Interview with Richard Wade, August 1992.
64. Interview with Steve Fulmer, May 1992.
65. Interview with FBI special agent Debbie Pierce, January 1993.
66. Interview with Richard Wade, August 1992.
67. Interview with FBI special agent Debbie Pierce, January 1993.
68. Ibid.

69. Interview with former FBI senior agent Joseph Krahling, April 1993.
70. Interview with Jimmy Whitener, August 1992.
71. Interview with Steve Fulmer, May 1992.
72. Ibid.
73. Interview with former FBI senior agent Joseph Krahling, April 1993.
74. Ibid.
75. Interview with FBI special agent Debbie Pierce, January 1993.
76. Interview with FBI special agent Phyllis Sciacca, December 1992.
77. Interview with Debbie Pierce, January 1993.
78. Interview with Richard Wade, August 1992.
79. Ibid.
80. The description comes from the transcript of a wiretapped conversation between William Parkin and Eugene Sullivan, April 30, 1987.
81. Based on interviews with William Parkin and a June 1988 federal affidavit for a search warrant for his home and office. Interviews conducted by Edward T. Pound.
82. June 1988 federal affidavit for a search warrant for William Parkin's home and office. Parkin and his family disputed the government's version of events.
83. Federal indictment of William Parkin, Teledyne Industries and five other individuals on bribery and other charges, January 1989.
84. Transcript of wiretapped conversation between William Parkin and George Kaub of Teledyne, July 1987.
85. Transcript of wiretapped conversation between Fred Lackner and Michael Savaides of Teledyne, March 1988.
86. Papers filed by prosecutors along with the guilty plea of William Parkin in federal district court in Alexandria, Virginia, March 1989.
87. Based on transcripts of federal wiretaps and several interviews with William Parkin, by Edward T. Pound.
88. Transcript of wiretapped conversation between William Parkin and Eugene Sullivan of Teledyne, March 1987.
89. Transcript of wiretapped conversation between William Parkin and Fred Lackner, February 1987.
90. Interview with Debbie Pierce, January 1993.
91. Ibid.
92. Interview with Bud Albright, November 1992.
93. Interview with Debbie Pierce, January 1993.
94. Interviews with Henry Hudson, February and October 1992.
95. Ibid.
96. Based on interviews with Steve Fulmer, Bud Albright and Henry Hudson.
97. Interview with former FBI senior agent Joseph Krahling, April 1993.
98. Robert E. Kessler, "Ex-LIer Heads Pentagon Probe," *Long Island Newsday* (September 5, 1988), p. 5.
99. Ibid.
100. Interviews with Joseph Aronica, September 1992.
101. Ibid.
102. Ibid.
103. Interview with Steve Fulmer, May 1992.
104. S. Lynne Walker, "Cubic, Wellborn Plead Guilty to Bribery," *San Diego Union and Tribune* (January 16, 1991), p. C1.
105. Interview with former NIS agent Mike Cox, May 1992.
106. Excerpt of wiretapped conversations filed with the guilty plea filed by Cubic Defense Systems, January 1991.

107. Based on an affidavit for a search warrant of Victor Cohen's residence, June 1988, and on court documents filed with the guilty plea of Cubic and the separate guilty plea of Victor Cohen, August 1991.
108. Ibid.
109. Court documents filed with the guilty pleas of Cubic, Loral and Cohen. Cohen declined to comment for this book.
110. Excerpts of wiretapped conversations filed with the guilty pleas of Cubic and Cohen.
111. Court documents filed with the separate guilty pleas of Loral Corporation, December 1989, and Louis Oberndorf, September 1992.
112. Ibid.
113. Interview with Joe Aronica, September 1992.
114. Court documents filed with the separate guilty pleas of Loral Corporation, December 1989, and Louis Oberndorf, September 1992.
115. Transcript of William Galvin's federal grand jury testimony, September 5, 1990.
116. Interview with Richard Wade, December 1992.
117. Interview with Mathew Walinski, April 1992.
118. Ibid.

Chapter VII

1. Interviews with Richard Fowler in October and November 1992, and in February and March 1993.
2. Ibid.
3. Ibid.
4. Ibid.
5. Ibid.
6. Based on documents Dick Fowler prepared for his defense lawyers.
7. Ibid.
8. Christopher Hanson, "Was It Espionage or Just Business as Usual," *Seattle Post-Intelligencer* (March 8, 1990), p. 5
9. Ibid.
10. Interview with Richard Fowler, November 1992.
11. Ibid.
12. Ibid.
13. Interview with Frank Caso, former Hughes marketing official, April 1993.
14. Interview with Richard Fowler, November 1992.
15. Christopher Hanson, "Network of Secrets," *Seattle Post-Intelligencer* (March 8, 1990), p. 1, corroborated by interviews with Richard Fowler and other former Boeing officials.
16. Memo from Thomas J. O'Brien, director of DIS, to Craig Alderman, Office of Deputy Undersecretary for Policy, dated May 29, 1987.
17. Interview with Richard Fowler, November 1992.
18. Interview with Henry Hudson, January 1990.
19. Hearing of the Congressional Joint Economic Committee, December 21, 1988.
20. Interview with Michael Costello, March 1992.
21. Interview with Richard Fowler, November 1992.
22. Interview with Richard Fowler, February 1993.
23. Andy Pasztor, "GTE Charged with Obtaining Records Illegally," *Wall Street Journal* (September 11, 1985), p. 3.
24. Andy Pasztor and Rick Wartzman, "How a Spy for Boeing and His Pals Gleaned Data on Defense Plans," *Wall Street Journal* (January 15, 1990), p. 1.

25. Andy Pasztor, "Grand-Jury Probe Jars the Close-Knit World of Electronic Warfare," *Wall Street Journal* (March 20, 1985), p. 1.
26. John M. Broder, "1984 Indictment: A Chilling Omen of Fraud Probe," *Los Angeles Times* (June 26, 1988), p. 1.
27. Pasztor, "Grand-Jury Probe Jars Close-Knit World of Electronic Warfare," p. 1.
28. Ibid.
29. Andy Pasztor, "Illegal Swapping of Defense Data Is Investigated," *Wall Street Journal* (October 3, 1985), p. 64.
30. Action Memorandum from Joseph Sherick to Defense Secretary Caspar Weinberger, May 21, 1985.
31. Interview with Richard Sauber, September 1992.
32. Based on interviews with Richard Sauber and Pentagon investigators, and a December 21, 1988, staff report released by the Congressional Joint Economic Committee's subcommittee on national security.
33. Interview with Richard Sauber, September 1992.
34. Broder, "1984 Indictment: A Chilling Omen of Fraud Probe," p. 1.
35. Andy Pasztor, "Criminal Charge Against GTE Recommended," *Wall Street Journal* (March 22, 1985), p. 5.
36. Pasztor, "Grand-Jury Probe Jars the Close-Knit World of Electronic Warfare," p. 1.
37. Kenneth L. Adelman and Norman R. Augustine, *The Defense Revolution* (San Francisco: ICS Press, 1990), p. 151.
38. William H. Gregory, *The Defense Procurement Mess* (Lexington, Mass.: Lexington Books, 1989), p. 174.
39. Interview with William Dupree, April 1992.
40. Caryle Murphy, "GTE Trial to Test Secrets Laws' Use," *Washington Post* (January 5, 1986), p. F1.
41. Tim Carrington, "Lockheed Concedes Security Was Lax at California Site, Sets Auditor Probe," *Wall Street Journal* (July 25, 1986), p. 6.
42. Tim Carrington, "Pentagon Finds Lack of Secrecy for Defense Jobs," *Wall Street Journal* (October 1, 1987), p. 38.
43. Edward T. Pound and Andy Pasztor, "Consulting Activities of Ex-Top Admiral Were Investigated," *Wall Street Journal* (July 25, 1986), p. 42.
44. Interview with DCIS agent Mathew Walinski, April 1992.
45. William J. Eaton, "Firms May Face Charges Tied to Defense Secrets," *Los Angeles Times* (December 22, 1988), p. 1.
46. Interview with Mathew Walinski, April 1992.
47. Interview with Michael Costello, March 1992.
48. Interview with Randy Bellows, March 1993.
49. Philip B. Heymann and Lance Liebman, eds., *The Social Responsibilities of Lawyers* (Westbury, N.Y.: The Foundation Press, 1988), p. 79.
50. Interview with Randy Bellows, March 1993.
51. Philip Shenon, "Justice Dept. Says It Was Wrong to Prosecute General Dynamics," *New York Times* (June 20, 1987), p. 1.
52. "General Dynamics, Beggs Cleared of Fraud Charges," *Aviation Week & Space Technology* (June 29, 1987), p. 25.
53. Interview with Randy Bellows, March 1993.
54. Interview with Randy Bellows, October 1993.
55. Interview with Randy Bellows, March 1993.
56. Based on interviews with Dick Fowler and with Max Franklin and Frank Caso, two former Hughes officials, and on testimony at Fowler's trial 1989 trial in Alexandria, Virginia, federal district court.

57. Based on testimony in Fowler's trial.
58. Interview with Mathew Walinski, April 1992.
59. Ibid.
60. Based on interview with Richard Fowler, October 1992, and Lozito's testimony at Fowler's trial.
61. Ibid.
62. Ibid.
63. Ibid.
64. Interview with Mathew Walinski, April 1993.
65. Based on interviews with Richard Fowler and the testimony of Kenneth Zike at Fowler's 1990 trial in Alexandria, Virginia, federal district court.
66. Testimony of Kenneth Zike at Fowler's trial.
67. Interview with Richard Fowler, November 1992.
68. Interview with Richard Fowler, March 1993.
69. Based on a memorandum written by lawyers for Debra Null, which summarized her questioning by Randy Bellows in July 1989.
70. Interview with Richard Fowler, October 1992.
71. Ibid.
72. Pasztor and Wartzman, "How a Spy for Boeing and His Pals Gleaned Data on Defense Plans," p. 1.
73. Interview with Mathew Walinski, April 1992.
74. Ibid.
75. Pasztor and Wartzman, "How a Spy for Boeing and His Pals Gleaned Data on Defense Plans," p. 1.
76. Based on notes prepared by Richard Fowler for his lawyers in 1989.
77. Interview with Mathew Walinski, April 1992.

Chapter VIII

1. Interviews with Richard Fowler, November 1992 and February and March 1993.
2. Based on interviews with Richard Fowler and court documents filed in his case in Alexandria, Virginia, federal district court.
3. Ibid.
4. Ibid.
5. Christopher Hanson, "Company Changed Its Tune," *Seattle Post-Intelligencer* (March 8, 1980), p. 4.
6. Duff Wilson, " 'The Fall Guy' Speaks Out," *Seattle Times* (January 14, 1990), p. 1.
7. Based on documents prepared by Richard Fowler for reporters and his defense lawyers.
8. Interview with Mathew Walinski, April 1993.
9. Interview with William Kasper, December 1989.
10. Tony Capaccio, "Boeing Document-Swap Web Widens," *Defense Week* (December 4, 1989), p. 1.
11. Bellows's interview of a Sanders official, summarized by Fowler's defense lawyers.
12. Interview with Max Franklin, March 25, 1993.
13. Ibid. (Today, Kasper claims he handled all documents "through the proper channels.")
14. Ibid. (IBM declined comment.)
15. Interview with Dick Fowler, October 1992.
16. Interview with Max Franklin, March 25, 1993.
17. Courtroom testimony of Paul Blumhardt at the trial of Frank Caso, a former Hughes official.
18. Interview with Randy Bellows, March 1993.

19. Wilson, " 'The Fall Guy' Speaks Out," p. 1.
20. Interview with Richard Fowler, October 1992.
21. Christopher Hanson, "Boeing Hired Me to Do What I Did," *Seattle Post-Intelligencer* (March 8, 1990), p. 1.
22. Courtroom testimony of Paul Blumhardt at the trial of Frank Caso.
23. Interview with Max Franklin, March 25, 1993.
24. Based on Gloria Mahaffey's testimony at Fowler's trial and on a summary of statements she made to investigators, prepared by Fowler's attorneys in 1989.
25. Gloria Mahaffey's testimony at Fowler's trial.
26. Summary of Gloria Mahaffey's statements to investigators, prepared by Fowler's attorneys.
27. Gloria Mahaffey's testimony at Fowler's trial.
28. Ibid.
29. Ibid.
30. Ibid.
31. Ibid.
32. Ibid.
33. Based on interviews with Mathew Walinski, May 1992 and April 1993.
34. Ibid.
35. Interview with Richard Fowler, March 1993. The government never pursued Watson for any wrongdoing, and he declines to talk about his dealings with Boeing or Boeing executives.
36. Interview with Max Franklin, former Hughes official, March 12, 1993.
37. Frank Lozito's testimony at Fowler's trial.
38. Ibid.
39. Ibid.
40. Ibid.
41. Interview with Frank Caso, April 1993.
42. Interview with Max Franklin, March 12, 1993.
43. Phil Jackson's testimony at Fowler's trial.
44. A summary of Phil Jackson's interview by Randy Bellows in July 1989, written by Jackson's attorneys.
45. Phil Jackson's testimony at Fowler's trial.
46. Ibid.
47. Based on Max Franklin's testimony at Fowler's trial, and on a summary of Phil Jackson's interview by Randy Bellows in July 1989.
48. Ibid.
49. Max Franklin's testimony at Fowler's trial.
50. Phil Jackson's testimony at Fowler's trial.
51. Linda Couture's testimony at Fowler's trial.
52. Based on interviews with Mathew Walinski, May 1992 and April 1993.
53. Based on interviews with Richard Fowler and Mathew Walinski, and on court documents.
54. Christopher Hanson, "Network of Secrets," *Seattle Post-Intelligencer* (March 8, 1990), p. 1.
55. Andy Pasztor, "Attempts to Streamline Pentagon Procurement Soften Amid Resistance of a Jealous Bureaucracy," *Wall Street Journal* (June 6, 1990), p. 30.
56. Deposition of attorney Marcus Topel in civil case filed by Frank Caso against Hughes Aircraft, in Los Angeles County Superior Court.
57. Interview with Randy Bellows, March 1993.
58. Interview with Max Franklin, March 25, 1993.
59. Wilson, " 'The Fall Guy' Speaks Out," p. 1.

60. Ibid.
61. Interview with Randy Bellows, September 1993.
62. Sharon Walsh, "Requisite for a Heavyweight; Bob Bennett Has the Moves and the Moxie to Be the Top Lawyer in Town," *Washington Post* (March 29, 1993), p. D1.
63. Kim Eisler, "Clark Clifford Needed a Damned Good Lawyer; So He Called Bob Bennett," *The Washingtonian* (March 1992), p. 66.
64. Ibid.
65. Frank Deford, "The Fabulous Bennett Boys," *Vanity Fair* (August 14, 1994), p. 85.
66. Walsh, "Requisite for a Heavyweight; Bob Bennett Has the Moves and the Moxie to Be the Top Lawyer in Town," p. D1.
67. Deford, "The Fabulous Bennett Boys," p. 85.
68. Ibid.
69. Ibid.
70. Suzanne Garment, *Scandal: The Culture of Mistrust in American Politics* (New York: Anchor Books, 1991), p. 135.
71. Interview with Mathew Walinski, May 1992.
72. Ibid.
73. Interview with Randy Bellows, March 1993.

Chapter IX

1. "Documents Detail Alleged Aerospace Bribes," *Aviation Week & Space Technology* (May 7, 1979), p. 24.
2. Ibid.
3. "Boeing Is Fined $400,000 for Hiding Fees," *Wall Street Journal* (July 1, 1982), p. 40.
4. Robert J. Serling, *Legend & Legacy: The Story of Boeing and Its People* (New York: St. Martin's Press, 1992), p. 412.
5. Interview with Henry (Bud) Hebeler, November 1992.
6. Serling, *Legend & Legacy*, p. 413.
7. Audit prepared by House staffers analyzing Boeing claims reviewed by the Defense Contract Audit Agency for fiscal 1979.
8. Duff Wilson, "Boeing Used Inside Information, Covered Up, Say 2 Fired Workers," *Seattle Times* (March 12, 1990), p. 1.
9. Ibid.
10. Eve Dumovich, *The Two Washingtons*, a publication of the Boeing Historical Archives (1991), p. 76.
11. Serling, *Legend & Legacy*, p. 426.
12. Ibid., p. 416.
13. Duff Wilson, "Not a Happy Chapter at Boeing," *Seattle Times* (May 2, 1990), p. 1.
14. Ibid.
15. Serling, *Legend & Legacy*, p. 416.
16. Wilson, "Not a Happy Chapter at Boeing," p. 1.
17. Serling, *Legend & Legacy*, p. 415
18. Duff Wilson, "Boeing Admonishes Eight in Probe of 1989 Defense Secrets Case," *Seattle Times* (April 28, 1993), p. 1.
19. Boeing's press spokesmen and the company's official historian declined to comment on the matter, and they wouldn't provide any assistance for this book. "The whole issue is something we want to put behind us and not rehash again," one spokesman said.
20. Wilson, "Boeing Admonishes Eight in Probe of 1989 Defense Secrets Case," p. 1.
21. Serling, *Legend & Legacy*, p. 415.

22. Susan Smith, "Recent Events Cast Cloud over Boeing, Industry Analysts Say," *Seattle Post-Intelligencer* (November 14, 1989), p. B6.

23. Editorial titled "Boeing Case: Need for New Ethical Goals," *Seattle Times* (November 15, 1989), p. 10.

24. Ralph Vartabedian, "NASA Admits Boeing Failed Cost Reviews," *Los Angeles Times* (July 28, 1994), p. D1.

25. Jeff Brazil, "FAA Considered Effect of 757 Ruling on Boeing Sales," *Los Angeles Times* (July 28, 1994), p. 1.

26. Summarized from Dumovich, *The Two Washingtons.*

27. Interview with Michael Costello, March 1992.

28. Ibid.

29. Les Blumenthal, "Former Boeing Employee Convicted," Associated Press (December 7, 1989).

30. Duff Wilson, "Fowler Not the Only Guilty One, Says Juror," *Seattle Times* (December 8, 1989), p. 1.

31. Ibid.

32. Based on interviews with Richard Fowler and summaries Fowler prepared after the trial.

33. Duff Wilson, " 'The Fall Guy' Speaks Out," *Seattle Times* (January 14, 1990), p. 1.

34. Excerpted from documents Fowler prepared before his sentencing.

35. Christopher Hanson, "Fowler Vows Not to Name Pentagon Sources," *Seattle Post-Intelligencer* (December 8, 1989), p. 1.

36. Interview with Richard Fowler, October 1992.

37. Ibid.

38. Ibid.

39. Interview with Randy Bellows, March 1993.

40. Interview with Frank Caso, April 1993.

41. Frank Caso's testimony at his trial in Alexandria, Virginia, federal district court, June 1990.

42. Interview with Max Franklin, March 1993.

43. Jonathan Peterson, "El Segundo, the Aerospace Child, Learns Price of Peace," *Los Angeles Times* (December 21, 1993), p. 1.

44. Nick Kotz, *Wild Blue Yonder: Money, Politics and the B-1 Bomber* (New York: Pantheon Books, 1988), p. 107.

45. Anthony Sampson, *The Arms Bazaar: From Lebanon to Lockheed* (New York: Viking Press, 1977), p. 211.

46. Jack Cheevers, "Still the Right Stuff; Edwards Air Base Defies Downsizing Trend," *Los Angeles Times* (July 20, 1994), p. 3.

47. Interview with Max Franklin, March 1993.

48. Interview with Frank Caso, April 1993.

49. Interview with Max Franklin, March 1993.

50. Summation of prosecutor Randy Bellows at Caso's trial.

51. Interview with Max Franklin, March 1993. An EIA spokesman says the organization isn't aware of any illegal document exchanges, adding that EIA "unequivocally condemns" them if they did occur.

52. Notes of interview with Thomas O'Brien, former director of the Defense Investigative Service, taken by Hughes lawyers. The document is part of Caso's civil case in Los Angeles Superior Court.

53. "Currie and Condor," *Aviation Week and Technology* (April 12, 1976), p. 10.

54. John W. Finney, "Eagleton Calls for Suspension of Pentagon Aide," *New York Times* (April 7, 1976), p. 10.

55. George Wilson, "Slowing Pentagon's Revolving Door," *Washington Post* (September 15, 1977), p. 1.

56. Based on Frank Caso's testimony at his trial, and on interviews with Caso in April 1993 and with Max Franklin in March 1993.

57. Interview with Max Franklin, March 1993.

58. Ibid.

59. Frank Caso's testimony at his June 1990 federal trial.

60. Interview with Frank Caso, April 1993.

61. Based on interviews with Frank Caso, his lawyers and prosecutor Randy Bellows.

62. Interview with Frank Caso, April 1993.

63. Sharyn Pinkstaff's testimony at Caso's federal trial. This chapter's depiction of the investigation and prosecution of Frank Caso and Hughes, including Caso's allegations concerning Currie, is based on court records, documents submitted into evidence, and interviews with the relevant parties.

64. Interview with Mathew Walinski, May 1992.

65. Randy Bellows's closing statement in Caso's federal trial.

66. Marcus Topel's deposition in Caso's civil case in Los Angeles Superior Court.

67. Interview with Randy Bellows, September 1993.

68. The Justice Department eventually decided against charging Wheelon or Hughes in the kickback case, but the investigation dragged on for nearly five years.

69. Marcus Topel's deposition in Caso's civil case and a separate interview with Topel, March 1994.

70. Interview with Randy Bellows, September 1993. Calder later testified that he relied on Frank Caso's explanations and had no independent knowledge of Currie's alleged dealings with Caso.

71. Frank Caso's testimony in his federal trial and interviews with Caso.

72. Ibid. Currie's lawyer disputed Caso's version, stressing that Calder's memos and courtroom testimony are inconsistent about the date of any such meeting.

73. Notes of interview of clerk Bennie Holmes by Hughes defense lawyers, March 1990.

74. James Calder's testimony at Caso's criminal trial.

75. Interview with Randy Bellows, September 1993.

76. Interviews with Randy Bellows and statements by Currie's defense lawyer.

77. Interview with Randy Bellows, March 1993.

78. Frank Caso's sworn testimony from his federal trial.

79. Based on Topel's deposition and other papers filed in Caso's civil suit.

80. Official transcript of Caso's federal trial.

81. Ibid.

82. Interview with Senator Carl Levin of Michigan, May 1993.

83. Andy Pasztor and Rick Wartzman, "Hughes Aircraft Chief Is Implicated Belatedly in Defense-Secret Case," *Wall Street Journal* (July 6, 1990), p. 1.

84. Letter from Herbert J. Miller, Currie's defense lawyer, February 25, 1994.

85. *Oversight of DOD's Management of Inside Information in the Acquisition Process,* Hearing Before the Subcommittee on Oversight of Government Management of the Senate Committee on Governmental Affairs, 101st Cong., 1st Sess., Feb. 24, 1989.

86. Malcolm Currie's interview with a group of defense correspondents in Washington, D.C., late 1991.

87. Interview with Mathew Walinski, May 1992.

88. Interview with Charles Welling, February 1993.

89. Excerpted from a draft of a letter Welling prepared for Fowler's sentencing hearing.

90. Included in a December 1989 letter from Richard Coupland to Judge Albert Bryan.

91. Interview with Mathew Walinski, May 1992.
92. Interview with Richard Fowler, July 1993.

Chapter X

1. Caspar Weinberger, *Fighting for Peace: Seven Critical Years in the Pentagon* (New York: Warner Books, 1990), p. 149.
2. Interview with John Lehman, December 1992.
3. Mark Thompson, "Paisley's Ties to Israeli Defense Contractor Investigated," *Dallas Morning News* (July 24, 1988), p. 1.
4. Interview with John Lehman, December 1992.
5. The overall size of the family's assets was disclosed in a civil suit involving its real estate holdings, filed in 1990 in Washington, D.C., superior court.
6. Interview with Melvyn Paisley, April 1993.
7. John F. Lehman, Jr., *Command of the Seas* (New York: Charles Scribner's Sons, 1988), p. 319.
8. Interview with Melvyn Paisley, April 1993.
9. Joe Pichirallo, " 'Extraordinary' Process Used to Buy Drones," *Washington Post* (July 28, 1998), p. A5.
10. Interview with John Lehman, February 1993.
11. Mark Thompson, "Paisley's Ties to Israeli Defense Contractor Investigated," *Dallas Morning News* (July 24, 1988), p. 1.
12. David Griffiths and Paula Dwyer, "The Navy's Drone Contract: Fair Bid or Fait Accompli?" *Business Week* (August 1, 1988), p. 30.
13. Interview with Richard Armitage, December 1993.
14. Memorandum from Melvyn Paisley to vice-chief of naval operations, December 1, 1985.
15. Court documents filed by prosecutors along with the guilty plea of Melvyn Paisley, June 1991.
16. Transcript of a portion of wiretapped conversation between Melvyn Paisley and William Galvin, August 3, 1987.
17. Excerpts of wiretapped conversations between Melvyn Paisley and William Galvin, including portions contained in court documents filed with Galvin's guilty plea.
18. Court documents filed by prosecutors along with the guilty plea of Melvyn Paisley, June 1991.
19. Interview with Melvyn Paisley, April 1993. In court filings by his lawyers after his guilty plea, Paisley maintained that his plans to bring on a second source were "totally contrary to the conspiracy's goals as alleged."
20. Excerpts of wiretapped conversations included in court documents accompanying the guilty pleas of William Galvin and Melvyn Paisley.
21. Ibid.
22. Edward T. Pound, "U.S. Sees New Signs Israel Resells Its Arms to China, South Africa," *Wall Street Journal* (March 13, 1992), p. 1.
23. Jim Mann, "U.S. Says Israel Gave Combat Jet Plans to China," *Los Angeles Times* (December 28, 1994), p. 1.
24. Indictment of Zvika Schiller and Uri Simhony, and court documents filed with the guilty plea of William Galvin.
25. Indictment of Schiller and Simhony.
26. Ibid.

27. Interview with Melvyn Paisley, April 1993.
28. Interview with John Lehman, December 1992.
29. Letter from Chester Paul Beach, the Defense Department's acting general counsel, to Congressman John Dingell, June 23, 1992.
30. Interview with Pam Bethel, March 1992.
31. Interview with Richard Sauber, September 1992.
32. Interview with Robert Powers, senior fraud investigator for the Naval Investigative Service, March 1992.
33. Jim Schachter and Mark Arax, "Defense Probe Focuses on No-Nonsense Foe of Waste," *Los Angeles Times* (October 11, 1988), p. 1.
34. Interview with Bud Albright, November 1992.
35. Bob Drogin and Glenn F. Bunting, "Earlier Allegations About Paisley Told," *Los Angeles Times* (June 26, 1988), p. 1.
36. Interview with John Lehman, February 1993.
37. Interview with Melvyn Paisley, April 1993.
38. November 1992 interview with Henry Hebeler, president of Boeing's aerospace subsidiary when the severance payments were determined, and an interview with T Wilson.
39. Court pleading filed in a civil suit filed by the Justice Department challenging the legitimacy of the severance payments.
40. Letter from Assistant FBI Director Milt Ahlerich to Senator Carl Levin of Michigan, dated August 9, 1988.
41. Interview with Phyllis Sciacca, December 1992.
42. Based on interviews with investigators and a detailed chronology prepared after the fact by Melvyn and Vicki Paisley.
43. Excerpt of wiretapped conversation between Melvyn Paisley and James Gaines, July 31, 1987.
44. Excerpts of federal wiretaps included in the Paisley chronology.
45. Interview with Melvyn Paisley, April 1993.
46. Copy of consultant agreement between Melvyn Paisley and Martin Marietta, dated July 27, 1987.
47. The quotation comes from an excerpt of a wiretapped conversation between Melvyn Paisley and William Galvin, April 1, 1987.
48. Interview with Steve Fulmer, May 1992.
49. Based on interviews with investigators and various court documents filed by the government.
50. Hearing of the House Appropriations Committee, March 19, 1987.
51. Based on interviews with Illwind prosecutors and investigators.
52. Excerpt of wiretapped conversation between Melvyn Paisley and Gloria Brown of Hercules Aerospace, April 2, 1987.
53. Excerpt of wiretapped conversation between William Galvin and Phil Sendel of Martin Marietta, April 9, 1987, and additional excerpt included in a July 15, 1988, memo to James Gaines from his defense lawyer.
54. William Galvin's federal grand jury testimony, August 1990.
55. Charges and other court documents filed in the 1991 criminal case against James Gaines in Alexandria, Virginia, federal court.
56. Based on excerpts of wiretapped conversations, draft indictments and draft informations prepared by federal prosecutors in the case against Gaines, the actual indictment filed against Gaines and entries in Melvyn Paisley's own chronology.
57. Excerpt of wiretapped conversation between Melvyn Paisley and James Gaines, January 25, 1988.
58. Excerpt of wiretapped conversation between Melvyn Paisley and James Gaines, April 7, 1987.

59. Interview with James Gaines, August 1992.
60. Excerpt of wiretapped conversation between Melvyn Paisley and William Galvin, April 28, 1987.
61. Excerpt of wiretapped conversation between Melvyn Paisley and William Galvin, April 30, 1987.
62. Excerpt of wiretapped conversation between Melvyn Paisley and William Galvin, April 28, 1987, part of which is taken from Paisley's own chronology.
63. Based on excerpts of wiretapped conversations; draft indictments and draft informations prepared by federal prosecutors in the case against Gaines; the actual indictment filed against Gaines; and entries in Melvyn Paisley's chronology.
64. Excerpt of wiretapped conversations between Melvyn Paisley and William Galvin, May 26, 1987.
65. Ibid.
66. Closing statement of Assistant U.S. Attorney Jack Hanly in the federal trial of James Gaines, March 1992.
67. Based on interviews with James Gaines and on chronologies Gaines prepared for his lawyer, in which he contends telling Paisley that he didn't want his son receiving a monthly retainer.
68. Based on Melvyn Paisley's chronology and excerpts of wiretapped conversation between Vicki Paisley and Dan McDonald, December 18, 1987.
69. Excerpt of wiretapped conversation between Melvyn Paisley and William Galvin, February 19, 1988, part of which is quoted in Paisley's own chronology.
70. Ibid.
71. Excerpt of wiretapped conversation between Melvyn Paisley and Bob Hood, September 23, 1987.
72. Excerpt of wiretapped conversation between Melvyn Paisley and Tom Young, September 28, 1987.
73. Excerpt of wiretapped conversation between Melvyn Paisley and Tom Young, September 30, 1987.
74. Based on Melvyn Paisley's own chronology and on an interview with Paisley in April 1993.
75. Excerpt of wiretapped conversation between Melvyn Paisley and James Gaines, October 16, 1987, part of which is quoted in Paisley's own chronology.
76. Interview with Melvyn Paisley, April 1993, and with United Technologies officials in 1995.
77. Excerpt of wiretapped conversation between Melvyn Paisley, William Galvin and Eugene Tallia, April 30, 1987, included in court documents filed by prosecutors with the guilty plea of Melvyn Paisley.
78. Court documents filed by prosecutors with the guilty plea of Melvyn Paisley and excerpts of wiretapped conversations included in Paisley's own chronology.
79. Ibid.
80. Based on Melvyn Paisley's chronology. Daniell has repeatedly declined to be interviewed.
81. Court documents filed by prosecutors with the guilty plea of Melvyn Paisley and excerpts of wiretapped conversations included in Paisley's own chronology.
82. Ibid.
83. Excerpt of wiretapped conversation between Melvyn Paisley and William Galvin, June 2, 1988, included in court documents filed with Paisley's guilty plea.
84. Court documents filed by prosecutors with the guilty plea of United Technologies.
85. Excerpts of wiretapped conversations between Melvyn Paisley and William Galvin, April 30, 1987, filed with the court along with Paisley's guilty plea. Portions also are included in expanded form in Paisley's own chronology.

86. Interview with Melvyn Paisley, April 1993.
87. Ibid.
88. Interview with Robert Powers, March 1992.
89. Interview with Melvyn Paisley, April 1993.
90. In its announcement of the plea bargain, United Technologies repeated language used in the court documents that prosecutors had "no evidence that any member of the board of directors of UTC was aware that UTC employees possessed the F404 pricing information." Eugene Tallia declined to be interviewed.
91. Open letter from Robert Daniell to UTC employees, August 28, 1992.
92. Open letter from Robert Daniell to UTC employees, December 15, 1989.
93. Based on interviews with Joseph Krahling and other current and former FBI agents involved in Illwind.
94. Ibid.
95. Ibid.
96. Interview with FBI agent Richard Wade, December 1992.
97. Based on interviews with Joseph Krahling and other current and former FBI agents involved in Illwind.
98. Interview with former NIS agent Mike Cox, May 1992.
99. Episode based on interviews with NIS agent Jimmy Whitener and with several current and former federal agents who declined to be identified.
100. Interview with senior NIS agent Cliff Simmen, March 1992.
101. Interview with Joseph Aronica, September 1992.
102. Interview with FBI agent Richard Wade, August 1992.
103. Interview with FBI agent Debbie Pierce, January 1993.
104. Ibid.

Chapter XI

1. Based on interviews with Charles Gardner and various federal investigators.
2. Interview with former NIS agent Mike Cox, May 1992.
3. Paul B. Carroll, "Unisys' Blumenthal to Resign as Chief," *Wall Street Journal* (January 26, 1990), p. B8.
4. Rankings contained in *Military Forum* magazine, August 1989 edition.
5. Based on documents filed by prosecutors in conjunction with the guilty pleas of Charles Gardner and Unisys in Alexandria, Virginia, federal district court.
6. Sentencing hearing for Charles Gardner in Alexandria federal district court, September 15, 1989.
7. Based on court documents filed by prosecutors along with the guilty pleas of Charles Gardner and Unisys, and on copies of investigative reports prepared by NIS agents.
8. Based on news reports, interviews with federal investigators and the May 1992 indictment of Republican congressman Joseph McDade of Pennsylvania by a Philadelphia federal grand jury. Congressman McDade's case is still pending.
9. William Nottingham and Ralph Frammolino, "Ex-Congress Aide's Ties to Sperry Corp. Probed," *Los Angeles Times* (July 7, 1988), p. 1. Also, the federal indictment of Congressman Joseph McDade in Philadelphia, May 1992.
10. Court documents filed by prosecutors along with Unisys's guilty plea.
11. Ibid.
12. Audio copy of a wiretapped conversation between Charles Gardner and a consultant before Illwind became public, but the exact date is unknown.
13. Court documents filed by prosecutors along with the guilty pleas of Unisys, John Roberts III, Robert Barrett and Joseph Hill.

14. Court documents filed by prosecutors along with the guilty pleas of Unisys and consultant James Neal.
15. Undated audiotape of wiretapped conversation between Charles Gardner and an associate, provided by a federal agent.
16. Interview with Steve Fulmer, May 1992, recounting Gardner's explanation.
17. Based on interviews with Charles Gardner in February and December 1993, and supported by interviews with other former Unisys executives and federal investigators.
18. Interview with Henry Hudson, November 1992.
19. Interview with former high-ranking Unisys executive, who declines to be identified in print.
20. Interviews with Henry Hudson, Joseph Aronica, Daniel Larkin, Michael Costello and other current and former federal investigators.
21. Interview with FBI supervisory agent Daniel Larkin, January 1993.
22. Craig Gordon, "D'Amato Law Partner: Senator Wasn't Involved," *Newsday* (April 27, 1993), p. 23.
23. Interview with Charles Gardner, February 1993.
24. Ibid.
25. Interview with Charles Gardner, December 1993.
26. Court documents filed by prosecutors along with the guilty pleas of Charles Gardner, James Neal and Unisys.
27. Court documents filed by prosecutors along with Unisys's guilty plea.
28. Court documents filed by prosecutors along with the guilty pleas of Unisys, Garland Tomlin, James Thompson, Frederick Carville and Steven Monas.
29. Ibid.
30. Interview with former NIS agent Mike Cox, May 1992.
31. Plea agreement between Unisys and federal prosecutors.
32. William Galvin's grand jury testimony, September 1990.
33. Ibid.
34. William Galvin's grand jury testimony, August 1990.
35. Interviews with Charles Gardner, February and December 1993.
36. Court documents filed by prosecutors along with the guilty pleas of Unisys and Melvyn Paisley.
37. Court documents filed by prosecutors along with the guilty pleas of Unisys, Melvyn Paisley and Victor Cohen.
38. Ibid.
39. Ibid.
40. Judson Gooding, "Protector of the American Fleet," *New York Times Sunday Magazine* (October 6, 1985), p. 37.
41. Court documents filed by prosecutors along with the guilty pleas of Unisys and Melvyn Paisley.
42. Ibid.
43. William Galvin's grand jury testimony, August 1990.
44. Interview with Charles Gardner, February 1993.
45. Interview with Charles Gardner, December 1993.
46. Court documents filed by prosecutors along with the guilty pleas of Unisys, Melvyn Paisley and James Neal.
47. Court documents filed by prosecutors along with the guilty pleas of Unisys and Melvyn Paisley.
48. Based on interviews with Vicki Paisley and federal investigators.
49. Court documents submitted by defense lawyers before Melvyn Paisley's sentencing.
50. Interview with Melvyn Paisley, April 1993.

51. Interview with Charles Gardner, February 1993.

52. Ibid.

53. Excerpts of wiretapped conversation broadcast by NBC News and then reported by the Associated Press in 1988.

54. David Johnston, "Chappell Tells of Contacts With Weapons Industry," *New York Times* (June 23, 1988), p. 20.

55. David Johnston, "Florida Congressman's Activities Seem to Interest Pentagon Investigators," *New York Times* (July 26, 1988), p. 19.

56. Dan Morgan and Eric Pianin, "Contractors Often Bypass Pentagon in Making Pitch," *Washington Post* (July 10, 1988), p. 1.

57. Interview with Steve Fulmer, May 1992.

58. Johnston, "Chappell Tells of Contacts With Weapons Industry," p. 20.

59. Susan F. Rasky, "Rep. Chappell Says Lies Are Used to Tie Him to Investigation," *New York Times* (June 22, 1988), p. 1.

60. Interview with James Gaines, August 1992.

61. Court documents filed with Unisys's guilty plea.

62. Interview with Charles Gardner, December 1993.

63. Andy Pasztor and Edward T. Pound, "Rep. McDade Indicted by U.S.," *Wall Street Journal* (May 6, 1992), p. 4.

64. Associated Press, Political Campaign Profiles, November 21, 1994.

65. Court documents filed by prosecutors along with the guilty plea of Unisys.

66. Robert E. Kessler, "Unisys Exec's Golf Talk Was Key Factor in Defense Probe," *Newsday* (November 14, 1988), p. 7.

67. Ibid.

68. Sara Fritz and William Nottingham, "Two Lawmakers Are Big Help to Defense Industry Friends," *Los Angeles Times* (July 18, 1988), p. 1.

69. Audio copy of a wiretapped conversation between Don Lynch and another consultant before Illwind became public, but the exact date is unknown.

70. Kessler, "Unisys Exec's Golf Talk Was Key Factor in Defense Probe," p. 7.

71. Eric Pianin and Dan Morgan, "Firm Relieved Chappell of Business Debt," *Washington Post* (July 1, 1988), p. 1.

72. Dan Morgan and Eric Pianin, "Defense Contractor Now Owns Chappell's Former Health Club," *Washington Post* (July 2, 1988), p. 10.

73. Eric Pianin and Dan Morgan, "Defense Firm Representative Provided Lodging for Chappell," *Washington Post* (July 18, 1988), p. 1.

74. Audio copy of a wiretapped conversation between Thomas Muldoon and another consultant before Illwind became public, but the exact date is unknown.

75. Eric Pianin, "Warner Campaign Donors Reportedly Reimbursed," *Washington Post* (August 10, 1988), p. 6. Also, court documents filed by prosecutors along with the guilty pleas of Unisys and John Roberts III.

76. Jonathan Rabinovitz, "D'Amato Tells of Arranging Senate Access," *New York Times* (April 29, 1993), p. B1.

77. Craig Gordon, "Armand D'Amato Trial Winds Down," *Newsday* (May 4, 1993), p. 7.

78. Craig Gordon, "D'Amato's Brother Gets Five Months in Prison," *Newsday* (November 16, 1993), p. 3.

79. Helen Dewar, "Ethics Panel Criticizes D'Amato For Letting Brother Use Office," *Washington Post* (August 3, 1991), p. 2.

80. Tom Bowman, "Dyson Linked to Lobbyist In Affidavit," *Baltimore Sun* (October 13, 1990), p. 1.

81. Court documents filed by prosecutors along with the guilty plea of Unisys.

82. Interview with NIS agent Jimmy Whitener, June 1992.

83. Interview with Charles Gardner, December 1993.
84. Christopher Callahan, "Search Warrant Reveals Engine Maker Had Competitor's Secrets," Associated Press (June 18, 1988).
85. Interview with FBI supervisory agent Daniel Larkin, January 1993.
86. Bowman, "Dyson Linked to Lobbyist in Affidavit," p. 1.
87. Memorandum from Fred Jenny to Unisys management, dated May 10, 1988.
88. Interview with Charles Gardner, February 1993.
89. Based on interviews with Charles Gardner, FBI agent Daniel Larkin and other investigators.
90. Audio copy of a wiretapped conversation between Don Lynch and another consultant before Illwind became public, but the exact date is unknown.
91. Interview with a former high-ranking Unisys executive who declines to be identified.
92. Memorandum from Frederick Jenny to the senior management of Unisys Defense Systems, December 11, 1987.
93. Memorandum from Frederick Jenny to selected Unisys executives, September 24, 1987.
94. Interview with Charles Gardner, December 1993.
95. Interview with Steve Fulmer, May 1992.
96. Interview with Curtis Hessler, former Unisys vice-chairman, July 1988. Charles Ruff declined comment.
97. Interviews with Joseph Aronica, Daniel Larkin and other federal investigators.
98. Interviews with former prosecutor Jonny Frank.
99. Audio copy of wiretapped conversation between William Galvin and Melvyn Paisley, April 30, 1987.
100. Excerpts of wiretapped conversations included in the federal indictment of Zvika Schiller and Uri Simhony.
101. Transcript of wiretapped conversation between William Galvin and Melvyn Paisley, May 12, 1987.
102. Transcript of wiretapped conversation between William Galvin and James Gaines, April 10, 1987.
103. Transcript of William Galvin's federal grand jury testimony, August 1990.
104. Court documents filed by prosecutors along with the guilty plea of Melvyn Paisley.
105. Based on written answers supplied by the Federal Bureau of Investigation and the Navy to Senator Carl Levin and other members of the Senate Armed Services Committee, July 1988.
106. Transcript of Richard Rumpf's federal grand jury testimony, April 1989.
107. Glenn F. Bunting, "Lehman Helped Paisley Retain Access to Secrets," *Los Angeles Times* (July 8, 1988), p. 1.
108. Audiotape of wiretapped conversation between Melvyn Paisley and James Gaines, May 4, 1987.
109. Norman Black, "Investigators Eye Dealings of Second Lehman Associate," Associated Press (June 18, 1988).
110. Interview with James Gaines, August 1992. Also, transcript of Richard Rumpf's federal grand jury testimony, April 1989, and interviews with John Brett.
111. Interview with James Gaines, November 1992.
112. Interview with NIS agent Robert Powers, March 1992.
113. Barbara Starr, "Webb Cites 'Duty to Keep My Own Counsel' on FBI Procurement Investigation," *Defense News* (July 1988), p. 14.
114. Transcript of wiretapped conversation between Melvyn Paisley and William Galvin, September 21, 1987.
115. Ibid.
116. Ibid.
117. Ibid.

118. Interview with FBI agent Richard Wade, August 1992.
119. Interviews with FBI agents Richard Wade and Debbie Pierce, and Illwind search plans passed out to agents in June 1988.
120. Interview with Joseph Aronica, September 1992.
121. Interview with Henry Hudson, November 1992.
122. Interview with Joseph Krahling, April 1993.
123. Interview with FBI agent Debbie Pierce, January 1993.
124. Interview with FBI agent Phyllis Sciacca, December 1992.
125. Interview with Steve Fulmer, May 1992.
126. Interview with John Lehman, December 1992; and with Melvyn Paisley, April 1993.
127. Based on interviews with Joseph Aronica, Richard Wade and several other federal investigators.
128. Interviews with former prosecutor Jonny Frank and former senior FBI agent Thomas Parker.
129. Interview with Joseph Krahling, April 1993.
130. Interview with former prosecutor Jonny Frank, December 1992.
131. Audio copy of a wiretapped conversation between Charles Gardner and another consultant before Illwind became public, but the exact date is not known.
132. Michael Arena et al., "The Favored," *Newsday* (December 19, 1990), p. 1.
133. Andy Pasztor and Charles W. Stevens, "Capital Dogfight," *Wall Street Journal* (July 27, 1989), p. 1.
134. Arena et al., "The Favored," p. 1.
135. Interviews with former prosecutor Jonny Frank and NIS agent Robert Watson, and court documents filed by prosecutors along with the guilty plea of John O'Brien.
136. Court documents filed by prosecutors along with the guilty plea and sentencing of John O'Brien.
137. Ibid.
138. Ibid.
139. Ibid.
140. Arena et al., "The Favored," p. 1.
141. Interviews with Jimmy Whitener, June and August 1992.
142. Interviews with Jimmy Whitener and Robert Watson.
143. Interviews with Jimmy Whitener, June and August 1992.
144. Ibid.
145. Interview with FBI agent Debbie Pierce, January 1993.
146. Interviews with Steve Fulmer, May 1992.
147. Interview with Henry Hudson, October and November 1992.
148. Interviews with Joseph Aronica and Henry Hudson.
149. Interview with Henry Hudson, October 1992.
150. Interviews with Joseph Aronica and Steve Fulmer.
151. The description of Gardner's confrontation by the FBI and the quotations are based on interviews with Charles Gardner, Richard Wade, Joseph Aronica and Henry Hudson.
152. Ibid.
153. Ibid.
154. Interviews with Charles Gardner and Richard Wade.
155. Ibid.
156. Ibid.
157. Interviews with Charles Gardner.
158. Ibid.
159. Interviews with Charles Gardner, Richard Wade and Joseph Aronica.
160. Interviews with Charles Gardner and Richard Wade.

161. Based on interviews with investigators and officials of United Technologies.

162. Based on interviews with Steve Fulmer and other investigators.

163. Ibid.

164. Based on interviews with investigators and Peter Stockton, former aide to Democratic congressman John Dingell of Michigan.

165. John M. Broder, " 'It's Still Business as Usual,' Despite Defense Fraud Probe," *Los Angeles Times* (June 15, 1989), p. 1.

166. Interview with William Parkin, August 1988, by Edward T. Pound.

167. Broder, " 'It's Still Business as Usual,' Despite Defense Fraud Probe," p. 1.

168. Interviews with James Gaines.

169. Interview with Thomas Muldoon, October 1992.

170. Robert E. Kessler, "L.I. Firm Raided by U.S. for Data," *Newsday* (July 9, 1988), p. 1.

171. Court documents filed by federal prosecutors along with the guilty plea of John Roberts III.

172. Ibid.

173. Interview with FBI agent Debbie Pierce, January 1993.

174. Ibid.

175. Interviews with Debbie Pierce and Steve Fulmer. The couple later maintained that she was merely chewing gum, but agents didn't believe them.

176. The description of the Oval Office meeting is based on interviews with Henry Hudson.

177. Edward T. Pound and Andy Pasztor, "Reagan Says Fraud in Pentagon Buying 'Understandable,' Asks Credit for Probe," *Wall Street Journal* (June 22, 1988), p. 4.

178. Maralee Schwartz, "Bush Shocked by Pentagon Inquiry," *Washington Post* (June 18, 1988), p. 11.

179. Knight-Ridder News Service, "Weapons-Buying Reforms Needed, Carlucci Says," *Harrisburg Patriot* (July 13, 1988), p. A3.

180. Philip Shenon, "Weinberger Says Bribery Inquiry May Show Reforms Are Necessary," *New York Times* (June 20, 1988), p. 1.

181. Helen Dewar and George C. Wilson, "Hill Leaders Demand Swift Justice," *Washington Post* (June 18, 1988), p. 1.

182. Tim Ahern, "Lawmakers Cite 'Good Old Boy' Network at Pentagon," Associated Press (June 19, 1988).

183. The opening statement of Representative Jack Brooks at a hearing of the national security subcomittee of the House Judiciary Committee, July 16, 1988.

184. Recounted by Henry Hudson in a speech he gave to the National Aviation Club, May 16, 1991.

185. Ibid.

186. Interview with Joseph Aronica, November 1992.

187. Interviews with Mike Cox, Jimmy Whitener and other current and former federal agents.

188. Interview with Richard Wade, December 1992.

189. Interview with former senior Pentagon criminal investigator Michael Costello, March 1992.

190. Interview with former senior FBI agent Joseph Krahling, April 1993.

191. Interviews with Joseph Aronica and Steve Fulmer.

192. Interview with FBI agent Phyllis Sciacca, December 1992.

193. Interview with FBI agent Daniel Larkin, January 1993.

194. Interview with Lawrence Garrett, August 1988.

195. Interview with former Pentagon general counsel Kathleen Buck, November 1993.

196. Sandra Sugawara, "Defense Probe Is Decried as A 'Lynch Mob,' " *Washington Post* (January 15, 1988), p. D2.

197. Robert F. Howe, "Pentagon Procurement System Called 'Outrage' by Judge," *Washington Post* (June 8, 1989), p. 4.
198. Interview with Debbie Pierce, January 1993.
199. Transcript of sentencing hearing for Charles Gardner, September 15, 1989.
200. Interviews with Richard Wade, Daniel Larkin and Charles Gardner.
201. Interviews with Charles Gardner, Thomas Muldoon and former FBI agent Thomas Parker.
202. Interviews with Charles Gardner, Thomas Muldoon and Daniel Larkin.
203. Transcript of sentencing hearing for William Galvin, September 21, 1990.
204. Interview with Robert Powers, March 1992.
205. Interview with Neel Patrick in 1993. The description of Paisley's decision to plead guilty is also based on interviews with Paisley, Joseph Aronica, Larry Barcella and others.
206. Interview with Joseph Aronica, September 1992.
207. Interview with Melvyn Paisley, April 1993.
208. Transcript of sentencing hearing for Melvyn Paisley, October 18, 1991.
209. Interview with Melvyn Paisley, April 1993.
210. Transcript of sentencing hearing for Melvyn Paisley, October 18, 1991.
211. Andy Pasztor, "U.S., Grumman Reach Accord In Pentagon Case," *Wall Street Journal* (November 23, 1993), p. 3.
212. Interview with former Pentagon inspector general June Gibbs Brown before the end of the Bush administration.
213. Ralph Vartabedian, "Cases of Defense Fraud Boom Amid Cutbacks," *Los Angeles Times* (March 26, 1995). p.1.
214. Ibid.
215. William H. Gregory, *The Defense Procurement Mess* (Lexington, Mass.: Lexington Books, 1989), p. 188.
216. Interviews with Henry Hudson in 1992 and 1993.
217. Andy Pasztor, "Defense Secretary Moves to Eliminate Budget Gimmicks," *Wall Street Journal* (June 15, 1989), p. B6.
218. Based on reports prepared by the General Accounting Office in March 1995 for the Secretary of Defense and various congressional committees.
219. Charles W. Hall, "Litton Industries Pleads Guilty, Closing Book on 'Illwind' Scandal," *Washington Post* (January 15, 1994), p. 11.

INDEX

Avco Corporation, 332
Avenger (A-12) bombers, 126–27, 131
AWACS (Airborne Warning and Control
    System) radar planes, 52, 75

B-1 bombers, 51, 271, 278
B-1B bombers, 273
B-2 Stealth bombers, 24, 56, 219, 270–71,
    272
B-17 Flying Fortress bombers, 50
B-29 Superfortress bombers, 50, 206
B-52 bombers, 52
Bahamas, 324
Baker, Bobby, 113
Baker, Howard, 313
Baker, James, 139
Bandar bin Sultan, Prince of Saudi Arabia, 85
Barcella, Larry, 105, 361–63
base closings, 365
Battle of the Bulge, 93
BCCI bank scandal, 252
BDM International, 144, 145, 146, 150, 156,
    158, 251, 303
    history of, 145
Bechtel Corporation, 67
Beggs, James, 223, 224, 226
Belgium, 93
Bell, Thomas D., 143
Bell Helicopter, 171
Bellows, Randy, 221–27, 231–32, 237–38,
    239, 241, 244, 246–49, 268–69, 289
    background of, 221–22
    Boeing plea agreement and, 253–56, 262
    Fowler indictment and, 250–51
    Fowler trial and, 265–66
    gynecologist prosecuted by, 262
    Hughes case and, 280, 282–87
    update on, 369
    workaholic habits of, 248
Bell XP-59A aircraft, 273
Bendix, 146, 157
Bennett, Robert S.:
    background of, 251–53
    Boeing work of, 253–56, 265
Bennett, William, 252
Bethel, Pam, 195–96, 299
Betti, John, 247
Blackbird (SR-71) aircraft, 272
Blumenthal, Michael, 363
Blumhardt, Paul, 237
Boeing, 30, 32, 38, 41, 42, 48–71, 72–74,

147, 157, 200, 204, 205, 225, 259, 288,
    290, 291
community power of, 102
in document acquisition, 37, 55, 59–63,
    69–71, 207–14, 219–20, 221, 225, 226,
    227–32, 239–56, 261, 270
and election of 1980, 41–55
Fowler dismissed from, 233–39
Fowler's document acquisition at, 207–14,
    219–20, 226, 227–32, 241–51, 255, 261,
    270
illegal documents plea agreement of,
    253–56, 257–64
illicit foreign payments of, 257–59
illicit library of, 240–41
Interior Department bidding dispute of,
    259–60
Lehman as consultant to, 74–76
Minuteman contracts of, 47–52, 59, 61,
    110, 206
1981 presidential transition and, 64, 69–71
one-on-one presentations at, 131
Paisley hired by, 96–97
Paisley's severance payment from, 302–3
Boeing 707 airliners, 75
Boeing 747 airliners, 48, 98, 264
Boeing 757 airliners, 51, 62, 263–64
Boeing 767 airliners, 51, 62
Boeing Applied Physics Laboratory, 96–97
Boileau, Oliver, 49, 97, 98
Boys and Girls Clubs of America, 259
Bradley, Omar, 92
Brady, James, 58, 59
Brazil, 14, 141
Brett, John, 338
"Brilliant Pebbles," 272
Brooks, Jack, 356
Brothers, Richard, 53
Brown, Harold, 45, 60, 61, 71
Bryan, Albert, 265
Bryant, Anita, 111
Bulge, Battle of the, 93
Burroughs Corporation, 320
Bush, George, 33, 82, 108, 127, 137, 162,
    252, 343, 366
    document raid briefing of, 354
    in election of 1988, 107
    on Illwind, 355
    Lehman's relationship with, 35, 67, 83, 162
    procurement reforms and, 247
    Tower nominated by, 360